W9-ADS-837

A Companion to Restoration Drama

Blackwell Companions to Literature and Culture

This series offers comprehensive, newly written surveys of key periods and movements, and certain major authors, in English literary culture and history. Extensive volumes provide new perspectives and positions on contexts and on canonical and post-canonical texts, orientating the beginning student in new fields of study and providing the experienced undergraduate and new graduate with current and new directions, as pioneered and developed by leading scholars in the field.

A COMPANION TO

RESTORATION
DRAMA

EDITED BY **SUSAN J. OWEN**

Copyright © Blackwell Publishers Ltd 2001
Editorial matter, selection and arrangement copyright © Susan J. Owen 2001

First published 2001

2 4 6 8 10 9 7 5 3 1

Blackwell Publishers Ltd
108 Cowley Road
Oxford OX4 1JF
UK

Blackwell Publishers Inc.
350 Main Street
Malden, Massachusetts 02148
USA

British Library Cataloguing in Publication Data

A CIP catalogue record for this book is available from the British Library.

Library of Congress Cataloging-in-Publication Data

A companion to Restoration drama / edited by Susan J. Owen.
    p. cm. – (Blackwell companions to literature and culture; 12)
   Includes bibliographical references and index.
   ISBN 0–631–21923–4 (alk. paper)
      1. English drama – Restoration, 1660–1700 – History and criticism – Handbooks, manuals, etc.
I. Owen, Susan J. II. Series.

PR691 .C66 2001
822'.409 – dc21

Typeset in 11 pt on 13 pt Garamond
by Kolam Information Services Private Ltd, Pondicherry, India
Printed in Great Britain by T.J. International, Padstow, Cornwall
This book is printed on acid-free paper.

Contents

About the Contributors

John Bull is Professor of Film and Drama at the University of Reading. He has directed a wide variety of classic and modern plays, including two of his own. His publications include *New British Political Dramatists, Stage Right: Crisis and Recovery in British Contemporary Mainstream Drama* and *Vanbrughh and Farquhar*, and he is currently working on a six-volume project, *British and Irish Dramatists Since World War II*. He is a past chair of the Standing Committee of University Drama Departments.

J. Douglas Canfield is Regents' Professor of English and Comparative Cultural and Literary Studies at the University of Arizona. He specializes in both English literature of the Restoration and early eighteenth century and comparative literature of the Southwest Borderlands. He is currently on a National Endowment for the Humanities fellowship to write *Tricksters and the Nation: On the Ideology of Revolution Comedy*.

Paul D. Cannan is an Assistant Professor of English at the University of Minnesota Duluth. He has published articles on seventeenth-century drama and dramatic criticism in the *Review of English Studies, Studies in Philology* and *Philological Quarterly*. He is currently completing a book manuscript on the emergence of an institution of criticism in late seventeenth- and early eighteenth-century England.

Mita Choudhury teaches cultural and media studies in the School of Literature, Communication, and Culture at the Georgia Institute of Technology. She is author of *Interculturalism and Resistance in the London Theater, 1660–1800: Identity, Performance, Empire* and co-editor of the forthcoming *Monstrous Dreams of Reason: Body, Self, and Other in the Enlightenment*. She also guest edited a special Spring 2001 issue of the *South Atlantic Review* titled *Being Global: From the Enlightenment to the Age of Information*.

Sandra Clark is Reader in Renaissance Literature at Birkbeck College, University of London, where she has taught for many years. She has published on Elizabethan popular pamphlets, the plays of Beaumont and Fletcher, Shakespeare (including an edition of Restoration adaptations of his plays), Webster, broadside ballads, and various other topics in early modern literature. She is currently working on a book about the representation of women and crime in early modern street literature.

Kirk Combe is an Associate Professor of English at Denison University specializing in Restoration and eighteenth-century British literature. In the early modern era, he has published on topics such as satire, drama and culture. His studies include in particular considerations of such authors as Rochester, Dryden and Shadwell.

Brian Corman is Professor and Chair of English at the University of Toronto. He has published articles on the plays of Behn, Centlivre, Cibber, Congreve, Dryden, Etherege, Shadwell, Tate and Wycherley. He is the author of *Genre and Generic Change in English Comedy, 1660–1710* (1993). He is currently working on a reception history of women novelists before Jane Austen. He is editor of the *University of Toronto Quarterly*.

Aparna Dharwadker was Associate Professor of English at the University of Oklahoma until autumn 2001, when she moved to a joint position in Theatre and the Languages and Cultures of Asia at the University of Wisconsin-Madison. Her recent work in early modern British and postcolonial drama has appeared in *Theatre Journal, Studies in Philology* and *The Eighteenth Century: Theory and Interpretation*. With fellowship support from the NEH and the AIIS, she is currently completing a book-length study of post-independence Indian theatre.

Don-John Dugas is Assistant Professor of English Literature at Towson University in Baltimore. He has published articles on Chaucer, Spenser, Milton, Rochester and the London book trade in 1709, and is completing a book-length project on the ways that performance and publication affected Shakespeare's popular reputation between 1660 and 1738.

Deborah Payne Fisk is an Associate Professor in the Department of Literature and Performing Arts at American University in Washington, DC. The author of numerous articles on Restoration theatre, she has edited *The Cambridge Companion to English Restoration Theatre* (2000) and has forthcoming a collection of *Four Libertine Plays from the Restoration* (2002). Professor Fisk also does dramaturgy and directing; currently she is the Humanities Project Consultant for the Shakespeare Theatre.

Todd S. Gilman is Librarian for Literatures in English at Yale University. He is currently completing a book-length manuscript called *Handel and London Theatre*, and is completing, correcting and editing the late John A. Parkinson's manuscript, *Thomas Arne: Master of a Scurvy Profession* (forthcoming). In collaboration with Peter Holman, he also contributed the entry on Thomas Augustine Arne to the *New Grove Dictionary of Music and Musicians*, second edition (2001).

Miriam Handley is a lecturer in English Literature at the University of Sheffield. She has published articles on Shaw and Chekhov and is currently writing a monograph on nineteenth-century stage directions.

Derek Hughes is Professor of English and Comparative Literary Studies at the University of Warwick. He is the author of *Dryden's Heroic Plays* (1981), *English Drama*, 1660–1700 (1996) and *The Theatre of Aphra Behn* (2001), and is the general editor of *Eighteenth-century Women Playwrights* (2001). He has also published on German opera, and is currently working on a comparatist study of representations of human sacrifice in literature and opera.

Paulina Kewes teaches in the English Department at the University of Wales, Aberystwyth. Her publications include *Authorship and Appropriation: Writing for the Stage in England, 1660–1710* and essays on Renaissance and Restoration drama, criticism, publishing history, Shakespeare, Dryden, Rowe and Rochester. She is currently writing a book on representations of history on the early modern stage.

Matthew J. Kinservik is Assistant Professor of English at the University of Delaware. His book, *Disciplining Satire: The Censorship of Satiric Comedy on the Eighteenth-century London Stage* (forthcoming), examines the effects of the Stage Licensing Act of 1737 on satiric comedy. He is currently working on a book about the sodomy and libel trials of the eighteenth-century actor and playwright, Samuel Foote.

Richard Kroll teaches at the University of California, Irvine. He has published extensively on Restoration and early eighteenth-century literature and culture. At present, he is working on a book about the relations between drama, the discourse of trade, political theory and physiology, of which his essay in this volume is part.

Edward A. Langhans is a Professor Emeritus of the University of Hawaii, where he taught drama and theatre for thirty-eight years after completing his doctorate at Yale University. He has published extensively on Restoration and eighteenth-century stagecraft and theatre architecture and was co-author of the sixteen-volume *Biographical Dictionary of Actors, Actresses, Musicians, Dancers, Managers and Other Stage Personnel in London, 1660–1800*. His current projects are David Garrick's promptbooks and Samuel Pepys on theatre.

Cynthia Lowenthal teaches in the English department at Tulane University and is currently Acting Dean of Newcomb College. Her research interests centre on late seventeenth- and eighteenth-century literature, with an emphasis on drama and the women writers of the era. She has just completed a study of the late seventeenth-century London playhouse and the strategies employed by playwrights to contain the excesses found in the creation of identities in early modern culture.

Robert Markley is Jackson Distinguished Chair of British Literature at West Virginia University, and editor of *The Eighteenth Century: Theory and Interpretation*. His books include *Two-Edg'd Weapons: Style and Ideology in the Comedies of Etherege, Wycherley, and Congreve* (1988) and *Fallen Languages: Crises of Representation in Newtonian England, 1660–1740* (1993). He is currently completing a book manuscript on European literature and trade to the Far East in the seventeenth and eighteenth centuries.

Jean I. Marsden is Associate Professor of English at the University of Connecticut. She is the author of *The Re-Imagined Text: Shakespeare, Adaptation and Eighteenth-century Literary Theory* and the editor of *The Appropriation of Shakespeare: Post-Renaissance Reconstructions of the Work and the Myth*. Currently completing a book on women and the Restoration stage, she has published widely on Restoration and eighteenth-century drama.

Jessica Munns teaches English Literature at the University of Denver. She is the author of *Restoration Politics and Drama: The Plays of Thomas Otway* (1995), and has co-edited a reader in Cultural Studies (1996) and a book on eighteenth-century dress codes (1999). She has written a large number of essays and book chapters on Restoration and eighteenth-century literature and is the editor of the journal *Restoration and Eighteenth-century Theatre Research*. She is co-editor of a forthcoming book on gender and power in early modern Europe and is working on a book on changing representations of power and authority on the English stage, 1660–1750.

Maximillian E. Novak is Professor Emeritus in the English Department of the University of California, Los Angeles. He has recently published a biography of Daniel Defoe, and has edited a volume of essays with Anne Mellor entitled *Passionate Encounters in a Time of Sensibility*. His edition (with Michael Seidel and Joyce Kennedy) of Defoe's *Consolidator* is to appear in 2001. He is currently working on a new book on the political contexts of Congreve's plays and other writings.

Susan J. Owen teaches in the Department of English Literature at the University of Sheffield. She is the author of *Restoration Theatre and Crisis* (1996) and *Perspectives on Restoration Drama* (forthcoming), as well as numerous articles and essays on Restoration drama, a piece on Andrew Marvell and a theoretical article, 'Chaos Theory, Marxism and Literature' (*new formations*, 1996). She has also edited *A Babel of Bottles: Drink, Drinkers and Drinking Places in Literature* (2000).

Laura J. Rosenthal is Associate Professor of English at Florida State University and author of *Playwrights and Plagiarists in Early Modern England: Gender, Authorship, Literary Property*. She is co-editor of the forthcoming *Monstrous Dreams of Reason: Body, Self, and Other in the Enlightenment* and is currently completing a study of prostitution and global commerce in eighteenth-century literature and culture.

Christopher J. Wheatley is the author of *Without God or Reason: The Plays of Thomas Shadwell and Secular Ethics in the Restoration* (1993) and *Beneath Ierne's Banners: Irish Protestant Drama of the Restoration and Eighteenth Century* (1999), the latter of which won the Rhodes prize for the best book on Irish literature in that year. He is editing a multi-volume *Dictionary of Literary Biography on Twentieth-century American Drama*, and is Professor of English at the Catholic University of America.

Preface and Acknowledgements

Long after the term 'Renaissance' in literary studies began to be interrogated, the term 'Restoration' was regarded as comparatively unproblematic. At the height of the revolution in Renaissance studies, the Restoration was regarded as a comparatively stable and conservative cultural yardstick against which to measure the cultural plurality of 'Renaissance' (or 'Early Modern' or 'Reformation') England.[1] The Restoration marked the end of Christopher Hill's 'Century of Revolution' and Restoration theatre was seen as culturally 'narrower' and more courtly than pre-Civil War theatre, reflecting the perceived re-establishment of order after the monarchy was brought back in 1660.

In recent years these views have been widely questioned and qualified, which is not to say that they are completely untrue. The fact there were only two licensed theatres in London meant that the Restoration audience *was* more dominated by royal and aristocratic tastes than the theatre of Shakespeare's time. This is reflected in the social composition of those immediately in front of the players: Shakespeare's 'groundlings' were replaced by an audience which contained many gentlemen and noblemen, seated on benches in the 'pit'. Yet the audience was by no means homogeneous. Humbler people sat in the galleries above the front tier of boxes, and people of 'middle rank' sat in the pit or the galleries or even took boxes themselves. Nevertheless, various factors might be supposed to have created a more culturally dominating experience for the audience than in earlier times. Restoration theatres were grander than theatres earlier in the century. Stage design was more elaborate, with a proscenium arch, and realistic sets made of painted wings, borders and shutters. Scenes could be changed by sliding moveable backdrops along grooves in the stage, shutters opened to stunning tableaux. Machines for enabling people to fly created exciting new possibilities, and there was increased use of music and spectacle. All this might have been supposed to contribute to a shift from critical engagement to passive consumption of the drama.

Yet there are contradictory aspects. In front of the proscenium arch, a forestage extended right into the pit. Most acting took place here. The forestage also allowed intimate exchanges with the audience in prologues and epilogues, the latter often spoken by actresses. The prologues and epilogues were spoken with an air of familiarity and were full of in-jokes. We know from Pepys's diary that he and others went to the theatre regularly, sometimes several times a week. They knew the actors and understood the theatre's conventions. Going to the theatre was a much more ordinary and everyday experience, and therefore less intimidating, than it can be in our own time. Nor was the audience respectfully silent. The candles remained lit throughout the performance, permitting flirting, the sale of everything from oranges to sexual favours, a ribald exchange of witticisms (by no means always connected to the play), and sometimes fights. The audience, in other words, were a theatre in themselves. Theatres did not really rank as 'high culture' in the Restoration. Plays rarely ran for more than six days, and were seldom extremely profitable. Actors were so poorly paid that many had second jobs. Authors got box office receipts on the third night, since published texts were usually cheap and shoddy and yielded little profit. Issues of cultural authority in the theatres were complex. This reflects a complexity in authority relations within Restoration society.

Restoration drama, like any cultural production following major social upheaval, has an immediacy and topicality which were to be gradually lost in the two centuries that followed. The theatre after 1660 was affected by big social contradictions, involving sex and gender, and political power. Everyone has heard of the so-called merry monarch and his mistresses, of whom Nell Gwyn is the best known. Under Charles II there was a burgeoning of libertinism. If John Wilmot, Earl of Rochester, was the most illustrious exponent, the chief practitioners were the Stuarts, Charles II and his brother and heir, James. The period after 1660 also saw the development of the sexual 'marketplace', ranging from prostitutes who catered for all tastes, to homosexual 'molly' houses, to a generalized fetishization of sexual characteristics. There are numerous references in the drama to homosexuality, sado-masochism and voyeurism, as well as libertinism and prostitution. However, there was also widespread moral disapproval of these developments. Even a royal supporter like Pepys notes the king's 'horrid effeminacy' (enslavement to women) and 'the viciousness of the Court' and 'contempt the King brings himself into thereby'. The king's promiscuity was often seen as a sign of political irresponsibility, as the arch-libertine Rochester himself noted: 'His sceptre and his prick are of a length, / And she may sway the one who plays with t'other / And make him little wiser than his brother'. When Rochester coined the designation 'merry Monarch' he was being sarcastic: Charles is 'A merry Monarch, scandalous and poor'. In Andrew Marvell's poem *Last Instructions to a Painter* the Kingdom appears to the recumbent Charles in allegorical female form and the king's response is to exploit it.

It is not surprising, therefore, that we encounter a contradictory attitude to sex in the drama. Constructions of gender were also thrown into crisis. As we shall see, this affected masculinity as well as female roles. It is enough here to mention the contradictory response of Dryden, who elevates the hero who 'weeps much, fights little, but is wondrous kind' in *All For Love*; but denigrates male 'effeminacy' in

Troilus and Cressida. For women, also, there were massive contradictions. Libertinism opened up a new freedom to assert sexual desire, but libertinism was itself a misogynistic philosophy, sanctioning desire for the male but not the female, and seeing women as prey. Women could for the first time become actresses and playwrights, a development of profound significance in the theatre, but they were often thought of as sexually available and morally compromised simply by their association with theatre and public exhibition. The actresses' changing room was open to the public. They were regarded as easy prey and it was hard for them to resist unwanted male attention. The first professional woman playwright, Aphra Behn, was always financially insecure and never really respectable. Behn's attitude to libertinism varies between indulgence, caution and criticism, and her plays are permeated by an awareness of the cost for women of sexual double standards. 'Breeches' parts for actresses embodied the contradiction for women: on the one hand, women could dress and fight as men; on the other, we know from contemporary accounts that the audience saw such parts as a chance to revel in the titillating sight of the actresses' legs.

These contradictions of sex and gender arise within a context of political contradiction. Despite the triumphant rhetoric and ostentatious rejoicing which accompanied the reassertion of royal control in 1660, the king soon came up against a crisis of authority. It was impossible to establish the ideological consensus, to obliterate the memory of the Interregnum, or to gloss over profound religious and political divisions in the nation. Charles faced criticism from the old Cavaliers for being too lenient towards former supporters of Cromwell; but he also faced growing mistrust from parliamentarians like Andrew Marvell for being soft on 'popery' and disposed towards 'arbitrary government' on the French model. Europe was in political and religious turmoil, and the depth of English anxieties about the Protestant succession and the parliamentary freedoms thought to be associated with it was reflected in the overwhelming electoral victories and mass support of the opposition to the government in the late 1670s and early 1680s. The Exclusion Crisis of 1678–83 almost erupted into another civil war. At this time party political division emerged for the first time in England, as royalist and parliamentarian factions hardened into Tories and Whigs. Ultimately these tensions were to explode in the revolution of 1688. The ejection of James II in 1688 was followed by significant reversals at the level of political ideology, law, constitution and foreign policy, and led to a changed culture.

Charles II took a keen personal interest in the theatre, and personally inaugurated the new genre of the heroic play. The assertion of royal control in the theatres also took the form of censorship and strict limits on theatrical outlets, since only two theatres were licensed (though plays could also be performed at court). Yet contradictions emerged in the drama's attitude towards royal authority, even during the early Restoration period of the ascendancy of the royalist heroic play. In the Exclusion Crisis, 'oppositional' tragedy develops and contradictions are evident even in plays in which dramatists were apparently straining every nerve to offer a royalist and Tory message. Censorship, while it may have worked to some extent to limit criticisms of the authorities in performance, did not stop publication. Even during the Exclusion Crisis play texts appeared in print uncensored, even when the play was banned from performance. In the 'bigger picture', all drama is permeated by anxieties about hierarchies of class and race. As J. Douglas Canfield has pointed out, 'the romance of empire' is 'a major subtext of Restoration tragedy...a subtext that moves into maintext after the Revolution [of 1688]' (Canfield 2000: 5).

This is not to say that dramatic shifts are entirely 'determined' by socio-political ones. The prevalence of tragicomedy after 1660, and the rise of tragedy in the 1670s, almost certainly had something to do with the changing political 'mood', but other questions need to be asked, and are addressed in this volume. Some of the chapters which follow explore directly the links between drama and politics, or issues of gender, race and class; others address questions about generic shifts, such as the movement from the satirical to the sentimental, and the important development of musical drama. The first section of this volume offers wide-ranging perspectives on Restoration theatre and society, locating the Restoration theatre as a performance space, and situating the drama in relation both to Restoration and more recent shifts in perspective. We examine the theatres themselves and survey the critical debates about what Restoration drama is and should be. We explore the new sexual climate and gender relations in the drama. We probe the drama's relationship with political issues and questions of race and social class. Contrary to widely held belief, the Restoration period was a time of dramatic variety, innovation and vitality. The second section of this volume introduces readers to that variety through explorations of different dramatic genres. The third section sheds new light on the work of the most significant dramatists, and on relationships between them. Criticism of Restoration drama has been uneven, and in this volume each contributor offers a unique perspective: there has been no attempt to homogenize or smooth out critical differences. On the contrary, our aim is to introduce the reader to the full range and diversity of criticism in this field as well as to the variety of the drama. For example, different perspectives on the Collier controversy are offered in different chapters. Dryden is looked at differently in chapter 12 on heroic drama, and in chapter 18 on Davenant and Dryden. Our aim is to provide an authoritative and stimulating guide to the diversity of drama at the end of the seventeenth century. Each contributor offers suggestions for further reading.

I would like to thank the University of Sheffield for granting me study leave in the autumn of 2000 during which I completed work on this volume, and the efficient editorial staff at Blackwell. As always, thank you to my daughters Alice and Jenny for their love and support.

NOTE

1   See, for example, Martin Butler's otherwise excellent *Theatre and Crisis* (1984); and Richard Kroll's critique in this volume (chapter 18).

REFERENCES AND FURTHER READING

In addition to the essays in this volume.

Albion 25, no. 4 (1993) contains an important debate by leading historians of the Restoration.

Botica, Allan Richard (1985). 'Audience, Playhouse and Play in Restoration Theatre, 1660–1710', D. Phil. thesis, Oxford University.

Braverman, Richard (1983). *Plots and Counterplots: Sexual Politics and the Body Politic 1660–1730*. Cambridge: Cambridge University Press.

Butler, Martin (1984). *Theatre and Crisis, 1632–1642*. Cambridge: Cambridge University Press.

Canfield, J. Douglas (2000). *Heroes and States: On the Ideology of Restoration Tragedy*. Lexington: University Press of Kentucky.

Chernaik, Warren (1995). *Sexual Freedom in Restoration Literature*. Cambridge: Cambridge University Press.

Downie, J. A. (1984). *To Settle the Succession of the State: Literature and Politics, 1678–1750*. London: Macmillan.

Harris, Tim (1997). 'What's New About the Restoration', *Albion* 29, 187–222.

Hill, Christopher (1961). *The Century of Revolution, 1603–1714*. London: Thomas Nelson.

Holland, Peter (1979). *The Ornament of Action: Text and Performance in Restoration Comedy*. Cambridge: Cambridge University Press.

Howe, Elizabeth (1992). *The First English Actresses: Women and Drama, 1660–1700*. Cambridge: Cambridge University Press.

Hume, Robert D. (ed.). (1980). *The London Theatre World, 1660–1800*. Carbondale: Southern Illinois University Press.

Hume, Robert D. (1982). 'The Nature of the Dorset Garden Theatre', *Theatre Notebook* 36, 99–109.

Love, Harold (1980). 'Who Were the Restoration Audience?', *Yearbook of English Studies* 10, 21–44.

Lowenthal, Cynthia (1996). 'Sticks and Rags, Bodies and Brocade: Essentializing Discourses and the Late Restoration Playhouse', in Katherine M. Quinsey (ed.), *Broken Boundaries: Women and Feminism in Restoration Drama*. Lexington: University Press of Kentucky, 219–33.

Owen, Susan J. (1993). 'Interpreting the Politics of Restoration Drama', *Seventeenth Century* 8, 67–97.

Owen, Susan J. (1996). *Restoration Theatre and Crisis*. Oxford: Clarendon Press.

Owen, Susan J. (1999). 'The Lost Rhetoric of Liberty: Marvell and Restoration Drama', in W. Chernaik and M. Dzelzainis (eds), *Marvell and Liberty*. London: Macmillan, 334–53.

Roach, Joseph (2000). 'The Performance', in Deborah Payne Fisk (ed.), *The Cambridge Companion to British Restoration Theatre*. Cambridge: Cambridge University Press, 19–39.

Scott, Jonathan (2000). *England's Troubles: Seventeenth-century English Political Instability in European Context*. Cambridge: Cambridge University Press.

Scouten, Arthur H. and Hume, Robert D. (1980). '"Restoration Comedy" and its Audiences, 1660–1776', *Yearbook of English Studies* 10, 45–69.

Straub, Kristina (1992). *Sexual Suspects: Eighteenth-century Players and Sexual Ideology*. Princeton, NJ: Princeton University Press.

Turner, James Grantham (1989). 'The Libertine Sublime: Love and Death in Restoration England', *Studies in Eighteenth-century Culture* 19, 99–115.

Turner, James Grantham (ed.). (1993). *Sexuality and Gender in Early Modern Europe: Institutions, Texts, Images*. Cambridge: Cambridge University Press.

Van Lennep, William (ed.). (1965). *The London Stage, 1660–1800*. Part I: *1660–1700*, ed. Emmett L. Avery and Arthur H. Scouten. Carbondale: Southern Illinois University Press.

Part I
The Drama in Context

1
The Post-1660 Theatres as Performance Spaces
Edward A. Langhans

Give actors the two boards and a passion that they say is all they need, and they will tear it to tatters to no avail unless they have a good play, a responsive audience and a workable performance space. This collective entertainment, as Jocelyn Powell has called it, cannot be really effective unless these interdependent elements of player, place, play and playgoer are properly balanced (1984: 15). It's a wonder, then, that great theatre ever happens at all, but it can and sometimes it does. Since a number of memorable plays came out of the Restoration period and stood the test of time, theatre then must have had some good things going for it. Indeed, it did, and it helped shape our modern theatre in some important ways.

We may think of Shakespeare's Globe and the plays written for it as the beginning of theatre as we now know it in English-speaking countries, but our roots may lie more in the theatre of Charles II. Shakespeare's sweeping, sprawling playwriting, the open-air, sceneryless playhouse and all-male company for which he wrote, and the variegated audience he appealed to are really not much like the standard professional theatre of today. It is to the Restoration we owe, for better or for worse, relatively small, roofed theatres, scenery, artificial lighting, actresses, small-scale drama – usually comedy that concerns itself chiefly with private rather than public matters, and audiences that are selective though not necessarily aristocratic, and educated though not always smart.

With the restoration of the monarchy in 1660 theatrical activity in London was not just revived but reinvented. Between then and the end of the century five different but similar theatres were in use: Vere Street (opened in 1660) and Lincoln's Inn Fields (1661), both converted indoor tennis courts seating perhaps 400, and then Bridges Street (1663), Dorset Garden (1671) and Drury Lane (1674), all larger and built from the ground up. It was touch and go financially for Restoration theatres, yet a remarkable number of good plays were written and produced in the space of some forty years. Side by side with new plays in Restoration London were regular revivals of old drama, including most of the best from Shakespeare's time. Doctored though many of them were, they worked effectively in small, roofed playhouses, before audiences they were not written for, and with scenic embellishments their authors never intended. To give them credit, Restoration managers set a pattern of attention to the drama of the past, and the tradition is still with us. At first they produced revivals because old plays were all that were available; they continued the habit because it pleased audiences and actors and was both good theatre and good business. There was also at the Restoration another novelty: actresses, for the first time in English public theatres, played the female roles, changing English drama forever. So much attention over the centuries has been given to the bawdiness of Restoration times that its importance as a period of reinvention and a transition from the old to the modern theatre is sometimes forgotten.

But we are in a pickle. No theatre from the period has survived, and we have only a few tantalizing scraps of evidence to help us: diaries, the observations of foreign visitors to Restoration playhouses, a little pictorial material, incomplete accounts and performance records, some promptbooks, and intriguing but sometimes baffling stage directions in plays written during the period. One of our sources is the diarist Samuel Pepys, an inveterate 1660s playgoer for whom the theatre was a mistress he was unable to resist. After eighteen years of Puritan suppression the theatres had to attract, in addition to the aristocracy, a new audience of middle-class, upwardly mobile types like Pepys, people who loved socializing and craved entertainment. But Pepys closed his *Diary* in 1669, before the best of Restoration drama was written. So this is shaky ground we're treading on, and we should proceed with caution. (Fortunately, there are several helpful guides to staging: Holland, Lewcock, Milhous and Hume, Muller, Muller-Van Santen, Powell, Rosenfeld, Southern, Styan, and Visser.) Our focus here will be on the features common to most of the Restoration playhouses: the scenic area and the working of scenes and machines; the forestage, where so much of the action in the best plays took place; and the auditorium, which was almost a performing space in itself.

The Scenic Area

The term scenic area is modern; Restoration playwrights in their stage directions often referred to the space behind the curtain line as the 'scene' – a word that can be misleading, since it was also used to designate a subdivision of an act in a play as well as the scenery itself. The scenic area and related spaces like offices, shops, rehearsal halls, dressing (tiring) rooms and a 'Green Room' (a lounge; called a 'Scene Room' in Pepys's day) occupied roughly half the building. Pepys made a backstage visit to the Bridges Street theatre in 1666, which should have told us all we wanted to know; he

> walked to the King's play-house, all in dirt, they being altering of the Stage to make it wider – but God knows when they will begin to act again. But my business here was to see the inside of the Stage and all the tiring roomes and Machines; and endeed it was a

sight worthy seeing. But to see their clothes and the various sorts, and what a mixture of things there was, here a wooden leg, there a ruff, here a hobby-horse, there a Crowne, would make a man split himself to see with laughing.... But then again, to think how fine they show on the stage by candle-light, and how poor things they are to look now too near-hand, is not pleasant at all. The Machines are fine, and the paintings very pretty. (19 March 1666)

Like many of our sources, Pepys left us dangling, but a few backstage tidbits are better than none. If he walked onto the stage at Bridges Street did he feel tipsy? He should have, for the floor was not level. Our terms upstage and downstage derive from the days when stages were raked – sloped gradually upward from front to back, conforming to the use of perspective in the scene painting.

If one goes backstage in a proscenium theatre of any vintage in any country – that is, a theatre with a picture-frame stage, like most Restoration and modern theatres – one finds behind the curtain an open space where scenery can be erected. In today's theatre a stage setting, representing a room, let's say, is usually like a box: painted flats forming three walls and the ceiling of the room, with one of the walls removed so we can sit out front and peep at the action. A typical setting is about 30 ft wide by 15 ft deep, and we view it through the proscenium arch (frontispiece), an opening roughly 30 ft wide and 15 ft high. During a performance we pretend that we are seeing real people in an actual room involved in a lifelike activity. In a Restoration theatre almost the same thing happened, for theatres then also had proscenium arches, scenic locales, an imaginary fourth wall and characters involved in dramatic situations. But Restoration scenery, though it might look like a box set from the auditorium (and in contemporary illustrations), was devised on an entirely different principle and used stage space in a very different way.

The locale – a room, forest, street, prison, battlefield, Heaven, Hell – would have been painted in perspective on a series of wings, shutters and borders. Wings were scenic flats or panels about 4 ft to 5 ft in width and of varying heights, three or four of them standing along each side of the acting area parallel to the curtain line, with open passageways between them. Shutters were a pair of wider flats butted together at the centre line of the stage, forming a back wall (backscene) part way upstage. Borders were horizontal scenic pieces stretching across the stage and suspended above each wing and shutter position. The three or four pairs of wings and their corresponding borders formed, as it were, a series of proscenia or picture frames, each successive set being smaller as one moved upstage, creating a perspective vista and at the same time masking the audience's view of the backstage area. The spaces between the sets of wings were for actor entrances and exits (in a forest scene, for example) or for catwalks hanging above the stage to give workers access to hanging scenery and flying devices. Properly painted in perspective to represent a room, such a setting looked for all the world like the real thing, just as a three-dimensional box set would – except this was painted on two-dimensional scenic pieces. It was all a trick, capable of deceiving audiences partly because of the painters' skill and partly because the scenery was lit only by candlelight, so its deceptions and imperfections could not be noticed from the auditorium. This setting made of wings, borders and shutters would not have been any wider or deeper than a box set, but it could do something the box could not: it could change in a twinkling.

Plays from the Restoration rarely confined the action to a single locale, for the English public theatre had long since thumbed its nose at the unities of time, place and action. Both old and new English plays regularly called for multiple locales, and when Restoration theatre managers committed themselves to using scenery in public theatre performances they had to provide for simple, swift changes. The system they adopted, common all over the Continent since the Renaissance and used earlier in the century in English court theatres, was simplicity itself. The wings and shutters just described slid onstage and off in grooves on the stage floor, with steadying grooves suspended from above. There were at least two complete sets of grooves, just an inch or so apart, at each wing and shutter position, so when one stage setting was slid offstage on each side, a second setting was revealed, already standing in the second grooves. When a third setting was required, the first would be pulled completely offstage, out of its grooves, and replaced by a third set.

The stage-floor grooves in which wings and shutters slid were either built up from the raked floor or cut down into it, and grooves for the shutters and for some of the wings ran almost the width of the stage. Some theatres, including perhaps Dorset Garden from our period, had slots in the stage floor instead of grooves; thrusting up through the floor and riding on wheeled carriages in the substage were ladders or poles, to which wings, shutters and other scenic units could be fixed. When the carriages were properly connected to a revolving cylinder, complete stage settings could be moved on and off mechanically.

Hanging above each wing and shutter position were two borders that could be raised or lowered, one for interior settings, showing a ceiling, and the other for exteriors, depicting the sky. If necessary, while a scene was being performed, stage-hands on catwalks could completely replace a set of borders. All these painted scenic units – wings, shutters and borders – were light, canvas-covered wooden frames about an inch thick. The borders may have been even simpler: unframed hanging cloths. A whistle signalled stagehands to move a complete setting on or off, and the change, almost always done in full view of the awed audience, would take about five seconds. It was such a marvellous scene-shifting system that it lasted until near the end of the nineteenth century, when three-dimensional stage settings became the fashion, and when, under bright new electric lighting, the old settings that depended so much on the painters' skill looked too much like painted scenery.

The diminishing height of the wings and shutters contributed to the sense of greater depth than a stage really had. Painters placed vanishing points in their designs well behind the back wall of the theatre, making the vista very gradual and allowing actors to work deep in the scenic area without distorting the stage picture. All this, in an age we do not associate with stage realism in the modern sense, was done to fool the audience into believing that what they were seeing was real, even though they knew all along, as we do, that theatre is a fiction for which we willingly suspend our disbelief – if the play and the performers can persuade us to do so.

The versatile wing-and-shutter system could also accommodate discovered scenes. If a stage direction in an old play says that the scene 'opens' or 'draws' or 'closes' or that a character is 'discovered in her chamber' or 'appears in bed', this did not require the lowering of the theatre's main curtain in order to set up a tableau. Instead, the shutters forming the back wall of a room setting, for example, would be drawn off to reveal a new locale in the 'inner' stage behind them. This new space was backed by yet another set of shutters – so that two discoveries in succession could be managed. Even Lincoln's Inn Fields theatre, built within the confines of a roofed tennis court, could have accommodated two such inner stages, each about 4 ft deep and 15 ft wide, towards the back of the scenic area. By the end of the 1600s theatres began using painted drops in place of or in addition to shutters. In narrow theatres shutters could not be used easily in the downstage part of the scenic area because of their width; they might hit the side wall of the building before they could be fully withdrawn from their grooves. Drops on rollers, on the other hand, could be suspended at any point along the depth of the stage, making it possible to create discovery spaces wherever they were needed.

Action could remain within such spaces or be moved downstage once the scene had begun and the locale had been established. Stage directions to 'Come forward' are sometimes placed after a page or so of dialogue, suggesting that the players were reluctant to remain too far upstage for too long. Action in the scenic area may have been about 20 to 30 ft from the nearest spectator, but the deeper reaches of the stage would surely not have been used at all if what was there could not be seen or heard.

We depend heavily on printed stage directions to help us reconstruct Restoration staging, but play texts may not always have been followed in performance, so one must read them warily. In the delightful letter-writing scenes in Wycherley's *The Country Wife* (1675, Drury Lane) the author seems to suggest that the bedchamber with the writing desk is discovered upstage, behind a pair of shutters that just drew open; if so, the fairly lengthy scenes would have been stuck there, for the desk is essential to the action. The King's Company may have decided that instead of a discovery, servants would, as directions in some plays show, simply bring the desk on as the scene changed, place it downstage, and come back to remove it when the scene was finished.

To handle various special effects, most stage floors had trap doors, large and small, some with ladders and others with rudimentary lifts. Stage directions in plays usually said only that a character or object 'rises' or 'disappears'; most playwrights left it to the stage technicians to decide which traps to use. Magical appearances might also be made by having an actor enter between the wings in an interior scene, thus seeming to walk through a side wall. Waves could be simulated by horizontal rotating or sliding pieces painted and shaped to resemble the sea.

More magical and daring than appearances from below or paintings of the ocean were flights above the stage. The simplest flying device was a rope running from offstage up to a pulley under the roof, across to another pulley above the stage, and down to a harness worn by an intrepid performer or a stand-in. Similarly, a platform with people on it, made to look like a chariot or masked with painted clouds, could be slung on ropes, also disguised as clouds, and lowered or raised. Foreign visitors to England were impressed with English scenes and machines. In his *Journal des voyages* in 1666 Balthasar de Monconys said, 'The scene changes and the machines are very ingeniously invented and executed' (26), almost as though the English were doing some things Continental technicians had not tried. From a performer's point of view, the scenic area was a treacherous part of the playhouse, full of things to trip over, get hung up on or fall into; for many of the paying customers it was a wonderland, the whole point of going to the theatre.

Presumably a seasoned author would not request a scenic effect that could not be handled by the theatre for which the play was written. Aphra Behn's successful farce *Emperor of the Moon* (1687, Dorset Garden) contains a sample of what playwrights sometimes asked for in works more dependent on spectacle than wit. Act 3 calls for a crane device that could move a flown object down and forward while opening like an umbrella, plus three other flying machines:

> [T]he Globe of the Moon appears, first, like a new Moon; as it moves forward it increases, till it comes to the Full. When it is descended, it opens, and shews the Emperor and the Prince. They come forth with all their Train, the Flutes playing a Symphony before him, which prepares the Song.... [*After the song*] A Chariot appears, made like a Half Moon, in which is *Cinthio* for the Emperor, richly dress'd and Charmante for the Prince, rich, with a good many Heroes attending. *Cinthio's* Train born by four Cupids. The Song continues while they descend and land. They address themselves to *Elaria* and *Bellemante*.... [*Later,*] A very Antick Dance. The Dance ended, the Front Scene draws off, and shows a Temple, with an Altar, one speaking through a Stentraphon [*speaking trumpet*] from behind it. Soft Musick plays the while. (63–4)

A page later, as if the stage were not crowded enough, '*two Chariots descend, one on one side above, and the other on the other side*' (65). The play concludes without any of the machines ascending, perhaps because there were not enough hands to move all the flying devices simultaneously. The models the English stage technicians could have used for such machinery were Nicola Sabbattini or Giacomo Torelli, both active on the Continent in the 1630s and 1640s (Hewitt 1958; Bjurström, 1962).

Extravagant technical demands have always been a challenge to stage technicians, who can usually figure out how the impossible can be accomplished. The genre of the day that depended most heavily on spectacular staging was the semi-opera, so called because the main characters were played by actors, not singers. Elkanah Settle's *The Virgin Prophetess; or, The Fate of Troy* (1701, Drury Lane) is loaded with wonderfully baffling specifics about scenery. Act 3, scene 2 is the Grecian Camp; after a few pages of dialogue

> The Scene opens and discovers *Paris* and *Helen* seated upon Thrones between the Scenes; &c. In the middle of the Scenes, and under the second Grand-Arch, a painted Curtain hangs down to the Ground, reaching upwards only thirteen Foot and the like width, the whole Prospect of the Roof of the Scenes being seen about Eleven Foot over it. —— Before this Curtain, upon two Rich Couches, lye two painted Cupids as big as the Life.

Then, after four lines spoken by Paris:

> Here a Symphony playes, and immediately the two Cupids start from their Couches, and flying up, take hold of the upper Corners of the Curtain and draw it up; two more Cupids of the same Bulk absconded [*hidden*] before behind the Couches rising with the Curtain at the two lower Corners.
>
> Here is discover'd a small set of Scenes, being 12 Foot high, and the like Breadth, consisting of three pair of Wings, and a flat Scene [*shutters*]; the Object being a Pallace of *Cupid*, with Blue Pillars, with Silver Bases and Capitals, hung round with Wreaths of Flowers, the inner Prospect terminating in Bowers, Fountains, &c.
>
> The Symphony still continuing, out of this set are drawn forth on each side, two more sets of Senes [*sic*] exactly Unison with the Inner set, the first set being no ways diminsht, and the whole three Prospectives now reaching to Twenty five Foot width. Here the Curtain advances [*rises*] yet higher, and discovers a fourth set of Scenes, over the middle set, in which Cupid sits in Glory; while from the sides of this set spring two Scenes, which cover the two outmost Pallaces. This Machine now filling the whole House, and reaching 24 Foot high, making so many Visto's [*vistas*] of Pallace-Work. (21–2)

Settle seems to be asking for sets of wings and shutters on at least two levels (as used earlier in the century by Inigo Jones in court masques), three vanishing points, and settings within settings, forming one large machine, revealed gradually by a rising curtain (Rosenfeld 1981: 47–8, 64–5). Exactly how it was all pulled off is anyone's guess. English stage machinists and designers, unlike their counterparts on the Continent, did not leave us detailed plans and explanations, perhaps because they wanted to keep their magical art a secret and not spoil the illusion by explaining it.

In addition to the elaborate spectacle described above, Settle also asked for song and dance, scenic transformations, transparencies, cut-out scenes, appearances from below the stage, the goddess Diana flying above, thunder, six white elephants (real? possibly; the eccentric Drury Lane manager had been negotiating for an elephant about this time), Heaven, Hell, Troy in all its splendour, Troy in flames and, to end it all, Helen's immolation. This production was puffed in the press for its technodazzle, delayed in production (because of staging problems?) and unable to draw the expected crowds. The unlucky manager Christopher Rich did not try anything like it again, though it must have seemed like a good idea at the time.

The scenic area, then, was the most elaborate and expensive performance space in a Restoration playhouse, even though many plays, including some of the best, did not exploit its capabilities. There seems to be a pattern in Restoration plays: the better the play, the fewer the stage directions involving technical theatre – as though the more accomplished playwrights, if they had a good play, did not want scenery to steal the scene.

The Forestage

The area between the curtain line and the front edge of the stage has been called the theatre, area, platform, proscenium (to indicate that it was before or in front of the scene) or apron. The modern term forestage avoids confusion and most accurately describes the space before the curtain in a Restoration theatre. The forestage provided actors, singers and dancers with a sizeable downstage, well-illuminated performance space, raked but free of grooves. It was a continuation of the scenic area yet separated from it by the imaginary curtain line, and though it was part of the auditorium, it was just as clearly an extension of the stage. It was a highly practical, versatile and purposely ambiguous space. Playwrights wanting to establish a locale but keep the action close to the audience could use the side walls of the forestage, with their entrance doors, instead of or in addition to the scenic area (Visser 1975: 59). When a locale was depicted by the scenery, the forestage was understood to be an extension of that place, and if the scene changed, the forestage became the new locale. When the curtain was down, the forestage was a neutral area, unless the speaker of a prologue or epilogue gave it a name. It was the actors' most useful and desirable performing space, though spectators could think of it as a piece of their part of the theatre. It served as a vital link between the audience and the performers, the auditorium and the stage, the playgoers and the play.

The forestage was a descendant, though altered, of the platform in public play-houses like the Globe and 'private' theatres like the Blackfriars, which was used by Shakespeare's company for winter performances. In 1660 the earliest of the Restoration playhouses, Vere Street, may have been patterned after the Blackfriars, for Vere Street is thought to have been set up in the Elizabethan/Jacobean manner with little or no scenery and with an acting platform perhaps 15 ft square thrusting into the audience's space, partly surrounded by spectators. Lincoln's Inn Fields in 1661 was equipped with wing-and-shutter scenery and, we think, had the first Restoration forestage: not a full thrust – for very few if any spectators would have had seats beside the stage – but a platform providing an acting space about 10 ft deep by 30 ft wide between the scenic area and the audience. Playwrights, players and patrons alike must have been satisfied with this acting area, for all three of the larger theatres, Bridges Street, Dorset Garden and Drury Lane, had sizeable forestages, measuring about 20 ft by 30 ft. Restoration actors thus had two different acting spaces, each with its own characteristics: the scenic area with its depth and sense of locale, and the forestage, a wide, open acting platform. Acting 'within the scene' must have been quite different from acting on the forestage: the first invited characters to use the scenery as an environment, while the second could divorce them from it, treating scenery as a decorative background.

We can only guess how performers used these two different performing spaces. *Hamlet*, considerably cut but not much altered, was a favourite of Pepys and many others when Thomas Betterton played the title part. The 'closet' scene with Hamlet and his mother could have been staged completely within a scenic representation of a chamber. No heavy properties would have been needed, though an illustration from Rowe's 1709 edition of Shakespeare shows a chair tipped over by Hamlet when he sees the Ghost; that piece of stage business was handed down to generations of actors during the eighteenth century. The picture has the Ghost within Gertrude's chamber; he may have entered between wing passageways, seeming to pass through the wall, and left through a scene door or the space between the first wings and the proscenium arch. Polonius could have hidden behind a curtain hanging at the first shutter position. A variant staging might have used the forestage for the Ghost and the scenic area for Hamlet and his mother. The Ghost could enter from a proscenium door, cross the forestage, and exit through an opposite door. The audience would see Hamlet and Gertrude upstage of the curtain line, in depth, as the Ghost moved across the forestage in a separate stage space, seen in width. Restoration playhouses provided players with interesting alternatives.

New Restoration productions normally began on the forestage, with a prologue to warm up the audience. The speaker(s) usually stepped before the curtain to establish a good rapport with the patrons, comment on topical matters, curry favour, plead for the poor playwright, or castigate spectators for their poor taste in playgoing and then beg them for their support. A paying customer willing to be criticized for his behaviour yet anxious to participate in the actor–audience undertaking that was to come obviously had an approach to theatre quite different from today's typical playgoer. The relationship back then between audience members and actors seems to have been like a family, and the actors must have understood just how far they could go before they upset their loved ones. At the conclusion of the prologue, the speaker(s) usually withdrew, the curtain was raised, the stage setting for the first act was revealed, and the performance began. The curtain would normally not fall until the end of the play unless a special tableau had to be set up behind it.

Primary access to the forestage was by permanent proscenium doors, at least one but more often two on each side of the stage, as Sir Christopher Wren's 1672–4 section drawing of a playhouse shows and as stage directions in plays confirm. (If a play seemed to call for three doors on each side, the actors could have used wing passageways or the space between the proscenium arch and the first wings.) In Wycherley's *The Country Wife* (1675, Drury Lane) the notorious 'china' scene must have been acted mostly on the forestage, with Quack behind a screen in the scenic area, observing Horner's success at playing musical doors. The forestage door assignments may have been:

Door #1, to outside Horner's lodgings.

Door #2, to Horner's chamber (lockable, on the opposite side of the stage from #1).

Door #3, to Horner's chamber the 'back way' (lockable, on the same side as #2).

Door #4, to another part of Horner's lodgings (on the same side as #1).

The doors were near the spectators, so people could follow the twists and turns of the action, and that same closeness was helpful for many of the asides delivered directly to the audience throughout the play.

Witty repartee in such plays as *The Country Wife* would have found in the forestage a perfect delivery platform. Actors could get as close to the audience as they wished, establishing whatever character–audience relationship was appropriate. The forestage must also have been ideal for the stage movements and gestures the players used, which, judging by manuals of the period, were probably what we would consider formal, conventional, dance-like – a series of changing configurations. Just as the scene-shifting system and technical capabilities of most of the Restoration playhouses invited the composition of spectacle plays, the forestage must have encouraged the kind of drama Wycherley, Etherege and Congreve wrote. The playwrights and the playhouses were made for each other – until the profit motive raised its ugly head.

Colley Cibber, who began his acting career at Drury Lane in 1690 and went on to be successful in management there, loved the forestage as an acting space because of its closeness to the audience. When he wrote an *Apology* for his life in 1740 he lamented the 1696 decision of the manager Christopher Rich, who, to seat more paying customers, cut back the forestage and replaced the lower doors on each side with boxes for aristocratic patrons. According to Cibber, the actors lost almost half the forestage.

> [W]hen the Actors were in Possession of that forwarder Space to advance upon, the Voice was then more in the Centre of the House, so that the most distant Ear had scarce the least Doubt or Difficulty in hearing what fell from the weakest Utterance: All Objects were thus drawn nearer to the Sense; every painted Scene was stronger; every Grand Scene and Dance more extended; every rich or fine-coloured Habit had a more lively Lustre: Nor was the minutest Motion of a Feature (properly changing with the Passion, or Humour it suited) ever lost, as they frequently must be in the Obscurity of too great a Distance: And how valuable an Advantage the Facility of hearing distinctly is to every well-acted Scene, every common Spectator is a Judge. A Voice scarce rais'd above the Tone of a Whisper, either in Tenderness, Resignation, innocent Distress, or Jealousy suppress'd, often have as much concern with the Heart as the most clamorous Passions; and when on any of these Occasions, such affecting Speeches are plainly heard, or lost, how wide is the Difference, from the great or little Satisfaction received from them? (Cibber 1889, 2: 84–6)

Windy Cibber exaggerated perhaps, and he couldn't refrain from delivering a lecture on acting, but he was justly concerned. The new stage boxes forced the players upstage, so they wouldn't seem impolite to the new stage-box patrons to their left and right. A sizeable strip of very important acting space had to be left unused. The players did not object to having physical distance placed between themselves and their spectators; that happened whenever they acted within the scenic area, and actors were used to it. But they did not want a gulf between themselves and their audience when they moved out onto the forestage. The actors had previously been able to go right up to the edge of the stage, close to their spectators and just where they wanted to be for asides and soliloquies. Money-minded Rich now denied them that. Further, the loss of two of the downstage proscenium doors meant that the staging of plays like *The Country Wife* had to be changed, with some entrances, exits and stage business forced willy-nilly into the scenic area.

Closely related to the forestage and its doors were the acting areas looking down on it, the lights illuminating it and the musicians posted near it. Above the proscenium doors on each side were acting spaces that could also serve for seating. References in stage directions to characters appearing 'above' or in windows were usually to these areas. Practical windows could have been built into scenic wings, but the permanent forestage features would have been safer for stage business involving ladders, climbing or jumping. Evidence in stage directions suggests that at Bridges Street the acting areas above the doors may have been windows indeed, while those at Drury Lane were balconies. As with many of the traditional physical features of these old playhouses, no two buildings would have been exactly alike.

Like moths drawn to a flame, performers must have been attracted to the forestage, not only because it was a splendid uncluttered acting space, but because that was where the best illumination was from chandeliers and footlights. As far as can be estimated, the amount of light a stage had back then was the equivalent of a 75 or perhaps 100 watt lamp (Mullin 1980: 74). That does not seem like nearly enough light for anyone to see by, but we are dealing here with people who regularly lived and worked under such conditions. The theatre lighting was sufficient for them. Hanging above the forestage were at least two chandeliers; similar fixtures were suspended from the ceiling of the auditorium, spilling some of their light onto the forestage, and there were sconces along the sides and back of the house, between the boxes, to augment the illumination from the chandeliers. Since performances were in the afternoons, daylight coming through the building's windows must also have helped. Onstage, in the scenic area, in addition to more chandeliers, candles with reflectors could be placed behind the wings, throwing light towards the centre of the stage. Though ways had been discovered to dim lights somewhat (lowering perforated canisters over flames or partially covering a footlight trough), dimming as we understand it was not possible; consequently, when a playwright called for a night scene, the audience settled, as in Shakespeare's time, for a character carrying a light of some sort, indicating darkness. But what should we make of stage directions in plays calling for the stage to be completely darkened? Candles and reflectors used behind the wings could have been rotated, throwing the light away from the acting area, and perhaps shields of some kind were lowered over some or all of the candles in the chandeliers above the scenic area if not the forestage as well. Even a partial darkening probably seemed startling to the spectators. This was, after all, an audience that accepted the convention of chandeliers hanging in the middle of a forest. More importantly, if they wanted to believe the stage was dark, it was. They were not as sophisticated as we are.

Music was an essential part of Restoration theatregoing. Musicians played before the show, during some intervals, and within acts as accompaniment for singers and dancers. Machine plays often had extensive musical sections, and works like Dryden's *Albion and Albanius* (1685, Dorset Garden) were proper operas, sung throughout. In the 1660s Pepys wallowed in theatre music, became an amateur musician because of it, and made friends with some of the best musicians of his day. Drawn to the theatres were the best English composers of the time, including, near the end of the century, Henry Purcell. Theatre managers, however, had trouble finding a place to put the band of instrumentalists. At Vere Street they seem to have been in an upper side box near the stage; at Lincoln's Inn Fields they may have been above the proscenium arch or over a forestage entrance door. Killigrew, according to Pepys on 8 May 1663, tried placing the musicians 'below' at Bridges Street – apparently in front of and partly under the stage, much to Pepys's displeasure, because the sound was distorted. At Dorset Garden, judging from illustrations in Settle's *The Empress of Morocco* (1673, Dorset Garden), the musicians had a home above the proscenium arch, a position similar to the music room in Elizabethan playhouses, though for *The Tempest* (1674, Dorset Garden) the band of more than twenty-four instrumentalists was placed in front of and below the forestage (Price 1979: 85).

The forestage, then, was at the heart of Restoration theatres. Its doors were crucial for most important entrances, exits and stage business associated with them; the illumination of the forestage drew the players to it; the musicians, wherever they were placed, were as close to the forestage as the managers could get them; and the acting area of choice for the players and playgoers was that valuable piece of stage real estate between the audience and the curtain line. Colley Cibber sensed that the forestage, because of its closeness to the audience and its appearance as part of the auditorium, was an invaluable part of the actor's character–audience relationship. He felt that anything that forced performers to retreat from their audience would damage a very precious bond actors wanted with their patrons. *Their* audience might become merely *the* audience.

The Auditorium

The 'house' in theatres of the post-1660 period had some common features that varied chiefly in size and shape from theatre to theatre. The audience occupied a cube roughly the same size as the cube encompassing the stage and backstage. There were normally three seating areas: pit, boxes and galleries, each designed for different social classes, with separate entrances and variant prices. The pit, what today we call the orchestra or stalls, had backless benches, placed rather too close together for real comfort when the house was full. Wrapping around the pit on three sides and forming a U, horseshoe or semi-circle, like a modern opera house but smaller, were one or two levels of boxes. These seated as many as twenty people each, with low partitions separating groups of patrons without cutting off their view of the stage. From the relatively few boxes on each side of the pit one could not see the stage fully, but the view of fellow patrons was excellent, which satisfied most people who chose to sit there. Above the tier(s) of boxes were one or two levels of open galleries, again wrapping around the pit and leaving some side seats with poor sightlines. However, seats for most of the spectators, the 'main audience', as Cibber called them, were laid out in a fan shape, with good views of the stage (Leacroft 1973: 89–99). The most distant spectators in the largest houses were probably only 60 ft to 70 ft from the stage. By comparison with the rebuilt Drury Lane theatre of 1794, which could accommodate a crowd of 3,600, Restoration playhouses were very cosy indeed.

The playgoers after the Restoration were not predominantly debauched aristocrats, as was supposed by Victorian critics who thought most of the plays of the time had no redeeming social value and could therefore not have been written for proper people. The great variety in the plays produced suggests an audience almost as mixed as that in Shakespeare's day, and Pepys found at the theatre many of the middle class like himself plus a growing number of 'citizens', 'prentices and servants, including some of his own, who came to performances with him. There were also courtiers and, often, the king and his entourage, but the upper classes seem to have made up a relatively small percentage of the audience; they were, however, a gorgeous lot to behold and understandably, when they attended, appeared to dominate the audience. Towards the end of the century, with royalty less addicted to theatregoing, the audience was less aristocratic. The anonymous satirical *Country Gentleman's Vade Mecum* in 1699 portrays a theatre attendance very like that recorded by Pepys decades earlier: the galleries full of citizens and their families plus servants, journeymen and apprentices; the pit peopled by 'judges, wits and censurers' along with 'squires, sharpers, beaus, bullies and whores', and the boxes decorated with 'persons of quality' (38–9).

There were important differences between Shakespearean and Restoration audiences, however, and they concerned the 'groundlings' to whom Hamlet refers. In the early theatres this lively class of playgoers, paying a penny to stand in the pit, were in the very midst of things and obvious to all; by Restoration times the cheapest places were moved to above and behind the occupants of the pit and boxes, almost out of sight if not out of mind or earshot. They paid a shilling for an upper-gallery seat, a price needed by the managers to cover production costs (especially for scenery, stagehands and lighting) but too high for poor folk. And so it remains today; the groundlings watch movies and television, and live theatre is thought of as for the elite. The Restoration redistribution of the audience space was the birth of auditoria as we now know them. Shakespeare would not understand.

Foreign visitors were both impressed and put off by London theatres. Most spent more time chiding the English for faulty playwriting than telling us what stage performances were like. But Samuel Chappuzeau in *L'Europe vivante* (1667) was quite taken with the music, dance, scenery, machinery and, of all things, the lighting: the

English troupes thought it a crime, he wrote, 'to use anything other than wax-light to illuminate the theatre or to fill the chandeliers with a material that might offend the sense of smell' (trans. Carole Hodgson, 215). When Cosimo III of Tuscany visited Lincoln's Inn Fields theatre (not Bridges Street, as was once thought) on 15 April 1669, one of his entourage, Lorenzo Magalotti, took notes. The pit was

> surrounded within by separate compartments in which there are several degrees [steps] of seating for the greater comfort of the ladies and gentlemen who, according to the liberal custom of the country, share the same boxes. Down below [in the pit] there remains a broad space for other members of the audience. The scenery is entirely changeable, with various transformations and lovely perspectives. Before the play begins, to render the waiting less annoying and inconvenient, there are very graceful instrumental pieces to be heard, with the result that many go early just to enjoy this part of the entertainment. (Orrell 1980: 6)

Henri Misson in his *Memoirs* in 1698 was struck by the lively behaviour of the pit patrons: 'Men of Quality, particularly the younger Sort, some Ladies of Reputation and Vertue, and abundance of Damsels that hunt for Prey, sit all together in this Place, Higgledy-piggledy, chatter, toy, play, hear, hear not' (1719, trans. Ozell, 219).

Back in the 1660s Pepys had regularly reported similar audience conduct. At one performance, of Beaumont and Fletcher's *The Maid's Tragedy* at the Bridges Street theatre on 18 February 1667, the diarist became so enthralled with Sir Charles Sedley's bantering with a masked lady that Pepys 'lost the pleasure of the play wholly, to which now and then Sir Ch. Sidlys exceptions against both words and pronouncing were very pretty'. Shadwell's *A True Widow* (1678, Dorset Garden) has a scene that takes place in a theatre, with audience members behaving obstreperously before and during a performance. Throughout the Restoration period there seems to have been (regularly? occasionally?) a show going on in the audience, as at a sports event. For many people, theatregoing was a social occasion: they could talk to friends, meet new people, criticize the play, make assignations, follow the plot, lose interest, get caught up, turn away, turn back, come, go, hear, hear not. It was all part of their afternoon at the theatre.

For the acting companies, playing to such spectators was a formidable challenge. Common sense would dictate that they should not present plays that had characters speaking directly to the audience, for surely that would encourage the audience to talk back. Yet Restoration plays, following the Shakespearean tradition, invited audience participation; direct address was written into most of them. There must have been a tacit agreement, sometimes broken, that spectators would enjoy the theatrical experience without disrupting it. For their part, Restoration actors had to keep audiences involved but at arm's length. When spectators got caught up in a performance, when their participation was not disruptive but supportive, then their reactions – such as applause or cheers after a well-delivered line – became an important part of the entertainment (Powell 1984: 14–19).

We play it safe. In a modern theatre, we dim the house lights, and customers quiet down, set their sights on the only thing they can now easily see, the stage, and become Peeping Toms. In Restoration days dimming the house was not possible, and no matter how carefully actors tried to control a performance, the playgoers could at any time tip the delicate balance.

What could capture such lively audiences? Scenic splendour, elaborate costumes and spectacular scenic effects often did. Titillating new plays that often satirized their own audiences also did, as did many old plays, retooled for the new playgoers. And it certainly would have taken strong, controlled, larger-than-life acting. Thomas Betterton, Pepys's favourite actor, had that power and magnetism, and he and his colleagues seem to have been capable, most of the time, of galvanizing the spectators into attention. When Pepys saw *Hamlet* on 31 August 1668 at Lincoln's Inn Fields he confessed to his diary that he was 'mightily pleased with it; but above all, with Batterton [*sic*], the best part, I believe, that ever man acted'. The anonymous *Laureat* in 1740 described the actor/character in detail:

> I have lately been told by a Gentleman who has frequently seen Mr *Betterton* perform this Part of *Hamlet*, that he has observ'd his Countenance (which was naturally ruddy and sanguin) in this Scene of the fourth Act, where his Father's Ghost appears, thro' the violent and sudden Emotions of Amazement and Horror, turn instantly on the Sight of his Father's Spirit, as pale as his Neckcloath, when every Article of his Body seem'd to be affected with a Tremor inexpressible; so that had his Father's Ghost actually risen before him[,] he could not have been seized with more real Agonies; and this was felt so strongly by the Audience, that the Blood seemed to shudder in their Veins likewise, and they in some Measure partook of the Astonishment and Horror, with which they saw this excellent Actor affected. And when *Hamlet* utters this Line, upon the Ghost's leaving the Stage, (in Answer to his Mother's impatient Enquiry into the Occasion of his Disorder, and what he sees) – *See – where he goes – ev'n now – out at the Portal*: The whole Audience hath remain'd in a dead Silence for near a Minute, and then – as if recovering all at once from their Astonishment, have joined as one Man, in a thunder of universal Applause. (31)

If that was the kind of acting Restoration theatres inspired, what an experience it must have been for playgoers. It is little wonder that Samuel Pepys could not stay away.

REFERENCES AND FURTHER READING

Bjurström, Per (1962). *Giacomo Torelli and Baroque Stage Design*. Stockholm: Almqvist and Wiksell.

Cibber, Colley (1740; 1889). *An Apology for the Life of Mr. Colley Cibber*, ed. Robert W. Lowe. 2 vols. London: Nimmo.

Hewitt, Barnard (ed.). (1958). *The Renaissance Stage: Documents of Serlio, Sabbattini and Furttenbach*. Coral Gables, FL: University of Miami Press.

Holland, Peter (1979). *The Ornament of Action: Text and Performance in Restoration Comedy*. Cambridge: Cambridge University Press.

Hume, Robert D. (1979). 'The Dorset Garden Theatre: A Review of Facts and Problems', *Theatre Notebook* 33, 4–17.

Hume, Robert D. (ed.). (1980). *The London Theatre World, 1660–1800*. Carbondale: Southern Illinois University Press.

Kenny, Shirley Strum (ed.). (1984). *British Theatre and the Other Arts, 1660–1800*. Washington: Folger Books.

Langhans, Edward A. (1981). *Restoration Promptbooks*. Carbondale: Southern Illinois University Press.

Langhans, Edward A. (1982). 'Conjectural Reconstructions of the Vere Street and Lincoln's Inn Fields Theatres', *Essays in Theatre* 1, 14–28.

Leacroft, Richard (1973). *The Development of the English Playhouse*. London: Eyre Methuen.

Lewcock, Dawn (1993–4). 'Computer Analysis of Restoration Staging', *Theatre Notebook* 47, 20–9 and 141–56; 48, 103–15.

Love, Harold (1980). 'Who Were the Restoration Audience?', *Yearbook of English Studies* 10, 21–44.

Milhous, Judith and Hume, Robert D. (1985). *Producible Interpretation: Eight English Plays 1675–1707*. Carbondale: Southern Illinois University Press.

Muller, Frans (1993). 'Flying Dragons and Dancing Chairs at Dorset Garden: Staging *Dioclesian*', *Theatre Notebook* 47, 80–95.

Muller-Van Santen, Julia Johanna Gertrud (1989). *Producing The Prophetess or The History of Dioclesian*. Amsterdam: University of Amsterdam.

Mullin, Donald (1980). 'Lighting on the Eighteenth-century London Stage: A Reconsideration', *Theatre Notebook* 34, 73–85.

Nicoll, Allardyce (1961). *A History of English Drama, 1660–1900. Vol. I: Restoration Drama, 1660–1700*. 4th ed. Cambridge: Cambridge University Press.

Orrell, John (1980). 'Filippo Corsini and the Restoration Theatre', *Theatre Notebook* 34, 4–9.

Pepys, Samuel (1970–83). *The Diary of Samuel Pepys*, ed. Robert Latham and William Matthews. 11 vols. Berkeley: University of California Press.

Powell, Jocelyn (1984). *Restoration Theatre Production*. London: Routledge and Kegan Paul.

Price, Curtis A. (1979). *Music in the Restoration Theatre*. Ann Arbor, MI: UMI Research Press.

Rosenfeld, Sybil (1981). *Georgian Scene Painters and Scene Painting*. Cambridge: Cambridge University Press.

Sheppard, F. H. W. (ed.). (1970). *Survey of London. Vol. 35: The Theatre Royal Drury Lane and the Royal Opera House Covent Garden*. London: Athlone Press.

Southern, Richard (1952). *Changeable Scenery*. London: Faber and Faber.

Styan, J. L. (1986). *Restoration Comedy in Performance*. Cambridge: Cambridge University Press.

Van Lennep, William (ed.). (1965). *The London Stage, 1660–1800*. Part I: *1660–1700*, ed. Emmett L. Avery and Arthur H. Scouten. Carbondale: Southern Illinois University Press.

Visser, Colin (1975). 'The Anatomy of the Early Restoration Stage: *The Adventures of Five Hours* and John Dryden's "Spanish" Comedies', *Theatre Notebook* 29, 56–69 and 114–19.

2
Restoration Dramatic Theory and Criticism
Paul D. Cannan

In the introduction to his still-useful edition of John Dryden's critical essays, George Watson warns his reader, 'Dryden's literary criticism must look odd to most who approach it for the first time' (v). Knowing that Samuel Johnson dubbed Dryden 'the father of English criticism', we expect the work of a pioneering genius. What we find, however, is a surprisingly cautious writer, who struggled through a series of now seemingly trivial debates while also attempting to humour the whims of a fickle audience. Dryden's 'oddities' are only manifested more clearly in the dramatic criticism of his contemporaries. Alexander Pope announced in *An Essay on Criticism* (1711) and the *Dunciad* (1728, revised 1742 and 1743) that the other major critics of the period – Thomas Rymer, John Dennis and Charles Gildon – were beneath contempt. The prevailing attitude towards late seventeenth-century dramatic critics and criticism has changed little since Pope's day. René Wellek, for example, begins his monumental *History of Modern Criticism circa* 1750, curtly dismissing earlier criticism as rudimentary and of little more than 'antiquarian' interest. Anyone who reads only snippets of late seventeenth-century dramatic criticism found in literary anthologies will almost certainly arrive at the same conclusion. The arcane debates these writers engaged in – is rhyme or blank verse more appropriate in serious drama? is the comedy of wit superior to the Jonsonian comedy of humours? – mean little to the modern reader, nor do they really help us understand the drama any better.

So why is late seventeenth-century English dramatic criticism important to the student of Restoration drama? First, this period marks the origin of literary criticism in England. Until well past 1700, an identifiable discipline of criticism simply did not exist: what criticism was, who should practise it and why it was worth practising were all contested questions. Part of the reason these critics seem to flounder so much is because they are searching for a critical voice. Determining how English criticism develops its own distinctive style and approach is essential to understanding the history of criticism to the present day. Second, underlying the critical debates of this period are questions that still have currency today. Should criticism be essentially

judicial? personal? scientific? historical? What is the connection between critical
theory and practice? Why do we need criticism, anyway? The purpose of this chapter
is to offer a roughly chronological account of the major debates the principal critics of
the period engaged in, while also identifying the more complex (and sometimes
surprisingly modern) issues surrounding them. Finally, at its best, this criticism can
be entertaining and even fun. Almost every critic writing during this period was
trying to make criticism accessible and appealing to a broad audience. Students who
take the time to read, in their entirety, Dryden's *An Essay of Dramatick Poesie* (1668),
The Rehearsal (1672), Rymer's *A Short View of Tragedy* (1693) and Jeremy Collier's *A
Short View of the Immorality and Profaneness of the English Stage* (1698) will be rewarded
with both a better understanding of late seventeenth-century dramatic theory and a
keener appreciation for English wit.

Any history of late seventeenth-century dramatic criticism must focus on the
achievements of John Dryden, while also recognizing the problems inherent in
doing so. Dryden has long been recognized as the most important critic of the period.
Indeed, his criticism is so clearly different in content and tone than anything
preceding it, critics since Samuel Johnson have honoured Dryden as their 'father'.
According to Johnson, Dryden was 'the writer who first taught us to determine upon
principles the merit of composition'. Even a cursory examination of Dryden's criticism
seems to substantiate this claim: Dryden frequently gave his readers critical tools –
borrowed from Aristotle, contemporary French critics, et al. – and showed his readers
how to *apply* these tools to the texts they read. But modern scholars have also often
exaggerated Dryden's influence at the expense of other, equally important critics
writing during this period. Dramatic criticism did not, of course, magically appear
after 1660 and Dryden was not the first person to write it. Earlier playwrights, most
notably Ben Jonson, addressed critical concerns in their play prefaces. Dryden's
criticism is also highly derivative. *An Essay of Dramatick Poesie* – his critical centre-
piece – is heavily indebted to Continental critics (particularly Pierre Corneille) and
contemporary literary debates. Dryden himself admitted in 'A Defence of an Essay of
Dramatique Poesie' prefaced to the second edition of *The Indian Emperour* (1668) that
the *Essay* 'is a little Discourse in Dialogue, for the most part borrowed from the
observations of others' (*Works* 9: 4). Similarly, 'The Grounds of Criticism in Tragedy'
prefixed to *Troilus and Cressida* (1679), Dryden's only other excursion into theoretical
criticism, is predominantly a redaction of the works of two influential contemporary
French critics, Jean Racine and René Le Bossu. As Johnson admits, much of Dryden's
criticism is also written primarily for the purposes of self-interest and self-promotion.
And Dryden is not really the appreciative critic Johnson wants him to be. Despite his
efforts to educate his audience, Dryden is more often a legislative critic, typically
more concerned with telling dramatists how to write plays than helping readers
discern the beauties of a text.

Dryden's criticism is also often unique. *An Essay of Dramatick Poesie* – generally
regarded by modern scholars as Dryden's most ambitious and important critical work
– is an anomaly of late seventeenth-century criticism. Indeed, in terms of content,

format and audience, there is nothing quite like it in the history of English dramatic criticism. Dryden composed this essay very early in his career, probably between the summer of 1665 and the autumn of 1666, while the theatres were closed on account of the plague. In it, he uses a conversation between four wits – Eugenius, Crites, Lisideius and Neander (typically but not always identified as, respectively: Charles Sackville, Lord Buckhurst; Sir Robert Howard; Sir Charles Sedley; and Dryden himself) – to explore three major critical controversies. After settling on the definition of a play as 'A just and lively Image of Humane Nature, representing its Passions and Humours, and the Changes of Fortune to which it is subject; for the Delight and Instruction of Mankind' (*Works* 17: 15), Crites and Eugenius argue over the dramatic practice of the ancients (primarily their adherence to the unities of time, place and action), Lisideius and Neander debate over 'whether we ought not to submit our Stage to the exactness of our next Neighbours [i.e., the French]' (*Works* 17: 33), and Crites and Neander spar over the limitations and virtues of rhyme in serious drama. For the student of late seventeenth-century criticism, this is an entertaining introduction to the literary debates of the period. Unfortunately, the modern reader will also be frustrated with the pedantry of the debates and the simplicity of the criticism. One modern scholar has even likened Dryden's detailed 'examen' – or critical analysis – of Jonson's *The Silent Woman* to a passable undergraduate essay. But the different critical issues that Dryden addresses do add up to more sophisticated arguments about the elevated mimesis required of dramatic representations (what Dryden calls 'Nature wrought up to an higher pitch' [*Works* 17: 74]) and literary history (particularly the relevance of Shakespeare, Jonson and Fletcher to contemporary dramatists). Perhaps the most interesting (albeit unanswerable) question raised by the *Essay* is what Dryden expected his audience to *do* with it. While the *Essay* sparked a number of debates (detailed below), it appears to have had little impact on dramatic practice or on how criticism was written. Accordingly, we need to acknowledge Dryden's unquestionable importance and impact, while also recognizing that he was not the *only* critical model available.

Much of the criticism Dryden produced in the 1660s and 1670s *is*, however, seminal in that it defines the subject matter, tone and rhetoric of a significant amount of the dramatic criticism written during the period. Dryden is largely responsible for popularizing in England the use of prefatory matter (i.e., extraliterary apparatus, such as dedications and prefaces) as a site for literary criticism. Very few book-length works of criticism were written in England in the late seventeenth century: Rymer's *The Tragedies of the Last Age* (1677) is really the first, original, *book* of English dramatic criticism. Rather, criticism typically appears in shorter – and more occasional – print formats, such as play prefaces and dedicatory epistles, prologues, epilogues, pamphlets, etc. Dryden wrote more prefatory criticism than any of his contemporaries, and, in doing so, set one standard for this genre of criticism. Dryden's prefatory rhetoric is characterized by its authoritative voice and emphasis on dictating artistic choices and anticipating objections. For example, in his first critical essay – 'To Roger, Earl of Orrery' prefixed to *The Rival Ladies* (1664), his first printed play – Dryden begins formulaically by writing a panegyric to Roger Boyle, Earl of Orrery, his social and artistic superior. But after heaping lavish praise on Orrery, Dryden turns, almost abruptly, to a detailed discussion of his own immediate critical concern – the advantages of rhyme over blank verse in serious drama. Four years later, with the publication of *Secret Love* (1668), Dryden felt sufficiently well established to offer his play to the public without a dedication, and in the preface exhibits even more confidence by justifying his role as poet-critic and countering objections to the play.

In the 1670s, Dryden continues this trend in his prefatory criticism by both brazenly challenging assaults on his artistic integrity and appending to his play texts lengthy and learned essays on genre, dramatic history and technique. In the preface to *An Evening's Love* (1671), Dryden detailed his theory of comedy; and 'Of Heroique Playes' and 'Defence of the Epilogue: or An Essay on the Dramatique Poetry of the Last Age', both attached to *The Conquest of Granada* (1672), addressed, respectively, his theory of serious drama and the inferiority of Elizabethan and Jacobean playwrights as literary models. If Dryden's prefatory pronouncements are scarcer after his comments on tragicomedy and audience taste in the dedication to *The Spanish Fryar* (1681), his authorial presence in them remains prominent. Even in the dedicatory epistle to his last play, *Love Triumphant* (1694), he admittedly digresses from his praise of James Cecil, fourth Earl of Salisbury, to address authorial concerns of composition and interpretation. While no other late seventeenth-century play-wright matched the output or assertive tone of Dryden's prefatory pronouncements, his influence is nevertheless clearly identifiable in the critical dedications and prefaces of important writers such as Aphra Behn, Nahum Tate, Thomas Southerne and William Congreve.

Dryden's use of prefatory matter as a high-profile platform for his artistic and critical agendas encouraged other writers to answer and attack him in their own play dedications and prefaces. Two famous, early examples of the use of prefatory matter as a battleground for literary controversies are Dryden's skirmishes with Robert Howard on serious drama and Thomas Shadwell on comic theory. Dryden and Howard had a close personal and working relationship: they became brothers-in-law in 1663, collaborated on *The Indian Queen* (first recorded performance 25 January 1664), and Dryden dedicated *Annus Mirabilis* to Howard in 1667. Yet the two writers clashed several times in the 1660s – often heatedly – over the appropriateness of rhyme in serious drama, the superiority of the ancients versus the moderns, and the usefulness of the Aristotelian unities in modern drama. Dryden instigated the debate in the dedication to *The Rival Ladies*; Howard replied in 'To the Reader' prefixed to *Four New Plays* (1665). Dryden continued the debate in *An Essay of Dramatick Poesie*, where he simulated (and cleverly manipulated) the controversy in the characters of Crites (Howard) and Neander (Dryden). Howard's angry reply in the preface to *The Duke of Lerma* (1668) was, in turn, answered by Dryden's very lengthy and mean-spirited last word in 'Defence of an Essay'.

The student of late seventeenth-century English criticism need only read Dryden's *Essay* to get the gist of the controversy. But the debate as a whole retains interest for the modern reader because both Dryden's and Howard's essays implicitly investigate a critical question that still retains currency today – who has interpretive control of the text? In contrast to Dryden, who believed that the audience should be familiar with the dramatist's art in order to understand a play properly, Howard argued that the audience is inevitably in control. In his epistle to *The Duke of Lerma*, Howard denounces Dryden's magisterial notions of authorship, particularly his dictating rules of composition in his prefatory matter in order to influence audience response: 'who ever wou'd endeavour to like or dislike by the Rules of others, he will be as unsuccessful as if he should try to be perswaded into a power of believing, not what he must, but what others direct him to believe' (Spingarn 1968, 2: 106–7). In fact, Howard believed so strongly in the interpretive control of the audience that he suggested the author cannot even assert the genre of a work: 'for in the difference of *Tragedy* and *Comedy*, and of [farce] it self, there can be no determination but by the Taste' (2: 106). Regardless of whether or not Howard was entirely serious, even the suggestion that genre might be open to interpretation represents a position Dryden could never accept. While Howard was not opposed to authorial presence in prefatory matter, he clearly believed that the author should never attempt to usurp interpretive rights, which always belong to the audience. In a sense, then, Howard is an early champion of reader-response theory.

Dryden's authoritarianism was also attacked in his high-profile prefatory skirmish with Shadwell over the form and function of English comedy – specifically, the superiority of the comedy of wit versus the Jonsonian comedy of humours. The source of the confrontation was Dryden's assertion in *An Essay of Dramatick Poesie* that Jonson was 'frugal' with wit, and that his wit falls short of Shakespeare and Beaumont and Fletcher. Dryden was not attacking Jonson here; indeed, he was using Jonson's example to argue for the superiority of English drama over the French, painstakingly demonstrated in the 'examen' of *The Silent Woman*. Similarly, Dryden claimed that in Jonson's dramatic criticism, 'we have as many and profitable Rules for perfecting the Stage as any wherewith the *French* can furnish us' (*Works* 17: 58). But Shadwell clearly took these comments as an affront to Jonson and his own dramatic practice, and as shameless self-promotion of Dryden's comedy of wit. In the preface to *The Sullen Lovers* (1668), Shadwell identified the failings of Dryden's comic theory by charging that he emphasizes wit at the expense of character:

> I have known some of late so Insolent to say that *Ben Johnson* wrote his best *Playes* without Wit, – imagining that all the Wit in Playes consisted in bringing two persons upon the Stage to break Jests, and to bob one another, which they call Repartie, not considering that there is more wit and invention requir'd in the finding out good Humor, and Matter proper for it, then in all their smart reparties. (Spingarn 1968, 2: 150)

Dryden replied in the preface to *An Evening's Love* by clarifying what he meant by 'wit' – which he defines as 'the sharpness of conceit' – and asserting once again that Jonson lacked it. In the preface to *The Humorists* (1671), Shadwell answered Dryden's preface by offering his most detailed account of his theory of humours. Responding to Dryden's claim that 'the chief end of [comedy] is divertisement and delight' (*Works* 10: 209), Shadwell expanded his argument to include the moral function of comedy. While Dryden asserted that comedy could not be as morally instructive as tragedy, Shadwell championed the more universal corrective powers of the comedy of humours,

> because the Vices and Follies in *Courts*, as they are two tender to be touch'd, so they concern but a few, whereas the Cheats, Villanies, and troublesome Follies in the common conversation of the World are of concernment to all the Body of Mankind. (Spingarn 1968, 2: 154)

Shadwell dropped out of the debate with *The Humorists*. In fact, in the dedication to *The Miser* (1672), he claims, 'I have resolved to take my leave of long Prefaces' – a promise he essentially kept. But Dryden explored many of the issues raised in the preface to *An Evening's Love* in more detail in the 'Defence of the Epilogue'. As the title suggests, the essay was written in response to criticisms of Dryden's controversial epilogue to Part II of *The Conquest of Granada*, where he dismissed the 'coarse' language of his Elizabethan and Jacobean predecessors for the refined tongue of the present day: 'Wit's now ariv'd to a more high degree; / Our native Language more refin'd and free. / Our Ladies and our men now speak more wit / In conversation, than those Poets writ' (*Works* 11: 201). But this essay was also the fulfillment of a promise he made in the preface to *An Evening's Love* to examine 'the difference betwixt the Plays of our Age, and those of our Predecessors on the English Stage' (*Works* 10: 202). As in his debate with Shadwell, Dryden cannot resist taking potshots at Jonson. A significant portion of the 'Defence of the Epilogue' is devoted to showcasing Jonson's egregious stylistic and grammatical errors in *Catiline*. (Incidentally, during this dissection of Jonson's play, Dryden introduces the grammatical 'myth' that a preposition is not something one should end a sentence with.) But the 'Defence' concludes with important comments on how contemporary dramatists should use the models of Shakespeare, Fletcher and Jonson. For example, with regard to Shakespeare, Dryden suggests: 'Let us therefore admire the beauties and the heights of *Shakespear*, without falling after him into a carelessness and (as I may call it) a Lethargy of thought, for whole Scenes together' (*Works* 11: 217). Dryden's essay on artistic progress here complements 'Of Heroique Playes', also prefixed to *The Conquest of Granada*, which documents the current age's contribution to serious drama. At the beginning of the second decade of the re-established theatre, Dryden recognized that new drama could either wallow in the mire of sloppy Shakespearean tragedy, stiff Jonsonian humour and banal French farce – or it could move forward. Both the 'Defence' and 'Of Heroique Playes' outline his prescription for this forward movement. Thus, the debate between Shadwell and Dryden provides insight into contemporary comic theory (something that playwrights did not explore in print again until the 1690s), and shows us how these writers came to terms with their past, and how they hoped to transmit the past in their own dramatic works.

Perhaps the most successful and best-known assault on Dryden's prefatory criticism is found in *The Rehearsal*. Written by George Villiers, second Duke of Buckingham, and a circle of wits in the 1660s and performed in December 1671, *The Rehearsal* was an attack on popular drama of the day. The satire takes place as two wits, Johnson and Smith, attend a rehearsal of a new heroic play by Bayes. While Bayes is a composite of a number of popular playwrights, he is instantly recognizable as Dryden. For example, a major target of Buckingham's satire is critical issues from every important dedication and preface written by Dryden from *The Rival Ladies* to *An Evening's Love*. In particular, Buckingham revels in ridiculing Dryden's ideas about the freedom of 'fancy' expressed in the preface to *Tyrannick Love* (1670) and his devaluation of plot in the preface to *An Evening's Love*. More broadly, the satire is an attack on pretensions of authors who, like Dryden, try to assert control over the interpretation of their text. Much of the humour in *The Rehearsal* concerns Bayes's absurd explanations of both the play at hand and his theories of dramatic composition and practice. Bayes's heroic drama is so cryptic that it is often comprehensible only to him: Johnson and Smith must frequently force Bayes to state his authorial intention overtly to make any sense of his 'new way of writing'. And occasionally the meaning of the play eludes even Bayes himself. Buckingham's point is that if a play is fundamentally flawed, no amount of authorial justification will help; in fact, an author's theoretical statements may even further obfuscate the meaning of the play. *The Rehearsal*'s pointed attack ridicules, then, not only an author's critical prescriptions but also the presumption in offering them to the audience. Interestingly, contemporaries frequently identified *The Rehearsal* as one of the period's most important works of criticism. In *A Short View of Tragedy*, Thomas Rymer even suggests, 'We want a law for Acting the *Rehearsal* once a week, to keep us in our senses, and secure us against the Noise and Nonsense, the Farce and Fustian which, in the name of Tragedy, have so long invaded, and usurp our Theater' (170). Given its emphasis on common sense, resistance to theory and lasting popularity, *The Rehearsal* is one of the most influential works of late seventeenth-century English criticism.

The success of *The Rehearsal* seems to have encouraged writers who were not dramatists to get involved in print critical debates. In 1673, four anonymous writers took advantage of increased access to print to pen pamphlets – collectively known as the Rota pamphlets – in an attempt to join the Shadwell–Dryden debate. Clearly inspired by *The Rehearsal*, two anti-Dryden pamphlets – *The Censure of the Rota* and *The Friendly Vindication of Mr Dryden* – turn Dryden's prefatory pronouncements against him. Both authors draw on the grammatical rules Dryden used to dismember Jonson in 'Defence of the Epilogue' to identify equally egregious stylistic errors in Dryden's drama, particularly *The Conquest of Granada*. Dryden found two supporters in *Mr. Dreyden Vindicated* and *A Description of the Academy of the Athenian Virtuosi*. The latter is a well-written defence that uses copious citations from Classical authority to dismiss Dryden's detractors. No doubt to the dismay of his adversaries, Dryden refused to be drawn into this pamphlet skirmish. In the dedication to *The Assignation* (1673), he only alludes to his anonymous critics in passing to declare, 'I have neither concernment enough upon me to write any thing in my own Defence, neither will I gratifie the ambition of two wretched Scriblers, who desire nothing more than to be Answer'd' (*Works* 11: 322). At their worst, the Rota pamphlets are silly and pedantic. Nevertheless, they retain an important place in the history of English literary criticism. They constitute the first extended pamphlet debate about drama (pamphlet controversies would soon become a common form of critical discourse). And they show how the rapidly growing London book trade enabled literary nonentities to match wits with the leading dramatists of the day.

The Rota pamphlets also represent the growing trend towards what would become one of the most popular genres of criticism during this period – burlesque criticism. Just as a literary burlesque mocks through comic exaggeration, burlesque criticism uses an exaggerated form of criticism to satirize the work under consideration. This genre is identified early on by the author of *A Description of the Academy*, who dismisses it as an illegitimate form of criticism: 'the Burlesque way of writing is the most hopeful to abuse a good Author, since the fantastick dress tickles the Reader, and makes him laugh whether he will or no' (Kinsley and Kinsley 1971: 107). The writer of burlesque criticism typically pulls quotations out of context and, often using inappropriate critical criteria, subjects the passages to witty ridicule. A detailed description of how burlesque criticism works is provided by Elkanah Settle, whose popular play, *The Empress of Morocco* (1673), was ripped apart line by line in *Notes and Observations on The Empress of Morocco* (1674), written collaboratively by Dryden, Shadwell and John Crowne. (Evidently Dryden's and Shadwell's mutual distaste for the upstart Settle allowed them to put their differences aside at least temporarily.) In his reply to this attack, *Notes and Observations on the Empress of Morocco Revised* (1674), Settle showed how the burlesque style is founded on the deliberate *misreading* of a text: the writer of burlesque criticism,

> either *implicitely* begs his Readers to believe the *Authors* meaning to be *thus*, or *thus*, contrary to their *Reason* or the Poets *design*, for his own purpose; or else by never taking notice of the *dependance* of what goes before, or what follows, gives a plausible argument against *this* or *that* expression, when the Props or all *sense* in a Discourse, *Connexion* and *Circumstance* are taken away. Or when these fail, tells you how *such* or *such* a thing may be *alterd* to be made Non-Sense. (11)

In direct opposition to the idea that the function of criticism should be (in Dryden's words) 'to observe those Excellencies which should delight a reasonable Reader' (*Works* 12: 87), burlesque criticism purposefully *distorts* the text and the author's meaning to suit the critic's purpose. While writers such as Dryden and John Dennis denounced the burlesque style of criticism, it was still employed by every major critic of the period, including Dryden and Dennis. Indeed, the popularity and rhetorical power of burlesque criticism is clearly manifested in three of the most important (and infamous) critical works of the period: Rymer's *Tragedies of the Last Age* and *A Short View of Tragedy* and Jeremy Collier's *A Short View of the Immorality and Profaneness of the English Stage*.

Rymer is best known today for using the techniques of burlesque criticism in his attack on Shakespeare in *A Short View of Tragedy*. By focusing on the improbabilities and indecorousness of *Othello*, Rymer produced some of the more outrageous statements in the history of Shakespeare criticism. Rymer finds, for example, the handkerchief's prominent role in the play highly implausible, and even wonders 'Why was not this call'd the *Tragedy of the Handkerchief?*' (160). Given Shakespeare's seemingly excessive reliance on the handkerchief as a dramatic device, Rymer reduces the moral of the play to, 'This may be a warning to all good Wives, that they look well to their Linnen' (132). Rymer's final assessment of *Othello* is blunt and unforgiving: 'There is in this Play, some burlesk, some humour, and ramble of Comical Wit, some shew, and some *Mimickry* to divert the spectators: but the tragical part is, plainly none other, than a Bloody Farce, without salt or savour' (164). If this is all we read of Rymer – and, indeed, this seems to be all that many modern critics *have* read – then George Saintsbury does seem justified in claiming, 'I never came across a worse critic than Thomas Rymer'. But a closer look at Rymer's work – particularly the method and purpose of his criticism – reveals him as an influential and respected critic.

One of Rymer's most important contributions to English criticism is that he, like Dryden, helped introduce cutting-edge French criticism to an English audience. But while Dryden assimilated French criticism into his own writing, Rymer's first published work was a translation of René Rapin's *Réflexions sur la poétique* (1674). This translation, published soon after the original appeared, was an act of remarkable foresight. Anything resembling a vogue for French criticism in translation did not occur until the 1680s, with the appearance of Nicolas Boileau's *The Art of Poetry* (1683; translated by Sir William Soames and revised by Dryden), Abbé D'Aubignac's *The Whole Art of the Stage* (1684), and Charles de St Évremond's *Mixt Essays* (1685). And while a few of Rapin's other works were published in the 1670s, *Réflexions* was regarded by contemporaries as the most useful. In 'The Authors Apology for Heroique Poetry; and Poetique Licence' prefaced to *The State of Innocence* (1677), Dryden praised Rapin's book as being 'alone sufficient, were all other Critiques lost, to teach anew the rules of writing' (*Works* 12: 89). But Rymer's real achievement is his preface. It is not just a generic introduction, but a thoughtful attempt to apply Rapin's formalist principles to English verse. In *Réflexions*, Rapin does not name or even allude to any English author, and his brief comments on English drama are dismissive. The primary purpose of Rymer's preface is, then, to fill a blank in Rapin: using the French critic's criteria, he assesses English heroic verse from Edmund Spenser to Dryden. Rymer then takes Rapin one step further. Without any elaboration he asserts the primacy of English drama: 'yet for the *Drama*, the World has nothing to be compared with us' (10). Finally, he compares ancient and modern descriptions of the night to argue for the superiority of modern English verse. As a result, Rymer's preface assumes a nationalistic fervour that is almost non-existent in Rapin's text.

The appearance in the summer of 1677 of Rymer's next work, *The Tragedies of the Last Age Consider'd and Examin'd by the Practice of the Ancients, and by the Common Sense of All Ages*, makes perfect sense in the context of the current trends in late seventeenth-century English criticism. Rymer's close analysis of three plays by Beaumont and Fletcher – *The Bloody Brother, A King and No King* and *The Maid's Tragedy* – is a contribution to two relatively long-standing and related controversies among play-wrights: the relationship between ancient and modern drama, and the extent to which playwrights of the 'last age' should serve as models. The full title of Rymer's work gives an accurate sense of his critical method. Following the French critics, Rymer analyses Beaumont and Fletcher's plays according to the formative elements of a literary work established in Aristotle's *Poetics*, particularly the quality of the fable (i.e., plot), character, thought and diction. He also offers detailed comparisons between the ancients and moderns, showing how playwrights such as Euripides and Seneca solved with greater artistry and tact the same dramatic problems evidenced in Beaumont and Fletcher. Following English critics such as Howard and Buckingham, Rymer also applies a great deal of weight to the criterion of common sense, even to the point of devaluing the status of the critic:

> And certainly there is not requir'd much Learning, or that a man must be some *Aristotle*, and *Doctor* of *Subtilties*, to form a right judgment in this particular; common sense suffices; and rarely have I known the *Women-judges* mistake in these points, when they have the patience to think, and (left to their own heads) they decide with their own sense. (18)

In particular, Rymer is concerned with common sense as it relates to decorum, probability and morality, a combination which causes him to produce some (by modern standards) surprising tenets. For example, with regard to the dramatic characterization of royalty in *A King and No King*, Rymer states: 'though it is not necessary that all *Heroes* should be Kings, yet undoubtedly all crown'd heads by *Poetical right* are *Heroes*' (42) and later 'I question whether in Poetry a King can be an accessary to a crime' (65). Largely on the basis of this kind of critical reasoning, modern scholars have little patience with this work, often assuming that the relative silence *Tragedies of the Last Age* met with is evidence it was essentially ignored. But Dryden admired it for its Classical learning, and drew up lines of possible argumentation against it ('Heads of an Answer to Rymer') in the end papers to his presentation copy of the book. And with the publication of *Tragedies of the Last Age*, Rymer rose from relative obscurity to become, as Dryden publicly dubbed him in 'The Grounds of Criticism in Tragedy', 'our English Critic' (*Works* 13: 234).

Rymer's next and last work of criticism – *A Short View of Tragedy; It's Original, Excellency, and Corruption. With Some Reflections on Shakespear, and Other Practitioners for the Stage* – is perhaps the most infamous text in the history of English dramatic criticism. Rymer begins his book abruptly by praising the introduction of the ancient chorus into modern French tragedy, adding, 'The *Chorus* was the root and original, and is certainly always the most necessary part of Tragedy' (84). And for two chapters Rymer ruthlessly attacks Shakespeare and *Othello* employing, in a far more scathing and relentless manner, the commonsense criteria of probability and decorum he had used on Beaumont and Fletcher's plays. Unlike the Rapin Preface and *Tragedies of the Last Age*, *A Short View of Tragedy* elicited a number of heated responses (the most notable from Dryden, Dennis and Charles Gildon), which many modern scholars have used to prove that Rymer's book was universally rejected. While there is no denying the severity of Rymer's comments on Shakespeare and the practical obstacles that faced the reinstatement of the ancient chorus on the modern English stage, Rymer's words need to be considered in the context of *A Short View of Tragedy* as a whole. Between Rymer's proposal for reinstating the ancient chorus (chapter I) and his attack on Shakespeare (chapters VII–VIII) are five chapters on the history of tragedy that are consistently neglected. As a detailed, developmental history of a literary genre, *A Short View of Tragedy* was unprecedented. Consequently, we need to consider *A Short View* seriously as a literary history, and determine how the ancient chorus, Shakespeare and *Othello* function in it.

Reading *A Short View of Tragedy* in its entirety quickly reveals the controlling thesis of Rymer's historical narrative: excellence in drama is always achieved when the connection between the government and the theatre is strong, and playwrights are subjected to some kind of outside scrutiny and control. For example, Rymer emphasizes the relationship between drama, religion and government in ancient Greek drama. In the conclusion to *A Short View*, Rymer even argues that the Greeks likened the drama to the law: 'At *Athens* (they tell us) the Tragedies of *Æschylus*, *Sophocles*, and *Euripides* were enroll'd with their Laws, and made part of their Statute-Book' (170). Similarly, Rymer attributes the success of French drama to the support it historically received from the government and, more recently, the regulatory control of the Académie Française. Rymer believed that this governmental support and regulation enabled French dramatists to match, and perhaps even challenge, the ancient stage: 'And now, if the *French* Theatre did not rise to equal the glory of the *Romans*, and Antient *Greeks*, it was not for want of Encouragement from the Government' (116). The relevance of these historical precedents and their connection to the reform of modern tragedy is clear: for tragedy to regain its former reputation and prominence, it would have to re-establish its connection to the state. Accordingly, *A Short View of Tragedy* should be read as an appeal for increased government support and regulation of the English stage. Given this context, Rymer's critique of *Othello* appears to illustrate the ill effects of an unsupervised and self-serving playwright. And, with the chorus, Rymer offers an aesthetically pleasing means of regulating both the production and reception of drama. As acerbic and impracticable as *A Short View of Tragedy* may be, it is an important, early exploration of two concerns that would quickly dominate English dramatic criticism: the regulation of the English stage, and the regulatory function of criticism.

The print controversy initiated by *A Short View of Tragedy* was instrumental in launching the careers of two major critics of the period – John Dennis and Charles

Gildon. Dennis is the first writer in England who seems to have consciously pursued a career as a critic. Dryden was, first and foremost, a dramatist; Rymer was a historian. Though Dennis's first efforts – *Poems and Letters upon Several Occasions* (1692) and *Poems in Burlesque* (1692) – show a desire to establish himself as a wit and a poet, Dennis published two works in 1693 that helped him earn his reputation as a critic: *Miscellanies in Verse and Prose* and *The Impartial Critick*. The preface to *Miscellanies*, Dennis's first major critical essay, features a relatively lengthy defence of burlesque verse against its principal detractors, Boileau and Dryden. *The Impartial Critick* is a rebuttal of Rymer's *A Short View of Tragedy*; but while Dennis attacked Rymer's proposed reintroduction of the chorus on the modern stage, he also touched on a whole range of critical problems, from the effects of climate on artistic temperament to various points on prosody. (Interestingly, Dennis only alludes to a future defence of Shakespeare, which was eventually supplied by Gildon.) More important, in *The Impartial Critick* Dennis addresses issues of propriety in critical discourse. Countering Rymer's privileging of common sense as the principal criterion in critical judgement, Dennis asserts, 'it is much more easie to find Faults, than it is to discern Beauties. To do the first requires but common Sence, but to do the last a Man must have Genius' (1: 13). The idea that a critic – like a poet – should have 'genius' was later picked up by Pope in *An Essay on Criticism*. And Dennis rejects Rymer's burlesque style of criticism, preferring instead 'the Didactick Stile' because it

> is a Stile that is fit for Instruction, and must be necessarily upon that account, pure, perspicuous, succinct, unaffected and grave.... It requires Succinctness, that its Precepts may be more readily comprehended, and more easily retain'd; and it requires Gravity to give it an Air of Authority, and cause it to make the deeper impression. (1: 16)

While Dennis lays down far more extensive critical precepts in *Remarks on Prince Arthur* (1696), *The Impartial Critick* marks a significant step in his attempt to formalize critical practice in England.

Dennis's efforts to establish rules and guidelines for criticism – in addition to the prodigiousness and ambition of his critical output – clearly distinguish him from any of his contemporaries. While much of the criticism written during this period is prefatory, Dennis wrote several major critical treatises, including *The Advancement and Reformation of Modern Poetry* (1701) and *The Grounds of Criticism in Poetry* (1704). *The Advancement* marked Dennis's introduction into serious, original criticism, and, as a proposal advocating religion in poetry, it represented a bold move for a relative newcomer. *The Grounds* is even more noteworthy as an unprecedented (albeit unsuccessful) attempt to solicit subscriptions for what Dennis intended to be a monumental critical work. In 'The Proposal' to *The Grounds*, Dennis indicates that the work will again promote religion in poetry, but will also include rules for judging all the major poetic genres and evaluative biographies of major English poets. While the project was never realized, his 'specimen' or sample instalment on *Paradise Lost* remains important in the history of Milton criticism. In his artistic output and unswerving devotion to the government, Dennis was fairly clearly setting himself up to be poet laureate. Despite two opportunities, in 1715 and 1718, Dennis was never granted the post. Because Dennis's critical endeavours effectively eclipsed his poetic efforts, his main significance in the history of literature is his role as the first professional literary critic in England.

Gildon's answers to Rymer in *Miscellaneous Letters and Essays, on several Subjects. Philosophical, Moral, Historical, Critical, Amorous, &c. in Prose and Verse* (1694) are representative of his contribution to the development of literary criticism during this period. Gildon's talent was commerical packaging – taking a hodgepodge of materials and assembling them into a marketable product. This skill was no doubt attributable to his literary background: instead of publishing books exclusively of his own words, he was a hack writer doing journalistic work and editing various publishers' projects. In particular, Gildon excelled in the genre of the poetical miscellany. Although miscellanies (collections of poems, letters, translated verse, etc.) had long been popular with the English reading public, the publisher Jacob Tonson demonstrated the inherent profitability of the genre with the success of *Ovid's Epistles, Translated by Several Hands* (1680) and *Miscellany Poems* (1684), printed in six parts over the next three decades. The miscellany format allowed Gildon to utilize his editorial skills while placing his original poetry – and soon his literary criticism – alongside the greatest writers of the day, both living and dead. Gildon's first collection, *Miscellany Poems upon Several Occasions* (1692), featured works by Congreve, Abraham Cowley, Matthew Prior and Robert Boyle. The collection begins with Gildon's own translation of André Dacier's *Preface sur les Satires D'Horace*. With *Miscellaneous Letters*, Gildon made his first significant contribution to literary criticism. This collection includes five critical essays by Gildon on current controversies – two on Rymer's *A Short View of Tragedy* – addressed to prominent literary figures such as Dryden, Congreve and Dennis. In 'Some Reflections on Mr. Rymer's Short View of Tragedy, and an Attempt at a Vindication of Shakespear, in an Essay directed to John Dryden', Gildon attacks Rymer's arguments at length by employing the critic's own satiric technique, consequently producing a far more complete and deliberately devastating refutation than Dennis's *The Impartial Critick*. More important than his actual attack, however, is Gildon's use of the fashionable miscellany format as a vehicle for his criticism. In doing so, he was clearly experimenting with the packaging and marketing of literary criticism to a broad, popular audience, something he would continue to do for the remainder of his career.

Dennis and Gildon were also involved in the print controversy sparked by the publication of Jeremy Collier's *A Short View of the Immorality and Profaneness of the English Stage: Together with the Sense of Antiquity upon this Argument* (1698), a long treatise that seemed to many to call for the abolition of the theatre. Collier was a non-juring clergyman, and a writer with a reputation as a controversialist. In the late 1680s and early 1690s, he wrote a series of pamphlets in support of James II and was imprisoned for his Jacobite sympathies. In an effort to identify the motivations for his attack on the theatre, Collier's opponents often alluded to the clergyman's past as a rabble rouser, even suggesting that a publisher 'bribed' him £50 to write *A Short View*. But the publication of Collier's book in 1698 makes sense given the current discussions among playwrights and reformers about morality in drama. In the early 1690s, a number of attacks on the theatre appeared, the most notable being James Wright's *Country Conversations* (1694) and Sir Richard Blackmore's preface to *Prince Arthur* (1695). Influential members of the theatre audience were also putting pressure on the Lord Chamberlain and the Crown in the mid-1690s to pass orders making sure the Master of the Revels and the theatre companies adhered to the censorship laws already in existence. As evidenced in their dedications, prefaces, prologues and epilogues, dramatists themselves were aware of problems with audiences being offended by the immorality of their characters and the offensiveness of their language. With what now seems like remarkable foresight (or cocksure goading), John Vanbrugh in the prologue to *The Provok'd Wife* (1697) even hoped, 'And that the satire may be sure to bite, / Kind heaven, inspire some venomed priest to write'.

While the time was clearly right for Collier's assault on the stage, what makes *A Short View* an important text in the history of English dramatic criticism is Collier's skill as a rhetorician and stylist. Collier's text belongs, of course, to a long history of anti-theatrical attacks; in England, Collier had antecedents in Stephen Gosson and William Prynne. But what distinguishes Collier from his reformist brethren is his rhetoric: instead of invoking tired religious polemics, he used dramatic criticism to attack the theatre. Clearly following Rymer's model, Collier combines theatre history, close readings of the texts and the burlesque style of criticism to demonstrate that modern playwrights are guilty of a whole slew of charges, principally gratuitous obscenities, abuse of the clergy and immoral characterization. The influence of Rymer is perhaps most evident in Collier's citations from Classical and Elizabethan and Jacobean playwrights to show how far modern playwrights have strayed from the 'norm'. In terms of language, some of Collier's passages seem like they are lifted straight from *A Short View of Tragedy*: with regard to Congreve's excessive language in *The Mourning Bride* (1697), Collier quips, 'This Litter of *Epithets* makes the *Poem* look like a Bitch over-stock'd with Puppies, and sucks the Sense almost to Skin and Bone' (34). And like *The Rehearsal*, Collier uses dramatists' own criticism against them. He frequently draws on statements from Dryden's preface to *An Evening's Love* – particularly the assertion that the primary purpose of comedy is to entertain – to substantiate his own claims about the moral depravity of modern comedy.

The decades-long pamphlet controversy sparked by *A Short View* is also important because it forced dramatists to articulate their theories of comedy in print, something that had not been done on such a grand scale since the Shadwell–Dryden prefatory debates. (Harold Love has identified a debate that occurred in the 1690s involving Dryden, Southerne, Congreve, Thomas Durfey and Gildon concerning the significance of wit versus plot in comedy; but this critical conversation was so subtle, at least in print, as to go undetected until Love's article.) Collier begins *A Short View* by establishing his moralistic definition of drama: 'The Business of *Plays* is to recommend Vertue, and discountenance Vice' (1). Despite various arguments about how morality is conveyed to the audience, almost every one of Collier's respondents accepted his definition, and even agreed that modern drama was in need of moral reformation. Consequently, having assented to the basic premise of Collier's argument, his opponents were never completely successful in refuting him. Dryden, who bore the brunt of many of Collier's arguments, conceded 'in many things he has taxed me justly', adding only 'in many places he has perverted my meaning by his glosses, and interpreted my words into blasphemy and bawdry of which they were not guilty. Besides that, he is too much given to horse-play in his raillery' (Dryden 1962, 2: 293). Vanbrugh and Congreve both wrote substantive pamphlet replies, respectively, *A Short Vindication of the Relapse and the Provok'd Wife* (1698) and *Amendments of Mr. Collier's False and Imperfect Citations* (1698). In arguing for the primacy of authorial intention over Collier's interpretation, these playwrights provide authorial commentaries that were unprecedented in content and detail. For example, in *A Short Vindication*, Vanbrugh offers a relatively in-depth assessment of the 'design' of *The Relapse* (61–71); and in *Amendments*, Congreve explains why Valentine's feigned madness in *Love for Love* (1695) is dramatically effective (55–6). But, despite the length of their responses, the gist of their refutations does not extend far beyond Dryden's claim that Collier was just playing with words. Although he spends some time attempting to counter Collier, Congreve finally admits the futility of arguing with him: 'very like the Controversie in *Ben. Johnson's Barthol. Fair*, between the *Rabbi* and the *Puppet*; it *is* profane, and it *is not* profane, is all the Argument the thing will admit of on either side' (46).

Among Collier's opponents, Dennis is one of the few writers to resist battling the clergyman on his own terms. Accordingly, Dennis's *The Usefulness of the Stage, To the Happiness of Mankind, To Government, and To Religion* (1698) is perhaps the most successful of the early responses to Collier. In it, Dennis deliberately avoids answering Collier's specific charges of the immorality and profaneness of the modern English stage, 'For no Man can make any reasonable Defence, either for the Immorality or the Immodesty, or the unnecessary wanton Prophaneness, which are too justly charg'd upon it' (1: 147). Instead, Dennis examines the broader, societal function of the theatre, and uses historical precedent to demonstrate 'That the Stage in general is useful to the Happiness of Mankind, to the Welfare of Government, and the Advancement of Religion' (ibid.). Dennis is clearly indebted to Rymer here, and his material on the Greek and Roman theatre reads like *A Short View of Tragedy*. In stark contrast to Rymer, however, Dennis employs in *The Usefulness of the Stage* the 'didactic' style he promoted in *The Impartial Critick*. As a result, his criticism is far more organized and systematic than any other late seventeenth-century English critic: it is not conversational like Dryden's, or informal and chaotic like Rymer's. Rather, Dennis's arguments are heavily forecasted, and broken down into sections that examine the 'reason' or logic of Collier's claims and his scholarship. While Collier's other critics expressed amusement over the clergyman's use of critical authority, Dennis showed how Collier misrepresented his scholarly citations just as he wilfully misinterpreted the play texts he scrutinized. *The Usefulness of the Stage* did not, of course, silence Collier, nor was it Dennis's last instalment in the controversy. But it remains an excellent example of one critic's attempt to formalize critical practice, and combat the vogue for burlesque criticism with the soberness of didactic criticism.

Collier and his supporters may have had little actual impact on how English comedy was written at the turn of the century; but the controversy sparked by *A Short View of the Immorality and Profaneness of the English Stage* can tell us much about the state of dramatic criticism during this period. That a clergyman with no connection to the theatre could use dramatic criticism to attack the stage and confound the leading playwrights of the day shows just how unsettled the discipline of criticism was in late seventeenth-century England. Collier challenged the idea of who could actually be a critic, and reaffirmed the rhetorical power of burlesque or satiric criticism. Out of the Collier controversy, however, emerged Dennis's infinitely more academic brand of didactic criticism. And Dryden's author-centred prefatory criticism had not vanished – this genre of criticism was still practised by playwrights such as Congreve, Colley Cibber and George Farquhar. But instead of regarding Dryden as the father of English criticism, and ignoring or dismissing critics like Collier and Dennis, we need to consider Dryden's achievements in the context of the contemporary challenges and alternatives to his critical model. The various strands of critical practice that constitute late seventeenth-century dramatic criticism were not really synthesized until Richard Steele's and Joseph Addison's critical essays in their famous periodicals, the *Tatler* (1709–11) and *Spectator* (1711–12; 1714). In these essays, the reader will instantly recognize the influence of Dryden, Rymer, Collier and Dennis. The modern reader will also probably find Steele's and Addison's criticism more accessible because it is more familiar – like much of the mainstream literary criticism written today, it is appreciative criticism geared towards a broad, popular audience.

REFERENCES AND FURTHER READING

Anthony, Sister Rose (1937; 1966). *The Jeremy Collier Stage Controversy, 1698–1726*. Milwaukee: Marquette University Press; New York: Benjamin Blom.

Barish, Jonas A. (1981). *The Antitheatrical Prejudice*. Berkeley: University of California Press.

Cannan, Paul D. (2001). 'A Short View of Tragedy and Rymer's Proposals for Regulating the English Stage', *Review of English Studies* n.s. 52, 207–26.

Crane, R. S. (1953; 1967). 'On Writing the History of Criticism in England, 1650–1800', *University of Toronto Quarterly* 22, 376–91. Rpt. in *The Idea of the Humanities*. 2 vols. Chicago: University of Chicago Press, 2: 157–75.

Dennis, John (1939–43). *The Critical Works of John Dennis*, ed. Edward Niles Hooker. 2 vols. Baltimore: Johns Hopkins Press.

Dryden, John (1956–). *The Works of John Dryden*, ed. Edward Niles Hooker, H. T. Swedenberg, Jr, et al. 20 vols in progress. Berkeley: University of California Press.

Dryden, John (1962). *Of Dramatic Poesy and Other Critical Essays*, ed. George Watson. 2 vols. London: Dent.

Engell, James (1989). *Forming the Critical Mind: Dryden to Coleridge*. Cambridge, MA: Harvard University Press.

Gelber, Michael Werth (1999). *The Just and the Lively: The Literary Criticism of John Dryden*. Manchester: Manchester University Press.

Harwood, John T. (1982). *Critics, Values, and Restoration Comedy*. Carbondale: Southern Illinois University Press.

Hume, Robert D. (1970). *Dryden's Criticism*. Ithaca, NY: Cornell University Press.

Hume, Robert D. (1976). *The Development of English Drama in the Late Seventeenth Century*. Oxford: Clarendon Press.

Hume, Robert D. (1999). 'Jeremy Collier and the Future of the London Theater in 1698', *Studies in Philology* 96, 480–511.

Kinsley, James and Kinsley, Helen (eds). (1971). *Dryden: The Critical Heritage*. New York: Barnes and Noble.

Krutch, Joseph Wood (1924; 1949). *Comedy and Conscience after the Restoration*. Rev. ed. New York: Columbia University Press.

Love, Harold (1973). 'Dryden, Durfey, and the Standard of Comedy', *Studies in English Literature 1500–1900* 13, 422–36.

Miner, Earl (1975). 'Mr. Dryden and Mr. Rymer', *Philological Quarterly* 54, 137–51.

Nisbet, H. B. and Rawson, Claude (eds). (1997). *The Cambridge History of Literary Criticism: The Eighteenth Century*. Cambridge: Cambridge University Press.

Pechter, Edward (1975). *Dryden's Classical Theory of Literature*. Cambridge: Cambridge University Press.

Rymer, Thomas (1956). *The Critical Works of Thomas Rymer*. Ed. and intro. Curt A. Zimansky. New Haven, CT: Yale University Press.

Spingarn, J. E. (ed.). (1908–9; 1968). *Critical Essays of the Seventeenth Century*. 3 vols. Oxford: Clarendon Press; Bloomington: Indiana University Press.

Trolander, Paul and Tenger, Zeynep (1994). '"Impartial Critick" or "Muse's Handmaid": The Politics of Critical Practice in the Early Eighteenth Century', *Essays in Literature* 21, 26–42.

Trolander, Paul and Tenger, Zeynep (1996). 'Criticism Against Itself: Subverting Critical Authority in Late-Seventeenth-Century England', *Philological Quarterly* 75, 311–38.

Watson, George (1962; 1986). *The Literary Critics: A Study of English Descriptive Criticism*. Rev. ed. London: Hogarth Press.

3

Theatrical Regulation during the Restoration Period

Matthew J. Kinservik

How were the London theatres regulated during the Restoration period? Who controlled the theatres, what sorts of control did they exercise, and how successful was their effort? This chapter will try to answer these very broad, basic questions. Finding answers to them is important because the tendency to regard Restoration drama as a libertine, anything-goes reaction against the Puritan past has proven as resilient as it is exaggerated. The Restoration period certainly was a time of greater freedom for the London theatres compared to the Interregnum, but this is not saying much. After an eighteen-year hiatus, any theatrical activity might seem liberated and liberating, yet a careful look at the Restoration theatre world shows that the freedom of the stage was qualified. From the censorship of scripts and published texts to the dictation of repertory decisions and personnel matters, the London theatres from 1660 to 1710 were subject to a striking range of regulatory pressures. Just as striking is the range of regulators, which included the reigning monarch, the Lord Chamberlain, the Master of the Revels, London municipal judges and grand juries, and private citizens who joined together in moral reform societies. The main goal of this chapter is to explain the many ways in which the Restoration theatre world was highly regulated.

When considering theatrical regulation, we tend naturally to think in terms of the most obvious and negative form of regulation: the suppression of play texts. Without discounting the importance of this type of censorship (indeed, this chapter will focus largely on it), I want to resist seeing it as the typical, or even the most important, form of regulation. Therefore, I offer two caveats. First, 'censorship' is not necessarily a negative term. While we use it nowadays to signify a repressive control of free speech, in the seventeenth and eighteenth centuries it was synonymous with 'regulation' and was almost universally regarded as a good and necessary thing – especially in relation to the theatres. Second, not all censorship is textual. The content of play texts certainly mattered to censors during the Restoration period, but of equal or greater importance were the questions of who would enact these texts, how they would do so, and in what theatres. If we limit ourselves to looking at just the suppression of play texts, we are privileging our contemporary interests in texts and free speech over the interests that animated theatrical people in the late seventeenth century. Instead, we must expand our current definitions of 'censor' and 'censorship' so that we can achieve the fullest and most accurate conception of theatrical regulation during the Restoration period.

The Censors

First things first: who was the government censor? At the time of the Restoration, Sir Henry Herbert thought he was. He had been the Master of the Revels to Charles I, and he made this a lucrative position by insisting that the theatres submit all new play texts to him for review prior to performance and charging a £2 per play fee (a hefty sum), whether he approved the play for performance or not. He seems to have licensed most plays without objection, but he occasionally 'reformed' a text by suppressing words and speeches, and in at least one instance, he threw a play into the fire because of its obscenity. When Charles II returned as king, Herbert successfully petitioned to have his old job back. However, he soon discovered that the Restoration theatre world was much different from the one that he had known before the Civil War. From 1660 to 1664, Herbert fought hard to assert his traditional control over the theatres, but was largely unsuccessful. His failure does not mean that the Restoration stage was freed from censorship; rather, it means that there were now many censors, not just one.

The most important questions to be decided after the Restoration involved not what sort of plays could be performed, but who could perform them, and by what authority. In August 1660, the king gave initial approval for the issuance of theatrical patents to Sir William Davenant and Thomas Killigrew, granting them the power to establish theatres, censor plays and silence any actors who refused to submit to their authority. In other words, the Master of the Revels was being pushed out of the public theatres. Herbert stood to lose not just his control over the theatres, but also his lucrative licensing fees. By December 1660, Davenant and Killigrew had succeeded in gobbling up the existing acting companies and stripping Herbert of his censorial powers over the public theatres.

Having obviously lost influence in the royal court, Herbert turned to the law courts. He sued Davenant and Killigrew for depriving him of the powers and emoluments of his office. He lost that suit, but won a subsequent case against Davenant alone. The result of all this wrangling – and only the barest of outlines is provided here – was that Davenant and Killigrew succeeded in establishing exclusive control over the London stage. However, they compromised with Herbert on the issue of censoring play texts, agreeing to submit plays to his review and pay him for the service. The fact that Davenant and Killigrew pulled out all the stops to establish monopoly control over the London stage but were willing to pacify Herbert with the licensing of play texts tells us something important: what really mattered was having control over the commercial stage, not the content of plays. So long as their control over the market was secure, the patentees were satisfied. Herbert's subsequent actions confirm the importance of making money over policing the content of plays. Rather than content himself with licensing plays, he sought to expand the jurisdiction (and fees) of his office by licensing acting companies outside of London, mountebanks and other travelling showmen, and printed plays. He often failed in these efforts, either because his orders were ignored or because he encroached on someone else's prerogative. For example, in 1660, Sir Roger L'Estrange was made the licenser of printed material, and when Herbert sought to license plays for publication, L'Estrange seems successfully to have asserted his authority over play publication.

Herbert remained Master of the Revels until his death in 1673, when he was succeeded by Thomas Killigrew. Four years later, Killigrew was replaced by his son, Charles. The younger Killigrew was a particularly ineffective censor whose tenure (1677–1725) is best remembered for the challenge to government control over the theatres led by Jeremy Collier and the moral reform societies beginning in the 1690s. I will discuss the Collier controversy in detail later, but must note here that the anti-theatrical campaign by the moral reformers represents the greatest threat to free expression in the theatres during this period. As I have suggested, the official censors were less concerned with controlling expression than they were with controlling acting companies and venues. By contrast, the moral reformers had no financial stake in the theatres. What they sought was either to clean up the stage or, better yet, to shut it down altogether. If one wishes to find a censor poring over play texts in search of objectionable material to delete, then one must ignore the official censors like Herbert and the Killigrews and turn instead to unofficial ones like Collier. This is not to say that the government was wholly uninterested in censoring the content of plays. As I will show, there were many instances of such government censorship between 1660 and 1710, but the fact remains that controlling the content of plays was neither a high nor a consistent priority for the government.

The Censorship of Play Texts

During the fifty years under consideration, only eighteen plays were suppressed – and many of them were performed either before or after suppression (see table 3.1). There was certainly a great deal of textual censorship that fell short of a total suppression, but with a few exceptions the record of these relatively minor acts of censorship is slim and not very interesting. For instance, existing manuscripts of plays read by Herbert offer some examples of his crossing out mild oaths like 'faith', as well as obscenities like 'pox' and 'arse'. But if we wish to find out what sort of content could really get a playwright into trouble with the censor, we need to look at the plays that were banned outright – and even then there is a frustrating amount of guesswork involved. There are two main reasons why we have difficulty determining the reasons for suppressing a Restoration play, both of which indicate the government's generally

Table 3.1　Plays suppressed, 1660–1710[a]

Title and date suppressed	Author
The Cheats (1663)	John Wilson
The Maid's Tragedy (1670s?)[b]	Beaumont and Fletcher
The Change of Crowns (1667)	Edward Howard
The Country Gentleman (1669)	Sir Robert Howard and Duke of Buckingham
Mr Limberham (1677/8)	John Dryden
The Massacre of Paris (1679?)	Nathaniel Lee
Lucius Junius Brutus (1680)	Lee
Richard II (1680)	Nahum Tate
Henry the Sixth, the First Part (1680/1)	John Crowne
City Politiques (1682)	Crowne
The Duke of Guise (1682)	Dryden and Lee
Cyrus the Great (1681?)	John Banks
The Innocent Usurper (1682?)	Banks
The Island Queens (1684)	Banks
The Spanish Friar (1686)	Dryden
The Patriot (1702)[c]	Charles Gildon
An Act at Oxford (1704)	Anonymous
The Quacks (1705?)	Owen Swiney

[a]　Many of these plays were, in fact, performed, either before or after suppression.
[b]　The evidence that this play was suppressed is conjectural and is still debated by scholars.
[c]　This is an adaptation of Lee's *Lucius Junius Brutus*.

lax attitude towards censoring plays. First, there were no explicit guidelines that distinguished licit from illicit content, and the censors seldom gave a careful explanation for why they banned a play (or any explanation at all). Second, the multiple layers of authority over the stage make it impossible in many cases to determine exactly who was responsible for suppressing a given play. Some plays were licensed by the Master of the Revels only to be suppressed later by his immediate superior, the Lord Chamberlain, or by the king. The system was unclear and the standards were inconsistent.

In some cases, the banning of a play had nothing to do with the text as written; rather, it was prompted by the text as performed. For instance, Edward Howard's *The Change of Crowns* (1667) was licensed by Herbert on 13 April 1667, and Samuel Pepys reported the premiere two days later (which suggests that rehearsals were occurring well before the licence was granted). John Lacy, one of Charles II's favourite actors, apparently ad-libbed some scandalous lines about influence-peddling at court that infuriated the king, who was in attendance. The company was silenced and Lacy was imprisoned. Fellow actor and another favourite of the king, Michael Mohun, soon obtained permission for the company to resume acting, but this play seems never to have been performed again (Bawcutt 1996: 103–4). This was a blow to the playwright, but ad-libbing was beyond his control. His text was licensed by the king's censor only to be effectively revoked by the king, and so Howard learned the hard way that just because a play was approved by the Master of the Revels, it was not necessarily free from further censorship.

An even more extreme example of this is the suppression of *The Country Gentleman* (1669). Sir Robert Howard wrote the play with assistance from George Villiers, second Duke of Buckingham. Buckingham added a scene that ridiculed his political opponents, Sir William Coventry and Sir John Duncomb, in the characters of Sir Cautious Trouble-all and Sir Gravity Empty, respectively. These inseparable fools are civil servants with an inflated sense of their own importance. However, Buckingham's satire was mainly aimed at Coventry, and it was effective not because it scored ideological points against him, but because it made him look absolutely ridiculous. Coventry had a special circular desk in his office that he could sit in the middle of and, by swivelling his chair around, file papers and attend to many items of business with great efficiency. He was proud of this desk and because he showed it off to visitors, it was well known. Buckingham wrote a scene that features two such desks, one each for Sir Cautious and Sir Gravity. In Act 3, the two men sit in the middle of their desks on swivelled chairs, racing each other to see who can locate his files the fastest. They spin wildly around on their chairs and shout out file names to each other when, to their mortification, they are discovered by Sir Richard Plainbred, the normative title character. The scene is silly and very funny. It would have been hilarious in performance, but it was never performed because Coventry got wind of it and managed to keep the play from the stage.

Presumably, the play was licensed by Herbert. It was in rehearsal at the King's Company when Coventry complained to Charles II about the impersonation. The king personally examined the text and, because the theatre removed the offensive scene, he allowed the play to be performed. Pepys records in his diary that Coventry 'told Tom Killigrew that he should tell his actors, whoever they were, that did offer at any thing like representing him, that he would not complain to my Lord Chamberlain, which was too weak, nor get him beaten, as Sir Charles Sidly [*sic*] is said to do, but that he would cause his nose to be cut'. This was not an idle threat. Just a month earlier, Sir Charles Sedley had hired assailants to beat Edward Kynaston for impersonating Sedley in another King's Company production, William Cavendish, Duke of Newcastle's *The Heiress* (1669). According to the play's editors, Arthur H. Scouten and Robert D. Hume, the threat of physical violence – not official action – led to *The Country Gentleman*'s not being performed. The king had approved the play, and so Coventry rightly considered a complaint to the Lord Chamberlain to be 'too weak' an option. The suppression of *The Country Gentleman* is a fascinating example of how contentious personal satire could be and how unofficial pressures were brought to bear on the theatres.

As these two examples indicate, several of the eighteen plays banned during the Restoration period were proscribed either by other government officials or by threats like Coventry's after being approved by the Master of the Revels. Many of these proscriptions occurred not because of ad-libbing, but because the plays were later determined to be too offensive to stage. Why is that? Were Herbert and the Killigrews permissive censors? Perhaps, but the main reason seems to be the absence of clear criteria establishing what a playwright could and could not write about. The patents granted to Davenant and Killigrew speak in only the vaguest terms about ridding plays of obscene and irreligious material. How to define 'obscene' and 'irreligious' was up to the Master of the Revels, but he could be overruled. Despite this vagueness, we can deduce some criteria from specific instances of suppression. Plays that ridiculed religion, real individuals and the government were the most likely to be banned. In particular, the censors were vigilant in protecting the *Christian* religion, *important* individuals and the *party in power* from satiric treatment on the stage.

A good example of these criteria, as well as the multiple levels of authority over the stage, is the suppression of John Wilson's *The Cheats* (1663). Wilson was a courtier and an ardent royalist, and his comedy expresses those sympathies quite clearly. Nevertheless, Herbert took great pains to excise what he considered to be inflammatory political and religious material before approving it for performance. Fortunately, Herbert's manuscript copy of this play survives, and the play text and Herbert's censorial markings were transcribed by Milton C. Nahm in his 1935 edition. Herbert followed his usual practice of crossing out single words that he found offensive, but the MS is unusual because it features several long passages that are marked for deletion, too. Most of the deletions concern the character of Scruple, a hypocritical non-conformist minister who debauches his female coreligionists, incites rebellion against the newly restored king, and betrays a total lack of principles when he considers conforming to the Church of England after being promised a living of £300 per annum. Although Scruple clearly is an object of ridicule, Herbert deleted a speech in Act 3, scene 5 in which he exhorts his fellow non-conformists not to forget the 'Good Old Cause' of the Puritan revolution. Either the irony was lost on Herbert or he thought that incitement to rebellion even by a negative character was too dangerous to permit. Similarly, Herbert objected to the lines in Act 2, scene 3 in which Scruple reassures Mrs Whitebroth that 'holy fornication' is no sin, nor is abortion when obtained in an attempt to cover up 'holy fornication'. As with the speech regarding rebellion, these sentiments seem to have struck Herbert as too outrageous to permit, regardless of their context.

Because the MS served as both Herbert's review copy and the theatre's prompt copy, we can assume that the censor's objections were honoured in performance. Even so, *The Cheats* fell victim to the objections of a 'faction' in the audience, according to its author. Apparently the abridged Scruple was still too offensive for some members of the audience. Their complaints reached the king's ears, but when a portion of the play was read to him, he found nothing objectionable. After protests persisted, Charles ordered that the play be suppressed until it was reviewed and further amended by the poets, Sir John Denham and Edmund Waller. This is odd. Strictly speaking, Denham and Waller had no business censoring plays – that was the job of the Master of the Revels and (frequently) his superior, the Lord Chamberlain. Some scholars have suggested that Waller was asked one other time to be a freelance censor for Charles II, resulting in Waller's adaptation of Beaumont and Fletcher's *The Maid's Tragedy*. However, the record is not as clear in this instance as it is in the case of *The Cheats*. Wilson's play regained the stage after Denham and Waller further cut back Scruple's part, and in spite of all this censorial 'reformation', the play remained a favourite for half a century. It underwent further censorship when L'Estrange reviewed it before approving publication in late 1663. His objections were few and he allowed many of the words and speeches Herbert deleted from the performance text to survive in print, including the two speeches mentioned above. This illustrates an important point about Restoration censorship: one had greater freedom of expression in print than on the stage. Because theatrical productions reached a mass audience and appealed not just to reason, but to the senses and emotions, they were considered to be more powerful than mere words on a page, and so they were more heavily regulated. When Charles Killigrew excised major portions of Thomas Shadwell's *The Lancashire Witches* (1681), Shadwell printed the banned speeches in italics to show what had been kept from the stage. This idea remains with us today when we bristle at any hint of press censorship, but happily submit to ratings and restricted access to movies and v-chips in our televisions.

The distinction between stage and press censorship can be seen most clearly during the years of the Popish Plot and Exclusion Crisis (1678–83). Half of the plays that were banned during the Restoration period were suppressed because they commented on the political turmoil during these years. However, the Licensing Act of 1662, which authorized press censorship, was allowed to lapse from 1679 to 1681, the most heated period of partisan activity before the Glorious Revolution of 1688. The political history of these years is complex, and literary scholars sharply disagree over the extent of topical commentary to be found in the plays of this time. Even so, there are some clear examples of partisan plays, and the most interesting one for our purposes is John Crowne's *City Politiques* (1683). While not entirely unproblematic in its use of Whig and Tory tropes, this play can confidently be considered anti-Whig – Crowne even calls himself a 'swingeing Tory' in the epilogue.

One might expect that a play like *City Politiques*, which castigates the king's political enemies as venal idiots and rebels, would be licensed straight away, but this was not the case. Charles Killigrew initially licensed the play on 15 June 1682, but then withdrew the licence after receiving an order from Lord Chamberlain Arlington on 26 June, saying that the king wished the play to be suppressed. Finally, on 18 December, Arlington sent another order to Killigrew, informing him that the king wished the play to be performed. The eighteenth-century critic, John Dennis, claimed that the Lord Chamberlain, secretly a Whig, was solely responsible for the prohibition made in the king's name. According to this theory, the king did not intervene until Crowne pleaded with him to have the play approved. If Dennis is right, then this is an unusual (and dangerous) instance of the Lord Chamberlain abusing his power in order to suppress a play he personally found to be politically objectionable. More recently, critics like Susan Owen have argued that production of

City Politiques was delayed by the Tories because they did not want to provoke the Whigs during the fall of 1682. During that time, the Tories were busy rigging the sheriffs' elections in London, thereby cementing their triumph over the Whigs. Crowne's play was performed only after the Tory triumph in the Exclusion Crisis was secure (Owen 1996: 99). The same explanation might apply to the banning of John Dryden and Nathaniel Lee's *The Duke of Guise* (1682), suppressed by the Lord Chamberlain on 18 July 1682, then, with the king's blessing, allowed to be performed by order of the Lord Chamberlain on 29 October. In any event, the suppression of *City Politiques* again illustrates the multiple and sometimes contradictory levels of authority over theatrical productions, this time in the overheated political atmosphere of the Exclusion Crisis.

When looking at censorship during the Restoration period, one is grateful for an event like the Exclusion Crisis because the political struggle lent some coherence to the process of licensing plays. The criteria became tidier: a play is either Whig or Tory. Of course, making this determination could be (and continues to be) very tricky, but at least the criteria seem logical and predictable. One can refer to the turmoil of the Exclusion Crisis to explain the suppressions of Nathaniel Lee's *The Massacre of Paris* (1679?) and *Lucius Junius Brutus* (1680); Nahum Tate's *Richard II* (1680); Crowne's *Henry the Sixth, the First Part* (autumn 1680?) and *City Politiques*; Dryden and Lee's *Duke of Guise*; and John Banks's *Cyrus the Great* (1681?), *The Innocent Usurper* (1682?) and *The Island Queens* (1684). Despite the seeming clarity of the criteria, the licensing process remained untidy during this period, and as Owen points out, many of these plays were initially licensed without any trouble (1996: 12). The lack of established criteria for censoring plays and the many layers of authority over the process are frustrating for the modern student, but they did not cause tremendous problems for the theatres of the period. The lax governmental oversight was occasionally a nuisance, but generally a good thing for the theatres. That ceased to be the case when the moral reform movement became a serious and persistent threat to the stage in the 1690s, challenging the authority of the Master of the Revels and precipitating a theatrical crisis that threatened the very existence of the public stage in London.

The Collier Controversy

The Collier controversy derives its name from Jeremy Collier, a non-juring clergyman who loved a good fight, especially in print. He was a Jacobite, and his loyalty to James II led to his refusal to take the oath of allegiance to William and Mary, which cost him his ministry. In 1696, he and two other ministers absolved Sir John Friend and Sir William Perkins on the gallows, where they were hanged for participating in the 'Assassination Plot' against William III. Collier's accomplices were jailed, but he fled, making him an outlaw. Given his precarious legal position, Collier became a surprisingly powerful and influential public figure with the publication of his famous book, *A Short View of the Immorality and Profaneness of the English Stage* (1698). His view of the stage is anything but short, and in this thick book he exhaustively analyses the works of many living playwrights, especially Congreve and Vanbrugh, to demonstrate the depravity of contemporary English drama.

Collier's tone is often harshly sarcastic, and so while his book is long, it is a lively and engaging text. It certainly engaged the interest of his contemporaries. *A Short View* instigated the most serious and lengthy public discussion about the legitimacy of the stage in English history. Scholars have been too dismissive of Collier, labelling him a Puritan (which he was not) and a failure since he did not succeed in abolishing the theatres. But this view ignores the fact that Collier's book started a debate that lasted more than two decades and included the publication of over one hundred responses, pro and con. It also assumes that the controversy was merely about abolishing the stage. While abolition seems to have been Collier's unstated goal, initially the debate focused on how to regulate the legal stage. Among other things, Collier accused playwrights of writing obscene and blasphemous dialogue and of rewarding vicious characters with success, thus subverting the true aim of drama, which Collier asserted in his first sentence:

> The business of *Plays* is to recomend Virtue, and discountenance Vice; To shew the Uncertainty of Humane Greatness, the suddain Turns of Fate, and the Unhappy Conclusions of Violence and Injustice: 'Tis to expose the Singularities of Pride and Fancy, to make Folly and Falsehood contemptible, and to bring every Thing that is Ill Under Infamy, and Neglect. (1)

Rhetorically, starting his attack on the stage this way was a brilliant decision because it cast his book as an effort to reform the stage, not abolish it. This maxim quickly gained broad acceptance, and both Collier's allies and his enemies invoked it repeatedly. Collier's enemies, particularly comic playwrights, thus were automatically at a disadvantage because they could not disavow the moral function of the stage, and yet they had the hard task of arguing that every line and every character in every play was meant to recommend virtue and discountenance vice. This was impossible, especially since Collier and his allies cleverly took scenes and speeches out of context in order to make them look as immoral as possible. Both functionally and theoretically, Collier's maxim became *the* censorship 'law' to which playwrights were subject at the turn of the eighteenth century. Indeed, the widespread acceptance of this maxim and the sheer number of positive and negative responses to *A Short View* established Collier as the *de facto* censor of the London stage.

That Collier could inhabit such a powerful cultural position is the result of his rhetorical prowess, the ineffectiveness of the state censor, and chance. Charles Killigrew was, by all accounts, a particularly incompetent Master of the Revels. Several decrees handed down by the Lord Chamberlain immediately preceding and following the publication of *A Short View* indicate that Killigrew was not adequately ridding the stage of 'Obsenityes & other Scandalous Matters & such as any wayes Offend against ye laws of God Good manners or the knowne Statutes of this Kingdom'.[1] These decrees are significant because they show that Killigrew was commanded to correct the very sort of abuses to which Collier's book called attention. In other words, Collier was competing with the Master of the Revels to be the representative of the laws governing the theatres. In this competition, he was assisted by the Society for the Reformation of Manners and the Society for the Promotion of Christian Knowledge (SPCK), private associations of pious citizens who sought to police the morals of the nation. The theatres were a main target of their efforts, and Collier was closely identified with the groups. Indeed, as late as 1712, the SPCK sought to commission Collier to write a tract against 'obscene ballads or songs' (Anthony 1937: 246). Together, Collier and the moral reformers railed against the theatres for over two decades, usurping many of the censorial functions of the Master of the Revels.

Despite the vehemence of the moral reformers' attacks and the warnings from superiors, Killigrew seems to have altered or suppressed only a few texts. When he excised the first act of Colley Cibber's *Richard III* (1699), Cibber claimed that Killigrew was merely assisting Collier in his campaign against the stage. Killigrew suppressed three plays entirely after the publication of *A Short View*. These include *The Patriot* (1702), an adaptation of Lee's *Lucius Junius Brutus*; *An Act at Oxford* (1704), banned after officials from the university protested; and Owen Swiney's *The Quacks*, an adaptation of Molière's *L'Amour médecin*, which was eventually performed at Drury Lane on 29 March 1705. In the preface to the printed version of *The Quacks*, Swiney suggests that his play might have been suppressed because the Queen's Theatre was planning to stage a different adaptation the following month, but he also hints that alleged personal satire in some scenes '*Alarm'd the Licencer*' and had to be cut. Like Cibber, he complains that Killigrew was an indiscriminate censor who '*generally destroys with as much Distinction as the old Woman in Don* Quixots *Library, and wou'd a sav'd no more of 'em, if it were not, that he is pay'd for Tolerating some*'. But this sounds like the complaint of a wronged author, and there is nothing to suggest that Killigrew was as severe a censor as Cibber and Swiney assert.

As was the case before the Collier controversy, most of the censorship of theatrical texts and prosecution of players in the early eighteenth century was done in spite of the Master of the Revels, not because of him. For instance, Thomas Durfey's *The Bath, or, The Western Lass* (1701) was apparently suppressed after its 31 May premiere because of obscenity in one scene. Presumably, Killigrew had licensed the play prior to performance. Nevertheless, according to Durfey's preface, the production was stopped 'by Superiour command . . . for taking the Poetical Licence of making the Mad man in my Scene Satyrically drink a Health'. The objection to this scene likely came from one of the 'sow'r Reformers in an empty Pit' who came to 'take Notes, and give Evidence 'gainst Wit' who Nicholas Rowe complains about in the epilogue to *Tamerlane* (1702). Rowe is referring to moral reformers who visited the theatres with notepads to copy down blasphemous and obscene dialogue which they then used as evidence in legal actions against the theatres and individual performers. Shortly after Durfey's play was suppressed, a grand jury (urged by the Society for the Reformation of Manners) had persuaded the Lord Mayor of London to prohibit plays at Bartholomew

Fair, and an informer had brought evidence against twelve members of the Lincoln's Inn Fields company 'for using indecent expressions in some late plays'.[2] The actors were fined £5 each on 16 February 1702 for using 'the most Abominable, Impious, Prophane, Lewd, Immoral Expressions, contain'd in their Plays'.[3] This may have been the culmination of an ongoing case in which Lincoln's Inn Fields players were charged with profanity and blasphemy on 12 October 1700 (Krutch 1949: 170–3). In a separate case, the actor John Hodgson of Lincoln's Inn Fields was individually fined £10 on 30 November 1700 for 'using prophanely and jestingly the Name of God upon the Stage'.[4] Also around this period, George Bright, of the same company, was fined £10 for speaking his part in *The Man of Mode*. These are very stiff fines when one considers that most actors were not paid more than 16*s* per acting day. In a petition to Sir John Stanley (secretary to the Lord Chamberlain), Bright asks for help paying the fine, pointing out that since the play was 'Lyconed & permited, ye said Bright did humbly conceive, y^t there was neither imorality or prophainess therein'.[5] Bright reminds the Lord Chamberlain's office that the Master of the Revels – not the moral reformers – is supposed to be the official censor. The successful prosecutions of the Lincoln's Inn Fields players demonstrate that Killigrew's judgement and authority were seriously undermined by these legal actions.

The Lincoln's Inn Fields company thus learned from experience that Killigrew's licence was insufficient protection against legal harassment. An undated petition to Queen Anne from several players provides a clear picture of how official regulation of the stage was being undermined in the courts. The petition reminds her that the Lord Chamberlain 'hath constantly restrained the acting of all new playes until they were first perused by the Ma:^{e} of the Revells who used to expunge whatever he thought unfitt to be acted'.[6] Under this system, the actors 'always thought they might safely act any play so perused & approv'd by the Ma^e of the Revells', until recent prosecutions proved otherwise. Since 'the prosecutors [i.e., the moral reformers]...are not satisfied with the method that hath soe long been used to prevent the Imorality of the Stage' the players ask the Queen to provide new directions for approving plays so that the actors are not 'misled' to act anything that could land them in court. This petition demonstrates an important point about theatrical censorship in the early eighteenth century: the theatres regarded the government censor as more an ally, albeit an ineffective one, than an enemy. The actors ask the government not to leave them alone, but to censor them in a way that screens them from prosecution on morals charges. Because of the moral reformers' successful legal harassment, the actors apparently felt that they needed protection from future legal action. Nor were the actors the only ones being threatened. In 1698, Narcissus Luttrell reports that the moral reformers were attempting to get injunctions against not just actors, but also Congreve and Durfey (for *The Double Dealer* and *Don Quixote*) and publishers like Jacob Tonson and Samuel Briscoe (Hume 1976: 434).

Queen Anne responded to the situation by ordering renewed vigilance about the morality of plays. On 15 January 1704, the Lord Chamberlain warned both companies not to act any play – old or new – or any song, prologue or epilogue without

Killigrew's approval.[7] He admonished the companies to submit play texts to Killigrew before they were broken into parts and rehearsed, so that his 'Censure & License' could be better observed, and to keep the licensed text 'safe by you for your Justification' in the event of a legal battle. The insistence that songs, prologues, epilogues and especially old plays needed to be licensed or relicensed is evidence of a desire to re-establish firm control over the theatres and prevent private citizens from bringing legal action against them. While the queen's moral sympathies may have been with the reformers, she was not willing to cede regulatory control of the theatres to them. Indeed, she did just the opposite. On 14 December 1704, she issued a licence to Congreve and Vanbrugh (two of the most grievous offenders of morality, according to Collier) for the Queen's theatre in the Haymarket. The licence explains that their new company was established 'for the better reforming the Abuses, and Immorality of the Stage', and the company is to operate 'under stricter Government and Regulations than have been formerly'.[8] The queen believed that the stage needed to be reformed, but she seems to have been determined that reformation would come from the royal court, not the law courts.

The turn of the eighteenth century was a precarious time for the theatres, and there was genuine fear that they would be closed again, as they had been during the Interregnum. That this did not happen is partly owing to the actions of the queen and her court, who came to the defence of the theatres and saved them from the legal campaign of the moral reformers. Ever since the establishment of fixed-location theatres in Shakespeare's day, acting companies had depended on the protection of the nobility from anti-theatrical forces in the city of London. What we see in the Collier controversy is the re-emergence of those anti-theatrical activists and the traditional response by the royal court. Shakespeare's company was called the Lord Chamberlain's Men (changed to the King's Men when James I assumed the throne). Davenant's and Killigrew's companies were called the Duke's Men and the King's Men, respectively, after the patronage of James, Duke of York (later James II), and Charles II. And in 1704, Congreve and Vanbrugh set up the Queen's theatre in the Haymarket, named after Queen Anne. These names were not merely honorific; rather, they signified a protective relationship between the noble patron and the acting company. During the Collier controversy – and especially between 1699 and 1701, when the legal actions against the actors were being pursued – this relationship was critical to the survival of the public stage.

Regulating Theatrical Business Practices

The close relationship between the court and the theatres during the Restoration period meant that the theatre business did not operate in a *laissez-faire* environment. Davenant and Killigrew knew that managing a theatre was a privilege, not a right. Indeed, once they were granted that privilege, they busied themselves by depriving everybody else of the opportunity to operate a public stage in London. While their theatres were private, capitalist ventures, unlike the Comédie Française (established in 1680), they nevertheless had to submit to the sometimes detailed oversight of their business by the Lord Chamberlain and others. The regulation of the theatres' business practices was pervasive, and a detailed account of the ways that the royal court dictated decisions involving the hiring and firing of actors, salaries and benefit night decisions, repertory choices and labour disputes would require another chapter. Allardyce Nicoll catalogues many such instances in his *History of English Drama* (1955, 1: 318–20, 360–85), and Milhous and Hume offer many more in their *Register of English Theatrical Documents, 1660–1730* and *Vice Chamberlain Coke's Theatrical Papers, 1706–1715*. For the purposes of this chapter, a few examples will serve to illustrate the extent and types of business regulation in the Restoration theatres.

The most important type of business regulation has already been discussed: allowing the formation and operation of a theatrical company. Charles II gave patents to Davenant and Killigrew and permitted them to stifle all competition. When the king licensed a third company under the direction of the old actor, George Jolly, the two patentees were permitted to cheat Jolly out of his enterprise. However, the court's favouritism to patentees was not total. When Christopher Rich and Thomas Skipwith, patentees of the United Company, antagonized the actors with their mercenary management, the actors took their grievances to the Lord Chamberlain. After failing to reconcile the two sides, the Lord Chamberlain permitted Thomas Betterton and his fellow actors to set up shop in a rival theatre in Lincoln's Inn Fields in 1695. Years later, Rich again ran foul of the Lord Chamberlain for mismanagement and suffered for it by having his Drury Lane theatre silenced in 1709. This was an extreme step, but prohibition is the flip-side of permission: the hand that gives can also take away.

Theatre managers were not the only ones who came to understand the dual nature of their relationship with the Lord Chamberlain. Actors, too, were subject to both rewards and punishments from the court. For example, on 20 December 1669, the Lord Chamberlain reprimanded two bailiffs for arresting Thomas Creek, a member of the Duke's Company, and hence a liveried (and protected) servant of the court. But as Nicoll points out, if actors were liveried servants of the court, then they were subject to arrest by order of the Lord Chamberlain, as happened to Jeremiah Lisle of the Duke's Company on 26 April 1670 for absenting himself from his duties to the company (Nicoll 1955, 1: 318–19, n. 7). Missing rehearsal or refusing to perform an assigned role obviously could have serious consequences for an actor. But actors were even regulated in the ways that they could perform their roles. We have already seen, in the case of John Lacy, how displeasing the king with offensive ad-libbing could lead to arrest. The case of Katherine Corey shows how a performer could become a pawn in court intrigue by virtue of her performance. On 15 January 1669, Pepys records that the Lord Chamberlain imprisoned Corey for impersonating his kinswoman, Lady Harvey, in a production of Ben Jonson's *Catiline*. Lady Castlemaine, the king's mistress, persuaded him to release the actress and command the play be performed before him, which it was, again with the impersonation of Lady Harvey.

Harvey's friends responded by pelting Corey with oranges and hissing her performance.

Unlike the previous examples, most of the regulation of the theatres was rather
mundane. The Lord Chamberlain's papers include orders to the theatres that they
eliminate the pushing and shoving for seats that generally took place when the doors
were opened; that they prohibit audience members from sitting on the stage during a
performance; and that they make sure that musicians remove their hats out of respect
for their noble patrons. Most often, the court's regulation of the theatre business
regarded labour disputes and money matters. For example, on 16 March 1665, the
Lord Chamberlain commanded actors in the King's Company to attend upon him in
his rooms at Whitehall and to bring their contracts with them, presumably to settle a
labour dispute with management (Nicoll 1955, 1: 299). In another instance, the
Lord Chamberlain ordered the United Company to re-engage Katherine Corey in
1689 after she had been involved in a plan to start a rival company. Ten years
later, during the season of 1697–8, the Lord Chamberlain ordered a suspension
of benefit performances at Lincoln's Inn Fields so that the company could devote
all its resources to paying off its sizeable debts. This order was the result of his
intervention in a dispute between John Verbruggen and the other actor-sharers in the
company.

Compared to Continental theatres of the time, the English stage seems to have been
very much a private enterprise. Had Charles II been more flush, perhaps the English
theatres would have enjoyed state subsidies on the French model. In Rochester's
words, Charles was a 'merry Monarch' who enjoyed the theatre (not to mention the
actresses), but he was also 'scandalous and poor', and so he could not support the stage
financially. While this gave theatre managers some autonomy, it also entailed great
financial risks on their part. And as the previous examples have shown, their business
was still subject to royal management even though they did not enjoy lavish royal
subsidies. Charles compensated for this by allowing Davenant and Killigrew exclusive
control over the public stage. Over the course of the next century and a half, this
private/public patent system continued to define the London stage, and when un-
authorized rival ventures emerged in the 1730s, the Stage Licensing Act of 1737
officially prohibited all theatres except those operating by virtue of royal patents or
licences, reasserting the Lord Chamberlain's control over the theatres.

Conclusions

The Licensing Act of 1737 was an effort to normalize and clarify the state's regulation
of the theatres, and in many ways it was needed because of the inadequacies of the
Restoration system described in this chapter. First of all, the law eliminated the
multiple levels of authority over the censorship of play texts. Despite Sir Henry
Herbert's efforts, the importance of the Master of the Revels steadily declined during
the eighteenth century. In his place, the Licensing Act made the Lord Chamberlain

the sole authority over the stage, and there was no appeal to his decisions. After 1737, every play text was reviewed and a copy retained by the Lord Chamberlain's office. Almost all of these copies are preserved, complete with the censor's markings, in the Larpent Collection of plays in the Henry E. Huntington Library. The Licensing Act was the most comprehensive and repressive censorship law in English theatrical history, and the Lord Chamberlain's office continued to license plays by virtue of this law until 1968.

The efficiency of the eighteenth-century system of textual censorship was a marked improvement over the Restoration one, which seems positively haphazard by contrast. But just because the earlier system was haphazard does not mean that it was without teeth. As we have seen, the government was able to crack down on political drama quite effectively during the Popish Plot and Exclusion Crisis years. The banning of nine plays in the space of just five years (not to mention the significant 'reformation' of others, like *The Lancashire Witches*) is proof that the state could control the freedom of expression in the theatres when it felt the need. And as the examples of the court's intervention in theatrical business matters show, the London stage was subject to a wide range of regulation, even if that intervention was not always predictable or tidy. Indeed, the very informality of theatrical regulation during the Restoration period is its defining feature: the system seems generally lax, but it permitted occasionally severe restrictions on the freedom of expression and the arbitrary dictation of business decisions. Given the haphazard nature of the state's control over the stage, we should not be surprised that the greatest threat to free expression – even to the very existence of the public stage – came from outside the government. What made the Collier controversy controversial was not merely the moral reformers' pamphlet attacks on the stage, but also their legal harassment of actors. Even before Collier published *A Short View*, the Lord Chamberlain was warning the Master of the Revels to scrutinize play texts more carefully. During the controversy, friends and foes of the stage both agreed that the current system of regulation had failed and needed to be fixed. That the government did not respond to Collier and the moral reformers by effectively reinvigorating official censorship is truly surprising. Instead, the system collapsed in 1715 when the actor-managers at Drury Lane stopped submitting play texts to the Master of the Revels altogether, arguing that Sir Richard Steele's patent for that theatre declared him the censor of its plays. From that point, the London stage continued to operate without systematic oversight by the government until the passage of the Stage Licensing Act of 1737.

NOTES

1   Lord Chamberlain Dorset's decree of January 1696 (Public Record Office, L.C. 7/1, f. 43); quoted in White (1931: 18). For the other decrees, see White (1931: 18–20); and see Milhous and Hume (1991), item nos 1523, 1556, 1557, 1602–4, 1607, 1753–5, 1763 and 1882.

2   See Milhous and Hume (1991), document nos 1667–8 for the ban on plays at Bartholomew Fair; nos 1674, 1679, 1681 and 1685 for the action against the Lincoln's Inn Fields actors. The quotation is from Luttrell (1857, 5: 111).

3   Quotation is from *The Proceedings and Tryals of the Players in Lincolns-Inn-Fields Held at the King's-Bench Bar at Westminster on Munday the 16th of February 1701/2* (London: J. Richardson, 1702); quoted in Milhous and Hume (1991), document no. 1679.

4   Quotation is from the *Flying Post* of 28–30 November 1700; quoted in Milhous and Hume (1991), document no. 1673.

5   Public Record Office, L. C. 7/3, f. 159.

6   Public Record Office, L. C. 7/3, f. 166.

7   Public Record Office, L. C. 5/153, f. 433.

8   Public Record Office, L. C. 5/154, f. 35.

REFERENCES AND FURTHER READING

Anthony, Sister Rose (1937). *The Jeremy Collier Stage Controversy, 1698–1726*. Milwaukee: Marquette University Press.

Barish, Jonas (1981). *The Antitheatrical Prejudice*. Berkeley: University of California Press.

Bawcutt, N. W. (ed.). (1996). *The Control and Censorship of Caroline Drama: The Records of Sir Henry Herbert, Master of the Revels 1623–73*. Oxford: Clarendon Press.

Clarke, W. K. Lowther (1959). *A History of the S.P.C.K.* London: SPCK.

Collier, Jeremy (1972). *A Short View of the Immorality and Profaneness of the English Stage* (London, 1698). Rpt. in *The English Stage: Attack and Defense, 1577–1730*, ed. Arthur Freeman. 50 vols. New York: Garland.

Freehafer, John (1965–6). 'The Formation of the London Patent Companies in 1660', *Theatre Notebook* 20, 6–30.

Hume, Robert D. (1976). *The Development of English Drama in the Late Seventeenth Century*. Oxford: Clarendon Press.

Hume, Robert D. (1999). 'Jeremy Collier and the Future of the London Theater in 1698', *Studies in Philology* 4, 480–511.

Krutch, Joseph Wood (1949). *Comedy and Conscience after the Restoration*. Rev. ed. New York: Columbia University Press.

Luttrell, Narcissus (1857). *A Brief Historical Relation of State Affairs, 1678–1714*. 6 vols. Oxford: Oxford University Press.

Milhous, Judith and Hume, Robert D. (eds). (1982). *Vice Chamberlain Coke's Theatrical Papers, 1706–1715*. Carbondale and Edwardsville: Southern Illinois University Press.

Milhous, Judith and Hume, Robert D. (eds). (1991). *A Register of English Theatrical Documents, 1660–1730*. 2 vols. Carbondale and Edwardsville: Southern Illinois University Press.

Nicoll, Allardyce (1955). *A History of English Drama, 1660–1900*. 4th ed. Cambridge: Cambridge University Press.

Owen, Susan J. (1996). *Restoration Theatre and Crisis*. Oxford: Clarendon Press.

Patterson, Annabel (1985). '*The Country Gentleman*: Howard, Marvell, and Dryden in the Theatre of Politics', *Studies in English Literature* 25, 491–509.

Staves, Susan (1974). 'Why was Dryden's *Mr. Limberham* Banned? A Problem in Restoration Theatre History', *Restoration and Eighteenth-century Theatre Research* 13, 1–11.

Weber, Harold (1996). *Paper Bullets: Print and Kingship under Charles II*. Lexington: University Press of Kentucky.

White, Arthur F. (1931). 'The Office of the Revels and Dramatic Censorship during the Restoration Period', *Western Reserve University Bulletin* n.s. 34, 5–45.

Williams, Aubrey (1975). 'No Cloistered Virtue: Or, Playwright Versus Priest in 1698', *PMLA* 90, 234–46.

Winton, Calhoun (1974). 'The London Stage Embattled: 1695–1710', *Tennessee Studies in Language and Literature* 19, 9–19.

Winton, Calhoun (1980). 'Dramatic Censorship', in Robert D. Hume (ed.), *The London Theatre World, 1660–1800*. Carbondale and Edwardsville: Southern Illinois University Press, 286–308.

4

Libertinism and Sexuality

Maximillian E. Novak

Leave this gaudy gilded stage,
    From custom more than use frequented,
Where fools of either sex and age
    Crowd to see themselves presented.
To Love's theatre, the bed,
    Youth and beauty fly together,
And act so well, it may be said
    The laurel there was due to either.

John Wilmot, Earl of Rochester,
'Song' (Vieth 1968: 85–6)

Rochester's connection between what was then called sexual conversation and the conversations heard on the Restoration stage and in the theatre was hardly unusual during the period, but it is suggestive of the ways in which libertine behaviour and ideas were intimately intertwined with stage presentation. It has sometimes been thought that the poem was written to the best actress of the Restoration, Elizabeth Barry, who was Rochester's mistress for a time. Such a possibility would hardly have surprised contemporary and later moralists. Indeed, the assumed relationship between social life and stage representation led to the general condemnation of Restoration comedy during the eighteenth and nineteenth centuries by critics such as Thomas Thornton, who, speaking of one of Otway's comedies, lamented its 'favourable reception with audiences whose minds were corrupted by habit and example, to a perfect relish of grossness and contempt of decency' (1813, 3: 99). Similar attacks upon the libertine nature of both the plays and the audience may be found in writers from Sir Richard Steele to Samuel Johnson. Although performances and editions of Restoration drama proliferated after 1920, some critics and moralists continued to have their doubts.

During the period following the Second World War to the 1980s the commonplace critical remark about Restoration comedy as well as much of the poetry and prose of the period was that, despite the fact that sex appeared to occupy an inordinately prominent and particularly vivid position in these works, they were not *really* about sex, but rather about more serious and important matters. A number of reasons might be found for this attitude. The influential attack upon the triviality of Restoration comedy by L. C. Knights in 1946 took on a momentum of its own that seemed to extend to the entire period.[1] In itself, Knights's critique was based on the arguments of Charles Lamb and other romantic critics to the effect that Restoration comedy had nothing to do with reality. Although Lamb was trying to remove the notion that these plays contained vicious sexual material, Knights turned the argument towards social concerns contending that the comedies failed to reflect the reality of their times in any meaningful way. During the 1960s, another form of anti-sex, anti-libertine interpretation made its appearance. David Vieth attempted to show that the poems of John Wilmot, Earl of Rochester, were actually attacking libertine attitudes in the name of traditional moral beliefs, and Aubrey Williams advanced a religious interpretation of Congreve (and by extension all Restoration comedy) that was extremely influential. His argument invoked a logic that went as follows: all serious thought during the Restoration was Christian thought; there was an obvious seriousness to these comedies; therefore they had to be read as essentially Christian documents. Critics such as Harriett Hawkins showed the flaws in Williams's argument, but it has continued to have its defenders decades after it was proposed.[2] Such thinking even spawned a computer study, which purported to show that true rakes were almost always punished; this despite the obvious problems with classification and definition which no computer could cure.[3] Its influence may be found even in such normally hard-headed critics as Robert Hume.[4] I think, however, that at this juncture we should be willing to admit what common sense would seem to dictate. Almost all of these plays are indeed about sex to a degree, and some of them are almost exclusively about sex.[5] The important question should be: why did sex seem so important to the period?

One answer is that it reflected the assertion of selfhood and power by the youngest members of society, beginning a trend that has continued until today. Like the poor couple observed in the act of sexual intercourse in Denis Diderot's *Jacques le fataliste*, sexuality was one thing that the young in this society had to themselves. For the most part, the years between 1660 and 1700 were not remarkably favourable towards the young. The doctrines of Thomas Hobbes preached an idea of absolute power of parents over their children, and although Hobbes was reviled for a variety of his views after 1660, not many critics focused their attacks on this aspect of his beliefs. The family, as conceived by one of Hobbes's most influential opponents, Richard Cumberland, may have been held together by natural social sympathies, but there is no sign that he did not believe in parental authority. Although there were the usual cases of disobedience, it was a patriarchal society in which both young men and women were usually kept under rigid control. The most famous rebel, the libertine poet John Wilmot, Earl of Rochester, was banished from the court on a number of occasions. Where the revolt was too excessive, punishment was likely to follow. Despite disapprobation directed at the young libertines and the playwrights who depicted them from moralists usually writing outside the sphere of the court and London, they clearly had some support from Charles II, whose private sexual libertinism was often in need of defence.

Finding the true origins of libertinism, like tracing the origins of any idea, is usually a futile task, but there is no question that its modern efflorescence began in seventeenth-century France in the circle around Théophile de Viau (1590–1626). He was sentenced to death in 1622 for his *Parnasse satyrique*, but the judgement was commuted to banishment. His poetry expressed the basic doctrines of libertinism: society was merely an artificial construct. Its laws were not to be taken seriously by those who understood that human beings had been tricked into accepting them. Marriage was just another burdensome, ill-conceived practice to be avoided at all costs. Life was to be experienced as much through the senses as through the mind, and the pleasures of the body taught far more truths than the learning promulgated by the universities. Since the young experienced the pleasures of the senses more fully than the old, they should ignore, as much as possible, the precepts delivered by those who could no longer experience the pleasures of life fully. Such understanding set the believers free from the conventions of society. They might use their freedom to indulge in the pleasures of the senses or, with Epicurus, decide that the highest pleasures were those of the mind. From a political standpoint, these beliefs might lead to a conservative attitude according to which it was understood that the masses of people could never grasp the liberty available to them, and that it was just as well to seek freedom among a small group while allowing the masses to obey the laws that enslaved them. On the other hand, it could lead to a radically democratic attitude – to a detestation of those who refused to enlighten the common people and subjected them to tyranny. In any case, no eighteenth-century government was willing to put up with too obvious a demonstration of libertine principles.

A second influence on libertinism in France was the rise of neo-Epicureanism under the leadership of Pierre Gassendi (1592–1655). This philosophic return to Epicurus and Lucretius brought with it none of the disapprobation of the group influenced by Théophile de Viau, but its emphasis on atomism and on empirical method might easily lead to materialism.[6] Thomas Hobbes was certainly influenced by Gassendi, and however his thought may be argued to allow for belief in a God, it was taken to uphold a purely material and mechanical cause for all human action. The combination of materialist thought and libertine concepts of the senses was a heady mixture in mid-century thought, especially since writers such as Isaac de la Peyrère and, eventually, Spinoza and Richard Simon were to throw doubt on the credibility of the Bible. Such doubts were already implicit in the writings of Théophile de Viau.

Of course the partially formalized attitudes of the libertines and the neo-Epicureans of France reflected interests in sexual freedom that were already apparent in English plays from the early part of the seventeenth century. For example, Mirabel in Francis

Beaumont and John Fletcher's *The Wild-Goose Chase* wants to sleep with every woman he encounters. Still, writers such as Sir William Davenant were very aware of the new *précieuse* attitudes towards love, which were the product of the literary salons of Paris. Why should he not have been aware of libertine attitudes as well? And despite a considerable degree of wildness in Fletcher's rakes, the real feel of Restoration comedy is not apparent before the plays of Thomas Killigrew. A follower of the future Charles II, Killigrew would have had no trouble encountering the libertine ideas when he was on the Continent. It is not difficult to understand why the impoverished followers of Charles would have been attracted by libertine ideals. Their sense of superiority as soldiers was eventually shattered by the victories of the parliamentary forces. They were uncertain if they would ever return to power in England, but they could at least flaunt their sexual powers as superior to the puritanical followers of Cromwell. They could not only shock these religious zealots by their actions, but they could experience the exhilaration of feeling that they belonged to a group of men and women who could assert, by their actions, their true sense of freedom from the conventions of society.

Thomas Killigrew's *The Parson's Wedding*, a popular play during the Restoration, shows clear signs of being written before the Interregnum, and however much it may have been revised, much of the play that was performed in 1641 remained. The central action of the play is based on a trick by which two rakes compromise the reputations of two women to the extent that they are forced to marry them. The bevy of rakes in the play is led by the Captain, who pronounces a libertine philosophy of sexual freedom. In addition to the rakish male characters, there are several women characters who were to become stock figures in later Restoration comedy: a hypocritical older woman, Lady Love-all, who has intercourse with any man who will make the slightest effort at a seduction, a witty young woman, Pleasant, and Wanton, a beautiful prostitute who announces her complete pleasure in her sexual freedom and preaches the virtues of libertinism. She attacks the economic forces that destroy the honesty of sexual relations. Which is worse, she asks, 'to let Love, youth, and good humor, betray us to a kindness, or to be gravely seduc'd by some aunt or uncle, without consideration of the disparity of Age, Birth, or Persons, to lie down before a Joynture' (134 [5.4]). True love, she argues, is the only important thing.

Some of the speeches in this play might have come directly from the work that became the source book for libertine attitudes, Francis Osborne's *Advice to a Son* (1656, 1658). Osborne's book was condemned by the authorities and burned by the public hangman for what was considered to be its immorality. He advised against marriage as a trap that would force a man to labour in the mines of sexual intercourse without true pleasure. Osborne had similar advice to women. If they could manage financially, they too should avoid marriage like the plague. For Osborne, the laws of society, particularly those governing marriage, were to be ignored as much as possible. They were part of the web of illusion that society had tricked its citizens into believing. Despite official condemnation during the Interregnum, Osborne's book remained popular and was frequently reprinted throughout the Restoration. Both the male rakes of Killigrew's play, such as the Captain, Jolly and Wild, and the female libertine, Wanton, assume attitudes towards sexual pleasure and the evils of marriage that are similar to those expressed in Osborne's work.

It should be noted that *The Parson's Wedding* is coarse fare indeed compared to the truly witty sexual comedies of the Restoration. It was a popular stage play, though the version that Samuel Pepys saw on the stage in 1664 must have been cut considerably from the lengthy version that appeared in the folio volume of Killigrew's plays published in that year. In some ways, it resembles what might be called the libertine picaresque, which flourished at mid-century and which allowed for considerable vulgarity – scenes of defecation as well as sex. The first part of Richard Head's *The English Rogue*, published in 1665, advanced a similar libertine doctrine for both men and women and, like *The Parson's Wedding*, put a high value on physical and social mobility. The term 'extravagant', sometimes applied to the witty rakes in such works, had meanings associated both with wandering and with striking and surprising actions. It is well to keep that in mind when considering another play by Killigrew – *Thomaso, or the Wanderer*. The hero, Thomaso, is described in Hobbesian terms as one who 'being bred with the wolf...grew wise enough to thrive in the forest' (321 [1.2]). Although Aphra Behn was later to give real power to Killigrew's play in her adaptation, *The Rover*, she also omitted many of the long speeches in which Angellica defends the freedom of women in love and in which Thomaso defends his libertine relationships:

> All the hony of Marriage but none of the sting, Ned; I have a Woman without that foundless Folly, of better or worse; there's a kind of Non-sence in that Vow Fools onely swallow; I can now bid my Friends well-come without Jealousie; Our vows are built upon kindness only, they stand & fall together; We neither load, nor enslave the mind with Matrimony; no laws, nor tyes, but what good Nature makes, binds us; we are sure to meet without false well-come, or dissembling smiles, to hide the Sallary of a sin, or elide the Fornication of a *Platonique* Friendship; Our knots hold no longer then we love; No sooner with a liberty but we take it. (346 [3.1])

Thomaso enjoys sex and does not fear violating laws of incest. Angellica, for her part, defies the custom that would scorn a woman who has sex outside of marriage. 'I prize my self as high for having enjoye'd a gallant man', she states, 'as you would do having won his sword, or a gallant woman's heart' (Part 2, 397 [1.1]). As in *The Parson's Wedding*, there are dreams of polygamy. Two of the rakes decide they will go to the Indies where they will have six wives each, 'smooth and comely beauties, naked truths, *Eves*, in the state of innocence' (453 [4.1]). And very predictive of the major comedies of the Restoration is the attack upon the country, where love is bestial and the behaviour of husbands physically disgusting. Yet the rendering of such matters tends more to the grotesque than the witty. In brief, it may be said that the often subtle and philosophic form of libertinism that flourished in France in writers such as Cyrano de Bergerac and J. Fr. Sarasin and which led to the free thought of the *philosophes* in the following century tended, in England, to exist on a far simpler level. Nevertheless, in both countries libertinism implied a belief in freedom of action, whether in the realm of the body or the mind.

Though Killigrew's plays focused strongly on sex, most of the new comedies performed during the years following the Restoration used such material in an incidental fashion. It was not until the emergence of the wits surrounding the court of Charles II as models of libertine behaviour and wit that such plays became popular. With the publication of *The Sullen Lovers* in 1668, Thomas Shadwell took the opportunity to complain about a new kind of comedy. As a follower of Ben Jonson, he defended the comedy of humour and character and attacked those who believed 'that all the Wit in *Playes* consisted in bringing two persons upon the Stage to break Jests, and to bob one another, which they call Repartie'. In the new comedies 'the two chief persons are most commonly a Swearing, Drinking, Whoring, Ruffian for a Lover, and an impudent ill-bred *tomrig* for a Mistress, and these are the fine People of the Play; . . . but their chief Subject is bawdy, and profaneness, which they call *brisk writing*'. Shadwell urged his fellow playwrights to avoid such writing as 'Indecent' (1: 11).

The particular playwright that Shadwell had in mind was unquestionably John Dryden. Although the character of Bayes in Buckingham's *The Rehearsal* (1671–2) was unquestionably a composite figure, Bayes's confession to the effect that when stuck for something to do, he simply wrote 'Bawdy' had to be aimed at Dryden. The characters of Celadon and Florimell in *Secret Love, or The Maiden Queen* (1667–8) engage in a great deal of banter about love and sex, but it was not until 1668 that Dryden produced his first pure sex comedy – *An Evening's Love, or The Mock Astrologer*. The couples in this play, men and women, are interested in pursuing their sexual adventures, and while everything ends up, innocently enough, in marriage, as in Killigrew's comedies, the characters advance libertine attitudes. Such comedies were becoming the norm. Libertines such as Lovemore in Thomas Betterton's *The Amorous Widow* (1670) pursue sexual seduction unremittingly throughout the play.

Nevertheless, it is easy enough to observe the change in sophistication and understanding between this play and Dryden's *Marriage A-la-Mode*, produced in 1671. Between that time and the 1670s, libertinism had gained a hold upon writers of comedy. As we have seen, libertine ideas had been available in both England and France and their usefulness for comedy should have been obvious. By the late 1670s these ideas were part of the culture of the court and the 'Town', associated with wits such as Sedley, Buckingham and Etherege, all of whom were playwrights. Wit was the most highly prized quality at the time, encompassing cleverness in conversation, physical actions and imagination.

The dissemination of libertine concepts throughout the culture, including libertine plays in the distinctly unaristocratic celebrations at the Lord Mayor's procession in London, is obvious enough in the literature of the 1660s, but these ideas received a powerful impetus from the writings of John Wilmot, Earl of Rochester. Young, handsome and a favourite of Charles II, his abduction of his future wife, Elizabeth

Malet, represented the kind of outrageous gesture that brought with it a degree of punishment and considerable admiration. His throwing over the king's sundial to the accompaniment of a witty observation on time was another example of an extravagant gesture displaying wit, while his wonderful disguise as a doctor (Bendo) specializing in the cure of venereal disease was accompanied by a brilliant announcement which called all of existence a product of illusion and masking.

Although his *Satyr against Mankind* appears to have been influenced by Théophile de Viau's 'Satyre première' in its celebration of the direct passions of animals and the equally powerful passions of the young, Rochester developed a far more subtle system, which extended to humans as social animals. Influenced by Hobbes's concept of the state of nature, a state in which humankind live in fear of the depredations of those willing to use their power against the weak, Rochester extended the state of nature into society itself, which he viewed as dominated by the 'knaves' – those who are willing to use their abilities to dominate the 'fools' of the society.

Rochester, then, exemplified the libertine ideal both in his writings and in his life. In his poetry he frequently played with ideas of experimental sex, including homo-sexuality, and did not hesitate to treat all bodily functions – menstruation, premature ejaculation, defecation – as entirely natural, as part of humankind's animal self. Rochester offered a kind of anti-intellectualism as an antidote to both the scholastic thought still practised at Oxford and Cambridge and the theoretical systems of the new philosophers who followed the lead of Descartes. The body, the passions, the will rule us better than an over-intellectualized response to experience. Whether Rochester actually had much to do with the obscene do-it-yourself orgy titled *Sodom*, it was certainly associated with his name, as were the many libertine poems that emerged alongside his genuine works, which appeared in the first printed volume of his writings published in 1680. Poems by other libertines such as Buckingham and Sedley were simply shuffled into the mix. For many contemporaries, Rochester *was* English libertinism. He became the model for the rakish protagonist of comedy and, as Count Rosidore, the subject of lament after his death in Nathaniel Lee's *Princess of Cleve* (1680, 1689). If Rochester sometimes turned his satire upon the absurd distor-tions of the libertine code, this did not mean that he was not an exponent of a proper form of libertinism. He and some of his friends managed to get into trouble by romping naked in the countryside, but the symbolism of the gesture should not be ignored. These men were asserting their freedom in a world filled with what they considered foolish rules – rules that ought not to apply to those who saw through the enchaining conventions of society.[7]

Sodom may be treated as a work of 'Rochester', in the same way as art historians designate anonymous paintings in the manner of Rembrandt as by 'Rembrandt'. *Sodom* is certainly a dramatic work, and although it could hardly be performed at a public theatre, it was widely known and circulated in manuscript. If one is to regard it as an artistic production rather than sheer sexual display, it may be treated as a parody of the rhymed heroic play which dominated serious Restoration drama up until 1677. Since the rhymed heroic plays usually posited a pair of idealistic lovers whose elevated sensibilities matched those in the French romances upon which they were often based, it was the job of the parodist to mock such a solemn treatment of love by creating a world of orgiastic sex. Hence the scene directions for the second act has:

> Six naked women and six naked men appear, and dance, the men doing obeisance to the women's cunts, kissing and touching them often, the women doing ceremonies to the men's pricks, kissing them, dandling their cods, etc. and so fall to fucking, after which the women sigh, and the men look simple and sneak off. *(136 {Act 2})*

Similar phallic and vaginal imagery accompanies the scene directions to several of the other acts. The plot, if it may be called that, has Bolloximian, king of Sodom, and his subjects punished with venereal disease for having turned to buggery and abandoned sexual relations with women. The ghost of his queen, Cuntigratia, appears at the end pronouncing doom upon him and his city. Defiant to the end, Bolloximian, leering at Pockenello, urges him to retire to a cavern, and 'There on thy buggered arse I will expire' (154 [Act 5]). The final scene resembles a number of supernatural scenes in Dryden's rhymed heroic plays, particularly Cuntigratia's

> Fire your bollocks singes,
> Sodom on the hinges.
> Bugger, bugger, bugger.
> All in hugger-mugger,
> Fire does descend.
> 'Tis too late to mend.
>   (153 [Act 5])[8]

As parody it is far from being as clever as some of Thomas Duffett's farces, and cannot be considered in the same class as Buckingham's *The Rehearsal*. It would be a mistake to find too much wit in it.[9] Its force lies in its outrageous flaunting of sexuality. Sexual desire drives every aspect of life in *Sodom*, and while that is a far cry from philosophic libertinism, it is certainly a part of the creed. Whatever Rochester's role in *Sodom*, he certainly revised John Fletcher's *Valentinian* before his death in 1680, a play which also involves a bisexual emperor and much incidental sexuality. In revising the play, Rochester centred the action on Valentinian's rape of Lucina, the wife of Maximus, and added a scene depicting Valentinian and his eunuch Lycus in a scene of sexual pleasure. The depiction of Valentinian's outrageous mistreatment of his Roman subjects may suggest that Rochester tended towards a politics of rights, obligations and freedom that was one aspect of libertine thought.

When Dryden came to write *Marriage A-la-Mode*, first performed in 1671, he dedicated his work to Rochester and to what he thought to be a new kind of wit whose ordinary conversation was superior to the witty dialogue in most comedies. In a telling statement, Dryden maintained that 'the best Comick Writers of our Age, will join with me to acknowledge, that they have copy'd the Gallantries of Courts, the Delicacy of Expression, and the Decencies of Behaviour, from your Lordship, with more Success than if they had taken their Models from the Court of *France*' (11: 221). The play itself, divided between an heroic action and a witty comedy, suggests the seeming necessity of extramarital sex for both men and women and even toys with the notion of an arrangement in which there might be a free exchange of sex between the two couples. Though Dryden shows sexual desire as conditioned by social pressures, he allows his young lovers to pursue it single-mindedly.

Objections to the court's toleration or approval of libertine ideals were not long in coming. In November 1670, Charles II began his long relationship with Louise de Kérouaille. She was French and had direct ties to Louis XIV. The sexual liaison began at a party that had some of the play-acting and masquerade associated with a libertine group known as the Roarers. Charles's relationship with Kérouaille brought severe criticism from some moralists identified with the country, and everything suggests that Charles was willing to accept a number of defences of his conduct from the writers of the time. These varied from a glorification of the sophistication of the city and court as opposed to the barbarity of the country to an argument on luxury as a superior and grand way of life for a monarch and his court – a way of life incomprehensible to ordinary people in the country. On the one hand, the writers of comedy ridiculed the country as never before; on the other, in tragedies such as Dryden's *All for Love*, Charles and Kérouaille (by this time Duchess of Portsmouth) might be celebrated as lovers comparable to Antony and Cleopatra.

In 1673, a series of works, many published by Allen Banks, staged the conflict between the old ways of the country and the new libertinism of the court and the wits of London. The author of *Remarques on the Humours and Conversations of the Gallants of the Town*, for example, expressed his annoyance at the new youth culture centred on the latest plays and the contempt for what the author considered the true and human values of the country. To the contrary, in associating with these new wits, 'if you cannot mock at Virtue and Prudence with a Mene of Scorn and Contempt, you will not be able to keep company with those *Heroes*'.[10] They are particularly contemptuous of marriage and of the traditions of the past. *Remarques upon Remarques: or a Vindication of the Conversations of the Town*, published in the same year, not only defended the new way of thinking but threatened the author of the original with punishment for possible rebellion against the government. Undismayed by this threat, the author of the original work returned to the attack in *Reflections on Marriage and the Poetick Discipline* (1673), once more defending marriage and attacking both the oddly idealized love in the heroic plays and the 'sordid' image of love in the comedies.[11] Among the many exchanges was *Gallantry A-la-mode* (1674), which contained a glorification of sexual intercourse in a manner reminiscent in its sensuality of Keats's *The Eve of Saint Agnes*.[12] Such works owed much to Ovid's *Amores*, a work that was extremely popular during the Restoration and provided much material for libertine playwrights and poets.

Thomas Shadwell's *The Libertine*, performed in June 1675, with its grotesque concept of the libertine as an arch-villain and criminal, may be seen as the strongest statement against what Shadwell saw as a kind of brutal nihilism that underlay libertinism. This is one of many theatrical pieces based on the theme of Don Juan, but in its moral and literary spirit it is as far away from the most famous of the lot, Mozart's *Don Giovanni*, as anyone could imagine. Whereas Mozart's hero-villain leaves us with a certain ambiguous admiration for his courage and energy, Shadwell's Don John and his friends are wholly despicable. Shadwell confesses that he drew his play from a variety of sources, including, obviously, the already renowned versions of Tirso de Molina and Jean-Baptiste Poquelin (Molière), but everything in his play was intended to draw a picture of the libertine that is utterly villainous and contemptible. If the result is an entirely contrasting view of good and evil that comes close to parody, Shadwell nevertheless presents a fairly thorough view of libertinism. He uses the key words 'wild' and 'extravagant' in describing the play in the prologue as being *'wild, and as extravagant as th' Age'* (3: 23). Don John's concept of 'Infallible Nature' is similar to that of the Marquis de Sade over a hundred years later – whatever exists is natural and whoever follows natural desire cannot be wrong. Don Antonio, who has tutored the entire group of libertines, has enabled his disciples to throw off the chains of their earlier education to discover the 'liberty of Nature'. Don John shows how well he has learned the libertine code:

> Nature gave us our Senses, which we please:
> Nor does our Reason war against our Senses.
> By Natures order, Sense should guide our Reason
> Since to the mind all objects Sense conveys.
> But Fools for shaddows lose substantial pleasures,
> For idle tales abandon true delight,
> And solid joys of day, for empty dreams at night
> Away, thou foolish thing, thou chollick of the mind,
> Thou Worm by ill-digesting stomachs bred:
> In spite of thee, we'll surfeit in delights,
> And never think ought can be ill that's pleasant.
>
> (3: 26 [1.1])

The end of life is pleasure, and reason exists merely to aid the senses. Following Hobbes's arguments, Don John argues a mechanical theory of the will ruled by the strongest desires. Shadwell clearly did his homework for presenting a philosophic basis for Don John and his libertines, but their indiscriminate rampage of murder and rape is mainly silly. Although the traditional ending with the statue of Don Pedro sending Don John to Hell must have been theatrically effective, many of the scenes, including the appearance of six of Don John's wives, must have bordered on the ludicrous. Shadwell's thuggish Don John is as far as anyone might imagine from wits such as Rochester and Etherege.

All of these disputes were, in many ways, merely preparation for the great libertine plays of 1675 and 1676, including William Wycherley's *The Country Wife*, George Etherege's *The Man of Mode* and Aphra Behn's *The Rover*. These plays are so rich in wit, satire and characterization that it is easy enough for a modern critic to forget their strong libertine thrust. Of course, the contemporary Christian moralist saw little but sexual licence, and we have to pay attention to such a viewpoint. Certainly Horner's pretended dislike of women, his supposed castration and his seduction of Margery Pinchwife have to be seen as embodying a libertine programme. The appeal to sexual liberty – particularly of married women – at the end of the play, while undercut by the deception of Pinchwife and the audience's pleasure in knowing that Horner's impotence is merely a ruse to trick husbands into believing that their wives are safe in his company, is convincing enough. Having failed in his efforts to find a mistress who will be true to him, Pinchwife marries Margery in the belief that she will remain ignorant and subservient. He brutalizes her throughout the play, and the audience rejoices in her discovery of sexual pleasure in her relationship with Horner, however short-lived such an affair must be. In the famous 'china scene', Horner manages to have intercourse with the wife of Sir Jasper Fidget while he is in the next room, and in one scene, the libertine ladies of the play confess that respectability is merely a mask for their lives of free sexual pleasure. If the women are satirized to an extent, it is only because society and its rules are shown to be a superficial disguise for the animal spirit in human beings.

Although Etherege had little interest in Wycherley's bitterly satiric view of society, his Dorimant, in *The Man of Mode* (1676), comes closer to the polished gentleman that many saw in the idealized figure of Rochester presented in the various dedications to him. Dorimant's affair with Mrs Loveit is ending, and his new relationship with Bellinda appears to be shortened by his instant sexual attraction to Harriet. Although modern audiences have become accustomed to scenes of sexual intercourse in the cinema, seeing Dorimant and Bellinda just after intercourse had to have a suggestive thrill for the Restoration audience. Dorimant's desire to possess Harriet is so great that he appears to be willing to marry her even if it means spending a month in the country, the equivalent of the terrible task set by the mistress of a knight in the old romances. Both Harriet and Dorimant feel a compelling physical force that draws them together, and the relationship between the women appears to be one of power. Harriet is also aware of her power over Dorimant and uses it with considerable cruelty. The stress on clothes in the figure of Sir Foppling Flutter only emphasizes the idea that, beneath our clothing, we function as passionate animals.

Behn was less inclined to such a hard view of sexual relations, but as Janet Todd has remarked, she too had absorbed the 'heady libertine concoction' (1: xxvi) brewed from Epicurus, Lucretius and Hobbes. The women in her comedies are vulnerable, and Angellica, the beautiful courtesan drawn to Willmore in *The Rover* (Part 1, 1677; Part 2, 1681) is unable to control her passionate attraction for him. Hellena, the 'virtuous' heroine, acts the role of a free spirit throughout the play, partly because she knows that the only way of getting Willmore to marry her is to pretend little interest in any commitment on his part. Behn's comedies tend towards presenting situations that are somewhat less fantastic than those involving Horner and Dorimant. Her women are certainly motivated by sexual desire, but they are often presented as having to trap a somewhat unwilling male. This was true as well of her poetry, in which she wrote of love from the standpoint of a woman who, as in her poem 'The Disappointment', often finds herself deprived of expected pleasure. And in a poem such as 'To the Fair Clarinda, Who Made Love to Me, Imagin'd More than Woman', like the poet Sappho with whom she frequently identified herself, she played with same-gender sex. She could be witty and satiric about love at times, but she was always an advocate for the pleasures that love might bring.

After this extraordinary beginning, libertinism in the drama tended to fall into somewhat coarser forms of sexuality – sex for its own sake. Abandoning the subtlety of Etherege and Behn, Thomas D'Urfey produced *A Fond Husband* in 1677, a comedy which ratcheted up the sexual scenes but tended to reduce them to farce. It was enormously successful, and Dryden followed this new pattern with *The Kind Keeper, or Mr Limberham* in the following year. Abandoning the subtlety and wit of *Marriage A-la-Mode*, Dryden allowed free licence to his characters, among whom is one who is suffering from a syphilis-induced form of insanity. There is no question that *The Kind Keeper* is a libertine play, but it is as far from philosophic libertinism as anyone could imagine. There was plenty of sex in plays such as Ravenscroft's *The London Cuckolds* (1681), but works of this kind belong to the category of sexual farce.

Thomas Otway's two comedies, *The Soldier's Fortune* (1681) and *The Atheist* (1683–4), did add something to sexual comedy in the way of Otway's particularly hard view of the relationships between men and women. In his tragedy, *The Orphan* (1680), the approach to sexual intercourse involves genuine feelings of disgust. Monimia, the heroine, who is victimized by male lust, becomes a pathetic, abused figure. Sexual pleasure seems to have given way to uncomfortable feelings of sadism. In *The Atheist*, particularly, the preaching against marriage that made up so large a part of Osborne's *Advice to a Son* seems to be obsessive. The character of Daredevil is hardly exemplary, but his remark to the effect that complaining about wives is foolish 'so long as there is Arsenick in the World' (2: 325 [2.1]) is not far from the norm of male opinion in the play. The pleasure of sexual intercourse seems tied up with various forms of voyeurism and revenge, and sexual gender seems suggestively fluid. Beaugard, one of the two rakes who appear in both plays, expresses a philosophy that is not far from traditional libertinism:

> grant me while I live the easie Being I am at pressent possest of; a kind, fair Shee, to cool my Blood, and pamper my Imagination withal; an honest Friend or two, like thee, *Courtine*, that I dare trust my Thoughts to; generous Wine, Health, Liberty, and no Dishonour; and when I ask more of Fortune, let her e'en make a Beggar of me. (2: 328 [2.1])

Yet the role given to sex seems more therapeutic than pleasurable. For Otway's men, sex emerges as an unfortunate urge that needs to be got rid of as easily as possible and without too much concern for the sufferings experienced by the victimized woman.

By the time one comes to the 1690s, libertinism has become a code that was hardly distinguishable from that of the gentleman. In the writings of Charles de Saint-

Evremond, a French libertine who passed his last years in London, Petronius became the ideal wit, and genuine love became something to which the libertine might aspire. On the stage, in the hands of Thomas Southerne, sexual relations became a matter of subtle struggles for power. The pro-feminist title, *The Wive's Excuse, or Cuckolds Make Themselves* (1691–2), suggests a sympathy for women married to bad husbands, and this theme continued throughout the comedies of the reigns of William and Mary and then William III. In Southerne's *Sir Anthony Love*, the female libertine defies convention by disguising herself in male attire to follow the man she loves. In general, Southerne's plays attempt a depiction of the relationships between men and women that is serious enough to make the comic element in some of his plays relatively slight.

Southerne was hardly the only writer to deal with the relationship between men and women in serious terms. John Vanbrugh, in *The Provoked Wife* (1697), attempted a balanced discussion of the problems of contemporary marriage, and in *The Relapse* (1696), he rejected Colley Cibber's move towards sentimental clichés in *Love's Last Shift* (1696) by returning Cibber's reformed rake to the status of a contemporary libertine. Vanbrugh's rakes are still willing to take sex where they can find it, but they are also capable of love. It is not easy, in teaching an undergraduate class, to explain why Mirabell in Congreve's *The Way of the World* (1700) is not something of a villain. He has had an affair with Mrs Languish and arranged a marriage for her with Mr Fainall when she feared that she might be pregnant. He certainly appears to like her, but he is not in love with her. He is definitely not going to marry her, though he will help her in every other way he can. He is not only attractive to women but he appears to like them.

Although one may read *The Way of the World* as a hard response to the attacks upon libertinism on the stage being mounted by Jeremy Collier, Mirabell was fairly typical of Congreve's rake-heroes. Bellmour in *The Old Batchelour* manages to seduce Laetitia, an all-too-willing wife of a citizen, but this hardly disqualifies him as the potentially excellent husband of Belinda. Similarly, Valentine in *Love for Love* is madly in love with Angelica, but he has had a recent affair that has left him with the care of a baby. All of this depends on the double standard that allows men this kind of liberty while disapproving of it in the heroine. If Congreve accepts this social convention, he nevertheless regards sex as a natural urge. The fools of Congreve's plays are those who try to pretend it does not exist or, as with Lady Wishfort in *The Way of the World*, attempt actively to suppress it.

Congreve's negative portrait of Maskwell, in his *The Double Dealer*, may be seen as a corrective to the older libertinism. Maskwell thinks nothing of having an affair with Lady Touchwood, the wife of his patron, and of trying to carry off Cynthia, who is engaged to his best friend Mellefont. He is savagely committed to his own self-interest, and his deceptions are less like those of Wycherley's Horner than betrayals that have potentially serious repercussions. Despite being raised to the status of a gentleman, he lacks the code of gentility that is now made part of a new form of libertinism. But much remains the same. Cuckolds deserve their horns, and the rakes who have sexual liaisons with women who are all too eager to oblige are scarcely to be considered reprehensible. In *The Way of the World*, the young widow Languish, now Mrs Fainall, is hardly to be disapproved of for having had an affair with Mirabell. It is her mother, Lady Wishfort, who married her daughter off to the unsuitable Mr Languish and who raised her according to a method that Jeremy Collier might have approved of, who is most to blame.

Jeremy Collier did not kill off libertinism on the stage with his *Short View of the Immorality and Profaneness of the English Stage* in 1698, but he was part of a trend towards reforming the morals of the nation. The Society for the Reformation of Manners, established during the 1690s, set as its goal the exposure and punishment of everything that its members considered to be vice. Actors were attacked by mobs, and the promptbooks reveal the degree to which plays were rewritten to suit the new moral atmosphere. The names of private citizens who were observed to frequent prostitutes or to be publicly intoxicated were printed up in 'Blacklists'.

Despite Vanbrugh's efforts, sentimental comedies and tragedies of sensibility were becoming the popular modes during the 1690s and into the next century. Libertines began to appear in literature as either villains, in the manner of Don John in Shadwell's *The Libertine*, or as somewhat pathetic figures. Libertinism did not die, despite being banished from stage presentations, but it had to fight a losing battle against sensibility, the dominant attitude of the eighteenth century. Samuel Richardson's Lovelace, the male protagonist of *Clarissa* (1747–51), embodies much of the wit and creative intelligence that made the libertine figure so attractive to the Restoration, but his inability to fully appreciate the serious sensibility of Clarissa suggests a flaw in his character and in libertinism itself. In some ways, sensibility absorbed libertinism by presenting itself both as a form of spontaneous behaviour based on direct emotion and as highly pleasurable – more pleasurable in its emphasis on benevolence and sympathy, so the argument went, than the individual hedonism of the libertine. Libertinism lived on, however, in one form or other. The desire for sexual freedom was not to be stifled permanently. As pornography it tended to go underground, to emerge in novels such as Cleland's libertine classic, *Fanny Hill* (1748). As an intellectual movement, its plea for liberty of thought and action ultimately fitted well with some aspects of Enlightenment thought, and in many ways it experienced a public re-emergence at the time of the French Revolution.

NOTES

1 In his essay, 'Restoration Comedy and Its Modern Critics', John Wain agreed with Knights and pronounced the comedies of the Restoration 'immoral' and 'the fever-chart of a sick society'.

2 In her *Likenesses of Truth in Elizabethan and Restoration Drama*, Hawkins analysed the combined sexual and religious imagery in a libertine poem by George Etherege by way of showing that the presence of religious language and doctrine in no way guaranteed religious meaning. Others, such as Anne Barton, showed the logical flaws in Williams's arguments.

3 Schneider (1971). For a critique of Schneider's work, see Harwood (1982), esp. 31–3.

4   Although Hume does not agree with Williams, he treats the argument with great respect. For a somewhat similar approach, see Weber (1986).

5   Recent works on libertinism and its influence have taken this attitude as a starting point. See Chernaik (1995) and also a variety of articles by James Grantham Turner, especially Turner (1995).

6   See Adam (1964: 15–16, 19–21). Although Gassendi maintained his beliefs as an orthodox Catholic, his disciples did not.

7   Rochester's deathbed reversion to Christianity through the efforts of Gilbert Burnet set the pattern for a theme that was essential to sentimental and melodramatic literature for the following centuries.

8   *Sodom* borrows more than its absurd ghost from the rhymed heroic play and the serious plays in blank verse that retained their basic form. The overreaching villain of these plays is usually a libertine in the form of a king or emperor who uses his power to obtain forbidden sexual pleasure through violent means.

9   Zimbardo (1998) is one of the few critics to find some redeeming artistic and intellectual value in this work.

10   (London, 1673), 39. Banks also published Francis Osborne's *Advice to a Son* and various libertine attacks upon marriage.

11   (London, 1673), 194. Among the exchanges, *Marriage Asserted* (London, 1674) accused the libertines of being republicans. Thus both sides accused the other of being against the monarchy. This author's target was *Congugium Conjurgium*, another anti-marriage Banks's publication of 1673. Though published under the name Seymar, this author saw it as a pseudonym for William Ramsey.

12   Of course the work is a 'Satyrical' narrative in which the protagonist progresses from his first sexual experience with a prostitute in the first section to his quarrelling with a whore in the last section. If these are both rendered in fairly realistic terms, the middle section, which is the largest, idealizes the passionate intercourse of the young lovers.

REFERENCES AND FURTHER READING

Adam, Antoine (1964). *Les Libertins aux XVIIe siècle*. Paris: Buchet/Castel.

Behn, Aphra (1996). *Complete Works*, ed. Janet Todd. London: Pickering.

Chernaik, Warren (1995). *Sexual Freedom in Restoration Literature*. Cambridge: Cambridge University Press.

Collier, Jeremy (1698). *A Short View of the Immorality and Profaneness of the English Stage*. London.

Dryden, John (1956–). *The California Edition of the Works of John Dryden*, ed. E. N. Hooker, H. T. Swedenberg, et al. 20 vols. Berkeley: University of California Press.

Harwood, John (1982). *Critics, Values, and Restoration Comedy*. Carbondale: Southern Illinois University Press.

Hawkins, Harriet (1972). *Likenesses of Truth in Elizabethan and Restoration Drama*. Oxford: Clarendon Press.

Hume, Robert (1983). *The Rakish Stage*. Carbondale: Southern Illinois University Press.

Killigrew, Thomas (1664). *Comedies and Tragedies*. London.

Killigrew, Thomas (1921). *The Parson's Wedding*, in *Restoration Comedies*, ed. Montague Summers. London: Jonathan Cape.

Knights, L. C. (1946). 'Restoration Comedy: The Reality and the Myth', in *Explorations*. New York: New York University Press, 131–49.

Novak, Maximillian (1977). 'Margery Pinchwife's "London Disease" and the Libertine Offensive of the 1670s', *Studies in the Literary Imagination* 10, 1–23.

Osborne, Francis (1656, 1658). *Advice to a Son*. London.

Otway, Thomas (1932). *Works*, ed. J. C. Ghosh. 2 vols. Oxford: Clarendon Press.

Reflections on Marriage and the Poetick Discipline (1673). London.

Schneider, Ben Ross (1971). *The Ethos of Restoration Comedy: The Reality and the Myth*. Carbondale: Southern Illinois University Press.

Shadwell, Thomas (1928; reissued 1968). *Complete Works*, ed. Montague Summers. 5 vols. London: Fortune Press.

Thornton, Thomas (ed.). (1813). *Works, by Thomas Otway*. London: T. Turner.

Turner, James Grantham (1995). 'The Libertine Sublime: Love and Death in Restoration Culture', *Studies in Eighteenth-century Culture* 24, 297–306.

Underwood, Dale (1957). *Etherege and the Seventeenth-century Comedy of Manners*. New Haven, CT: Yale University Press.

Vieth, David (ed.). (1968). *The Complete Poems, by John Wilmot, Earl of Rochester*. New Haven, CT: Yale University Press.

Wain, John (1956). 'Restoration Comedy and Its Modern Critics', *Essays in Criticism* 6, 367–85.

Weber, Harold M. (1986). *The Restoration Rake-Hero: Transformations in Sexual Understanding in Seventeenth-century England*. Madison: University of Wisconsin Press.

Williams, Aubrey (1979). *An Approach to Congreve*. New Haven, CT: Yale University Press.

Wilmot, John, Earl of Rochester (1993). *Complete Poems and Plays*, ed. Paddy Lyons. London: J. M. Dent.

Zimbardo, Rose (1998). *At Zero Point: Discourse, Culture, and Satire in Restoration England*. Lexington: University of Kentucky Press.

5

The Restoration Actress
Deborah Payne Fisk

English and Continental Actresses in the Seventeenth Century

'Women-Actors, notorious whores.' So reads an index entry to William Prynne's mad, rambling invective against the theatre, *Histrio-Mastix*, also known as *The Players Scourge, or Actors Tragædie* (London, 1633). Prynne intones his strong feelings about 'women-actors', all of them, in his eyes, *'notorious impudent, prostituted Strumpets'* (214), in dissonant keys throughout the volume. It was Prynne's bad luck that the publication of *Histrio-Mastix* coincided with the appearance of Queen Henrietta Maria and her ladies-in-waiting in a court masque, Walter Montagu's *Shepherd's Paradise*. Since women were not permitted to act on the public stage, the Star Chamber assumed, not without reason, that Prynne targeted the thespian queen and her ladies. He lost the trial for libel and sedition and suffered an enormous fine, a year's imprisonment and the mutilation of his ears.

Such was the state of theatrical (and political) affairs in England prior to the Civil War. As *l'affaire Prynne* suggests, attitudes towards women acting on stage were nothing if not schizophrenic. Noblewomen could perform in court theatricals and women and girls from 'good families' in private household entertainments. Milton, for instance, wrote the charming masque *Comus* to celebrate the Earl of Bridgewater's appointment in 1631 to the Lord Presidency of Wales; and it was understood that his daughter, the fifteen-year-old Alice Egerton, would play the part of the Lady. Commercial theatre, however, was until 1661 entirely forbidden to English women harbouring professional ambitions. This was not the case in most European countries. In Spain, women were performing professionally by 1587, nearly seventy-five years earlier than in England. Except for a short period in the 1590s when the Council of Castile banned women from the stage, actresses were an accepted, albeit regulated, part of Spanish theatre (McKendrick 1989: 49). Laws compelled actresses to be married, but the same demand was made of actors, who were expected to have their wives with them at all times, even on tour.

In Italy, the *commedia dell'arte* – which featured women prominently in *lozzi*, a kind of improvisational skit – used actresses from the outset. The same was true of Italian opera, where female performers not only commanded a large following but made more money than the composers. Even Cavalli, who earned far more than other Venetian composers, received 300 scudi (or 450 ducats) for a commissioned opera, the same salary paid to an ordinary female singer. The very best singers would earn twice that amount, confirming that performers, especially women, were the most important members within the opera hierarchy (Rosand 1991: 223). The press further heightened the status of star performers. Anna Renzi, often considered the first 'diva', was extolled in a special volume published in her honour, *Le glorie della signora Anna Renzi romana* (Venice, 1644). The book features encomiastic poems, descriptions of her roles and a long laudatory essay that provides, in exquisite detail, an account of the diva's every note, word and gesture during performance. As Ellen Rosand notes, these singers, so beloved by their public, similarly exercised enormous power over the opera repertory: 'all of Renzi's roles were clearly tailor-made for her by composers and librettists intimately acquainted with her abilities' (1991: 233).

In France, women acted in provincial theatre beginning in the late sixteenth century, travelling with the itinerant bands of players that roamed the countryside. Once the Confrérie de la Passion yielded the Hôtel de Bourgogne – the only all-purpose playhouse in Paris – to the professional companies by the early seventeenth century, actresses found themselves welcome in the nation's capital as well. French women helped to establish companies: Madeleine Béjart founded the Illustre Théâtre with Molière in 1643. Actresses were shareholders within the companies; in 1665 they held five out of twelve shares in Molière's troupe (Howarth 1997: 153). Samuel Chappuzeau, whose *Le Théâtre français* (1674) provides an invaluable glimpse of the workings of the seventeenth-century French stage, claimed that 'both sexes share in the authority of their state, women being as useful as men, if not more so, and they contribute and vote on all matters of general concern' (Howarth 1997: 186). According to Chappuzeau, the high rate of intermarriage between actors and actresses accounted for the unusual degree of authority accorded to this particular group of early modern women.

Roman Catholic nations, such as Italy, France and Spain, accepted actresses far sooner than Protestant nations did. England was not the only Protestant country to deny women access to the commercial stage: not until 1655 did a Dutch woman receive an appointment to act in the Amsterdam municipal theatre. Protestant suspicion of the stage – and particularly of the women acting on it – also surfaced in countries torn by religious wars. While theatre in Paris included famous Catholic clerics, such as Cardinal Richelieu and the Abbé d'Aubignac, among its apologists, Huguenot reformers cried down the sins of the stage, counting actresses foremost among iniquities. Jansenists, those Calvinist-minded Catholics, also attacked the theatre. Pierre Nicole made apparent his anti-theatrical sentiments in *A Discourse against Plays and Romances* (1672). Like Prynne, he considered actresses a particular abomination.

In part, the Protestant suspicion of actresses can be attributed to the usual sanctions against display and ostentation, whether in everyday life or religious liturgy. Protestants and Catholics also disagreed on essential aspects of sin and redemption; and this divergence undoubtedly fuelled their respective attitudes towards female performers. Spectators in predominantly Catholic cultures, such as France, Spain and Italy, could view actresses – even lust after them – with relative impunity since, from the time of the Council of Trent, traditional Catholic theology defined sin as a human act requiring the exercise of both intellect and will. Since concupiscence, or desire, was considered part of human nature, it only posed a threat if reason or the will was overcome. While most theologians advised their flock to avoid temptations that might occasion sin, they nonetheless distinguished between desire and the deed itself. With regard to actresses, one might look but not touch. By contrast, the Puritan emphasis on sincerity – on a correspondence between the inner and outer self – rendered desire far more dangerous. As Jonas Barish observes, for the Puritan, 'all one's acts would be directly revelatory of one's essence' (1981: 94), thereby collapsing the Catholic separation between concupiscence and a sinful *action*.

For this reason, Puritans also distrusted the actor's art of impersonation. The actor pretends to be other than himself, effectively participating in lies, and thus shatters the necessary correspondence between inner essence and outward manifestation at the core of Puritan belief. This peculiarly theatrical form of insincerity, which accounted for the traditional suspicion of performers, was especially damaging to actresses since it belied female chastity: how did one assess the purity of an actress personating an adulteress? If rendered convincingly, then logically the *rôle* must proceed from an inner moral flaw. The mutability essential to the actor's art was equally damaging to women. Actresses played queens, noblewomen and gentlewomen; they overreached social origins, transforming themselves on stage as they never could in real life. Actresses also used this protean ability to represent boys; and by violating the concept of absolute identity, they once again contravened the desired equivalency between inner self and outer manifestation. For Puritan moralists, as Barish notes, even distinctions of dress expressed essence and could no 'more be tampered with than that essence itself' (1981: 92). In a traditional hierarchical society, such as seventeenth-century England, a woman assuming male identity (and the concomitant masculine privileges) was far more threatening than a man putting on female identity. For once, the customarily prolix Prynne put it succinctly: 'Secondly, admit men-Actors in womens attire, are not altogether so bad, so discommendable as women Stage-players' (215).

Differences in training, as well as in the organization of the acting companies, also kept English actresses from the stage far longer than their Continental sisters. Because European companies were based on a family model, actresses were seen through the bifocal lens of profession and kinship. The high rate of intermarriage between French actors and actresses sometimes resulted in a company where virtually everyone was related. Thus, an actress on the French stage was not merely an available young woman on display but part of a prominent family of actors. She was somebody's wife, sister, daughter or cousin; and that familiarity – and one might consider briefly the etymological overtones here – rendered her less dangerous. In Scarron's *Roman comique*, Mlle de la Caverne describes how her social identity derives from this very fusion of family and profession: 'I was born a player, the daughter of a player whose parents have always said to have been in the same profession' (as cited in Mongrédien 1969: 199). In Italy, companies comprised of family members, such as the Gelosi or Fideli, dominated the early years of the *commedia dell'arte*. Within the *commedia* troupes, a tradition of training arose not unlike that in Kabuki or Noh theatre whereby parents trained their children – in this instance, daughters as well as sons – in the art of acting.

The apprentice system that dominated the training of English actors prior to the Civil War made it virtually impossible for women to 'break into' commercial theatre. In the adult companies, boys entered their bonds between the ages of ten and thirteen, training for several years in women's parts before graduating to be hired men and perhaps even sharers (Gurr 1992: 95). The apprentice system in the early modern period was, of course, confined solely to men. Women did occasionally enter guilds, but their membership usually derived from the death of a husband. The other source of English actors came from the children's companies. Originally affiliated with the choir schools, such as St Paul's, the boy companies had by 1600 become commercial ventures. The boys were bound to the master of the company and their training, according to Andrew Gurr, appears to have been more rhetorical than that of the male apprentices in the adult companies (1992: 96). Like apprenticeship, the choir schools favoured boys exclusively. Women would have to wait until the Restoration to make their first appearance on the commercial stage.

The First English Actresses

The closing of the theatres for eighteen years between 1642 and 1660 eradicated these traditional avenues of entry into the acting profession. The boy companies, already unfashionable by the 1620s, were never revived after the Restoration; and the adult companies no longer existed as discrete entities to be reconstituted in full after 1660. The players who managed to survive the Civil War were absorbed into two new licensed acting troupes: the King's Company, headed by Thomas Killigrew, and the Duke's Company, headed by William Davenant. Because a theatrical culture had to be created immediately, the new managers could not afford merely to reinstate the 'old ways' – too many pieces were missing. Moreover, both Killigrew and Davenant had seen Continental innovations during their respective exiles abroad; and both men were eager to incorporate these innovations, including actresses, into the new companies.

Standard accounts attribute the advent of actresses after 1660 either to Charles II's predilection for pretty women or to his years of exile abroad, when he saw women perform on the commercial stage. J. L. Styan, for instance, says that 'King Charles II was also responsible for the appearance of *the actress* on the English stage' (1996: 245). The original patent to Davenant and Killigrew (dated 21 August 1660) never mentions actresses, despite Styan and John Harold Wilson's claims to the contrary (1958: 4). Actresses are first mentioned in a petition dated 13 October 1660 in which Michael Mohun and several actors complain to the king that Killigrew suppressed all of their performances until 'wee had by covenant obleiged our selues to Act with Woemen a new Theatre and Habitts according to our Scaenes' (Bawcutt 1996: 235). More specific mention of actresses is made on 5 November 1660 in the 'Articles of Agreement between the players and Davenant' (Bawcutt 1996: 236). The articles stipulate that the actors who had been performing at Salisbury Court would, after one week's warning, 'remove and Joyne with the said Henry Harris and with other men and women prouided or to be prouided by the sd Sir Wm Davenant' (Bawcutt 1996: 238). The articles further give seven shares of the company to Davenant and his assigns in order 'to mainteine all ye Women that are to performe or represent Womens parts in the aforesaid Tragedies Comedies Playes or representacons' (Bawcutt 1996: 238).

That both of these documents predate by a good fourteen months the *revised* royal patents issued to Davenant and Killigrew on 15 January 1662 – which do indeed mention actresses – suggests strongly that the request for actresses originated within the theatre companies, not the government. The revised patents repeat the language of the original documents and acknowledge the various concessions made by the two theatre managers that might justify their monopoly over the theatrical marketplace. The patents also give Davenant and Killigrew permission to employ actresses:

> And we do likewise permit and give leave that all the women's parts to be acted in either of the said two companies from this time to come may be performed by women, so long as these recreations, which by reason of the abuses aforesaid were scandalous and offensive, may by such reformation be esteemed not only harmless delights, but useful and instructive representations of human life, by such of our good subjects as shall resort to see the same. (Fitzgerald 1882, 1: 77)

The language of morality notwithstanding – and reformist rhetoric frequently disguised the more pecuniary motives of the theatre managers – it is important to understand that the theatre managers considered actresses essential to modernizing the stage. In Killigrew's patent they are mentioned in the same breath with 'a new Theatre and Habitts'. Both theatre managers were admittedly self-conscious about theatrical innovation. Killigrew in 1667 boasted to Samuel Pepys how 'the stage is now by his pains a thousand times better and more glorious then ever heretofore' (8: 55). He went on to enumerate the improvements: wax instead of tallow candles, more civilized behaviour from spectators, nine or ten musicians rather than a paltry two or three fiddlers, no rushes tossed hastily onto the stage, even the king in attendance. Davenant's fascination with the latest theatrical novelties is similarly well documented (Milhous 1979: 15–25, *passim*). The first actresses stepped onto the English stage because the two new managers wanted to surpass their predecessors and to rival Continental theatre, not because of morality and certainly not because of the more prurient interests of the monarch.

Some critics question whether the new actresses had anything to do with a desire for heightened naturalism; the companies themselves, however, saw female performers as a marked improvement over earlier conditions of staging. In Thomas Jordan's *A Royal Arbor of Loyal Poesie* (London, 1663) is the prologue he wrote for a revival of *Othello* on 8 December 1660, the first known appearance of an actress. In it he jokes about the average age of the actors, specifically the problem in having 'men act, that are between / Forty and fifty, Wenches of fifteen'. He also notes their inappropriate build: 'With bone so large, and nerve so incomplyant, / When you call *Desdemona*, enter Giant' (22). The prologue to an early revival of Ben Jonson's *The Alchemist* (n.d.) similarly worries about men personating women's parts: 'What? are the Fellows mad? / Who shall *Doll Common* Act? Their tender Tibs / Have neither Lungs, nor Confidence, nor Ribs' (London, n.d.). Even later in the Restoration, companies periodically threatened recalcitrant spectators with the grim prospect of boy actors. To the men in the audience who would seduce talented actresses away from the theatre, the epilogue to Nathaniel Lee's *The Rival Queens* (London, 1677) threatens: 'For we have vow'd to find a sort of Toys / Known to black Fryars, a Tribe of chopping Boys: / If once they come, they'l quickly spoil your sport' (65).

Theatre traditions that cast boys in female roles typically use some sort of distancing device, be it spatial or stylistic, to overcome the inherent difficulties in having boys impersonate women. The Theatre of Dionysus in Athens, one of the largest of the Greek theatres, seated upwards of 30,000. Even the much smaller theatre at Epidaurus seated 6,200 spectators in 300 BC. A century later an upper landing would allow for over 12,000 spectators. The Hellenistic theatres were larger still. The Elizabethan playhouse, although intimate by the standards of ancient theatre, nonetheless dwarfed the Restoration playhouse. A boy performing Cleopatra in the 3,000-person-capacity Swan or Globe might well succeed, particularly if we consider that even the groundlings, although pressed close to the stage, were positioned to see ankles better than faces. As we know from the reconstructed Globe theatre in London, spectators standing in the pit would have had to tilt their heads back since the stage was considerably higher than their natural sightlines. The Swan's stage was about 4 feet 8 inches high; the Red Lion was 5 feet high, roughly the same height as the Globe. If one contrasts these dimensions with the extraordinary intimacy of the Restoration playhouse – in the early years roughly the same size as a modern tennis court – the drawbacks to casting boys becomes apparent.

Transvestite theatre traditions also use convention to create distance. In Asian and Greek theatre, stylized intonation – which obscures differences between male and female voices – shapes the delivery of language. The performers in Peking Opera chant an archaic dialect according to strictly codified rules, and Noh drama uses a fourteenth-century court dialect that was already remote by the seventeenth century. Elaborate costuming, make-up and masks designate the gender, class and occupation of the dramatic character. A convincing portrayal of a woman in Kabuki drama proceeds from an understanding of these conventions; and, indeed, spectators judge the actor's performance on how well he enacts a stylized representation rather than the behaviour one might expect from a 'real' woman. What we know of Elizabethan acting styles suggests they were similarly bound by convention; as Andrew Gurr notes, 'theatrical shorthand in the conventions of action that mimed the internal passion must have been essential to the Elizabethan actor' (1992: 103).

Restoration theatre, by contrast, habitually emphasizes a social specificity that invokes everyday life and manners. Names of streets, taverns and fashionable locales saturate the dialogue of Restoration comedies, and spectators enjoy cosy jokes about coteries and cliques. Prologues and epilogues allude to contemporary events at court. Changeable scenery also encourages this sort of specific social identification. Although companies recycled painted flats from one production to another, a scene of the Pall Mall can only represent itself and therefore limits the sort of imaginative leaps possible in Shakespeare's wooden 'O'. This new commercial theatre of social specificity demanded a certain level of naturalism that rendered boy actors obsolete. Clearly, notable exceptions exist. In 1660, before actresses were permitted on the stage, Pepys claimed that the strikingly pretty Edward Kynaston 'made the loveliest lady' he had ever seen on stage (1: 224). According to Colley Cibber, ladies of quality were having Kynaston, 'so beautiful a Youth', accompany them in coach rides to Hyde Park (1968: 71). We might remember, however, that Pepys in 1660 had no basis for comparison: he had never seen a woman act and therefore might very well consider Kynaston the 'loveliest' stage woman to date. And Cibber's anecdote discloses the singularity of Kynaston's feminine beauty: court ladies, charmed by his prettiness, have him on display as an exotic, a sort of coveted pet, precisely because his looks were *not* typical of most boys. If one grants Davenant and Killigrew some degree of theatrical understanding, their desire to employ actresses from the outset in all likelihood proceeded from an intuitive grasp of the new conditions that obtained at the Restoration.

Given these changes, it should not surprise that most actresses came from the 'middling ranks' where they would have acquired the social skills to represent a wide range of female characters. They needed, of course, to be literate; and literacy in the seventeenth century presupposed an education the poor could ill afford. Nell Gwyn's mother, according to contemporary lampoons, was reputed to be a prostitute or an orange woman (that is, a woman who made her living by selling oranges to spectators in the playhouse), but she was a notable exception. Women from titled families, the other end of the social spectrum, were equally rare. More typical were women like Rebecca and Anne Marshall, born to the chaplain to Lord Gerard and his wife Elizabeth, née Dutton, the illegitimate daughter of John Dutton (Highfill et al. 1973–93, 10: 106). Mary Davis was either the illegitimate daughter of Colonel Charles Howard, son of Thomas, Earl of Berkshire, or the daughter of a blacksmith who lived near the Howard estate (Highfill et al. 1973–93, 4: 222). Elizabeth Barry, who would become the greatest actress of the Restoration stage, was born to the barrister Robert Barry. Anne Bracegirdle was the offspring of gentry fallen on hard times – in the words of Oldys, 'a gentlewoman of so good an extraction' (1814: 26). Sarah Cooke's mother was a vendor of herbs and her aunt was the governess of the maids of honour to the Duchess of York (Highfill et al. 1973–93, 3: 473). According to William Oldys, Anne Oldfield was 'on her mother's side . . . well descended' (1814: 3). Her father, who had a commission in the guards from James II, ran through his estate, leaving his widow and daughter in impecunious circumstances. Colley Cibber claimed that Charlotte Butler was the daughter of a 'decay'd Knight' (1968: 93). Most actresses were born – at least those we know about – to 'respectable' families, but a decline in family fortunes (and with it, the prospect of a good marriage dowry) necessitated some form of employment. The daughter of a barrister might resent going into service, but becoming an actress eluded these class overtones, precisely because it was an anomalous social space, one that had never before existed in England.

Women made their way to the stage through several avenues. Several cryptic references to 'nurseries' – acting schools for the young – crop up during the first two decades of the Restoration. Very little is known about them, including whether or not they trained girls as well as boys (Van Lennep 1965: xxxviii–ix). William Oldys recounts two instances of actresses discovering fledgling performers. Elizabeth Barry and Anne Bracegirdle took such a liking to Mary Porter's portrayal of the fairy queen at Bartholomew Fair, they insisted Betterton admit her into the company. Thereafter, adds Oldys, 'they treated her with the most tender indulgence' (1814: 55). Margaret Saunders, whose acting career was cut short by a 'very violent Asthmatical indisposition', was brought to Drury Lane by Anne Oldfield (Oldys 1814: 143). Most women hoping to act had to apply first hand to one of the two houses, a procedure parodied in Henry Neville Payne's comedy, *The Morning Ramble, or, the Town-Humours* (London, 1673). Merry and Townlove, two rogues on the lam, intend to liberate four 'Gentlewomen' arrested by the Constable and Watch. The fourth woman of the group claims she is 'a very good Gentlewoman both born and bred; I am a Presbyterian Ministers Daughter', one who has

> a great mind to be a Player, and have offer'd my self to both Houses, and truly most of the sharers have had me severally at their Chambers to try me, and they all say, I do very well; but 'tis the Envy of the women already there, that fearing I should out-do e'm, keep me out, as I was told by two or three of the hired men of the Duke's House, with whom I have been to Night, and spent all my money, but I do not doubt to find Friends to bring it about, for there are two or three Persons of Quality have undertaken it. (25)

This passage reveals something of the urgency felt by young women hoping for a career on the stage. This erstwhile minister's daughter has spent money, perhaps even bestowed personal favours, upon shareholders (who would have had particular influence) and then 'hired men' (the full-time actors). That avenue exhausted, she nonetheless believes friends will 'bring it about', including 'two or three Persons of

Quality'. This final statement discloses the other means of gaining employment in the theatre: through recommendations or introductions. Nobility, of course, were especially influential in this regard. Charles II recommended Charlotte Butler to the Duke's Company (Cibber 1968: 93–4). The Earl of Rochester supposedly put forth Sarah Cooke's name to the King's Company (Highfill et al. 1973–93, 3: 474); and, in an often-told but perhaps apocryphal story, asked Davenant to reinstate Elizabeth Barry after she had undergone tutoring at the Earl's country seat (Oldys 1814: 15–17). Whatever the means of access, Payne's comedy suggests that by 1673, competition for places was keen.

The Daily Life of the Actress

Actresses worked very hard for their wages. Customarily, the players laboured six days a week for roughly thirty-five weeks out of the year. They rehearsed in the morning, performed at the playhouse in the afternoon, and sometimes acted again at Whitehall in the evening. The repertory system placed additional demands on their 'spare' time. Frequent revivals of what the prompter John Downes called 'Old Stock Plays', that is, plays written before the Civil War, in addition to productions of new plays meant that actresses were constantly memorizing lines (Downes 1968: 8). Their mnemonic abilities must have been considerable. Revived plays rarely kept the boards for more than two or three days, the same run expected for a new play of middling interest. If a new production proved popular with audiences, it might run for over a week, as did Thomas Shadwell's *The Sullen Lovers* (1668), which was performed for twelve consecutive days (Wilson 1958: 35). Both companies mounted between forty and sixty productions each season. Given these numbers, an actress could expect to perform several roles over the course of a month, in addition to singing and dancing if the play or the *entr'acte* entertainment asked it of her. In the early years of the Restoration, these demands must have seemed especially onerous to the inexperienced actresses, and Pepys mentions several performances that were 'wronged by the womens being much to seek in their parts', a complaint that lessened over time (2: 8).

Previous theatre historians have averred that 'the women's wages were significantly lower than the men's', a statement based solely on the salary disparity between Elizabeth Barry and Thomas Betterton (Howe 1992: 27).[1] Given the historic imbalance between male and female salaries, one might very well infer that seventeenth-century actresses were also underpaid, but such an inference differs from a stated 'fact'. Betterton and his wife Mary Saunderson, another leading player with the company, *jointly* earned £5 weekly to Barry's 50s, which means that individually all three players earned the identical salary (Pepys 2: 41, n. 4). As Betterton's career progressed, he acquired responsibilities that would account for additional monies. After Davenant's death in 1668, Betterton co-managed the Duke's Company with Mary Davenant. Betterton went on to manage the United Company in 1682 and Lincoln's Inn Fields in 1695. Additionally, he taught young actors and functioned as a

'Monitor in a Schole to looke after rehearsalls' (Milhous 1979: 28). Without extant Restoration account books, it is difficult to know salary ranges conclusively. Barry's weekly salary of 50*s* appears to be commensurate with the wages paid to senior actors, according to *An Apology for the Life of Colley Cibber*, one of our few sources of information. Unpaid for the first nine months of his apprenticeship, Cibber went on salary at 10*s* weekly. A hireling would expect to earn between 30*s* weekly, as Cibber did in 1694–5, and 40*s* weekly, as did Thomas Dogget in 1693 (Van Lennep 1965: ciii). The maximum salary was 50*s* weekly. As Judith Milhous notes, even after 1700 'the annual salary for a senior actor amounted to something between £80 and £150' (1979: 14). Actresses, like actors, could earn more money if they were talented. The theatre manager Thomas Killigrew declared to Pepys that 'Knipp is like to make the best actor that ever came upon the stage, she understanding so well. That they are going to give her 30£ a year more' (8: 55).

If an actor eventually held one share in the company, he might expect to augment his salary by roughly £66 a year, assuming the theatre took in an average of £35 a day (Milhous 1979: 14). There is some evidence to suggest that prominent actresses had become shareholders by the late 1670s. In the prologue to Durfey's *The Virtuous Wife* (London, 1679), the great Restoration actress, Elizabeth Barry, pouts that '*Underhil, Jevan Currier, Tony Lee,* / *Nokes,* all have better Characters than me' (A2ʳ). Barry threatens to 'throw up her Parts' until dramatists write her better roles, but, soothed by Nokes and Leigh, ultimately decides against losing her 'share' in the company (A2ᵛ). Certainly by 1695 actresses were active shareholders: Anne Bracegirdle, Elizabeth Barry and Elizabeth Leigh held three shares of Lincoln's Inn Fields to the men's five shares. Actresses also earned extra money from the annual benefit performance given in their honour; on 28 September 1668, Pepys records that 'Knepp's maid comes to me to tell me that the women's day at the playhouse is today, and that therefore I must be there to encrease their profit' (9: 320). The company benefit died out as the individual benefit performance became more popular towards the end of the century. According to Cibber, it was Elizabeth Barry who 'was the first Person whose Merit was distinguish'd, by the Indulgence of having an annual Benefit-Play, which was granted to her alone, if I mistake not, first in King *James's* time, and which became not common to others, 'till the Division of this Company, after the Death of King *William's* Queen *Mary*' (92).

Actresses contended with the indignities besetting any performer: indifferent (or hostile) audiences, loutish admirers and vocal critics. The Lord Chamberlain's records contain numerous proclamations against backstage tumult. Although the proclamations periodically banned 'persons of quality' from going into the attiring rooms or behind the scenery, abuses persisted (Wilson 1958: 28). Obsessive fans, then as now, could terrify or degrade an actress. Rebecca Marshall, who was employed at the King's Company, had particular trouble in this latter regard. In 1665 she complained to the Lord Chamberlain of being molested by one Mark Trevor 'as well upon the Stage as of[f]' (Highfill et al. 1973–93, 10: 107). The following year a ruffian, probably hired by Sir Hugh Middleton, flung faeces in Marshall's face and then disappeared (Highfill et al. 1973– 93, 10: 107). A far more disturbing occurrence happened in 1692 to Anne Bracegirdle when she refused marriage from Captain Richard Hill, an ardent fan. Her suitor blamed William Mountfort, another actor in the company, for his failure. After an unsuccessful attempt at abducting Bracegirdle, Hill ran his sword through Mountfort – who did not even have time to draw. Mountfort died the following day, and Bracegirdle, deeply shocked by the turn of events, stayed away from the theatre for nearly three months (Highfill et al. 1973–93, 2: 272).

Because of their equivocal social status – half servant and half professional – actresses were prey to the darker impulses of their superiors. This was equally true for actors. Pepys on 20 April 1667 recounts a dispute between Edward Howard and John Lacy that became violent. The diarist marvelled that Howard, who had received 'a blow over the pate' from Lacy, 'did not run him through', but concluded the actor was 'too mean a fellow to fight with' (8: 173). Pepys records another incident on 1 February 1669 involving Edward Kynaston. Sir Charles Sedley, deeply affronted by Kynaston's impersonation of him in a play, hired 'two or three that assaulted him – so as he is mightily bruised, and forced to keep his bed' (9: 435). It was a week before Kynaston could act again. Nobility sometimes used performers as pawns in court feuds. Katherine Corey, who had imitated Lady Harvey's mannerisms in a revival of Jonson's *Catiline*, found herself imprisoned by the Lord Chamberlain (Pepys 9: 415). The Countess of Castlemaine, no friend to Lady Harvey, sprung Corey from prison and, according to Pepys, ordered 'her to act it again worse then ever the other day'.

To be fair, some of the performers invited enmity. Lacy had already been committed to the porter's lodge and the King's Company temporarily shut down because of his inflammatory performance in Edward Howard's *A Change of Crownes*. Nonetheless, Lacy cursed the playwright – a member of the eminent Howard clan – saying 'he was more a fool then a poet', thus precipitating the ensuing quarrel (Pepys 8: 173). And while violence can never be condoned, one wonders how much Rebecca Marshall contributed to the problems with Trevor and Middleton. She was nothing if not obstreperous. Pepys reports a screaming match in which Marshall called Nell Gwyn 'my Lord Buckhursts whore' (8: 503). On 16 January 1668 a Hannah Johnson went to court against Marshall for reasons unknown; the following year, on 5 November 1669, Marshall sued the theatre concessionaire ('Orange Moll') for abusing her. On 18 May 1672 Marshall was again embroiled in a dispute, this time for debt (Highfill et al. 1973–93, 10: 107). Hardly a paragon of restraint herself, it should not surprise that Marshall clashed with women and men alike, including her admirers.

Taken in isolation, these few incidents depict the theatre as a very grim place indeed, the attiring rooms a virtual maze of predatory suitors and the stage door a haven for violent misfits. Contemporary accounts, however, convey the pleasures the theatre held for actresses and actors. Because of its collective nature, the theatre has always been an especially social milieu; and Pepys records numerous instances of actresses chatting, bantering and flirting, often assuming a raucous air that unnerved the poor diarist utterly. At one point he professed to be shocked by 'how lewdly they talk', but in the next breath admitted that 'to see how Nell cursed for having so few people in the pit was pretty' (8: 463). At moments such as these, Pepys appears torn between propriety and defiance, perhaps even enjoying a vicarious moment of contumacy through the brassy Nell Gwyn. In his diary we also glimpse something of the easy camaraderie typifying the theatre: Pepys sitting backstage, happily munching on fruit given to him by Nell Gwyn while running lines with Elizabeth Knepp for her role in *Flora's Vagaries* (8: 463). Arguably, the theatre gave seventeenth-century women an unusual degree of freedom, including the freedom to be impudent.

The very social fluidity that sometimes resulted in problems with their 'betters' had its flip side in providing actors and actresses an entrée to elite circles denied to more established professions. For Colley Cibber, this was one of the great attributes of the acting profession – that the actor is 'receiv'd among People of condition with Favour; and sometimes with a more social Distinction, than the best, though more profitable Trade he might have follow'd, could have recommended him to' (52). Had they been 'eminent Mercers' or 'famous Milliners', queries Cibber, 'though endow'd with the same natural Understanding, they could have been call'd into the same honourable Parties of Conversation?' (52). In rare cases, a man might 'make a name for himself' that would allow upward mobility later in life, should he desire such a thing. It is difficult to imagine a seventeenth-century milliner, even the most 'famous' of her profession, as Cibber observes, entering the drawing rooms of London as a social equal. Women customarily derived their social rank (and the accompanying privileges) from their fathers, husbands or lovers. Acting was singular among the occupations available to women insofar as it permitted them to enter polite society on the basis of individual achievement and consummate skill.

Actresses and the Repertory

It would take several years to develop a new generation of playwrights capable of imagining parts for flesh-and-blood women rather than the piping boys of the Renaissance stage. In the meantime, the stock of pre-Commonwealth plays – the Shakespeare, Jonson, Beaumont and Fletcher – that entered the Restoration repertory were reworked to produce suitable roles for women. As Michael Dobson notes, 'the other factor which transformed the pre-war corpus, equally affecting the unadapted repertory no less than the adaptations which it often stimulated, was the advent of the female player' (2000: 45). Lines were added and characters were adjusted to accommodate the new actresses. When the number of female roles in an 'Old Stock' play were insufficient, they were created, as occurred with several of the Shakespeare plays adapted for the Restoration stage.

In Thomas Shadwell's redaction of *Timon of Athens* (London, 1678) the roles of Evandra, played by Mary Saunderson Betterton, Melissa, played by Ann Gibbs Shadwell, and Chloe were created anew. Shadwell does far more than toss the actresses a few additional lines: he creates a tense rivalry between Evandra and Melissa that requires subtle manoeuvring and emotional expression. The respective characters are sketched vividly, giving Mrs Betterton and Mrs Shadwell splendid possibilities for theatrical display. Evandra, who has pledged herself to Timon without benefit of marriage, speaks movingly of her plight early in the play and then shows her single-minded devotion in the final acts. Melissa, who regards her admirers as little more than acquired baubles, exults in her various schemes. The addition of female characters not only softens the misogynist tone of the original script but also deepens Timon's character, giving him an opportunity to exhibit more finely nuanced emotions than unthinking generosity or raving anger.

John Dryden and William Davenant similarly added female characters to their redaction of *The Tempest* (1667): Dorinda, a second daughter to Prospero, and Sycorax, sister to Caliban. The role of Hippolito, according to the prologue, was also performed by an actress because of the 'dearth of Youths' in the Duke's Company, as was Ariel. Dryden and Davenant created several new speeches for the characters, including exchanges in which Prospero's daughters describe meeting men on the island for the first time.[2] They express their desire more forthrightly than the retiring Miranda in Shakespeare's original script, but Prospero still keeps the lovers apart 'lest too light / Winning make the prize light' (3.5.40–1). Nahum Tate, in his notorious reworking of *King Lear* (1681), enlarged the role of Cordelia for the superb Elizabeth Barry and invented the part of Arante, a servant. By creating a romance between Cordelia and Edgar, Tate hoped to render her 'Indifference and her Father's Passion in the first Scene probable'.

In these few examples emerge some of the dramatic possibilities occasioned by the presence of actresses. Old scripts had to be rewritten or enlarged to accommodate women in the two acting companies, but dramatists also seized the opportunity to use additional female characters to 'improve' the plays. While one might grimace at Tate's final product, his intention is perfectly understandable: to give Cordelia and her father sufficient motivation for their opposition in the opening scene (a scene which even today bedevils directors and actors). The expansion of Cordelia's role not only gave Barry more to do on stage but also allowed Tate to 'solve' a critical problem in the play. Dryden and Davenant's decision to award a second daughter to Prospero, in addition to the creation of Hippolito, permitted them to tackle another textual difficulty: Prospero's irritable, curmudgeonly behaviour. This device gives Prospero several opportunities to answer humorously Miranda, Dorinda and Hippolito's eager questions about the opposite sex. Of men, Dorinda exclaims, 'I would stroak 'em and make 'em gentle, / Then sure they would not hurt me', to which Prospero quips, 'You must not trust them, Child: no woman can come / Neer 'em but she feels a pain full nine Months' (2.4.109–12). The overall effect is to soften the edges of his character, making Prospero's decision in 5.2 to bury all past crimes 'in the joy of this / Blessed day' less precipitous than in the original script.

When revising the old repertory and penning new plays, playwrights inevitably confronted issues of sexual and psychological difference. Much has been made of the 'novelty of the female body as a specular and frequently disempowered object' on the Restoration stage (Rosenthal 1996: 207). Breeches roles – which proliferated in the period – are thought to be little more than visual peep-shows, the form-fitting pants showing off rounded calves and slim ankles. Other critics have stressed the staging of sexual violence against women, especially 'a new emphasis on the representation of rape' (Marsden 1996: 185). Certainly the spectacle of the suffering virtuous woman, popular in the tragedies and pathetic plays of the 1680s and 1690s, depended upon a female interiority that was associated with the body: bared breasts, dishevelled hair, terrified eyes. Plays such as Aphra Behn's *The Rover* (1677), Thomas Otway's *The Orphan* (1680) or John Dryden's *Amphitryon* (1690) all, for instance, include scenes of ravishment. There is also, as Jean I. Marsden observes, a voyeuristic element: 'these scenes present rape as both violent and intensely erotic' (1996: 186). Other critics consider the prologues and epilogues to plays, which actresses from the 1670s on delivered in increasing numbers, as little more than advertisements for their sexual availability (Howe 1992: 98; Rosenthal 1993: 4–5).

Some of these generalizations need to be qualified. Prologues and epilogues treated an enormous range of subjects; actresses delivering these set pieces bantered with audiences, scolded critics, castigated unresponsive spectators, promoted the play, defended the writer and debated politics. Given that some 1,200 prologues and epilogues are extant from 1660–1700, and that no more than 2 per cent eroticize the actress, it strains credulity to characterize them as sexual advertisements for available females.[3] A prologue delivered by an actress before Charles II, perhaps in the spring of 1672, suggests that the 'sexually available actress' was more of a theatrical convention than a reality:

> We are less careful, hid in this disguise;
> In our own Clothes more serious, and more wise.
> Modest at home, upon the Stage more bold,
> We feign warm Lovers, tho our Breasts be cold.
> For your diversion here we act in Jest;
> But when we act our selves, we do our best.
>   (Waller 1690: 53)

What one finds in the prologues and epilogues from this forty-year period, as might be expected, is the actress performing a variety of social and theatrical functions. To appease hostile audiences a young girl might deliver the epilogue, as happened with Otway's *Don Carlos* (London, 1676): 'Yonder's the Poet sick behind the Scenes: / He told me there was pity in my face, / And therefore sent me here to make his peace' (67). At other moments, the actresses took a far more martial stance on behalf of the poet or the play. Mrs Lee (Lady Slingsby), still in her disguise as a soldier, 'Offers to Draw' against anyone damning Settle's *The Conquest of China by the Tartars* (A4[r]). Elizabeth Barry, who played the Woman Captain in Shadwell's play of the same name, functions as his champion, declaring she will 'assert his cause' (A4[r]). Sometimes the actresses made apparent their differences with the men in the acting company, as occurs in the prologue to John Smith's *Cytherea* (London, 1677). The actress playing

Venus, who 'descends in a Chariot drawn by Doves', declares 'The Lady-Players say this Author's Pen / Writes something worth my pains – but not the men' (A3ʳ). At other moments they advocated partisan politics, as did Mrs Cook in the epilogue to Southerne's *The Loyal Brother* (London, 1682). During the Exclusion Crisis, Elizabeth Barry proved an especially popular speaker of partisan prologues and epilogues. And actresses were fully capable of directing ribaldry against men in the audience or even their fellow actors, taunting their sexual insufficiency. Barry, in the epilogue to Lee's *Lucius Junius Brutus* (London, 1681), tells the men, 'Know we have born your impotence too long' and then mocks their 'monstrous Judgment' in regard to the stage. They are, according to Barry, like a fumbling old keeper, full of 'midnight storming / For your all talking, and your noe performing' (74). Rebecca Marshall in the prologue to Killigrew's *The Parson's Wedding* (London, 1672) reveals the actresses have 'prevail'd again' upon the poet 'to give us our Revenge upon the men' in the company: 'Our tricks, our jelting hath been often told, / They nere were tax'd for impotent, and old' (3).

The representation of sexual violence against women, while abhorrent, existed well before the Restoration period. Jacobean theatre, as recent studies have shown, revelled in violence against women. The presence of actresses did not suddenly give birth to stage violence against women; but actresses did make possible a more physical, less abstract, representation. This is true of Restoration drama in general, which tends to underscore the materiality of the female body, as if to emphasize the authenticity of the actress playing the part. The prologue to the Dryden/Davenant *Tempest* warns the audience that the actress playing Hippolito will not be transformed into a woman at the end of the play. If spectators want 'To find her woman, it must be abed', presumably after the performance proper. In William Wycherley's *The Plain Dealer* (1676), which borrows elements from *Twelfth Night*, Fidelia's femininity is established when a stage direction stipulates that Vernish *'pulls off her peruke and feels her breasts'* (4.2.379). Female authenticity is also underscored when male characters itemize delectable body parts; for instance, in Sir George Etherege's *The Man of Mode* (1676), Medley catalogues Harriet's attributes for Dorimant in an oft-cited passage:

> . . . a fine, easy, clean shape; light brown hair in abundance; her features regular; her complexion clear and lively; large, wanton eyes; but above all, a mouth that has made me kiss it a thousand times in imagination – teeth white and even, and pretty, pouting lips, with a little moisture ever hanging on them, that look like the Provins rose fresh on the bush, ere the morning sun has quite drawn up the dew. (1.1.126–33)

Only a theatre that employs actresses can sustain such repeated references to women's breasts, lips and shoulders, even their scent; significantly, theatre traditions that use boy actors to play female roles tend to produce scripts that direct the spectator's focus away from an embodied specificity to an abstracted ideal. This is equally true of male roles. Plays written for the Greek, Noh or Renaissance stage simply do not have speeches detailing the glories of the male or female body in erotic or highly physical terms. Even Cleopatra, the most lusty of Shakespeare's women, expresses her sexual longing for the absent Antony in terms of his body's movement, not the particularized body itself: 'Stands he, or sits he? / Or does he walk? or is he on his horse? / O happy, happy horse, to bear the weight of Antony!' (1.5.19–21). A theatre of female impersonation cannot afford the implicit comparison between a material, 'authentic' male body and an artificially represented female body; thus, the language of Greek or Noh drama directs the viewer towards the manifestation of movement or emotion – what the body *produces*, not what it *is*.

Even on the Renaissance stage, playwrights are chary of physical description that might overly emphasize the reality of the boy actor rather than the fiction of the female character he impersonates. Perhaps the best-known moment of physical cataloguing occurs in *Twelfth Night* when Olivia haughtily lists her glories for Viola: 'item, two lips, indifferent red; item, two grey eyes, with lids to them; item, one neck, one chin, and so forth' (1.5.233–4). Notice the implicit androgyny of this description: necks and chins rather than breasts, grey eyes rather than a woman's soft curves. Red lips remain the only specifically gendered body part; and their colour is easily remedied by stage make-up. Even this description is unusual; Shakespeare typically refrains from writing passages that call attention to the appearance of his female characters. We know, for instance, very little about the features of comic heroines such as Portia, Rosalind, Viola, Hermia and Helena. When a character, such as Lady Macbeth, makes explicit the femininity of her body, she does so in the past tense or in a conditional clause. Of the 'babe' Lady Macbeth nursed in the past, she 'would, while it was smiling in my face, / Have plucked my nipple from his boneless gums / And dashed the brains out' (1.7.56–8). These lines encourage the spectators to imagine a lactating female body that relates to the boy actor impersonating Lady Macbeth through memory only.

In Restoration theatre, an insistent emphasis on the female, as well as the male body, accentuates sexual difference. Nemours in Nathaniel Lee's *The Princess of Cleves* (London, 1681?) enumerates to Marguerite the most tantalizing bits of her body: 'a skin so white and soft', 'beauteous dimples', 'hands, arms, and breasts', and 'pleasures that must be without a name' (4.1.166–70). The play also eroticizes the male body. Tournon entices Celia and Elianor – both bored with their husbands – with the prospect of two lovers, the first who 'has eyes as black as sloes – you can hardly look on 'em – and a skin so white, and soft as satin with the grain', and the second with 'such a straight bole of a body, such a trunk, such a shape, such a quick strength' (2.2.166–71). To ensure that Celia will put this male body to good use, Tournon underscores its sexual prowess: 'He will over anything he can lay his hand on, and vaults to admiration' (2.2.172–3). Indeed, male characters in Restoration plays are often rated in fairly harsh physical terms, particularly the older men who would secure young attractive wives. In Thomas Otway's *The Soldiers' Fortune* (London, 1680), Lady Dunce, forced to marry Sir Davy seven years earlier by her parents, endures Sylvia's description of the 'charming animal', her husband:

'Tis an unspeakable blessing to lie all night by a horse-load of diseases – a beastly, unsavoury, old, groaning, grunting, wheezing wretch, that smells of the grave he's going to already. From such a curse and hair-cloth next my skin, good heaven deliver me! (1.2.6–10)

Lady Dunce goes her friend one better, pointing out Sir Davy's 'incomparably odious' person, his stinking breath ('one kiss of him were enough to cure the fits of the mother'), his fondness for garlic and chewing tobacco, and his penchant for wearing fouled linen (1.2.35–41).

Actresses also affected the subject matter of new plays. Jean I. Marsden contends that because of actresses, Restoration drama 'devoted new attention to the subjects of family, love and marriage, a development closely linked to the definition of women as inhabitants of the private or domestic sphere and their exclusion from the public world of politics and commerce' (1991: 43). This shift to love and domesticity found expression in dramatic forms such as tragicomedy or the pathetic play. Comedy registered the impact of actresses quite differently, as plays showed – sometimes in uncomfortable detail – dissatisfied wives married to doddering, philandering or just plain cruel husbands. Female desire was expressed explicitly in plays like Wycherley's *The Country Wife* (1675), Thomas Durfey's *A Fond Husband* (1677) or Aphra Behn's *The Lucky Chance* (1686); and female characters often claim for themselves, at the very least, the right to choose husbands, if not sexual partners should the husband fail to please. Hellena's injunction to her sister in Behn's *The Rover* – 'let's ramble' – with all of its sexual overtones, serves as a slogan for the lively heroines who grace these comedies.

Playwrights wrote parts that played upon the particular strengths of actresses within the companies. Some actresses became known for a particular kind of role and had a clear impact on the evolution of dramatic form. Nell Gwyn, reputedly weak in tragedy, nonetheless possessed comedic skills so impressive that playwrights scrambled to show them off in the 'gay couple' comedies written in the 1660s. Gwyn performed with her lover Charles Hart in several such plays: James Howard's *All Mistaken* (1665) and *The English Monsieur* (1663); Richard Rhodes's *Flora's Vagaries* (1663); the Duke of Buckingham's redaction of Fletcher's *The Chances* (1667); and Dryden's *Secret Love* (1667). Sometimes parts were fashioned to appearance; as actresses aged, they moved into different kinds of roles. Of Elizabeth Bowtell, Edmund Curll, in *The History of the English Stage* (London, 1741), says 'she was low of Stature, had very agreeable Features, a good Complexion, but a Childish Look. Her Voice was weak, tho' very mellow; she generally acted *the young Innocent Lady* whom all the Heroes are mad in Love with' (21). Several times she was coupled with Rebecca Marshall, who played the villainess to Bowtell's innocent. After 1670 Mrs Bowtell turned to a wider range of parts befitting her maturity: cuckolding wives and tragic heroines, especially meek, virtuous women caught up in larger forces, such as Cyara in Lee's *The Tragedy of Nero* (1674). For versatile actresses, playwrights wrote a wide range of roles. Mary Lee (later Lady Slingsby) would throughout her career play virginal ingenues or martial women, for instance, Eugenia in Edward Howard's *The Six Days Adventure* (1671) versus Amavanga in Elkanah Settle's *The Conquest of China by the Tartars* (1676). Elizabeth Barry, the most famous actress of the late seventeenth-century stage, excelled in tragedy, but her abilities were such that she could play almost anything, from ingenue, to jealous mistress, to villainess, to wife or widow.

Some Final Thoughts

It is something of a commonplace that society regarded actresses to be little more than whores, a topic I have addressed elsewhere (Payne 1995: *passim*). Suffice it to say that attitudes ran the gamut of opinion. As might be expected, the authors of acerbic lampoons accused actresses of promiscuity and, in some cases, of trading sex for money. Robert Gould, Tom Brown and the anonymous lampooner who wrote *The Session of the Ladies* (London, 1688) all attacked the actresses in the nastiest of terms. Gould in *The Play-House, A Satyr* characterizes the actresses thus: 'All *Paint* their Out-sides and all *Pox* within' and 'Divested of the *Robes* in which they're Cas'd, / A *Goat's* as sweet, and *Monkey's* are as Chast' (Summers 1964: 311). *The Session of the Ladies* describes 'chestnut-maned Boutell, whom all the Town fucks' (2^r). The vitriol of these writers, as I have argued especially in regard to Robert Gould, may very well have proceeded from their own embattled position in the literary marketplace, a position that structurally paralleled the actresses' (Payne 1995: 19–22). Whatever the motive, whether jealousy or spleen, lampooners and satirists indulged the childish pleasure of attacking their victims through sexuality.

That some actresses, like Nell Gwyn or Moll Davis, left to become mistresses is indisputable. To say that only one-quarter of the eighty known actresses led 'what were considered to be respectable lives' (Howe 1992: 33) or that 'the actresses' sex lives really were fairly unorthodox' (Maus 1979: 602) seems quaintly Victorian. Social historians, such as Lawrence Stone, have shown that in the sixteenth and seventeenth centuries 'unmarried English women enjoyed what was by European standards a quite exceptional freedom to conduct their own courtship rituals', which included, up to the gentry, the choice to 'grant limited or even full sexual favours to their suitors' (1995: 12). Most of the actresses who reportedly enjoyed sexual freedom were not 'kept' in the manner of a Nell Gwyn but, like Elizabeth Barry, continued to work and earn their livelihood over a long career. Others, like Mary Saunderson Betterton, Elinor Leigh or Anne Gibbs Shadwell, were married to fellow actors or playwrights. *The Session of the Ladies* may very well have touted Bowtell's sexual infamy, but her will tells quite a different story: she died a rather grand old lady (Milhous 1985: 130–1). Bowtell married into respectable gentry (and, indeed, her own family, as indicated by the estate of a maternal uncle, were also decidedly well off). Whether or not she benefited from the generosity of lovers, as Curll alleged, is simply unknown. She did profit from various family inheritances. Mrs Bowtell acted sporadically over a twenty-five-year period; after retiring from the stage in 1696, she appears to have lived a comfortable country existence in Middlesex. When Bowtell died in 1715, she left an estate worth over £800 that included, among other things, East India bonds, lottery orders, a 100-guinea ring, silver, china and a portrait of a sister (replete with the family coat of arms). She requested burial in Winchester Cathedral 'in the manner I have ordered it to my Executrix' (130).

Because so little material evidence exists for seventeenth-century actresses, we risk gross generalizations on the basis of a few scraps of scurrilous writing. Bowtell's will hints at a woman eminently concerned with the trappings of respectability, a far cry from the town slut enshrined in *The Session of the Ladies*. Perhaps, like Moll Flanders, Bowtell sowed her wild oats in youth and acquired gentility later in life (although her stolidly gentrified origins suggest otherwise). Whatever Bowtell's trajectory, the theatre afforded her and other women the freedom to earn a living, to have lovers, to enjoy themselves. That very autonomy may have been what so threatened the satirists; within the local culture of the theatre, the actresses were admired for their professionalism. It should not surprise that the highest praise comes from play-wrights, fellow actors and early chroniclers of the theatre. Dramatists were especially fulsome. Thomas Shadwell, whose play *The Humorists* (London, 1671) had 'met with the clamorous opposition of a numerous party', not to mention poor acting, credits Mrs Johnson with its rescue: 'This of mine, after all these blows, had fall'n beyond Redemption, had it not been revived, after the second day, by her kindness (which I can never enough acknowledge) who, for four days together, beautified it with the most excellent Dancings that ever has been seen upon the Stage' (Van Lennep 1965: 178). William Joyner praised Mrs Bowtell's performance as Aurelia in *The Roman Empress* (London, 1671), 'which, though a great, various, and difficult part, was excellently performed' (A2^v). Dryden, in his preface to *Cleomenes*, echoed 'what the Town has generally granted, That Mrs. *Barry*, always Excellent, has, in this Tragedy, excell'd Herself, and gain'd a Reputation beyond any Woman whom I have ever seen on the Theatre'. Thomas Southerne in the dedication to *Sir Anthony Love* (London, 1691) commended Mrs Mountfort's interpretation of the eponymous hero: 'as I made every Line for her, she has mended every Word for me; and by a Gaity and Air, particular to her Action, turn'd every thing into the Genius of the Character' (A2^r). In the preface to *The Comical History of Don Quixote*, Part II (London, 1694), Thomas Durfey extolled Mrs Bracegirdle's performance of Marcella ('so incomparably well sung and acted ... that the most envious do allow, as well as the most ingenious affirm, that 'tis the best of that kind ever done before') and praised Mrs Verbruggen's 'extraordinary well acting' in the role of Mary the Buxom (Van Lennep 1965: 436).

Despite claims that the actress's sexuality 'became the central feature of her professional identity as a player' – supposedly a preoccupation of contemporary critics – early accounts of the theatre focus far more on an actress's talent on the stage than her skill in the bedroom (Howe 1992: 34). Often cited is John Downes's inimitable quip about Moll Davis's charming delivery of a song raising 'her from her Bed on the Cold Ground, to a Bed Royal' (24) as well as his equally memorable remark how Mrs Davenport, Mrs Davis and Mrs Jennings 'by force of Love were Erept the Stage' (35).

Less remarked is the praise he bestows throughout *Roscius Anglicanus* on the skill of actresses: of Davenant's *The Rivals*, 'all the Womens Parts admirably Acted' (23); of Dryden's *Sir Martin Mar-all*, 'All the Parts being very Just and Exactly perform'd', especially 'the last Act at the Mask, by Mr *Priest* and Madam *Davies*' (28); of Betterton's *The Woman Made a Justice*, 'Mrs. *Long, Acting* the Justice so Charmingly; and the Comedy being perfect and justly *Acted*, so well pleas'd the Audience, it continu'd *Acting* 14 Days together' (30); of Otway's *The Orphan*, the part of Monimia (as well as the roles of Belvidera in *Venice Preserv'd* and Isabella in *The Fatal Marriage*) 'gain'd her the Name of Famous Mrs. *Barry*, both at Court and City; for when ever She *Acted* any of those three Parts, she forc'd Tears from the Eyes of her Auditory, especially those who have any Sense of Pity for the Distress't' (37–8); of the Dry-den/Lee *Oedipus*, 'This Play was Admirably well *Acted*; especially the Parts of *Oedipus* and *Jocasta*: One by Mr. *Betterton*, the other by Mrs. *Betterton*' (37); of Betterton's *The Amorous Widow*, Mrs Betterton performed her role 'so well, that none Equall'd her but Mrs. *Bracegirdle*' (30); of Durfey's *Don Quixote*, 'Mrs. *Bracegirdle* Acting, and her excellent Singing in't' (45); and of Congreve's *The Way of the World*, 'Madam *Bracegirdle* performing her Part so exactly and just, gain'd the Applause of Court and City' (45).

Colley Cibber echoes similar accolades for Elizabeth Barry, Mary Saunderson Betterton, Elinor Dixon Leigh, Charlotte Butler, Susanna Percival Mountfort Verbruggen, Anne Bracegirdle and Anne Oldfield, listing their finest roles and noting their particular gifts. William Oldys, Edmund Curll and other early chroniclers of the stage devote the bulk of their pages to acting, not to sexual gossip. When as historians of the theatre we focus critical attention on the actress's 'specularized body' to the exclusion of her artistry, we merely reinscribe the salaciousness of a Robert Gould. To uncover 'unconscious structures' of oppression is one thing; to overlook evidence that calls into question easy stereotypes quite another. Breathing life into words in a way that convinces and moves audiences has always posed a challenge, even for the most skilled of performers. That actresses lacking a tradition of training could so quickly master the notoriously difficult demands of Restoration language should command far more attention than is credited. The distinguished actor Simon Callow observes that

> Restoration comedies demand the most exhausting kind of acting: sustained thinking. Shakespeare with his glorious word-music and the unfailing pulse of his rhythms provides the actor with an emotional wave; the lines have a sort of momentum which bears you along with them. They *give* you energy. But Restoration comedy demands that the brain, as well as the heart and senses, of the actor is fully engaged. These plays live in the play of ideas, which can only be achieved by thinking through each line. (1991: 13–14)

'Thinking through each line' suggests some of the creative work Restoration actresses performed. While Restoration acting styles, especially in tragedy, might seem excessively mannered to modern eyes, performers nonetheless did then what they have always done: use their artistry to make audiences believe them. Given the cool, analytical quality of many Restoration comedies, the challenge for actors and actresses to use their intellect as well as their emotions was particularly great. Nonetheless, Betterton's remark of Barry, that 'I have frequently observ'd her change her Countenance several Times as the Discourse of others on the Stage have affected her in the Part she acted', or Southerne's comment of how Mrs Mountfort 'by a Gaity and Air, particular to her Action, turn'd every thing into the Genius of the Character' show just how successful the better performers could be. Moreover, these examples also underscore the dynamism of Restoration acting: the performers were not just talking heads who stood and declaimed in 'tones'. Both actresses perform a verb that completes the dramatic action: Barry 'changes' her countenance as she responds to other actors, and Mountfort 'turns' the gaiety arising from the action into character-ization. Actresses who take their art seriously – and from all evidence, most Restor-ation actresses did – exert and control performance energy. They pace language in such a way as to balance spontaneity with predictability; they accelerate or decelerate events, building them into a coherent sequence; and they fill space so that ordinary movements assume extraordinary significance. Actresses are active agents who 'do' something to the script to make it come alive in performance; they are not merely specularized, sensationalized or otherwise sexualized objects. By its very nature, acting could not but give early modern women a sense of agency: the chance to earn money, the freedom to have pleasure and, above all else, the power to do things with words.

NOTES

1   I too fell into the trap of assuming that wages were lower for actresses by not double-checking Howe's source for this statement when I was writing a previous article on actresses. See Payne (1995: 17). Maus similarly claims that 'all the evidence suggests that . . . actresses were never as numerous or as well-paid as their male colleagues' (1979: 600).

2   Laura J. Rosenthal contends that 'The Restoration *Tempest* demonstrates a high degree of self-consciousness about the gender of the actors and confronts the erosion of earlier forms of patriarchal authority' (1996: 208). Both of these assertions are highly questionable. Rosenthal locates self-consciousness about gender in the 'sexually indefatigable Hippolito', concluding that 'while Pros-pero's daughters comically and seductively discuss their cravings for a husband, Ferdinand battles Hippolito over his (her) uncontained desires' (ibid.). Because Hippolito was played by an actress, probably Jane Long, this character is read as manifesting unbridled *female* desires – desires so dangerous they must be murdered by Ferdinand. Nowhere in the *dramatis personae* is it specified that the role be performed by a woman; as the prologue makes clear, the paucity of young male actors (cleared out because of the Second Dutch War) necessitated the casting of a woman in the role, a substitution they were 'forc'd to'employ'. In effect, Rosenthal reads the conditions of a particular performance, not the script. Furthermore, extension of the same logic would dictate that every desiring female on the Renaissance stage would in actuality be expressing male passion since the roles were played by boys. As for the erosion of 'patriarchal authority', Prospero stage manages the action

as much in this version as in the original, including the meetings between his daughters and their suitors.

3   In my previous article, I stated that fewer than 1 per cent of prologues and epilogues 'mention either the sexual availability of the speaker or actresses in general' (Payne 1995: 23). If the category of 'sexual availability' expands to include innuendo – for instance, a speaker's remark about her enticing legs – then the number swells to 2 per cent.

REFERENCES AND FURTHER READING

Barish, Jonas (1981). *The Antitheatrical Prejudice*. Berkeley: University of California Press.

Bawcutt, N. W. (ed.). (1996). *The Control and Censorship of Caroline Drama: The Records of Sir Henry Herbert, Master of the Revels 1623–73*. Oxford: Clarendon Press.

Callow, Simon (1991). *Acting in Restoration Comedy*. New York: Applause Theatre Books.

Cibber, Colley (1740; 1968). *An Apology for the Life of Colley Cibber*, ed. B. R. S. Fone. Ann Arbor: University of Michigan Press.

Dobson, Michael (2000). 'Adaptations and Revivals', in Deborah Payne Fisk (ed.), *The Cambridge Companion to English Restoration Theatre*. Cambridge: Cambridge University Press, 40–51.

Downes, John (1929; 1968). *Roscius Anglicanus*, ed. Montague Summers. New York: Benjamin Blom.

Fitzgerald, Percy Hetherington (1882). *A New History of the English Stage*. 2 vols. London: Tinsley Brothers.

Gurr, Andrew (1992). *The Shakespearean Stage 1574–1642*. 3rd ed. Cambridge: Cambridge University Press.

Highfill, Philip H., Jr, Burnim, Kalman A. and Langhans, Edward A. (eds). (1973–93). *A Biographical Dictionary of Actors, Actresses, Musicians, Dancers, Managers and Other Stage Personnel in London, 1660–1800*. 16 vols. Carbondale: Southern Illinois University Press.

Howarth, William D. (ed.). (1997). *French Theatre in the Neo-classical Era, 1550–1789*. Cambridge: Cambridge University Press.

Howe, Elizabeth (1992). *The First English Actresses: Women and Drama 1660–1700*. Cambridge: Cambridge University Press.

McKendrick, Melveena (1989). *Theatre in Spain 1490–1700*. Cambridge: Cambridge University Press.

Marsden, Jean I. (1991). 'Rewritten Women: Shakespearean Heroines in the Restoration', in Jean I. Marsden (ed.), *The Appropriation of Shakespeare: Post-Renaissance Reconstructions of the Works and the Myth*. New York: St Martin's Press, 43–56.

Marsden, Jean I. (1996). 'Rape, Voyeurism, and the Restoration Stage', in Katherine M. Quinsey (ed.), *Broken Boundaries: Women and Feminism in Restoration Drama*. Lexington: University Press of Kentucky, 185–200.

Maus, Katharine Eisaman (1979). '"Playhouse Flesh and Blood": Sexual Ideology and the Restoration Actress', *ELH* 46, 595–617.

Milhous, Judith (1979). *Thomas Betterton and the Management of Lincoln's Inn Fields 1695–1708*. Carbondale: Southern Illinois University Press.

Milhous, Judith (1985). 'Elizabeth Bowtell and Elizabeth Davenport: Some Puzzles Solved', *Theatre Notebook* 39, 124–34.

Mongrédien, Georges (1969). *Daily Life in the French Theatre at the Time of Molière*, trans. Claire Eliane Engel. London: George Allen and Unwin.

[Oldys, William] (1814). *The History of the English Stage*. Boston: William S. & Henry Spear.

Payne, Deborah C. (1995). 'Reified Object or Emergent Professional? Retheorizing the Restoration Actress', in J. Douglas Canfield and Deborah C. Payne (eds), *Cultural Readings of Restoration and Eighteenth-century English Theater*. Athens: University of Georgia Press, 13–38.

Pepys, Samuel (1970–83). *The Diary of Samuel Pepys*, ed. Robert Latham and William Matthews. Berkeley and Los Angeles: University of California Press.

Rosand, Ellen (1991). *Opera in Seventeenth-century Venice: The Creation of a Genre*. Berkeley: University of California Press.

Rosenthal, Laura J. (1993). ' "Counterfeit Scrubbado": Women Actors in the Restoration', *The Eighteenth Century* 34, 3–22.

Rosenthal, Laura J. (1996). 'Reading Masks: The Actress and the Spectatrix in Restoration Shakespeare', in Katherine M. Quinsey (ed.), *Broken Boundaries: Women and Feminism in Restoration Drama*. Lexington: University Press of Kentucky, 201–18.

Stone, Lawrence (1995). *Uncertain Unions and Broken Lives: Marriage and Divorce in England 1660–1857*. Oxford: Oxford University Press.

Styan, J. L. (1996). *The English Stage: A History of Drama and Performance*. Cambridge: Cambridge University Press.

Summers, Montague (1934; 1964). *The Restoration Theatre*. New York: Humanities Press.

Van Lennep, William (ed.). (1965). *The London Stage, 1660–1800*. Vol. 1. Carbondale: Southern Illinois University Press.

Waller, Edmund (1690). *The Second Part of Mr. Waller's Poems*. London.

Wilson, John Harold (1958). *All the King's Ladies: Actresses of the Restoration*. Chicago: University of Chicago Press.

6
Masculinity in Restoration Drama

Laura J. Rosenthal

Even though the study of masculinity as a distinct and historical category has only recently attracted major attention, the representation of men has been among the most controversial aspects of Restoration drama. Men in the comedies have shocked audiences and critics by their apparent callousness, their sexual voraciousness and their resistance to marriage. Villains in the tragedies share these faults in addition to their often-sadistic violence, while the heroes can appear merely bombastic. By contrast, others have admired the sexual energy, razor wit and brilliant machinations of men in the comedies, as well as the integrity and complexity of the men in the tragedies. Whether admired or despised, the distinctiveness of masculinity on the Restoration stage cannot be denied.

While historians have long acknowledged the significant social changes during the period and the changes in constructions of the feminine, too often masculinity has been understood as something that transcends history. But while men have long enjoyed certain privileges over women of their own class, the terms of gender division and even the idea of gender itself have been anything but stable. Restoration drama documents a small revolution in what it meant to be a man in at least four major ways: first, males lost the assumption of absolute authority over women and children in their families *as fathers*; second, European men began to understand themselves as a group *as men* in a way that the overwhelming force of rank would not previously have allowed; third, the capacity to rise through money destabilized certain status-based associations of masculinity; and fourth, increasing global travel and commerce that brought Europeans into contact with a range of peoples helped construct masculinity as part of a racial and ethnic identity as well. But while the plays distinguish men from each other through a variety of subtle assumptions about age, class and race, the comedies – and to some extent the tragedies as well – defined male difference perhaps most explicitly through sexuality. Formations of masculinity on the Restoration stage, of course, emerged in the context of broad social and political changes explored elsewhere in this volume in greater detail. Nevertheless, I will briefly touch on these changes and how they shaped Restoration masculinity before turning to the plays.

The Restoration

Charles II returned from exile to a country that had authorized the execution of his father. While the English Revolution had tremendous consequences for the political order in general, it also had particular consequences for the age's construction of masculinity. In fact, the question of the relationship between the king's authority over his people and a father's authority over his family became an important debate in the Restoration. John Locke and Sir Robert Filmer articulated opposing positions on this matter. Filmer's *Patriarcha*, written to defend Charles I, was reprinted in the context of the Exclusion Crisis. In this essay, Filmer argued that a king rules his people by exactly the same authority that a father rules his family. In this traditional form of patriarchalism, each father becomes a small king of his own family, holding absolute authority over them and at the same time owing complete protection to them. This does not mean, however, that pre-Restoration England demanded women's complete subjugation to men. In practice women had considerable responsibility – some historians, in fact, have argued that the end of the seventeenth century marked a sharp *decline* in options for women (Clark 1968). Legal, social, religious, philosophical and medical doctrine, however, assumed a non-negotiable hierarchy between men and women.

John Locke contested Filmer's *Patriarcha* in his *Two Treatises of Government*. In these essays, Locke attacked Filmer for his equation of masculine domestic authority with royal authority, separating a public sphere from the private in a way that Filmer had not. Locke argued that while a man derives his authority over his wife from nature, the king derives his authority over the people through an implied contract with them. Thus if the king violates the trust of the people, the people have the right to question his authority. Locke specifically argued against Filmer's analogy between the absolute authority of the king and the absolute authority of the father. Filmer, he pointed out, ignored the authority of mothers in his scheme, who shared responsibility for the children with the father. Further, Locke insisted that parents only maintain absolute power over their children until those children reach an age at which they can make decisions for themselves. Instead of absolutism, Locke advocated the natural rights of self-ownership, property ownership and ownership of the products of one's labour. As a result, Locke has been admired by some feminists for his critique of Filmer and for the way his *Treatises* open up the possibility of equal rights. At the same time, other feminists have pointed out that Locke's division of the public from the private and insistence on male authority in the private sphere laid the ground-work for a different kind of gender inequality. Locke, in other words, separates *natural* authority, which husbands hold over wives simply by the law of nature and natural differences between men and women evident in the garden of Eden, from *political* authority, which is contractual and thus negotiable. Thus in Locke, the decreased importance of birth in some ways created an increased importance in gender.

    While some historians have recently argued that Locke's advocacy of contractarian-ism was still radically outside of the mainstream of political thought, the *Treatises* themselves can still be read as symptomatic of the ways masculinity began to change at the end of the century. As Susan Staves has shown in *Players' Scepters*, playwrights, like political writers, also explored analogies between the authority of the king and the authority of the father or husband. Women on stage begin to suggest, she argues, that if the people had some right in choosing their monarch, then a woman had some right in choosing her husband. Staves's insight helps explain why the plays so often show men, often in poignant and hilarious ways, on tenuous, shifting ground: anxiety in the plays about cuckoldry and female disobedience in general suggested that the culture no longer took patriarchalism for granted.

Gender

Yet there are other ways in which masculinity changed even more radically. Thomas Lacquer, Thomas A. King and Michael McKeon have in different ways suggested that the early eighteenth century marked the emergence of the modern category of gender itself; that is, as King argues, only in the late seventeenth and early eighteenth centuries did men begin to see themselves as a group *as men*. These arguments have a precedent in those of feminist historians who have questioned the extent to which it is useful at all to talk about 'women' as a group before the Restoration when rank and status were such powerful forces. Clearly Queen Elizabeth had far more in common with male aristocrats than with female agricultural labourers. Nevertheless, this insight has only recently been extended to thinking about men. Filmer's version of patriarchalism did not entitle men equally to authority *as men*, but rather emphasized the rigid hierarchies between them. With the general discourse of rights, contract and possessive individualism, however, this possibility began to emerge. But while Locke's sense of universal self-ownership may have planted the seeds for claims to general human equality, the late seventeenth century demonstrably retained – or reinvented – gendered and other hierarchies. Carole Pateman, in fact, has argued that what happened in the late seventeenth century was not the fall of patriarchy, but rather a rearrangement of male authority from *paternal* patriarchy to *fraternal* patriarchy. Paternal patriarchy accepted the father as the absolute authority over his wife and children; fraternal patriarchy insisted on the basic equality of all (reasoning, non-slave, adult, European, propertied) men in the public sphere, but defined these men as full citizens in a way that their wives and sisters were not. Thus masculinity itself, among other factors but in distinction from rank *per se*, defined citizenship. Further, many scholars have argued that as a result the public sphere became the domain of masculinity and the private sphere the domain of the feminine. This rough and generally defensible division, however, should not obscure the importance of men in the private sphere (Maurer 1998) and women in public. While conduct books insisted on the importance of women in upholding the reputation of households and families (Armstrong 1987), husbands and fathers nevertheless maintained considerable authority over their wives and daughters (Staves 1990). Still, there were also women who achieved authority in the public sphere as writers, shopkeepers, philosophers, merchants and scientists. The theatre constituted a unique opportunity for women's participation in the public sphere, both posing risks and offering opportunities. Theatre had long been associated with disreputable elements of society. Some critics attacked actresses as prostitutes, for not only did these critics understand the public attractiveness of some women as suggesting their public availability, but they also associated the women on stage with the prostitutes who apparently met their clients at the theatre. Nevertheless, the theatre was one of the very few – if not the only – public institutions that virtually guaranteed the high-profile employment of women.

Theatre as Public Institution

While Restoration drama spoke to a less diverse audience than did the plays of Shakespeare and incorporated some elements of private court theatre, it nevertheless remained firmly in the commercial marketplace. The coffee houses that developed in the late seventeenth and early eighteenth centuries created a male public sphere that excluded women; in the theatre, on the other hand, men and women operated in the public sphere together as audience members, performers and writers. While women certainly wrote plays before the Restoration, nearly all of the plays performed in public had been written by men. But in the early decades of the Restoration, Aphra Behn became one of the most popular playwrights; in the 1690s, several other women playwrights launched their careers. Given this integration of women performers and women writers, some critics have observed that commercialization itself offered particular opportunities to and advantages for women. But in noting the new participation of women in theatre as actors, writers and even managers, we must also acknowledge the sometimes astonishing release of misogyny that accompanied these changes in plays and satires of the age (Nussbaum 1984) as well as the gender hierarchies that the eighteenth century established. As I have argued elsewhere in greater detail, it seems that since the evidence supports both observations (of women's success in the marketplace *and* of the gender-specific challenges they faced), we need a more balanced model than either simple progress or simple decline (Rosenthal 1996: ch. 1).

But what did this mean for men? Even in the Restoration with its range of sexual possibilities and permutations, options for men seemed to be narrowing. While a certain level of homoeroticism had been more or less standard on the Renaissance stage with boys playing the women's parts, that particular kind of gender fluidity had become constrained by a presumed consistency between the gender of the actor and the gender of the character. Preening gradually became unmanly. Kristina Straub has argued that the Restoration stage marked a transition from an earlier power dynamic in which the object of the gaze held authority to the emergent eighteenth-century dynamic in which power belonged to the spectator. Thus the position of spectatorship became masculine, while the position of the object of the gaze became a feminized one. As a result, acting could compromise a man's masculinity and even lead to rumours about his sexuality. Like women, male actors also became stereotyped by their bodies, with the odd-looking ones limited to comical roles. Male actors clearly had some advantages over their female colleagues: the better ones earned admiration and respect as artists in ways less readily available to the women. While their sexuality could come under suspicion, they were probably on the whole less vulnerable to this kind of attack than women. Earning money through public display did not associate them with prostitution as it did the women; they could more readily move into management positions and were more likely to write for the stage as well as act on it. Nevertheless, the women on stage attracted a great deal of attention unavailable to the men. Some productions, in fact, ignored men completely and cast all parts with women actors. Thus, men who trod the boards not only worked closely with women but also placed themselves in situations increasingly defined as feminine. Some, like Colley Cibber, who specialized in fop roles, seemed to recognize this and turned it to their advantage. All male actors, however, had to negotiate this complex combination of authority, admiration and yet potential compromise to their masculinity.

Court Influence

While Restoration theatre was a public, commercial institution, the influence of the court should not be underestimated either. Particularly in the early part of the Restoration, Charles II and the court culture influenced the kinds of masculinity displayed on stage. Charles's philandering became legendary and acquiring mistresses fashionable. He became lovers with both Nell Gwyn and Moll Davis after watching them act. Courtiers imitated their king, and the plays themselves frequently featured plots around male rakishness. Rakes on stage sometimes implicitly flattered the king and his court by representing royalist men as sexually desirable (Markley 1995). The use of stage rakes could also be an expression of loyalty to the Crown by mocking the conservative sexual morality advocated by the Puritans. But as we will see when we turn to the plays, stage rakes were not necessarily entirely positive. Many who supported the king found his sexual behaviour disturbing, and critics accused him of ignoring affairs of state for the affairs of his bedroom (Weber 1995). Male sexual prowess sometimes became a metaphor for effective political or masculine authority in general, but this relationship was often illustrated through impotence, cuckoldry and other forms of sexual failure.

Sexuality

The undeniable fascination with sexuality itself on the Restoration stage has been variously explained as a reaction against the reign of the Puritans but also as a continuation of Puritan prurience (Thompson 1979, for example). But given the major changes in male identity as described above, perhaps it is time to reconsider this relationship. Religious movements had long proscribed sexual behaviour. But if men were beginning to form a self-understanding as a group across status positions, then it would make sense that sexuality would become a defining factor in this emergent masculinity. Indeed, Randolph Trumbach has argued that by the early eighteenth century, a third gender had appeared in the form of the sodomite, the despised outsider to dominant masculinity against whom heterosexual men could define themselves. But while traditional (paternal) patriachalism was dissolving in the Restoration, a stable fraternal patriarchy with a hegemonic male heterosexual identity had not yet fully replaced it either. This transition could very well have contributed to the flurry of pornography, the fascination with prostitutes and the style of comedy in which most problems and solutions revolved around sexuality. (Tragedy explored masculinity as well, but not always in such explicitly sexual terms as the comedy.) Comedy, of course, has long explored sexual desire. Few other periods, however, explore it with such explicitness or expose such profound anxiety or ambivalence. And while questions of sexuality in literature so often revolve around women, those questions in the Restoration address masculinity as least as – if not more – powerfully.

Restoration drama – especially comedy – defined masculinity primarily through sexuality; masculine types are generally sexual types. Historians of sexuality have suggested that while long-term, monogamous relationships between men of equivalent status may have been uncommon, the seventeenth century tolerated sexual relationships between men and boys (see King forthcoming: introduction). This possibility, as Thomas King argues, depends on a model in which gender has not yet emerged as a primary social category and other social hierarchies prevailed. Some Restoration poetry suggests that men still eroticized masculine hierarchical relationships: John Wilmot, Earl of Rochester, for example, represented the sexual appeal of boys as well as women. The plays, however, suggest that male effeminacy, which was beginning to be associated with sodomy (King forthcoming; McKeon 1995; Trumbach 1998), had become a subject of both fascination and ridicule.

But just because Restoration drama begins to mock male effeminacy does not mean that it does not represent desire between men. The emerging fraternal patriarchy of the Restoration compelled men to direct their sexual desires towards women, but relationships with each other remained extremely important – although most acceptably in ways that suppressed any sexual element. Eve Kosofsky Sedgwick has described this pattern as *homosocial*: much of a man's social world consisted of men, but erotic or intimate feelings towards those men had to be channelled through the medium of a woman. For example, in Restoration drama men frequently try to cuckold each other, which on the surface suggests the simple desire for sex with a woman who happens to be married. But as Sedgwick has pointed out, cuckolding is something that a man does to another man; cuckolding establishes through the medium of a woman a relationship between two men that expresses dominance or even desire for intimacy that cannot be expressed any other way. Thus, men in Restoration plays pursue married or engaged women not only in spite of their previous attachments, but also sometimes *because* of those attachments.

While some men in these plays relentlessly pursue a variety of women, many seek marriage as well as or even instead of affairs. Men in the tragedies often fall profoundly and passionately in love; men in the comedies, however, sometimes see marriage as a restraint on their pleasure. Nevertheless, Restoration England, like so many cultures, established kinship networks through exogamy – that is, by marriage outside the family. Gayle Rubin has described this practice as 'the exchange of women', for families will offer a daughter in marriage in order to connect themselves with another family. Women thus come to inhabit the contradictory position of being objects of exchange between families but also human beings in their own right. This tension provides the plot for numerous comedies in which a relative insists on a young woman's marriage to someone she finds unacceptable. Men find themselves in this position as well, however. While relatives sometimes try to compel them to marry against their inclinations, often men (and women) are willing to accept lucrative matches without passionate love. This can strike modern readers as cynical; we must keep in mind, however, that these plays were written before the hegemony of bourgeois domesticity. Some plays accept the need for practical concerns in marriage, some plays pit desire against interest, and some plays both raise and avoid this problem by having this conflict turn out to be some kind of misunderstanding.

Class and 'Race'

The significance of class – or, more precisely for the Restoration, social rank – cannot be underestimated. While the tragedies draw large-scale distinctions between royalty and pretenders, aristocrats and commoners, the comedies often rely on subtle distinctions between men of leisure and men of business. We even find this conflict between playwrights themselves, for the elite amateurs considered themselves superior to the working professionals. As noted earlier, finance and mercantile capitalism destabilized distinctions in status during the Restoration. Merchants and businessmen gained more power and prestige, competing in both social and economic terms with the established gentry. The new economy brought a variety of world cultures to the attention of Londoners on an unprecedented scale. Global commerce may have influenced the comedies in more subtle ways, but it shaped the entire meaning of many of the tragedies. The tragedies frequently explore conflicts over colonial rule and trade routes; in the process, they suggested different versions of masculinity intersected by racial and national differences.

The Plays

Thus far, I have discussed the larger cultural shifts in masculinity. In the rest of this chapter, I will illustrate these conflicts through particular representations on stage. No essay could cover all the permutations of masculinity during this period. Nevertheless, by looking at various character types, I will attempt to touch on several of the problems suggested by the discussion above.

Aphra Behn's *The Rover* displays a wide range of masculine possibilities particular to the Restoration. We might first notice the absence of fathers, for Behn sets the plot in motion through Don Pedro's usurpation of paternal authority. At first Don Pedro tries to persuade his sister Florinda to follow their father's will and marry Don Vincentio, a wealthy old merchant. Their sister Hellena bluntly expresses the horrors of this possibility: Don Vincentio repulses the young women not only because of his age, but because global travel and trading for slaves have associated him with 'third world' rather than European masculinity (Hellena calls him 'Don Indian' [162]). To underscore the point that trading in African people contaminates the trader, Hellena compares the marriage market to the slave market, although not with the usual gender configuration: 'He thinks he's trading to Gambo still, and would barter himself (that bell and bauble) for your youth and fortune' (162). While later drama will struggle to lionize the merchant, here global commerce undermines male sexual attractiveness. With Don Vincentio so firmly rejected through his racialized mercantile associations, Don Pedro then insists that Florinda marry *his* choice, Don Antonio. Young, handsome and rich, Don Antonio proves harder to make a case against, except that Florinda has already given her heart to the English cavalier Belville. Thus while Don Pedro attempts to exert his masculine authority over his sisters, the plot involves not just Florinda's rebellion against her brother but Don Pedro's rebellion against his father. Don Pedro suggests to Florinda that the absence of their father offers the perfect opportunity quickly to marry Don Antonio and thus avoid Don Vincentio. Further, the death of Don Pedro's uncle, Angellica Bianca's former lover, creates the conflict between Don Pedro and Don Antonio when Angellica places herself back on the sexual market. The conflict of the younger men over Angellica Bianca, which ends up also involving Willmore as a suitor and even Belville because he fights in disguise on Don Antonio's behalf, constitutes a kind of Oedipal plot in which the 'brothers' fight over the surviving lover of the 'father'. (Of course, none of them actually killed Don Pedro's uncle as a true Oedipal plot would require, but Don Pedro had desired Angellica Bianca long before his uncle's death.)

The Rover also shows masculine identity intersected by nationality in the implicit comparisons between the Italian men and the English cavaliers. The play compares Pedro's rigid concerns with money, honour and family status to the apparently more

English value of love, represented by Belville. Belville stands out in this play filled with men seeking prostitutes for his companionate ideas and monogamous desire. While many of the English men pursue several women, Behn's creation of the one male character devoted to the same woman throughout the play suggests romantic monogamy as a particularly English masculine possibility. Blunt and Willmore both seek affairs with local women, but Belville in some ways disturbs local authority most directly by wishing to marry Florinda. Yet the play crucially ends not with his secretive marriage to Florinda, but with Don Pedro's acceptance of this alliance after his disappointment in Don Antonio. In order to earn this acceptance, Belville must undertake a journey through the complexities of the male homosocial order where the obstacles to his happiness lie. Belville accidentally joins the fight over Angellica Bianca when he takes Willmore's side in a sword fight against Don Antonio. Later in the play Willmore injures Don Antonio, which prevents him from keeping his appointment to duel Don Pedro over Angellica. Thinking Belville the injurer after Willmore runs away, Don Antonio nevertheless forgives him and then asks him to fight Don Pedro in disguise. Belville agrees, thinking that this will give him the opportunity to fight for Florinda's honour. He defeats Don Pedro, spares him at Florinda's request, and would have married her at that instant disguised as Don Antonio had not Willmore let the cat out of the bag. Nevertheless, Belville's willingness to fight for Florinda's honour earns him Pedro's respect, whereas Don Antonio's interest in Angellica Bianca and failure to keep his appointment to duel make him a less worthy potential husband. Thus Belville's emotional trials in this play have little directly to do with Florinda, for their feelings for each other stay the same from beginning to end. Rather, his challenge lies in winning the affections of Don Pedro and respect in his apparently more traditional sense of masculinity. Since Belville secretly marries Florinda without Pedro's approval first, there must be more at stake in getting this approval than simply a means to the woman. Pedro's change of heart towards Belville seals the homosocial circuit of the play, for without it there could be no happy ending.

The companionate ideal may organize Belville's desires, but Behn presents it as one among many possible configurations of male sexuality. Don Pedro, at least initially, values men for their status; he pursues the courtesan Angellica Bianca, who clearly gains some of her appeal for having been the lover of his powerful uncle. The eponymous Rover – Willmore – seeks to seduce any woman he meets. The rakish Willmore is one of the play's most appealing characters – witty, passionate, attractive, full of life and reckless sexual energy. Behn defines Willmore's character through his sexuality and his irresistibility to most women; sexual desires, inclinations and skills distinguish one man from another more than anything else in this play and so many others. While Belville seeks one woman, Willmore connects with three different ones: the spunky yet virginal Hellena (Florinda's sister, who pursues Willmore to escape the convent); the beautiful courtesan Angellica Bianca, also pursued by both Don Pedro and Don Antonio; and finally Florinda, whom he mistakes for a prostitute and attempts to rape. Behn's portrayal of Willmore is complicated: his vitality often upstages the more sentimental Belville; his appetite for sex seems endless, as the other characters often note in amazement, and unlike some other Restoration rakes he does not appear to seduce women for the purpose of humiliating their husbands or male relatives. In fact, he lands in Naples seeking prostitutes, the seduction of whom would, at least in theory, only strengthen the homosocial network since it demonstrates heterosexuality without transgressing against male property. His enjoyment of prostitutes, however, is limited by his lack of funds; unlike Pedro or Antonio, he cannot possibly offer Angellica the high price she requires. But Willmore has another limitation as well. While Belville has an ability to assess the status and sexuality of most of the women he meets, Willmore comes across as remarkably oblivious. Sometimes he resembles the fool Blunt, whom I will discuss next, more than his sophisticated cavalier friends. This obliviousness also leads him, often inadvertently, to disrupt the male homosocial network in ways that sometimes prove almost fatal.

Willmore's combination of penury, sexual attractiveness and sexual appetite end up making him quite similar in some ways to the prostitutes in this play (Rosenthal 1996: ch. 3). Male heterosexual prostitution is not unusual in Restoration writing: Behn has a male character trade sex for money in *The Lucky Chance*, and Lyric in Farquhar's *Love and a Bottle* pays off his landlady with sex. Men are just as likely to marry for money as women in the plays; Willmore, in fact, makes his choice of Hellena over Angellica only after he learns of her financial value. Along the way, however, his adventure ends up disturbing the homosocial network, but not intentionally. Perhaps worst of all, he almost rapes Florinda when he takes her for a prostitute as she waits outside for Belville. Belville, of course, is outraged, and when Willmore pleads that he did not know the woman was Florinda, Belville wonders 'If it had not been Florinda, must you be a beast – a brute? A senseless swine?' Willmore also expresses his contempt for Angellica Bianca even as he pursues her. 'Yes, I am poor', he tells her, 'but I'm a gentleman. / And one that scorns this baseness which you practise; / Poor as I am, I would not sell myself.' But of course, the discovery of Hellena's fortune makes her more attractive as a marriage partner.

If Behn's Willmore, in spite of (or perhaps because of) his occasional brutality, frequent drunkenness and obliviousness represents the successful rake, Blunt represents the failed rake. While Willmore achieves the male fantasy of free sex from a prostitute due to his overwhelming powers of attraction, Blunt gets the opposite. He thinks that Lucetta loves him, but in fact with the help of her pimp she takes his money without even giving him sex. He vows revenge on all women and, like Willmore, tries to rape Florinda. When he discovers Lucetta's cheat, Blunt calls himself a 'dull believing English country fop', another male type developed in different ways by other plays. Blunt has in common with other stage fops a kind of insufficient or alternative masculinity. He lacks the heterosexual allure of Willmore and his vanity makes him an easy target for Lucetta and her pimp. The play ends in the visual joke of Blunt 'dressed in a Spanish habit, looking very ridiculously' (245); throughout the Restoration, fops would become notorious for their sartorial excess.

Much later in the century, Congreve's *Way of the World* offers a different kind of rake more consistent with, as Richard Braverman has shown, the emergence of contractarianism over absolutism. While Willmore seems to have inborn gifts that render him irresistible to most (but not all) women, and Horner from Wycherley's *The Country Wife* (to which I will next turn) has an inborn talent for pleasing women sexually (although in both cases the playwrights complicate their rakes with a dark side), Congreve's Mirabell, Braverman argues, uses contracts rather than strictly inherent value and attractiveness to attain his sexual goals. Mirabell not only negotiates the personal terms of marriage with Millamant, but he saves the day at the end by producing a prior contract made with Mrs Fainall. But this does not mean that women and men contracted with each other as equals. In fact, *The Way of the World* clearly shows that Mrs Fainall, as a married woman, could not control her own assets except by entrusting them to another man, whose honesty she would then become entirely dependent upon. The play, in fact, shows the vulnerability of both Mrs Fainall and Lady Wishfort in a contract society quite poignantly. Nevertheless, while Willmore sees the offence to Belville and not Florinda as the reason he should not have tried to rape her, Mirabell, as Richard Braverman has argued, actually shows some ability to negotiate and compromise with Millamant herself.

But while men in Restoration comedies often distinguish themselves through their sexual vitality, the plays just as often characterize them by sexual inadequacy. Male impotence, in fact, provides the plot for Wycherley's *The Country Wife*, in which Horner pretends that venereal disease has left him a 'eunuch' in order to gain easier access to other men's wives and female relatives. While Willmore does not seem to intend to disturb the homosocial network through his sexual adventures, Horner's motives are more complicated. He states at the beginning that he has had no trouble seducing women, but invents this trick to get at *particular* women attached to *particular* men. In short, he wants to seduce women in the higher ranks of society for reasons that seem to have as much to do with the husbands as with the women. Horner wants to cuckold – something, as Eve Sedgwick has pointed out, a man does to another man through the medium of a woman. Thus his sexual play with Margery Pinchwife draws its pleasure from not just the act itself but the enraged response of her husband. For this reason, though, Horner cannot fully satisfy his desires with the Fidget ladies since the male involved – Sir Jasper Fidget – believes the story about Horner's impotence. In this plot, Horner's feigned impotence ultimately becomes both literally and metaphorically genuine. Greeting Horner's trick as an opportunity, the Fidget ladies make Horner their private sex toy, using him to satisfy themselves until he is all used up. Metaphorically, the now-enforced secrecy of his sexual ability renders him impotent as well, for he finds that he cannot cuckold Sir Jasper without Sir Jasper's open knowledge of his sexual 'conquests'.

While libertines combine sexual mastery with sexual vulnerability, fops perform different kinds of sexual and gender variations. Like libertines, individual fops both fulfil recognizable types and exhibit particular characteristics. While characters occasionally accuse a woman of foppery, the identity generally serves as a type of masculinity (as the name of the play, *The Female Fop*, like the phrase 'male nurse', suggests). The fop's outstanding characteristic is excess: a giant wig, too much lace, exaggerated gestures, copious theatricality. In some ways the fop parodies an outdated form of masculinity. In the early seventeenth century, for example, male courtiers expressed their power through expensive clothes designed to draw the gaze. In the Restoration and eighteenth century, however, the politics of the gaze were changing. Simpler clothes became fashionable for men; elaborate dressing and thus attracting the gaze became feminized pursuits (Kuchta 1993). In a contract as opposed to an authoritarian society, women needed to make themselves as desirable as possible in the marriage market through, among other things, their appearance. The fop, however, comically approximates the behaviour of the old-fashioned courtier and the contemporary woman. Thus he becomes associated with both femininity and an increasingly criticized aristocratic mode (McKeon 1995). While fops in Restoration drama commonly court women, their association with effete aristocrats and femininity in general associated them with sodomy as well – a transgression rumoured to be popular among aristocratic men. But understanding the way fops mimicked aristocratic behaviour only tells part of the story, for often this mimicry marks the distance between a play's true gentleman and a country bumpkin trying to be suave. Thus as much as fops try to be fashionable, they overshoot the mark and thereby inadvertently reveal their humble origins to those in the know. Behn describes Blunt as 'an English country gentleman': he lacks the urban sophistication of his friends. He is easily flattered and duped; he eroticizes being looked at rather than looking. When Lucetta glances his way, he concludes: 'I have beauties which my false glass at home did not discover' (170). Significantly, the last visual joke of the play involves Blunt appearing on stage 'dressed in a Spanish habit, looking very ridiculously' (245).

But a better example of the type than Blunt and perhaps the most famous fop of the Restoration is George Etherege's Sir Fopling Flutter from *The Man of Mode*. The contrast between Sir Fopling Flutter and Dorimant demonstrates the complex ways in which class intersects with masculinity and male sexuality in the Restoration. In order to compare them at all, however, we must begin by noting their similarity. Both men want to be 'men of mode', but understand somewhat different things by that term. While the play satirizes Sir Fopling's obsession with clothes and fascination with himself in the mirror as both trivial and effeminate, it nevertheless has a long opening scene in which Dorimant dresses himself as he gossips with his friends and pumps a bawd for information about a new heiress in town. Clearly Dorimant sees himself as just as much an aesthetic object as a desiring subject in a way that would soon become less acceptable for men: he takes great care with his appearance and charms, planning to use both of them to attract and marry an heiress who will repair his fortune. Like Willmore, there is a sense in which Dorimant also trades his body for money in the heterosexual marketplace. Neither of these men shows any lasting interest in women without sufficient fortune, no matter how much they may enjoy having sex with them, although, interestingly, the sequel *Rover II* kills off Hellena and finds Willmore engaged in a more equal and less financially based romance with a prostitute. While

Etherege's play, especially in the light of *Rover II*, presents perhaps a more cynical view of male heterosexual desire, both plays assume the inherent sexual attractiveness of these dispossessed but well-born men and show men with no compunctions about using their sexuality to repair their fortunes.

Fopling Flutter differs from Dorimant in both personal terms and terms of status. While Dorimant moves through the world as one 'to the manor born', Sir Fopling Flutter only recently came into his fortune. Like Blunt, he is a country bumpkin trying to fit in with the sophisticated elite men of the town. While masculinity changes through the century to the point that male preening begins to suggest effeminacy and even sodomy, in this play the difference between Dorimant and Flutter lies in their preening skills and not the preening itself. But even *The Man of Mode* shows this change in masculinity on the horizon, for the satire of Flutter circles back to some sharp satire on Dorimant himself. Nevertheless, Dorimant clearly possesses an excellent fashion sense, an irresistible body and finely tuned amorous skills. Flutter, on the other hand, consistently overshoots the mark: he wears too much lace, he spends too much time looking at himself in the mirror and he seems deficient in the arts of love. His problem is not too much attention to fashion, but in some ways not enough attention compared to Dorimant's years of self-cultivation. Dorimant's ability, however, appears to be inborn. While Sir Fopling Flutter, like many other fops, shows a class outsider attempting to imitate the manners of his betters, fops also come to suggest the excess of the aristocracy itself. Whatever the social origin of the individual fop, his manners and tastes satirize aristocratic masculinity that encouraged men to understand themselves as cultivated objects of the gaze when in the middle class this position was increasingly assigned to women. While men in the eighteenth century did not entirely renounce their preening, the increasingly powerful middle class defined masculinity in terms consistent with the emerging capitalist economy. Libertinism came under suspicion as a dangerous distraction from business, and even sometimes as a violation of a code of chastity that some thought should apply to men as well as to women. The libertine in Restoration drama almost always belonged to an elite class, even if he had been impoverished. Labouring-class men or men of business who drank and whored as much as the libertine would have had a hard time surviving. *The Man of Mode* explicitly and satirically recognizes this disparity early in the play when Dorimant reprimands his shoemaker for practising vices that should be reserved for the elite classes. Etherege's scene between Dorimant and his shoemaker shows a consciousness that different classes defined virtue in different ways; the scene both revels in and satirizes the dissolution of the aristocracy.

Arguments for male chastity held little force on the early Restoration stage, unless in the context of a romantic commitment. But by the end of the century, those who spoke for the reform movement demanded restraint for men as well as women. John Dunton's *Nightwalker*, for example, tells the story of a male reformer who visited prostitutes in an attempt to 'rescue' them. While on the surface women seem to be the object of reform, most of the stories that these prostitutes tell suggest that their unhappy fates resulted from male iniquity. *Nightwalker* treats female sexual transgression with surprising tolerance, but male philandering with little sympathy. *Night-walker* certainly does not challenge the 'fraternal patriarchy' (Pateman 1988) emerging at the beginning of the eighteenth century, for it represents women as victims of male callousness rather than as full social agents. Rather, it suggests a collective male responsibility for the preservation of female chastity and female lives (Maurer 1998). For a man to seduce a woman in *Nightwalker* becomes less an offence against her father than a threat to the emergent bourgeois family that needs women to become wives and mothers.

Nevertheless, heterosexual male chastity remained controversial well into the eighteenth century. Henry Fielding comically explored it in his novel *Joseph Andrews*, in which a young male servant resists the advances of his mistress. Female prostitution, by all accounts, flourished. Randolph Trumbach has argued that the eighteenth century tolerated prostitution because it emerged as an important way for men to demonstrate their heterosexuality and thus difference from the sodomite, the despised third gender. Yet the late Restoration also saw an intense anti-prostitute reform movement. Jeremy Collier and others in the late seventeenth century attacked the theatre as immoral, associated the seductiveness of actresses with prostitution and objected that the theatres had become places for prostitutes to meet clients. Collier also thought that the plays themselves encouraged lascivious behaviour. Congreve and others defended the stage, but some of the playwrights responded by creating tamer versions of sexuality in their work. Thus by the end of the seventeenth century male heterosexual purchase of commercial sex or support of long-term mistresses was neither completely forbidden nor entirely condoned. In part because of this contradiction in expectations for male sexuality, prostitution became one of the most talked-about and written-about social issues of the Restoration and eighteenth century.

I have spent most of this chapter addressing the comedies in the Restoration because those are the plays most likely to appear on a syllabus and in contemporary productions. Further, in some ways the comedies exemplify the conflicts and variety of possibilities available in masculinity more clearly than the tragedies, for comedy has always explored human sexuality. Nevertheless, the tragedies deserve attention as well. George Haggerty has recently argued that Dryden's *All for Love* and many other Restoration tragedies are organized around passionate male–male love that does not necessarily refer to sexual activity. Close attention to the language of male affection for each other certainly reveals rhetoric indistinguishable from the way men pledge their love to women in Restoration tragedy. Haggerty's work complicates the standard observation that men in Restoration tragedy tend to face a conflict between love and honour, for this love can be for a man as well as for a woman. But while sexuality most significantly distinguishes men from each other in the comedies and also remains central to the tragedies, other distinctions tend to prevail. Restoration tragedy explicitly explores racial, ethnic and national differences (and similarities) between men. I have already touched on the ways in which Behn takes advantage of perceived cultural differences between Italian men and English men. In the tragedies, however, this can often be a central issue in the context of the nascent British empire. Sir William Davenant's play, *The Cruelty of the Spaniards in Peru*, for example, makes the commonly used suggestion that English colonialism proceeded with less violence and more respect for the natives than the colonialism of the other nations. Near the end of the Restoration period, Thomas Southerne adapted Aphra Behn's novel *Oroonoko* into a play of the same name that became one of the most popular tragedies of the eighteenth century and tells the story of a slave rebellion in the New World. Southerne's play, which arguably participates in the emergent racism of his culture and does not entirely condemn slavery, articulates the degradation of enslavement in terms of compromised masculinity. Oroonoko, an enslaved African prince, suffers most acutely when his status renders him helpless to rescue his white wife from rape. Like Joseph Addison's *Cato* (1713), Southerne's *Oroonoko* defines masculinity through both a transracial romance and a passionate male friendship. The prevalence of colonial settings and exploration of masculinity through racial, ethnic and national difference in Restoration tragedy demands more attention and research.

Finally, we cannot leave the topic of masculinity in Restoration drama without at least briefly thinking about the controversies it has stirred up. To summarize in extremely broad terms that must necessarily omit interesting exceptions, from the middle (or even early part) of the eighteenth century until the middle of the twentieth, many critics found male sexuality of the Restoration, with its frequent definition through libertinism and cuckoldry, to be offensive, mostly because it appeared to encourage unchaste behaviour and disrespect for the male obligation to uphold female chastity. While the historical burden of chastity has tended to fall to women, the burden of protecting that chastity has fallen at least in part to men; some writers, however, have genuinely objected to male promiscuity as well. Perhaps even more than male promiscuity itself, critics have found the calculating, unsentimental and acquisitive view that so many male characters in Restoration drama take offensive. These men commonly make little pretence of a relationship between sex and love, and thus their pursuit of pleasure as its own end has troubled some readers. Rejecting this moral critique, new generations of critics in the second half of the twentieth century, perhaps inspired by their own sexual revolution, began to argue for these plays as psychologically insightful and/or celebratory of human sexuality. Feminists, however, soon pointed out that the plays tend to celebrate *male* sexuality, often at the expense of female sexuality. Many pointed out that the sexuality in these plays and in their performance took the particularly modern form of the visual fetishization of the female body, a possibility that earlier English theatre, with boys in women's roles, could not accomplish in quite the same way (Diamond 1989). Queer theorists complicated this view by arguing that the individual supposedly empowered male spectator could never actually live up to the phallic power he was supposed to hold (Straub 1992; Weber 1995) – hence the emphasis in these plays and in Restoration culture in general on male sexual inadequacy. Kristina Straub has also looked at the ways in which the male actor, as the object of the gaze, came under suspicion for his own sexuality. Thus masculinity in Restoration drama has been read as sex-positive or prurient; liberated or misogynistic; rapacious or castrated; homo-erotic or homophobic; nationalistic or cosmopolitan.

I cannot resolve these conflicts in the space of this chapter, but clearly we need to keep thinking about them. The comedies are among the most riveting in the English language because they explore, among other things, both the bright and the dark sides of the period's conceptions of male and female sexuality in so many of their complexities. While they often use sexuality as a way of representing politics and social transformations, they also can demystify gender and sexuality – and sometimes even class and race – in a way that rarely appears in the later drama. And while they clearly emerge from a society struggling to maintain male domination in the wake of serious challenges to traditional patriarchy, in the process they challenge some fundamental assumptions. Let us take the famous 'china' scene and drinking scene in *The Country Wife* as an example of this. In brief, Horner has begun affairs with the Fidget ladies by convincing Sir Jasper that he can't have sex at all. When drunk, the ladies reveal that their show of sexual virtue only masks their nearly insatiable desires. In the 'china' scene, one lady after the other keeps demanding sex from Horner until he has no more 'china' to give. Now one could see this as misogynistic, in the sense that the playwright suggests that all claims to female virtue are hypocritical and that women's lust reduces them to a kind of animalistic desire. There is indeed something disturbing about the way Wycherley represents these ladies. On the other hand, one could argue that these ladies have hoisted Horner with his own petard, so to speak. Since Horner cannot reveal his scheming he can never reap the full homosocial rewards for his plot. Thus these women have trapped Horner, forcing him to meet their sexual desires with apparently little consideration for *his* pleasure. He has thus inadvertently reduced himself to their sex toy; he serves rather than conquers; he, rather than any of the ladies, has become objectified. While no example of equal and tender heterosexual desire, this scene may offer a rare instance of unabashed female pleasure, albeit closeted and frankly shocking to Horner. Such scenes alone are worth the price of admission.

REFERENCES AND FURTHER READING

Armstrong, Nancy (1987). *Desire and Domestic Fiction: A Political History of the Novel*. New York: Oxford University Press.

Braverman, Richard (1995). 'The Rake's Progress Revisited: Politics and Comedy in the Restoration', in J. Douglas Canfield and Deborah C. Payne (eds), *Cultural Readings of Restoration and Eighteenth-century English Theater*. Athens: University of Georgia Press, 141–67.

Canfield, J. Douglas (1997). *Tricksters and Estates: On the Ideology of Restoration Comedy*. Lexington: University Press of Kentucky.

Canfield, J. Douglas (1999). *Heroes and States: On the Ideology of Restoration Tragedy*. Lexington: University Press of Kentucky.

Canfield, J. Douglas and Payne, Deborah (eds). (1995). *Cultural Readings of Restoration and Eighteenth-century English Theater*. Athens: University of Georgia Press.

Clark, Alice (1919; 1968). *Working Life of Women in the Seventeenth Century*. New York: A. M. Kelley.

Diamond, Elin (1989). '*Gestus* and Signature in Aphra Behn's *The Rover*', *ELH* 56, no. 3, 519–41.

Haggerty, George (1999). *Men in Love: Masculinity and Sexuality in the Eighteenth Century*. New York: Columbia University Press.

King, Thomas A. (forthcoming). *Queer Articulations: Enacting Masculinity and Difference in Early Modern England*. University of Wisconsin Press.

Kuchta, David (1993). 'The Semiotics of Masculinity in Renaissance England', in James Grantham Turner (ed.), *Sexuality and Gender in Early Modern Europe: Institutions, Texts, Images*. Cambridge: Cambridge University Press, 233–46.

Lacquer, Thomas (1990). *Making Sex: Body and Gender from the Greeks to Freud*. Cambridge, MA: Harvard University Press.

McKeon, Michael (1995). 'Historicizing Patriarchy: The Emergence of Gender Difference in England, 1660–1760', *Eighteenth-century Studies* 28, 295–322.

Markley, Robert (1995). ' "Be Impudent, Be Saucy, Forward, Bold, Touzing, and Leud": The Politics of Masculine Sexuality and Feminine Desire in Behn's Tory Comedies', in J. Douglas Canfield and Deborah C. Payne (eds), *Cultural Readings of Restoration and Eighteenth-century English Theater*. Athens: University of Georgia Press, 114–40.

Maurer, Shawn Lisa (1998). *Proposing Men: Dialectics of Gender and Class in the Eighteenth-century English Periodical*. Stanford: Stanford University Press.

Nussbaum, Felicity (1984). *The Brink of All We Hate: English Satires on Women, 1660–1750*. Lexington: University Press of Kentucky.

Pateman, Carole (1988). *The Sexual Contract*. Stanford: Stanford University Press.

Rosenthal, Laura J. (1996). *Playwrights and Plagiarists in Early Modern England: Gender, Authorship, Literary Property*. Ithaca, NY: Cornell University Press.

Rubin, Gayle (1975). 'The Traffic in Women: Notes on the "Political Economy" of Sex', in Rayna R. Reiter (ed.), *Toward an Anthropology of Women*. New York: Monthly Press, 157–210.

Sedgwick, Eve Kosofsky (1985). *Between Men: English Literature and Male Homosocial Desire*. New York: Columbia University Press.

Staves, Susan (1979). *Players' Scepters: Fictions of Authority in the Restoration*. Lincoln: University of Nebraska.

Staves, Susan (1990). *Married Women's Separate Property in England, 1660–1833*. Cambridge, MA: Harvard University Press.

Straub, Kristina (1992). *Sexual Suspects: Eighteenth-century Players and Sexual Ideology*. Princeton, NJ: Princeton University Press.

Thompson, Roger (1979). *Unfit for Modest Ears: A Study of Pornographic, Obscene, and Bawdy Works Written or Published in England in the Second Half of the Seventeenth Century*. Totowa, NJ: Rowman and Littlefield.

Trumbach, Randolph (1998). *The Sex and Gender Revolution. Vol. 1: Heterosexuality and the Third Gender in Enlightenment London*. Chicago: University of Chicago Press.

Weber, Harold (1986). *The Restoration Rake-Hero: Transformations in Sexual Understanding in Seventeenth-century England*. Madison: University of Wisconsin Press.

Weber, Harold (1995). 'Carolinean Sexuality and the Restoration Stage: Reconstructing the Royal Phallus in *Sodom*', in J. Douglas Canfield and Deborah C. Payne (eds), *Cultural Readings of Restoration and Eighteenth-century English Theater*. Athens: University of Georgia Press, 67–88.

7

Images of Monarchy on the Restoration Stage

Jessica Munns

> Then Courts of Kings were held in high Renown,
> E're made the common Brothels of the Town:
> There, Virgins honourable Vows receiv'd,
> But chast as Maids in Monasteries liv'd:
> The King himself to Nuptual Ties a Slave,
> No bad Example to his Poets gave:
> And they not bad, but in a vicious Age
> Had not to please the Prince debauch'd the Stage.
> John Dryden, translation of Chaucer's 'The Wife of Bath's Tale', ll. 61–8

Monarchy and theatre were closely connected during the early modern period in England. A court official, initially the Master of the Revels, scrutinized plays for indecent, irreligious or treasonable materials, and great courtiers patronized theatre companies. Monarchy had lost much of its numinous medieval sacerdotal ethos but gained the splendour of Renaissance showmanship. Henry VIII invested in spectacular pageant tournaments and Elizabeth I turned the realm into a stage with her elaborate progresses through England. Indeed, in a Renaissance commonplace, she drew attention to the theatricality of her position, famously stating 'We Princes are set on stages, in the sight and view of all the world duly observed' (Neale 1965, 2: 119).

The stage and the glittering world of the court were made for each other: they reflected back on each other and confirmed each other's validity. But it was also an uneasy relationship. Dramas did not always flatter monarchs; indeed, given the literary conventions of the period, tragic dramas tended to present negative as well as positive images of monarchy. Poetic decorum demanded that high dramas only happen to high personages and since drama involves conflict, the plays depicted good rulers deposed, murdered, rebelled against and misled, as well as those who were tyrannical, lustful and foolish. Despite censorship, the dramas of monarchy were often critical of royal politics and policies as well as adulatory. Indeed, the theatres provided a forum for discussing the nature of royalty and rulership, and the relations of subjects and sovereigns – compelling issues for monarchical realms.

The early Stuart monarchs made less use than their Tudor predecessors of the public spectacles of rulership; however, they formalized the relationship between theatre and court when they gave their names to leading companies, and masques and plays were a regular feature of court entertainment. Nevertheless, this did not ensure the production of sycophantic dramas. In the court, academic and public theatres the processes of investigating, celebrating and admonishing monarchs continued. Martin Butler has shown that theatre remained intensely political and deeply concerned with definitions of right rule during the reign of Charles I. The romance pastoral dramas that were particularly favoured by Queen Henrietta Maria and her circle did not simply flatter the queen but were also vehicles for criticisms of the king's policies. As Butler points out, 'romance and high politics are related activities; they share a vocabulary of "courtship," "intrigue," and "service"' (1984: 28). The public theatres similarly reflected the political tensions and conflicts of the 1630s and in either arena the dramas of tyrant kings provided a dramatic staple.

The closing of the theatres from 1642 to 1660 necessarily limited performance; plays, however, were occasionally performed illegally, and there were also private theatricals, masques were performed at the court of Oliver Cromwell, and by 1656 Sir William Davenant was permitted to perform musical dramatic entertainments. Moreover, as Dale B. J. Randall has demonstrated in *Winter Fruit: English Drama 1642–1660*, whether they could be performed or not, plays continued to be written. Closet drama flourished along with tragedies written by dramatists supporting or denouncing the Commonwealth, or by anxious unallied writers who variously depicted monarchs as benevolent, as weak or vicious, and as tyrant usurpers. The political traditions of English drama were sustained and, indeed, fostered by the experience of civil wars and the Commonwealth and Protectorate.

Monarchy Restored

The restoration of the monarchy was greeted with great public enthusiasm, and pageants presented to the king glossed over the past to glorify the resumption of royalty in England. In 1660, for instance, John Tatham, rapidly turning his talents from civic celebrations for Cromwell's London, to royal pageant, concocted *London's Glory represented by* TIME, TRUTH *and* FAME . . . *on the 5th day of July 1660 in the 12th year of his Majestys most happy reign*. Time, courtesy of the Skinners' Company, expressed a certain embarrassment at having been 'a property to slaves'. Truth, representing the 'untainted Clothiers', wished that Charles should 'live long and happy and Encrease', and Fame, on behalf of the Grocers, assured Charles that 'in yourself You are a History / A volume bound up for Eternity'. Charles was welcomed back to his formerly rebellious capital with traditional concepts of monarchy as dynastic and eternal embodied in the idea of Charles not merely as a part of history, but as History itself, moving forward towards Eternity. This was also a concept of history that buried the inconvenient years of Commonwealth and Protectorate. In the newly opened theatres, however, the King's and the Duke's Companies, performing (eventually) at the Theatre Royal Drury Lane and Dorset Garden, respectively, obsessively re-enacted the recent past.

During the 1660s a number of plays were written by gentlemen amateurs with court connections, and Roger Boyle, Earl of Orrery, who received royal encouragement to write his pioneering heroic plays, helped to establish usurpation and restoration as dominant dramatic topics. *The Generall* (written *c*.1661; King's, 1664), was Orrery's first attempt at a rhymed heroic drama and is a thinly disguised drama of recent events, depicting a powerful general (George Monck renamed Clorimun) who turns against the usurper he had served and restores the rightful monarch. Orrery's *Henry the Fifth* (Duke's, 1664), although written later, was performed before *The Generall*. Decked in the coronation robes lent to the company for the occasion, the play was a huge success. The tale of a noble warrior king, wild in his youth but responsible as he assumes majesty, and restored to his French possessions, provided a more elegant analogy than the better-known and intrinsically more complex and less 'heroic' events of 1659–60. As Braverman notes, Orrery set his play 'within the framework of a mythical past' and 'it was far easier to extol the restored monarchy by recounting the heroics of Henry V than those of Charles II' (1987: 41). Derek Hughes has drawn attention to the social conservatism of Orrery's dramas in which 'individuals are entirely contained and expressed within a society that orders their existence' and within which 'their nature is fully expressible in social signs'. Above all, this applies to the 'Sacred Name' of king (1996: 33).

Elevated figurations of monarchy are usual in the new dramas of the 1660s that followed Orrery's model and the imperative to put a 'spin' on recent history by replaying the drama of usurpation and restoration. In Dryden's dual-plot comedy, *Marriage A-la-Mode*, the usurping monarch of the 'high' plot employs the language of divine right as he resigns his throne to the rightful (and magnanimous) heir, Leonidas:

> Oh, had I known you could have been this King,
> Thus God-like, great and good, I should have wish'd
> T'have been dethroned before. 'Tis now I live,
> And more than reign: now all my joys flow pure,
> Unmixed with cares, and undisturbed by conscience.
>
> (5.208–12)

The two male 'low'-plot characters, Rudophil and Palamede, spend all their time trying to seduce each other's wife and fiancée; however, when duty calls, they display their loyal mettle and come to the support of the legitimate heir, Palamede even declaring his willingness to die in the attempt: 'no subject e'er can meet a nobler fate, than at his sovereign's feet' (5.198). In *Heroes and States*, Douglas Canfield states that 'the relationship between subjects and kings in these plays [heroic dramas by Orrery and Dryden] is depicted as ideally one of reciprocal trust. Not only must subjects remain loyal, but kings are bound too' (2000: 8).

However, despite the obvious political and cultural project for a royally restored and patronized theatre to celebrate kingship restored, or gloriously functioning, the ideals of reciprocity and trust between subjects and sovereigns, or descriptions of monarchs as 'God-like', were rapidly replaced by more ambiguous figurations. The second chapter of Derek Hughes's study, *English Drama, 1660–1700*, offers a clear account of the plays, comic as well as tragic, that worked through the master-trope of the 1660s, usurpation and restoration. As he shows, simple glorification of the restoration of legitimate monarchs was rapidly problematized.

In Dryden's and Sir Robert Howard's *The Indian Queen* (King's, 1664), the ruler to be restored, Montezuma, is a virtual outsider, a noble but uncivilized prince who must learn, with difficulty, to exchange primal freedom for civilization. The sequel play, by Dryden alone, *The Indian Emperor* (King's, 1665), shows, in effect, the drawbacks of such an exchange, as well as increased concern with royal sexuality. Montezuma is now in love with Almeria, the daughter of the defeated usurping Indian Queen, who hates him and plots against him. 'Love', Montezuma declares, 'rules my heart and is your Monarch's King' (2.1.6). But love is not a very good king for a monarch: this is a drama of demoralized and defeated majesty. Dryden's *Conquest of Granada*, Parts 1 and 2 (King's, 1670–1), offers an even more nuanced version of the restoration plot. The Christian monarchs, Ferdinand and Isabella of Spain, are surrounded by loyal subjects and magnanimous in the victory that restores them to the throne of Granada. That victory, however, is won through treachery and Ferdinand misreads ambition for loyalty when he makes the scheming Lyndaraxa his regent in Granada (Part 2, 5.252–3). The hero, Almanzor, an outsider who declares that 'I alone am King of me' (1, 1.206), disturbs the concept of kingship through lineage rather than ability, as well as pitting natural virtues against the hierarchies and corruption of courts.

Although Orrery's *Mustapha* (Duke's, 1665) has a usurpation and restoration plot, the restoration of the virtuous Christian Queen of Hungary to the throne the Sultan Solyman had taken from her, the play is less driven by the topic of royal restoration than by the dilemmas and dangers faced by the hero, Mustapha. His father, the Sultan Solyman, is jealous of his military success; his stepmother lusts after him. As he is led to his death, Mustapha doubts if it is virtuous to submit to an unjust power: 'Can I my Duty shew when I do ill, / Unjustly yielding to a Father's will?' (5.210–11). Solyman, who is misled rather than evil, and certainly less crafty than the Hungarian queen's counsellor, the Cardinal, concludes the play sadly resolving, 'I will to Beauty ever shut my Eyes'. The frailties of the ruler, especially sexual frailties that warp judgement, become an increasingly insistent dramatic topic. In 1668 Samuel Pepys was disturbed by an instance of *lèse-majesté* in Sir Robert Howard's *The Great Favourite; or, The Duke of Lerma* (King's). He noted in his diary that the play was 'designed to reproach the king with his mistresses . . . I was troubled by it, and expected it should be interrupted'. The play, however, was more particularly an attack on the king's chief counsellor, the Earl of Clarendon, the scapegoat for the failure in the Dutch War.

Nevertheless, Pepys was surely correct in seeing that the presentation of a king who merely has to have a pretty woman pass in front of him to overturn his previous policies was scarcely flattering. Lerma, who faces disgrace and banishment, decides to prostitute his daughter Maria to the king, musing as he sends her off, 'There go the Spells must catch the King' (1.29), and he is not wrong. The young king, though not bad, is eminently seducible and has no sooner set eyes on Maria than he rescinds the dying wish of his father that Lerma be banished and restores him and his faction to even greater power than before. As Lerma smugly remarks when flattering courtiers return to ingratiate themselves with him, there is 'Such a Magnetick power's in a King, / Where he but kindly touches, others Cling' (1.1.263–4). The power of the monarch is not disputed – but it is shown to be easily subject to manipulation. The realm and the monarch are saved from Lerma's machinations; but not by any self-control or political intelligence on the part of the king. Rather, Maria, who is both virtuous and intelligent, contrives to save her virginity without imperilling her father, and rival counsellors manage to outmanoeuvre Lerma.

Douglas Canfield has pointed out that, rhymed or unrhymed, the heroic play 'was not just a genre spawned by the restoration of Charles Stuart'. He cites plays such as William Whitaker's *Conspiracy; or, The Change in Government* (1680) and Thomas Southerne's *The Loyal Brother* (1683) as examples of the mode lasting deep into periods of political crisis (2000: 9). Undoubtedly, many of the characteristics of heroic drama survived into later decades. However, as the 1660s waned and in the following troubled years, what alters is the role of the monarch in these plays. Hughes notes as he draws to the conclusion of his survey of drama in the 1660s that 'increasingly, serious dramatists turned from the celebration of restored authority to reflection upon the problems inherent in the exercise and very nature of power' (1996: 78). Reformed and heroic monarchs, such as Henry V, or merely weakly amiable ones, such as Philip in *The Great Favourite*, were replaced by tyrannical, hysterical and frequently entirely mad monarchs. When their siblings and courtiers pay respect to them, their loyalty glorifies their adherence to a tough theory of loyalty and obligation to a monarch. However, loyalty to a mad or bad monarch can also illustrate the dangerous nature of a system of rule vulnerable to the happenstance of the ability and moral nature of a singular individual.

'Pageant Princes'

Dryden helped to set the new trend for plays centred on extravagantly bad rulers with *Tyrannick Love* (King's, 1669). The (usurping) emperor, Maximin, moves from dismissing the power of the senate to appoint rulers – 'That Senate's but a name: / Or they are Pageant Princes which they make' (1.1.36–7) – to tyrannical oppression and, finally, total insanity. After Maximin's serio-comical demise – sitting on top of the body of the man who has fatally wounded him and repeatedly stabbing it – the good general Porphyrius is acclaimed emperor by the army. However, he turns the honour down: 'Two Emperours at *Rome* the Senate chose, / And whom they chuse no *Roman* should oppose' (5.1.661–2), enunciating with approval a concept of elective monarchy and a limitation of powers. The early 1670s are filled with tyrant plays, and as well as delinquent kings these frequently featured bloodthirsty, lustful and ambitious female rulers. In Elkanah Settle's *Empress of Morocco* (Duke's, 1673) the main villain is the empress of Morocco, who has murdered her husband and goes on to arrange for her son's murder so that she can place her lover on the throne. As she explains, 'My will's my King, my pleasures are my Gods' (4.3), in a line that deploys the language of divine right monarchy to express libertine contempt for either kingship or religion. Such reductive language is a commonplace of scheming villains who consider monarchy merely in terms of the freedoms and pleasures it enables or prevents them from enjoying. 'Majesty!', exclaims the lustful queen of Sparta in Thomas Otway's *Alcibiades* (Duke's, 1675),

> . . . what's that?
> Th'ill natur'd pageant mockery of fate;
> When her ungrateful sportive pow'r she'd show,
> To barr us of the benefits below.
>
> (2.144–8)

Lustful queens offered, perhaps, a particularly exciting and 'safe' way to present images of irresponsible monarchy, faction-driven courts and civil disorder.

More generally, villain dramas also presented opportunities for spectacular scenes, executions, masques and musical visions, which were very much in fashion and particularly featured by the Duke's Company with its new and technologically advanced Dorset Garden theatre in operation by 1673. The vogue for tyrant plays is, in many ways, just that – a vogue. Performed drama must always be responsive to audience desires and boredom. The relatively small audience pool shared between the two Restoration theatres meant they were always obliged to compete and to seek to draw audiences through innovation. However, the new trend that replaced the essentially 'happy' dramas of royalty restored with melodramatic depictions of monarchy in disarray was also very much the product of a rising generation of professional dramatists who emerged in the 1670s.

These writers, such as Aphra Behn, Thomas Shadwell, Nathaniel Lee, Otway and Settle, were dependent on courtly and aristocratic patronage, but were not drawn from the court. They did not share the obsession with retelling the traumas of the Civil War and Interregnum and were not invested in glorifying and mythologizing the fact of restoration. They were also coming onto the scene well after the euphoria that marked the accession of Charles II. Their representations of monarchs and their courts recall Jacobean melodrama rather than Caroline pastoral, and more topically, their plots reflect current political concerns. John Wallace has warned against the search for 'dark allegories' in Restoration literature (1969: 266) and R. D. Hume (1998) reissued this warning with respect to Restoration and early eighteenth-century opera. Douglas Canfield has also pointed out that one cannot assume that 'every portrait of a flawed monarch was an attack on Charles II or an instance of "antimonarchism"' (1985: 236). The preponderance of such portraits may not indicate a personal attack on the ruling monarch (although some clearly do), or an attack on monarchism. However, they reopened in the public sphere of the playhouse the great seventeenth-century debate begun a generation earlier, over the nature, limits, rights, duties and obligations of monarchy. These included the obligation to produce a legitimate and Protestant heir to the throne.

By the 1670s, the number of the king's illegitimate children and the unpopularity of his French mistress, Louise de Kérouaille (created Duchess of Portsmouth in 1676), had seriously impaired royal dignity. The king's wife, Catherine of Braganza, was no longer expected to have children, so that Charles's sexual irregularity was not merely a topic for scandalized gossip but a cause for national anxiety. His brother, the Duke of York, was heir presumptive and his marriage in 1673 to an Italian Roman Catholic princess, Mary d'Este, Duchess of Modena, raised fears for his religious convictions. These were confirmed when he refused to take the Test Act of 1673 and resigned from his post as Lord High Admiral. The king's sexual adventurism had already provoked plays cautioning against lustful infatuations that weaken regal judgement. By the 1670s mild cautions were replaced by public ridicule. When an equestrian statue of Charles was erected in London in 1675, it soon acquired a placard reading 'Haste, post-haste, for a mid-wife' (Hutton 1991: 338). The previous year Andrew Marvell's *Upon His Majesty's Being Made Free of the City* (1674) portrayed the king as an unruly foreign-bred apprentice who 'spends all his days / In running to plays', and his nights in 'reveling, drinking, and whoring'.

No other plays were as outrageously iconoclastic as *Sodom; or the Triumph of Debauchery*, possibly by John Wilmot, Earl of Rochester, probably dating from the early 1670s and certainly never publicly staged (until performed at the Edinburgh Festival, 2001). However, its themes – a monarch given over to sexual excess, the extinction of the royal family, a land left in decline and at the mercy of a foreign monarch – were common. In *Sodom*, the king, Bolloximian, weary with 'cunt', proclaims that buggery may be used 'O're all the land, so cunt be not abused' (1.1.68–70). For all its obscenity, *Sodom's* politics of monarchy and sexuality are quite conventional. When sodomy rules, disease and sterility stalk the land, and in the final act, the court physician begs the king to rescind his declaration:

> To Love and Nature all their rights restore,
> Fuck no men, and let buggery be no more.
> It does the *propagable end destroy*,
> Which Nature gave with pleasure to enjoy.
> (5.44–7, my emphasis)

Insofar as *Sodom* is a satire on the condition of monarchy in the 1670s, the implication is not that Charles is a sodomite, but rather that he is given over to sexual excess and also sterile where he ought to propagate – the marriage bed. Charles may have been living 'long' and 'happy', but he had failed to provide that legitimate 'Encrease' those who welcomed him back in 1660 wished for and expected.

With considerably less vulgar violence than in *Sodom*, dramas of the 1670s replayed themes of regal impotence and monarchic irresponsibility as obsessively as the previous decade had revisited the topic of glorious restorations. Realms have not so much lost their monarch as have a monarch whose heirs (as in Orrery's *Mustapha*) are pitted against each other, monarchs who have murdered their heirs, or realms where legitimate monarch and heirs are all murdered. Both in Settle's *The Empress of Morocco* and *The Conquest of China by the Tartars* (Duke's, 1674), the legitimate succession is wiped out and the throne passes to one who, if not of the ruling family, is more worthy. Aphra Behn entered the fray with *Abdelazer; or the Moor's Revenge* (Duke's, 1676), where a lustful queen, on the lines of the empress of Morocco, turns her husband against his loyal brother. She then conspires with her lover and murders her husband and tries to exterminate her own sons. Nathaniel Lee early specialized in dysfunctional royal families with Nero in the play of that name (King's, 1674) madly wiping out his family. In *Gloriana; or, the Court of Augustus Caesar* (King's, 1676) he presents a family riven by dispute over the succession with two claimants: Caesario, Julius Caesar's son by Cleopatra, and Augustus, his son by adoption. Augustus plays out the lustful ruler as he attempts to rape Caesario's beloved Gloriana. Lee's *Mithridates* (King's, 1678) presents a ruler who is an aged, lustful, incestuous rapist, one of whose sons unsuccessfully rebels against him and another he murders. He leaves behind him a 'Royal Race of Little Ones' (5.359), but their eventual inheritance is dubious and at the mercy of the victorious Roman general, Pompey. In Otway's *Alcibiades* the ruler, Agis, is singularly ineffectual, and is, indeed, depicted by his queen as an impotent fool who, like most husbands, can only 'ignorantly with Loves Magick play.../ raise Spirits they want pow'r to lay' (2.159–60). The queen has the king killed, and when she has eventually dispatched herself, as well as several other people, the throne is left to the virtuous son of the ambitious general who aided her. He, however, is unwilling to assume the role of king and is more concerned about what to do with his regicidal father and where to find his mistress, who has disappeared in the chaos. The effect of the ending is not so much to show that evil has run its course and order is restored as to suggest a kind of dynastic entropy.

In Otway's next tragedy, *Don Carlos* (Duke's, 1676), the play opens with the heir to the throne, Don Carlos, exclaiming

> Curse! What's obedience? A false Notion made
> By Priests, who when they found old Cheats decay'd,
> By such new Arts kept up declining Trade...
> (1.1.14–16)

Such lines might be expected to issue from the villain, but Carlos is no villain, just deeply angered by the fact that his father has just married his betrothed. King Philip of Spain is not precisely a villain either, but he is cruel and selfish, and morally, if not legally, incestuous in marrying the woman who was to be his daughter. He is then consumed with jealousy of his son and his wife. Philip, indeed, is rebuked by his half-brother, Don John, who tries to point out to him that monarchy is not just a question of exercising power over others, but over oneself: 'Be something less a man, and more a King' (5.1.64). This is not advice the jealous king can take: he has his son and his wife murdered, and the horror of the act drives him insane – in the final moments of the play the stage direction has him running 'off raving'.

In Dryden's *Aureng-Zebe* (King's, 1676), which was an important model for the royal family-in-disarray play, a succession crisis between the sons of the Mughal emperor, described in the opening lines as 'Rebels and Parricides!' (1.1), is complicated by the lusts of the emperor for Indiamora, beloved by his loyal son Aureng-Zebe, and the empress for her stepson, Aureng-Zebe. After the last filial rebellion is defeated, that of Morat, the emperor abdicates, in the circumstances quite sensibly but significantly dispensing with primogeniture. He bypasses his elder sons to enthrone Aureng-Zebe, who is the play's hero, yet, as Hughes and Braverman have pointed out, there is a question mark over whether Aureng-Zebe will be up to the task, or even a significant moral improvement on Morat (Hughes 1981: 149; Braverman 1987: 134).

Charles Davenant's operatic *Circe*, a verse couplet play (Duke's, 1677), also presents a dysfunctional royal family, a weak and lustful king and the extermination of the legitimate succession. Circe, the enchantress, married to Thoas, King of Scythia, plans to wed her son Itacus to Osmida, Thoas's daughter by a previous wife, thereby ensuring the succession for her line. Itacus, however, is in love with Iphigenia, high priestess of Diana Taurica, with whom Thoas is also in love. Despite his adulterous desire, Thoas, like Agis in *Alcibiades*, is less marked by lust than impotence. Circe, for instance, describes him as a 'Pageant Monarch', and complains 'He fills my Bed as idly as the throne' (Act 2, p. 16). When Circe is caught out herself with a young lover, she unites the topics of monarchical incompetence, impotence *and* promiscuity as she mocks the angry king:

> How like the Love of thy declining Age!
> How boasting! But how feeble is thy rage.
> Prince without Pow'r! Go languish in despair,
> Ridden by all——
> Thy Favourites, and imposed on by the Fair.
> (Act 4, p. 41)

Circe's lover, Orestes, is of course also a member of a murderous royal family – and a matricide – who goes mad and stabs himself and Circe. Meanwhile, her son Itacus has also died, as has Osmida, thus exterminating the direct heirs to the Scythian throne, and the question of who will succeed the aged Thoas is left unresolved. Davenant, in fact, manages to present two dysfunctional royal families, that of Greece as well as that of Scythia, where doomed or weak kings have failed to secure their realms.

Dryden and Lee's *Oedipus* (King's, 1678) offers a particularly acute version of the succession crisis play complicated by regicidal patricide and incest. Patricide, inclinations towards patricide, a monarch's fears, justified or not, that his heir contemplates the crime and a father's murderous inclinations towards his heirs, feature extensively in the serious dramas of the 1670s. The frequency with which these topics are raised suggests an unease, conscious or not, with the very system of patrilineal monarchy that involved the necessity for a male heir, and then the son's eagerness to inherit and the father's fear of his son. Incest is also a repeated theme, often combined with the heir-murdering topic, as mimetic desire compels the ruler towards the woman his son loves and wishes to marry and, therefore, symbolically to emasculate him. Doubtless there is a strong element of fashion as dramatists strove for more and more sensational materials, but there is also a sense that as dramatists work through the tropes and topics of the drama of monarchy, what surfaces is a regressive and primitive concept of monarchy. The early plays celebrating monarchy and the restoration of order were superseded by the dramas of a ruler's unruly desires: monarchy emerges as the *fons et origo* of a system of disorder.

Plays where the succession is not in doubt – Otway's *Titus and Berenice* (Duke's, 1676); John Crowne's two-part *Destruction of Jerusalem* (King's, 1676); and Nahum Tate's *Brutus of Alba: or, The Enchanted Lovers* (Duke's, 1678) – depict rulers who struggle against the necessity of putting the public good above private inclination. Failure to subordinate pleasure to power also informs the group of Alexander and Antony plays, which depict the hero-ruler unable or unwilling to accept his responsibilities. Lee's *The Rival Queens* (King's, 1677), Sir Charles Sedley's *Antony and Cleopatra* (Duke's, 1677), John Banks's *The Rival Kings* (King's, 1677), Samuel Pordage's *The Siege of Babylon* (Duke's, 1677) and Dryden's *All for Love; or, The World Well Lost* (King's, 1677) all depict hero-rulers at their point of decline. The Alexander plays, drawing on La Calprenède's *Cassandre*, and the two Antony plays, based on Shakespeare, are similar in their account of the unruly last days of empire. Unlike Dryden's later play, Sedley concentrates on Antony's failures – naval disaster, licentiousness, impolitic neglect of his wife's bed, extravagance and 'Asiatic' tyranny – criticisms that echo contemporary complaints against Charles II. As Octavius Caesar points out:

> The Asians now with double Taxes prest
> His slothful Days and drunken Nights detest;
> Buffoons and Players chiefly have his ear;
> He dares not the free tongues of *Romans* hear.
> To marry Whores to Fencers is his Sport,
> And with his issue throng his loathed court
> . . .
> Now lewd *Cytheris* has a greater Train,

Than his own Mother or his Wife maintain.
From such a Foe as this what can we fear
In whom all symptoms of lost pow'r appear.

(3.1, p. 20)

Agrippa makes the moral for princes:

Example is a living Law, whose sway,
Men more than the written Laws obey.
Princes of all men therefore shou'd take care
How in their manners they the Crowd ensnare.

And he goes on to express wonder at Antony's 'dotage' on Cleopatra – a passion that reverses all laws of power and nature:

Women should sit like idle Passengers,
While the tall ship some able Seaman steers
    . . . was it ever seen
A Woman rul'd an Emperor till now?
What Horse the Mare, what Bull obeys the Cow?

(3.1, p. 21)

Like the Antony plays, the Alexander plays depict the hero-ruler in decline. In the *Rival Queens*, Lee presents the stereotypes of the 'foreign' queen – the fierce Roxana and the gentle Statira – who between them unman Alexander and encourage his deviation from national, Macedonian mores – conquest and success. In selecting Antony or Alexander as heroes, the writers chose to dramatize a ruler past his prime, and who is given over to irresponsible and 'foreign' luxury. In the case of the Antony plays, the hero is defeated, if not by a better man, by a more controlled man, while Alexander's death without heirs plunges his territories into war. Banks's play concludes with the deaths of Alexander and Ephestion and news of rebellion; Lee's play ends in chaos and with the legendary words of the dying Alexander bequeathing his empire: 'To him that is most worthy' – the opening words of an imperial bloodbath.

'Religious Broyles'

By the late 1670s, England and her theatres had new topics to contend with and dramatize. In September 1678 Titus Oates revealed (and concocted) information about a Jesuit plot to murder the king and impose Catholicism on England, which led to a period of profound crisis. The dramatic responses to the period when the king manoeuvred to protect his throne and its succession to his brother James have been thoroughly discussed in a number of recent works. Canfield has argued that in political dramas, 'the royalist code of loyalty to a rightful monarch, however weak or indulgent, wrong or unfortunate, is strenuously maintained' (1985: 238). However, as Susan Owen has shown in her meticulous account of drama during this period, the degree of strenuousness varied. Dramas expressing anxiety over the twinned fears, Roman Catholicism and arbitrary power, were written and staged, and, Owen argues, even the royalist dramas failed to 'paper over ideological cracks' but rather revealed the 'constructed nature of late Stuart ideology' (1996: 19). After surveying tragedies written during 1679, Hughes concludes that the serious drama was 'predominately anti-court, even when...the exhortation is to loyalty' (1996: 273). In the plays following that year, Hughes finds dramatists exhibiting pessimism 'about royal and patriarchal authority' and 'depressed' and 'chilling' representations of restorations of royal authority (1996: 275, 281).

Shakespeare's plays, especially his 'Wars of the Roses' history plays, provided writers with models for dramatizations of civil conflict and challenges to kingly authority. However, even when offering warnings against such challenges, the subject matter could be too close for comfort. Nahum Tate's *History of Richard the Second* was banned in December 1680, and when the King's Company tried to perform it under another name, *The Sicilian Usurper*, the theatre was closed in punishment. No matter how much Tate improved the character of Richard II or made Bolingbroke repent of his crime of usurpation, this clearly was no time to present a play that depicted a successful usurpation. John Crowne's *The Misery of Civil-War* (Duke's, 1680), whose prologue draws attention to the 'Religious Broyles' of the period, is an adaptation of parts of Shakespeare's *2 Henry VI* and *3 Henry VI*. His play was staged, but as Owen states, it 'contains some residual anxieties' with regard to its royalism (1996: 76). In *The Misery of Civil-War* Crowne also has to deal with usurpation and regicide, but cleverly contrives sympathy for all claimants to the throne. Shortly before his murder Crowne's saintly Henry VI is visited by the ghost of Richard II, who explains carefully that the line of Bolingbroke usurped the throne and have regretted it ever since. A kindly white-clad spirit then urges 'Religious Henry' not to 'think thyself unkindly us'd' since 'Heaven' merely 'takes away what is not thine' (Act 5, p. 68). The spirit assures Henry that though he will suffer for this ancestral deed, once dead he will enjoy the company of his murdered son and experience 'exalted joy' (Act 5, p. 68). Crowne condemns usurpation, and also seeks to palliate the unnerving depiction of regicide. Edward IV, the 'lawful King' (Act 3, p. 38), is depicted as womanizing but basically capable.

In an extraordinary scene the Earl of Warwick and Duke of Gloucester berate Edward for having spent the night of his father's death with a woman. Edward responds haughtily with a speech that the first audiences must have understood as the best defence that could be made for their own king's sexual promiscuity. 'A King', Edward informs them loftily, 'is a strong Tower on a high Rock', though he agrees he has a 'heart' that 'to beauty lies too open'. He admits that he 'fell into an ambuscade of beauty' and 'deep in Love, I lay some hours last night', adding 'which of you wou'd not have done the same?', and goes on to point out that Warwick too is fallible on this count (Act 3, pp. 39–40). The best defence seems to be that the king is no more promiscuous than his great subjects, and that despite falling into an 'ambuscade of beauty' for a few hours, Edward has also been busy about the business of state, sending 'Commissioners / To Henry to demand the Crown of him' (Act 3, p. 41). Edward has a mistress, Lady Eleanor Butler, whom by any standards he treats very caddishly once he has instead fallen in love with Lady Grey, whom he proposes to marry (later, by mistake, he kills Lady Eleanor in battle when she is disguised as a man). Edward defends his decision to marry Lady Grey, which breaks off the politically advantageous marriage Warwick had arranged for him with a daughter of the king of France, with a series of angry questions that assert his kingly will:

> Why may not this fair Lady be a Queen?
> But she's a Subject, *England* will not like it.
> And the *English* Nation, like the Sea it governs,
> Is bold and turbulent, and easily mov'd,
> And always beats against the shore, that bounds it.
> What? is the people free and not the King?
> Not free where every Slave is free, his bed?
>
> (Act 4, pp. 50–1)

It is rather striking that the assertion of royal authority is that a monarch should have the right to be 'free' in 'bed'.

For dramatists opposed to royal policy and fearful of a Catholic succession, the current monarch could be attacked directly in anti-Catholic dramas, and indirectly by way of nostalgic celebrations of Queen Elizabeth I – 'sole Protector of our Lives, Fortunes, and Religion' (*The Coronation of Queen Elizabeth, with the Restauration of the Protestant Religion: or, the Downfall of the Pope*, Southwark Fair, 1680). It is perhaps a not very obscure irony that the most positive images of royalty come not from Tory poets seeking to support a troubled monarchy but from Whig writers happily opposing it with propagandistic images of a national icon. Royalist dramatists had a hard job. Otway, undoubtedly a loyal royalist, provided support through negative images of republican states: Rome in a state of violent civil disorder in *Caius Marius* (Duke's, 1679), and a corrupt and weak Venetian republic in *Venice Preserv'd* (Duke's, 1682). He seems to have been unable to present positive images of monarchy. His pastoral tragedy, *The Orphan* (Duke's, 1680), is set in the home of Acasto, a loyal supporter of the king (of Bohemia). Acasto, however, is depicted as so disgusted by the king's court that he has not only retired to the country but also refuses to let his restless sons serve at court.

Following the period of political crisis (1679–82) that had seemed to threaten civil war, it was easier to praise royalty, once again restored to full authority. Dryden's *Albion and Albanius* (United, 1685), with music by Louis Grabu, is an operatic allegory of the Restoration and crisis years, featuring Albion – Charles II – and Albanius – the Duke of York – which reasserts monarchical power and right in traditional terms. The immediate years after the political crisis and the unification of the theatres in 1682 are thin in new drama generally, and the trend was understandably away from contentious political materials. However, Rochester's *The Tragedy of Valentinian* (United, 1684), based on the play by Beaumont and Fletcher, portrays a corrupt ruler, Valentinian, who rapes Lucina, the chaste wife of his general Maximus. Valentinian is then murdered – while disporting himself with his young eunuch lover – and Maximus assumes the purple. This is a singularly unflattering depiction of a cynical and sensual monarch, yet, as R. D. Hume has pointed out, the play was performed at court, an indication perhaps that dramas of royal lust and violent deposition no longer troubled a confident monarch (1976: 364).

The Royal Touch

Whatever the image of monarchy on the theatrical stage, in verse satires, broadsheets and in polemics, on a wider national stage belief in the divine powers of a king continued. As Marc Bloch pointed out in his classic study *The Royal Touch* (1923), Charles II performed this ritual of touching most assiduously. Charles had started performing the ritual, believed to cure sufferers of 'the King's Evil', scrofula, before his restoration. Bloch tells of 'an ingenious merchant' who 'ran organized tours by sea for the English and Scottish scrofula sufferers to the Low Country towns where the prince had his meager court' (1961: 210). As he points out, 'figures give us some idea of Charles II's popularity as a healer', and he calculates that over the course of his twenty-five year reign about 100,000 sufferers were touched (1961: 221). The royal touch, as Bloch also points out in the course of his study, was early on divorced from any particular king, so the character and morals of a ruler were not significant: it was the sacerdotal ethos of the role, not the personality of the incumbent, that mattered. Charles's enthusiasm for touching may have been an indication of his deep belief in that sacerdotal ethos, or may have been fed by his realization that his monarchy needed whatever support it could find. Harold M. Weber suggests that by the end of Charles's reign, and particularly after the Duke of Monmouth's employment of the touch during his western progress in 1680, the royal touch was 'irrevocably cheapened' (1996: 81). However, if belief in a divine monarchy waned gradually in the nation, the image of royalty on stage is only hedged with divinity during the early years of the Restoration. Thereafter royalty is enmeshed in a double structure: the structure of plays whose tragic plots, no longer restating the miracle of restoration, depend on representations of royal fallibility, and the structure of an increasingly crisis-driven national politics. The images of royalty that emerge on stage as a result of this long period of crisis and debate are not merely of monarchs too fond of women, madly tyrannical or weak, but rather of monarchs who are always themselves part of larger systems that they imperfectly understand or control.

In one of the first plays of monarchy and history, John Bale's Protestant political allegory *King John* (*c*.1534, 1561), King John opens the play with a very kingly description of his role, lineage and function:

> John, King of England, the chronicles doth me call.
> My grandfather was an emperor excellent;
> My father a king by succession lineal;
> . . .
> I have worn the crown and wrought victoriously;
> And now do purpose, by practice and by study,
> To reform the laws and set men in good order;
> That true justice may be had in every border.
>
> (1.9–11, 18–22)

Appealed to by Widow England who faces all sorts of problems, King John rather effortlessly expels Sedition, Clergy, Dissimulation, Private Wealth and other unsavoury characters. Clearly a great deal happens politically and culturally (including Shakespeare), to complicate and sophisticate the idea of the king as font of law, justice and good order. Above all a king, Charles I, was executed after being put on trial and judged by his own subjects. The representations of monarchs and monarchy on the English stage could never be the same again. Loyally and royally, many Restoration dramatists deplored regicide and usurpation, and celebrated restorations; however, the very vehemence of their efforts revealed the vulnerability of their project. As Susan Owen puts it, 'plays which agitate so hard on behalf of the dominant ideology expose the fragile nature of that ideology precisely in the fact that such agitation is necessary' (1996: 19).

The monarchs who pace the Restoration stages (or run across it raving) are not isolated figures: they live in courts where they are fooled by favourites, by ambitious statesmen, and beguiled by 'beauty'. Often offstage, but by the 1680s increasingly present, there are also other voices and opinions to be taken into account – the rabble, the mob and the people outside the palace – whose opinions, however much they are represented as foolish, cannot be ignored. Regal power is shown as challenged by the energy and action of subjects – by women, legally powerless, but empowered by royal lust, by younger sons, by 'people' and 'Senate', and by those 'worthy' men who emerge from outside the royal circle or from its lesser ranks to assume power. Indeed, frequently bloodthirsty, lustful and wilful, or, alternatively strangely weak, impotent and imposed upon, monarchs are beginning to look like anachronisms. No more than the actual monarch do Restoration stage monarchs appear as 'a History / A volume bound up for Eternity', but like their subjects, they are subject to history.

In an anonymous poem printed in 1684 – the period of Charles's second restoration to power – to commemorate a statue of the king erected in the Royal Exchange by the Society of Merchant Adventurers, the statue-king addresses his people in blunt terms:

> Look Britain, our established king survey
> See how the assaults of faction are in vain.
> My Race, Heaven's Choice o'ere Albion still must reign
> If from no other source your love will spring
> Let interest reconcile you to your king
> Know your own interest and Obey your king!

The statue was wrong; the number of years ahead for the Stuart monarchy was distinctly limited. But more significant is the mixture of arrogant assertion with an acknowledgement of the possibility of unpopularity. The location of the statue and its sponsors are also significant: the monarch may not be loved, divine or very glorious, but he's in power and business interests prefer that to civil strife. Yet another force – merchant wealth – is entering the stage of English politics and with it new topics, concerns and ideology. Hereafter, although dramatists continue to depict monarchs and courts, occasionally running into trouble with censors, the image of monarchy is not so much threatening or redeeming as romantic, 'historical' and picturesque. The violent, vexed and anxious images of monarchy on the Restoration stage mark the end of a dramatic era. That era began with plays like John Bale's, in which England's destiny and well-being were dramatized in terms of the monarch. It concludes as the dramatizations of the monarch spiralled out to include personality, religion, politics, family life and sexual habits, and, in the process, revealed the ruler as less than 'God-like', definitely human and unlikely to 'set men in good order'. Increasingly, the drama and image of monarchy ceased to speak urgently to a nation as much concerned with its 'interests' as the nature of its imported rulers.

REFERENCES AND FURTHER READING

All play citations are taken from editions listed here.

Bale, John (1965). *King John*, in *Elizabethan History Plays*, ed. William Armstrong. Oxford: Oxford University Press.

Bloch, Marc (1923; 1961). *The Royal Touch*, trans. J. E. Anderson. New York: Dorset Press.

Boyle, Roger (1937). *The Tragedy of Mustapha*, in *The Dramatic Works of Roger Boyle, Earl of Orrery*, ed. William Smith Clark II. 2 vols. Cambridge, MA: Harvard University Press, vol. 1.

Braverman, Richard (1987). *Plots and Counterplots: Sexual Politics and the Body Politic in English Literature, 1660–1730*. Cambridge: Cambridge University Press.

Butler, Martin (1984). *Theatre and Crisis 1632–1642*. Cambridge: Cambridge University Press.

Canfield, J. Douglas (1985). 'Royalism's Last Dramatic Stand: English Political Tragedy, 1679–89', *Studies in Philology* 82, no. 2, 234–62.

Canfield, J. Douglas (2000). *Heroes and States: On the Ideology of Restoration Tragedy*. Lexington: University Press of Kentucky.

Crowne, John (1680). *The Misery of Civil-War*. London: Printed for R. Bentley and M. Magnes.

Davenant, Charles (1677). *Circe*. London: Printed for Richard Tonson.

Dryden, John (1956–92). *The Works of John Dryden*, gen. eds Edward Niles Hooker and H. T. Swedenberg, Jr. 20 vols. Berkeley: University of California Press.

Fisk, Deborah Payne (ed.). (2000). *The Cambridge Companion to Restoration Theatre*. Cambridge: Cambridge University Press.

Howard, Robert (2000). *The Great Favourite, or The Duke of Lerma*, in *Restoration Drama: An Anthology*, ed. David Womersley. Oxford: Blackwell.

Hughes, Derek (1981). *Dryden's Heroic Plays*. London: Methuen.

Hughes, Derek (1996). *English Drama, 1660–1700*. Oxford: Clarendon Press.

Hume, R. D. (1976). *The Development of English Drama in the Late Seventeenth Century*. Oxford: Clarendon Press.

Hume, R. D. (1998). 'The Politics of Opera in Late Seventeenth-century London', *Cambridge Opera Journal* 10, no. 1, 15–43.

Hutton, Ronald (1991). *Charles II, King of England, Scotland, and Ireland*. Oxford: Oxford University Press.

Munns, Jessica (1995). *Restoration Politics and Drama: The Plays of Thomas Otway, 1675–1683*. Newark: University of Delaware Press.

Neale, J. E. (1965). *Elizabeth I and her Parliaments, 1584–1601*. 2 vols. London: Jonathan Cape.

Otway, Thomas (1932; reprinted 1968). *The Works of Thomas Otway*, ed. J. C. Ghosh. 2 vols. Oxford: Clarendon Press.

Owen, Susan J. (1996). *Restoration Theatre and Crisis*. Oxford: Clarendon Press.

Pepys, Samuel (1970–83). *The Diary of Samuel Pepys*, ed. Robert Latham. 11 vols. Berkeley: University of California Press, vol. 9.

Randall, Dale B. J. (1995). *Winter Fruit: English Drama 1642–1660*. Lexington: University Press of Kentucky.

Van Lennep, William (ed.). (1965). *The London Stage, 1660–1800*. Part I: *1660–1700*, ed. Emmett L. Avery and Arthur H. Scouten. Carbondale: Southern Illinois University Press. All performance dates are taken from this work.

Wallace, John (1969). 'Dryden and History: A Problem in Allegorical Reading', *ELH* 36, 265–90.

Weber, Harold M. (1986). *The Restoration Rake-Hero: Transformations in Sexual Understanding in Seventeenth-century England*. Madison: University of Wisconsin Press.

Weber, Harold M. (1996). *Paper Bullets: Print and Kingship under Charles II*. Lexington: University Press of Kentucky.

Wilmot, John, Earl of Rochester (1993). *Complete Poems and Plays*, ed. Paddy Lyons. London: J. M. Dent.

8

Restoration Drama and Politics: An Overview

Susan J. Owen

Politics had a profound effect on both the form and the content of Restoration drama. Yet this is a subject about which misconceptions abound. Here are some examples of common critical fallacies: that Restoration drama is effete and courtly, lacking any political 'guts' and vitality (old-fashioned, but surprisingly persistent); that drama was largely apolitical until the Popish Plot and Exclusion Crisis led to sudden politicization; that in so far as the drama was political, it was mainly royalist and Tory; conversely, that the only drama of real interest in this period is that which prefigures the rise of Whig and/or bourgeois drama; that anti-Catholic drama is not political; that political commentary in the drama is incidental and occasional, rather than sustained and central. What follows is not an attempt to engage head-on with these mistaken notions. Rather, it is (I hope) a clear and concise survey of Restoration drama's engagement with politics and the effect of politics on the drama from 1660 to the end of the Exclusion Crisis. After that, there was (not completely but to all intents and purposes) a lull until the Williamite revolution of 1688.

The immediate effects of the Civil War, Interregnum and Restoration of 1660 can be seen in the satirical comedies of the early 1660s. Often, these comedies deal explicitly with the events of the Interregnum from a royalist point of view. Examples are John Tatham's *The Rump* (1660), Abraham Cowley's *The Cutter of Coleman Street* (1661), Robert Howard's *The Committee* (1662) and John Lacy's *The Old Troop* (1664). There are also political tragicomedies set in the Interregnum, such as the anonymous *Cromwell's Conspiracy* (1660) and Robert Howard's *The Usurper* (1664). These plays satirize parliamentarians and hypocritical upstart Puritans, and offer the Restoration of 1660 as a happy ending and a source of hope. What is at stake in these plays is property. The satire of upstart Puritans has a bitter edge because they have expropriated the estates of the loyal but impoverished Cavalier heroes. In Cowley's *The Cutter of Coleman Street*, for example, the royalist Colonel Jolly must scheme to recover his confiscated estate by marrying the widow of the low-class, Puritan soap-boiler who bought it; and he also plots against his niece and ward to get her property. Howard's

The Committee has two royalist colonels whose estates have been sequestered and two wards whose guardians are trying to misappropriate their property. These plays have a strong element of class warfare. The Restoration of 1660 is portrayed as turning the world the right way up and restoring property to those whose natural superiority entitles them to possess it. The Cavaliers are also naturally sexy, whereas the Puritans are unattractive and hypocritically lustful. For example, in *The Cutter of Coleman Street* Cutter marries the Puritan widow's daughter Tabitha by pretending to be a Puritan himself; but his wife is pleased and titillated when, on their wedding night, he reverts to Cavalier dress and behaviour.

However, even at this early stage there is some evidence of political contradictions or fault-lines. For example, the emphasis on property is rather double-edged: later, it was to become a weapon in the Whig arsenal, and accounted for the popular appeal of the Whigs during the Exclusion Crisis, when there seemed to be a threat to property from what Andrew Marvell called 'Popery and Arbitrary Government'. Another contradiction in the satirical comedies arises ironically from the very heart of their comic appeal: the Cavaliers' trickery – the Cavaliers seem at times both heartless and unscrupulous. Poets like Dryden in 'Astrea Redux' were trying desperately to portray the Restoration as a divinely ordained and sacred moment in history. The comedies provide a more realistic and irreverent portrayal of royalists and a more pragmatic and materialist representation of the issues at stake. John Wilson's city comedy *The Cheats* (1663) even attracted adverse attention from the censor. Wilson's play offers a critical portrayal of hypocritical, lustful and avaricious city Puritans; but also rather cynically depicts universal corruption which taints even impoverished royalists. Even more irreverent is Lacy's *The Old Troop*, in which satire of Puritan upstarts coexists with an extremely cynical depiction of Cavaliers as plunderers and libertines. Idealized values of honour, truth, fidelity and service are made a mockery of, and, as an unscrupulous Lieutenant tells a prostitute in Act 1, the general principle of mankind is not friendship but the desire for other people's property.

Political reference is also evident in the serious plays of the 1660s, most of which may be classed as tragicomedies. Tragedy is rare before the late 1670s, when its development is connected to the sharpening political division in the nation. In the 1660s it was more important to stress that the restoration of the monarchy had offered a happy ending to the dire events of the 1640s. Dominant themes are the evils of usurpation and the redeeming and regenerative effects of restoration of the true king (Hughes 1996: ch. 2; Maguire 1992: *passim*). The heroic drama of the 1660s is explicitly royalist in intention. Charles II, an admirer of the French heroic drama of Corneille, and of French heroic romance, encouraged the genre, suggested what the dramatists should write, lent costumes and attended performances. The plays celebrate royalism, usually in the form of the restoration of the true king. The dilemmas of love and honour, and personal versus public good, which exercise the heroes of the Earl of Orrery (early master of the genre) are similar to those which faced English people before 1660: private royalism versus the public duty of adapting to Cromwell's regime for the sake of peace; or private self-interest in 'selling out' to Cromwell versus a public political duty of oppositional royalism. The tensions are usually resolved through royalist celebration of beneficent (and inherently superior) kingship which reminds us of the genre's origins in the early Stuart court masque. (Other influences on the genre include Corneille's heroic plays, French heroic romance, the English 'hero' play from Marlowe onwards, Caroline *précieuse* drama, the tragicomedies of Beaumont and Fletcher, and Davenant's opera, *The Siege of Rhodes*.)

However, again, as with the comedies, there are political contradictions, even in royalist heroic drama. As in the comedies, these contradictions have to do with the portrayal of royalists, and in this case of royalty itself. For example, Charles II was a notorious liar, whose bad faith caused some problems for his supporters as well as his opponents. In John Dryden's two-part heroic masterpiece, *The Conquest of Granada* (1670–1), the near-tragedy is precipitated by the angry vacillations of King Boabdelin, and the play thus dramatizes the need for kings to keep their word, as well as for subjects to keep their loyalty. A more fundamental ideological difficulty arises from the heroic ethos itself. The heroic plays celebrate a grandiose courage, on the model of some of Marlowe's larger-than-life protagonists, or Chapman's Bussy D'Ambois. Thus it is said of Almanzor, hero of Dryden's *The Conquest of Granada*:

> Vast is his courage, boundless is his mind,
> Rough as a storm and humorous as wind;
> Honour's the onely Idol of his Eyes:
> The charms of Beauty like a pest he flies:
> And rais'd by Valour, from a birth unknown,
> Acknowledges no pow'r above his own.
>   (Part 1, 1.1.253–8)

Charles II found the play's celebration of heroic aspiration extremely congenial. But this relates precisely to the source of the problem. Charles's own heroic aspiration was to emulate his powerful, absolutist cousin, Louis XIV of France. This was what Marvell exposed and denounced in his book-length pamphlet, *An Account of the Growth of Popery and Arbitrary Government in England* (1677); and it was also what created the tensions which were to explode in the Exclusion Crisis. In the heroic plays, grandiosity in the king can easily come close to tyranny (or arbitrary government). This is clear in the heroic plays of Nathaniel Lee and Elkanah Settle in the 1670s, in which super-villains and tyrants use the same kind of rant as Dryden's super-heroes. Indeed, even within Dryden's own oeuvre, a tyrant like Maximin in *Tyrannick Love* (1669) can seem close to a super-hero like Almanzor in the *Conquest of Granada*. A different contradiction arises when heroic aspiration is located in the subject rather than the king, precisely because heroic aspiration often seems incompatible with absolute loyalty to the sovereign. This is particularly true of Almanzor, who defies the king: 'Obey'd as soveraign by thy Subjects be, / But know that I alone am King of me' (Part 1, 1.1.205–6).

Contradictions in heroic drama are successfully contained and do not break the bounds of royalism. For example, in *The Conquest of Granada* the tension about royal high-handedness is dealt with by offering an ideal of Christian kingship in Ferdinand of Spain, who wins the ultimate victory. The contradiction about heroic aspiration in a subject is dealt with by having Almanzor turn out to be a nobly born Spaniard who was lost at birth and brought up as a Moor; and by having the power of King Boabdelin whom Almanzor defied turn out to be illegitimate. Royalism in the drama is still firmly in the ascendant and heroic drama successfully papers over ideological cracks; but there is residual tension, both about royal arbitrariness and about the problems of subjects' loyalty. These tensions resurface in the drama of the Exclusion Crisis when dramatists have to work far harder to contain and assuage them.

Moreover, there are some plays in the 1660s in which contradictions come close to breaking the bounds of royalism, especially after 1666. At this time, Charles began to lose the confidence of the political nation, following plague, fire, soaring taxes, misconduct of the Second Dutch War and fraternization with the Catholic Louis XIV (Pincus 1996: 343–440). The libertinism of the royal brothers Charles and James also caused concern, even to royalists like Samuel Pepys. The king's French Catholic mistresses were thought a bad influence. The fact that Charles had many bastards but no legitimate heir was also a problem, especially after the Catholicism of James became widely suspected. In the theatres political tensions are apparent in the drama. For example, Robert Howard's *The Great Favourite* (1668) attacks the king's chief minister Clarendon, but also seems critical of the king. The play's king is amorous, just like the libertine Charles II. He is also weak, and easily manipulated by the villain. This play prefigures the fraught and contradictory royalist tragedy of the Exclusion Crisis, in which the depiction of royal faults almost overwhelms the possibility of heroic loyalty.

A few plays were actually banned. Edward Howard's comedy, *The Change of Crowns* (1667), satirizes court corruption and the sale of offices. The play was suppressed when John Lacy, who played the part of a country gentleman who comes to court to purchase office, developed the potential for savage satire of the court in improvised speeches (leading to a physical fight between actor and author). Another comedy, *The Country Gentleman* by Robert Howard and the Duke of Buckingham (1669), goes further in using country virtue as a site of opposition to corruption and francophilia at the centre of power. Bumptious civil servants replace the upstart Puritans of royalist comedy. Critics usually attribute the banning of this play to its rude portrayal of contemporaries, especially the Treasury Commissioner, Sir William Coventry. However, the depiction of country virtue is a striking feature, in sharp contrast to the treatment of the country in Cavalier comedy as a site of dullness and folly (though a precedent for *The Country Gentleman* may be found in the positive treatment of country values and satire of effeminacy and francophilia in James Howard's *The English Monsieur*, 1663). Buckingham and Robert Howard were associated at this time with the developing political opposition, and were keen to ally with the 'Country party' in Parliament (so called due to its wide support among country MPs). Their agenda included opposition to James and to Clarendon, investigation of naval and fiscal mismanagement, a Protestant foreign policy and toleration of

Dissenters, who were condemned by royalists as the descendants of Interregnum Puritans, and became a base of support for the Whigs. Buckingham was again to make political use of country virtue as a critique of the courtly excess in *The Rehearsal* (1671). His oppositional use of country values prefigures Shadwell's explicitly Whiggish treatment of a virtuous country gentry in *The Lancashire Witches* in the Exclusion Crisis. Shadwell's own *The Humorists* (1670) had to be withdrawn after it caused offence with its excoriating satire of aristocratic degeneracy, a theme which Shadwell was to develop in Whiggish vein in the Exclusion Crisis in plays like *The Woman-Captain*.

In the 1670s divisions in the political nation deepened following Charles's Declaration of Indulgence in 1672, which offended as much by its 'arbitrary' use of royal prerogative as by its toleration of Catholics and Dissenters. James's public admission of Catholicism and marriage to the Catholic Mary of Modena in 1673 caused parliamentary remonstrances and public outcry. Charles had made a secret treaty with Louis XIV in 1672, agreeing in exchange for French money to convert his country to Catholicism using French troops if necessary. Although this was not public knowledge, there was widespread suspicion, as is clear from a reading of Marvell's political history of the 1670s in *An Account of the Growth of Popery and Arbitrary Government*. It was Louis XIV's influence which prompted Charles to engage in the Third Dutch War, despite widespread desires (and parliamentary urging) for a Protestant foreign policy directed against France. The war remained unpopular despite Dryden's attempt to whip up support for it in his propaganda play, *Amboyna* (1672). Anti-court satirical verses proliferated and oppositional pamphlets began to liken the 1670s to the 1640s (Owen 1999).

In this decade, contradictions deepen within royalist drama, and a dramatic rhetoric of opposition continues to develop. This is true even in libertine comedy, once thought to be apolitical, or only incidentally political. In the 1660s the rake had been a Cavalier figure, carrying out the royalist goal of cuckolding and outwitting upstart Puritans. The 1660s Cavalier plays his part in the reinstatement of social order through a resumption of his property and rank which parallels the monarch's restoration to the throne. In what Maximillian Novak has called the 'libertine offensive of the 1670s', the libertine becomes a predatory cynic. In an increasingly divided nation, the rake becomes associated with a civilized court, as against the country, which is portrayed as barbaric and dull. The rake's assertion of Cavalier values becomes abrasive. As Richard Braverman puts it, 'in spite of a manifest contempt for heroic idealizations, he nonetheless held fast to courtly-aristocratic values, none of which was more important than his eroding autonomy that mirrored the predicament of the Crown' (1995: 150). Thus, though the libertine's triumphs and humiliations are sexual and social, they have a political resonance. The libertinism of the Stuart brothers reinforces this; and indeed the king had a liking for libertine comedy. An all-conquering rake such as Horner in Wycherley's *The Country Wife* is a kind of sovereign. The libertine is certainly not just a champion of sexual freedom, for he does not extend to women, or to men outside the court milieu, the freedoms he demands for himself (Hume 1977). Of course there are contradictions. Whilst the rakes of royalist libertine comedy can seem just as unscrupulous as their 1660s forebears, their wit and sexiness disarm the audience as well as the other characters and make it hard to condemn them. This is not to say that the playwrights wholeheartedly endorse a predatory libertinism: far from it. Few plays go so far as to extol libertinism outright. Libertine comedies convey varying degrees of scepticism about the new ethos of the Stuart court. There may even be moral warnings to the Stuarts in some plays. Yet these mostly remain tensions at the heart of royalism rather than factors in opposition to it.

However, the treatment of libertinism in some plays does develop an oppositional dimension. The rake can become a tyrant, enslaving others to his appetites, just as he is enslaved by them himself. Savage satire of the 'heroic libertine' develops a political, anti-court dimension in comi-tragic plays such as Shadwell's *The Libertine* (1675) and Lee's *The Princess of Cleve* (1682?). These plays depict monstrous, predatory, ruthless and devouring libertines, who know no moral constraints whatsoever, and whose outrageous behaviour passes all bounds (Owen 1996: ch. 5). Another play, *Sodom*, probably by Rochester and probably written by 1676, though not performed, offers thinly disguised satire of Charles in the person of the sex-mad King Bolloximian (Elias 1978; Weber 1995). Bolloximian's declaration of indulgence of universal buggery parodies Charles's 1672 declaration of religious toleration; and his special relationship with King Tarsehole of Gommorah caricatures Charles's with Louis XIV. Bolloximian is described as having 'fuckt and bugger'd all the land' (42); just as at the end of Marvell's satirical and oppositional poem, *Last Instructions to a Painter*, Charles II is shown as confronting his kingdom (which appears to him at night in allegorical female form) and wanting to screw it, literally and figuratively. Bolloximian's universal buggery, which brings his land to destruction, is a satiric transformation, but also a *reductio ad absurdum* of the inordinate sexuality which contemporaries saw as unnatural, unmanly and politically disastrous. His perversions also represent the unnatural political condition of England. As he degenerates into a tyrant, and as he threatens in Act 5 to invade Heaven and bugger the gods, it is not far-fetched to suggest that sodomy, in effect, becomes a metaphor for Charles's 'popery and arbitrary government'.

Thus it is clear that tensions were running high even before the outbreak of the Popish Plot scare and resultant near-hysteria in the autumn of 1678, and that the drama was politicized even before the Exclusion Crisis. The Popish Plot and Exclusion Crisis did not (contrary to popular critical belief) lead to sudden politicization of a previously apolitical culture. The Crisis did, however, sharply intensify both political divisions in the nation and political engagement in the drama (Owen 1996; Kenyon 1974). This led to three important shifts in dramatic form and content: a change in comedy, the development of tragedy and the rise of the sentimental.

In comedy there is a sharp break in 1678/9. Sex comedy goes into eclipse, following the astonishing failure of a series of sex comedies by major writers in the spring of 1678. Then, as political crisis grips the nation, there is a virtual cessation of comedies: only one in the 1678/9 season. That one, *The Feign'd Curtizans* (1679) by Aphra Behn, is a sign of what is to come: a revival of satire of upstarts and Puritans, coupled with a celebration of upper-class good taste across national boundaries. Behn's play associates Whiggish anti-popery and patriotism with Puritan sexual hypocrisy, folly, pretension, philistinism and low-class money-grubbing. This sets the tone for a new wave of political comedies which employ methods and modes reminiscent of 1660s comedy to attack the Whigs.

The fact that the Whigs were especially strong in the city of London offered an ideal opportunity to graft royalism onto city comedy. We can see this in two plays of 1679/80: *The Revenge* (1680), probably by Behn, and Otway's *The Souldier's Fortune* (1680). *The Revenge*, an adaptation of Marston's *The Dutch Courtesan*, is so called because of the central revenge plot against a cheating wine seller who is ridiculously Puritan and patriotic, and credulously anti-popish. In *The Souldier's Fortune* royalism takes the form of 'cuckolding the Whig'. The Tory Reaction period of 1681–2 sees a boom in city comedies which satirize Puritans and Whigs: examples are the anonymous humours comedy *Mr. Turbulent*, D'Urfey's *Sir Barnaby Whigg*, Ravenscroft's *The London Cuckolds* (all 1681), Behn's *The City Heiress* (1682) and Crowne's *City Politiques* (1683). Other comedies attack the Whigs by direct reference to their Interregnum predecessors. Behn is in the forefront with *The Round-Heads* (1681), an adaptation of Tatham's *The Rump*. D'Urfey quickly follows with *The Royalist* (1682). Both plays are set in the Interregnum, invoke a mythologized memory of republican villainy and royalist heroism, and end with the Restoration, in the fashion of plays of the 1660s. Royalist idealization is greater and the contradictory elements of cynicism rather less than in the 1660s, presumably because the distance of twenty years has lent a rosy-tinted perspective; or perhaps because Tory dramatists are working harder in the Exclusion Crisis to do a job of ideological work.

Tragicomedy is rarer in the Exclusion Crisis than in the early Restoration, but there are some notable royalist examples. In *The Young King* Behn develops topical themes which she had explored in *Abdelazer* (1676): a divided royal family and the dangers of tampering with the succession because of religious or superstitious scruples. Dryden's *The Spanish Fryar* offers a moderate royalism. The play harks back to the 1660s, ending on a note of reconciliation, as the old king is miraculously restored and the true prince is united in marriage with the usurper's daughter (Owen 1994). William Whitaker's *The Conspiracy* (1680) also recalls the values of the 1660s. Whitaker revives the defunct form of the royalist heroic play in rhyming couplets and the 1660s tragicomic model of regicide followed by restoration. Possibly the most fervent and wholehearted royalist play of the Exclusion Crisis, *The Conspiracy* offers a spectacle of an exemplary royal couple resembling the idealized Charles I and Henrietta Maria, beset by demonic regicides and rebels. The rebels are guilty of rabble-rousing, arrogance, arbitrariness, hypocrisy, religious zeal and atheism together, lying, lust, presumption and fanatical cruelty (all characteristics which were to be associated with rebellion in Tory tragedy). The rebels succeed in killing the Sultan, but are routed in their turn by exemplary royalist heroes who manage to restore the royal couple's son to the throne.

Royalist comedies are quite well known, but oppositional comedy is perhaps less familiar. Whig comedy reserves for Catholics the satire which Tory comedy directs at Puritans. *Rome's Follies; or, the Amorous Fryars*, performed at a private house in autumn 1681, and published with a dedication to the Whig leader Shaftesbury, reverses the paradigm of Tory comedies by associating hypocritical rampant sexuality with Catholic friars rather than Puritans. The friars cuckold deluded parishioners and absolve a man who has had sex with a goat. Shadwell's *The Lancashire Witches* (1680) reverses the model of Tory comedy in a different way. Shadwell associates with the Catholic priest Tegue the qualities which Tory dramatists associated with Puritans: self-interest, changeability and flexibility of conscience. More controversial is the character of Smerk, a popish Anglican priest whose fanatical anti-Puritanism mirrors the anti-popery which is satirized in Tory comedies. Smerk is also a low-born upstart who presumptuously censures the follies of the Whig gentleman who employs him. The Whig gentry are moderate, cultured and civilized, the wise defenders of English Protestant tradition. In terms of sexual politics, this comedy also reverses the Tory norm: it is the papists and their apologists who are hypocritically lustful. Whiggery is anti-patriarchal, guarantees the liberties of the Protestant Englishwoman and ensures freedom of choice in marriage. The play ends on a note of harmony based not on the values of 1660, but on the country gentry (and Country party) values of old-fashioned decency, moderation, patriotism, Protestantism, charity, hospitality and good sense (Owen 1996: ch. 6; Munns 1996).

Protestant tradition is also celebrated in the anonymous *The Coronation of Queen Elizabeth*, performed at the London fairs in the summer of 1680. In this anti-Catholic black farce the Pope compacts with devils, eventually flees to England when the corruption of his church outrages the local population, and is literally burned by trusty English artisans who thereby secure the safety of the realm while their social superiors are busy fighting the Armada. Queen Elizabeth is grateful for their loyalty, a pointed contrast to Charles's different sentiments towards his politically concerned subjects. The use of Elizabethanism as a criticism of Charles was prevalent in Whig propaganda. Elizabeth in the play is humble before God, concerned for the whole 'commonwealth' of England, and vigilant in combating Catholicism at home and abroad. The comparison with Stuart 'popery and arbitrary government' is sufficiently pointed.

Possibly even more significant than the effect of the Crisis upon comedy is its influence on tragedy. Just as the Exclusion Crisis was foreshadowed by growing social divisions, so the development of political tragedy had slightly earlier antecedents. It was the Crisis, however, which brought the new form to fruition. Henry Neville-Payne's *The Siege of Constantinople* (1674) foreshadows the tragedies of the Exclusion Crisis in its use of blank verse, its political topicality and its peculiar combination of royalism with scepticism and pessimism. The wicked, plotting Chancellor, modelled on opposition noblemen such as the Earl of Shaftesbury, was a model for subsequent villains of Tory tragedy; but Payne's play also evinces what was to become typical unease about the problems caused by unruly royal desire and caprice. The tension between the ruler's desires and political necessity is also central in Sedley's *Antony and Cleopatra*, Lee's *The Rival Queens* and Dryden's *All For Love* (all 1677). Sedley's treatment of the issue prefigures Whig tragedy. His Antony is a critical portrait of Charles II, blind to the way in which his foreign mistress manipulates him, and inappropriately merciful and severe at the wrong times. The battle of Actium is a critical depiction of Charles's unpopular Third Dutch War. As in later Whig drama, the Roman republic is viewed with nostalgia, while the common people are treated kindly and Antony is glad to be set right by them. Poet laureate Dryden's *All For Love*, as might be expected, treats the ruler's unruly passion for an unpopular foreigner more sympathetically. The proto-Whiggish values of Roman civic virtue and respect for law are treated correspondingly more negatively. Meanwhile, Alexander in Lee's *The Rival Queens* is an ambiguous figure, somewhere in between the hero and tyrant, the tragic lover and the libertine.

As tragedy develops, and polarization in the nation deepens, it is possible to discern rival Tory and Whig dramatic paradigms. This is not to say that the dramatists found it easy to take sides, but that it is possible to identify a dramatic rhetoric of partisanship. However, evidence of difficulty is found in the fact that Tory tragedies, following Payne's *Siege of Constantinople*, often seem rather fraught, offering a some-what hollow royalism, shot through with contradictions. Examples are: John Crowne's *The Ambitious Statesman; or, the Loyal Favourite* (1679), Tate's *The Loyal General* (1679), Otway's *The Orphan* (1680) and *Venice Preserv'd* (1682), Dryden and Lee's *Oedipus* (1678) and Dryden's *Troilus and Cressida* (1679). Tory tragedies tend to idealize heroic absolute loyalty, to place a high value on 'quietism' (Owen 1996: 4), and to demonize rebellion. Whig factionalism, legalism and patriotism are satirized. In place of the positive value Whigs place on the nation, liberty and law, Tory plays privilege class values. Whereas in comedy this takes the form of satire of the Whiggish citizen-merchant class, in tragedy rebels (or Whigs) are depicted as dangerous rabble-rousers who incite an unruly mob which they cannot then control. The king and (loyal) nobility possess an inherent social superiority, and there may be a privileging of aristocratic bonds across national boundaries, as against national bonds. Whig anti-popery may also be satirized as credulity and superstition, and the satiric focus is shifted to Puritans and Dissenters, who may be likened to papists. Tory tragedies can make powerful use of family themes, drawing upon Tory ideologue Sir Robert Filmer's political association of absolute monarchy and patriarchal authority: the violation of the family by rebels and ambitious plotters mirrors subversion in the state. Rebellion may be associated with lust, rape, sexual hypocrisy and female unruliness. Contradictions often arise, and are overdetermined to a greater or lesser extent by the need for unity against the paramount threat of disorder and potential civil war emanating from ambitious noblemen, factious malcontents or rebellious plebeians.

A major contradiction arises from the inherent difficulty in dramatizing Tory quietism convincingly. However much moral and political force the idea of absolute loyalty is felt to have, there is something unconvincing about the spectacle of 'quiet' heroes like Vendosme in *The Ambitious Statesman* or Theocrin in *The Loyal General*. The heroes of avowedly royalist or Tory plays are often masochistic, passive and paralysed by a sense of the difficulty of right action. If absolute loyalty is to be heroic, it must be tested and found true even in the face of vitiated kingship. Yet there is also something troubling from a royalist point of view about the spectacle in play after play of royal faults which correspond with the faults of the Stuart brothers as even the most tolerant contemporaries perceived them. In the Tory tragedies listed above we find royal lies, ineptitude, passivity, misrule, 'effeminacy' and excessive mercy towards the kingdom's enemies, which are all failings for which Charles was criticized; arbitrariness, rage and self-centredness, considered to be faults in James; and lust and (quasi-)Catholicism, perceived faults of both. There are times when the assertion that the monarch will rule well if the people will be quiet and courtiers constant rings distinctly hollow. If the radical alternative was unthinkable for loyal playwrights, conformity is a bleak prospect too, especially for Otway, whose plays offer little more reassurance than that misfortune might be endured. Loyalty without hope of reward is a stifling ideal when loyal heroes must annihilate themselves in conformity with the ideal of absolute obedience to kings who do not deserve or value it.

Even family values, a powerful Tory ideological counter then as now, can be problematic. Problems were posed for the Stuarts by the disparity between Filmerian ideology and the perceived reality: Charles I was virtuous but politically impotent, so unable to be a good father to the nation, and Charles II was unable to be a good father literally in terms of securing the succession with a legitimate son, or figuratively in his conduct as leader of the nation. The most famous Tory tragedy, Otway's *Venice Preserv'd*, aims to problematize republicanism by a negative depiction of the Venetian senate. One senator abases himself in sexual sadomasochism; another is a bad father whose cruelty precipitates the main tragedy. However, the spectacle of bad fatherhood in the microcosm, even if intended to dramatize the evils of republicanism, resonates uncomfortably for royalists. The Exclusion Crisis was a crisis of fatherhood: Charles had no legitimate son, was considered to have scattered his seed irresponsibly throughout the land and to be over-indulgent towards his illegitimate son, Monmouth. The play's moral against cruel fatherhood, summed up in the last lines as Senator Priuli warns 'bid all cruel fathers dread my fate', is the wrong moral from the Tory point of view. Tory ideology places the burden of political responsibility on the son or subject, not the father/king.

Another important dramatic trend at this time was a vogue for politicized adaptations of Shakespeare's tragedies and history plays. Sedley and Dryden, as we have seen, adapted *Antony and Cleopatra* as *Antony and Cleopatra* and *All For Love*, respectively, and Dryden also adapted *Troilus and Cressida*. Otway adapted *Romeo and Juliet* in a Roman setting as *The History and Fall of Caius Marius* (1679). Crowne's *The Misery of Civil-War* (1680) and *Henry the Sixth, the First Part* (1681) were adaptations of the *Henry VI* trilogy. Tate offered *The History of King Richard II*, *The History of King Lear* (both late 1680 or early 1681) and *The Ingratitude of a Common-wealth* (1681), an adaptation of *Coriolanus*. These plays foreground the dangers of rebellion, rabble-rousing, mob rule, faction, ingratitude and civil war. The dangers of banishment and exclusion may be stressed, with clear application to the fate of James, banished by Charles in response to pressure from the Whig-dominated Parliament which also wished to exclude him from succession to the throne. Tate's Coriolanus, in particular, bears a strong resemblance to James. Various alterations in the plays are aimed at arousing pity and fear for England's royal brothers. In *The Ingratitude of a Common-wealth*, for example, the characters of Virgilia and Volumnia, and their relationships with the hero, are sentimentalized. Both pity and fear (as well as incredulity!) are aroused at the end as horror succeeds horror: Coriolanus cannot die until he has witnessed the wounding and threatened rape of his wife by Aufidius, the torturing of his little son and the mad ravings of Volumnia, who has been driven demented by the boy's sufferings. The appearance on stage of the boy's mangled body and his pathetic dying speech add a further touch. Crowne in *The Misery of Civil-War* uses horrors to create a moralized spectacle: in 3.2 soldiers are shown robbing and tormenting peasants and raping their daughters. The peasants have only themselves to blame for they have railed seditiously in ale houses instead of living 'honestly and quietly'. The soldiers repeatedly sneer 'How do you like Rebellion?' Then the lesson is driven home as 'The Scene is drawn, and there appears Houses and Towns burning, Men and Women hang'd upon Trees, the Children on the tops of Pikes' (3.3, p. 36).

Like royalist tragedies, the Shakespeare adaptations show varying degrees of anxiety about rulers' ineptitude, lust, bad fatherhood or intransigence. Even when the dramatists are straining every nerve 'to Recommend Submission and Adherence to Establisht Lawful Power, which in a word, is *Loyalty*', as Tate puts it in his Dedication to *The Ingratitude*, they do not succeed. Tate works hard to exculpate his hero and to demonize 'the busie Faction of our own time . . . those Troublers of the State that out of private Interest or Mallice, seduce the Multitude to ingratitude, against Persons that are not only plac't in Rightful Power above them; but also the Heroes and Defenders of their Country'. Yet his improvement of Coriolanus/James does not really work: nothing can assuage the uncomfortable resonance of a man in league with his country's enemies, Volscian or French, and making war on his own people. There was enough apparent criticism of James in the play for it to be revived as an anti-Stuart piece after the rebellions of 1715 and 1745.

Whig tragedies fall into several types. Some, like Whig comedies, rely for their force on anti-Catholicism. Anti-Catholic plays offer a mirror-image of Tory plays, attributing to 'papists' all the qualities which Tories attributed to rebels: ambition, arrogance, arbitrariness, hypocrisy, lying, plotting, secret atheism and secret lust, presumption, fanatical cruelty and even rabble-rousing. A precursor of Whig anti-Catholic tragedy is Thomas Shipman's anti-Catholic *Henry III of France* (1672). Shipman's depiction of the horrors of Counter-Reformation Catholicism, and his unease about royal supineness in the face of it, foreshadow Lee's explicitly Whiggish banned play, *The Massacre of Paris* (1679?). In Lee's play the hero is a Protestant patriot who resorts to arms to defend the true religion in the face of Catholic duplicity and ferocity and royal corruption. With obvious topical application, a weak king called Charles is manipulated by evil Catholics through a manipulative woman (Catherine de Medici). A similar image of female monstrosity is used to demonize Catholicism in Settle's *The Female Prelate* (1680), in which the ambitious, cruel and lustful Pope Joan typifies the horrors of popery. Lee's *Caesar Borgia* shows popish ambition and tyranny rampant in Rome in a way which reflects the particular anxieties and events of the Popish Plot scare, and concludes with the moral, drawn by Machiavel:

> No power is safe, nor no Religion good,
> Whose Principles of growth are laid in Blood.
> (5.3.371–2)

Atrocities in these plays, arousing pity and terror, rival anything in *The Misery of Civil-War* or *The Ingratitude of a Common-wealth*. In *The Massacre of Paris* the hero is literally torn apart by a papist-inspired mob. In *Caesar Borgia*, as in Tate's *The Ingratitude*, there is the 'mangling' of a little boy (Borgia's much-loved bastard son) and a descent into madness, this time by the protagonist himself, as the demands of popish Machiavellian villainy prove too much to execute or endure. *The Female Prelate* offers moralized spectacles. For example, in Act 3 the persecuted hero Saxony is taken into a chamber where the scene opening 'discovers variety of Hereticks in several Tortures' (p. 40). In Act 4 the imprisoned heretics set the prison on fire and the ghost of the old Duke of Saxony, murdered by Pope Joan in her youth, writes 'MURDER' on the wall in 'bloudy fire' (4.3, p. 50); and in Act 5 'The Scene opens, and discovers a Stake and Faggots, with Priests with Lighted Torches to kindle the Fire, and the Rabble hurrying Saxony to the Fire' (5.2, p. 70).

Even plays which are not explicitly anti-Catholic rely for their effect on quasi-papist atrocities. For example, in Lee's *Lucius Junius Brutus* (1680) the royalist plotters who try to undermine the fledgling Roman republic are in league with treacherous priests, and most of Act 4 is devoted to atrocities as royalist conspirators and priests engage in bloodthirsty ranting, and burn, crucify and consume their victims. Anti-Catholicism was popular with the audience, though not with the authorities. Lee's *The Massacre of Paris* was banned at the instigation of the French ambassador, and he had difficulty in getting a licence for *Caesar Borgia* (though *The Female Prelate* had a good run, possibly due to the titillation of a female villain).

Anti-Catholicism is definitely a Whig ideology, despite the fact that Tory drama-tists sometimes made concessions to the widespread anti-Catholic sentiment. But not all Whig tragedies work by demonizing Catholicism. The twin evils for the Whigs were, in Marvell's phrase, popery and arbitrary government, and some plays focus on the latter to celebrate heroic resistance to tyranny or republican virtue. Good examples are two Roman plays, Bancroft's *The Tragedy of Sertorius* and Lee's *Lucius Junius Brutus*. These plays celebrate godliness, parliamentary institutions, the rule of law, the common good and the ability to put political obligations before personal ones. *Lucius Junius Brutus* was banned after a few days' performance for 'Scandalous Expressions and Reflections upon ye Government'; hardly surprising since it depicts the expulsions of the corrupt, libertine and tyrannical monarchy and the founding of a glorious republic. Other plays, such as Lee's *Theodosius* (1680) and Settle's *The Heir of Morocco* (1682), offer more coded discussions of bad kingship and loyal opposition, though still with a Whiggish slant.

The third and final aspect of the dramatic resonance of the Exclusion Crisis is to accelerate the rise of the sentimental (the subject of chapters 14 and 17 in this volume). The reason for this is that both Tory and Whig playwrights use sentimentalized, suffering characters to dramatize the horrors of rebellion and republicanism, and tyranny and popery, respectively.

What we have seen, then, is that the relationship between Restoration drama and politics was a fruitful one. Political engagement is productive of dramatic diversity. We have also seen that contradictions within royalist drama are not always successfully contained and that there is a significant body of oppositional drama. It is also clear that Restoration drama was not the worse for its political nature. On the contrary, the immediacy and intensity of the drama's engagement with politics contributed to significant transformations in dramatic form and content, and gave the drama its vitality.

REFERENCES AND FURTHER READING

Braverman, Richard (1987). 'Libertines and Parasites', *Restoration* 11, 73–86.
Braverman, Richard (1993). *Plots and Counterplots: Sexual Politics and the Body Politic in English Literature, 1660–1730*. Cambridge: Cambridge University Press.
Braverman, Richard (1995). 'The Rake's Progress Revisited: Politics and Comedy in the Restoration', in J. Douglas Canfield and Deborah C. Payne (eds), *Cultural Readings of Restoration and Eighteenth-century English Theater*. Athens: University of Georgia Press, 141–68.
Canfield, J. Douglas (1997). *Tricksters and Estates: On the Ideology of Restoration Comedy*. Lexington: University Press of Kentucky.
Canfield, J. Douglas (2000). *Heroes and States: On the Ideology of Restoration Tragedy*. Lexington: University Press of Kentucky.
Corman, Brian (1993). *Genre and Generic Change in English Comedy, 1660–1710*. Toronto: University of Toronto Press.
Elias, Richard (1978). 'Political Satire in *Sodom*', *Studies in English Literature* 18, 423–38.
Hughes, Derek (1996). *English Drama, 1660–1700*. Oxford: Clarendon Press.
Hume, Robert D. (1976). *The Development of English Drama in the Late Seventeenth Century*. Oxford: Clarendon Press.
Hume, Robert D. (1977). 'The Myth of the Rake in Restoration Comedy', *Studies in the Literary Imagination* 10, 25–55.
Jose, Nicholas (1984). *Ideas of the Restoration in English Literature*. London: Macmillan.
Kenyon, J. P. (1974). *The Popish Plot*. Harmondsworth: Penguin.
Maguire, Nancy Klein (1992). *Regicide and Restoration: English Tragicomedy, 1660–1671*. Cambridge: Cambridge University Press.
Markley, Robert (1988). *Two-Edg'd Weapons: Style and Ideology in the Comedies of Etherege, Wycherley, and Congreve*. Oxford: Clarendon Press.

Munns, Jessica (1995). *Restoration Politics and Drama: The Plays of Thomas Otway, 1675–1683*. Newark: University of Delaware Press.

Munns, Jessica (1996). ' "The Golden Days of Queen Elizabeth": *The Lancashire Witches* and the Politics of Nostalgia', *Restoration* 20, 195–216.

Neill, Michael (1983). 'Heroic Heads and Humble Tails: Sex, Politics, and the Restoration Comic Rake', *Eighteenth Century: Theory and Interpretation* 24, 115–39.

Novak, Maximillian E. (1977). 'Margery Pinchwife's "London Disease": Restoration Comedy and the Libertine Offensive of the 1670s', *Studies in the Literary Imagination* 10, 1–23.

Owen, Susan J. (1994). 'The Politics of John Dryden's *The Spanish Fryar; or, the Double Discovery*', *English* 43, 97–113.

Owen, Susan J. (1996). *Restoration Theatre and Crisis*. Oxford: Clarendon Press.

Owen, Susan J. (1999). 'The Lost Rhetoric of Liberty: Marvell and Restoration Drama', in Warren Chernaik and Martin Dzelzainis (eds), *Marvell and Liberty*. London: Macmillan, 334–53.

Pincus, Steven (1996). *Protestantism and Patriotism: Ideologies and the Making of English Foreign Policy, 1650–1668*. Cambridge: Cambridge University Press.

Todd, Janet (ed.). (1996). *Aphra Behn Studies*. Cambridge: Cambridge University Press.

Weber, Harold M. (1995). 'Carolinean Sexuality and the Restoration Stage: Reconstructing the Royal Phallus in *Sodom*', in J. Douglas Canfield and Deborah C. Payne (eds), *Cultural Readings of Restoration and Eighteenth-century English Theater*. Athens: University of Georgia Press, 67–88.

Weber, Harold M. (1996). *Paper Bullets: Print and Kingship Under Charles II*. Lexington: University Press of Kentucky.

9
Restoration Drama and Social Class
Aparna Dharwadker

Drama, Criticism and the Subject of Class

In *The Political Unconscious*, Fredric Jameson describes Marxism as the only system that can offer 'an adequate account of the essential *mystery* of the cultural past' because it assimilates the history of human society to 'the unity of a single great collective story' – the history of class struggle (1981: 19–20). The criticism produced by the current poststructuralist, neo-Marxist and new historicist orientations of early modern studies, however, considers class not as the ultimate subject of history but as a key element in the critique of ideology, which reveals how literature (as institution and genre) serves the interests of a dominant culture, social group or gender. Such criticism typically claims to uncover meanings that lie hidden beneath the surface, and the validity of its interpretive procedures does not depend on whether authors and audiences in a given period are *conscious* of the workings of ideology. Thus the editors of *The New Eighteenth Century*, the collection of essays which most clearly signals the turn towards theory in eighteenth-century studies, include 'the formation of a broad and systematic critique of ideology, and . . . a new interdisciplinarity concurrent with and attendant upon such a critique' among 'the most productive new directions' for the field (Brown and Nussbaum 1987: 20). This programme has in turn been criticized for privileging 'abstractions' like race, class, gender and power, and for recycling predictable readings (see Damrosch 1992: 4, 135), but it does represent the direction that recent discussions of class have taken.

Restoration drama stands in a curiously anomalous relation to this rediscovery of class in eighteenth-century studies, for two reasons. First, the Restoration is a historical period in which a variety of theoretical, polemical and rhetorical discourses not only *acknowledge* but actively *underscore* the importance of social categories in cultural production. Class undergirds drama due to the strong symbolic and practical connections between the theatre and the Stuart monarchy, and the counter-revolutionary turn in Restoration society, which creates a predisposition towards royalist ideology, aristocratic norms and elite forms, particularly during the first two decades of Charles II's reign. The well-known prologue to the first play performed before Charles at Whitehall maintains that 'They that would have no KING, would have no *Play*: / The *Laurel* and the *Crown* together went, / Had the same *Foes*, and the same *Banishment*'. Since king and stage were also restored together in 1660, theatre becomes, in royalist rhetoric, the cultural institution uniquely suited to the celebration of monarchy and courtly values. A number of early Restoration authors also invoke the figure of *theatrum mundi* to describe stage performance as the most effective antidote to the disruptions of recent history. In a special epilogue for a court performance of *Cutter of Coleman Street* (1661), Abraham Cowley claims that his anti-Puritan comedy neutralizes the 'Tragick Follies' of the Interregnum, and rightly degrades characters who had held an absurdly high station 'On the World's Theatre not long ago'; in the epilogue to *The Usurper* (1664), Edward Howard describes his tragedy as 'A Record of all such Loyalty; / That after long Contests, did safely bring / Subjects to Rights, and to his Throne our King'. In another direction, the desire to elevate the social tone of drama above Renaissance models and invent cultural forms adequate to the new order is evident in the principal Restoration dramatic genres, including Spanish romance, the rhymed heroic play, upper-class wit comedy, split-plot tragicomedy and royalist tragedy. Given theatre's involvement in the material, ideological and social effects of a royalist restoration, the consciousness of class pervades Restoration discourse about dramatic authorship, the theory and practice of dramatic genres, the construction of author–audience relations, and the formation of theatre institutions.

Second, ahistorical generalizations precisely about the class characteristics of Restoration dramatic and theatrical culture are the mainstay of the singular 'critical tradition' which begins with Sir Richard Blackmore and Jeremy Collier at the end of the seventeenth century, and determines the literary–popular reception of Restoration drama for two centuries. The eighteenth- and nineteenth-century attacks on the drama's immorality and artificiality – by Richard Steele, Joseph Addison, Samuel Johnson, Thomas Macaulay, Charles Lamb, William Hazlitt, Alexander Beljame and others – constitute a body of writing in which the complex symbolism of class in Restoration theatre and society is gradually flattened out and assimilated into the Whig interpretation of history. John Harwood points out that 'the conflation of drama and society into a single nauseating phenomenon is a central ploy in the attack on Restoration comedy' (1982: 5), allowing critics to dismiss the plays as exclusive representations by, for and about a corrupt and self-indulgent ruling class. Hence Johnson characterizes Restoration theatres as 'mansions of dissolute licentiousness'; Macaulay insists that the plays appealed to 'the most deeply corrupted part of a corrupted society'; and even in the early twentieth century, Allardyce Nicoll claims that the audience 'for whom the poets wrote and the actors played were the courtiers and their satellites' (1952: 7; see also Love 1980: 21; Harwood 1982: 3–5). These abstractions reduce 'Restoration drama' to a single genre – comedy – and reduce 'Restoration comedy' further to a single type – the 'licentious' comedy of a few practitioners like Etherege, Wycherley, Otway, Behn and Vanbrugh. Although the tradition of moral criticism and semantic reduction appears impossibly remote from the recent theoretical and critical concerns of Restoration studies, it is relevant to the issue of class for two reasons: it shows the extent to which Restoration drama was susceptible to exclusive identification with the ruling class; and for nearly two centuries, it was influential enough to push this drama beyond the margins of acceptability.

In relation to Restoration drama, therefore, the category of social class functions both *synchronically*, as the basis of late twentieth-century ideological critique, and *diachronically*, as an aspect of the period's understanding of itself, and its subsequent representation by (mainly unsympathetic) historians and critics. This implicates the subject of class in historical event, social change, political symbolism, topical polemic, critical rhetoric and dismissive generalization to an extent that is particularly difficult to negotiate in theory and criticism. Indeed, class issues were more or less marginal to the postwar critical movement that re-established the historical specificity and heterogeneity of Restoration drama through varieties of historical, formalist, biographical and textual scholarship. Only in the last two decades has the work of critics like Laura Brown, J. Douglas Canfield, Eve Kosofsky Sedgwick, Robert Markley, Deborah C. Payne, Laura Rosenthal, Nancy Klein Maguire and Susan J. Owen reconsidered class in relation to Restoration dramatic form, language, style, political ideology, theatre culture, authorship and audience response (see References and Further Reading). Most of these critics assert that the relative uniformity of social setting in Restoration drama does not denote ideological or cultural homogeneity: if literary form 'includes ideology', both form and ideology in Restoration drama appear to be either self-critiquing or the objects of contemporary critique. As Robert Markley comments, 'to assume, as a working principle, that late-seventeenth century drama exhibits a single conservative ideology or that it describes a linear, evolutionary course from a decadent aristocratic culture to a semi-enlightened bourgeois society is to exchange Macaulay's fictions for Aubrey Williams' (1988: 138). Restoration drama studies has to acquire the same nuanced understanding of social class that the Restoration itself possessed.

The successive parts of this chapter consider some major aspects of the discourse of class in Restoration drama, and some late twentieth-century critical positions related to them. In the next two sections I discuss the class characteristics of the Restoration theatre and audience, and the explicit relation between class, dramatic genre and authorship after 1660. The two following sections deal respectively with varieties of comedic and serious drama, and the concluding section considers the significant reorientation in the relation of class to representational forms at the end of the seventeenth century.

Theatre and Audience

The shift from patronal to commercial relations, which defines theatre as a competitive, popular and public institution, occurs in England at the end of the sixteenth century, creating the contradictory languages of patronage and commerce in drama that Kathleen McLuskie considers symptomatic of 'the vital cultural accommodation to a new economic and social system' (1991: 61). However, the disruption of professional theatre for religio-political reasons during the Puritan Interregnum, and its restoration through royal patent grants in 1660, are events that again radically alter the forms of institutional organization, the nature of patronage, the culture of performance and the terms of theatrical discourse in the Restoration. The symbolic bond between theatre and monarchy, recognized in the naming of the two patent monopoly companies after the king and his brother, also translates into various forms of legal, financial, political and even aesthetic control. Thomas Killigrew's company, the King's Servants, 'were technically part of the royal household; they took an oath of loyalty at the Lord Chamberlain's office, were privileged to wear His Majesty's uniform, and ranked as "Gentlemen of the Chamber"' (Sharp 1909: 35). Both companies performed often at court, received gifts in cash and kind, and catered to the courtly circle by cultivating genres like Spanish romance and the rhymed heroic play; less benignly, they were subject to supervision and censorship by the Lord Chamberlain, and were often at the financial mercy of defaulting patrons, including Charles II.

To some extent, critical descriptions of the Restoration theatre as 'ultramonarchist' (Nicoll 1952), 'essentially a Court theatre' (Boswell 1966) or a 'court toy managed by courtiers' (Jones 1996) are problematic because they literalize the rhetoric and symbolism of the period. But the theatre established in 1660 is indubitably a 'closed system' which circumscribes authors, performers and texts within limited competitive boundaries, and maximizes the importance of class relations and hierarchies (see Hume 1976: 16–22). In 1682, when at Charles II's insistence the two monopoly theatres merge into the United Company, even the element of limited competition disappears until Thomas Betterton's move to Lincoln's Inn Fields in 1695. Deborah C. Payne describes the late seventeenth-century theatre environment as 'a marketplace of generalized exchange...[which limits] transactions of "pure" exchange (in the theatre, this translates into direct payment for varying and competing kinds of entertainment), usually through two strategies: institutionalization of various titles or entitlements, and specifications on social interaction and access to positions' (1991: 138–9). Every major feature of the Restoration theatrical system – the exclusive patent grants to courtier-playwrights, the control of the repertory through division and ownership of old and new plays, the regulatory role of theatre managers – depends on the institutionalization of limitations. The Renaissance distinctions between court, elite and popular performance, which correspond to social divisions, thus become inoperative in the Restoration: the public theatres are not really popular, while popular forms of theatre develop elsewhere, in the Lord Mayor's shows and the annual London fairs. Moreover, while in Renaissance popular theatre a sort of democracy of professionalism effectively excludes courtiers and gentlemen from authorship, after 1660 courtly and titled authors like Sir William Davenant, the three Howard brothers, the Earl of Orrery, the Duke of Buckingham and the Duke of Newcastle compete with professional playwrights like Shadwell, Dryden, Behn, Otway, Lee, Crowne, Durfey, Tate and Settle for the *same* general and courtly audiences.

The effect of these changed conditions on playgoing is a closely debated issue in postwar criticism, since 'the myth of the Restoration audience' as a narcissistic upper-class coterie is one of the most enduring legacies of the prolonged Whig reaction to Restoration drama. By invoking the audience persistently and extensively in pro-logues, epilogues, printed addresses to the reader and metatheatrical plays, Restor-ation playwrights certainly make their viewers and readers an intrinsic part of their craft. The problem is that of relating the 'implied audience' of authorial discourse to the socio-economic phenomenon of spectatorship in such a way as to uncover an historically plausible 'real audience'. As Harold Love argues persuasively, 'the recur-ring charges . . . of severe social restrictiveness, domination by the court, and attendant moral corruption' cannot be taken literally because they are historical generalizations based ultimately on the playwrights' own rhetorical, occasional and context-dependent discourse (1980: 21). On the other hand, inferences about the audience based on theatre finances, demographic data, urban geography, non-theatrical sources and social practices are also tentative, not decisive. 'Evidence' about the audience's class characteristics must come from both kinds of sources – authorial constructions as well as more objective data.

Among the forms of authorial address, published dedications naturally display the greatest self-consciousness about economic relations and class differences among authors and patrons. In the figural language that sublimates the convention's monet-ary basis, playwrights usually describe their work as a form of presumption or folly that needs the patron's support, indulgence and protection (sometimes literally). They invoke the idea of the nobility's unconditional generosity to explain such an inher-ently unequal exchange, but the cleverer playwrights also claim that patrons need the transaction as much as authors in order to fulfil a vital class role. In dedicating *The Old Batchelour* (1693) to Charles Clifford, son of the Earl of Burlington and Cork, Congreve argues that without authorial transgressions,

> Power would have nothing to do, and good nature no occasion to show itself; and where those virtues are, 'tis pity they should want objects to shine upon. I must confess this is no reason why a man should do an idle thing, nor indeed any good excuse for it, when done; yet it reconciles the uses of such authority and goodness to the necessities of our follies, and is a sort of poetical logic, which at this time I would make use of, to argue your Lordship into a protection of this play.

This rhetorical turn binds patrons and authors, occupying different rungs on the social ladder, in a relationship of reciprocal obligation. The dissimilar class back-grounds of Restoration *playwrights*, however, also vary the content of dedications in unpredictable ways. The courtly Wycherley dedicates *The Plain Dealer* (1676) 'To My Lady B—' (Mother Bennet, a notorious London Madam) to mock what he sees as the empty conventions of the form, and to express his preference for a prostitute over 'the ladies of stricter lives' who would 'make nonsense of a poet's jest, rather than not make it bawdy'. Addressing real patrons, professional playwrights like Behn, Dryden, Shadwell and Otway cannot afford to deviate into such irony.

In other Restoration forms of oral and printed address the stratifications of audience are broadly social – wits, gallants, fops, cits, 'the Ladies', to name a few – but by emphasizing qualities like discrimination, judgement and virtue in the audience, Restoration playwrights avoid a narrow determinism based on class. In the *Essay of Dramatick Poesie* (1668) Dryden's alter-ego Neander dismisses the judgement of 'the multitude' as a 'mere lottery', but courts the approval of the 'mixed audience of the populace and the noblesse' for rhymed heroic drama. Sir Car Scroope's prologue to *The Man of Mode* (1676) conceives of the audience as an undifferentiated collective and chides it for neglecting home-grown English comedy in favour of gaudy foreign wares. Perhaps most suggestively, in the preface to *The Humorists* (1671) Shadwell separates the 'Men of Wit and Honour', who have no rigid class associations, from two kinds of 'rabble': the 'rabble of little People' who are delighted by slapstick and farce, and 'the higher sort of Rabble (as there may be a rabble of very fine people in this illiterate Age)', who 'are more pleased with the extravagant and unnatural actions[,] the trifles, and fripperies of a Play, or the trappings and ornaments of Nonsense, than with all the wit in the world'. In contrast, authorial addresses attached to political drama are intensely class conscious, because characterizing political divisions along class lines and linking them to the theatrical reception of plays develops into a crucial Restoration convention. The epilogues to both John Tatham's *The Rump, or A Mirrour of the Late Times* (1660) and Abraham Cowley's *Cutter of Coleman Street* (1661) choose to imagine an audience consisting entirely of loyal Cavaliers, and revel in the absence of guilty and disruptive fanatics. During the Exclusion Crisis, Tory drama demonizes London's merchant citizens as a social class because, as Susan J. Owen explains, 'the citizen-merchant class...had formed a base of support for parliamentarians in the interregnum and now played a central role in opposition to the monarchy' (1996: 151).

The authorial rhetoric of extra-textual addresses thus clearly indicates that stratifying the audience along social lines and manipulating its response is an important dimension of theatrical experience in the Restoration. To attempt an historical reconstruction of the 'Restoration audience' in its entirety, recent critics have relied on reasonable inferences based on a variety of contemporary data. In essays that have appeared since the late 1960s, Emmett L. Avery, Harry W. Pedicord, Arthur H. Scouten and Robert D. Hume, and Harold Love argue that the Restoration theatre did not belong exclusively to any one group. Its audience was socially less diverse than during the Jacobean and Caroline periods, especially from 1660 to 1672 when the court of Charles II dominated theatrical culture, but it was in no sense a coterie. According to more than one estimate, approximately 5 to 7 per cent of the total population of late seventeenth-century London (about 20,000 to 30,000 people) attended the theatre in any given season, making it an institution that was neither exclusive nor truly popular. Love describes this 'real' audience as consisting of not one but multiple coteries, and makes a suggestive comparison between the Restoration theatre and the Restoration city, 'conceived as a number of distinct and independent territories within which it was possible for people from a wide range of backgrounds to find their own local sense of belonging and their own local mode of participation' (1980: 43). To sum up, Restoration conventions for conceptualizing and characterizing the audience turn out to be socially more restrictive than the audience itself.

Genre and Authorship

Laura Rosenthal observes that 'no genre illustrates the significance of literary property as a *cultural* category quite so much as drama', which by the late seventeenth century had long been recognized as both an elite and a popular art (1996: 6). Restoration drama is unusual even in the terms of her discussion because the specialized nature of the theatrical marketplace, and changes in the membership of the dramatic profession, make class an *explicit* referent in the discourse of genre and authorship. Restoration playwrights and theorists of drama are the first to explicitly acknowledge the social properties of genre, and to explain authorial choices by reference to specific social alignments and purposes. Broadly speaking, playwrights like Dryden and Robert Howard endorse the promotion of upper-class values through 'new' varieties of tragedy, romance and heroic drama, while others, like Shadwell and Buckingham, endorse the universality of the 'traditional' genre of comedy, especially in its canonical Jonsonian forms. In the case of authorship, the vital conceptual distinction is between privileged amateurs who write for pleasure but want the prestige of participating in the culture of 'dramatic poesy', and lay professionals who depend on patronage and popular success for survival in the theatre. Both groups of authors acknowledge the relation of genre to social class: their disagreement is over how drama promotes social values, and what values it ought to promote. The debate unfolds, moreover, in a context in which 'professional authorship' and the pressures of the theatrical marketplace are already well-recognized phenomena.

The class-based division between serious and comedic genres appears most clearly in the cluster of interrelated documents that represent the first important initiatives in Restoration dramatic theory: Howard's prefaces to *Four New Plays* (1665) and *The Duke of Lerma* (1668); Dryden's *Essay of Dramatick Poesie* (1668), *Defense of an Essay* (1668) and preface to *An Evening's Love* (1671); and Shadwell's prefaces to *The Sullen Lovers* (1668) and *The Humorists* (1671). Howard's use of class criteria in his two prefaces seems to be the least deterministic, since he links the different degrees of elevation among genres to the principles of 'naturalness' and 'decorum' rather than to social rank or status. The issue for him is not what is most elevated or comes most easily to the author, but what 'is most proper for the subject he writes upon'. Hence, where language is concerned, '[t]he easier dictates of nature ought to flow in comedy', while in 'serious subjects' language 'ought to be great and easy, like a high-born person that expresses greatness without pride or affectation'. Comedy in this scheme is 'lower' than serious drama only in terms of subject matter, not value. In contrast, Dryden's concern with 'refining' literary forms leads him to create a class system of genres as much on the basis of a social and cultural as a literary hierarchy. His dedication to *The Rival Ladies* (1664) claims that only the 'excellence and dignity' of rhyme will enable England to keep up with the 'polished and civilized nations of Europe', because as a medium it makes great subjects possible in drama. The rhymed heroic play then appears at the top of Dryden's hierarchy because its 'argument', its 'medium' and its 'characters and persons' are all consistently 'great and noble', whereas in Jonsonian humours comedy (which Thomas Shadwell promotes as the best model for his time), the language, characters and situations are uniformly low and crude. In the *Essay of Dramatick Poesie* Neander balances the competing claims of prose comedy and serious poetic drama by considering

> what is nearest to the nature of Comedy, which is the imitation of *common* persons and *ordinary* speaking, and what is nearest the nature of a serious play: this last is indeed the representation of Nature, but 'tis Nature wrought up to an *higher* pitch. The plot, the characters, the wit, the passions, the descriptions, are all *exalted* above the level of common converse, as *high* as the imagination of the poet can carry them, with proportion to verisimility. (Emphasis added)

Predictably, the only variety of comedy Dryden supports is the 'Comick stile' of John Fletcher, which became, as Robert Markley shows, the mainstay of Cavalier attempts to 'identify a standard of "disinterested" gentlemanly conversation as the "proper" or "correct" model for readers and audiences to emulate' (1988: 61).

Shadwell counters Dryden's aristocracy of genres with a meritocracy – an alternative system based not on exclusiveness and refinement but universality and cultural utility. In his two important early prefaces he reaffirms the canonical status of Jonsonian humours comedy within the received tradition of *English* drama, and aggressively socializes the elements that for him constitute the 'life' of comedy – wit, humour and satire. In Shadwell's view, wit is not the skilful repartee of comic *characters* but an intellectual quality in the *author* that allows him to observe and select appropriate objects of attack within his social world. Humour is the quality of disequilibrium that makes contemporary character types vulnerable to attack. Although defined literally as a natural obsession – a 'Byas of the Mind, / By which with violence 'tis one way inclin'd' – in Shadwellian satiric comedy humour is more often an affectation acquired purely for social effect by those 'who are not Coxcombs by Nature but with great Art and Industry make themselves so' (dedication to *The Virtuoso* [1676]). Wit is therefore the enabling faculty, humour the social substance and satire the end of social comedy. For Shadwell, the very topicality and ordinariness of comedy demonstrate its superiority to tragedy, since 'the Vices and Follies in *Courts* (as they are too tender to be touch'd) so they concern but a few; whereas the Cheats, Villanies and troublesome Follies, in the common conversation of the World, are of concernment to all the Body of Mankind' (preface to *The Humorists*). Finally, comedy accomplishes the culturally important task of reformation more effectively, because where tragedy subjects 'Vices and Fopperies' to hatred or oblivion, 'here we make them live to be despised and laugh'd at, which certainly makes more impression upon men, than even death can do' (preface to *The Humorists*).

These arguments about genre in Shadwell's early criticism accomplish several important shifts in relation to class. First, he effectively diverts attention away from social or moral 'lowness' as the defining condition of comedy by emphasizing the 'common' and 'general' qualities of the genre: comedy is socially useful precisely because it is accessible across class boundaries. Second, he avoids the usual reductive clichés about 'popular' responses in the theatre by asserting that taste and judgement can be corrupt regardless of class. Third, he establishes the interdependence of class, genre and authorship more clearly than any other early Restoration playwright by arguing that certain 'high' genres project narrow cultural prejudices onto literature. All these aspects of the debate over genre are thematized with remarkable complementarity in two early Restoration plays – Shadwell's *The Sullen Lovers* (1668) and Buckingham's better-known *The Rehearsal* (1671) – which move the tension between the comic and heroic modes, and between professional and amateur authorship, from the sphere of theory and polemic into the sphere of performance.

In *The Sullen Lovers* the attack centres on a trio of upper-class poetasters – Sir Positive At-all, Woodcock and Ninny – who assume that the privileges of class extend automatically to authorship, and that the expression of particular class interests legitimizes genre. Sir Positive and Ninny have chosen literary authorship as their primary identity, and the heroic mode in drama and poetry – 'the fashionable way in writing' – as the 'natural' expression of their nobility. Since their authorial identity is appropriated as a class prerogative rather than earned under competitive conditions, court society in the play is reduced to a mock-marketplace where the fools impose texts endlessly on a captive audience, and demand a legitimation they cannot have. In the real theatrical marketplace Sir Positive insists that mere clerks in the eighteen-pence gallery cannot damn his heroic flights, or exercise their rights as auditors 'when Gentlemen write'. Greatness of birth guarantees him greatness as an artist, and also entitles him to an 'aristocratic immunity' from criticism.

Shadwell develops the social aspects of this argument further by casting the problem of authorship in terms of the dichotomy between professionals and amateurs. In the preface he states that 'Men of Quality, that write for their pleasure, will not trouble themselves with exactness in their *Playes*; and those, that write for profit, would find too little encouragement for so much paines as a correct *Play* would require'. Within the play the fools make it clear that the freedom not to be 'exact' is one of the privileges of gentility, but this freedom also implies that amateurish 'Men of Quality' will never excel at their craft. The play's female misanthrope, Emilia, asks bluntly if it is not ridiculous to see 'Gentlemen of 5000 *l.* a year write Playes, and as Poets venture their Reputations against a Sum of Money, they venture theirs against Nothing? Others learn Ten years to play o' the Fiddle and to Paint, and at last an ordinary Fiddler or Sign-Painter that makes it his business, shall out-do 'em all'. By having his courtiers claim an exclusive right to every form of scientific, professional and artistic knowledge on the basis of their class, Shadwell gradually broadens his satire to question the role of social hierarchy in determining the new cultural conditions, for the production of literary works in particular and the acquisition of knowledge in general.

Performed three years after *The Sullen Lovers*, Buckingham's *The Rehearsal* is the first substantial Restoration play about the institution of professional theatre, and engages fully with the effects of material and social relations on the theatrical marketplace through its metatheatrical structure. The professional playwright Bayes has abandoned the 'common pitch' for the 'grand design' of heroic drama, which he intends for 'some persons of Quality, and peculiar friends of mine, that understand what Flame and Power in writing is: and...do me the right...to approve of what I do'. Bayes's pursuit of greatness violates the established norms of dramatic construction and the structure of the audience's expectations, but the alienation that the actors and the two dramatized spectators, Johnson and Smith, feel towards his play is a matter of class as well as classical authority, since nothing in the play's artificially elevated (and therefore ridiculous) narrative of kings, heroes and goddesses has meaning for them. The metatheatrical format of Buckingham's play therefore shows the playwright at odds with the performers, who eventually abandon the rehearsal; cultivated viewers, whose ironic commentary forms the core of Buckingham's critique; and his own fragmentary drama, which collapses entirely due to his vulgarity, ignorance and social inexperience.

Both *The Sullen Lovers* and *The Rehearsal* therefore satirize heroic drama, but from opposite ends of the social spectrum. For Shadwell, the upcoming professional, the heroic mode represents the narcissistic fantasies of the class of privileged amateurs; for Buckingham, the privileged amateur, the same mode represents the compromises and limitations of professionalism. As a dramatized character, Bayes is the obsequious author who writes for 'Persons of Quality' and struggles 'to oblige the Auditors by civility'; Sir Positive *is* the person of quality who stages conflicts of love and honour because they enhance his own courtly status, and exacts deference from his less privileged auditors. By representing heroic drama as a form of indulgence for a specific class, both Shadwell and Buckingham use the social in addition to the aesthetic as a primary category of judgement, and their plays present class and authorship as virtually inseparable categories in the process that transmutes drama into cultural capital. Comedy, the genre of 'prose and sense' both these playwrights advocate, is also the most overtly social genre, but in the Restoration it raises and resolves the problems of class in interestingly diverse ways.

Social and Political Comedy

There is considerable agreement in modern criticism that the best-known Restoration genre – the verbally dazzling, mannered, satirical social comedy of Etherege, Dryden, Wycherley, Otway, Behn, Southerne, Congreve, Vanbrugh and Farquhar –

is homogeneous in terms of class and ideologically conservative. The distinctive frictions of this form involve inequalities not of class but gender (men against women), social success (self-serving town wits against fops and country bumpkins), virtue (self-possessed young heiresses against cast-off mistresses, hypocritical wives and jealous guardians) and intelligence (cultivated young men against libertine posers). The vast majority of these characters – normative and negative – belong to the same privileged ranks. There are few outsiders to question or radically disrupt class boundaries, and only two notable groups of characters outside the dominant social fold: servants, whose function as facilitators and confidantes occasionally accommodates the perception that they have more virtue and intelligence than their betters; and citizens, whose conventional comic function as gulls and cuckolds darkens into cupidity and treason in royalist political drama.

Two decades ago, John Loftis had argued that reaction against the Civil War experience, the nature of the Restoration theatrical monopoly and the Lord Chamberlain's close supervision of the stage kept 'egalitarian thought' out of Restoration drama, producing a deliberately conformist world view:

> The fact that the dramatists...accepted the traditional class relationships as the condition of life (even when they wrote about non-European societies) provides a measure of their conservatism and that of the relatively affluent audiences for which they wrote.... [T]hey show little inclination to question the justice of a distribution of wealth and privilege in patterns determined by social rank and, beginning under the Hanoverians, success in commerce. (1980: 254)

In a 1997 study, J. Douglas Canfield echoes this position to observe that Restoration comedy 'underwrites the same ideology, the same natural right of the English aristocracy – from peers to the gentry – to rule because they are superior in intelligence (wit) and natural parts, and because they have been bred to rule' (1997: 1). Although some female protagonists in the plays of Behn, Shadwell and Southerne attempt to destabilize patriarchy and inheritance through promiscuity, on the whole marriage 'presents no threat to status hierarchy and...guarantees the continuation of an aristocratic order in which power and property continue to be safely transmitted through genealogy' (1997: 33).

The strategies of containment used in the representation of servants and cits, the two groups of peripheral characters whose relationship to the centre is based specifically on class *differences*, appears to confirm the conservatism of mainstream social comedy further. If Restoration servants transcend their function as facilitators and actually 'speak', the most they wish for or enact is a parody of the life of gentility. In Etherege's *The Man of Mode*, the shoemaker asserts his right to be wicked because 'men of quality' must not be allowed to 'engross the sins o' the nation'; in his marriage he claims to have arrived at the exact balance of indifference and hate that marks a gentleman's relations with his wife. Mirabell's servant Waitwell in *The Way of the World* (1700) can mimic the aristocracy well enough to impersonate Sir Rowland and court Lady Wishfort, but once the masquerade is over he knows he will have to 'recover my acquaintance and familiarity with my former self...and fall from my transformation to a reformation into Waitwell'. Perhaps one of the most intricate plays on class occurs in Farquhar's *The Beaux' Stratagem* (1707). When Archer reveals to the landlord's daughter Cherry that he is a well-born younger son forced by circumstances to disguise himself as a footman, she offers him marriage and two thousand pounds in the certainty that 'any gentleman who could bear the scandal of wearing a livery' would rather marry a social inferior than continue to endure the humiliations of poverty. Despite a strong sexual attraction, Archer refuses the offer precisely because his class pride gets in the way – and Cherry finds her proper station in life as the heiress Dorinda's maid at the end.

The gulling and cuckolding of cits by witty gallants is a plot formula devised to contain a more unmanageable threat – the growing power of capital and its quest for autonomy in a society ideologically recommitted to the values of inherited rank and wealth. Sir Nicholas Cully in Etherege's *The Comicall Revenge* (1664), Mr Jorden in Ravenscroft's *The Citizen Turn'd Gentleman* (1672), Sir Davy Dunce in Otway's *The Souldier's Fortune* (1680), Sir Cautious Fulbank in Behn's *The Lucky Chance* (1686) and Fondlewife in Congreve's *The Old Batchelour* are bankers, magistrates and aldermen; their sexual and intellectual inadequacies are directly proportionate to their economic and political clout. Ravenscroft's *The London Cuckolds* (1681), which has not one but three City fools with adulterous wives, is oddly apolitical for its date; but Crowne's *City Politiques* (1683) adjusts the formulae of sex-farce exactly to the topical details of the Popish Plot and Exclusion Crisis, and develops the most effective parallel in Tory comedy between civic and sexual politics. In Canfield's view, cit-cuckolding in Restoration comedy is a form of class warfare that 'aggressively reinscribes aristocratic ideology, and does so, in Foucault's terms, not only through *language* but the *body-language* of stage performance, and indeed, through *bodies* themselves...[which] become the contested ground for class dominance and, ultimately, symbols of the contested estate of England itself' (1997: 76–7).

These conservative elements in Restoration comedy do not, however, preclude other perspectives which reveal class as a locus of conflict in various *kinds* of comedies produced in this period. First, the notion of 'intra-class' rather than 'inter-class' warfare does not account sufficiently for the absence of genuine reconciliation or closure in mainstream social comedy. The libertine, witty or humane comedies of Wycherley, Congreve, Farquhar et al. are morally ambivalent towards their self-interested protagonists, and unsparing in their ridicule of affectation, hypocrisy and stupidity among the very ranks whose privileged culture is their *raison d'être*. Among recent critics who have offered more complex accounts of the workings of ideology, Laura Brown begins with a conventional definition of major comedy as 'dramatic social satire' that is 'ordered by a set of aristocratic social determinants' (1981: 28). But she regards the centrality of libertine philosophy, and the 'turn to satire in this period of a reinstated but economically and socially transfigured aristocracy', as signs of irresoluble social contradictions:

> Dramatic social satire...is the formal expression of a peculiarly vexed and conflicted
> ideology, fundamentally conservative in its allegiance to traditional values and to the
> status quo, but daringly radical in its exposure of the hypocrisy, the immorality, and the
> materialism of the society it must finally accept. (1981: 42)

Robert Markley argues that the exaggerated concern after 1660 with the distinction
between true and false wit is a way of suppressing the problem of social inequality, but
the plays of a 'wit' like Wycherley do not rationalize privilege: rather, they 'describe a
complex and profoundly ironic attempt to accommodate a radical practice to a
conservative ideology; they exhibit an insistent, embattled anti-authoritarianism
that questions the ability of any discourse – including the playwright's own – to
stabilize moral, social, and ideological values' (1988: 138–9). Charles H. Hinnant
suggests that the trading and professional classes are treated with contempt in
Restoration comedy to enforce the 'centrality of the gentry and the aristocracy', but
the 'political economy of consumption', extended to sexual pleasure on one hand and
to an emergent consumer culture on the other, 'destabilize[s] any clear-cut distinctions between high and low, politeness and vulgarity, courtier and "cit".... What
unites gallant and tradesman in a hierarchy of getting and spending is an acquisitive-
ness that is associated not with property ownership but with the pleasurable consumption of objects, persons, and experiences' (1995: 78–9). Such interpretive turns
decisively disrupt the older idea of complicity between the playwright and his or her
imperfect social world.

The second caveat regarding the idea of class uniformity involves an intermediary
genre, occupying the middle ground between the Hobbesian ambivalences of courtly
comedy and the explicit class conflicts of topical comic drama. Best represented by
plays like Shadwell's *The Sullen Lovers* (1668), *The Virtuoso* (1676), *The Lancashire
Witches* (1681) and *The Squire of Alsatia* (1688), and Buckingham and Howard's *The
Country Gentleman* (1669), this genre embodies an alternative social vision that is
essentially political but independent of specific political crises (this is in part true
even of *The Lancashire Witches*, the vitriolic and much-censored Whig comedy of the
Exclusion Crisis period). The plays posit a vital socio-political role for the aristocracy
and gentry, and satirize all those forms of conduct – sexual licence, prodigality,
misanthropy, parental tyranny or absenteeism, intellectual and artistic dilettantism,
religious superstition – that prevent these classes from fulfilling their responsibilities
to family, society and nation. That similar objects of attack appear in Shadwell's best-
known *tragedies*, *The Libertine* (1675) and *Timon of Athens* (1678), points to the
consistency of his ideological position across genres and contexts. The political
cornerstones of this ideology are Protestantism, parliamentary tradition and the
national interest; its cultural priorities are companionate marriage, the proper education of children (both male and female), the cultivation of virtue and the responsible
stewardship of estates. In representing these values the playwrights abandon subtlety
for the simple dialectic of satire and example: the 'exemplary country gentleman' Sir
Richard Plainbred versus the 'caballing fools' Sir Cautious Trouble-all and Sir Gravity

Empty in *The Country Gentleman*, or Sir William Belfond versus Sir Edward Belfond in *The Squire of Alsatia*. In the topical *Lancashire Witches*, Shadwell's variation on the country house theme, it is even more important for Sir Edward Hartfort to reassert his authority as master and father, and rescue his family from the ruinous interference of his popish chaplain Smerk, and the Irish impostor Teague who is masquerading as a priest.

The third caveat about the representation of class involves context-specific differences within the genre of comedy. In Restoration political comedy – the anti-Puritan plays of the early 1660s and the Whig and Tory plays of the Exclusion Crisis period – the ironic conformism of social comedy is replaced by full-blown class antagonisms. Retaining its generic concern with contemporary society, political comedy renders ideological differences as class warfare, and hence focuses on the *social* consequences of political crisis. Royalist political comedies like Robert Howard's *The Committee* (1662), John Wilson's *The Cheats* (1663), Thomas Durfey's *The Royalist* (1682) and Aphra Behn's *The Roundheads, Or The Good Old Cause* (1682) are ideologically similar to mainstream social comedy inasmuch as they support the hierarchical position of the traditional ruling class. But their method is mainly that of straightforward affirmation, not ambivalence and irony. On the other hand, an oppositional Whig comedy like *The Lancashire Witches* attacks the ruling class for specific political-cultural failures, and offers a kind of critique that is *uncommon* in mainstream comedy. Topical intentions, and the vigour of both Tory and Whig politics during the Exclusion Crisis, thus dislodge any sense of sameness and modify the attitudes of both conformity and irony.

Early Restoration anti-Puritan comedies like Abraham Cowley's *Cutter of Coleman Street* (1661), Howard's *The Committee* and Wilson's *The Cheats* are modelled on pre-Civil War city comedy, but they accommodate the two great movements of the mid-seventeenth century – the ascent of the Puritan to a position of unprecedented political and social power, and the corresponding descent of the royalist into political obscurity, personal danger and material loss. These playwrights therefore represent the Puritan Interregnum first and foremost as a radical transformation of the social order made possible by institutionalized theft: the sequestration, composition and sale of 'malignant' estates. Their Puritan characters are no longer 'fools who have gone mad on religion' but the 'new gentry' who have unfairly gained access to a style of living entirely beyond their birth and breeding, and exercise power solely for personal gain. The comedies therefore centralize the experience of royalist dispossession and disempowerment within a sweeping, reductive political critique. Puritan power is shown to be short-lived because it is an illegitimate appropriation of royal authority, and ludicrous because it violates the established social hierarchy. Furthermore, the significance of this socio-political perspective on Puritanism outlasts its original historical context, because fictions of royalist dispossession make a striking comeback in the Tory comedies of the Exclusion Crisis period. Some of these later plays, such as *The Royalist* and *The Roundheads*, revive the Commonwealth setting as a reminder of past injustices that would reappear in the present if the Whigs were allowed to prevail in the issue of succession. Others, such as Durfey's *Sir Barnaby Whigg* (1681) and Behn's *The City Heiress* (1682), are set in the present, but create Commonwealth connections to explain the seditious and disloyal behaviour of Whig knights like Sir Barnaby and Sir Timothy Treat-All. In short, the transgressions of class and gender represented by the mid-century Puritan state still possess enough cautionary value for supporters of the monarchy in the 1680s to shape political theatre during the Exclusion Crisis.

Serious Drama: The Heroic Play, Tragicomedy and Tragedy

The subject of class has a particularly complex relation to Restoration serious drama because of the non-realism of the form, the assimilation of form to a specific, conflicted political history, and the intrinsic but not entirely consistent correspondence between politics and class in the seventeenth century. Christopher Hill describes the Civil War as a class war in which, according to contemporary accounts, 'a very great part of the knights and gentlemen of England . . . adhered to the King', while 'the smaller part . . . of the gentry . . . and the greatest part of the tradesmen and freeholders and the middle sort of men' sided with Parliament (Hill and Dell 1969: 240–1). Three decades later, the Exclusion Crisis was again perceived as a contest between the court and the landed aristocracy on one hand, and Parliament and City interests on the other. Royalist comedy simplifies these allegiances by equating the Puritan or Whig position with the fanaticism, hypocrisy, greed and rebellion of social upstarts. But between 1642 and 1688, England goes through irreversible social and political changes brought about successively by revolutionary anti-monarchism, counter-revolutionary absolutism and Protestant loyalism, and is poised at the end of the century to alter the balance of power in Europe and join the race for colonial markets. As inherently political works in elite genres, Restoration serious plays translate these socio-political conflicts into historical or invented 'fictions of authority', creating qualitatively different variations on the relation of ideology to experience.

It is worth re-emphasizing here that the status of tragedy in the hierarchy of literary genres has a social function in the Restoration, while its formal and affective features are modified substantially by the needs of a specific political history. Unlike the variation between 'high' (Fletcherian) and 'low' (Jonsonian) modes in comedy, the uniformly high modality of serious dramatic forms invests them with special significance in a period that is concerned with creating and maintaining a culture of high civility. As Dryden's dedication of *The Conquest of Granada* to the Duke of York suggests, the highest recommendation of 'heroic poesy' is that it has 'always been sacred to princes, and to heroes'. But tragedy's thematic involvement in the *misfortunes* of the great, and its affective emphasis on the emotions of pity and fear, are largely incommensurate with Restoration objectives. The dominant Renaissance (mainly Shakespearean) models of tragedy, with their characteristic fusion of historical engagement and transcendent humanism, disappear after 1660. The pre-eminent early Restoration genre is tragicomedy, defined so as to include heroic drama and Spanish romance as well as split-plot and double-plot plays which juxtapose serious and comic (high and low) elements. Nancy Klein Maguire argues that the affective mixture of sadness and mirth in tragicomedy is exactly suited to a period of royalist resurgence that mourns the 'martyrdom' of Charles I while rejoicing in his son's return to the throne. 'In tragicomic rituals re-enacting regicide and restoration', Maguire notes of the 1660s playwrights, 'they promoted kingship in the new circumstances by exonerating themselves of the execution of Charles I while celebrating the restoration of his son' (1992: 3). In contrast, during the Exclusion Crisis period when serious plays debate the Tory and Whig positions energetically and the outcome is uncertain until late 1682, the characteristic dramatic form is tragedy.

In one perspective, then, tragicomedy of the 1660–71 period appears to be a seamless, virtually unchallenged expression of class ideology – an elevated and more affecting version of the anti-Puritan comedy of the same decade. Yet this description would be at odds with the political actualities of the Restoration compromise, and the paradoxical 'contamination' of class categories *within* some drama. Owen describes the royalist heroic play of the 1660s as an attempt to 'paper over ideological cracks . . . which, in its very artifice, reveals the constructed nature of late Stuart ideology' (1996: 19). Similarly, Maguire emphasizes the avoidance of 'inherent and obvious contradictions' in the royalist drama of Charles's reign: 'For both psychological and political reasons, an ideal monarchical order continued to be celebrated, but the culture recognizes the order as mythic, and hence the myth no longer operates as a motivating force' (1992: 162). The non-English, non-contemporary settings of rhymed heroic plays like *The Indian Queen* (1664), *The Indian Emperour* (1665) and *The Conquest of Granada* (1670–1), and their massive discursive engagement with the antithetical claims of honour, loyalty and love, represent the most determined Restoration efforts to transfer the qualities of heroic poetry to drama. But in Dryden's plays, unlike Orrery's, the heroic code is not pristine or absolute, because it often accomplishes the same ends as its baser opposite. Of course, observing the same ethos from the outside, an unsympathetic courtier-playwright like Buckingham denies heroic drama any serious cultural value at all.

The heroic play maintains its ambivalences while remaining within an elite world, but in other forms of tragicomedy an inferior social world also intrudes directly (and sometimes inexplicably) into the representation. While seventeenth-century genre theory both attacks and defends tragicomedy for the *affective* mixture of mirth and sadness which allows serious plays to end happily, many Restoration versions of the genre offer a mixed *society* as well. In Edward Howard's *The Usurper: A Tragedy* (1668), the title character Damocles admits that he has 'no Name, / No Birth, no Images: Nothing in Annalls / To Speak the Glory of one Predecessor', and is therefore 'too feeble to sustain a Crown'. In the opposite camp, Parmenio, the son of a senator, desires death because his father and his estate are already lost. The 'class war' aspect of political comedy thus enters the thematic of political drama as well. The more radical forms of social mixing occur in tragicomic plays with double-plot or split-plot structures. In Howard's *The Change of Crownes* (1667), the main plot involving not one but two usurpers is interwoven with the fool Asinello's unsuccessful efforts to buy a position at court. John Lacy's satiric improvisations in the comic role were all too successful, because Charles II personally ordered the play's discontinuation, despite its loyalist theme of a double restoration. In Dryden's *Marriage A-la-Mode* (1671), marriage resolves the romantic as well as political problems of two young lovers, the fisherman Leonidas and the peasant girl Palmyra, who turn out to be the children, respectively, of Sicily's rightful king and the usurper Polydamas. In the comic (but courtly) second plot, two couples – one married, the other engaged – consider the constraints of marriage and the problem of sexual boredom in the manner of 1670s sex comedy, but remain faithful and enter the main plot by helping to bring about Leonidas's restoration at the end. That the play's heroic characters are reduced to a low station in life while the comic figures are courtly suggests the deliberate, though hardly subversive, manoeuvring of social positions in this mixed genre.

During the Exclusion Crisis years, serious drama most often takes the form of historical tragedies based on Greek and Roman subjects as well as Shakespeare's history plays and tragedies. Since these plays refract everyday political reality through allegory and historical analogy, they invoke class indirectly, in the social motivations that underlie their competing fictions of kingship, loyalty, civic order and the responsibilities of state. In keeping with general critical trends, however, scholars no longer regard the serious plays of 1679–83 as unmediated or unqualified expressions of ideology. Canfield's influential earlier view, that political tragedy of the 1679–89 decade was 'royalism's last dramatic stand', strenuously maintaining 'the royalist code of loyalty to a rightful monarch, however weak or indulgent', has given way to criticism that recognizes the nuances of dramatic response to the complex and confusing issues of the crisis. A play may support kingship but not absolutism (Dryden's *Troilus and Cressida*, 1679), or absolutism but not Catholicism (Banks's *Vertue Betray'd; or, Anna Bullen*, 1680); present both king and usurper as flawed (Tate's *The History of King Richard the Second*, 1680); criticize an indecisive king (Dryden and Lee's *The Duke of Guise*, 1683); or present domesticity as a comforting but failed antidote to the corruptions of politics (Lee's *Lucius Junius Brutus*, 1680, and Otway's *Venice Preserv'd*, 1682). The period of Tory triumphalism is limited to 1682–3, and not all major Tory playwrights participate in it.

In addition to the range of positions within 'Toryism', Susan Owen has argued for 'the existence of a vigorous and specific Whig dramatic language [as] a useful counter to assumptions about the hegemony of royalism in the Restoration' (1996: 6). As noted earlier, this language is transgeneric, and during the Crisis it allows for the emergence of an interestingly circular 'political language' of class:

> Themes of order and disorder find inverse reflection in Shadwell's plays and those of his Tory opponents. The ideal for Shadwell, threatened by Popery and the Tory faction within the Church of England and the court, is a hierarchical society based upon

English Protestant and parliamentary tradition. For Tory dramatists the ideal, threatened by upstart cits who want to meddle in affairs of state and either ape or interfere with the sexual pleasures of their betters, is a society based upon the hegemony of royal rule and aristocratic taste. The charges of credulity, superstition, hypocrisy, changeability, and monstrosity, applied by Tories to rebels, are associated by Shadwell with papists and their apologists. (Owen 1996: 198)

The confrontation between these positions, and their substantive if unequal expression in drama, are defining features of the Crisis period. After the merger of the two monopoly companies in 1682, theatre emerges from a state of dormancy only in 1688 – the year in which the decisive end of divine right kingship irrevocably changes the future language of class, political as well as dramatic.

The Decade of Transition

As a genre devoted to the social present, the resurgent comedy of the 1690s offers the most extensive and complex insights into the effects of cultural realignments on dramatic representation. What is remarkable about this decade is the modified revival of Caroline comedic modes even as Whig attacks on the culture of wit begin to take serious shape. The Jonsonian humours tradition continues, *mutatis mutandis*, in the last five comedies of Thomas Shadwell (1688–92). Dryden's *Amphitryon* (1690), Southerne's *Sir Anthony Love* (1690) and *The Wives' Excuse* (1693), and the first plays of Congreve and Vanbrugh – *The Old Batchelour* (1693) and *The Relapse* (1696), respectively – are major works in the sex-comedy mode (Vanbrugh's play was in fact written specifically to mock the emphasis on sentiment and reform in Colley Cibber's very successful *Love's Last Shift* [1695]). Congreve's *The Double Dealer* (1693) follows a classical satiric structure, while *Love for Love* (1695) and *The Way of the World* (1700) are wit comedies with serious love interests. W. M.'s *The Female Wits* (1696) and Vanbrugh's *Aesop* (1697) are metatheatrical. With the partial exception of Shadwell, major comedy in the 1690s also retains its ambivalent, satiric-affirmative focus on the privileged classes, although its wits are more humane than cynical, and plays like *The Wives' Excuse, The Relapse, The Way of the World* (1700) and especially Farquhar's *The Beaux' Stratagem* (1707) deal seriously with the problem of companionate marriage. By shifting the setting from London to the countryside, Farquhar's best-known play also revises the simplistic town–country oppositions of courtly comedy, and draws the landed country gentry more substantially into the ideological frame.

The thematics of tragedy after the Revolution are more predictable, since political and constitutional changes are once again allegorized in disparate representations of kingship. In Whig tragedy, as Derek Hughes notes, 'monarchy and justice are no longer irreconcilable', and 'the problem of the criminal monarch loses its complexity' (1996: 358, 359). Dryden's two major tragedies, *Don Sebastian* (1689) and *Cleomenes* (1692), deal with displaced and defeated royalty in a cultural environment which, unlike the 1660s, does not recognize the idea of divine right even as a myth. While Dryden remains within a predominantly European context, a more radical cultural reorientation takes place in the tragicomedies of Behn and Southerne, which overlay class issues with those of race and colonialism in their geographically dispersed versions of post-Revolution England – the colony of Virginia in Behn's *The Widow Ranter* (1689), and Surinam in Southerne's *Oroonoko* (1695, a split-plot version of Behn's novella). The playwrights' argument, familiar from Tory drama of the Exclusion Crisis period, is that the bonds of class transcend those of nationality and now race: with the end of the heroic age in England, the virtues of majesty are displaced onto racial others, such as the Indian King and Queen in *The Widow Ranter*, and the 'royal slave' Oroonoko in Southerne's play. In both plays, the brutality and treachery of the English characters (colonialists, slave-traders, fortune-hunters) is inseparable from the new class language of mercenary calculation which opposes and destroys nobility wherever it exists. Indeed, playing on the Virginia setting, Dryden's prologue to *The Widow Ranter* describes plays themselves as commodities that are brought in 'from every foreign shore', and ought to succeed because the sparks have 'ventures in our vessel's lading'. From this language of consumption to the 'business' of imprisonment, hanging and death in Gay's *The Beggar's Opera* (1728) is merely a matter of time, and the realization that secularized forms of authority at home are also irredeemably corrupt.

Underlying the specifics of dramatic composition in the 1690s, however, is the growing expectation that drama should have a constructive rather than deconstructive cultural programme, and although this position affects both comic and serious forms, it is least compatible with the Caroline modes in comedy. The idea that the culture of wit is self-serving, elitist and therefore unproductive pervades the attacks by Sir Richard Blackmore which initiate the critique of comedic satire and wit in the mid-1690s. In the *Essay Upon Wit* he argues that

> tho the Gentlemen of a pleasant and witty Turn of Mind often make the industrious Merchant, and grave Persons of all Professions, the Subjects of their raillery, and expose them as insipid Creatures, not supportable in good Company; yet these in their Turn believe that they have as great a right, as indeed they have, to reproach the others for want of Industry, good Sense, and regular Oeconomy, much more valuable Talents than those, which any mere Wit can boast of.

In *A Satyr Against Wit*, the self-styled 'man of wit' is described as 'an idle, wretched Fool of Parts, / That hates all Liberal and Mechanick Arts'.

Robert Martin Krapp rightly describes the Blackmore controversy as one of those 'moments of historical understanding when writers have consciously undertaken to change the type of literature which was being written, in order to make it correspond more closely with changed social relations' (1943: 80). By the end of the century, this shift in the class alignments of literature has the effect of emphasizing and promoting, rather than questioning, the identification of genre with class interests. Both Jeremy

Collier and Steele are outraged by the satiric comedy of their time not only because it is immoral, but because its immoralities are practised by men and women of quality. Collier asserts in *A Short View* (1698) that '[t]o put *Lewdness* into a Thriving condition, to give it an Equipage of Quality, and to treat it with Ceremony and Respect, is the way to confound the Understanding, to fortifie the Charm, and to make the Mischief invincible'. Steele's strongest objection to *The Man of Mode* as 'the Pattern of Gentile Comedy' is that its 'Characters of Greatest Consequence', Dorimant and Harriet, are 'Low and Mean', and Dorimant is morally indistinguishable from the shoemaker (a curious reversal of the shoemaker's own aspirations!). Since these authors consider the state of theatre and literature vitally important to the national interest, their ideal of comedy moves firmly towards the reformed, 'liberal mirth' of Steele's *The Conscious Lovers* (1722), which creates exemplary upper-class characters and displaces the verbal and sexual antagonisms characteristic of satiric comedy onto the servants Tom and Phillis. In tragedy, the crucial shift comes in the dedication to *The London Merchant* (1731), where George Lillo makes as strong a case for the accessibility of this genre as Shadwell had done for comedy some sixty years earlier. Bourgeois tragedy should be accepted, Lillo argues, because tragedy can be 'the instrument of good to many', and would not lose any of 'its dignity by being accommodated to the circumstances of the generality of mankind'. During the course of seven decades after the Restoration, the specific class appeal of a genre thus ceases to be a disqualification and becomes a distinct advantage.

REFERENCES AND FURTHER READING

Boswell, Eleanor (1932; reprinted 1966). *The Restoration Court Stage, 1660–1702*. New York: Barnes and Noble.

Brown, Laura (1981). *English Dramatic Form, 1660–1760: An Essay in Generic History*. New Haven, CT: Yale University Press.

Brown, Laura and Nussbaum, Felicity (eds). (1987). *The New Eighteenth Century: Theory, Politics, English Literature*. New York: Methuen.

Canfield, J. Douglas (1985). 'Royalism's Last Dramatic Stand: English Political Tragedy, 1679–1689', *Studies in Philology* 82, 234–63.

Canfield, J. Douglas (1997). *Tricksters and Estates: On the Ideology of Restoration Comedy*. Lexington: University Press of Kentucky.

Damrosch, Leo (ed.). (1992). *The Profession of Eighteenth-century Literature*. Madison: University of Wisconsin Press.

Harwood, John (1982). *Critics, Values, and Restoration Comedy*. Carbondale: Southern Illinois University Press.

Hill, Christopher and Dell, Edmund (1969). *The Good Old Cause: The English Revolution of 1640–1660*. 2nd ed. London: Cass.

Hinnant, Charles H. (1995). 'Pleasure and the Political Economy of Consumption in Restoration Comedy', *Restoration: Studies in English Literary Culture, 1660–1700* 19, 77–87.

Hughes, Derek (1996). *English Drama, 1660–1700*. Oxford: Clarendon Press.

Hume, Robert D. (1976). *The Development of English Drama in the Late Seventeenth Century*. Oxford: Clarendon Press.

Jameson, Fredric (1981). *The Political Unconscious*. Ithaca, NY: Cornell University Press.

Jones, Marion et al. (1976; reprinted 1996). *The Revels History of Drama in English. Vol. 5: 1660–1750*. London: Routledge.

Krapp, Robert Martin (1943). 'Class Analysis of a Literary Controversy: Wit and Sense in Seventeenth-century Literature', *Science and Society* 10, 80–92.

Loftis, John (1980). 'Political and Social Thought in the Drama', in *The London Theatre World, 1660–1800*. Carbondale: Southern Illinois University Press, 253–85.

Love, Harold (1980). 'Who Were the Restoration Audience?' *Yearbook of English Studies* 10, 21–44.

McLuskie, Kathleen (1991). 'The Poets' Royal Exchange: Patronage and Commerce in Early Modern Drama', *Yearbook of English Studies* 21, 53–62.

Maguire, Nancy Klein (1992). *Regicide and Restoration: English Tragicomedy, 1660–1671*. Cambridge: Cambridge University Press.

Markley, Robert (1988). *Two Edg'd Weapons: Style and Ideology in the Comedies of Etherege, Wycherley, and Congreve*. Oxford: Clarendon Press.

Nicoll, Allardyce (1952). *A History of English Drama, 1660–1900. Vol. 1: Restoration Drama, 1660–1700*. 4th ed. Cambridge: Cambridge University Press.

Owen, Susan J. (1996). *Restoration Theatre and Crisis*. Oxford: Clarendon Press.

Payne, Deborah C. (1991). 'Patronage and the Dramatic Marketplace under Charles I and II', *Yearbook of English Studies* 21, 137–52.

Rosenthal, Laura J. (1996). *Playwrights and Plagiarists in Early Modern England: Gender, Authorship, Literary Property*. Ithaca, NY: Cornell University Press.

Sedgwick, Eve Kosofsky (1985). *Between Men: English Literature and Male Homosocial Desire*. New York: Columbia University Press.

Sharp, R. Farquharson (1909). *A Short History of the English Stage*. London: Walter Scott.

10

Race, Performance and the Silenced *Prince of Angola*

Mita Choudhury

> It is always the goal of the ideological analysis to restore the objective process, it is always a false problem to wish to restore the truth beneath the simulacrum.
>
> Baudrillard (1994: 27)

Apatosaurus, Brachiosaurus, Diplodocus and Dimetrodon are spectacular points of reference in the vast template of our collective, prehistoric past, an elaborate simulacrum that has become visually familiar and a natural expression of our global identity. Through books, museums of natural history and, even more compellingly, on TV and on the giant screen, we have come to see and experience and touch and feel the prehistoric creatures that occupied our space once upon a time. Particularly for first-world children, the deadly have become dear and the carnivores have become cuddly. Indeed, the branding, packaging and marketing mechanisms in the dinosaur industry have been so refined that the manipulations of demand and supply seem inconsequential, if not entirely invisible.

But the naming of these at-once strange and all-too-familiar creatures embeds a covert reference to the much more recent past when the Anglo-American civilization derived its strength, if not its identity, from a Greco-Roman foundation. In 1841, as is well known, Sir Richard Owen invented the term 'dinosaur' – and that 'invention' led to the re-creation and a sort of de-fossilization of the creatures that died millions of years ago. Since the concept of 'history' and the idea of 'the Greeks' seem to be subliminally linked, one can see why 'Compsognathus' or 'Tyrannosaurus' inevitably invoke a familiar ring even though in the act of pronouncing these names the past is made delectably difficult and impenetrable, but also *naturally* so. The contact zone between now and the Mesozoic era lies at least in this instance in ancient Greek taxonomy that legitimizes our curiosity and links it with the concept of scientific discovery and all its overlapping European applications, beginning most forcefully in the Enlightenment. This is just a simple way to say, as I will do implicitly here, that the past is always recuperated from the vantage point of the present – and its complex, evolving subjectivities – and that the present therefore always looms large in the past (rather than just the other way around). Discovery, creation, representation, naming, identifying, interrogating and so on are seldom just that, seldom pure and motiveless; likewise, there is no motiveless interpretation (Felperin 1991: 78).

Meaning and Methodology

The post-industrial, post-capitalist phenomenon of re-creating and marketing the dinosaur is not just a metaphor but a useful framework for evaluating, as I do here, the mechanisms of demand and supply that were so integral to eighteenth-century theatrical representations of the (distant) Other. As with the theatre then, and more recently with new media or digital technologies, the mechanisms of demand and supply and the strategies of packaging and image-building are inevitably linked with issues of 'shared pleasures' that intersect seamlessly with the dynamics of power and hegemony. The spectral pleasures derived from witnessing and gazing at the Other in an eighteenth-century performance environment may be hard to re-create or recuperate and therefore largely speculative, but in retrospect at least this narrative, or this dinosaur, demands theoretical intervention.

However, the nuances in the naming of the dinosaurs are neither universally visible nor generally significant. For one thing, significance or lack of it lies at the source, in the gaze and in the perception that gives objects of inquiry their identity and sometimes their names. Who speaks is therefore almost more important than what is said. 'Names that signal ethnicity (like all other names and like language in general) acquire or fail to acquire significance – causally, ironically, catastrophically – depending on whether or not (and how) people read one another and themselves in terms of such names', Sabine I. Gölz observes. Pointing to her own isolation on an American campus and the tenacious grip of her German ethnicity, she goes on to argue that names can provide both comfort and a sense of danger. The comfort is derived by those whose lives are seemingly distanced from the scenes of crime, those who consider themselves to be the witnesses rather than the perpetrators-cum-defendants (Gölz 1998: 50–1). Gölz's analysis makes clear that the business of identity is hopelessly entangled in systems of identification that position into camps of pro and anti not only those, in her narrative framework, who survived the Second World War, in its immediate aftermath, but also their distant descendants in postmodern America. Identity, seldom stable and secure, is always subject to systems of identification that emerge from a complex interplay of race, class, ethnicity and other markers of difference.

'But what is ethnicity? Why are so many members of the profession fascinated by it? Why has it become a political force in ways of talking about (and criticizing) the study of literature and culture?' When Sander Gilman raised these questions in the prestigious *PMLA* issue devoted to 'ethnicity' in 1998, he was not so much heralding a new movement as giving voice and space to a concept that had already acquired a certain cachet, legitimacy and even urgency. Ethnicity is largely a North American concept, Gilman points out, having definite roots in the Civil Rights Movement, but, he goes on to add, similar movements and impulses can be seen and felt throughout the UK (Gilman 1998: 19–20). In the forefront of discussions on ethnicity as well as on Gilman's list appear the names of (followed by brief blurbs about) those whose interventions are well known: Hardeep Kohli, Dinesh D'Souza, Homi Bhabha, Linda Hutcheon and so on (Gilman 1998: 20). Whether the *PMLA* is mainstream or elitist, whether its essays are too 'trendy' or 'fusty' (Banta 1998: 14), the fact is that it has a very large readership which is buoyed by a very large membership. As a result, in the recent past the shifts in demand and supply have led to the dislocation of the traditional placements of margin and centre. Marginal voices – the act of criticism outsourced – have come to acquire the power and force of hegemonic discourse and at least for the time being this revisionist instinct has found its niche.

Symptomatic perhaps of a more exclusive membership, mainstream discourse in eighteenth-century theatre studies has been profoundly insular, and by that I mean profoundly disinterested in the ideological underpinnings of shared pleasures, particularly when those pleasures derive from the invocation of racial or ethnic differences. Disciplinary boundaries, I believe, play a vital role in limiting the fields of inquiry and sustaining myths of controlling and documenting information; compartmentalization and the resultant divides necessitate the erasure of that which is someone else's concern and provides methodological and ideological routes of escape. Pointing to this systemic pattern of evasion, Elizabeth Bohls asks the following question in the context of her study of *Frankenstein*: 'What is it about the disciplinary definition that entitles scholars and teachers of English literature in North America to conserve a certain cultural heritage – our portfolio, so to speak – that has been so effective in blocking the fact of empire and its domestic ramifications out of our field of vision as we study and teach the imperial era' (Bohls 1994: 23)? Those who have studied the theatre, its audiences and its unfolding history tended to be those who looked upon that past as their own heritage – a heritage to unearth, publicize and celebrate. Among scholars of the eighteenth century, theatre historians in particular mined the past for information and for new ways of cataloguing a 'tradition', a history, they rightly argued, in which theatricality must be seen as playing a vital role. This archaeological instinct not only prevailed but gained momentum and authority and produced spectacular results: *The London Stage* and *The Biographical Dictionary*. Two of the most invaluable resources without which we would all be severely handicapped, these paved the way for more work using the same methodologies. But this archival enterprise can flourish *without*, to use Graham Holderness's words, 'a powerful analysis of ideological and institutional production' (1991: 156). Immersed in facts and statistics, the theatre archaeologists in the latter half of the twentieth century were seldom compelled to delve into or contemplate the realms beyond the strictly textual or directly theatrical. In theories of the eighteenth-century theatre too an unselfconscious, unreflexive subjectivity prevailed. Scholars have discussed class consciousness and explored other ideological angles but for the most part without acknowledging the implications of the overlapping trajectories of class *and* race, gender *and* race, and the structures of power that emerge as a result particularly in the context of empire. John Gay's *Beggar's Opera* (and its unpredictable but huge success on the eighteenth-century stage) does not allow one to ignore class as a defining element in the play and the world that it mocks. But what about the sequel, *Polly*, and its curious departure from the known into the relatively unknown and, according to Gay, deliberately absurd realms peopled by characters with unpronounceable names?

Robert Alan Canfield, one among a handful who have studied *Polly* in depth, has recently argued that far from presenting a radical departure from the European ethos, Gay merely uses Polly to present a bourgeois solution that is rooted in the notion of the noble savage. Canfield goes on to argue that instead of subverting the rhetorics of seventeenth-century colonialism and capitalism, Gay only manages to reaffirm their central premise. Moreover, he suggests, the savage, functioning as Ariel, is recast as Cawwawkee and remains like Ariel a wish-fulfilling fantasy that encapsulates a variety of European philosophies pertaining to revolution, freedom and enlightenment (Canfield 2001). This approach to *Polly* is not just revisionist or postcolonial or even necessarily the only way to read the play; it does, however, raise the question that I raise later: can this theatre be radical or autonomous enough to challenge the fundamental assumptions of the culture that creates a demand for it?

Questions such as these cannot be raised nor adequately addressed in an atmosphere that some eighteenth-century scholars attribute to an overwhelming resistance to theory in the field (Nussbaum and Brown 1987). Others point out that theatre studies enjoys the status of a foster-child in eighteenth-century studies (Canfield and Payne 1995). The resistance to the language of postcolonial discourse more often than not tends to be a resistance to oppositional thinking. And this way of thinking has traditionally been identified with third-world scholars or immigrants or minorities or someone 'Other' whose primary identity lurks in the periphery of the English-speaking world. But the robust growth of postcolonial studies and the number of scholars engaged in it seem to suggest that oppositional intervention in this vein is no longer as culture-specific as it might have been at the beginning, some fifteen or twenty years ago. Inevitably, however, when 'theory' is conflated with oppositional discourse – or that which challenges the historiographical foundations of Western traditions and heritages – theory can legitimately be seen as disruptive and destabilizing.

Disruptive, oppositional, anxiety-ridden discourse, first fuelled by liberal feminism and gradually by several postmodernist approaches as well as through postcolonial discourse, made a slow and almost reluctant entry into the field of eighteenth-century theatre studies. According to Graham Holderness, in Shakespeare studies, the inevitable point of contrast and comparison, '[t]his motivation towards self-exposure – which derives from a theoretical rejection of the pseudo-objectivity characteristic of traditional forms of criticism, from a methodological acknowledgement that a criticism committed to disclosing the ideological infrastructure of cultural works cannot operate by concealing its ideological problematic, and from a "post-modernist" preoccupation with meta-discourse – has featured strongly in specifically focused feminist writing, but in other areas has remained relatively undeveloped' (1991: 153–4). The reasons for this tendency are not hard to find: from among the ranks of the marginal emerge patterns of resistance to oppressive or essentialist frameworks and agendas.

In eighteenth-century studies, considerable attention has been paid to the 'ideological infrastructures' of the print medium which has been a formidable rival to performance practices. Particularly in the wake of Michael McKeon's impressive tome on the novel, there seems to be a renewed interest in eighteenth-century prose fiction locating it as the site where social forces, albeit unstable, come most powerfully into play. 'Has literary theory granted the novel too much cultural and social power altogether, a power it is bound to cede or has already ceded to visual narrative?' Cora Kaplan's broad question about literary studies (2000: 13) posits a scenario that is exactly opposite to the one we find in eighteenth-century studies. The revolution in narrative theory today has been galvanized by performance, film and television studies as well as by the equally dynamic and perhaps more seductive approaches to the new media. A shift is therefore inevitable – a shift that dislocates the elevated status of the novel (an ascendancy that Mary Poovey and others have traced back to the beginning of the nineteenth century) and replaces it with the media of visual and virtual pleasures. But the eighteenth-century precursor of film and television, the theatre – popular entertainment that defied class and gender divides, 'mass' entertainment that was not reliant upon literacy or access to libraries – remains historically undertheorized and therefore also marginalized. Seen as a repository of bourgeois ideologies in the more radical readings of it, this theatre is retrospectively seen, nonetheless, as being curiously impervious to global forces and the kind of interculturalism that is associated with trade, commerce, colony and narratives of travel and discovery. But how can indigenous location and content based upon local knowledge be expanded to accommodate the more complex trajectories of interculturalism?

The general critical tendency is to scrutinize the plays whose titles flag them as playing with foreign characters and distant domains: *The Indian Emperour, Aureng-Zebe* (Dryden), *Ibrahim, the Illustrious Bassa* (Settle) and so on. But the scripts that reside more explicitly within the local – the scripts that most self-consciously proclaim to be indigenous stimulants evoking empathy or compassion or laughter or titillation for indigenous spectators – are more often than not the scripts that are worth exploring. Take, for instance, the diary of Samuel Pepys, which has been invaluable for reconstructing the theatrical seasons immediately following the Restoration. Pepys's random references to the theatre were not just part of a private register useful from our perspective for reconstructing the offerings of a given theatrical season or to study the emergent patterns of public and private domains. Pepys's haphazard references to the theatre constitute a larger signifying system that links England's naval challenge and global identity with its metropolitan, cultural imaginary at a significant moment in nation building. This consumer, this spectator, was also an 'actor' and a master naval strategist. His leisure activities and surreptitious dalliances in the theatre allow us to reflect upon the ways in which the imperial consciousness coexists with a desire for the collective experience of the theatre and its self-indulgent and self-validating mechanisms.

Joseph Roach's recent work is perhaps the most compelling example of how far the study of eighteenth-century performance practice can and should go. In *Cities of the Dead*, he demonstrates the infinite potential for theorizing and politicizing the early modern public sphere in which performance and ritual are an integral part, and this he accomplishes by juxtaposing 'living memory as restored behavior against a historical archive of scripted record' (1996: 11). Commenting on Thomas Betterton's burial in Westminster Abbey and Steele's eulogy in the *Tatler* to this great Shakespearean actor, for instance, Roach explains the role of performance and the creation of a new imagined community thus:

> Benedict Anderson stresses the role of printed media in the vernacular, particularly the newspaper, in the formation of modern national consciousness out of dynastic, feudal, and sacred communities.... [T]he burial of an actor, a practitioner of a despised profession, in the cathedral of English dynastic memory suggests a cultural use of marginal identities to imagine a new kind of community. Attending such a ritual performance as a friend of the deceased, Steele the pioneering journalist grasped – or created – its significance as national news. (1996: 17)

More than anything else Roach's study demonstrates the methodological pitfalls of setting up artificial barriers between the print and performance media, between the theatre and the cathedral, between the actor and the writer, between memory and restored behaviour. Sketching a vast performance arena that cuts across geographical, psychological and material divides – with 'walking in the city' serving as both method and metaphor – Roach captures the impulses of an early modern, global culture where circum-Atlantic performance practices challenge and dismantle the rigid frameworks of disciplinarity that we invoke to recall the past.

Pleasures, Passions and the Power of a Mute Performance

Witnesses, perpetrators, gullible spectators, voyeurs and bystanders all instinctively recognize the power of blackness even as it plays, very marginally, in their peripheral visions. This may be one way to understand the paucity of blackness on the eighteenth-century British stage but also its very persistent and durable interest in one towering figure: Othello's successor, Oroonoko. The purpose of this section is not to examine how Aphra Behn's colonial fantasy, *Oroonoko* (1688), survives on the London stage but, with a backward glance, to see how it was reconfigured at the very end of the eighteenth century, by whom and to what effect. The visual and sensual elements of Behn's novella are so naturally aligned to the dramatic and theatrical impulses that its subsequent dramatic renditions remain smooth and the narrative's resistance to

generic change is minimal. Focusing on the three versions of the Oroonoko story –
first by Behn and then most immediately by Thomas Southerne (1695) and much
later by Dr John Hawkesworth (1759) – Suvir Kaul observes that '[t]he form of the
heroic tragedy . . . is [Behn's] generic strategy for the retelling of a tale of slavery and
culturally-specific cruelty as a story of heroism and transcultural nobility'. Kaul goes
on to argue that 'Southerne's decision to change Imoinda into a white woman
responds to the dynamics of interracial desire that energize the telling of Behn's
tale'. And 'in Hawkesworth's emendation of Southerne, we have a final cleansing
of the disturbing excesses of the Oroonoko story, so that it safely, *rationally*,
reaffirms the superiority of English self-conception in the language of transcultural
empathy' (1994: 80–1). The cultural environment that shaped Hawkesworth's intervention and his revisionist instinct are indeed, as Kaul and others have suggested,
tempered by the cultural environment that is most forcefully epitomized by the
voyages of Captain Cook, Alexander Dalrymple, Jean de Lery, Bernal Diaz and their
ilk.

John Ferriar's interest in this narrative – my focus here – introduces a whole new
dimension to this discussion because he is a witness who refuses to identify with the
perpetrators. Ferriar's interest in race and difference arises from his oppositional
stance, his very outspoken denunciation of slavery, and his sincere efforts to rescue
Oroonoko from the clutches of Southerne's vision and to restore if not re-create this
hero as a motivating and inspirational symbol for the abolitionists. But renamed as he
is in this version, Ferriar's 'Prince of Angola' remains tethered to an inherited system
of meaning that cannot escape the tenacious grips of a by then sustainable simulacrum.

The concluding lines of the epilogue to *The Prince of Angola* (1. 788) are a poetic
rendition of the concluding segment of the preface to the play and are as follows:

> You, whose kind Breasts at Tales of Sorrow melt,
> You, who can pity griefs you never felt,
> With Wealth, unharden'd, who can stoop to trace
> A Brother's Features in the Negro's Face;
> Commerce for you shall ope' her richest Stores,
> The hidden Wealth of yet-neglected Shores;
> And, proud to fill the heaven-directed Sail,
> Shall grateful Afric' breathe a spicy Gale.
> But other Hopes your pious Toils engage,
> That mock the Plaudits of the mimic Stage.
> Sure, that to bless the glorious Work begun,
> The sole unerring Judge shall say, WELL DONE–

Substantially longer than the epilogue, the preface is also a unique document of social
philosophy, ostensibly written to promote the agenda of the 'Manchester Society for
Procuring the Final Abolition of the Slave Trade'. The writer's passion is unmistakeable and the message is clear: commerce is a 'pious' means towards securing economic

prosperity; 'other Hopes' should neither compromise nor contaminate the 'heaven-directed' enterprise. With an apparently clear sense of means, ends and purpose, Ferriar sketches a broadly humanist approach to the problem in the preface thus:

> The friends of the African must consider their task as but begun. For even should the justice of the Legislature provide the Redress we hope, in the speediest manner predictable, tho' the evils of the Africans would be diminished, by removing our share of the dreadful guilt, yet much oppression would continue to be exercised on them, by other European nations. . . . Nothing less can be desired than a suppression of this systematic inhumanity, throughout Europe. (1788: ix)

Ferriar's concerns transcended the immediate contexts of the British slave trade to seek a European referendum on the subject so that 'all the professors of Christianity' could make abolition their common cause. His reference to France's commitment to this cause (specifically the French *Code noir*, of which there was no equivalent in Britain) may be strategic – designed to introduce an element of competition – but not entirely an exaggeration.

The works of French social theorists such as the Abbé Raynal and Denis Diderot – both of whom dealt extensively with issues of commerce and slavery and made indelible contributions to the anti-slavery literature of the eighteenth century – had been in circulation for more than fifteen years by then. As is well known, Diderot had established an inflexible link between immorality and continuous travel. As Anthony Pagden points out, Diderot believed, for instance, that 'the faceless European traveler has, in a sense, reversed the journey that his ancestors once made from the state of nature to civil society. By traveling through space, he has gone backwards in time; by going from Europe to America or India or the Pacific, he has also gone from civility to savagery' (1995: 134). Whether positioned in a French or British metropolis, whether championing the cause of commerce or advocating the benefits of a life lived in *civitas*, the most progressive European thinker associated civility with Europe. In this sense Ferriar was no different from Diderot. And on the subject of commerce and his perception of its idealized and ideal role, one that they saw as being separate from colonialism, he was no different from David Hume (who considered foreign trade and commerce absolutely essential for the financial well-being of civil society). Ferriar's point about the native/European capacity for theatrical empathy – 'You, whose kind Breasts at Tales of Sorrow melt' – is a romantic echo of Diderot's more cynical sentiments regarding the blindness to the African plight: 'In the silence of the study, or in the theater, every conceivable human misery was capable of reducing every educated European man and woman to tears. Except one. In the end . . . it seems that "it is only the fatal destiny of the unhappy negroes which is of no interest to us"' (Pagden 1995: 139).

Convinced of the theatre's capacity to induce passionate responses, Ferriar summons *The Prince of Angola* to the sites of commerce that *Oroonoko* had inhabited in order to weed out the weak and what he considered to be the blemished 'conduct of the Old

Play': the 'nearly six pages of tedious declamation' (iii) in the fifth act. Ferriar's implicit faith in the power and, more importantly, the effectiveness of the theatrical medium is a faith shared by 'some active friends of the cause'. Together, they

> *imagined* [emphasis mine], that by assembling a few of the principal topics, in a dramatic form, an impression might be made, on persons negligent of simple reasoning. The magnitude of the crime, by dispersing our perceptions, sometimes leaves nothing in the mind but a cold sense of disapprobation. We talk of the destruction of millions, with as little emotion, and as little accuracy of comprehension, as of the distances of the Planets. But when those who bear with Serenity, of depopulated Coasts, and exhausted Nations, are led by tales of domestic misery, to the sources of public evil, their feelings act with not less violence for being kindled by a single spark. When they are told of the pangs of an innocent creature, forced to a foreign country in want of everything, and in subjugation to an imperious stranger; of the anguish caused by violated ties, and unchecked brutality; of the mother fainting under her task, and unable to supply her neglected infant; of the aged abandon'd to want, and the sick compelled to exertion, by the lash; nature will rise up within them, and own her relation to the sufferers. (i)

The activists believed in the power of performance, the potential of a spectacular display of inhumanity and hubris, to elicit responses that would spill over from the theatre to the streets and ultimately lead to the destruction of the malignant forces of corruption that engendered slavery.

The Prince of Angola has a streamlined plot unhampered by what Ferriar calls the 'wretched scenes' (ii) of Southerne's underplot; Widow Lackitt is converted to a 'woman' who appears briefly in the beginning; and the depravity of the colonists is summarized in a short dialogue between the woman (consumer) and the Captain Driver (the supplier). Oroonoko is promptly introduced on stage in Ferriar's version without the prevarications that Southerne's play begins with. As in Southerne's version, however, the Captain relates the circumstances of Oroonoko's capture – how he got Oroonoko's attendants 'dead drunk' and then how he 'secured' the prince – even as the slaves are ushered on to the stage. In both versions, 'Black Slaves, Men, Women, and Children pass across the Stage by two and two; Aboan, and others of Oroonoko's Attendants two and two: Oroonoko last of all, in Chains' (Southerne, 117; Ferriar 1788: 6). The first portrait of the slaves, as they are supposed to appear on stage, remains the same: they are on display, mute and chained. In the exchanges that follow, both versions invert tradition and received opinion by emphasizing the white man's propensity for betrayal and the black man's propensity for honesty, integrity and so on. And following Southerne, Ferriar shows that even though Oroonoko tears off his 'pomp' and dons his 'slavish habit', he is the quintessence of the noble savage; likewise, even though Blandford is one of the whites, he distinguishes himself by saying that 'we are not monsters all' (Southerne, 119; Ferriar 1788: 8). The self-reflexive European, aware of his shortcomings, aware of what he was before the Fall and what he has now become, is sensitive and can make amends.

Towards the beginning of Aphra Behn's *Oroonoko*, recall that she describes the Indians as being in a prelapsarian state of innocence: 'They are extreme modest and bashful, very shy, and nice of being touched. And though they are all thus naked, if one lives for ever among them, there is not to be seen an indecent action, or glance; and being continually used to see one another so unadorned, so like our first parents before the Fall, it seems as if they had no wishes; there being nothing to heighten curiosity, but all you can see, you see at once, and every moment see; and where there is no novelty, there can be no curiosity' (1992: 76). In Behn's romantic reverie, the stark presence of 'unadorned' nature stands in sharp contrast to civilization. Unhampered by evasive intrusions that seek to conceal beauty and thus to excite curiosity, this natural nakedness transforms and uplifts the origin of the civilized gaze. This idea is picked up consciously or unconsciously in the later dramatizations and injected with the 'loss of innocence' angle: Oroonoko first appears dressed as a prince. The planters, never having seen royalty in chains and particularly – by implication – black royalty, 'pull and stare at Oroonoko'. This is novelty, this sight invokes curiosity. Blandford 'turns them away', shattering the gaze inspired by novelty and curiosity: 'What wou'd you have there? You stare as if you never saw a Man before. Stand further off' (Southerne, 119; Ferriar 1788: 7). But this is not just any man. Aphra Behn's intuitive understanding of the magnetism of novelty that is the instigator of curiosity finds expression in Southerne's dramatization, which is reproduced without revision by Ferriar. In performance, one would imagine, the first still of Oroonoko in chains and, subsequently, the other characters' gawking mimics the spectatorial impulse, 'acting out', as it were, the spectator's 'idea of a slave'. Stripped of his status and his princely robes, the Southerne-Ferriar Oroonoko prepares to assume his new role as slave by donning his slavish habit with the following defiant words:

> Tear off this pomp and let me know myself:
> The slavish habit best becomes me now,
> Hard fare and whips, and chains may overpow'r
> The frailer flesh, and bow my body down:
> But there's another, nobler part of me,
> Out of your reach, which you can never tame.
>   (Southerne, 119; Ferriar 1788: 8)

In their 'unadorned' if not naked states, both the Indians and Oroonoko reveal a facet of humanity that European culture had forfeited long ago for tasting the forbidden fruit. In Behn's vision of this state of innocence, 'it seems as if they had no wishes'. 'They' had no desire; they were instinctively decent. It follows then – the dramatizations echo Behn's corollary – that 'they' are 'out of . . . reach' – distant – so much so that the European 'can never tame' them. However, authorial idealism exits swiftly, and even inadvertently (immediately after the noble thoughts of a free and distant 'native' are expressed), and dramatic realism thunders in: following the emotional and heroic outburst from Oroonoko quoted above, Blandford 'presumes' to call him Caesar (Southerne, 119; Ferriar, 1788: 8).

In an impressive essay about the 'globalization of Western face-naming strategies' in the eighteenth century, Kay Flavell examines the contemporary rhetorics of 'national physiognomies' that combine science and pseudo-science to produce a hierarchical scheme that is then used to link physical attributes to mental and moral capacity. 'By grounding the sublime within a Greco-Roman representative tradition, it was then an easy matter to claim that European male bodies looked most godlike – and, therefore, contained the most sublime moral and spiritual essence – and to locate Asians and Africans on the descending scale' (1994: 11). The recuperation of the Roman 'Caesar' and the renaming of Oroonoko as Caesar is a theatrical gesture designed to convert the slave into a European potentate. Appearance is not just the exclusive domain of the physiognomist. Appearance is quintessentially a visible, palpable, theatrical presence, a performance that can be manipulated and altered to suit a myriad motives and themes.

Mechanisms of Evasion, Perils of Resemblance

About 'Othello's Identity,' Jyotsna Singh observes that 'we cannot really "speak of [Othello as he is]", for his "otherness" as a black man cannot be contained within the dominant, Western fantasy of a singular, unified identity'. Consequently, Singh points out, Othello does not have access to his own identity since it is configured through European colonial discourses (1994: 287). But the connotations of Caesar reverberate perhaps more powerfully than 'Othello' even as the oxymoron 'royal slave' takes shape – making Oroonoko somewhat more vulnerable than his predecessor to a flauntingly arbitrary system of naming and hierarchization.

Ascribed in the image of his predecessor, Oroonoko too is made to accommodate contradictory roles (Singh 1994: 288). His body is both adorned and unadorned; his body is frail and strong; he is both slavish and noble. Oroonoko claims that 'honest black / Disdains to change its color' and almost in the same breath he says he is ready to be led: 'Where must I go? Dispose me as you please' (Ferriar 1788: 8; slightly different version in Southerne, 119). Imperious one moment, submissive the next, this tragic hero dances schizophrenically to different white-hued tunes. Or, more to the point, this tragic hero's agency and simultaneous lack of it remain locked in the performance of an emancipatory aesthetic that must, willy-nilly, confront and accommodate the realism that is its premise, the realism that engenders the emancipationist's cause.

In Behn's colonial fantasy, Oroonoko first kills Imoinda because he cannot think of leaving 'his lovely Imoinda a prey, or at best a slave, to the enraged multitude' (1992: 135). Behn does not witness this episode, which is related to her by Oroonoko after the fact. In 'their notion', Behn explains as a preface to this killing, 'wives have a respect for their husbands equal to what any other people pay a deity, and when a man finds any occasion to quit his wife, if he love her, she dies by his hand' (1992: 135–6). Behn's otherworldly portrait of marital bliss in *Oroonoko*, etched elaborately in the scene of Imoinda's death, is produced by the author's unblinking gaze at the agent of death: Oroonoko 'with a hand resolved, and a heart breaking within, gave the fatal stroke, first, cutting her throat, and then severing her, yet smiling, face from that delicate body, pregnant as it was with fruits of tenderest love. As soon as he had done, he laid the body decently on leaves and flowers.... But when he found she was dead, and past all retrieve, never more to bless him with her eyes...his grief swelled up to rage; he tore, he raved, he roared, like some monster of the wood, calling on the loved name of Imoinda' (1992: 136). The author chooses what to witness.

Behn does not witness Oroonoko's death either, leaving this gruesome sight to her mother and sister (1992: 140) – her closest female relatives, their eyes gazing at her dying hero. This ceremonial death was supervised by one from beyond another border: Banister, 'a wild Irishman...a fellow of absolute barbarity, and fit to execute any villainy, but was rich' (1992: 139–40). The Irishman whipped Oroonoko, tied him to a post, and fit a big fire into which the executioner and others threw chopped parts of his body. 'They' hacked off his arms and cut him into quarters that were then sent to different plantations (1992: 140). The author does not witness the 'frightful spectacles of a mangled king' (ibid.). Behn hopes, in the concluding line of her 'true history' that her 'pen is considerable enough to make his glorious name to survive to all ages' (ibid.). The authorial refusal to witness the deaths – a deliberate 'distancing', an unconscious denial – coalesces with an authorial refusal to superimpose a moral perspective on the brutality of the ending, or indeed on the brutality of slavery. Southerne remains true to Behn's preference for a 'romance of empire', which is his main plot, while creating a subplot whose grotesque rendition of life on the plantation seeks to provide a sharply contrasting background to the grandeur of the tragedy and the trials and tribulations of a larger-than-life hero.

John Ferriar, however, was not concerned with Behn's distancing or historicizing technique and the resultant myopia in the novella version; his focus was on the earlier *dramatizations* and the disjunction in them between image and message: 'Although the incidents appeared even to invite sentiments adverse to slavery, yet Southern, not contented with refusing them, delivered by the medium of the Hero, a grovelling apology for slave-holders, which Hawkesworth has retained.' The 'material changes' that Ferriar made were designed to manipulate not so much the image (of slavery) nor the sentiments (adverse to slavery) but the effect on the spectator. Southerne had catered to the 'gross and depraved audience of that time' (ii), while Ferriar envisaged addressing a different audience almost a century later – an audience, he believed, that was ready and willing to accommodate the twin forces of spectacularity and morality. In retrospect, Ferriar's revisionary vision/version, despite his intentions, is neither radical nor that different because although he changed much of the 'form' of the play, he did not do much to change the 'substance' of it. Oroonoko and the white-washed Imoinda of Southerne's creation retain centre stage. With fewer words and a less ambiguous friend in Blandford, they are the focus of Ferriar's radical act. Trapped within the walls of the originary performance, Ferriar's challenge to the establishment comes in the form of didactic passages and, despite his sincere commitment to the cause, the shift from a romantic illusion of the noble savage to a realistic, hard-headed look at the cause of the tragic ending of the noble savage – this shift – only helps to reify the quondam hero, the image of the noble savage and his troubling legacy.

A brief glance at the endings of the two versions helps to clarify my criticism of Ferriar. Southerne's concluding scene is very long-winded, sentimental and full of pathos, compared to the one that Ferriar wrote. But notice that Behn's villains (the Irishman, for instance) are strategically effaced in Southerne's version after one clear reference to the governor as being the villain (172). Immediately following, the specific identification of the forces of evil, or at least one source of it, is generalized, as Oroonoko laments 'Villain's the common name of Mankind here' (ibid.). There is a systemic failure that is linked to the 'here' or Surinam. Thereafter, Imoinda talks about 'Heav'n and Earth our Foes!' and Oroonoko refers to 'the great . . . angry Pow'rs' (173), to 'those stars, which are my Enemies' (175). The target is not only defused but destroyed; the villain becomes an abstract, wrathful force that occasionally assumes plurality in references to 'these cruel Men' (174), but most often they remain 'Enemies' – formless, faceless and thus beyond reproach. The lengthier laments of the lovers are sentimental outpourings: 'I submit my self / To their high pleasure, and devoted Bow / Yet lower, to continue still a Slave' (174). The tragic hero is hopelessly entangled in an emotional outburst provoked by a chimerical source of evil that is made to recede further and further into the background as the concluding scene winds tediously towards the bloody end. Death is put off repeatedly for '*He drops his Dagger as he looks on her, and throws himself on the Ground*' or because '*She takes up the Dagger, he rises in haste to take it from her*'. These parenthetical stage directions punctuate the final farewell, after which Imoinda '*Stabs herself*' (177–8). It is this emphasis on 'passion' and, consequently, the popularity of the play among the female members of the audience that made Southerne's *Oroonoko* a success in its initial run and became, subsequently, one of the most frequently performed plays on the eighteenth-century stage. Robert Jordan and Harold Love remind us that 'it is the power of the work over the passions that became dominant in the critical comments that proliferated at mid [eighteenth] century'. The appropriation of the play towards the end of the eighteenth century by anti-slavery activists represents, according to Jordan and Love, a 'distorted view of the work'. 'It is likely that at the time of writing it Southerne was already cultivating one of the richest slaveowners in the West Indies, Christopher Codring-ton, a potential patron', Jordan and Love concede, but 'there is no contradiction between such an act and his authorship of *Oroonoko*, for the play's concern is not primarily with the tragedy of slavery but with the tragedy of the noble prince enslaved' (Jordan and Love 1988: 95). Jordan and Love's interpretive strategy maintains the distinction that Southerne and the other playwrights wished to make. The individual slave is separate from the larger category of the slaves. I would argue that Oroonoko's passion (as a lover, as an exiled prince, as one who gives up *his* empire) is precisely the act of evasion – a simulation of passion – that, in retrospect, implicates the tragedy of slavery in the tragedy of the noble prince enslaved.

Consistent with his propagandist agenda, Ferriar streamlines the ending and provides a target of attack: 'There is no hope of mercy from these Christians', Oroonoko concludes (1788: 50) and Imoinda agrees, recalling the 'wild passions of the governor' (1788: 51) from whose sexual aggression Blandford protects her. In Southerne's version, Imoinda stabs herself; Oroonoko cannot go the distance. In Ferriar's version – designed to weed out the passion, the endless ending – he stabs her. In a provocative outburst just before Imoinda's death, Ferriar's Oroonoko expresses revulsion at the thought of killing Imoinda thus:

> Must I deface this idol of my heart?
> . . .
> No! Come destroyers of my wretched race,
> Come with your fires, your steel, and every engine
> Your savage industry has form'd to pain:
> Let me feel all, so Imoinda live.
>
> (1788: 51)

Oroonoko positions himself as a racial Other while the emblems of industrial development (the connection between the rise of industry and commerce and slavery) are presented as the instruments of death. A straightforward indictment of slavery is predictably voiced by Blandford, who, from the very beginning, is the conscience-keeper, the voice of authorial ideology. The last lines of the play are thus given to him:

> A desp'rate deed, and fatally achiev'd
> But you [To Stanmore, &] who mutely eye
>   this scene of horror,
> Curse not the erring arm – the guilt is ours;
> For deed like these are slav'ry's fruit; the chain
> Any bloody whip bring punishment upon us.
>
> (1788: 52)

As a character, Blandford is deadly dull; and the overall tone of Ferriar's ending is deadeningly didactic.

Unsurprisingly, neither Blandford nor Ferriar was able to communicate the anti-slavery message to an audience: there is no record of a performance of Ferriar's play. Indeed, towards the end of the century there seems to have been a direct correlation between the play's topicality and its lack of popularity. The injection of anti-slavery propaganda into the play led to its prohibition in the slave-trading port of Liverpool (Jordan and Love 1988: 95–6) – an insignificant footnote in theatre history but a significant record of achievement, nonetheless, for dissidence. However, stripped of his romantic aura and placed on an ethical bully pulpit, the hero loses his lustre. In performance, the appropriation of Behn's vision has varying results depending on the degrees of reliance upon the 'spirit' of her colonial engagement. Behn's distancing technique is part and parcel of her perception of a hazy, hot, surreal and romantic haven in distant Surinam. This perception – this authorial lens – is borrowed by and remains the basis for Southerne's version, which is hugely successful; and her 'slavish' attraction for Oroonoko paves the way for Ferriar's entrapment, his naive hopes for the theatre's ability to transform and liberate, his dreams of a free slave.

In an astute analysis of the modern American novel, Toni Morrison describes the phenomenon of 'romancing the shadow' and points to issues that are central to my argument here. She rejects the simplistic formulation 'that romance is an evasion of history (and thus perhaps attractive to a people trying to evade the recent past)'. Instead, she is 'more persuaded by arguments that find in it the head-on encounter with very real, pressing historical forces and the contradictions inherent in them as they came to be experienced by writers. Romance, an exploration of anxiety imported from the shadows of European culture, made possible the sometimes safe and other times risky embrace of quite specific, understandably human, fears.... Romance offers writers not less but more; not a narrow a-historical canvas but a wide historical one; not escape but entanglement' (Morrison 1992: 36–7). The celebrated passion of Oroonoko is very much akin to the 'nature as subject matter, a system of symbolism, a thematics of the search for self-valorization and validation' that the modern American writers wrote about and that Morrison comments on (Morrison 1992: 37). Oroonoko's passion – captured so effectively in Southerne's diction and style, which were also praised by his contemporaries – is the passion of an unrestrained, prelapsarian being in the state of nature. Behn's originary vision of colonial contact, however romanticized and however historicized, particularly due to her distancing and evasive tactics, is the 'very head-on encounter with real, historical forces' that Morrison talks about. And it is the imaginative rendition of this encounter – vividly expressed through sights, sounds, smells, textures, tones and shades of 'natural' attraction and repulsion – that invites the ritualistic persistence with which her story is repeatedly recuperated in performance.

In performance – the medium in which Behn's 'history' was ritualized in the eighteenth century – the message that tends to get conveyed is often the message that the spectator wants to receive. If the marketability of any product depends upon the extent to which the producer is able to *accommodate* the demand of the consumer, the producer – or the playwright, the director, the visionary, the political activist – has very little autonomy or power to affect change. Ferriar's failure was directly linked to his ethno-political stand that stood in sharp contrast to the bourgeois sensibilities that guided and motivated theatrical production and colonial discourse. In his masterful analysis of the relationship between reality and simulation or lack of it, Jean Baudrillard contemplates the complex nature of 'the double' thus:

Of all the prosthesis that mark the history of the body, the double is doubtless the oldest. But the double is precisely not a prosthesis: it is an imaginary figure, which ... haunts the subject like his other, which makes it so that the subject is simultaneously itself and never resembles itself again, which haunts the subject like a subtle and always averted death. This is not always the case, however; when the double materializes, when it becomes visible, it signifies imminent death. (1994: 95)

The double that Ferriar wished to create – the Prince of Angola – never really resembled anything or anyone and 'its' death was a foregone conclusion because its function was so anachronistic and therefore not sustainable. There was never a 'real' Oroonoko, but there was a real narrative. Failing to accommodate the evasive tactics of his predecessors, Ferriar more than any one else before him exposes the narrative's (Behn's, Southerne's, Hawkesworth's) head-on encounter with reality, its marketing strategies, the mechanisms of its demand and supply, the inflexibility of its packaging principle, and ultimately the reasons for its success.

NOTE

I would like to thank Bucknell University Press for giving me permission to reprint here part of the epilogue from my book, *Interculturalism and Resistance in the London Theater, 1600–1800: Identity, Performance, Empire* (2000).

REFERENCES AND FURTHER READING

Banta, Martha (1998). 'Primal Needs, Primary Concerns', *PMLA* 113, no. 1 (January), 7–18.

Baudrillard, Jean (1994). *Simulacra and Simulation*, trans. Sheila Faria Glaser. Ann Arbor: University of Michigan Press.

Behn, Aphra (1992). *Oroonoko*, in *The Rover and Other Works*, ed. Janet Todd. New York: Penguin.

Bohls, Elizabeth (1994). 'Standards of Taste, Discourses of "Race", and the Aesthetic Education of a Monster: Critique of Empire in *Frankenstein*', *Eighteenth-century Life* 18, no. 3 (November), 23–36.

Canfield, J. Douglas and Payne, Deborah (1995). *Cultural Readings of Restoration and Eighteenth Century Theater*. Athens: University of Georgia Press.

Canfield, Robert Alan (2001). 'Something's Mitzen: Anne Bonny, Mary Reed, *Polly* and Female Counter Roles on the Imperialist Stage', *South Atlantic Review* 66, no. 2 (Spring), 45–63.

Felperin, Howard (1991). '"Cultural Poetics" Versus "Cultural Materialism": The Two New Historicisms in Renaissance Studies', in Francis Barker, Peter Hulme and Margaret Iversen (eds), *Uses of History: Marxism, Postmodernism and the Renaissance*. Manchester: Manchester University Press, 76–100.

Ferriar, John (1788). *The Prince of Angola*. Manchester: J. Harrop.

Flavell, Kay (1994). 'Mapping Faces: National Physiognomies as Cultural Prediction', *Eighteenth-century Life* 18, no. 3 (November), 8–22.

Gilman, Sander L. (1998). 'Ethnicity–Ethnicities–Literatures', *PMLA* 113, no. 1 (January), 19–27.

Gölz, Sabine I. (1998). 'How Ethnic Am I?', *PMLA* 113, no. 1 (January), 46–51.

Holderness, Graham (1991). 'Production, Reproduction, Performance: Marxism, History, Theatre', in Francis Barker, Peter Hulme and Margaret Iversen (eds), *Uses of History: Marxism, Postmodernism and the Renaissance*. Manchester: Manchester University Press, 153–77.

Jordan, Robert and Love, Harold (eds). 1988. *The Works of Thomas Southerne*. 2 vols. Oxford: Clarendon Press.

Kaplan, Cora (2000). 'Millenial Class', PMLA 115, no. 1 (January), 9–19.

Kaul, Suvir (1994). 'Reading Literary Symptoms: Colonial Pathologies and the Oroonoko Fictions of Behn, Southerne, and Hawkesworth', *Eighteenth-century Life* 18, no. 3 (November), 80–96.

Morrison, Toni (1992). *Playing in the Dark: Whiteness and the Literary Imagination*. New York: Vintage Books.

Nussbaum, Felicity and Brown, Laura (eds). (1987). *The New Eighteenth Century: Theory, Politics, English Literature*. New York: Methuen.

Pagden, Anthony (1995). 'The Effacement of Difference: Colonialism and the Origins of Nationalism in Diderot and Herder', in Gyan Prakash (ed.), *After Colonialism: Imperial Histories and Postcolonial Displacements*. New Jersey: Princeton University Press.

Roach, Joseph (1996). *Cities of the Dead: Circum-Atlantic Performance*. New York: Columbia University Press.

Singh, Jyotsna (1994). 'Othello's Identity, Postcolonial Theory and Contemporary African Rewritings of *Othello*', in Margo Hendricks and Patricia Parker (eds), *Women, Race, and Writing in the Early-Modern Period*. New York: Routledge, 287–99.

11

Restoration Drama after the Restoration: The Critics, the Repertory and the Canon

Brian Corman

By 1710, most of the important writers of Restoration drama had either died or stopped writing for the stage. (The most notable exceptions are Centlivre, Cibber, Rowe and Steele.) So had most of the critics who had first written about that drama. In a mere four years, the last Stuart monarch, Queen Anne, died, and the throne was inherited by her Hanoverian cousin, George I, a non-English speaker with little interest in the theatre. The theatres had grown progressively larger in the fifty years since the Restoration, acting styles had changed with a new generation of actors, audiences continued to grow and diversify; it is hardly surprising that the plays, too, changed with the times. It is important to remember that art forms and the critical responses to them are no more static than other social or political institutions, a point too often overlooked by those who wish to make sweeping generalizations about the theatre of the Restoration and eighteenth century. By 1800, Restoration drama was for the most part gone and forgotten. A core of plays was still in print; very few were still performed. How Restoration drama reached this state of neglect, and the gradual renewal of interest that developed in the twentieth century, is the subject of this chapter. The reception history of Restoration drama, like that of any performance art, must be measured with reference both to its place in the judgements of critics and to its place in what we now call the canon and the performance repertory. A canon is usually formed through the evaluation of literary critics, the decision of publishers to print or reprint, and, more recently, by the place of the work in question in university curricula. The repertory is measured mainly by frequency of performance and augmented by responses to those performances by theatre critics. The relationship between canon and repertory is symbiotic: successful performance stimulates interest from literary critics and publishers, and a high profile in the canon challenges actors and directors to bring texts to life on stage. Before looking specifically at the canon and the repertory, I shall begin with the criticism.

Critical History

Collier and the reform movements of the 1690s set the tone and agenda for much of the critical debate for the next 250 years. The Restoration debate about the proper way for a play to achieve its moral function had shifted to a debate about whether or not a play in fact met the moral standards of English society. The reformers failed to close a theatre that they considered immoral, but they succeeded brilliantly in establishing the dominant methodology for critics over the next many generations. For example, the traditional, Aristotelian–Jonsonian view that comedy imitates characters worse than we are in order to provide us with negative examples was rejected in favour of the more Platonic–Christian view that comedy should provide clear role models whose characters embody unequivocally the moral standards of the audience, that is, the prevailing standards of eighteenth-century Britain.

The new moral standards informed a range of issues and responses. Some of Collier's most intense righteous anger was fuelled by the presence of swearing (taking God's name in vain) and at representations of the clergy in a less than flattering light. And in issues of this sort, his success was both quick and lasting. But cleaning up the language and removing comical clergymen did not resolve the fundamental objections of the Collierites. What are the appropriate qualities to expect from heroes and heroines on stage? How much deviation from the ideal is to be tolerated? That is, are monarchs to be seen allowing their personal desires to subvert their political judgement? Can a heroine be allowed independence from patriarchal authority? Is she to reveal any indication of sexual desire? What is the appropriate language for comedy? For tragedy? And, increasingly, how bound should playwrights be by notions of poetic justice, the artistic imitation of the working of God's providence, to meet the moralists' demands that good people be rewarded and bad people punished on stage?

These basic issues, the objects of representation, the language of that representation, the formal requirements of that representation, and the pleasure and instruction that should result, of course, are the issues that have intrigued critics since Aristotle. The terms of their discussion and the answers they propose continue to change, as they have done over the past 200 years. Collier's answers remained on the critical agenda for some time to come, but while Collier was responding to the dominant plays of his own time, subsequent critics soon thereafter were responding to the plays of a rapidly receding past. It became increasingly difficult, in other words, to see Restoration plays as active threats to the political or moral well-being of the nation. And with the rise of historicist criticism in the later eighteenth century, they could also be safely distanced as the products of a distinctly different age.

Distance did not soften the hostility of every critic. William Popple, Francis Gentleman and Edmund Burke are examples of critics who remain unequivocally opposed to Restoration drama on moral principle. Nor did the growth of bardolatry help the cause of Restoration dramatists. As Shakespeare became the national poet, his faults were increasingly ignored or denied, but the same generosity of spirit did not extend to other writers. It was as if Shakespeare's superiority required the denial of merit in the competition. Still the best critics realized that the issues were far more complex than these simple solutions suggest, and that the grey areas were far more numerous and far more interesting than those that could be reduced to black and white. The best critic provides the best example. Samuel Johnson asked the same critical questions and applied the same critical standards to Shakespeare that he later applied to the dramatists of the Restoration. In his 'Preface' to his edition of Shakespeare, Johnson writes that

> his first defect is that to which may be imputed most of the evils in books or men. He sacrifices virtue to convenience, and is so much more careful to please than to instruct that he seems to write without any moral purpose. (*Works* 7: 71)

It is hardly surprising, then, that the critic who could question Shakespeare's moral purpose would have similar doubts about the dramatists of the Restoration. But Johnson is also interested in the merits of this drama (as he is in Shakespeare's), merit demonstrated by the ongoing approval it receives from the public. Any play that has survived a hundred years of scrutiny has, for Johnson, passed the test of time, or, in our terms, has entered the canon. The critic's job, in dealing with canonical texts, is, in part, to explain the source of their staying power.

When Johnson turns to the plays of the Restoration, his evaluations take into account the complexities of all the critical issues he identifies. *Venice Preserv'd*, Otway's

> last and greatest dramatick work...still continues to be one of the favourites of the public, notwithstanding the want of morality in the original design, and the despicable scenes of vile comedy with which he has diversified his tragick action.... The striking passages are in every mouth; and the public seems to judge rightly of the faults and excellencies of this play, that is the work of a man not attentive to decency nor jealous for virtue; but one who conceived forcibly and drew originally by consulting nature in his own breast. (*Lives* 1: 245)

When he turns his attention to the comedies of Congreve, Johnson strikes the same balance. He makes no attempt to downplay their deficiencies, declaring, 'The general tenour and tendency of his plays must always be condemned' (*Lives* 2: 222). But like Otway, Congreve has remained a great favourite for a long time and Johnson, though somewhat grudgingly, identifies the causes:

> Congreve has merit of the highest kind; he is an original writer, who borrowed neither the models of his plot, nor the manner of his dialogue.... His characters are commonly fictitious and artificial, with very little of nature and not much of life. He formed a peculiar idea of comic excellence, which he supposed to consist in gay remarks and unexpected answers; but that which he endeavoured, he seldom failed of performing. His scenes exhibit not much of humour, imagery, or passion: his personages are a kind of intellectual gladiators; every sentence is to ward or strike; the contest of smartness is

never intermitted; his wit is a meteor playing to and fro with alternate coruscations. (*Lives* 2: 228)

Both the natural Otway and the artificial Congreve, writers of genuine merit, are nonetheless found morally deficient, a 'fault' no more to be excused by the 'want of morals, or of decency' (*Lives* 1: 243) of late Stuart England than the 'barbarity' of Shakespeare's 'age' excused it in him. Congreve wrote at a time when 'irreligion and licentiousness' were 'taught at the public charge'. Johnson will not allow the relativism of historicist argument on so crucial an issue: 'it is always a writer's duty to make the world better, and justice is a virtue independent of time or place'.

Moral objection to Restoration drama remained strong in the eighteenth century. A central concern to even the enlightened and judicious Samuel Johnson, it was a much cruder measure in the hands of lesser critics. It is not surprising, then, that the critical reputation of these plays was at best mixed, and that little effort was made to reassess the value of plays that, over time, had fallen from the canon or the repertory. But with Johnson, the full range of critical issues that has informed debate and discussion ever since is in play: the basic dialectical relationship between pleasure and instruction; the relationship of the plays to the society that produced them and its relevance to pleasure and instruction; the plays as belated and inferior to those of Shakespeare; and the relationship between performance and critical evaluation or appreciation of the plays as works of dramatic art. None of these issues, of course, begins with Johnson, but it is in his criticism that they are formulated as complex issues without simple, reductive or dogmatic solutions, that is, with Johnson, the questions are formulated and the terms set for the critical debates that have followed.

Where Johnson differs from most of the critics who followed him (or, for that matter, preceded him) is in his ability to contemplate both the moral and the aesthetic dimensions of Restoration drama. He is no special friend of the plays, but neither is it his goal to ban or suppress them. Supporters of Restoration comedy in the next several generations built their case on one of Johnson's negative assessments of Congreve's characters, that they are 'fictitious and artificial'. That very artificiality formed the basis of Charles Lamb's famous defence of Restoration comedy from the ongoing attacks of the moralists:

> I feel the better always for the perusal of one of Congreve's greatest comedies. . . . They are a world of themselves almost as much as fairyland. . . . The Fainalls and the Mirabels, the Dorimants and the Lady Touchwoods, in their own sphere, do not offend my moral sense; in fact they do not appeal to it at all. . . . They have got out of Christendom into the land – what shall I call it? – of cuckoldry – the Utopia of gallantry, where pleasure is duty, and the manners perfect freedom. (1935: 127)

By emphasizing the artificiality of Restoration comedy, Lamb is able to remove it from moral consideration; for him, the comedies exist in a world so totally distant from ours that moral questions simply do not apply. His approach gained momentum from the support of other major Romantic critics like Hazlitt and Leigh Hunt until Hunt's polemical 1849 edition of *The Dramatic Works of Wycherley, Congreve, Vanbrugh and Farquhar*, complete with reprinted essays by Hazlitt and Hunt, received the devastating review from Macaulay that undid all the work previous generations had done to make Restoration drama respectable again. Macaulay's objection was to the assessment of the plays as artificial. He insisted that they quite effectively mirrored the society of their time, a society that was fundamentally corrupt and immoral. As such, they could not be excused as amoral but must be condemned as immoral. And Macaulay's view carried the Victorian day.

It was not until the turn of the new century, under the influence of the 'art for art's sake' criticism of the aesthetes and decadents of the time, that another serious challenge was mounted against the hegemonic authority of the moralist critics. Probably the central text in this new campaign was John Palmer's *The Comedy of Manners* (1913). Palmer challenged Macaulay not for his assertion that 'the comic plays of the Restoration were a reflexion of the morals and manners of the Restoration' (1913: 18), but for the conclusions he drew from that assertion. For Palmer, 'the excellence of Restoration comedy is, in fact, directly due to the honest fidelity with which it reflects the spirit of an intensely interesting phase of our social history' (1913: 22). For all his acknowledgement of the wit of the comedy and of the need to recognize it as the product of a particular moment in English history, Macaulay insists on judging – and condemning – the comedies on their deviance from 'the standards of 1849' (1913: 24). In response, Palmer urges that the plays be enjoyed for their adherence to and reflection of a very different time. The pleasure they offer is limited by the narrowness of its source; here the measure is, of course, Shakespeare, who is never limited by time or place. But it is nonetheless a legitimate pleasure, and one which will not corrupt the morals of an early twentieth-century audience.

Palmer's approach was followed and developed by many others, critics like Henry Ten Eyck Perry, Kathleen Lynch and Bonamy Dobrée. The arguments of the 'manners' critics were even to appear in works such as Joseph Wood Krutch's *Comedy and Conscience after the Restoration* (1949), a work which explains – quite sympathetically – the context for the triumph of Jeremy Collier. Krutch follows Palmer, against Collier and most of the other moralists, including Johnson, in blaming the lapses in the comedy on the times:

> As immoral as it was brilliant. . . . The credit for the brilliance of the plays of the time of Charles and William belongs largely to the genius of the writers. The perversity of their tone must be charged to the spirit of the age. (1949: 1, 13)

If a critic like Krutch, one with strong moral principles, could accept the central premises of the 'manners' critics and refuse to blame the writers for capturing accurately the spirit of the age, what was an old-style moralist to do? L. C. Knights's response was to reject the 'manners' premise, and instead return to the argument of Lamb, but to a very different end. He argues that it is the non-dramatic prose writers of the Restoration who best capture the full spirit of the age: the dramatists, writing merely for the aristocratic members of their society, produced an account of it so limited and non-representative as to warrant Lamb's 'artificial'. (His other comparative measure is the far more representative drama of the early seventeenth century, most notably, of course, Shakespeare.) Knights then claims – disingenuously, I would argue – that the problem with this artificial drama is not that it is immoral, but that it is 'trivial, gross, and dull' (1946: 149). To be as uninteresting and irrelevant as Knights finds all of Restoration drama is to minimize its moral impact – it can hardly be the threat to public well-being that Collier found it – but it hardly removes the plays from the realm of moral discourse where Knights in fact finds them wanting.

Most critics in the second half of the twentieth century rejected the readings of both the 'manners' critics and the latest versions of moralists. A critic like Palmer attempted to evade moral condemnation of the plays by fixing them in a remote time, making them powerless to infect us because of their very otherness. Some critics of the 1950s and 1960s found themselves defending the plays because the problems they address are the very same ones we still face. For Norman Holland, the plays of Etherege, Wycherley and Congreve have 'real intellectual substance'; moreover, 'that substance comes surprisingly close to our twentieth-century world view' (1959: 8). Holland's argument, in short, is that these are 'the first modern comedies', and that they thus have a special significance for us that repays attention. As it became increasingly difficult for Restoration drama to shock or outrage its late twentieth-century audiences, it became easier to return to its cultural origins in the intellectual and social issues of the late seventeenth century. Particularly influential were Dale Underwood's study of libertine philosophy as a guide to understanding the serious questions embodied in the plays, and John Harrington Smith's and Thomas H. Fujimura's analyses of social and sexual mores that must be understood to make sense of the comedies. For the first time in their critical history, the need to attack or defend the plays because of their putative threat to the audience no longer determined the debate. Many of the critics continued to address questions of morality, but only after considering a wide range of relevant issues. The results were most often supportive of Holland's thesis: the plays deserve renewed attention because they address issues of importance to us today.

The critics who were demonstrating the relevance of Restoration drama were writing at a time when academic criticism was dominated by formal and structural approaches to literature. Those approaches had less impact on drama studies in general, and Restoration drama studies in particular, than they had on most other literary genres. But the critical climate that was favourable to a more nuanced understanding of the culture of the Restoration also fostered diachronic study of the plays: it was no longer necessary to keep them under critical quarantine. Restoration playwrights were well aware of the fact that they were not the first to write for the stage, and twentieth-century critics were again free to place their works in a tradition that did not begin in 1660 – or end in 1710. One result was the renewed opportunity to declare the superiority of Shakespeare. But more interesting questions also emerged as critics like Northrop Frye placed the plays in his transhistorical theory of all literature. Frye is able to subordinate the moral questions to the structural because of 'the principle that dramatic structure is a permanent and moral attitude a variable factor in literature' (1957: 176). He is thus able to cite Congreve's *Love for Love* as an exemplary comedy for its representation of the 'comic Oedipus situation in which the hero replaces his father as a lover'. Such timeless, mythic qualities explain 'the occasional "naughtiness"' of the comedy as much as its explicit treatment of 'marital infidelity'. Similarly,

> a theme which would be recognized in real life as a form of infantile regression, the hero pretending to be impotent in order to gain admission to the women's quarters, is employed in Wycherley's *Country Wife*, where it is taken from Terence's *Eunuchus*. (1957: 180–1)

The 1960s also brought the appearance of *The London Stage* with its calendar of daily performances throughout the period. The sheer diversity of activity in the theatres uncovered by the editors was the major impetus for a reconsideration of the history of the drama. The editors themselves, William Van Lennep, Emmett L. Avery and Arthur H. Scouten, and those who have profited from their efforts – and their lessons – such as Robert D. Hume, Richard Bevis, Derek Hughes, Frances M. Kavenik and the author of this essay, have attempted to rewrite the history of the drama to include plays frequently ignored by earlier critics. The data collected by the editors of *The London Stage* called for new, better-informed, histories, histories facilitated considerably by no longer having to be organized around a response, usually defensive, to the moralist attack. And they have profited, too, from the case for the relevance of the plays to our time, a case that has diminished the need for the other recurring apology – for being inferior to Shakespeare.

The generation of critics who promoted Restoration drama as 'modern' saw its relevance in shared social, political and cultural concerns, but they saw no need or reason to break down the difference between the late seventeenth century and the late twentieth. The otherness of Restoration drama was not at issue. Since the feminist critics of the 1970s, however, that otherness, too, has come under critical scrutiny. Poststructuralist theory and the new historicism and political and cultural criticism it has fostered start with very different assumptions about the relationship between past and present. When a play is part of its context and that context is a retrospective construct, the relationship between past and present becomes relative, contingent and unstable. If the past is a construct of our own making, we must become more self-conscious and self-reflexive about our designs on those constructs. (The same principles, of course, can apply to the criticism of Restoration drama, as Simon Shepherd has demonstrated in a 1996 survey.) But since the result will, in any event, be a construct of our own making, we are free to (or have no choice but to) create that construct in our own image. For recent critics, that image is most often political with a focus on power relations especially as they are manifested around issues of gender, race and class. And at this point, the criticism has once again come full circle with the appearance of a new group of moralists who can justify the relevance of a Restoration play only by its contribution to a political agenda for our time. The goal of this criticism is to replace ideologically conservative readings with those written to achieve desired political ends. The analytical methods and the ideological ends are very much of the twenty-first century, but Jeremy Collier could well feel at home with the programme and its advocates.

Repertory

Collier and the moral reformers also set the terms for the evolving canon and repertory after the Restoration. The most immediate response, both from playwrights and actors, was to remove offensive language and satiric portrayals of the clergy. Congreve himself purged his plays of most of the swearing in the original editions when he edited them for the *Works* of 1710. And Vanbrugh rewrote the scene in *The Provok'd Wife* (1697; revised 1706) where the drunken Sir John Brute blasphemes in a stolen clergyman's gown; the revision substitutes a purloined gown of his wife's. When the playwrights themselves were unavailable to make these required, if cosmetic, changes, the actors made the changes for them. Failure to do so could – and did – result in fines, closures and even imprisonments. The threat of legal and criminal action was usually sufficient to force the acting companies to police themselves. And self-censorship by playwrights and actors alike proved the most effective, ongoing method for enforcing what would today be called community standards. Few plays that were to hold the stage remained untouched. *Venice Preserv'd*, one of the most popular and highly regarded tragedies throughout the eighteenth century, was performed without its 'Nicky–Nacky' scenes early in the new century. Those scenes, with their explicit representation of sado-masochistic sexuality, remained unacceptable for stage performance until the revivals of the early twentieth century. More severe treatment was the fate of most other plays written during the reign of Charles II, both in the study and on stage, though the most common form taken by their diminishing fortunes was neglect.

One of the most fruitful distinctions to emerge from the increased attention to Restoration drama since the appearance of *The London Stage* is that between the plays of the Carolean period (1660–85) and those of the following twenty-five years (for which no equivalent name yet exists). It is important to recognize the differences as well as the similarities in the plays of the fifty years between 1660 and 1710; those differences are detailed in many of the essays in this volume. They were also apparent to the early audiences of Restoration drama, and they inform much of its reception history, though that history varies significantly by dramatic genre.

Tragedy was consistently the most respected of the genres, but comedy was always the most popular. And it is with comedy that the generational contrast is especially noteworthy. The most popular Carolean comic writers, Behn, Dryden, Etherege,

Howard, Shadwell, Tuke and Wycherley, were unable to hold the stage within a few years of the death of Charles II. Whether it was because of changing aesthetic or cultural or performance values – and it was almost certainly all three – eighteenth-century audiences did not support performances of most Carolean comedies; the result was their exclusion from the repertory. This is in stunning contrast to the next generation of playwrights, Centlivre, Cibber, Congreve, Farquhar, Steele and Vanbrugh, who dominated the repertory for most of the eighteenth century, despite the opposition – pointedly strong opposition in the cases of Congreve and Vanbrugh – of Collier and the moralists. Even granting that cosmetic changes were made to their plays, the success of their comedies is remarkable. As Shirley Strum Kenny has noted, 'with the exception of Shakespeare, no group of plays then or now can compare with such virile longevity' (1976: S7).

Tragedy had a very different reception history, with far fewer tragedies entering the repertory. Those from the first fifteen years following the Restoration had short lives as performance pieces, but with the appearance of Otway, Lee and Banks in the mid-1670s, a new kind of tragedy, one quickly embraced by Dryden, became the model for the tragedies that were able to remain repertory pieces for at least the next hundred years. Shakespeare's tragedies increasingly dominated the stage, but those of Otway, Lee and Rowe were to tragedy what the post-Carolean playwrights mentioned above were to comedy. The other genres had different histories again, but in almost every case, Carolean favourites did not remain on the eighteenth-century stage. Nowhere is this more evident than in the case of the heroic play, enormously popular in the 1670s but unable to hold its popularity to the end of the reign of Charles II. Even the best of the heroic plays, Dryden's, lost their appeal to audiences very quickly. The other major dramatic form, split-plot tragicomedy, had nearly but not quite as short a life after the Restoration. Few tragicomedies were written after 1685; *Oroonoko* is the only noteworthy exception. And very few were performed in the eighteenth century. The reason is probably tied to the fate of the heroic play as the best of the tragicomedies, again Dryden's, combine a heroic plot with a comic plot. The comic plots were always the favourites, and a number of them were extracted from their full texts in order to keep them viable as stage pieces. Colley Cibber's *The Comical Lovers* (1707), an amalgam of the comic plots of two of Dryden's tragicomedies, *Secret Love* and *Marriage A-la-Mode*, provides a particularly interesting early example.

Just as Restoration playwrights looked back to the plays of the early seventeenth century for material to adapt or recycle, so their eighteenth-century counterparts depended on them to provide plots, characters and ideas for 'new' stage pieces. This long-standing tradition of adaptation or appropriation is best known in Shakespeare studies since Shakespeare has attracted far more interest from scholars than any other writer. Adaptation was normally motivated by the opportunity to salvage good theatrical material from a text that had lost – or never had – a place in the repertory. Occasionally condemned as plagiarism, adaptation was accepted by theatre managers and audiences alike as a legitimate source of popular entertainment. Adaptations were sometimes praised as improvements on their sources: Buckingham's *The Chances* (from

Fletcher's play of the same name) and Dryden's *All for Love* (from Shakespeare's *Antony and Cleopatra*) are especially prominent Restoration examples. More common was a level of acceptance manifested in repertory status without critical acclaim. Because so few non-Shakespearean adaptations have been studied, it is easy to overlook the survival of many Restoration plays in eighteenth-century (and occasionally later) adaptations. There are dozens of these adaptations, often by major playwrights, and often with very successful stage histories. Comparison with the source text in most cases reveals detailed evidence of the particular aspects of Restoration drama that became unacceptable to later audiences. Attention to their dates of composition allows still more precise analysis of the history of theatrical values and taste. In other words, these adaptations ensured survival, but only survival of a sort. A list of prominent examples would include: Isaac Bickerstaffe's *The Plain Dealer* (1765; from Wycherley's play of the same title) and *The Capture* (1765; from Dryden's *Don Sebastian*); Hannah Cowley's *A School for Greybeards* (1786; from Behn's *The Lucky Chance*); Charles Dibdin's *Jupiter and Alcmena* (1781; from Dryden's *Amphitryon*); David Garrick's *Isabella; or The Fatal Marriage* (1757; from Southerne's *The Fatal Marriage*) and *The Country Girl* (1766; from Wycherley's *The Country Wife*); John Philip Kemble's *Love in Many Masks* (1790; from Behn's *The Rover*) and *Alexander the Great* (1795; from Lee's *The Rival Queens*); and Richard Brinsley Sheridan's *A Trip to Scarborough* (1777; from Vanbrugh's *The Relapse*). Like Tate's *King Lear* or Cibber's *Richard III*, even the best of these plays are not likely to please audiences or readers who admire their source texts, but they remain at the very least important documents in the history of Restoration drama, and like *All for Love* or Dryden and Davenant's *The Tempest*, the best of the plays have considerable interest beyond what is generated by their connection to their sources.

By the end of the eighteenth century, the performance of Restoration drama was reduced to a handful of plays, and that number further dwindled through most of the nineteenth century. The late Victorian/Edwardian renewal of critical interest in the plays and the accompanying new editions of the plays (see below) provided the climate required for stage revivals, at first by limited-audience stage societies and, gradually, by major theatre companies and university theatre groups throughout the English-speaking world.

Most of the early revivals were staged by the Mermaid Society, the Stage Society and the Phoenix Society. Each of these societies shared the prevailing views of turn-of-the-century aesthetes like Edmund Gosse and John Addington Symonds who created the interest necessary to mount even small-audience productions of plays that had not been staged for two hundred years. The tastes of their audiences were captured by the *Times* reviewer, A. B. Walkely, who enthused over the 1904 Mermaid revival of *The Way of the World* as an ideal choice for 'pleasure-seekers'. He explains:

> I say pleasure-seekers advisedly. For it is the primary business of dramatic entertainments, old and new, to entertain. A classic is a classic not because it is old, not (as Stendhal petulantly said) because it pleased our grandfathers, but because it pleases us. (1907: 304)

Walkely's call to pleasure did not instantly win over all critics. Many critics condemned the early revivals as elitist fare performed for an audience that wished to see itself as members of an aristocratic society, a society these critics saw as immoral and dull. They were not impressed by the attempt to glamorize values they found all too decadent. And theirs were the values that prevailed. The societies failed to generate a large, sustaining audience for their productions, and died out with the coming of the Great Depression.

Interest in Restoration drama, and in most cases this means interest largely in the comedies, did not, however, die with the societies. But new approaches to their performance were essential to achieve a wider commercial appeal. The breakthrough came with Nigel Playfair's series of revivals at the Lyric, Hammersmith. Playfair's productions reached a more inclusive audience by removing the offensiveness many viewers had found in the earlier productions, and by emphasizing the genial, good-natured, farcical and unthreatening qualities of the plays, all in a highly artificial, stylized presentation that reinforced a safe distance between audience and stage. Playfair's success, along with Allan Wade's at the Everyman theatre in Hampstead, paved the way from suburban triumphs to still more impressive triumphs in the West End, New York and beyond.

Productions of Restoration comedy, though never frequent, have remained constant since Playfair. His artificial style dominated subsequent productions until the 1960s when a more realistic style was introduced, one that allowed those productions to emphasize the aspects of the plays that had until then been neglected, that is, the social, moral and cultural issues that continue to provide the greatest appeal to readers, critics and directors today. The new production styles also allowed for an emphasis on the darker, more satiric aspects of the plays. The breakthrough event for this more engaged approach was William Gaskill's 1963 National Theatre production of Farquhar's *The Recruiting Officer*, a production heavily inspired by Brecht. It is important to remember that for all the successes of the past century in returning Restoration drama to the active repertory, those successes have been limited to a small number of plays by a still smaller number of playwrights. The overwhelming number of productions have been of plays by four playwrights: Congreve, Farquhar, Vanbrugh and Wycherley. Behn, Buckingham, Cibber, Dryden, Etherege, Otway, Ravenscroft and Shadwell have had more limited success. Since repertories are always works-in-progress, the one near-certainty is that this repertory will continue to change, develop and expand.

Canon

The dramatic repertory is a performance canon, which, in the case of Restoration comedy, overlaps considerably with the literary canon. Plays that remain in the repertory have a leg up on others for a place in the literary canon, though there are some plays, farces are an obvious example, that succeed better in performance than in the study or classroom. More common is the play that maintains critical interest but fails to interest an audience. For Restoration drama, this holds for anything but comedy. It is especially pronounced for serious drama, whether tragedy or the heroic play. Even the most canonical plays, say *All for Love* and *Venice Preserv'd*, are rarely to be seen on stage, and they fare far better than *The Conquest of Granada*, *The Orphan*, *The Rival Queens*, *Tamerlane* or any other likely candidate. While repertory status is easily measured, canonical status is more complicated. For the first two hundred plus years, the indicators of the canon for Restoration drama are almost exclusively evaluations by critics and availability in print. Here the judgements are no longer collective: even when Restoration drama reached its critical nadir, some plays were preferred to others and some plays remained in print (though most did not). Critics, unlike theatre managers, held tragedy in higher esteem than the other genres, but compared to the past fifty years, there was remarkably little criticism of any drama. Most serious critics focused on poetry, and those interested in the drama were most interested in theoretical issues, not practical criticism (unlike the moral critics whose primary interest was often practical – though rarely literary at all).

The true canon makers in the eighteenth and nineteenth centuries – and little has changed since then – were the editors and publishers of anthologies of plays. The large-scale publishing of anthologies was delayed in England by perpetual copyright laws. Thomas Johnson got around those laws by publishing his *Collection of the Best English* Plays (1711–12, and later, enlarged editions) in The Hague. The first edition consisted of plays entirely from the period 1660–1710, with the exception of Shakespeare and Jonson. Later editions added new plays, so that by the 1720–2 edition, about 70 per cent of the plays were from the Restoration period. Johnson includes Banks, Buckingham, Cibber, Crowne, Dryden, Etherege, Farquhar, Granville, Howard, Killigrew, Otway, Rowe, Shadwell, Southerne, Trapp, Vanbrugh and Wycherley. The surprising omissions are Centlivre, Lee and Steele. Many of these playwrights did not retain canonical status later in the century; additions are few and far between.

The great age of British anthologies begins with John Bell's successful challenge of perpetual copyright. Bell's *British Theatre* (1776) and Rivington's rival *New English Theatre* established a tradition of anthologies of best plays that lasted over a hundred years. The taste informing these anthologies reflected the stage repertory in the age of Garrick. Over half the plays in Bell and Rivington are from the Restoration, but only a small minority are Carolean. Congreve, Vanbrugh, Cibber, Farquhar, Centlivre and Steele are the dominant comic writers; Dryden, Otway, Congreve and Lee hold pride of place among the tragic writers.The retirement of Garrick, however, seemed to accelerate the inevitable pace of change to the canon. Bell added thirty-six plays to his collection in 1791; they were not Restoration plays. A mere 16 per cent of the plays in Elizabeth Inchbald's influential 1808 collection are from the Restoration, and similar, if less dramatic, reductions are to be found in the 1811 *British Drama* and in Richard Cumberland's popular 1817 collection. By the time of Oxenberry's 1823 *New English Drama*, the Restoration is reduced to 6 per cent. The momentum to exclude Restoration plays reaches its extreme in the collection published by John Dicks. Dicks issued two out-of-copyright plays a week for several years. Around 1883 he produced a catalogue of 1,189 'universally recognized' titles, each manifesting 'the innate beauty of these offsprings of genius'. In a list far too generous and inclusive to be called canonical, Dicks could find room for but twenty-eight titles by the following few Restoration playwrights: Centlivre (3), Cibber (4), Congreve (4), Dryden (1), Farquhar (4), Lee (1), Otway (3), Rowe (4), Steele (1) and Vanbrugh (3). And a few of these plays – the total is barely 2 per cent – were written slightly after 1710.

Just as Restoration drama seemed on the verge of extinction, it was rediscovered by a handful of late Victorian critics, critics generally at odds with the dominant values of their time. The most influential was Edmund Gosse, whose 1881 *Cornhill Magazine* article on Etherege paved the way for the recovery of much long-forgotten Carolean drama. A. Wilson Verity's 1888 edition of Etherege's *Works* made him accessible once again to the reading public. Verity's edition complemented the far more influential, high-profile work of Havelock Ellis and his colleagues in the 'Mermaid Series' of 'The Best Plays of the Old Dramatists' in 'unexpurgated' editions. The enormous success of this controversial series had a major impact on the emerging sense of the canon of Restoration drama. The list of Mermaid playwrights is quite conservative: Congreve, Dryden (two volumes), Farquhar, Otway, Shadwell, Steele, Vanbrugh and Wycherley, but it helped ensure that Restoration plays in general, and Carolean plays in particular, would recover a place in the authorized histories of English drama. The Mermaid recovery project aroused strong opposition, so much so that the editors chose to reprint Macaulay's hostile review of Hunt in the editions of both Congreve and Wycherley as a kind of moral health warning to endangered consumers. Montague Summers met similar opposition to his handsome, scholarly editions of Behn, Congreve, Dryden, Farquhar, Otway, Vanbrugh and Wycherley a generation later, and though they did not reach the popular readership of the Mermaids (they were far more costly, and they were issued in limited editions), they did provide much-needed library copies of most of the canonical playwrights.

The Mermaids remained in print well into the twentieth century; several of the volumes sold well in much later paperback reprints. They also demonstrated the viability of collections of Restoration plays in the marketplace, informing a number of small, highly successful anthologies aimed at the 'general reader' early in the new century. Just as Georgian taste had determined the canon of the early anthologies, Edwardian taste determined the canon that continues to form the core of current lists of the most important Restoration plays.

Gosse's Everyman volume 'from Dryden to Farquhar' (1912) reprinted *All for Love*, *The Country Wife*, *The Way of the World*, *Venice Preserv'd*, *The Beaux' Stratagem* and *The Provok'd Wife*. His volume was soon followed by very similar selections in the World's Classics and Modern Library. All three were reissued in paperback, to be joined by more recent clones from publishers like Penguin and Signet. They in turn have since been joined by similar collections aimed expressly at the academic market, now the largest target audience for canonical literature. The impact of the academic market emerged in the 1920s with a series of textbooks constructed for North American classroom use – early recognition that canon-making had become largely a university-based activity. Seven important anthologies appeared in the 1920s and 1930s with the same small list of playwrights: Dryden, Buckingham, Wycherley, Etherege, Lee, Otway, Shadwell, Congreve, Cibber, Vanbrugh, Farquhar, Rowe and Steele. The only one still in print today, George Winchester Stone's lightly revised edition of George Henry Nettleton and Arthur E. Case's *British Dramatists from Dryden to Sheridan* (1939; revised 1969) remains the only comprehensive classroom anthology available, a fact that has inhibited changes to the canon long desired by specialists in the field.

A century of scholarship devoted to the plays of the Restoration has produced a far more comprehensive view – and appreciation – of the full range of the drama of the period. New, scholarly editions of out-of-print and neglected writers have made it possible for critics to reassess and revise the Edwardian canon they inherited. Three kinds of plays in particular have already achieved near-canonical status (a far cry, it must be said, from bestseller status). The first is a group of dark social comedies, comedies of a kind that were not particularly successful when they first appeared, but have much to offer us today. Michael Cordner's recent anthology, *Four Restoration Marriage Plays* (World's Classics), has made some of the best of these plays available to the wide reading public: Lee's *The Princess of Cleves*, Otway's *The Soldier's Fortune*, Dryden's *Amphitryon* and Southerne's *The Wives' Excuse*. Sandra Clark's *Shakespeare Made Fit* (Everyman) provides a similar function for the second group of plays, Shakespearean adaptations. Her collection includes the most popular of the Restoration adaptations, *All for Love*, the Dryden–Davenant *Tempest* and Nahum Tate's *King Lear* as well as John Lacy's *Sauny the Scot* (from *The Taming of the Shrew*), Cibber's *Richard III* and selections from Otway's *Caius Marius* (from *Romeo and Juliet*). The third and far more comprehensive group consists of plays by women, so noticeably excluded from the Edwardian canon. Anthologies by Katharine Rogers (Meridian), Paddy Lyons and Fidelis Morgan (Everyman), and others have reprinted plays by Behn, Pix, Manley and Centlivre, establishing a significant presence in an emerging new canon of Restoration plays.

Canons by their very nature are unstable beings: they are constructed to meet the needs of their makers and thus cannot be of limitless duration. Even when the canon in question is of a literature that has been largely neglected, even when it is the product of an institution as conservative as the English theatre, it is subject to the same kinds of changes as other literary canons. The last generation of criticism has challenged the Edwardian canon to the point that it no longer holds sway. Plays that have not been performed since the early eighteenth century, even plays that did not survive as stage pieces beyond their initial productions, have been mounted successfully in the full range of theatres, from academic to regional to mainline. The first comprehensive anthology of Restoration plays since the eighteenth century, David Womersley's *Restoration Plays: An Anthology* (Blackwell), appeared in 2000. It brings together eighteen of the great hits of the period in a single, accessible volume: *The*

Adventures of Five Hours, The Great Favourite, or The Duke of Lerma, The Conquest of Granada, The Rehearsal, The Country Wife, The Plain Dealer, The Man of Mode, The Rover, All for Love, Lucius Junius Brutus, Venice Preserv'd, Love for Love, Love's Last Shift, The Relapse, The Way of the World, The Recruiting Officer, The Beaux' Stratagem and *The Busie Body.* And the first new comprehensive anthology of Restoration and eight-eenth-century plays in sixty years is scheduled to be released by Broadview Press (J. Douglas Canfield, general editor) in summer 2001. It is a much larger collection (thirty plays from 1660 to 1710 plus post-1710 plays by Manley and Centlivre), and (in contrast to Womersley's) it is a collection designed to challenge earlier canons: *The Rump, The Committee, Henry V, The Old Troop, Marriage A-la-Mode, The Careless Lovers, The Country Wife, The Man of Mode, The Rover, The Fond Husband, All for Love, A True Widow, Friendship in Fashion, Lucius Junius Brutus, The Unhappy Favorite, Venice Preserv'd, The Princess of Cleves, City Politiques, The Lucky Chance, Sir Anthony Love, Amphitryon, Oroonoko, Love's Last Shift, The Relapse, Tamerlane, The Way of the World, The Beau Defeated, Love at a Loss, The Fair Penitent* and *The Beaux' Stratagem.* It will be interesting to see how it contributes to the new canon that is so clearly an active work-in-progress. Interest in the plays as stage pieces and as literary texts is stronger than it has been for well over two hundred years. The twenty-first century shows no sign of reversal of that interest in the near future.

REFERENCES AND FURTHER READING

Bear, A. (1972). 'Restoration Comedy and the Provok'd Critic', in H. Love (ed.), *Restoration Literature: Critical Approaches.* London: Methuen, 1–26.
Bevis, R. (1997). 'Canon, Pedagogy, Prospectus: Redesigning "Restoration and Eighteenth-century English Drama"', *Comparative Drama* 31, 178–91.
Child, H. (1926). 'Revivals of English Dramatic Works, 1919–25', *Review of English Studies* 2, 177–88.
Corman, B. (1986). 'Johnson and Profane Authors: The *Lives* of Otway and Congreve', in P. Korshin (ed.), *Johnson after Two Hundred Years.* Philadelphia: University of Pennsylvania Press, 225–44.
Corman, B. (1992–3). 'What is the Canon of English Drama, 1660–1737?', *Eighteenth-century Studies* 26, 307–21.
Corman, B. (1997). 'Restoration Studies and the New Historicism: The Case of Aphra Behn', in W. G. Marshall (ed.), *The Restoration Mind.* Newark: University of Delaware Press, 252–71.
Frye, N. (1957). *Anatomy of Criticism: Four Essays.* Princeton, NJ: Princeton University Press.
Harwood, J. T. (1982). *Critics, Values, and Restoration Comedy.* Carbondale: Southern Illinois University Press.
Holland, N. N. (1959). *The First Modern Comedies: The Significance of Etherege, Wycherley, and Congreve.* Cambridge, MA: Harvard University Press.
Holland, P. (1979). *The Ornament of Action: Text and Performance in Restoration Comedy.* Cambridge: Cambridge University Press.
Hume, R. D. (1982). 'English Drama and Theatre 1660–1800: New Directions in Research', *Theatre Survey* 23, 71–100.
Johnson, S. (1905). *Lives of the English Poets*, ed. G. B. Hill. 3 vols. Oxford: Clarendon Press.
Johnson, S. (1968). *The Yale Edition of the Works of Samuel Johnson*, ed. Arthur Sherbo. 'Preface to Shakespeare' in ibid., *Vols 7 and 8: Johnson on Shakespeare.* New Haven, CT: Yale University Press.

Kaplan, D. (1995). 'Representing the Nation: Restoration Comedies on the Early Twentieth-century London Stage', *Theatre Survey* 36, 37–61.

Kavenik, F. M. (1995). *British Drama, 1660–1789*. New York: Twayne.

Kenny, S. S. (1976). 'Perennial Favorites: Congreve, Vanbrugh, Cibber, Farquhar, Steele', *Modern Philology* 73, S4–S11.

Kewes, P. (1998). *Authorship and Appropriation: Writing for the Stage in England, 1660–1700*. Oxford: Clarendon Press.

Knights, L. C. (1946). *Explorations: Essays in Criticism, Mainly on Literature of the Seventeenth Century*. London: Chatto and Windus.

Krutch, J. W. (1949). *Comedy and Conscience after the Restoration*. New York: Columbia University Press.

Lamb, C. (1935). *The Complete Works and Letters*. New York: Modern Library.

Markley, R. (1983). 'History, Ideology, and the Study of Restoration Drama', *The Eighteenth Century: Theory and Interpretation* 24, 91–102.

Markley, R. (2000). 'The Canon and its Critics', in D. P. Fisk (ed.), *The Cambridge Companion to English Restoration Theatre*. Cambridge: Cambridge University Press, 226–42.

Palmer, J. (1913). *The Comedy of Manners*. London: Bell.

Shepherd, S. (1996). 'Bawdy, Manners and the English National Character', in S. Shepherd and P. Womack (eds), *English Drama: A Cultural History*. Oxford: Blackwell.

Styan, J. L. (1986). *Restoration Comedy in Performance*. Cambridge: Cambridge University Press.

Taney, R. M. (1985). *Restoration Revivals on the British Stage (1944–1979): A Critical Survey*. Lanham, MD: University Press of America.

Van der Weele, S. J. (1978). *The Critical Reputation of Restoration Comedy in Modern Times up to 1950*. 2 vols. Salzburg: Institut für Englische Sprache und Literatur.

Walkely, A. B. (1907). *Drama and Life*. London: Methuen.

Part II
Kinds of Drama

12

Heroic Drama and Tragicomedy

Derek Hughes

Dryden

In the winter of 1670–1, the King's Company gave the first performance of John Dryden's fourth rhymed heroic play, the two-part *The Conquest of Granada*. Dryden's previous heroic play, *Tyrannick Love* (1669), about the martyrdom of St Catherine, had featured a rantingly bombastic and egomaniac villain. In *The Conquest of Granada*, rant and extraordinary self-assertion were transferred to the hero, Almanzor, a powerful warrior brought up outside civilization and for a long time incapable of comprehending its demands.

The Conquest of Granada set up a controversy that has persisted to the present day, even if it is now only the preserve of specialist scholars. Although records of performances are sparse, the play was clearly successful. Mary Evelyn, the wife of the diarist, saw it, her only reservation being that it might represent unrealistic patterns of virtue (Van Lennep et al. 1960–8, 1: 177). But it was also attacked, in pamphlets such as Richard Leigh's *The Censure of the Rota on Mr Driden's Conquest of Granada* (Oxford, 1673) and the sarcastically titled *Friendly Vindication of Mr Dryden From the Censure of the Rota by his Cabal of Wits* (Cambridge, 1673), which mocked the alleged linguistic absurdities of this play (and others) and the lawlessness of its hero (*Drydeniana* 1974). These attacks were answered in [Charles Blount], *Mr Dreyden Vindicated* (London, 1673) and the anonymous *A Description of the Academy of the Athenian Virtuosi* (London, 1673). Comic dramatists (notably Dryden's rival, Thomas Shadwell) parodied and jeered at heroic rant, and Dryden was caricatured on stage: as Drybob in Thomas Shadwell's *The Humorists* (1670), as the Tutor in Joseph Arrowsmith's *The Reformation* (1673) and – most woundingly – as Mr Bayes in *The Rehearsal* (December 1671), a collaborative theatrical skit whose chief author was one of the greatest noblemen in the country, George Villiers, second Duke of Buckingham. The titular rehearsal is of an absurd play whose central character is – in clear parody of Almanzor – the boastful superhero Drawcansir. *The Rehearsal* was long in the making, its original target was not Dryden, and it parodies plays by many other authors (including Aphra Behn, who had recently made her debut with two tragicomedies). In the finished version, however, the main target was obviously Dryden (the name Bayes alludes to his status as poet laureate), and the actor who took the role, John Lacy, took some trouble to imitate his mannerisms.

When *The Conquest of Granada* was published, early in 1672, Dryden already felt obliged to defend his creation and himself, and indeed does so at three points: in the dedication, in a substantial prefatory essay, 'Of Heroique Playes', and in a postscript, where he pedantically elaborated criticisms of the language of Shakespeare and his contemporaries, first made in the epilogue to Part 2. Dryden had alluded to the success of 'Heroick Plays' in his dedication of his second such play, *The Indian Emperour* (1665) (*Works* 9: 23), but in 'Of Heroique Playes' he mounts an elaborate theoretical justification of the genre, not only defending the use of rhyme ('Heroique verse') in drama, which he had done before, but explaining the literary lineage of Almanzor and of the play as a whole. From previous English drama, Dryden cited only one precedent: Sir William Davenant's rhymed semi-opera, *The Siege of Rhodes*, the original version of which had been staged in 1656 (its status as a musical entertainment exempting it from the Puritan ban on theatrical performances). Dryden was more concerned with locating his creation in the tradition of European non-dramatic heroic writing. He alludes briefly to the possibility that Davenant 'heighten'd' his characters after the example of Corneille (*Works* 11: 9), but his main point of reference is the epic. '[A]n Heroick Play', he declares, 'ought to be an imitation, in little of an Heroick Poem' and, citing the opening lines of Ariosto's *Orlando Furioso*, he asserts that its main subjects should be 'Love and Valour' (*Works* 11: 10). When he embarked on the defence of Almanzor (*Works* 11: 14–17), he continued to invoke the epic, providing his hero with a three-stage literary pedigree which commenced with the first epic hero of all: Achilles in the *Iliad*. The two other literary forebears are Rinaldo in Tasso's *Gerusalemme Liberata* (clearly modelled, as Dryden indicates, on Achilles), and Artaban, one of the heroes of La Calprenède's enormous prose romance, *Cléopâtre* (1647–56), whom Dryden states, with less justification, to have been modelled on both.

For the modern reader, one of the main questions about *The Conquest of Granada* is that of how we are to judge Almanzor: is he to be admired, ridiculed, or subjected to a complex and divided assessment? The genealogy which Dryden provides gives us less guidance than we might wish. *Orlando Furioso* is famously ambiguous in its treatment of the heroic. Rinaldo provides a critical Christian reconsideration of the figure of Achilles, re-enacting the latter's quarrel with his leader and secession from the army, but outgrowing the flaws of his model in ways that invite specifically Christian assessment. Artaban, who (like Almanzor) *'unthrones Kings, overthrows Monarchies, and makes Empires depend on the point of his Sword'*, is not critically portrayed, and Dryden did take plot lines (at times almost verbatim) from the huge heroic romances that La Calprenède, Madeleine de Scudéry and her brother George churned out. Although La Calprenède wrote at a time of political upheaval in France, however, *Cléopâtre* is a work of pure escapism. However unrealistic it seems to us, *The Conquest of Granada* is a play about political events and ideas, about civil war, usurpation and restoration, addressed to an audience that had lived through all three. The unthroning of kings was not to be portrayed lightly.

Achilles was a variously interpreted hero. The Penguin translation of Aristotle's *Poetics* contains the judgement that Homer portrayed him as 'decent' (Dorsch 1965: 52), but this is one way of interpreting a very garbled and corrupt passage in the Greek text, which in the sixteenth and seventeenth centuries was variously elucidated, to produce very different assessments of Achilles's character: as a mixture of goodness and harshness, as a pure embodiment of goodness, or as a pure embodiment of harshness (Hughes 1981: 175–6, n. 50). Dryden rather muddied the waters in a retrospective discussion of *The Conquest of Granada* in 'The Grounds of Criticism in Tragedy', an essay prefixed to his adaptation of Shakespeare's *Troilus and Cressida* (1679), when both the political situation and his own artistic outlook were very different from those of 1670. For this discussion, he used a work of epic theory which had not been available to him when he wrote *The Conquest of Granada*, René Le Bossu's *Traité du Poëme Epique* (1675). Arguing that the hero of a play need not be '*a perfect character of virtue*', he writes that it is only '*necessary that the Hero of the Play be not a Villain*' (*Works* 13: 232), and goes on to cite approvingly Le Bossu's precept that the poet's first step should be to choose the fundamental moral of his work: '*as namely*, Homer's (*which I have Copy'd in my* Conquest of Granada) *was, that Union preserves a Common-wealth, and discord destroys it*' (*Works* 13: 234). Since the withdrawal of Achilles from the Greek side is the root cause of the disunity in the *Iliad*, this automatically implies an unfavourable assessment of Achilles, and indeed Le Bossu is extreme in his hostile interpretation of Achilles's character. It is probably safest to take this passage as a record of how Dryden's view of his own creation changed. It reminds us, however, of the political seriousness of his plays, and of the complexity of the body of epic practice and theory to which he was appealing.

For many years there was a sterile debate about the origins of the heroic plays, the chief candidates for the honour of primary source being the epic, the French prose romance, the idealistic drama of Platonic love current in Charles I's reign, and the plays of Beaumont and Fletcher. All these influences played an important role, and it is unnecessary and even meaningless to suggest that one dominated to the exclusion of the others. Dryden demonstrably uses plots from the prose romances, at times following the English translations almost verbatim, though he generally gives ironic twists to the material. The idealization of friendship popular in the Caroline period survived on the early Restoration stage, and influenced Dryden (though he tends to portray friends who fall short of the theoretical demands of their ideal). The fashion for rhyme was doubtless influenced by Corneille, some of whose works were staged in translations (most notably, Katherine Philips's translations of *La Mort de Pompée* and *Horace*, the latter completed after her death by Sir John Denham), though Corneille's dramaturgy exercised little influence on the content or construction of British plays. And we have to take very seriously

Dryden's claim to have been influenced by the epic. Renaissance poetic theory decreed the epic to be the noblest form of poetry: *Paradise Lost* was published in 1667, and Dryden hoped – vainly – that his own career would be crowned by the production of an epic. In the 1650s, moreover, the fascination with the epic form produced an outpouring of epics in France and Italy that was impressive in quantity, if nothing else. Interestingly, the best of these epics, by Girolamo Graziani, was entitled *Il Conquisto di Granata* (1650). Dryden borrowed nothing from it, though he would certainly have known of it, for it is warmly praised in the preface of another epic, George de Scudéry's *Alaric* (1654), from which he borrowed, almost verbatim, a plot line for *The Indian Emperour*. Despite his close verbal debt to his source, however, he changes Scudéry by giving his hero a secretive and ultimately destructive preoccupation with personal honour.

The European epics of the 1650s generally followed the precedent of Tasso's *Gerusalemme Liberata*, retaining the military or questing themes of Homer and Virgil, rejecting elements of their pagan morality (particularly any possible idealization of Achilles), and creating an interplay between the inadequate values of the pagan heroic tradition and the newer ideals of Christian military heroism, particularly as expressed in missionary warfare against non-Christian nations. *Paradise Lost* is exceptional (though not unique) in its complete rejection of heroic action, pagan or Christian. With Tasso and his imitators, however, we always know where we are: who is meant to be right, and who wrong. Dryden's characters have often provoked uncertainty or resistance, initially from critics (from Buckingham onwards) who felt that they demanded admiration for amoral violence and linguistic absurdity, more recently from a minority of scholars who recognize the aesthetic problems that they pose, but feel that Dryden cannot have created the problems inadvertently. This is still a controversial area; my own view is that at least some of the problems are deliberately created. Our response to the rhetoric of Almanzor's boasts is inevitably subjective, but we can say with reasonable objectivity that he repeatedly fails to fulfil them. On the battlefield, he is unstoppable. Within the confines of the city, he constantly trips up: his promises of good behaviour are repeatedly broken, and he is even physically vulnerable. One of his most famous and stylish boasts is his 'Stand off; I have not leisure yet to dye' (Part 1, 1.1.232), which he utters when the Moorish king orders his execution. It is important to remember, however, that when he makes the boast he has no capacity to fulfil it: he is overpowered and physically helpless, and is only spared on the intercession of the king's brother. The very different hero of Dryden's next and final heroic play, the moralistic Aureng-Zebe, shows another kind of gap between profession and performance. When his father disinherits him and attempts to steal the woman he loves, he ostentatiously refuses his followers' offer to join him in a rebellion, only to reveal in an aside that he thinks he can gain his ends without the embarrassment of disloyalty, by bombarding his father with reminders of how much he has done for him. The refusal to rebel remains commendable, but the private (initially mistaken) calculation shows a character more human and fallible than appears in the public facade. Aureng-Zebe's life is a non-stop attempt to do the right thing or strike the right pose; but neither the world nor his own motives are quite what he would wish.

Another fairly objective test is to look at the way in which Dryden handles his sources in the prose romances. These are generally long and intricate, and one very simplified example must suffice. In *The Indian Emperour* (1665), which portrays Cortez's conquest of Mexico, Cortez falls in love with Montezuma's daughter Cydaria, who is loved by a morally flawed Indian, Orbellan. Orbellan makes his way to the Spanish camp in order to assassinate Cortez and is detected, but not before he has secured a promise of protection from the unsuspecting Cortez. When Cortez discovers the truth, he keeps his word to the extent of escorting Orbellan from the camp, but then promptly challenges him to a duel, unwilling to 'strain Honour to a point too high' (3.3.7). When he wounds Orbellan, he regrets the honour that forbids him to kill him, but his frustration is short-lived, for he promptly mounts an attack on the town and kills Orbellan there. This is hardly deep-dyed villainy, but neither is it high principle. Cortez likes the idea of honour, but is constantly irked by the practice of it, in a way that the character on whom he is here based does not. The Orbellan plot reworks and rearranges elements from La Calprenède's *Cassandre* in the account of the rivalry of Arsaces (really Artaxerxes, prince of Persia) and Arsacomes for the hand of the princess of Scythia. In La Calprenède the duel does not strain the limits of a promise; Arsaces unhesitatingly spares and secures medical aid for his rival; he *delays* attacking the town; and, when he does attack, he spares Arsacomes (Hughes 1981: 160–2). Dryden's alterations consistently show the compromising of ideals that are flawlessly upheld in his source.

It is more difficult to evaluate the strained and hyperbolic language of some Dryden characters, and it is unlikely that a single explanation will solve all the phenomena. Dryden could at times write badly, and in later life confessed to doing so in his heroic plays. At the same time, the nature and limitations of language were, as always, topical subjects, and he and other dramatists were keenly interested in them. It was frequently maintained that the rebellion against the Crown had been sustained by a fraudulent perversion of the proper meaning of language, 'subversion', for example, becoming '*reformation*' (South 1823, 4: 206). Political and religious concerns with the abuse of language mingled with concerns emerging from the growth of experimental science, which fostered a belief that for millennia men had explained natural phenomena by empty verbal formulae corresponding to nothing in the real world, such as Aristotle's accident and substance. The philosopher Thomas Hobbes emphasized that linguistic meaning depended on agreed social compact, that linguistic abuse could give rise to dangerous intellectual and political error, and that the shared public medium of language could easily splinter into private systems of meaning. The existence of private linguistic systems within the shared public discourse fascinated Restoration dramatists. If Dryden may at times simply be writing badly, there are other times when he is clearly examining the nature and even the origin of language. In his tragicomedy *Marriage A-la-Mode* (1671), for example, the scatty social climber Melantha acquires her day's supply of French words by learning them from her maid, whom she rewards with items of cast-off clothing. We witness the development of an idiosyncratic language, but also one whose meanings are not internalized, and whose tokens are acquired by contract with an outside party.

In the heroic plays, also, there are times when Dryden focuses on moments of linguistic crisis and transition. The native Americans of *The Indian Emperour* are, in their original state, almost without metaphor, a condition that is all the more remarkable because we have already seen the Spaniards responding to the unfamiliar landscape with some wildly strained imagery. For example, Cortez imagines the genesis of the new continent in terms of the inhibited formalities of a Spanish pregnancy: it is 'As if our old world modestly withdrew, / And here, in private, had brought forth a new' (1.1.3–4). Here, the linguistic strain arises because the Spaniards are trying to translate things outside their previous experience into a language which is necessarily limited by that experience. There is a complementary moment when Montezuma's son Guyomar reports the approach of the Spanish fleet (his first ever encounter with ships), awkwardly applying words from his acquired stock of experience to an unknown and uncomprehended object (the ships are, for example, 'floating Palaces' [1.2.111]). This is the moment at which the Indian culture invents metaphor, in a fumbling attempt to put into language something that lies outside their acquired linguistic experience. At points such as this, Dryden is clearly addressing the limitations of language as an intermediary between the isolated individual consciousness and the collective world outside.

The Renaissance epics are attempts to translate ancient heroic genres into a Christian moral scheme. It is doubtful whether Dryden in the 1660s and 1670s was a Christian (though, obviously, he was later in life). He appears at this stage rather to have been a deist: that is, to have believed in a rational and benevolent divinity, but to have rejected the idea that there were revealed truths that were specific to Christianity, such as atonement through the Crucifixion. In 1674 he wrote a stage adaptation (never performed) of the greatest Christian epic, *Paradise Lost*, and (remarkably) completely jettisoned all its Christian elements. There is not even the most indirect reference to the Son of God or to the Crucifixion, and God's requirements of man are the standard deist ones of praise, prayer and penitence. Dryden's earlier tragedy *Tyrannick Love* also handles a traditionally Christian theme, the martyrdom of St Catherine. Again, however, there is no reference to Christian revelation, and it is at least possible to see St Catherine as a ruthless religious zealot, achieving her martyr's crown whatever the cost and danger to others.

In *The Indian Emperour* and *The Conquest of Granada* Dryden handled the conventional epic theme of Christian conquest, but in both – and especially in the earlier play – it is handled with some reservation. *The Indian Emperour* emphasizes the Aztec practices of human sacrifice, treating them as part of a religion that sees human life and identity as inseparably and organically implicated in the cosmic natural cycles of decay and generation. The Spaniards, however, arrive at comparable levels of religious atrocity by a different cultural route. They have a culture of measurement, and of economic equivalence (whereas the Indians – unhistorically – have neither abstract measurement nor economic infrastructure), and by the end of the play the Spaniards' advanced culture of numeric and economic categories has led them, too, to perform human sacrifice, torturing Montezuma and his high priest in an attempt to get them to reveal the whereabouts of Montezuma's gold. The bodies of the victims are removed from their sympathetic oneness with the cycles of nature, becoming passive, isolated items in an economic transaction. All that Christianity has done is to provide a new intellectual system for an old barbarity.

A potent influence upon Dryden was Thomas Hobbes, a *bête noire* to Christians but a great stimulus to sceptical intellectuals. Appalled by the chaos of the British Civil War, he had endeavoured to devise a science of stable government: most famously in his *Leviathan* (1651). His starting point was an entirely materialistic view of man. The human body consisted of moving material particles, and thought, reason and desire were the products of their motions. Because man was constitutionally a creature of restless material desire, he was naturally in a state of competition and hostility with his fellows: the state of nature, prior to civilization, would have been a state of total war, not only without any material security, but without any right or wrong, since there was no civil authority to impose ideas of right and wrong. Man entered into civil society in order to escape from the horrific consequences of his own unbridled nature, contracting away his natural rights in exchange for the security of a political state. This is one of many occasions on which Hobbes turns received terminology and teaching on its head. Aristotle had taught that man formed civil societies because he was naturally a political animal, but Hobbes explicitly disagreed. For him, there is a paradox at the heart of civilization: man forms societies because he is anti-social; civilization arises from man's natural propensity to savagery. This paradox is one of the major topics of Restoration drama, heroic and comic.

Hobbes saw absolute monarchy as the most stable form of government: the subjects were bound by the social covenant, but not the monarch, whose power was so absolute that he even had the authority to determine which books of the Bible were canonical in his kingdom. Indeed, Hobbes denied that it was possible to have any verifiable assurance that a text or command was divine in origin. He thus combined an extreme defence of secular power with extreme moral and religious scepticism: man was matter, not spirit, the mechanistic workings of his constitution left him with no free will, divine revelation was unknowable, and doctrines and moral principles generally deemed universal were in fact variable matters of local legislation. Perhaps with justice, he was accused of atheism.

In many ways, Dryden's early plays show a receptive, if critical, engagement with the ideas of Hobbes, and he informed John Aubrey that he admired him and used his doctrine in his plays (Aubrey 1898, 1: 372). As already indicated, he was fascinated with the problem of how an individual, idiosyncratic consciousness can use language as a transparent medium of universally agreed meanings. In the dedication to his early comedy, *The Rival Ladies* (1664), he contemplated the possibility that man might be a materially driven automaton, and he was fascinated with the proposition that man in his archetypal state was an egocentric savage. Almanzor, the turbulent hero of *The Conquest of Granada*, is (we finally discover) the nephew of the king of Spain, but he was brought up outside the limits of civilization, and he has to undergo a very protracted and erratic education in the existence of realities and values that are independent of his desires. Dryden's first heroic play, *The Indian Queen* (1664), written in collaboration with his brother-in-law, Sir Robert Howard, has a similar character in the young Montezuma, debarred from his rightful throne by usurpation, brought up outside civil society, initially unruly and chaotic in his character, but finally restored as the just and temperate ruler of Mexico. The parallel to Charles II's experiences is obvious; but, of the many sycophantic celebrants of Charles's return, few portrayed him as a noble savage in need of civilization. Heroic literature of the Renaissance and the seventeenth century tends to portray a transcendence of the personal, and the fulfilment of the self in some national or Christian ideal. In Dryden, the heritage of the Hobbesian savage is a persistent and disruptive one.

Early Restoration Tragicomedy

The heroic element in Restoration drama, then, was the subject of much contemporary controversy, and of an essay by Dryden on the nature and genesis of the heroic play. In this essay Dryden is defending his own plays, with passing reference to *The Siege of Rhodes*, but this narrowness of focus has not deterred scholars from writing more generally about the Restoration Heroic Play, sometimes imagined as a fairly consistent and stable genre which dominated the Restoration stage from 1660 until the late 1670s. It is undoubtedly true that a fashion for rhymed tragedy persisted from the Restoration until 1677, but beyond that many distinctions and qualifications need to be made.

Dryden dedicated his second play, the intrigue comedy *The Rival Ladies* (1664), to the Earl of Orrery, an important figure in the administration of Ireland. In the 1660s, Orrery achieved some success as a tragedian, acting upon the king's suggestion that he write a play in rhyme, after the French fashion. One of his serious plays, *Mustapha* (1665), held the stage for some time, and is mentioned by Dryden in 'The Grounds of Criticism'. Dryden does not mention Orrery in 'Of Heroique Plays', but modern scholars have with some reason felt justified in seeing his works as part of the heroic phenomenon. There is no evidence, however, that Orrery wished to create a drama based on the classical epic; rather, the values of his plays perpetuate the idealization of friendship and Platonic love common in court-oriented drama of the Caroline period. For example, a common Orrery situation (with plenty of pre-Restoration precedents) is for two friends who love the same woman to put friendship before love, to the extent that each will urge the loved one to marry the other. Heroic self-denial in love is also a principal theme in Davenant's *The Siege of Rhodes*, in which the Turkish Sultan Solyman the Magnificent behaves nobly towards the Christian warrior Alphonso, despite being in love with his wife. This transcendence of personal desire is the very thing that eludes Dryden's more passionate heroes.

The idealism of Orrery's plays has a political point, the heroes' subordination of individualistic passion to calm reason corresponding to the triumph of order and social responsibility over rebellion in the justly ordered state. In his first play, the tragicomedy *The Generall* (written in 1661, performed in Dublin in 1662 under the title of *Altemera*, and first performed in London in 1664), a usurper's seizure of power in the kingdom is paralleled at a personal and mental level by his desire at one point to rape the heroine (love for her being, indeed, the motive for his usurpation); conversely, the hero who restores legitimate power internally re-enacts his defeat of subversion, triumphing over his own unruly desires by renouncing the heroine, whom he unrequitedly loves, and reuniting her with her lover.

The political dimensions of Restoration serious drama have received sustained attention only over the last thirty years, most plays being previously discussed with quite astonishing blindness to their political import. Yet most serious plays of the 1660s, and many of the comedies, portray or allude to the restoration of Charles II. In its outline, *The Generall* clearly corresponds to the events of early 1660: a general initially connected with the usurping forces turns against them and restores the rightful king, as George Monck had done in Britain. Here, however, the resemblance ends. There are no allusions to the grievances which led to the Civil War, about unparliamentary government, arbitrary taxation or denial of religious freedom. The characters are judged simply by their confirmity to the ideals of love and honour, and even the usurpation of a throne is motivated by unrequited love. The complex conflicts and fissures of a developing early modern society are erased and translated into a fictitious feudal system, unified by simple personal bonding: friendship, loyalty, love.

If Orrery simplified seventeenth-century political realities in his art, however, he exemplified them in his life. Like others, he held high political office both under Charles II and Cromwell, and had even taken a leading part in urging Cromwell to assume the crown. Plays such as *The Generall* (and his later tragedy *Tryphon* [1668]) do acknowledge the moral difficulties of men who feel obligations to a usurper, yet at the same time their conflicts are trivialized by their predictable, formulaic reduction to issues of love and honour. As Susan Staves has recognized, a drama in which characters negotiate perplexing mazes of love and honour provides an escape from the compromises and tergiversations that Orrery and others had actually performed (1979: 52).

A number of plays from the 1660s have affinities with Orrery's. Edward Howard, brother of Sir Robert, resembled Orrery in writing a play that clearly allegorized the Restoration, *The Usurper* (1664). Orrery's second play was *The History of Henry the Fifth* (1664; not indebted to Shakespeare), in which the hero's recovery of the French crown acts as another example of restored legitimacy. With similar relevance, John Caryll wrote a non-Shakespearean play about the deposition of the usurping Richard III, *The English Princess* (1667). To term such works heroic plays is, however, to stretch beyond usefulness a term to which Dryden, its originator, gave a very specific and narrow meaning. Without resorting to over-simplifying categories, however, one can say that most serious drama of the 1660s deals with idealized forms of human conduct in the realms of honour, friendship and love; it mostly ends happily; and it bears some relationship to the cycle of usurpation and restoration through which Britain had recently lived. Nancy Klein Maguire has, indeed, argued that the tragicomic form of early Restoration reflects the larger tragicomedy of state: the atonement of Charles I's execution in the phoenix-like restoration of his son (Maguire 1992).

The Cavalier dramatists' glorification of friendship and Platonic love reflected the values that Queen Henrietta Maria had sought to establish in Charles I's court. Such values could scarcely have been more remote from the cynicism and promiscuity of his son's milieu. The king's conduct brought him into widespread disrepute, and a sense of malaise was heightened by the catastrophes of the mid-1660s: plague in 1665, fire the following year, and humiliation in the Second Dutch War in the year after that. Although plays representing the Restoration continued to be premiered until 1671, by the mid–1660s drama – even heroic drama – can have an admonitory tone, portraying sexually unwise kings, and ending tragically. In Orrery's *Mustapha* (1665), Solyman the Magnificent is deceived by his second wife into executing his loyal eldest son and endangering his succession. In *The Indian Queen*, the young Montezuma had been a vigorous hero, triumphantly restored to his ancestral throne. In its sequel, *The Indian Emperour*, he is enfeebled by unwise love, his folly contributing to the destruction of his kingdom. Dryden also started to display an intellectual scepticism about the Restoration myth: the king of Spain in *The Conquest of Granada* is a ruthlessly pragmatic politician whose first move on regaining Granada is to install the villainess as his client ruler.

In movement from *The Generall* to *Mustapha* we see a movement from tragicomedy, in one of its senses, to a more tragic view of politics. *The Generall* is an entirely serious play in which the virtuous characters are saved from imminent or apparent death (at one point, the heroine does seemingly die). Another sense of tragicomedy, however, is of a play which combines a serious (though happily ending) main plot with an important comic subplot. Such drama, too, was characteristic of the early Restoration, the leading practitioner was again Dryden, and it enabled exploration of the relationship between the heroic myth of the Restoration and the contemporary reality. Some of these plays, such as Etherege's first play *The Comical Revenge* (1664), are primarily dominated by the comic ethos: although the heroic characters of *The Comical Revenge* live according to self-denying principles akin to those of Orrery's heroes, the principles are here stultifying, and the heroes are rescued from them by a boisterous representative of the new festive order, Sir Frederick Frollick.

If such plays (another is James Howard's *All Mistaken* of 1665) are primarily comedies, Dryden's two split-plot plays from the early Restoration create a more balanced relationship between mundane pragmatism and the struggle to maintain ideals. In *Secret Love* (1667) a queen stifles her love for one of her subjects (Philocles), allows him to marry the woman he loves, and enters on a reign of lonely spinsterhood; but the realization that the queen loves him complicates the hero's feelings for his loved one, and gives a slight ambiguity to their final happiness. Ambitious love for the queen prompts another subject, Lysimantes, to rebel and imprison her, and although the free-and-easy courtship of the comic lovers, Celadon and Florimell, provides a lively contrast to their ruler's painful self-denial, it does not offer an escape route (unlike Sir Frederick's lifestyle in *The Comical Revenge*). The playful infidelity of Celadon and Florimell is unavailable to the queen and not translatable into the terms of other lives; it becomes troubling when it is reflected in the momentary tarnishing of Philocles's love for his future wife. Moreover, it is significant that not only Lysimantes but both Philocles and Celadon, the heroic and the comic lover, partici- pate in the rebellion against the queen (Philocles because he resents and does not yet understand her obstruction of his marriage). The play leaves us with an unresolved conflict between the queen's exemplary political virtue, whose cost is lifelong sexual unfulfilment, and the less contained sexuality of the three heroes, each of whom is associated with rebellion. Whereas Etherege's Sir Frederick humanizes the social order, the conduct of Dryden's heroes implies that rebelliousness and sexuality are linked and inescapable aspects of male nature.

The most complex split-plot play of this period is another by Dryden, *Marriage A- la-Mode* (1671), one of the last plays to deal with the subject of restoration until the revival of the topic during the last years of Charles's reign. In the serious plot Leonidas, true heir to the throne of Sicily, has been brought up as the son of a fisherman. Early in the play, he is wrongly identified as the son of the reigning usurper. The error corrected, he returns to being a fisherman's son, is privately identified as the true king, and finally manages to declare his identity publicly as he is on the point of being executed. His perceived identity is constantly fluid, and his problem (not totally overcome) is to attain some consistency of character amidst the changing external formulations of his self. In the complementary comic plot, two bored couples seek to enjoy each other's partners. The problem here is the mirror-image of Leonidas's: not how to stabilize a fluid identity but how to elicit variety from unending sameness. One man has tried to compensate for the tedious immutability of his wife by serial sexual fantasy, successively imagining her in bed as every beauty in Sicily. The marriage falters when all attractive women have been used up. Although the restoration of the king is accomplished, Leonidas's changes of persona do raise the question of what kingli- ness is and where it lies: public reaction to him is so geared to the role of the moment as to forbid any impression of an instinctive reverence for true royalty, and Leonidas's own character changes subtly with his changes of role. In a sense, the paralysing sameness of role that is so irksome in the comic plot would be more useful to the king, and the king's perceptible shifts of role would be more useful to his libertine subjects.

Tragicomedy was the genre in which Aphra Behn made her debut. She was by far the most prolific dramatist of the 1670s and 1680s, writing approximately twenty plays, in which she provides an unusually sophisticated and comprehensive survey of the development of patriarchal society. The early tragicomedies trace male suprema- cism back to its origins in feudal society: a society sustained not by idealized male bonding (as in Orrery) but by a trade in women as military prizes (as in her first performed play, *The Forc'd Marriage* [1670]). Starting with her second performed play,

The Amorous Prince (1671), which provides frank criticism of a philandering ruler, she moves on to a peacetime aristocracy, where attractive males exploit women with their wealth, and finally (in her comedies) to a bourgeois economy, where the exploiting males are old and impotent, having only the power of money. *The Young King*, first performed (probably) in 1679 but by her own account her first play, is a tragicomedy of restoration. One plot strand, loosely (and probably indirectly) derived from Calderón's *La vida es sueño* (*Life is a Dream*), portrays a prince who has been denied his ancestral throne because of prophecies about his future tyranny, and has been brought up a prisoner. Although he has had no cultural inducements to machismo, he nevertheless grows up as a pure, undiluted man, a tangle of aggression and rapist lust, at first far more of a Hobbesian savage than Almanzor or the young Montezuma. He is reformed and restored, but to portray the restored king as initially a tangle of brute lusts is to celebrate restoration in strangely muted terms, and Behn gives quite disturbing stress to the ignorance and banality of the restoring mob.

Heroic Drama in the 1670s

Split-plot tragicomedy went out of fashion after 1671, giving way to unmixed social comedy. Simultaneously, serious drama changed, as a result of separate but interacting factors. One was that plays about the Restoration had simply outlived their topicality. Another was the success of *The Conquest of Granada*. A hoary myth maintains that *The Rehearsal* so successfully ridiculed heroic drama as to drive it off the stage, but in fact imitations of Dryden only started to appear in the 1670s, after *The Conquest of Granada*, but also after *The Rehearsal* (Hume 1976: 290–1). There was a deluge of Conquest, Siege and Destruction plays, such as Elkanah Settle's *The Conquest of China* (1675) and John Crowne's two-part blockbuster, *The Destruction of Jerusalem* (1677), though these change and diversify the heroic play: if Dryden is different from Orrery, Dryden's epigones are different from him and each other. Another factor was the appearance of a new generation of dramatists, and a final one was growing fear of, in Andrew Marvell's phrase, popery and arbitrary government. It had long been clear that Charles's queen, Catherine of Braganza, was not going to provide him with an heir, and that (barring remarriage or the legitimizing of one of Charles's bastards) the succession would devolve upon Charles's authoritarian, inflexible and stupid brother James, Duke of York, whose defects were reinforced by the dangerous virtue of military courage. In 1672 Charles aroused public disquiet by entering upon another war with Protestant Holland, in alliance with the absolutist Catholic monarch Louis XIV. Then, in 1673, James made public what was already an open secret: that he was a Catholic convert, and that the country faced the succession of a ruler of alien and absolutist principles.

These various factors produced a marked shift in the character of drama. Plays about the Restoration petered out (though they reappeared in the Exclusion Crisis of 1678–81, when opposition to James's succession reached its height). What follows is drama about the problems of an uncertain succession. An early example is Elkanah Settle's *Cambyses* (1671), set in ancient Persia, in which the heroic principles of virtuous characters leave them divided in allegiance between two equally unsatisfactory claimants to the throne: the titular tyrant, who has murdered his younger brother, and an impostor pretending to be that brother. Finally, both die, and the succession goes, not to the candidate who is next in line, but to the one who would be the best ruler. An example of how individual principle is now deluded and manipulated by corrupt public authority is the exemplary self-denial of one of the heroic characters, Theramnes: he has sworn not to reveal that a letter was written by his king, and continues to honour his oath even when the letter turns out to be a forgery designed to make him appear false to the woman he loves. This is not far from what an Orrery hero would have done: a character in *Tryphon* scrupulously observes an oath to help the titular usurper in his love, even after discovering that they both love the same woman, and feels considerable political obligations to the *de facto* ruler. The twist in Settle is that Theramnes has been taken in by a complete fraud, and that the obligations which he so punctiliously honours are illusory.

A characteristic of Settle's plays is that they explore the moral and epistemological enigmas that bedevil justice in an absolute monarchy. What happens when the ruler who is the arbiter of justice is, in any sensible construction of the term, a criminal? The problem is not only one of practical response to the situation but of fundamental definition: if the king is the arbiter of justice, by what standards beyond himself *can* he be termed a criminal? The situation of the criminal ruler dominates Settle's plays, and generates imbroglios in which the roles and rituals of justice become hopelessly confused. In one scene in *Cambyses*, for example, a heroine formally approaches the impostor king for justice, unaware that he is himself the criminal on whom she seeks judgement. Later, a death sentence imposed by a further criminal usurper is prevented when, in a rather ludicrous reversal of judicial roles, the executioner turns out to be a virtuous hero in disguise. Settle was a confused writer whose best creations are his lists of extras (*Cambyses* calls for 'Villains, Ghosts, Spirits, Masquers, Messengers, Executioners, Guards, and Attendants'), but his very confusions register the bewilderment of the early 1670s, when anxiety about the intentions of the Stuart regime was neither channelled nor inhibited by a clearly formulated alternative. When that alternative did emerge, during the attempts to exclude James from the succession in favour of Charles's eldest illegitimate son, the Duke of Monmouth, he was one of the leading Exclusionist dramatists, though he changed sides with unusual unattractiveness when Exclusion was defeated.

Disquiet about the succession is evident even in Dryden. In 1680–1, he emerged as the most memorable defender of James's cause, but his last heroic play, *Aureng-Zebe* (1675), shows the succession going to the best candidate, after the elimination of two elder claimants with suspiciously James-like characteristics. One is brave but unforgiving (1.90–1), the other 'a Bigot of the *Persian* Sect', who 'by a Foreign Int'rest seeks to Reign' (1.94–5): probably an allusion to James's Catholicism, and to his association with France. As indicated above, Aureng-Zebe is not quite a paragon. He has the flaws of the rigid idealist: destructive intolerance and lack of self-knowledge. But he is the best that is on offer, and he is not initially the first in line.

If Settle portrays confusion confusedly, there is more purpose in the works of the two best tragedians to make their appearance in the 1670s, Nathaniel Lee and Thomas Otway. Both were instrumental in moving serious drama beyond rhymed tragedy, and both found their mature voices in doing so, though it is their early plays that concern us here. Otway's first heroic play, *Alcibiades* (1675), portrays a disjunction between individual codes of honour and the public sphere in which they are pursued. Its hero has the traditional ideals of love and honour, but they are erratic in operation, and are at odds with their social setting: Alcibiades has been exiled from his native Athens for sacrilege, and is displaying his prowess and honour on the side of his country's enemies (he exemplifies a widespread concern with dislocation and isolation in the drama of this period). He is also disastrously out of touch, carelessly consoling an amorous villainess by saying that he would love her were it not for her husband and his mistress, and thereby (predictably) prompting her to murder both.

What is particularly striking in the drama of this period is a fascination with the figure of the lustful or rapist tyrant. In drama of the 1660s, usurpers attempt rape; now, legitimate rulers can attempt it, and sometimes succeed. The tactful criticism of royal sexuality in plays such as *Mustapha* has been replaced by violent outrage. One cannot crudely say that all lustful stage rulers are direct representations of Charles II, but the portrayal of stage royalty in the 1660s had been visibly linked to the cult of the king (Charles loaned his and his brother's coronation suits to the theatre for a revival of Davenant's *Love and Honour* [1661] and for Orrery's *The History of Henry the Fifth* [1664]). The diminishing celebration of the king, and the growing portrayal of tyranny, inevitably suggests a change of climate. Otway's second play, *Don Carlos* (1676), resembles Dryden's earlier *Aureng-Zebe* in having an elderly, sexually oppressive monarch, who covets his son's mistress. In *Aureng-Zebe*, however, the conflicts are finally resolved. In *Don Carlos* they are insoluble (Carlos even plans to join a rebellion against his father), the play ends in catastrophe, and the king goes mad.

Otway remained loyal to the monarchy, though gloomily so. Nathaniel Lee's early plays, by contrast, are particularly hostile to the Stuart regime, until the tide of events (and the banning of his plays *The Massacre of Paris* and *Lucius Junius Brutus*) converted him. Lee is so preoccupied with the sex-mad tyrant that, in *Gloriana* (1676), he even turns the emperor Augustus into one. More traditionally, he also portrays Nero in this way, in *The Tragedy of Nero, Emperour of Rome* (1674), a comprehensive destruction of the clichés of early Restoration tragicomedy. The son of the previous emperor (Claudius) and true heir to the throne, Britannicus, is not restored, but goes mad and is killed, and the play concludes with the deposition of the ruling dynasty by an outsider, Galba (who, historically, was himself to be quickly deposed). A conventional image of the Restoration had been the return of Astraea, goddess of justice, who according to classical myth had fled the earth at the beginning of the Iron Age (Ovid, *Metamorphoses* 1.150). Virgil's celebration of the return of the Golden Age in *Eclogue* 4.6 had been quoted on one of the arches which adorned Charles's coronation procession, and Dryden's panegyric on the Restoration, *Astraea Redux*, derived its name from the myth of Astraea's return. Lee, however, depicts a world from which Astraea has again departed: observing Nero's pride and cruelty, a character exclaims 'where is Astrea fled?' (2.3.90); significantly, the exclamation coincides with the moment at which Nero resolves on Britannicus's death, and where the possibility of restoration is snuffed out. The existence of plays such as *Nero* and *Don Carlos* should make us wary of the old cliché that Restoration audiences revelled simultaneously in a serious drama of extreme idealism and a bawdy comic drama of unparalleled cynicism. Full-blown sex comedy did not emerge until 1674–5. Although the best plays of the 1660s were, naturally, still being performed at that time, idealism had largely disappeared from new tragedies: the tragic contemporaries of the sex-comedy heroes were the lustful tyrants, or the men of principle who were out of touch with the murky cynicism around them.

Obviously, drama of the mid-1670s has many strands, and not all stage rulers were sex-mad egomaniacs. Some, such as Titus in John Crowne's *The Destruction of Jerusalem*, heroically renounce foreign mistresses (as Charles failed to do with the Duchess of Portsmouth). A very different, yet extremely topical, play is Henry Neville Payne's *The Siege of Constantinople* (1674), which contains clear portrayals of a number of political figures, including Charles, James and the Earl of Shaftesbury, who was now clearly moving into opposition to James. The play is loyalist, and its royal brothers have exemplary sex lives, but it nevertheless portrays royal weakness, for the Byzantine emperor is destroyed by benevolence, and by trusting (and mistrusting) the wrong people. Payne's approach is the reverse of Orrery's, in that he analyses specific conflicts in some detail, and a consequence is that abstract schemes of love and honour retreat into the background. The most overt debt to earlier heroic drama is in the general Justiniano (an unfair caricature of Count Schomberg, who was sent by Louis XIV to command British troops in the Third Dutch War), who resembles Almanzor in being a bombastic foreign ally. Justiniano, however, is a mere poseur and a mercenary, who will not fight without pay: the economics of political conflict, so strikingly banished from Orrery's world, are here central. *The Siege of Constantinople* clearly has its roots in the heroic play, yet in almost every respect apart from its royalism it reverses Orrery's procedures. It portrays not the rebirth of England but its reduction to a client state, and it does so with attention to the impenetrable maze of deception and profiteering in which politics is conducted.

'The Restoration Heroic Play' is not, then, a single, monolithic phenomenon. Overall, one may distinguish three stages: Davenant and Orrery; Dryden, who deals sceptically with the values, and the political events, that Orrery simply endorses; and the host of new dramatists who take their lead from *The Conquest of Granada* but transform drama to reflect the growing sense of political crisis. In some ways, the quantity of Siege, Conquest and Destruction plays gives a false impression of theatrical fashion: these are often short-lived plays by minor or immature dramatists, with no ideas of their own and nothing better to do than to imitate the successes of their betters. Drama changes when Lee and Otway find their voices, when Dryden changes direction, and when the political crisis of 1678–81 turned diffused anxiety into focused, if rapidly shifting, partisanship.

REFERENCES AND FURTHER READING

Aubrey, John (1898). *'Brief Lives', Chiefly of Contemporaries*, ed. Andrew Clark. 2 vols. Oxford.
Barbeau, Anne T. (1970). *The Intellectual Design of John Dryden's Heroic Plays*. New Haven, CT, and London: Yale University Press.
Canfield, J. Douglas (1984). 'The Ideology of Restoration Tragicomedy', *ELH* 51, 447–64.
Canfield, J. Douglas (1989). *Word as Bond in English Literature from the Middle Ages to the Restoration*. Philadelphia: University of Pennsylvania Press.
Cannan, Paul D. (1994). 'New Directions in Serious Drama on the London Stage, 1675–1678', *Philological Quarterly* 73, 219–42.
Dorsch, T. S. (trans.). (1965). *Classical Literary Criticism*. Harmondsworth: Penguin.
Dryden, John (1956–). *The Works of John Dryden*, ed. Edward Niles Hooker, H. T. Swedenberg, Jr, et al. 20 vols in progress. Berkeley: University of California Press.
Drydeniana: 'The Censure of the Rota' and Elkanah Settle (1974). The Life and Times of Seven Major English Writers. Drydeniana, 5. New York and London: Garland.
Hughes, Derek (1981). *Dryden's Heroic Plays*. London and Basingstoke: Macmillan.
Hughes, Derek (1996). *English Drama, 1660–1700*. Oxford: Clarendon Press.
Hume, Robert D. (1976). *The Development of English Drama in the Late Seventeenth Century*. Oxford: Clarendon Press.
Jose, Nicholas (1984). *Ideas of the Restoration in English Literature, 1660–71*. London and Basingstoke: Macmillan.
Kirsch, Arthur C. (1965). *Dryden's Heroic Drama*. Princeton, NJ: Princeton University Press.
Lee, Nathaniel (1954–5). *The Works of Nathaniel Lee*, ed. Thomas B. Stroup and Arthur L. Cooke. 2 vols. New Brunswick, NJ: Scarecrow Press.
Maguire, Nancy Klein (1992). *Regicide and Restoration: English Tragicomedy, 1660–1671*. Cambridge: Cambridge University Press.
Munns, Jessica (1995). *Restoration Politics and Drama: The Plays of Thomas Otway, 1675–1683*. Newark: University of Delaware Press; London: Associated University Presses.
Rubidge, Bradley (1999). 'The Code of Reciprocation in *The Conquest of Granada*', *Restoration* 23, 31–56.
South, Robert (1823). *Sermons Preached upon Several Occasions*. 7 vols. Oxford.
Staves, Susan (1979). *Players' Scepters: Fictions of Authority in the Restoration*. Lincoln, NB, and London: University of Nebraska Press.
Van Lennep, William, Avery, Emmett L., Scouten, Arthur H., Winchester Stone, Jr, George and Beecher Hogan, Charles (eds). (1960–8). *The London Stage, 1660–1800*. 5 parts in 11 vols. Carbondale: Southern Illinois University Press, vol. 1.
Wallace, John M. (1980). 'John Dryden's Plays and the Conception of a Heroic Society', in Perez Zagorin (ed.), *Culture and Politics: From Puritanism to the Enlightenment*. Berkeley: University of California Press, 113–34.

13
Restoration Comedy
J. Douglas Canfield

If the Renaissance is the Golden Age of English comedy, the Restoration is the Silver. Restoration comedy is famous for its shimmering dialogue, its wit, its elegance of manners, its daring portrayal of sexual intrigue. But it is also rich in folk exuberance, often manifesting in farce. And it is deeply political and sometimes quite nasty.

One might say of classical occidental comedy that it puts the right couple to bed at the end. Such is true because European society has been since time immemorial patriarchal. Power and property are conveyed through patrilineal genealogy. Aristocracies must reproduce themselves as the rightful class to rule, and thus they must control reproduction so couples with the right breeding, both literally and metaphorically, inherit the estates. This process of cultural reproduction must cloak itself in the rhetoric of naturalness: aristocrats have the right to rule because they are superior by birth.

In Restoration England, the aristocracy had this same general concern. But it had concerns particular to its own time. It had just emerged from a fight for its life in the English Civil Wars and sought to relegitimate itself. So it portrayed itself as superior in every way to its opponents, whom it caricatured as self-interested cits from London or self-enamoured parvenus and pretenders invading the fashionable Town and Court in Westminster or Country boobies lacking the sophistication of their Cavalier cousins. These Beautiful People of their time reaffirm their right of succession by manifesting the necessary *élan* to ridicule their opponents, on the one hand, and, on the other, to perpetuate their estates through the good breeding of the gay, insouciant couples who inevitably marry at the end. As the Restoration yields to the Revolution, however, comedies begin to portray a bourgeois morality wherein the superior are so by merit, by good nature. For if Britannia is to rule the world, She must allow her *nouveaux riches* into both her seats of power and her ideology of superiority.

The majority of Restoration comedies perform the cultural work of relegitimation, and I call these *social* comedies, that is, comedies that socialize threats, both explicit and implicit, to the hegemonic ideology of the restored Stuarts and their court party.

In the 1660s Cavalier wits and witty women conspire, as in Sir Robert Howard's *Committee* (first performed 1662), to win back for dispossessed Cavaliers their estates sequestered by the Roundheads and their factors during the Interregnum, which factors are roundly satirized. In the 1670s, comedy seems less overtly political, but it is still concerned with trickery and estates and cultural superiority. Witty women socialize potent young men so that their sexual energy serves the cause of cultural reproduction. Three of the best of this kind of comedy are John Crowne's *Country Wit* (1675), Sir George Etherege's *Man of Mode; or, Sir Fopling Flutter* (1676) and Aphra Behn's *Rover; or, The Banished Cavaliers* (1677). The names of two of the protagonists indicate their sexual excesses (Ramble and Willmore) and that of the third his potential (Dorimant, suggestive of *dormant*, French for 'sleeping'). All three espouse a libertine ethic opposed to spousals and favouring promiscuity as natural to the human species. All three meet women as resourceful and desirable as they, with whom there is no taking up without, as one of Etherege's characters expresses it, 'church security'. Behn's waggish Hellena, who refuses to have her sexuality sequestered in a nunnery, responds to Willmore's plan to love and leave with an effective rejoinder condemning a double standard that leaves her 'a cradle full of noise and mischief, with a pack of repentance at my back'. Her image, however witty, nonetheless reminds us of the nasty future for fallen women in her culture: she and her bastard were likely to be turned out of doors and forced to beg. But Hellena and the others, heiresses all, manage to awaken a new awareness in the 'souls' of their rakes, so much so that they are willing to be so unfashionable as to marry. Ramble, who has used portraits to gain access to mistresses, now swears to make no images but his own – through reproduction with his new bride. Willmore agrees to Hellena's terms and is accepted by her noble brother as himself inherently noble (despite his loss of his estate in the Interregnum), especially because he has loyally served his prince and helped preserve the Estate of England. And Dorimant appears, incredibly, to be willing to 'keep a Lent for a mistress' – courting her in the 'dismal' country – 'in expectation of a happy Easter', that is, resurrection to his rightful role as lord of the manor on Harriet's inherited estate.

However 'dismal' and unfashionable the Country, it is the locus of the estates that support the conspicuous consumption of the aristocracy in the Town, a reality that these plays obfuscate as they portray the pursuits of the leisured class as if their wealth were unattached to the labour of their tenants. The economic reality surfaces when prodigals like Dorimant must marry to mend their squandered estates. Often, as in *The Man of Mode*, gentry have come to London not just for the fashionable residence in the Town but to negotiate the business of estates. Harriet's mother, Lady Woodvile, has come for the purpose of marrying her heiress daughter to the son of a country squire, Young Belair. But in these three comedies in particular and much of Restoration comedy in general, the young women – and sometimes the young men as well – refuse to accept their parents' or guardians' choice. Yet they do so at great risk, for they can lose their inheritances or marriage portions. Harriet falls in love with Dorimant at first sight and insists to her disapproving mother that she will marry no other – but that she will never marry without her consent either. Young Belair loves elsewhere too, and by chance his father falls in love with his beloved. It is a constant threat in such comedy that a widower or a widow might remarry, beget another child, and thus dispossess the current heir-apparent. So the witty young gentry of these plays become tricksters and manage to obtain their own choice complete with parental blessing at the end. And the older generation must sometimes perforce retire from reproduction and yield to the younger. Crowne's Christina and Etherege's Harriet resist parental choice, reform the rakes of their desires, and finally win parental approval. Behn's Hellena's sister Florinda escapes an arranged marriage, but by leaving the safety of her father's house runs the risk of abduction and rape until she is at last united with her brave English colonel in a marriage blessed by her guardian brother.

An important part of these and most comedies is discipline. If a major action is to unite the right, aristocratic couple(s) at the end, another is to satirize opposing groups from the Country and the City (of London) and from the Town itself. This discipline through satire performs the work not only of caricaturing old and continuing enemies from the Civil Wars (Roundheads, Puritans, cits) but of obfuscating the Town's necessary economic relations with both Country and City, the latter, as the centre of commerce, especially with increasingly important colonies, being the source of new money for the rebuilding of estates and the expansion of agriculture (*engrossment*, often through *enclosure* of common land). In Behn's play, the banished Cavaliers of its subtitle are dependent on Ned Blunt, a country squire who did not, apparently for expediency's sake, lose his estate in the Interregnum, and Blunt is mercilessly tricked and beaten and stripped – as if in denial of still necessary Cavalier connections with the Country. In Crowne's play, the title itself is an oxymoron: the country sow's ear Sir Mannerly Shallow cannot be made into a silk purse. And in Etherege's play, the affected parvenu Sir Fopling Flutter lacks the breeding and grace of a real gentleman like Dorimant – although he does constitute a threat if the ladies, showing no discrimination, are attracted to him. So Dorimant must engineer Sir Fopling's discipline at the hands of his mistress Loveit.

For the discipline of Puritans and cits we should look to comedies of the 1660s, where they are relentlessly satirized, beaten, tricked in a theatre controlled by the victors in the wars. But especially we should look to the cit-cuckolding plays, where Cavalier rakes, in a kind of generalized *droit du seigneur*, seduce the wives of citizens with impunity. These plays begin increasing in number as the Restoration compromise begins to crumble, particularly over the principle of succession, for Charles II produced no legitimate male heir and his Catholic brother, James, Duke of York, became heir-presumptive. So in the late 1670s, as England reeled towards the Popish Plot and then the Exclusion Crisis, the discipline of the ruling class's – or better, ruling oligarchy's – enemies became more strident. The most aggressive comedy around the time of the Plot was John Leanerd's *The Rambling Justice; or, The Jealous Husbands* (1678); around the time of the Crisis, Crowne's *City Politiques* (postponed by censors until 1683). All of these plays feature in-your-face cuckolding that the husbands are forced finally to accept. The import is that their persons, portrayed as imperfect, impotent, dull, are no match for the perfect bodies and wits of the class designed by nature to rule, who have the right of the *seigneur* sexually to dominate their inferiors and deposit with them their bastards. As the wacky servant Bramble says to his superannuated master Sir Arthur Twilight in Leanerd's play, being cuckolded with brazen impunity is 'an Hereditary possession' of cits. Florio in Crowne's play infiltrates the centre of seditious Whigs by pretending conversion from promiscuity to Puritan piety. As he bends the Podesta's (in effect, Lord Mayor's) wife over and gazes on her exposed bosom, he triumphs, 'I will come ashore on these white cliffs' – a metaphor designed to remind us that Tories and Whigs in the 1680s contend for the same prize as Cavalier and Roundhead in the 1640s: the White Cliffs of Dover, a metonymy for the Estate of England.

Aside from these two dominant actions of Restoration social comedy, those in which witty women land their men and witty men discipline their political rivals by cuckolding them, there are other actions. There are plays featuring mature women, often widows, who also manage affairs in order to man their land, like Lady Wealthy in James Howard's *English Mounsieur* (1663), Lady Pleasant in William Cavendish, Duke of Newcastle's *Humorous Lovers* (1667) and Mrs Hadland of *The Counterfeit Bridegroom; or, The Defeated Widow* (1677). There are plays in which young men sans portfolios, especially younger brothers, trick their way into marriage with attendant estates, as in Roger Boyle, Earl of Orrery's *Guzman* (1669), Francis Fane's *Love in the Dark; or, The Man of Bus'ness* (1675) and Behn's *City Heiress; or, Sir Timothy Treat-All* (1682). One last important action of social comedy is the trickster tricked, for example, in the very interesting *Sir Salomon; or, The Cautious Coxcomb* (1670) by John Caryll. The title character plans to trick his old friend, an 'Indy-Merchant', out of his rich daughter, left to Sir Salomon's wardship while the merchant expands his fortune abroad, and to beget upon her an heir to displace his prodigal son, Single. Sir Salomon's name may indicate Puritan origins, perhaps one who purchased a baronetcy; howbeit, he is not only ungenerous (in the sense of *noblesse oblige*), he is downright vicious, as he attempts to have his rival for the daughter beaten to death by his servants. That rival's name is not accidentally Peregreen, the falcon that is a metonym for the aristocracy. But Sir Salomon has overreached himself, signing over his estate to his intended wife, who ends up the wife of Peregreen. As her husband, Peregreen now owns the deed and generously, nobly renders it back to its rightful owner, the prodigal son, who marries the daughter of a rich cit. Especially interesting here is the union of Town wits with daughters of City and Indies merchants: an acknowledgement of the growing dependence of England's aristocracy on the wealth of the colonial metropolis London was becoming – even as the play underwrites the value of aristocratic *generosity*.

So not even Restoration social comedy, in its cultural work of relegitimation, presents a seamless garment of Stuart aristocratic ideology. But there are comedies that split the seams even further, Restoration *subversive* comedy. Edward Ravenscroft's *Careless Lovers* (1673) is a perfect foil to Etherege's *Man of Mode*. The rake Careless eschews marriage, spouting the typical libertine ethic of natural promiscuity. His fellow Town wit Lovell predicts Careless will come round at last and be socialized into marriage, and the play seems to set up this expectation, as Careless becomes enchanted by and engaged in a contest of wits with the irrepressible Hillaria. Hillaria outrageously beats a foppish suitor of her cousin and even threatens her uncle with a beating if he continue to force his will upon the young women. Dressing as a waggish wit herself, Hillaria attracts Careless's mistresses and whores away from him, and the two finally engage in a scene of exchanging terms in an agreement that usually ends in a traditional marriage, with the centrifugal energy of the rake usually centripetalized. But in Ravenscroft's play, this proviso scene arranges for post-marital promiscuity on the part not just of the rambling Careless, but Hillaria herself: she expects him to be a father to all her children and not ask who begot them; he expects her to be a nurse to all his children, including his bastards; she demands he not quarrel with her gallants but instead befriend them; he demands she befriend his mistresses and even hold the door for them. Such an arrangement, of course, would scramble the eggs of legitimacy – a legitimacy at the heart of succession of estates and even of the Estate of England. One of the suggestions during the Exclusion Crisis was that Charles and Parliament simply declare the king's bastard son, the Duke of Monmouth, the legitimate heir.

A small handful of comedies feature not so much inter- as intra-class warfare: Town wits who cuckold not cits but fellow wits in a subversion of ruling-class solidarity that threatens to rend that class's ideology asunder. The best of these are written by William Wycherley and Thomas Otway. Wycherley's *Country Wife* (1675) is probably the most infamous play of the Restoration, for the trickster Horner, obsessed with conquering women of high quality, whether they are married or not, publishes the rumour that he is a eunuch so that he might have access to them with impunity. It was a play that apparently outraged audiences, for Wycherley implies that upper-class morality masks hypocrisy, that every woman, aristocrats included, is at heart a rake (as the satirist Alexander Pope was to express it). These women are portrayed as desiring affairs with men of their own class instead of having to resort to the servant class! The central scene of the play stages the deliverance over to Horner by husbands and an old lady of Horner's desirable women so that they might fulfil their transgressive desires – in Horner's own lodgings in the virtual presence of these guardians of honour. The dominant of these women, Lady Fidget, married to a knight who is preoccupied with business at court, retires to Horner's bedroom supposedly to examine some rare china. When her husband shouts to her that Horner is coming around to the back door of the chamber, she delightfully invites Horner to come in to her any way he will. Such in-your-face cuckolding the audience cannot dismiss as mere class dominance, for if these are women of quality, whose constant complaint is that *birth* ought to count for something (that is, to attract Town lovers of quality), then their adultery and fornication threaten not only legitimacy of birth, of patrilineary, but the very rhetoric of an ideology filled with the pure vessels of conveyance of power and property.

Nor are Horner's antagonists all fools. In his effort to cover his affair with the country wife of the title, he nearly crosses swords with his fellow Town wit Harcourt, who pursues her sister-in-law to keep her from marrying a fop. Horner's way out is to pretend his assignation was with the sister, Alithea, and not the wife, Margery. Each Cavalier threatens to defend his interest in his lady. The conflict is resolved by lies and hypocrisy, and although the play ends partly with typical hymeneal celebration of the union of the witty Harcourt and Alithea, it also ends with Horner unexposed, unpunished – his very potent danger ungelded.

Otway's *Friendship in Fashion* (1678) devastatingly treats the breakdown of aristocratic codes of friendship and marital chastity. Goodvile, an intelligent and thoroughly competent wit, married to an attractive and equally witty lady, has not been socialized by marriage but continues to chase women, attempting to pawn off his cast mistresses (one of them his cousin Victoria) onto his supposed friends. Two of these friends, Truman and Valentine, determine to punish him for his breaches of faith by diverting Victoria onto a bumpkin and by winning Goodvile's wife and intended new mistress for themselves, respectively. Goodvile is so infuriated, he brings home whores to whom he intends to grant his wife's privileges of ownership and stewardship, thus threatening the very manor system itself.

The play pulls back from its brinkmanship, however, for Mrs Goodvile and Truman pretend nothing ever happened, and Goodvile is forced to take them at their word. Yet the cynicism of his last lines of the play about keeping wives away from 'Balls and Masquerades' reveals that the ending, notwithstanding its celebration of the marriage of Valentine and Camilla, only plasters over deep fissures in class solidarity.

Mrs Goodvile belongs to a small subset of Restoration comic witty heroines who get away with sexual transgression. The best and most interesting of these – because the most independent and threatening – were created by Behn, Thomas Shadwell and Thomas Southerne. Behn's Lucia of *Sir Patient Fancy* (1678) and La Nuche of *The Second Part of the Rover* (1681) are parasites. Lucia marries the title character for money to support herself and her libertine but penurious lover, Wittmore. She manipulates her hypochondriac husband until she can escape with wealth he has stashed for her; to be exposed and turned out of the marriage before she secured that wealth would, as she says aside, call her wit into question. Sir Patient is powerless to prove she has robbed him, and he must live with the fact that he is the proverbial cuckolded cit. But Lucia does provide him with his own escape from the marriage through annulment, and Behn has him at the end convert from stodgy and hypocritical Puritanism to gay Cavalierism. Lucia, who has mistakenly lain with another young man than her lover, goes off scot free to live with Wittmore on the proceeds of their scam.

Similarly, Behn's La Nuche is a parasite: she is a whore who wins the widower Willmore to a free way of life. Along the way she attacks traditional, conventional modes of reproductive economy, a system that demeans truly 'noble' illicit love and makes an aristocratic man a 'slavish Heir to estate and Wife, born rich and damn'd to Matrimony'. Though La Nuche eschews the slavery of prostitution as well, she and

Willmore, like Lucia and Wittmore, create no radical alternative economy but must remain parasites on the dominant economy of estates and heirs.

Shadwell's Lady Cheatly in *A True Widow* (1678) escapes into financial security through marriage to a wealthy cit. A widow whose husband's estate was stolen away, she revenges herself by pretending to be, in effect, an investment broker of significant means and talents. But she signs her securities in disappearing ink. In short, she is not a sexual but an economic trickster. Men normally control the economic world, whether of estates or trade, but Lady Cheatly asserts an agency that controls her world. When her steward attempts to reassert male control by blackmailing her, she arranges for him to be transported to the colonies. When miraculously he escapes and returns, she takes final refuge in marriage to the wealthy Maggot, who is 'governable' and who promises to manipulate the law for her benefit.

The most outrageous of these naughty women tricksters is Southerne's eponymous heroine of *Sir Anthony Love; or, The Rambling Lady* (1690). Sir Anthony is in reality Lucy, a young woman probably of the lower gentry whose mother sold her into white slavery. Having escaped from her keeper, Sir Gentle Golding, she pursues her lover Valentine to France, where she dresses and acts like a man with the best of them. She abets other women who seek at least freedom of choice in marriage, and she tricks other tricksters. She seems to do all for the sheer love of wit. She tricks Sir Gentle into marriage and a permanent settlement. And at the end of the play, after helping put other young lovers to bed, she avoids socializing herself, plans to continue a life of freedom and pleasure, including having sex with Valentine, though he is now married to Florante. Along the way, she has confused gender roles by out-machoing the men and status roles by deflating pretensions to inherited nobility. The most interesting figure for the resultant fluidity and lubricity is the homosexual abbé, who concludes the play by offering a thousand extra crowns to the niece who brings him the first boy! Sir Anthony's world has turned the aristocratic world upside down and threatened it with class and gender instability. As Sir Anthony says, she and her ilk make 'all the year a Carnival' – a world of play and *jouissance* that threatens established order.

One of the most remarkable – and least remarked – aspects of Restoration comedy is its folk exuberance. From 1660 to 1690 boisterous low-life figures tumble over and off the stage. These are not the satiric butts of disciplinary satire but folk tricksters who represent bodily and societal excess that cannot be contained and that demand representation and voice. Sometimes they are excrescences of plays whose high plots are social; sometimes they take over whole plays and make them subversive.

The 1660s were particularly rich in such characters, from Cutter and Worm in Abraham Cowley's *Cutter of Coleman Street* (1661) to Teague in Howard's *Committee* to Captain Bilboe and Titere Tu in John Wilson's *Cheats* (1663) to the subtitle character in John Lacy's *Old Troop; or, Monsieur Raggou* (1664). The type is perpetuated in such memorable figures as Footpad from the Duke of Newcastle's *Triumphant Widow* (1674), the title character of Behn's *False Count* (1681) and Trappolin in Nahum Tate's *Duke and No Duke* (1684). Even as they carry out some of its discipline, these male folk figures mock the pretensions of the aristocracy, particularly its rhetoric, and they often imitate its Town wits in winning for themselves women and even minor estates, thus moving up in social status. At the same time, they are a levelling force, exposing the hypocrisy of the aristocracy and revealing a world where all are cheats, tricksters, con men, and where sex, despite obfuscation, is an act of animal energy and renewal performed amidst the very detritus of existence.

Matching these male figures of folk misrule are similar female figures, from the clever women servants like Lucy in Wycherley's *Country Wife* or Peg in John Dover's *The Mall; or, The Modish Lovers* (1674); to bawds like Joyner and Mrs Crossbite in Wycherley's *Love in a Wood; or, St James's Park* (1671) or Sabina in Thomas Porter's *The French Conjuror* (1677); to whores like Lacy's Dol Troop in *The Old Troop*, the second Constantia in the Duke of Buckingham's *The Chances* (1667), and the 'family' of prostitutes in Dryden's *Mr Limberham; or, The Kind Keeper* (1678); to tricksters who are at the centre of their plays, like the infamous – and historically real – Mary Moders (Carleton) in Porter's *Witty Combat; or, The Female Victor* (1663?), or the fortune teller/ grave robber who gives her name to Edward Ravenscroft's *Dame Dobson; or, The Cunning Woman* (1683), or the dissembling Strega (the witch), the amorous old woman of Thomas Duffet's play of that name (1674). The title character from Thomas Thompson's *Life of Mother Shipton* (1662?) articulates as rationale for lower-class female transgression in Restoration society the argument from the necessity to escape poverty: 'Why am I so low then when others are so high? Why do I court the ground when others in their glorious pinacles grasp the sky? . . . *Directly or indirectly I will find a way, To make me rich*'. In the world of estate-getting and perpetuating, the young Mother Shipton represents the dispossessed.

If *social* comedy is the major subset of Restoration comedy and *subversive* comedy a minor but substantial one, there is one other even smaller but significant subset, *comical satire*. Comedies end in celebration, renewal, reproduction: of a new generation, of the political economy of the status quo ante (though sometimes with some alterations). Even if, as in subversive comedy, there are centrifugal elements, endings are still festive. All of these comedies contain satirical elements as well, especially as disciplinary devices. But some plays called comedies do not conclude in celebration and renewal. They conclude in either a draconian poetical justice or in no resolution at all, leaving the foolish or vicious behaviour to continue unabated.

Most of these satires are *corrective*; that is, they provide a clear standard by which to judge aberrant behaviour. Three good examples of this category during the Restoration are Shadwell's *Woman-Captain* (1679), Behn's *Lucky Chance; or, An Alderman's Bargain* (1686) and Thomas Durfey's *Fool's Preferment; or, The Three Dukes of Dunstable* (1688). Shadwell's and Durfey's plays satirize especially libertine wasteful extravagance. Stewards of estates lament their masters' squandering of them in the pursuit of either pleasure or preferment at court. Shadwell's title character serves as a delightful disciplinarian, chastising her Puritan husband for stealing estates, among other things, and rakehells for selling them off bit by bit to cits and whores. Having gained financial independence from her husband, this woman who has masqueraded as a captain remains single at the end of the play, a lone scourge whose agency has whipped transgressors. Durfey's faithful servant Toby continually articulates the standard of proper estate husbandry, first to his wayward master Cockle-brain, then to Cockle-brain's uncle Grub, both of whom throw caution – and wealth and even wives – to the wind chasing the title of duke. Even Toby becomes infected with social climbing and tries to become a duke as well. Durfey's play ends with poetical justice administered by an agent of the king: the three would-be dukes are humiliated and return home chastened, if grumbling.

Behn's play is perhaps the most interesting of these corrective satires. Two of its plots have to do with chastising cits for interfering with the matching of witty, gay couples. But the third plot chastises a Town wit for violating the person of his beloved. Gayman's betrothed has been forced by financial exigencies to marry Sir Cautious Fulbank in Gayman's absence. Gayman wins a night with her in a card game (the *lucky chance* of the title). But when she discovers who he is, she is furious with him for raping her liberty of person. She has told him throughout that if she wanted to cuckold her husband she would, but not so much morality as personal, aesthetic choice keeps her from doing so. Gayman has not honoured that right to choose, and thus he violates her personal tranquillity, her 'Quiet'.

A small handful of these satires are *menippean* or *absurdist*; that is, they pull the rug out from under ostensible standards of judgement and leave us with mere words, words, words. Two of these plays occur at the beginning and the end of the Restoration proper, and one occurs smack in the middle. Durfey's *A Fond Husband; or, The Plotting Sisters* (1677) seems on the surface a typical cit-cuckolding play. The Town wit Rashley cuckolds the foolish Bubble with his attractive wife, Emilia, right in Bubble's own house. His fellow wit, Ranger, and Bubble's sister, Maria, try again and again to expose the adultery to the credulous Bubble, discoursing of the immorality in traditional, Christian terms, as if Emilia were as bad a 'Devil' as Eve, the arch-transgressor. Emilia's wit is superior to Maria's, however, and the audience's expectations of poetical justice are frustrated throughout. Instead, we seem to be invited to admire the outrageousness of this sublimely gay couple – especially because Ranger's and Maria's motivations are complicated by their own desires and jealousies. Finally, not as the result of Ranger's and Maria's plotting but strictly by accident, the couple is discovered *in flagrante delicto*, and Emilia for the first time in her life is at a loss for words, her impudence shamed. Yet just when we expect Durfey to draw a moral, Maria, instead of attributing the denouement to the Heaven she has so often invoked, attributes it merely to 'chance', and Ranger decides to abet rather than oppose fashionable adultery.

John Tatum's *Rump; or, The Mirrour of the Late Times* (1660) ushers in the Restoration (which actually occurred after the play was performed) with a satire on Cromwell's generals who have seized power, forced out Cromwell's son and the remaining Rump Parliament of the title (which they have to recall almost immediately), and established themselves as the Committee of Safety to rule England. Throughout the play they are exposed as unfit to rule because of their pettiness, their appropriation of public funds to pay off their supporters, and above all, their complete lack of loyalty. Concurrently, their wives expose themselves as unfit as well, and as preoccupied with status. The most delightful woman character in the play is Phyllis, waiting woman to the lead general's wife, who has her own status aspirations. And the most delightful male character is the Champion apprentice, who leads the common folk of London in rebellion against their oppressors. They look to General Monck to save the City, preserve liberties and sponsor the election of a free Parliament. The audience expects, in the celebration of the final ousting of the generals and the Rump by roasting rumps in the streets of London, a poetical justice that re-establishes order and hierarchy. But who carries out the change? Soldiers, who have been characterized throughout as callous, immoral opportunists. So when the generals, their wives and Phyllis must resort to being street vendors in the end, Phyllis declares that whatever the change of state, 'If any gentleman take me up, I am still' – just as the soldiers have declared 'While We are here, We are here; when We are gone, We are gone'. 'Words are but wind', opines Phyllis: whatever the regnant ideology, it's all the same. The politicians, the soldiers, the poor are always with us: the people endure.

Dryden's *Amphitryon; or, The Two Sosias* (1690) takes the old story of Jupiter's impersonating Amphitryon to seduce his wife Alcmena – an adultery justified by the resultant child, Hercules, who rids the world of evils – and gives it an absurdist twist. Perhaps moved by the absence of God's justice anent the usurpation of England's throne from its legitimate heir (as he saw it), right after William III's final and conclusive victory over James II at the Battle of the Boyne, Dryden managed to have produced a play portraying the Father-God as amoral power justifying supplanting of all sorts, in effect, through sheer desire. To his (bastard) sons Phoebus Apollo and Mercury, Jupiter declares that what he wills is fate, and particularly the latter points out the speciousness of Jupiter's theodicy.

Dryden's treatment of this incredibly subversive theme is not heavy-handed, however, but amazingly light, funny, ludic. He availed himself of the two greatest comic actors of the time – James Nokes and Anthony Leigh – to play the two Sosias of the subtitle, one of them an impersonation by Mercury, and their hilarious antics serve, in their cumulative effect, to toss high culture, with its official morality now abrogated by Jupiter, into a cocked hat. The doubling of Sosia destabilizes identity itself, and the result is a folk acceptance of the vagaries of power as the folk themselves collectively endure – in this case by recommending that Amphitryon accept fate and turn it to account by figuring that Jupiter merely gets his sexual leavings.

After the Revolution of 1688–90 comedy still concerns tricksters and estates, but a new kind of trickster emerges, one portrayed as ultimately a worthy steward of the new Nation. Let me call Revolution comedy those comedies produced between Revolution and the Union Act linking England and Scotland in 1707. Perhaps the best example of a Revolution comedy in which the right couple overcome obstacles in order to be matched and inherit is William Congreve's *Love for Love* (1695). Valentine Legend has squandered his allowance in the pursuit of his beloved Angellica, niece and ward of the astrologically preoccupied Foresight. Valentine's father, Sir Samuel, outraged at his son's prodigality, acts to disinherit him and supplant him with his younger brother, the seafaring Ben.

As in other Revolution comedies, the object of discipline includes not just a mistaken or perverse parent but parvenus and superannuated would-be lovers and especially those rapacious cits who continue to acquire aristocratic estates: hence Valentine's dun, Trapland. Valentine thinks he can sign over his inheritance for a settlement that will allow him to pursue Angellica, but neither his father nor Trapland has any intention of letting him off the hook. When Valentine finally realizes the seriousness of his (financial) situation, upon advice from his fellow trickster Scandal, he feigns madness – for two reasons: so he is *non compos mentis* and therefore cannot make over his inheritance, and so he can win sympathy from Angellica, whose aloofness is taken as the cause of his madness. She, however, discovers he feigns and plays him 'Trick for Trick', pretending she never loved him. His generosity in relinquishing his inheritance in order to make her happy, as he believes, in a marriage to his brother finally demonstrates his worth.

What is manifest in Valentine is worth without inheritance, without birth, as it were. Angellica's highest desideratum in a man is 'good Nature and Sense', and here we have underscored a new optimum: not the *wit* of Restoration comedy. Valentine's plots fail. Instead, *generosity* has been subtly redefined to have less to do with birth, with the *genealogy* that produces *gentlemen*, than with essential moral goodness, benevolence. Like the down-and-out younger brother Aimwell in George Farquhar's *Beaux' Stratagem* (1707), who is rewarded for his generosity, in not taking advantage of the desirable, well-born and financially well-endowed Dorinda, by fortuitously inheriting his brother's title and estate, Valentine joins estates possessed by those who merit them by morality more than wit and energy and heritage.

Congreve and Farquhar both wrote popular plays that socialize the sexual energy of more conventional Town wits: *The Old Batchelour* (1693) and *The Constant Couple; or, A Trip to the Jubilee* (1699), respectively, although the original ending of the latter includes sentiments Ranger, Dorimant and Willmore would never utter. When the inveterate rake Sir Harry Wildair discovers that he has been tricked into thinking this play's Angellica a prostitute, he makes the following offer: 'If chastest, purest Passion, with a large and fair Estate, can make amends, they're yours this Moment'. Instead of Harriet's witty scepticism about mistrusting the first signs of repentance in one, like Dorimant, long-hardened in sin, Angellica's response emphasizes new keywords: 'I'm pleas'd to find my Sentiments of you, which were always *Generous*, so generously answer'd'. Prompted by success to write a sequel in which Sir Harry is on the loose again, thinking his wife dead, Farquhar concludes the play that carries his name as the title quite differently from how Behn concludes her sequel to *The Rover*: Sir Harry, reunited with his wife, proceeds to regale us with 'the definition of a good Wife, in the Character of my own'.

In other words, though critics have tried to keep the comedies of Congreve and Farquhar out of the category *sentimental*, their comedies belong with those of Shadwell and Colly Cibber, with the difference being one of degree and not of kind. For sentimental comedy is a term critics use, really, to characterize *bourgeois* comedy, that based upon an ethos of benevolence, the theory of which was supplied by Anthony Ashley Cooper, third Earl of Shaftesbury. Shadwell's *Squire of Alsatia* (1688) moves a rake into a marriage at the end, but he is radically different from Dorimant. He has never used an oath as the price of admission to his mistresses' favours. He asks himself how a 'good natur'd man' could cast aside such mistresses, but insists, 'I must' – a phrase he repeats when he decides to marry. For the same necessity of patriarchy obtains: society must reproduce itself; the best couples must be put to bed. What has changed is the definition of *best* – and to some extent, the nature of trickery.

Cibber's 'Good-natur'd', abandoned wife wins back the rakish wit Loveless employing *love's last shift*, as announced in the title of his famous and popular play (1696): her trick is the old Shakespearean one of substituting herself in bed, although the trick has been psychologized, novelized. The ideal couple has not only been put back to bed, but Amanda has learned how to please her husband well enough to keep him there. So it is not only stoic 'Reason' that centripetalizes Loveless but a bit of Epicurean fleshly delight as well. Loveless has come to merit the mending of his own estate and the joining of it to Amanda's by his acknowledgement of the superiority of 'Virtue' – not untested but tried in the furnace of 'warm Desires'.

That which must be socialized in Revolution comedy is just as much centrifugal women as men: coquettes, like Cibber's Lady Betty Modish in *The Careless Husband* (1704), Shadwell's Gertrude in *Bury Fair* (1689), Crowne's Julia in *The English Frier; or, The Town Sparks* (1690) and Congreve's Millamant in *The Way of the World* (1700). Lady Betty articulates the issue perhaps most explicitly: she does not want to relinquish 'Power'. But as Lady Easy tries to teach her, Lady Betty must learn to surrender gracefully and with 'good Humour' to the inevitable, that is, society's need to reproduce itself through those couples of 'good Nature' and 'Generosity'.

Plays featuring intra-class rivalry, which are subversive in Restoration comedy, are not so in Revolution comedy: here rivals are roundly defeated by superior morality. Plays like *The Way of the World*, Congreve's earlier *Double Dealer* (1693) and Farquhar's *Twin Rivals* (1702) pit good-natured protagonists against malevolent antagonists who are brothers or erstwhile friends. Like Shadwell's *Squire of Alsatia* or Cibber's *Careless Husband*, the plays move out of earlier tragicomic romance towards later melodrama. They present the trickster tricked, but outwitted not so much by wittier protagonists as by themselves. No one is a match for Congreve's double-dealing Maskwell. He is a Machiavellian parasite on the verge of dispossessing the rightful heir to Lord Touchwood's estate, the lord's nephew Mellefont. But Maskwell has miscalculated the passion of the termagant Lady Touchwood, who out of spite reveals all in the nick of time. Lord Touchwood rewards 'Virtue and wrong'd Innocence' by joining Mellefont and the nubile Cynthia in a hymeneal embrace.

Farquhar's Benjamin Wou'dbe, who would usurp his twin brother Hermes's estate by suborning witnesses to swear to his prior birth, is another Machiavel, a Hobbist:

'The World has broke all Civilities with me; and left me in the Eldest State of Nature, Wild, where Force, or Cunning first created Right.... My Brother! What is Brother? We are all so; and the first two were Enemies'. To him morality exists to keep the masses in control. Hermes and his friend Trueman devise a trick to get Benjamin out of Hermes's town house (possession being nine-tenths of the law), but sheer accident delivers into the mistaken servant Teague's hands letters that incriminate the major witness so that she reverses her testimony. Hermes's right is vindicated, luckily, but the play has vouchsafed him poetical justice as not only the elder but the more moral of the brothers – and the better husband too, in both senses of the word, for he not only wins the right girl, he knows how to husband his estate for maximum productivity for the good of the Nation.

Congreve's Mirabell in *The Way of the World* defeats the 'Malice' of Fainall through his own agency, on the other hand, because he can play a final trump card: in his bourgeois virtue of prudence he has protected his former mistress, the young widow Arabella, who has married Fainall out of fear of pregnancy to Mirabell, by hedging her bets. Reading Fainall's character aright, he negotiates a deed of trust to protect Arabella's jointure from her new husband. When Fainall tries to blackmail his mother-in-law Lady Wishfort by revealing Arabella's former affair with Mirabell (in order to get more money to support himself and his mistress Marwood), Mirabell silences him by producing the deed of trust. Like many of the protagonists of Revolution comedy, Mirabell has been a rake in the past, but his behaviour in the play, though puckish, has never been 'downright' vicious. Once again, 'Generosity' and 'good Nature' are key value terms. Mirabell bests Fainall because he possesses them – plus the circumspection that makes him not only a worthy adversary but a prospective good husband and husbandman. No lurking Horner he.

So the protagonists of Revolution social comedy are noteworthy more for their moral character than their pedigree; moreover, though often they are legitimate heirs to country estates, sometimes their playwrights, even as they continue to satirize citizens, go out of their way to portray positively *hauts bourgeois* – bankers, merchants – like Mr Rich in Mary Pix's *Beau Defeated* (1700), who even threatens the effete beau of the title with a sword, or Fairbank in Farquhar's *Twin Rivals*, who, according to Hermes Wou'dbe, merits a title more than many a peer. Notice, too, that evil or effete peers are increasingly satirized, even as tradesmen are admitted into the ranks of the moral and worthy. The new oligarchy justified itself *vis-à-vis* the decadent old (Stuart) aristocracy as it attempted to consolidate power by welcoming *nouveaux riches*.

Are there no *subversive* Revolution comedies? There are certainly subversive elements that refuse to be contained, like the strain Lady Brute's severe frustration with her marriage to Sir John, in the aptly named *Provok'd Wife* by Sir John Vanbrugh (1697), puts on the hymeneal closing of Heartfree's marriage with Bellinda. Or the subversive folk energy of Sergeant Kite, who (especially as the mock fortune-teller) steals the show in Farquhar's *Recruiting Officer* (1706) and whose energy is mustered in the service of the crescent power of Great Britain as it asserts itself both on the Continent and in the colonies (even as that energy masks the displacement of the poor off the land because of enclosure and engrossment, and their susceptibility to impressment into the military service of that power).

But the most subversive comedy is probably Farquhar's *Beaux' Stratagem* in its fantasy-concluding divorce on the grounds of mutual incompatibility. No-fault divorce would wreak havoc with patrilineal succession of power and property. Some critics try to put realistic restraints on the divorce at the end, arguing it is just a separation and that Mrs Sullen cannot marry again. But clearly Farquhar suggests that, since Archer offers to redeem Mrs Sullen's portion when the French count won't, he intends to join his newly acquired ten thousand pounds with hers and marry her. Thus her reproductive power will not be sequestered but unleashed to scramble the eggs of the new ruling oligarchy. Moreover, Archer's earlier line that he and Aimwell, penurious younger brothers, 'are the Men of intrinsick Value, who can strike our Fortunes out of our selves' in a way subverts the compromise ideology of the new oligarchy by undercutting worth by birth absolutely.

Southerne and Vanbrugh wrote *corrective satires* about bad marriages: *The Wives' Excuse; or, Cuckolds Make Themselves* (1691) and *The Relapse; or, Virtue in Danger* (1696). In both plays the women protagonists stand out in agonized relief at the end. Vanbrugh's Amanda has failed to contain the sexual energy of the supposedly converted Loveless of *Love's Last Shift*, who carries on an affair with her best friend, Berinthia, right in their own town house. Moreover, she herself is tempted to have an affair with Berinthia's former lover, Worthy. Although Amanda finally resists Worthy, and although he appears to be temporarily converted to her virtue, there is no resolution to her dilemma, and she is excluded from the hymeneal dance at the end. Unlike the concluding hymeneal of *The Provok'd Wife*, this one is totally cynical. For the marriage is not between a typical Restoration gay couple but rather between a younger brother, who has outwitted a Country bumpkin, and the bumpkin's rich daughter – whom he does not love, who he expects will give all the beaux of Town a merry chase, while he will just take the money and run. The Masque of Cupid and Hymen at the end is a cynical celebration of marriage because it enables sexual promiscuity with impunity. The moral standard of the play – 'The robe of virtue is a graceful habit' – hangs over the ending like an epitaph.

The one sure candidate for *menippean* or *absurdist* satire would seem to be Durfey's three-part *Comical History of Don Quixote* (1694–5). Like the original, the play contains romance elements, lovers whose constancy is finally rewarded. But the romantic itself is undercut by Don Quixote's imagination, crazed as it is by books, romances. The play is overwhelmed by folk humour. Sancho is all body, all belly, preoccupied with food and the avoidance of pain; his wife and daughter are preoccupied with ephemeral concerns, including their bodies and sexual satisfaction. But the comedy is more than just folk-subversive.

Sometimes we sense that we are in a corrective satire, where the norms are obvious. There is a delightful Durfeyan song about his favoured theme of preferment, wherein a labourer and his wife conclude that deserting the village for the court is a sleeveless errand: 'Ambition's a Trade, no Contentment can show'. Another song contrasts artificial Town women with natural Country girls. Another bit mocks and ironically praises at the same time the 'sort of Cattle they call Citizens' for enduring cuckolding in order to make away with estates. Gines de Passamonte, erstwhile galley slave and now disguised as a puppet master, has a show satirizing the English in general: 'Then I've a third, and please ye, upon an English Plot, 'tis call'd, English Men Satisfied; or, the Impossibility; 'Tis plaguy Satyrical, it makes 'em the verriest Maggots; the mearest Shatterbrains, for it shews, that neither Monarchy nor Commonwealth, nor Pope nor Protestant, nor War nor Peace, nor Liberty nor Slavery, nor Marrying nor Whoring, nor Reason nor Treason, can satisfie a right Englishman'. Sometimes, however, satire on the English serves the purpose of galvanizing public support for King Billy and his wars, as when the Knight of the Screech-Owl, who has bested Don Quixote, makes everyone listen to a song about how the French will invade England. The song is juxtaposed to one praising England's 'Genius' for protecting 'the *British* state' from foreign foes.

Yet at the end of part three, Don Quixote inserts into his will the following provisions: 'I give my chiefest Quality, my Knight Errantry, to the veriest Ideot amongst my Countrymen, that he may have it in his Head to conquer Kingdoms; and that he may be heartiley drubb'd about it as I have been. . . . I bequeath my Valour, which in me was but a worse sort of Itch, to all the Cowards and faint-hearted in the Armies abroad, that they may fight with one another to the end of the World, without knowing why or wherefore'. The earlier chauvinism is undercut by the absurdity of war.

Sometimes Don Quixote can lucidly seem to provide bearings, as when he lectures Sancho on the values of conscience and decency. But these he discusses in the context of a Machiavellian 'Morallity', which Sancho, as future governor of his island, should cultivate even if he has it not, 'if it were for nothing but to be a Screen, that people might not pry too much into his Religion': once known for a moral leader, he might in reality be an atheist, it won't matter.

Perhaps Gines is right when he says of himself and his fellow criminals, '[W]e are no more Rogues than the rest of Mankind; all the World are Rogues, and deserve the Galleys as much as we'. If he is right, how discriminate? So he recommends the life of a thief: 'Ah, of all Trades a Rogue is the most pleasant; They may talk of Merchants with their subtle Bargains; of Shopmen with falacious Weights, and Measures; of Gamesters with false Dice, Lawyers with Lying; but for the Wit and Pleasure of Mystery, the Ingenious, the right true modell'd Thief, is the delightful function in the World'. Thief as trickster, trickster as thief.

The playwright seems to be the ultimate trickster, for he concludes the play with Don Quixote dismissing everyone, leaving all sorts of loose ends untied and uncertainty concerning his own fate, for he may either sleep or die. Most curiously, the final song of the play, at the very end, is a dialogue between folk brother and sister, who've been told they can't lie together any more. They defiantly decide to continue to kiss till they inevitably learn why that's all they can do. In other words, morality, especially sexual morality, is socially constructed in defiance of nature. The last couple to leave the stage are the recently married Basilius and Quitteria. But the Masque of Hymen in celebration places Hymen's song between those of Joy and Discord and concludes in a dance 'representing the Happiness and Unhappiness of Marriage'. Right in the middle, Hymen sings,

> The vast Universe I sway,
> Humane Kind my Laws obey:
> By a Power that equals Fates,
> I give Honours and Estates.

Marriage has nothing to do with the spiritual; the spiritual, the entire socially constructed ideology, merely reinforces the political economy of transferring 'Honours and Estates'. Here revealed is the underlying rationale for both Restoration and Revolution comedy: only the ethos has been changed to protect the powerful.

REFERENCES AND FURTHER READING

Bernbaum, Ernest (1915). *The Drama of Sensibility: A Sketch of the History of English Sentimental Comedy and Domestic Tragedy, 1696–1780*. Boston and London: Ginn.

Braverman, Richard (1993). *Plots and Counterplots: Sexual Politics and the Body Politic in English Literature, 1660–1730*. Cambridge: Cambridge University Press.

Brown, Laura (1981). *English Dramatic Form, 1660–1760: An Essay in Generic History*. New Haven, CT, and London: Yale University Press.

Canfield, J. Douglas (1997). *Tricksters and Estates: On the Ideology of Restoration Comedy*. Lexington: University Press of Kentucky.

Canfield, J. Douglas and Payne, Deborah C. (eds). (1995). *Cultural Readings of Restoration and Eighteenth-century Theater*. Athens: University of Georgia Press.

Corman, Brian (1993). *Genre and Generic Change in English Comedy, 1660–1710*. Toronto: University of Toronto Press.

Ellis, Frank H. (1991). *Sentimental Comedy: Theory and Practice*. Cambridge: Cambridge University Press.

Gill, Pat (1994). *Interpreting Ladies: Women, Wit, and Morality in the Restoration Comedy of Manners*. Athens: University of Georgia Press.

Holland, Norman (1959). *The First Modern Comedies: The Significance of Etherege, Wycherley, and Congreve*. Cambridge, MA: Harvard University Press.

Holland, Peter (1979). *The Ornament of Action: Text and Performance in Restoration Comedy*. Cambridge: Cambridge University Press.

Hughes, Derek (1996). *English Drama, 1660–1700*. Oxford: Clarendon Press.

Hughes, Leo (1956). *A Century of English Farce*. Princeton, NJ: Princeton University Press.

Hume, Robert D. (1976). *The Development of English Drama in the Late Seventeenth Century*. Oxford: Clarendon Press.

Kenny, Shirley Strum (1977). 'Humane Comedy', *Modern Philology* 75, 29–43.

Loftis, John (1959). *Comedy and Society from Congreve to Fielding*. Stanford: Stanford University Press.

Markley, Robert (1988). *Two-Edg'd Weapons: Style and Ideology in the Comedies of Etherege, Wycherley, and Congreve*. Oxford: Clarendon Press.

Milhous, Judith and Hume, Robert D. (1985). *Producible Interpretations: Eight English Plays 1675–1707*. Carbondale: Southern Illinois University Press.

Nicoll, Allardyce (1952). *A History of English Drama, 1660–1900. Vol. 1: Restoration Drama, 1660–1700*. 4th ed. Cambridge: Cambridge University Press.

Owen, Susan J. (1996). *Restoration Theatre and Crisis*. Oxford: Clarendon Press.

Pearson, Jacqueline (1988). *The Prostituted Muse: Images of Women and Women Dramatists 1642–1737*. London: Harvester.

Rothstein, Eric and Kavenik, Frances M. (1988). *The Designs of Carolean Comedy*. Carbondale: Southern Illinois University Press.

Schneider, Ben Ross, Jr (1971). *The Ethos of Restoration Comedy*. Urbana: University of Illinois Press.

Sherbo, Arthur (1957). *English Sentimental Drama*. East Lansing: Michigan State University Press.

Smith, John Harrington (1948). *The Gay Couple in Restoration Comedy*. Cambridge, MA: Harvard University Press.

Staves, Susan (1979). *Players' Scepters: Fictions of Authority in the Restoration*. Lincoln: University of Nebraska Press.

Weber, Harold (1986). *The Restoration Rake-Hero: Transformations in Sexual Understanding in Seventeenth-century England*. Madison: University of Wisconsin Press.

14

Tragedy and Varieties of Serious Drama

Jean I. Marsden

To understand Restoration tragedy, one must first understand what the playwrights and audiences meant by the term as well as the many diverse influences that shaped the serious drama of the later seventeenth century. For writers such as Dryden and Lee, Otway and Rowe, tragedy was an inclusive concept that implied a certain *gravitas* of action although not necessarily a tragic ending. While fatal endings still dominated and were viewed as a higher form of drama, the umbrella term 'tragedy' applied to almost any form of serious drama, so much so that John Dryden made a distinction which would be easily recognizable to his contemporaries when he referred in 'The Grounds of Criticism in Tragedy' (1679) to 'that inferior sort of Tragedies which end with a prosperous event' (1984: 233). To Restoration writers, tragedy was the most exalted form of drama, and it was also the subject of the hottest critical debates. Although comedies outnumbered tragedies on the stage, tragedy stirred more critical debate, first because writers deemed it more worthy of discussion, and second, because of the implications of its subject matter. With its depiction of the struggles of kings and princes, tragedy allowed for significant political commentary, which at times made it a dangerous literary pastime.

Writing after an eighteen-year hiatus during the Civil Wars, Restoration play-wrights sought to establish a distinct dramatic tradition, one which was manifestly British yet which avoided the 'barbarisms' of earlier writers. Perhaps the most obvious influence on the tragedy of the Restoration was that of the drama of the earlier seventeenth century, especially the tragedies of Shakespeare and Fletcher (Ben Jonson, while a respected forefather, was known primarily for his comedies). Writers were familiar with the works of earlier playwrights and often mined their plays for material. The qualities playwrights saw as distinctly British (and therefore admirable) in these earlier dramas were the 'liveliness' of the representation, the strength of characterization (especially in Shakespeare's works) and the variety of the action; in Dryden's *Essay of Dramatick Poesie* (1668), one of the earliest critical discussions of drama, the ideal drama is described as 'a just and lively image of human nature'.

Despite the praise for the previous generation, Restoration tragedy represented a significant break from drama written before the theatres closed in 1642. While Restoration playwrights respected the work of their predecessors, they frequently found these earlier tragedies faulty, the plots too convoluted and the language often arcane. Even while praising the works of Renaissance playwrights (Shakespeare, Dryden writes, 'had the largest and most comprehensive soul' of all poets), Restoration writers sought to separate themselves from the previous generation. Looking for models of more refined drama, they turned to another literary tradition, the drama of seventeenth-century France.

Many Restoration writers had become familiar with the French stage during the Interregnum, when theatres in London were closed. Some, such as Thomas Killigrew, manager of one of the two patent houses, even spent time in France with the exiled Charles II. To a new generation of playwrights, French literature provided a more regular and modern style of tragedy, and they looked to the great French dramatists of the later seventeenth century, Corneille and especially Racine, whose works were repeatedly translated and adapted for the English stage. In contrast to the bold and often violent drama of the English Renaissance, the neoclassical drama of seventeenth-century France emphasized decorum and restraint. Bloodshed occurred offstage, and passion was represented through beautifully controlled language. Plotting was also more controlled, without the abundance of subplots which characterized much of earlier English drama. The precepts which governed French drama were known generally as the 'Rules' and provided a benchmark for judging the propriety of plays, both tragedies and comedies. Drawn in part from Aristotle's *Poetics*, these rules were famously articulated by Rapin, whose works were also widely read in England.

The 'Rules' called for unity of action (a single plot without the distraction of subplots), unity of place and unity of time. Ideally, a play should take place in real time, or at most during the course of one day, and in one setting, although this stricture could be stretched to include a general area such as a city (but not the radical change in locale seen in a play such as *Antony and Cleopatra* or *The Winter's Tale*, which also violated the unity of time because of its sixteen-year gap between Acts 3 and 4). French tragedy, however, followed the precepts so closely that often a single room served as the location for the action and all characters were tied strictly to the play's main action. These rules produced what was known as 'regular drama', as opposed to the works of Shakespeare and other sixteenth- and early seventeenth-century playwrights, which were sometimes faulted for being 'irregular'. In addition to these major precepts, French critical theory advocated a doctrine of decorum, which prohibited violence on stage and dictated specific behaviour amongst the characters represented. Under these rules, characters should behave according to their rank or social class. As Rapin stated, 'the most general Rule for painting the *Manners* is to exhibit every person in his proper *Character*. A *Slave*, with base thoughts, and servile inclinations. A *Prince*, with a liberal heart and *air* of Majesty. A *Souldier*, fierce, insolent, surly, inconstant', and so on (1674: 36).

French drama and French literary theory undoubtedly produced a significant influence on Restoration serious drama. But the extent of this influence can be – and too often has been – overestimated. While English writers admired the cohesion and clarity of French drama and even adopted the principle of the three unities in many of their own tragedies, they had no intention of slavishly imitating the French style of drama. With few exceptions, English writers faulted the French for writing overly formulaic drama, plays which some claimed were 'boring', 'insipid' and even 'absurd'. In the eyes of British writers, the extreme care with which the French adhered to the rules made their plots too thin, their characters seemingly passionless and their dramas too uniform overall. Richard Flecknoe, a minor poet and playwright, observes that many English plays are 'faulty', but continues, 'if the French have fewer [faults] than our English, 'tis because they confine themselves to narrower limits, and consequently have less liberty to erre' (Flecknoe 1664). Likewise, Charles Gildon writes of the French that their '*Genius* as well as Language is not strong enough to rise to the Majesty of Poetry, [and thus they] are easier reduc'd within the Discipline of Rules'. Their works are more regular, he concludes, 'yet I never yet met with any Englishman who wou'd prefer their Poetry to ours' (Gildon 1694: 91). Often fuelled by nationalism, these attacks contrast the 'servile' nature of the French with the more 'manly' British; Dryden even sets his paean to British drama in the *Essay of Dramatick Poesie* against the backdrop of a naval battle in which the English emerge victorious. Near the end of the century, when Thomas Rymer attacked English playwrights and specifically Shakespeare, comparing them unfavourably with 'ancient' dramatists such as Socrates and Euripides, John Dennis, Dryden and a number of their contemporaries spoke out against the rules and in favour of the more irregular but varied English drama. Not surprisingly, the characteristics noted by critic-playwrights appear in the tragedy of the Restoration which is consistently less controlled, more violent and more spectacular than that of France.

Restoration dramatists hoped to write tragedy which retained the vigour of their predecessors as well as the best elements of the French neoclassical drama, with the ideal goal a 'just and lively' drama that would be both instructive and entertaining. They saw themselves as distinct both from their predecessors and from their French contemporaries. Seeking to retain the variety of action and character that typified English drama, they also sought to make their own tragedies more correct. The result was orderly tragedies which lacked the excesses of Renaissance drama but which still maintained the English fondness for violent action, spectacle and bloodshed. These general concerns remained central throughout the Restoration even while the specific subject matter of tragedy shifted from the imperial in the first decades after the Restoration to a more inward focus on the domestic realm as the century closed.

Grandeur to Horror: Serious Drama, 1660–80

The first decades of serious drama after the Restoration were characterized by visual and verbal grandeur. Playwrights sought to represent greatness, both of virtue and of evil, in the characters and design of their drama, drawing their plots from history, romance and epic. Eugene Waith (1971) describes the plays of these years as representing an admiration of greatness, greatness of character, of action, of ideals. Making use of the opportunities for spectacle provided by sliding scenery and elaborate stage effects, playwrights set their dramas in grand locales and embellished them with scenes of storms and pagan ceremonies. By the end of the 1670s, however, playwrights and their audiences began to question the certainties of heroic action, and, as drama became darker in tone, the grand spectacles of the early Restoration evolved into scenes of horror and destruction.

During the early 1660s, the two patent theatre companies produced few original tragedies; most of the serious drama staged was either a translation or adaptation of contemporary French drama, such as Katherine Philips's translation of Corneille's *Pompée*, which was staged in Dublin in 1663 and later that year in London, or an adaptation of earlier English tragedy, such as Sir William Davenant's adaptation of Shakespeare's *Macbeth* (1664). As playhouses and companies became more established, more new tragedies appeared. By the mid-1660s, playwrights such as Dryden and his brother-in-law, Sir Robert Howard, were writing serious drama in the form of the rhymed heroic play. This movement, discussed in depth in chapter 12, also merits consideration in the context of the development of tragedy in the Restoration. The heroic plays, labelled tragedies by their authors, were serious drama on a grand scale. Often set in exotic locales such as India, the Aztec empire or Moorish Spain, they featured larger-than-life characters with larger-than-life emotions, often an impassioned and epic struggle between the abstract forces of love and of honour. Dryden's Almanzor in *The Conquest of Granada*, Parts 1 and 2, perhaps the best known of all heroic play characters, is a good example of these elevated and often fantastic figures, a man whose high standards of honour (as well as his passionate love for the beautiful Almahide) cause him to shift alliances several times. Almanzor himself declares his singularity in terms of an innate sense of liberty, that most English of all values:

> Obey'd as Soveraign by thy Subjects be,
> But know, that I alone am King of me.
> I am as free as Nature first made man
> 'Ere the base Laws of Servitude began
> When wild in woods the noble Savage ran.
>
> (1, 1.1.205–9)

He is a man above all forms of servitude, even to a king, although such radical individuality changes when he finally encounters a proper Christian ruler at the end of Part 2. Villains were equally grandiose, displaying almost impossible degrees of evil to be offset by the heroes' virtues. Characters such as Dryden's Maximin in *Tyrannick Love; Or the Royal Martyr* (1669), Behn's Abdelazer or Settle's empress of Morocco display an almost endless capacity for lust and violence.

As such heightened figures would suggest, the scope of the action in the serious drama of the early Restoration is heroic rather than psychological. In a play such as Dryden and Howard's *The Indian Queen* (1664), the action is propelled by the characters' conflicting loves and ambitions. The play centres on the heroic Montezuma and his love for Orazia, daughter of the Ynca of Peru. Rebuffed by the Ynca despite his feats in war, Montezuma gives his services to the usurping Indian Queen Zempoalla in order to capture his love. This ploy goes astray when the queen falls in love with Montezuma. Assisted by the noble Acasis he frees Orazia, and then the two reluctantly fight to prove their love. The rationale given by Acasis provides a fine example of the idealized motivations which guide characters in heroic drama; despite their respect for each other, they must fight to the death:

> Our Lives we to each others Friendships owe;
> But Love calls back what Friendship did bestow:
> Love has its Cruelties, but Friendship none;
> And now we fight in Quarrels not our own.
>   (4.2.41–4)

In the end, the usurper is vanquished, the rightful queen regains her throne and the lovers are united. The lofty nature of the action is enhanced by Dryden and Howard's use of spectacle in the form of bloody altars, singing spirits and the appearance of the God of Dreams. *The Indian Queen's* clarity of characterization and scope of action is typical of serious drama in the early decades of the Restoration. With its prosperous conclusions, belief in ideals and overall lack of cynicism, serious drama of this period reflects a more general optimism still present in Restoration England, before political turmoil and contention over the succession darkened drama during the later 1670s and early 1680s.

Like the action, the language of the plays is elevated and even epic. Notably, the plays are written in heroic couplets; Dryden's defence of rhymed drama in the *Essay of Dramatick Poesie* (1668) was directed at plays such as *The Indian Queen* and *The Conquest of Granada*. In the *Essay*, he argues that rhyme was not only more elevated than blank verse, and thus suited to the elevated ideas of heroic drama, but even that it was 'nearest the nature of a serious Play' because "tis Nature wrought up to an higher pitch' and everything in serious drama should be elevated above 'common converse' (1971: 74), as in the examples cited above. Because of this association of the couplet with heroic drama, the gradual elimination of rhyme in serious drama is often used to track the demise of the heroic play. Even Dryden eventually bid a public farewell to the heroic couplet in the prologue to his final heroic drama, *Aureng-Zebe* (1676), where he confesses that he 'grows weary of his long-loved mistress Rhyme'. Such absolute distinctions are obviously too neat, as drama continued to incorporate elements of the heroic plays throughout the 1670s, as in Thomas Shadwell's *The Libertine* (1675), for example, which not only contains scenes written in verse but presents a villain-hero whose overweening lust links him to the villain-heroes of earlier heroic plays.

The ascendancy of the heroic play was short-lived. Its sometimes stilted verse and overwrought, formulaic plots became fodder for burlesques by playwrights such as Duffet and Buckingham, who emphasized the unrealistic and absurd qualities of the form. By 1676, the reign of the heroic play was all but over, and tragedy began to take on a new form. No longer written in rhyme but in blank verse, serious drama also displayed significant changes in plot, characterization and mood. Keeping the grand settings and spectacles of the heroic plays, tragedies in the mid-to-later 1670s began to feature more deeply flawed heroes, whose weaknesses made them more human than exaggerated figures such as Almanzor. Along with the movement away from broad idealized action came a corresponding shift in tone; after 1675, serious drama displays a noticeably darker mood, which would deepen as the decade drew towards an end. The plays are often troubling, with heroism seemingly absent. These changes can be traced in part to the darkening political situation in England during the mid-to-later 1670s. The Restoration 'honeymoon' was over, and questions about the succession to the throne as well as Charles II's libertinism and its effect on his rule were stirring throughout the country. These concerns were to come to a head in the wake of the Popish Plot, but they were latent even in the years before 1679 and are reflected in the movement away from the optimism and expansive view of the heroic play. Instead, tragedy becomes increasingly topical and politically suggestive as the decade draws to a close.

Shifting away from the emphasis on idealized abstractions as motivations for action, playwrights employed a more psychological approach to characterization. In plays such as Nathaniel Lee's *The Rival Queens* (1676) and Dryden's *All for Love; Or, the World Well Lost* (1677), the heroes struggle with their own weaknesses. These plays, with their similar plots of a man caught between two women, emphasize the flaws in the heroes, along with, and sometimes instead of, their heroic qualities. In *The Rival Queens*, Lee depicts the final days of Alexander the Great. The 'rival queens' are Alexander's two wives, Roxana and Statira; Alexander has broken his vows to Statira by returning briefly to the passionate Roxana, who stands in the position of his cast-off mistress. *All for Love*, a retelling of the story of Antony and Cleopatra, portrays Antony wavering between his mistress Cleopatra and his wife Octavia; the first represents love and passion, the second, duty. In contrast to a figure such as Almanzor, whose struggles to satisfy both love and honour only serve to make him greater, Dryden's Antony fails because his conflicts cannot be reconciled. While the setting in these plays is still empire, it is neither so exotic nor so grand as the new world represented in *The Indian Queen* or the Moorish kingdoms in *The Conquest of Granada* or *The Empress of Morocco*. Instead, playwrights present us with scenes such as the banquet in Act 4 of *The Rival Queens*, where Alexander's magnificence becomes a means for Lee to display his character's weakness. While the scene contains a spectacular entertainment of singing and dancing, its main focus is Alexander's hubris: he insists on his godlike nature as the son of Jove and stands above his commanders as they kiss the ground at his feet. The scene's splendour, epitomized by Alexander's Persian garments, serves to represent the moral bankruptcy of Alexander's court rather than the grandeur of the characters and their actions.

A similar dynamic appears in Otway's *Don Carlos, Prince of Spain* (1676). Although written in rhyme, the play has no other similarities to the heroic drama. Otway's tragedy provides no spectacle and no sweeping action, instead presenting an almost claustrophobic picture of betrayal and irrational emotion. Don Carlos, heir to the throne of Spain, is in love with his father's wife, who was previously betrothed to him. Deeply infatuated, he cannot hide his feelings for the queen, and his passion is used by a corrupt minister to drive the king into a fit of jealousy which results in the deaths of both Don Carlos and the queen, and in the king's eventual madness. Only the king's brother is left at the end of the play exclaiming, 'Despair! how vast a Triumph hast thou made?' (5.500). With death and despair triumphing, the certainties which buttressed the drama of the early 1670s seem far away. The heroes of these plays tend to be weak rather than heroic, like Dryden's Antony vacillating between two women and two worlds. Even Otway's Don Carlos, whose affections remain fixed on one object, has no control over his emotions and actions. As plays such as *Don Carlos* suggest, the reappearance of the tragic rather than the 'prosperous' ending represents growing moral uncertainty, especially regarding questions of authority and power.

In the years following the Popish Plot, the ambiguities of plays such as *The Rival Queens* and *All for Love* intensified into tragedies of political doubt and horror. While the Plot itself was in reality not a threat to England's autonomy (see chapter 8 for details), it incited increased fear of the effects of Catholicism within the government; this translated into intense propaganda against Catholicism by opponents of Charles II's government and dire warnings of civil war by Tory supporters of the government. The anti-Catholicism stimulated by the Popish Plot generated attempts to exclude from the throne Charles II's brother James, who had made his connections to the Catholic Church public. These uncertainties in the public sphere made their way into the serious drama of the period, as playwrights on all sides used tragedy to express their views. With its representation of the fate of princes and empires, tragedy was the perfect forum for political debate, a fact not lost on playwrights – nor on government censors. During the years 1679–82, when the Exclusion Crisis was at its height, the number of new tragedies increased dramatically, as did the number of adaptations of Shakespeare's serious drama. Political views ranged from the virulent anti-Catholicism of Lee's *Lucius Junius Brutus* and *Caesar Borgia* to John Crowne's transparently titled *The Misery of Civil-War* (1680), an adaptation of Shakespeare's *2 Henry VI*, equally vehement in its Tory sympathies. The censors were also busy during these years. Lee's *Lucius Junius Brutus* was suppressed by the Lord Chamberlain's office after a short run because of 'very Scandalous Expressions & Reflections vpon ye government'. Nahum Tate's adaptation of *Richard II* met the same fate, despite the author's attempt to defuse the play's political liabilities by setting it in the Mediterranean and giving it a new title (*The Sicilian Usurper*). Simply the act of representing the overthrow of a rightful monarch, no matter how evil the usurper is made to seem, was a dangerous business during this age of heightened political awareness.

On the stage, these political controversies were made more vivid through the lavish use of horror in the form of visual effects. Where plays from the early 1670s relied on grand spectacles of scenic display, the later, more intense dramas employed graphic displays of bloodshed to make their arguments more emphatic. For example, Nathaniel Lee's Whiggish attack on absolute monarchy in *Lucius Junius Brutus* gains force from the lurid representation of atrocities, most notably in Act 4, where Lee parodies the symbolic sacrifice of the Catholic mass. In Lee's play, the human sacrifice is real:

> The scene draws, showing the sacrifice: one burning and another crucified; the *Priests* coming forward with goblets in their hands, filled with human blood.

The bluff republican Vinditius comments on the scene, making explicit its connections with the Catholic rite of transubstantiation:

> *Vinditius* [*from window*]: O the gods! What, burn a man alive! O cannibals, hellhounds! Eat one man and drink another!... What, drink a man's blood! Roast him and eat him alive! A whole man roasted! Would not an ox serve the turn? Priests to do this! O you immortal gods! For my part, if this be your worship, I renounce you. No; if a man can't go to heaven unless your priests eat him and drink him and roast him alive, I'll be for the broad way, and the devil shall have me at a venture. (4.120–9)

Writing from the opposing view, John Crowne in *The Misery of Civil-War* uses graphic scenes of bloodshed and destruction to bring home to his audience the horrors of civil war and rebellion against the (rightful) monarchy. Again, the means used to make this point is through the graphic depiction of iniquities.

> The Scene is drawn, and there appears Houses and Towns burning, Men and Women hang'd upon Trees, and Children on the tops of Pikes.
>
> 1 & 2 *Country Girls*: Oh Heaven! have mercy on us! have mercy on us!
> 1 *Souldier*: Now Rogues, how do you like Rebellion?

In both these examples, although the point of view differs radically, the means of representation is similar: shocking scenes presented to the audience's view followed by observations which make their political import unmistakeable.

In the dark plays of the late 1670s and early 1680s, it is difficult to find a play which ignores the politics of horror. Even a play such as Nahum Tate's pro-monarchy adaptation of *King Lear*, in which both Lear and Cordelia survive in a paean to the 'King's blest Restauration' (*King Lear* 5.6.119), keeps in the shocking scene of Gloucester's blinding by the pro-revolutionary Regan and her husband. The violence of these plays and their copious use of bloodshed in order to shock the audiences not only link them to the political events of the Restoration, but also tie them to the English tradition of violence seen in the Jacobean tragedies of the earlier seventeenth century.

By 1680, the world of tragedy was dark, littered with broken vows and betrayals, symbolic of a larger disillusionment with a world which had seemed so promising in the first years after the Restoration. Despite figures such as Cleopatra, Roxana and Statira, the tragedies of the 1670s present a male-centred world in which heroes struggle less against fate than against their own personal weaknesses and increasingly inhabit a universe in which there are no moral certainties. Otway's *Venice Preserv'd* (1682), the greatest tragedy of the later seventeenth century, documents the bleak vision of the age. In Otway's play, the well-meaning but weak Jaffeir wavers between love for his wife and loyalty to his friend Pierre, and between upholding the senate in order to 'preserve' Venice and joining a rebellion which vows to scour the corruption from Venice's government by destroying it. Jaffeir's indecision mirrors that of heroes such as Dryden's Antony, and he inhabits a world in which all options appear equally corrupt. The play's pessimism is deep-seated; even the purest of emotions, friendship and marital love, lead to betrayal and ultimately to death. Very much a play of its time, *Venice Preserv'd* also marks the form tragedy was to take in the following decades in its depiction of Belvidera, one of the most vividly realized female characters in Restoration drama. A complex figure who is neither as exalted as an empress nor as exaggerated in her emotions as characters such as Lee's and Dryden's queens, she is central to the play's action and, crucially, evokes pity for the pathos of her death.

Pathos and She-Tragedy: Serious Drama after 1680

The political turmoil which shaped the drama of the later 1670s and early 1680s also resulted in a sharp decrease in the number and variety of new drama in the following decade. As Aphra Behn noted in the Prologue to *The Feign'd Curtezans* (1679), political upheavals resulted in poor theatre attendance, 'The Devil take this cursed plotting Age, / 'T has ruin'd all our Plots upon the Stage', and in 1682, the struggling King's Company collapsed. For the next thirteen years, plays were staged by a single company which relied largely on stock plays; few new tragedies were to appear before the mid-1690s. Those which were staged began to introduce qualities uncommon in the violent, male-centred plays of the previous decade. Instead of horror, the tragedy of the 1680s emphasized pathos and perhaps most notably shifted its emphasis from the hero to heroine, usually a virtuous woman beleaguered and overwhelmed by sorrows.

Writing of the drama of the 1680s, Robert Hume describes the pathetic play as 'the one important new mode established in the early eighties' (1976: 350), and the use of pathos as a dominant dramatic device became the most significant development in the serious drama at the end of the seventeenth century. Praising Mary Pix's *Ibrahim, Thirteenth Emperor of the Turks* (1698), which uses pathos extensively, critic and playwright Charles Gildon notes that the play regularly brings tears into the eyes of the audience, 'which is the true End of Tragedy' (1699: 111). The source of these tears, in *Ibrahim* and elsewhere, is the suffering of an innocent woman. In the seventeenth century, men might rave under the effects of oppression, but their roles in drama were defined as active rather than as passive. Women, on the other hand, were expected to cultivate passive virtues such as patience and humility. In drama, the almost inevitable result of such qualities was an inability to escape suffering. As the heroine of one such play relates, 'Do! Nothing, for I am born to suffer' (*The Fatal Marriage* 2.2.66). In these plays, female suffering becomes the central spectacle, replacing the grand panoramas of empire and scenes of atrocities. In these 'she-tragedies' (the term was coined by Nicholas Rowe, who wrote two of the most popular plays of female suffering), the action revolves around a central female character who suffers for most of the play and dies pathetically at the end. Often, the female protagonist unwittingly commits some sort of a sin, usually sexual in nature, which results later in her suicide, murder or madness. The pathos these scenes of suffering and madness generate takes the place of the horror and heroism found in the male-centred plays of earlier decades. At a time when moral certainties were undercut, it provides serious drama with a new authenticity of emotion.

The genesis of this movement can be traced to Otway's popular tragedy, *The Orphan* (1680). While Otway's play, like those of his contemporaries, reflects a concern with the political events around him in its representation of an ordered family (symbolic of an ordered state) falling into chaos, it was more memorable to contemporary audiences for its vivid picture of a woman whose distress moved all who saw her. Unlike the dramas of earlier decades, *The Orphan* is intimate rather than grand; its characters have in fact chosen to live a life away from the potential corruption of court and power. The story centres on the nobleman Acasto, his two sons Polydore and Castalio, and his ward, the orphaned Monimia. Polydore and Castalio both love Monimia, and this love acts to separate the two brothers, for Castalio does not inform his brother that Monimia returns his love. Instead, he feigns indifference and even urges Polydore to court the reluctant Monimia. This secrecy proves deadly. The two lovers marry, and Polydore, overhearing them plan their wedding night, misinterprets both his brother and Monimia's intentions and takes his brother's place in Monimia's bed, thus causing the unsuspecting maiden to commit both adultery and incest. The mistake is revealed, causing unhappiness to all but especially to Monimia, who agonizes over her sin and ultimately drinks poison, dying pathetically in the final act. It was this pathos, what the seventeenth and eighteenth centuries referred to as 'distress', which captured the imagination of Restoration audiences. Seen as the greatest tragedian of his age, Otway was often described as 'next to Shakespeare' in his ability to excite the passions, even exceeding Shakespeare in his depiction of female characters such as Monimia and Belvidera. The spectacle of sexual transgression, suffering and ultimate death was to become a defining element in the wave of she-tragedies which emulated Otway, each combining sexual spectacle with often exaggerated displays of female suffering.

A second important figure in the development of she-tragedy and later seventeenth-century drama is John Banks, whose four last plays centre on the sufferings of women whose love is thwarted by duty or treachery. While the conflict between love and honour was familiar from the heroic plays of the 1670s, Banks shifts the focus to female protagonists, depicting not simply the conflict but the misery which it causes.

His plays, *The Unhappy Favorite; Or, the Earl of Essex* (1681), *Vertue Betray'd: Or, Anna Bullen* (1682), *The Innocent Usurper* (1683) and *The Island Queens: Or, the Death of Mary Queen of Scotland* (1684, later *The Albion Queens*), focus on women in England's past (even *The Unhappy Favorite* takes as its subject Elizabeth's passion for Essex). While two of Banks's tragedies, *The Innocent Usurper* and *The Island Queens*, were originally banned because of their political implications, both *Vertue Betray'd* and *The Unhappy Favorite* quickly became popular favourites, designed to exploit possibilities of women as both erotic objects and generators of pathos. *Vertue Betray'd*, for example, depicts Anne Boleyn as a virtuous woman, forced to abandon her love for young Piercy and marry Henry VIII. Once on the throne, she is quickly cast aside by the king and slandered by her enemies. She goes to the block a Protestant martyr, her innocence discovered only after her death. The play depicts no heroic action, only the articulated unhappiness of its heroine. As Elizabeth Howe notes, by the mid-1680s, 'female suffering has become the whole subject of tragedy' (1992: 122).

The pattern of female suffering as dramatic spectacle established in the plays of Otway and Banks was to prevail until the end of the century and into the early eighteenth century. After the dearth of tragedies in the later 1680s and early 1690s, there was a resurgence of serious drama in the mid-1690s, assisted by the fine acting of tragedians such as Elizabeth Barry and Thomas Betterton. The renewed interest in tragedy was also a function of London once again having two playhouses; in 1695, Thomas Betterton, Elizabeth Barry, Anne Bracegirdle and several other prominent actors left Drury Lane to establish a new company. The presence of two theatre companies meant more new plays, and in particular more new tragedies as the new company's talents were especially strong in serious drama. Playwrights responded to the increased demand with a host of new plays, most trading on the current popularity of she-tragedy.

The re-emergence of tragedy was spurred by another event even before the formation of Betterton's company: the success of one of the finest Restoration she-tragedies, Thomas Southerne's *The Fatal Marriage; Or, The Innocent Adultery* (1694). *The Fatal Marriage* is Southerne's masterpiece, a dark picture of a good woman who, driven to extremes, makes a fatal mistake. Drawing on Aphra Behn's novel *The Nun, Or, the Fair-Vow-Breaker*, Southerne uses only the bare outline of the story of a woman who breaks her religious vow in order to wed and later commits bigamy. Where Behn focuses on the breaking of vows and the implications of such an act, Southerne relegates his character's experience as a nun to the margins, focusing instead on her inadvertent bigamy, the 'fatal marriage', and its consequences. In Behn's novel, the title character kills both husbands with spirited ingenuity. In Southerne's play, there are no murders; instead, his character is tormented with guilt and slips into madness, stabbing herself in her frenzy. Southerne's changes to Behn's plot not only reflect prevailing motifs in tragedy but also were to influence future practitioners of the genre. More even than the plays of Otway and Banks, *The Fatal Marriage* centres on the prolonged misery and even degradation of its female protagonist as, like Monimia, Southerne's Isabella innocently commits a sexual sin. Overwhelmed by poverty, she marries only to protect her son. The play's final acts detail her response to the ill-timed arrival of her beloved first husband, her recognition of her sin, her descent into madness and eventual death. The pain is lightened only by Southerne's incorporation of a comic subplot. Even with the inclusion of the subplot, the play is unparalleled in its representation of female suffering. (In the mid-eighteenth century, David Garrick stripped the play of its comic elements, leaving Isabella's fate unrelentingly tragic; in this form the play was cited for the almost excessive distress the suffering of its heroine caused to the audience.) While few playwrights were to imitate Southerne's use of comedy, many would emulate his emphasis on Isabella's distress, and especially the representation of a sexually compromised female protagonist.

Another important component of *The Fatal Marriage*'s success was its use of two outstanding actresses, Elizabeth Barry and Anne Bracegirdle. The role of Isabella was written for Barry, who had also created such notable roles as Monimia, Belvidera and Anna Bullen, while Bracegirdle played the role of Victoria in Southerne's subplot. Soon the two actresses would come to define the form of tragedy; Barry was renowned for her ability to represent passion and yet to wring tears from even the stoniest audience, while Bracegirdle's forte was embodying passive feminine virtue; for nearly twenty years the two actresses would influence the representation of women in serious drama. The pairing of Barry and Bracegirdle became particularly predominant after the success of William Congreve's only tragedy, *The Mourning Bride* (1697). In this she-tragedy, Barry played the passionate Queen Zara, whose inappropriate love for the hero, Osmyn, ultimately results in her death. Bracegirdle, by contrast, represented the title character, the mournful, helpless Almeria. In the decade to follow, playwrights created parts for the two actresses, reiterating the roles each played in *The Mourning Bride*. Inevitably, Barry was the passionate, sometimes sinful, woman, while Brace-girdle was cast as her virginal counterpart. The popularity of the form was contagious as dual-heroine tragedies appeared at the rival Drury Lane theatre as well as in Betterton's company and continued until Bracegirdle retired from the stage in 1707.

By the end of the century, tragedies, although increasing in number, were largely familiar permutations of the she-tragedy formula; only a handful of the serious dramas staged were successful enough to be revived. Most depicted the travails of an innocent woman, often the victim of incest or rape, whose anguish ultimately leads to her death. The plots are often lurid, with rape and incest commonplace. Only rarely did plays break away from this pattern. One of the few was Southerne's *Oroonoko* (1695), one of the most enduringly popular tragedies of the 1690s and, like *The Fatal Marriage*, adapted from a Behn novel. In Southerne's hands, Behn's story of a heroic African prince who is tricked into slavery, performs amazing feats and is ultimately betrayed, is compressed into an account of Oroonoko's experiences in the British colony of Surinam. Like *The Fatal Marriage*, Southerne includes a comic subplot in his tragedy, but unlike his early play, the play's action centres on a heroic figure, the princely Oroonoko, and only to a secondary degree on Oroonoko's wife, Imoinda. (In practical terms, the absence of a large female role may also have been dictated by the dearth of skilled tragic actresses in the Drury Lane company so soon after the departure of Barry and Bracegirdle.) Southerne's tragedy is unusual in its use of a male figure as the central focus of tragedy; despite his disenfranchised status, Oroonoko remains noble and daring throughout the play, never sinking into pathos (even Imoinda is stronger than the average doomed heroine of late seventeenth-century drama). Nonetheless, the tragedy does obey the demand for refinement voiced in Southerne's prologue, where the playwright argues that 'The Buskin with more grace should tread the Stage, / Love sigh in softer Strains, Heroes less Rage'. Oroonoko is a lover as much as he is a royal leader, and much of the play's final act is dedicated to his despair over losing Imoinda, the lovers' joy at reunion, and their final wrenching farewells as they decide to kill themselves rather than to live as slaves.

The distinctive nature of Southerne's tragedy can be seen clearly when compared with another ostensibly male-centred play, Nicholas Rowe's *Tamerlane* (1700). Rowe's second play, *Tamerlane* is an overt Whig drama, emphasizing the justness of Tamerlane in contrast to the libertine absolutism of Bajazet, meant to represent Louis XIV (it would frequently be revived on dates important to the Whig party, such as the anniversary of the coronation of George I). Although expressly designed as a paean to William III, *Tamerlane* includes many of the familiar elements of she-tragedy, including the dual-heroine plot, and the rape and subsequent death of the more passionate heroine, played by Elizabeth Barry. While the focus to some extent shifts away from the Barry and Bracegirdle figures, they are still central to the drama and provide the necessary context for Tamerlane's (English) justice. Despite its political overtones, *Tamerlane* is nonetheless tied more closely with the literary traditions of the past than with any future dramatic innovations. Only in his next play, *The Fair Penitent* (1703), would Rowe begin to experiment with the form and content of tragedy.

The Fair Penitent provides a fitting conclusion to a discussion of Restoration tragedy as it creates a bridge between seventeenth-century conventions of pathos, and even sensation, while introducing ideas that would become central in eighteenth-century drama. Chief among Rowe's innovations is his emphasis on a more domestic sphere of tragedy. Where the heroic dramas and tragedies of the earlier Restoration had centred around the exploits of kings and emperors, with idealized figures such as Dryden's Almanzor whose actions shaped nations, Rowe looked into the heart of the family. Claiming to show his audience 'Men and Women as they are', Rowe avoided the broad scale of action that had characterized most Restoration tragedy. In his words,

> Therefore an humbler Theme our Author chose,
> A melancholy Tale of private Woes:
> No Princes here lost Royalty bemoan,
> But you shall meet with Sorrows like your own.
>
> ('Prologue')

While Rowe's characters remain part of the upper class (the depiction of middle- and lower-class tragic figures would wait until George Lillo's *The London Merchant*

[1738]), their concerns centre on events within the family, the 'private Woes' cited by Rowe. The plot, taken in part from Massinger and Field's earlier *The Fatal Dowery* (c.1630), involves a misguided marriage and the calamity that results from it. Before the play opens, the heroine Calista has lost her virginity to Lothario; she loves him, but marries Altamont in accordance with her father's wishes. In form, the play is much like the she-tragedies which had dominated the stage – and indeed, Rowe was to go on to write *The Tragedy of Jane Shore* (1714), one of the most popular she-tragedies. Calista, however, lacks the pathos of an Isabella; she questions her fate at the hands of men and ends her life in an almost heroic fashion after mourning the death of first Lothario, and then her father, Sciolto. The play's action rarely strays beyond the walls of Sciolto's garden, and the characters are absorbed by their personal sorrows. Rowe's innovations appear more clearly when comparing *The Fair Penitent* and Otway's *The Orphan*, a play also set within the confines of the family. Although intimate in action, Otway's play is clearly set within the context of the public; the characters have retreated from the corruptions of court, yet nonetheless corruption penetrates their country seclusion. By contrast, the world of Rowe's characters is shaped entirely by personal relationships.

This concern with the private over the public was to become a crucial component of drama in the eighteenth century, although Rowe's innovation did not have an immediate effect on the tragedies which followed. But in contemporary commentaries on the theatre, it was this play which critics cited as the turning point in the conception of tragedy as not simply a chronicle of the fall of kings, but of 'humbler Theme[s]' of commonplace sorrows. The movement towards woman-centred drama can be seen not only as the first step towards domestic drama, but as the most distinctive development in the tragedy of the later Restoration. Too often denigrated as sentimental and effeminate, the movement from the heroic to the domestic demonstrates not simply a shift in literary sensibilities. At the end of the century, tragedy's transition from a focus on action to one on emotion, that of the characters and of the audience, reflects a broad-based social change in which the personal, interior and subjective were to become central to the culture at large.

REFERENCES AND FURTHER READING

Backscheider, P. (1993). *Spectacular Politics: Theatrical Power and Mass Culture in Early Modern England.* Baltimore: Johns Hopkins University Press.

Braverman, R. (1993). *Plots and Counterplots: Sexual Politics and the Body Politic in English Literature, 1660–1730.* Cambridge: Cambridge University Press.

Brown, L. (1981). *English Dramatic Form, 1660–1760: An Essay in Generic History.* New Haven, CT: Yale University Press.

Brown, L. (1982). 'The Defenseless Woman and the Development of English Tragedy', *Studies in English Literature* 22, 429–43.

Canfield, J. D. (2000). *Heroes and States: On the Ideology of Restoration Tragedy.* Lexington: University Press of Kentucky.

Canfield, J. D. and Payne, D. C. (eds). (1995). *Cultural Readings of Restoration and Eighteenth-century Theater*. Athens: University of Georgia Press.

Dobree, B. (1929; reprinted 1954). *Restoration Tragedy, 1660–1720*. Oxford: Clarendon Press.

Dryden, J. (1668; 1971). 'Essay of Dramatick Poesie', in *The Works of John Dryden*, vol. 17, ed. Samuel Holt Monk. Berkeley: University of California Press.

Dryden, J. (1679; 1984). 'The Grounds of Criticism in Tragedy,' prefixed to *Troilus and Cressida, Or, Truth Found too Late*, in *The Works of John Dryden*, vol. 13, ed. M. E. Novak and G. R. Guffey. Berkeley: University of California Press.

Flecknoe, R. (1664). *A Short Discourse of the English Stage*. Published with *Love's Kingdom*. London.

Gildon, C. (1694). 'Some Reflections on Mr. *Rymer's Short View of Tragedy* and an Attempt at a Vindication of *Shakespeare*, in an Essay directed to *John Dryden* Esq.', in *Miscellaneous Letters and Essays*. London.

Gildon, C. (1699). *The Lives and Characters of the English Dramatick Poets. Also an Exact Account of all the Plays that were ever yet printed in the English Tongue; their Double Titles, the Places where Acted, the Dates when printed, and the Persons to whom Dedicated; with Remarks and Observations on most of the said Plays. First begun by Mr. Langbain, improv'd and continued down to this Time, by a Careful Hand*. London.

Hagstrum, J. H. (1980). *Sex and Sensibility: Ideal and Erotic Love from Milton to Mozart*. Chicago: University of Chicago Press.

Ham, R. G. (1931). *Otway and Lee: Biography from a Baroque Age*. New Haven, CT: Yale University Press.

Howe, E. (1992). *The First English Actresses: Women and Drama, 1660–1700*. Cambridge: Cambridge University Press.

Hughes, D. (1996). *English Drama, 1660–1700*. Oxford: Clarendon Press.

Hume, R. D. (1976). *The Development of English Drama in the Late Seventeenth Century*. Oxford: Clarendon Press.

Marshall, G. (1975). *Restoration Serious Drama*. Norman: University of Oklahoma Press.

Munns, J. (1995). *Restoration Politics and Drama: The Plays of Thomas Otway, 1675–1683*. Newark: University of Delaware Press.

Owen, S. J. (1996). *Restoration Theatre and Crisis*. Oxford: Clarendon Press.

Quinsey, K. (ed.). (1996). *Broken Boundaries: Feminist Readings of Restoration Drama*. Lexington: University Press of Kentucky.

Rapin, R. (1674). *Reflections on Aristotle's Treatise of Poesie, Containing the Necessary, Rational, and Universal Rules for Epick, Dramatick, and other sorts of Poetry. With Reflections on the Works of Ancient and Modern Poets, and their Faults Noted*, trans. T. Rymer. London.

Rothstein, E. M. (1967). *Restoration Tragedy: Form and the Process of Change*. Madison: University of Wisconsin Press.

Staves, S. (1979). *Players' Scepters: Fictions of Authority in the Restoration*. Lincoln: University of Nebraska Press.

Waith, E. M. (1971). *Ideas of Greatness: The Heroic Play in England*. New York: Barnes and Noble.

15

London Theatre Music, 1660–1719

Todd S. Gilman

England boasts an impressive heritage of instrumental music, and especially music drama composed for the London theatres from the Restoration of Charles II (1660) until 1719. Throughout this period music was more central to English drama than it had ever been previously, and the last forty years of the seventeenth century to the first two decades of the eighteenth comprise a period of substantial innovation for English music drama of all kinds. Every Restoration drama (to *c*.1705) and many early eighteenth-century English dramas, from tragedy to tragicomedy, to comedy, to farce, from masque to opera – all together well over 600 stage works – incorporated music in performance. Even in plays that had no singing, a group of musicians would begin with two instrumental suites, the first music and second music, performed while the audience gathered. The musicians were seated aloft in the music room, in what we would call the orchestra pit, or on the stage itself. The first and second music would be followed by an elaborate overture (played after the speaking of the prologue from the stage), then (in many cases) a 'curtain tune' to accompany the raising of the curtain; once raised, the curtain usually remained up until after the epilogue. Between the acts the musicians played act tunes (short instrumental pieces). These men also played any music needed to accompany scene changes and dancing within the play.

Through extensive collaboration, Restoration and early eighteenth-century London-based dramatists including John Dryden, Thomas Shadwell, Peter Anthony Motteux, Thomas Durfey, William Congreve, George Granville, Joseph Addison, John Hughes, Colley Cibber, Lewis Theobald and John Gay, along with composers including Matthew Locke, John Banister, brothers Henry and Daniel Purcell, Pelham Humfrey, Jeremiah Clarke, Godfrey Finger, John Eccles, Richard Leveridge, John Christopher Pepusch, John Ernest Galliard and George Frideric Handel, together produced the period's finest and most popular works. Some of the extant works are enjoying a renascence today, thanks in part to a growing interest in historically informed productions that feature not only contemporary musical instruments and baroque performance practice, but also the costumes, staging, dancing and scenery that the dramatists, composers, actors, musicians and singers of the period would recognize. The celebrations and festivals commemorating Henry Purcell in 1995 (the tercentenary of his death) – notably fully staged productions of the Dryden/Purcell semi-opera *King Arthur* in Stockholm, Paris, London and Boston – positioned English Restoration music drama front and centre in the public consciousness to a degree that many productions of the more traditionally operatic *Dido and Aeneas* have been unable to manage. So popular was *King Arthur*, in fact, that it was resurrected in London two years later in a semi-staged version by William Christie and Les Arts Florissants.

Still, for now at least, *Dido and Aeneas*, Nahum Tate and Henry Purcell's masque of the 1680s, can claim to be the best-known musico-dramatic work of the period. Its reputation is well deserved, as is that of Gay and Handel's masque *Acis and Galatea* from the end of the period (1718), but neither work was written for the public theatres (our immediate concern) and, as *King Arthur*'s success demonstrates, other examples merit reconsideration. Highlights of surviving theatre music include scores for Shadwell and Locke's semi-opera *Psyche* (1675); Betterton and Purcell's semi-opera *Dioclesian* (1690); the Anonymous/Purcell semi-opera *The Indian Queen* (1695); and Purcell's two musical adaptations of Shakespeare: the semi-operatic *Fairy Queen* (1692) and the masque in *Timon of Athens* (1695). To these we might add post-1700 achievements such as Eccles's settings of Congreve's masque *The Judgment of Paris* (1701) and all-sung opera *Semele* (1707); (?)Weldon's resetting (*c.*1712) of the semi-opera *The Tempest* (1674); Galliard's settings of Hughes's all-sung opera *Calypso and Telemachus* (1712) and Theobald's masque *Pan and Syrinx* (1718); and Pepusch's masque music – for Cibber's *Venus and Adonis* (1715), Barton Booth's *The Death of Dido* (1716) and Hughes's *Apollo and Daphne* (1716).

Solo songs that originated in the theatres and then migrated to song collections have fared better overall: Henry Purcell's 'Music for a while', 'Retir'd from any mortal's sight', 'Let the dreadful engines' and 'From rosie bow'rs'; Eccles's 'Oh! take him gently', 'Releive, the fair Belinda said' and 'A soldier and a sailor'; Daniel Purcell's 'Morpheus thou gentle god', 'Underneath a gloomy shade' and 'Fixt on the fair Miranda's eyes'; Simon Pack's 'The larks awake the drowzy morn'; and William Croft's 'I hate a fop that at his glass'. Among the surviving instrumental works, classical music audiences today know Henry Purcell's suite from Aphra Behn's tragedy *Abdelazer, or The Moor's Revenge* (1695), particularly the D minor rondeau, which Benjamin Britten adopted as the theme for *The Young Person's Guide to the Orchestra*, Op. 34, but could they hear them they might also enjoy Purcell's lesser-known suites for Elkanah Settle's *Distressed Innocence, or The Princess of Persia* (1690), John Crowne's *Married Beau, or The Curious Impertinent* (1694) and the revival (?1692) of Shadwell's *Libertine* (1675); Locke and Robert Smith's suite from the original setting of the semi-operatic *Tempest* (1674); and the manuscript miscellany of act music by Locke, *The Rare Theatrical* (*c.*1685).

A comprehensive discussion of London theatre music between 1660 and 1719 must take some account of the influence of French opera under Louis XIV and, especially, the centrality of Italian opera. Restoration England's primary foreign models for vocal and instrumental music were French, not least because Charles II himself had spent years at the French court during his exile. Charles also sent Banister, Humfrey and Betterton to France to study her musical and theatrical practices, appointed French musicians such as Louis Grabu to high posts, saw half a dozen French operas brought to his court and the public theatres, and tried to establish a French-language Royal Academy of Music in the 1670s (Luckett 1977: 128–9).

In 1660 Charles granted Giulio Gentileschi the opportunity to bring a company of Italian musicians to London who would perform operas, and to build a theatre suitable for staging them. Thomas Killigrew, patentee of the King's Company, had similar ambitions and persuaded Charles to establish a King's Italian Musick. Ian Spink remarks that 'Vincenzo and Bartolomeo Albrici were already in service by 1665, and three others – of whom Giovanni Sebenico is the best known – were engaged the following year. In due course Giovanni Battista Draghi arrived, and the castrato Girolamo Pignani' (1986: 204). Charles also paid for Humfrey's travel to Italy for musical training. The Italian operas did not materialize in London until decades later, but they exerted a palpable influence from abroad, and in 1705 Motteux and Clayton's *Arsinoe*, 'an Opera after the *Italian* manner. All-sung' began a vogue for the exotic sorceress that continues today (Luckett 1977: 126–7).

By 1719 the Italian opera had gained a clear if temporary advantage (in popularity, not financial solvency) over native music drama, evidenced by the founding in 1719 of the Royal Academy of Music as a truly distinct enterprise that lasted nearly a decade (Milhous and Hume 1999). Still, virtually all distinctly English musico-dramatic genres perfected during the Restoration – constantly and creatively updated throughout the early eighteenth century and beyond – held their own against foreign incursions and proved more consistently profitable than the Italian opera. In other words, contrary to received wisdom native music drama continued to develop and thrive after Henry Purcell's untimely demise in 1695.

As noted, every performance in the Restoration theatre incorporated a substantial amount of instrumental music specially composed for each play, including music preceding the performance, between acts (sometimes also between scenes) and for any dances. Beyond the minimum, varieties of Restoration theatre music can be divided into four categories: (1) music in the spoken play – comedy, tragedy or tragicomedy – incorporating songs and other musical pieces within the drama; (2) the organic and/or independent masque, a short (usually one-act) but substantial musical interlude featuring singing (both solo and choral) and dancing and performed in costume in front of scenery; (3) the semi-opera or dramatic opera, a five-act tragedy, comedy or, least often, tragicomedy, based on an allegorical, mythological or supernatural theme, incorporating numerous masques or musical scenes but with the speaking and singing characters nearly always separated; and (4) the all-sung or Italianate English opera, modelled formally on its Italian counterpart/predecessor but attempting a higher poetic standard, especially greater dramatic integrity and a stronger connection

between text and music. The dialogue is conducted in recitative, a declamatory kind
of singing of Italian origin, which Congreve adeptly described in his introduction to
Semele as 'a more tuneable Speaking; its Beauty consists in coming near Nature, and in
improving the natural Accents of Words by more Pathetick or Emphatical Tones'.
Recitative alternates with airs (in Italian, arias), emotionally charged tableaux composed in strophic (a-a-a) or da capo (a-b-a') form.

Spoken Play

Restoration comedy, tragedy and tragicomedy – their significant generic differences
notwithstanding – share many varieties of music. For example, the practice of using
music for banquet scenes, coronations and weddings typifies all dramatic genres from
the late sixteenth century. Mad songs, also traceable to the Renaissance – Ophelia
delivers the best-known snatches in *Hamlet* (1600) – appear in Restoration tragedy
and comedy alike, from Thomas Porter's *The Villain* (1663) to Durfey's three-part
Comical History of Don Quixote (1694–5). Still, we may posit some distinctions
regarding music along generic lines. On the whole music in the comedies serves as
entertainment. Comedies often feature characters singing, playing or listening to
others play an instrument (as for a serenade). Some have choruses, pantomimes
and/or dances. Restoration tragedies, by contrast, more often use music to enhance
pathos: songs in tragedy tend to intensify expressions of love, melancholy, worry
and consolation, or to underscore scenes of villainous seduction or death, at times by
means of symbolic lyrics. Moreover, in tragedy, unlike comedy, it is often supernatural
personages who do the singing. An act song for Katherine Philips's *Pompey* (1663),
'From lasting and unclouded Day', which Pompey's ghost sings to comfort his widow
Cornelia, is one of the best integrated and most effective (Price 1979: 62).

Instrumental music in tragedy often serves to elevate the tone of processions,
prophecies, charms and incantations, or religious ceremonies for Christian, Greek,
Roman, Indian or druidic rites (sacrifices and funerals, for example). As in modern
films, tragic instrumental music also imparts a mood of impending doom to bloody
battles and other dire affairs. With a few exceptions, musically speaking Restoration
tragicomedies resemble tragedies rather than comedies.

Curtis Price's *Music in the Restoration Theatre* (1979) and *Henry Purcell and the London
Stage* (1984) remain the best studies to date of music in the Restoration spoken play;
any subsequent discussion of the subject (including this one) owes much to his. In the
earlier book Price distinguishes between paradramatic and dramatic music according
to a piece's function within its play. Paradramatic music is introduced for aesthetic
reasons alone. Dramatic music is music whose omission would create a noticeable gap
in the play. Dramatic music can itself be subdivided into atmospheric music (which
enhances emotional situations or prepares for scene changes) and organic music (which
tells the audience something important about a character or situation) (Price 1979: 3).

Since theatre music followed no formula, these categories cannot be considered mutually exclusive, as Price admits (1979: 2–3)

Paradramatic music includes dances, such as the one concluding Sir George Etherege's comedy *The Man of Mode* (1676), and lyrics unconnected to the action, such as Laura's in Act 5, scene 1 of Crowne's comedy *The English Friar* (1690): 'Come, sing the song I like!' she commands Airy, who obliges with 'I once had virtue, wealth, and fame'. A familiar example that combines paradramatic song and dance occurs in Act 3, scene 15 of Congreve's popular comedy *Love for Love* (1695). Ben, a sailor, sings to Mrs Foresight, Mrs Frail and Scandal the bawdy song (set by Eccles), 'A soldier and a sailor', about the rivalry of four lecherous men for the hand of a nubile maid. Ben introduces the song by means of a dubious connection to his listeners, claiming it 'was made upon one of our ship's crew's wife; . . . mayhap you may know her, sir. Before she was married, she was called buxom Joan of Deptford'. The song ended, Ben continues, '"If some of our crew that came to see me are not gone, you shall see that we sailors can dance sometimes as well as other folks." (*Whistles*) "I warrant that brings 'em, an they be within hearing." [Enter SEAMEN] "O, here they be – and fiddles along with 'em. Come my lads, let's have a round, and I'll make one." *Dance*'.

Melancholy songs offer the most effective instances of atmospheric music. These generally occur in tragedies, and Athenais's death wish in Act 5, scene 1 of Lee's *Theodosius* (1680) occasions the most exceptional example. Forced to marry the villainous Roman emperor, Athenais decides to poison herself during her maid's performance of 'Ah cruel bloody fate', Henry Purcell's first song for the theatre, concerning a pastoral nymph who sacrifices herself to be reunited with her dead lover. Atmospheric music can also accompany soliloquies, again especially in tragedies. Dryden was particularly fond of this means of inspiring or reflecting pathos. In Act 4, scene 1 of *Aureng-Zebe* (1676), the eponymous hero ruminates to 'Soft Musick' on his impending doom, 'Distrust, and darkness, of a future State, / Make poor Mankind so fearful of their Fate. / Death, in itself, is nothing; but we fear / To be we know not what, we know not where'. Similarly, in Act 1, scene 1 of *All for Love* (1678), Antony calls for music to relieve his sorrow, '"Give me some Musick; look that it be sad: / I'll sooth my Melancholy, till I swell, / And burst my self with sighing – [*Soft Musick*. / 'Tis somewhat to my humor. Stay, I fancy / I'm now turn'd wild, a commoner of Nature; / Of all forsaken, and forsaking all; / Live in a shady Forrest's Sylvan Scene, / Stretch'd at my length beneath some blasted Oke; . . . More of this Image, more; it lulls my thoughts." [*Soft Musick again*'. Discoveries, the revelation of scenes hidden behind the curtain or a pair of shutters, also employ atmospheric music: in Act 4 of Delarivier Manley's *The Royal Mischief* (1696), Levan Dadian's new lover Homais treats him to the following spectacle: 'The *Curtain* flys up to the sound of Flutes, and Hoboys, and discovers the River *Phasis*, several little gilded Boats, with Musick [i.e., instrumentalists] in them; a walk of Trees, the length of the House; Lights fixed in Chrystal Candlesticks to the Branches; several Persons in the walk, as in Attention' (Price 1979: 7–9).

Lyrics that contribute to characterization comprise one kind of organic music. A classic example from a comedy occurs in Congreve's *The Way of the World* (1700). In Act 3, scene 1 Marwood and Millamant, rivals for Mirabell's affections, spar wittily over their relative charms. Marwood, the older of the two, seems to be winning when Millamant calls for a song, peremptorily denying that the lyrics have any bearing on the present situation, 'You shall hear it madam – not that there's any great matter in it, but 'tis agreeable to my humour'. Yet the song, 'Love's but the frailty of the mind', argues that the only reason to pursue a lover is the attendant joy of beating the competition. As the concluding couplet (endlessly repeated and embellished in Eccles's impish setting) has it, 'If there's delight in love, 'tis when I see / That heart which others bleed for, bleed for me'. By means of this song Millamant, the more successful suitor and the one Mirabell chooses, gains the advantage while also revealing her otherwise hidden ruthlessness.

One other variety of dramatic music for spoken plays deserves mention: the Restoration mad song. As noted, mad songs occur equally in comedies and tragedies of the period to *c*.1703. It is admittedly difficult to generalize about their precise dramatic function; for mad songs often only verify what the audience already knows and so are not organic. Still, some mad songs function organically, as when the audience first learns of a character's derangement through song. Price demonstrates how Purcell's song for Cardenio in Durfey's *Comical History of Don Quixote, Part I* marries music and action to an extent rarely accomplished elsewhere:

> In 'Let the dreadful engines', his first utterance in the play, one learns that Cardenio, like King Lear, is tormented by the realization of his own insanity.... [Purcell] reacted to the violent changes of mood and unbridled imagery with a series of reflex-like responses: wild, thrashing *secco* recitatives; a truly pathetic and lyrical air; jocular, earthy ballads; and highly ornamented declamations. Yet the diverse elements somehow fit together coherently. The most obvious order imposed on the poetic chaos is a symmetrical tonal scheme.... The grand design – major/minor tonic followed by major/minor dominant – reinforces the underlying drama. F major represents Cardenio's brash exterior, manifested at the beginning by cosmic delusions of grandeur and at the end by a devil-may-care dismissal of all women as scolding, money-grabbing witches. His inner despair is depicted in the F minor sections; C major is reserved for brief moments of towering rage; and C minor is the key of the pathetic aria placed at the emotional core of the song when Cardenio recalls his lost youth. (1984: 211)

Moreover, fine distinctions concerning the atmospheric and organic function of mad songs lose some of their force in the light of the songs' role as theatre. Certain actresses and actors who doubled as singers – Anne Bracegirdle, Mrs Hodgson, Mrs Hains and Richard Leveridge, for example – became renowned for their performances of mad scenes, and mad lyrics inspired Restoration composers to their greatest heights. Small wonder that such consummately theatrical songs, with their wildly contrasting 'affects' and corresponding alternations between dissonant recitatives and melodious airs and ballads, frequently appear in concerts and recordings today as miniature music dramas in their own right.

In fact, concerning mad songs Eccles might be said to have surpassed Purcell in theatrical cogency, though not aesthetically. 'I burn, my Brain consumes to Ashes', which Bracegirdle sang as Marcella in *The Comical History of Don Quixote, Part II* (1694), instantly outshone Purcell's contributions. Following Purcell's death in 1695, Eccles continued to write mad songs for Bracegirdle, and a particularly fine example occurs in Banks's tragedy *Cyrus the Great* (1696). In Act 4, scene 1 Lausaria (Bracegirdle), whose unrequited love leads to madness, enters 'Distracted, drest like Cupid, with a Bow and Quiver, follow'd by her Women'. After singing 'O take him gently from the Pile', she sends an arrow whizzing by Cyrus and totters off the stage to die. Other fine examples of Eccles's mad songs include 'Restless in thought', which Hodgson sang in the anonymous comedy *She Ventures and He Wins* (1696); a duet for 'two Madmen' – 'Come let us howle some heavy Note' – composed for *The Duchess of Malfey*, a revival of the Jacobean revenge tragedy; 'Find me a lonely Cave', sung by Hodgson in *The Villain* (1694); and three songs from Motteux's 1701 semi-operatic adaptation of John Fletcher's *The Mad Lover*: 'Must then a faithful Lover go?', 'Cease of Cupid to complain' (both for Bracegirdle) and 'Let all be gay' (sung by Hodgson).

Many comedies, tragicomedies and tragedies incorporate extended musical scenes in performance. These are variously designated 'entertainments', 'entry dances', 'banquets', 'shows' and 'masques' in the playbooks. In order to avoid confusing them with the organic/independent masques discussed below I refer to all such scenes – i.e., any musical scene short of a full-blown masque – as 'entertainments'. These are usually paradramatic, and Congreve's *Way of the World* is perhaps the best-known comedy to incorporate this variety: in Act 4, scene 2, Lady Wishfort invites Sir Roland to join her, 'Call in the Dancers. – Sir Roland, we'll sit if you please, and see the Entertainment'. Another paradramatic entertainment in a popular comedy of the day occurs at the end of Aphra Behn's *The Rover* (1677).

A typical example of a paradramatic entertainment in a tragicomedy occurs in a discovery scene in Act 3 of Shadwell's *The Royal Shepherdess* (1669). The nobility in the play are treated to this frolicsome pastoral song and dance episode: 'SCENE draws, the Shepherds and Shepherdesses are discover'd lying under the Shades of Trees, at the appearance of the King and Court; one arises and sings as follows, *In Stilo recitativo*'. The shepherd soloist sings four verses of the song, 'Shepherds awake, the God of day does rise', during the refrains of which a chorus of his fellows joins in. Then 'the Shepherds and Shepherdesses take hands round, and Dance, as they sing the following Song ["Thus all our Life long we are frolick and gay"], and at the end of the Song they fall into the Figure they must dance in'.

An unusual organic entertainment in a tragicomedy occurs in Act 3, scene 1 of Dryden's *The Rival Ladies* (1664). A musical scene is staged to honour the wedding of Julia and Don Rodorick, but Don Rodorick seems to have abandoned his fiancée at the altar. Just then, Cupid, accompanied by music, 'descends in swift Motion, and Speaks' of how Venus 'Has, by my Aid, contriv'd a black design, / The God of Hell should Ravish *Proserpine*: / Beauties, beware; *Venus* will never bear / Another *Venus* shining in her Sphere'. After some impressive flying effects involving Venus, Ceres, Phoebus (Apollo) and Mercury, Cupid addresses Julia directly:

> The Rival Deities are come to woo
> A *Proserpine*, who must be found below:
> Would you (fair Nymph) become this happy hour,
> In name a Goddess as you are in pow'r,
> Then to this change the King of Shades will owe
> A fairer *Proserpine* than Heav'n can show.

Julia, further flattered by her betrothed's sister Angellina (disguised as a man, Amideo), joins a dance of the gods. Then, as the stage direction indicates: 'Towards the end of the Dance, *Rodorick* in the Habit of *Pluto*, rises from below in a black Chariot all Flaming, and drawn by black Horses; he Ravishes *Julia*, who personated *Proserpine*, and as he is Carrying her away, his Vizard falls off: *Hippolito* [another woman in male disguise] first discovers him'. Hippolito screams in protest, provoking Rodorick – assisted by the dancers playing Phoebus and Mercury! – to draw his sword and attack Julia's defenders. The action integrated into the entertainment proves central to the plot and characterization of the play, and the allegory of the rape of Proserpine reinforces the connection.

An atmospheric entertainment occurs in the incantation scene in Act 3, scene 1 of Dryden and Lee's tragedy *Oedipus* (1678). Peter Holman demonstrates how the music by Henry Purcell for a revival *c*.1692 works particularly effectively. Tiresias the blind soothsayer and two priests invoke the ghost of Laius to discover who killed him:

> they begin by addressing the 'sullen powers below', describing their unpleasant activities in a mixture of declamatory solos and tutti invocations [performed by alto, tenor and bass soloists, two violins and continuo]. Then the first priest persuades Laius to rise by singing the famous ground-bass air 'Music for a while' [which] uses an arpeggiated ground with a simple rising bass in dialogue with an interlocking tenor. . . . The two strands creep upwards in an unpredictable mixture of chromatic and diatonic movement, portraying the eerie and inexorable rise of the dead king, while the melodic line soothes him with a series of gently descending phrases. As in a number of Purcell's late ground basses, the return to the home key after a series of modulations coincides with a return to the opening words and music, which gives it something of the character of a da capo aria. (Holman 1994: 216)

Act 4, scene 1 of Crowne's tragedy *The Ambitious Statesman, or The Loyal Favourite* (1679) contains an uncommon organic entertainment. The Dauphin and Louize, sitting in state, are 'entertain'd with music and dancing'. While the entertainment proceeds, the Duke of Vendosme 'sees the *Dauphin* Caressing *Louize*'. Although she still loves the Duke, after hearing rumours of his infidelity Louize has agreed to marry the Dauphin. A song given during the entertainment, 'Long long had great Amintor lain', recapitulates the characters' actions and motivations: despite her love for him, Celia (Louize?) cruelly disdains the weeping Amintor (the Duke?), or as the choral refrain confides, 'Yet all the while fair Celia prov'd, / So haughty, so cruel, she secretly lov'd'. Another organic entertainment can be found in Act 2 of Henry Neville Payne's *Othello*-inspired tragedy *The Fatal Jealousie* (1673): a grotesque performance by singing and dancing gypsies (reminiscent of an antemasque from the Jacobean court masques described below) provides the context for a prediction of Don Antonio's future: like those of the witches in *Macbeth*, the gypsies' words come true in the end (Price 1979: 28–34).

Masque

The Restoration theatre masque, along with its counterpart performed at the second Charles's court, developed from Tudor and Stuart masques performed at court or private houses for special occasions from as far back as the early sixteenth century right up to 1659. The Tudor and Stuart masques, in turn, bear the influence of two prior forms: (1) the Italian *masquerie* that Henry VIII (himself a masquer) imitated at court as early as 1512, and (2) the disguising, a masked dance (popular at most of the courts of Europe as well as in England) based on an allegorical or mythological theme and boasting speaking and singing actors as well as elaborate spectacle. The disguising – which was performed in England from the beginning of the fifteenth century – evolved for its part from the tradition of mumming, or masked dance pantomime.

The Renaissance court masque flourished from Tudor days through the unstable last years of the reign of Charles I. During the Civil Wars, additional masques were composed, notably James Shirley, Matthew Locke and Christopher Gibbons's *Cupid and Death* (1653, revised 1659), but stylistically these are nearly identical to their immediate predecessors. In order to grasp the theatre masques that began to appear shortly after Charles II's return from exile in 1660, then, we must look back to the earlier court masques.

Based on allegorical or mythological themes and boasting dancing, poetry, music, costumes, and eventually elaborate scenery and stage machines, the court masque peaked under James I and his queen, Anne of Denmark. A devoted patron of the arts as well as a skilful dancer, Anne commissioned the many artists, poets and musicians who devised these sumptuous entertainments, the culmination of which was always the 'revels': the masquers descended from the stage to dance with members of the audience. Although poets as talented as Thomas Campion, Francis Beaumont, George Chapman and Samuel Daniel penned texts for these productions, the poet laureate Ben Jonson and stage architect Inigo Jones mounted the quintessential court masques with composers including Alfonso Ferrabosco II, Thomas Lupo, Nicholas Lanier and Robert Johnson.

Jonson and Jones's collaborative efforts to 1631 showed a strong Continental influence resulting from the latter's excursions abroad. Jones visited Italy twice (at some time between 1598 and 1601, then from 1613–14), Denmark in 1603 and France in 1609. The Teatro Olimpico at Vicenza, begun by Palladio in 1580 but not completed until 1585 under Vincenzo Scamozzi (with whom Jones met and exchanged ideas), served as the crucial Continental model for the illusionist perspective scenery and flying machines Jones was to bring to the English masque. Thanks to Jones, the English court stage, caught in a time warp in scenic development since the Reformation, finally equalled and in some respects surpassed its Continental rivals (Rosenfeld 1973: 17).

Jonson and Jones mounted each of their thirty masques between 1605 and 1631 for special occasions such as births and marriages. The usual places of performance were the Great Hall or Banqueting House at Whitehall. Contemporaries greatly admired the increasingly cunning stages, scenery and machines. In the earlier masques Jones accomplished his scene changes via the *machina versatilis* or 'turning machine', which rotated to reveal a different scene and hidden masquers on the opposite side. One such example was a globe created for *Hymenaei* (1606). Seeming to hover above the stage, in Jonson's words, it 'stood, or rather hung (for no Axell was seene to support it) and turning softly discouered the first *Masque*'. Later, elaborate sets of moveable flats that could be fitted into shutters (the *scena ductilis*) or lowered from flying galleries became the norm.

Each of these early court masques consisted of two parts: the first half humorous, the second, serious. The former consisted largely of burlesque dances – 'anticks' or 'antemasques' – performed by grotesque figures such as satyrs, witches or apes, who set off the main masque. While the music for the second half would be formal 'art' music specially composed by the leading court musician(s), the burlesque music was more free-wheeling: popular ballads, catches and quick and lively dances from jigs and voltas to galliards, corantos and almains were the typical fare. The Jonson/Jones/ Ferrabosco *Masque of Queenes* (1609), presented at the Banqueting House in honour of Queen Anne, set the standard of the masque for some years, in part because it introduced the antemasque. An interesting connection between the Jonsonian masque and the Restoration variety further substantiates its influence: the twelve witches who sing and dance the antemasque in Jonson's *Queenes* appear to have served as the model for their Restoration counterparts from the operatic *Macbeth* to Purcell's *Dido and Aeneas* (Plank 1990). The Jonson/Jones/Ferrabosco II/Robert Johnson *Oberon, The Faery Prince* (1611), in which the young Henry, Prince of Wales played the title role, proved another landmark: no fewer than seventy-five musicians, divided by function, performed that New Year's Day, including twenty lutenists of the Royal Lutes and Viols who apparently doubled as Fairies while accompanying Oberon's magical dancing!

In 1631 Jonson and Jones quarrelled over whether poetry or spectacle was the soul of the masque, and Jones made sure that Jonson was denied any further opportunities in that art; Jonson retaliated with his famous verse 'Expostulation'. Caroline court masques became increasingly extravagant visually, but were also even more expensive to mount and dramatically incoherent. This unlucky turn of events had at least one extremely positive result: Sir William Davenant (later patentee of the Duke's Company, which developed many of the innovations associated with semi-opera), Jones, his pupil John Webb, and a French composer in the service of Henrietta Maria, Louis Richard, created *Salmacida Spolia* (1640), the last masque staged before the Civil Wars. *Salmacida Spolia* was a technical marvel and featured more than twenty antemasques; Davenant writes that it was 'generally approved of, especially by all the strangers [i.e., foreigners] that were present, to be the noblest and most ingenious that hath been done here in that kind'.

Still, the most instructive surviving prototype of the Restoration theatre masques was mounted just before Charles II's coronation: *Cupid and Death*. The dancing master Luke Channen (or Channell) first presented *Cupid and Death* on 26 March 1653 to honour the visiting Portuguese ambassador. It was revised in 1659 for a performance at the Military Ground in Leicester Fields. The surviving music (from the later performance) is mostly by Locke, whose recitatives, much more substantial than those of earlier composers such as William Lawes, constitute a true innovation. By ingeniously combining the angular English declamatory style with the more emotional Italian idiom, Locke succeeds in giving 'the various emotional phases' of *Cupid and Death* 'a much greater intensity of expression' than Lawes had managed (Dent 1965: 87).

The plot, fuller and better integrated than prior examples, derives from Aesop's fable of the title characters' exchange of arrows. A variation on earlier Stuart masques, *Cupid and Death* comprises five acts or 'entries'. Each 'entry', in turn, consists of a suite of dances – almain and courant, saraband, jig or galliard – and a sequence of solo song, recitative or duet (or some combination of these), followed by or interspersed with short chorus(es). Each of the first three entries has dialogue, but thereafter music and dance take over. Like the court masques, *Cupid and Death* culminates in a dance of the principal characters, but unlike the court masque the humorous and serious portions alternate throughout.

Some private masques were attempted after 1660, mainly in schools, and *c.*1682 John Blow mounted a production of *Venus and Adonis* at court. Holman argues that this work 'belongs to the private masque tradition in that it was performed partly by amateurs – Venus and Cupid were played by Charles II's mistress Moll Davies and their young daughter Lady Mary Tudor – and that there was much dancing' (1994: 198). Although modern audiences consider Tate and Purcell's *Dido and Aeneas* an opera, it was obviously modelled on *Venus and Adonis* and is more accurately designated a masque.

Consistent with the private and court masques, the public theatre masques written for Restoration comedies were usually conceived as autonomous units with no necessary connection to the larger play. Also like their private counterparts they boasted scenes of singing and dancing in exotic locales, their characters usually allegorical or symbolic personifications taken from classical mythology or British legend. Edward Ravenscroft's three-act farce, *The Anatomist, or The Sham Doctor* (1697), makes no pretence of integrating the musical part, featuring a theatre within a theatre in which actors and playhouse audience together enjoy Motteux, Finger and Eccles's masque, *The Loves of Mars and Venus*. George Powell and Thomas Morgan's masque *Endimion The Man in the Moon*, interpolated into *The Imposture Defeated* (1697), is similarly set apart. Other masques unrelated to their comedies (or tragicomedies) include Jeremiah Clarke's *The Four Seasons, or Love in Every Age*, performed after the last act of the semi-opera *The Island Princess* (1699); Dryden, Daniel Purcell and Finger's *Secular Masque*, interpolated into Sir John Vanbrugh's adaptation of Fletcher's *The Pilgrim* (1700); Granville and Eccles's *Peleus and Thetis*, in Granville's *The Jew of Venice* (1701); and Motteux and Eccles's *Wine and Love* and *Acis and Galatea*, for a revival of Fletcher's *The Mad Lover* (1701).

Restoration tragedies that had substantial masques usually integrated them quite skilfully. These include *Orpheus and Euridice* in Settle's *The Empress of Morocco* (1673); *The Rape of Europa by Jupiter*, for a revival of Rochester's revision of Fletcher's *Valentinian* (1694); *The Loves of Mars and Venus*, interpolated into Ravenscroft's *The Anatomist, or The Sham Doctor* (1696); and *Ixion*, in Ravenscroft's tragedy *The Italian Husband* (1697). Robert D. Hume notes that *Ixion* constitutes 'an exact thematic anticipation of the catastrophe into which it leads' (1984: 80). The masque of Cupid and Bacchus in Shadwell's *Timon of Athens* is uncommon as a substantial masque in a Restoration tragedy that is unrelated to the larger drama, but Shadwell inherited the masque from Shakespeare.

Orpheus and Euridice provides the finest example of an integrated masque in a Restoration tragedy. *The Empress of Morocco* itself can be characterized as one of many seventeenth-century analogues of the late twentieth-century exploitation film. Settle seems to have derived the plot from earlier English revenge tragedies and their variations, particularly *Hamlet*, as well as the gruesome Latin tragedies of Seneca. Composed of strained rhyming couplets that Dryden, Shadwell and Crowne stingingly dismantled in their *Notes and Observations on The Empress of Morocco* (1674), the play concerns the machinations of the ruthless Queen Mother Laula (the empress), and her secret lover Crimalhaz. Before the play opens these two have poisoned her husband, and now they intend to kill her son Muly Labas, who has just taken over the throne.

At the end of Act 4 Laula and Crimalhaz present the masque. Muly Labas is to play Orpheus and his young queen Morena, Euridice. However, Laula, pretending to take Morena into her confidence, tells the young queen that it is Crimalhaz who is to play Orpheus, in which disguise he intends to ravish Morena and kill her husband: 'Then will he rudely snatch you from the place, / And basely force You to his foul Embrace. / And at that instant, Your dear Lord shall Bleed / By Murderers appointed for the Deed'. During the performance, then, just as Laula intends that she do, Morena stabs and kills her own husband, falling into a dead faint when his mask is lifted. As Price notes, this episode constitutes 'a startling departure from the orderly presentation of a courtly entertainment. In no other play of the period does one find such an elaborate masque so closely related to its play' (1979: 31). The surviving music for the first performance, by Locke, also merits attention: although its somewhat stilted recitatives would seem passé to a contemporary witness from, say, Venice, Michael Burden argues that the music 'resists all temptations to obvious text painting and vulgar effects, and relies on a consistent creation of atmosphere, exemplified by the subtle chromatic writing as Orpheus gently feels his way into Hades' (1995: 72).

The action of the masque itself adds still another level of cynicism to this deeply cynical play. Orpheus, whose very entrance instantly calms Hell's tortured souls, asks Pluto to return Euridice. Pluto balks at the effrontery of a mere mortal until Proserpine mollifies him. Euridice comes forth, whereupon Orpheus sings, 'For this signal Grace to the World I'le declare, / In Heaven Earth and Hell Loves Pow'r is the Same. / No Law there nor here, no God so Severe, / But Love can Repeale, and Beauty can Tame'. A chorus repeats Orpheus's song, then an antemasque follows featuring 'several infernal Spirits, who ascend from under the Stage'. Only then does Morena/ Euridice stab Muly Labas/Orpheus; contrary to the lyric, Settle implies, even after the ultimate adversary has been overcome and lovers reunited, disaster awaits.

Shortly after the turn of the century, when mounting new plays playwrights abandoned the interpolated masque in favour of the masque as a separate entity. Occasionally a masque filled an evening on its own, as was the case with the four separate settings of Congreve's *The Judgment of Paris*, performed at Dorset Garden in the spring of 1701. Composed on the occasion of a 'Musick Prize' competition sponsored by 'several Persons of Quality' for 'the Encouragement of MUSICK', these productions were anomalies in many ways, not least because John Weldon – only 25 years old and a virtual unknown from Oxford – took first prize over Eccles, whose Italianate score recalls the beauties of Purcell's *King Arthur*. (Daniel Purcell took third prize; Finger, fourth.) Additionally, far greater forces than usual were amassed and the stage specially outfitted for the performances. Eccles's orchestra, for example, normally comprised about twenty instrumentalists who, transplanted to Dorset Garden, would ordinarily have sat in the pit; yet just after the first performance, Congreve implies to a friend that the orchestra was greatly expanded and sat on the stage:

> The number of performers, besides the verse-singers [i.e., soloists], was 85. The front of the stage was all built into a concave with deal boards; all which was faced with tin, to increase and throw forwards the sound. It was all hung with sconces of wax-candles, besides the common branches of lights usual in the play-houses. . . . The place where formerly the music used to play, between the pit and the stage, was turned into White's chocolate-house; . . . the whole expence of every thing being defrayed by the subscribers.

Fortunately, the three Englishmen's music survives (Walsh printed Eccles's and Purcell's in full score; the Moravian Finger's is lost). Weldon's – never printed – is the most original contribution, but as Stoddard Lincoln argues, the native scores have much in common:

> They all employ essentially the same orchestral forces: strings with oboes doubling the violins, recorders, trumpets and continuo. Most of the arias make use of solo obbligato

instruments, and there is a conscious attempt to characterize the goddesses by means of orchestral colouring. Venus sings to the recorders, Athena to the trumpets, etc. Typically English is the use of a florid arioso, rather than recitative, which alternates with the airs. Harmonically, the chord progressions are purely functional and the part-writing is essentially diatonic. (1972: 1080)

The survival of three scores written at the same time to the same high-quality libretto provides us unique and valuable insight into the compositional techniques of English theatre musicians at the turn of the eighteenth century.

The Judgment of Paris aside, however, masques composed in the early eighteenth century were generally presented as afterpieces to spoken plays. Not only did after-pieces serve as an added attraction to soften the blow of raised ticket prices, but on the strength of these offerings theatre managers could now justify charging latecomers to the mainpiece half-price 'after-money'. By 1714–15, competition between Lincoln's Inn Fields and Drury Lane led to a marked increase in new masques, including some of the genre's most influential works. For example, Gay and Handel's *Acis and Galatea* – composed for a private performance at the home of the future Duke of Chandos at Cannons Park in the summer of 1718 – took its inspiration mainly from the Cibber/Pepusch *Venus and Adonis* and the Hughes/Pepusch *Apollo and Daphne*.

Semi-opera

The Dorset Garden theatre, which opened in 1671, encouraged the Duke's Company under Betterton to expand masques over the course of the next two decades to the extent that, in combination with their parent plays, they became a distinct genre. Though many of his predecessors and contemporaries were satisfied with the word 'Opera' or the phrase 'English Opera' when referring to these works, Dryden, con-scious of the difference between these works and their Italian and French predecessors, invented the phrase 'Dramatick Opera', first used for the title-page of *King Arthur* in 1691. Looking back from 1728 an elderly Roger North referred to them somewhat disparagingly as 'ambigue enterteinements' and 'Semioperas, for they consisted of half Musick, and half Drama'. More recently Judith Milhous coined the phrases 'multi-media spectaculars' and 'Dorset Garden spectaculars' (Milhous 1984). Others prefer 'dialogue opera'; I have settled on North's semi-opera because it seems the most descriptive and readily understood today while negotiating between historicity and critical distance.

Like masques, semi-operas drew themes from Greek mythology and ancient legend and boasted increasingly elaborate scenes and machines seldom reusable for straight plays. Small wonder that they were notoriously expensive to produce and required doubling and sometimes tripling admission prices. For a complete list of semi-operas see the appendix to this chapter; the keystones include Davenant, Locke and Robert Johnson's adaptation of Shakespeare's *Macbeth* (c.1663); Shadwell, Locke and others' adaptation of Shakespeare's *The Tempest* (1674); Shadwell, Locke and Draghi's *Psyche* (1675); Dryden and Purcell's *The Prophetess, or The History of Dioclesian* (1690) and *King Arthur* (1691); and the Anonymous/Purcell *Fairy Queen* (1692) and *Indian Queen* (1695). Granville, Eccles and Corbett's *The British Enchanters* (1706) also merits discussion, for although it was in some ways old-fashioned (Granville wrote the text in the 1680s), music and drama are more integrated here than in many previous semi-operas. Moreover, lasting twelve nights it surpassed Giovanni Bononcini's all-sung opera *Camilla* (which survived ten) and 'even threatened the future of the Italian opera enterprise in London' (Price 1987: 122–3).

Macbeth

The history of the operatic *Macbeth* (*c*.1663) – characterized by its three interpolated Hecate scenes performed from the Restoration through the 1870s – has proven controversial, but we now know most of the facts. Shakespeare's play as he wrote it (the version familiar to modern audiences) requires very little music: an alarm for a battle scene and a flourish preceding a grand entrance. Yet Davenant appears to have altered Shakespeare's text at least twice, first in 1610 for a court performance (this version appears in the First Folio of 1623), and then after the Restoration. For the 1610 version Davenant borrowed song words from Thomas Middleton's play *The Witch* (*c*.1610), and Robert Johnson almost certainly supplied the music. Davenant completely rewrote Macbeth *c*.1663; here he doubled his earlier musical requirements by adding a longer operatic scene in Act 2, where the witches utter a prophecy concerning Macduff and Lady Macduff. For this version Davenant commissioned new music from Locke, who may have incorporated some of Johnson's earlier pieces. This was the version that Samuel Pepys saw nine times from 5 November 1664 and deemed 'one of the best plays for a stage, and a variety of dancing and music, that ever I saw'. It was also this version or an augmentation of it to which John Downes, the Duke's Company's prompter, referred somewhat ambiguously as having been revived – or possibly augmented with yet more music by Locke – at Dorset Garden in 1673: 'Being drest in all it's Finery, as new Cloath's, new Scenes, Machines, as flyings for the Witches; with all the Singing and Dancing in it:... it being all Excellently perform'd, being in the nature of an Opera, it Recompenc'd double the Expence; it proves still [*c*.1706–8] a lasting Play'. Davenant's semi-operatic *Macbeth* was set to music again by Eccles and Finger about 1695, then by Leveridge in 1702. Leveridge's music – not Locke's, as scholars thought for a long time – is the so-called Famous Music that featured in virtually every production of *Macbeth* from 1702 until the 1870s (Moore 1961b; Fiske 1964).

The Tempest

The 1674 Dorset Garden *Tempest*, a second semi-operatic adaptation of Shakespeare, vies with *The Island Princess* (1699) for the title of most popular English theatre work before John Gay's *The Beggar's Opera* (1728) (Hume 1984: 81). Working from the 1667 Dryden–Davenant adaptation of Shakespeare's *Tempest*, Shadwell added the song 'Arise, ye subterranean winds', extended the devils' dialogue in the Act 2 masque, and wrote an original masque of Neptune and Amphitrite in Act 5. Pietro Reggio set the song; Humfrey, the dialogue and masque. Price aptly describes the adapters' operatic genius:

> Taking Ariel's songs as a point of departure, [they] allowed the new musical scenes to grow naturally from the plot, which was modified specifically for this purpose. For example, the masque of devils in II.iii is meant to nettle Alonzo and Antonio for their usurpation; it is a graphic representation of their guilty consciences. And in an episode joining the spoken and musical worlds of the drama, Ferdinand expresses his sorrow in song, while Ariel sings the echoes. (Price 1984: 204)

Milhous shows how Betterton's two spectacular scene changes comprising the finale contributed to the opera's novelty. (*The Tempest* was one of the first English stage works to employ French-style machinery, moving Dorset Garden instantly into the limelight.) Following the fanciful masque of Neptune and Amphitrite, 'for the first time in the opera the merely human characters see Ariel fly, and [we see] not only their wonder but . . . the liberated Ariel soaring before the rising sun. Spirits had flown . . . in *Macbeth* – but here Betterton had found a way to relate trick and theme' (Milhous 1984: 47).

While clearly a lavish production, *The Tempest* seems not to have broken the bank, and its popular and commercial success had much to do with Betterton's subsequent promotion of opera at Dorset Garden (although as Downes noted, 'not any succeeding Opera got more Money'). *The Tempest* also occasioned the first English libretto to be issued in the theatre for a performance – *Songs and Masques in The Tempest* – and featured singers from the Chapel Royal, whom Charles II lent in a singular display of confidence. Shadwell might be forgiven for his boastful epilogue written for the premiere: 'From [France] new arts to please you, we have sought / We have machines to some perfection brought, / And above 30 Warbling voyces gott. / Many a God & Goddesse you will heare / And we have Singing, Dancing, Devills here'.

Psyche

Shadwell and Locke wrote *Psyche* (1675) shortly after *The Tempest* with the help of Draghi. Of her premiere Downes noted that *Psyche* 'came forth in all her Ornaments; new Scenes, new Machines, new Cloaths, new *French* Dances: This Opera was Splendidly set out, especially in Scenes; the Charge of which amounted to above 800*l*. . . . It prov'd very Beneficial to the Company; yet the *Tempest* got them more Money'. In spite of the greater overall success of its predecessor, *Psyche* is the more influential of the two in the history of English opera. Price notes that *Psyche* was 'an immensely innovative and daring' undertaking: 'The first English musical extravaganza without a tap-root in the Stuart masque or the early Restoration play with music, it comes closer to true *dramma per musica* [i.e., drama by means of music, the normal term for opera since the second third of the seventeenth century, an ideal proposed by Count Bardi's late sixteenth-century Florentine Camerata] than any of Purcell's theatre works except *Dido and Aeneas*' (1984: 296). It was the first dramatic musical score printed in England (a handsome quarto, albeit compressed and minus Draghi's dances and other instrumental music), served as the model for Purcell's semi-operas, and came the closest of any work to a full-length all-sung native opera before Congreve and Eccles's unacted *Semele*.

Shadwell based *Psyche* on the 1671 French *tragédie-ballet Psyché* of Molière, Corneille, Quinault and Lully, the text and music of which Betterton may have brought back with him from Paris. The story concerns the love of Cupid and Psyche, which Psyche's jealous sisters Aglaura and Cidippe attempt to thwart by calling on Venus. Edward J. Dent notes that Shadwell 'had the makings of a really good librettist; he could imagine an essentially musical situation, and make his play lead up to it as a dramatic climax' (1965: 115).

Robert Etheridge Moore offers a nice glimpse of *Psyche*'s charms:

> The opening of the third act (as well as that of the fifth) is beholden to the antimasque with Vulcan and the Cyclops singing at their forge in Cupid's golden palace, following up with a Bacchanalian dance. Before the most genuinely operatic movement of the work [that in which Psyche is saved from suicide], occurs an elaborate episode in which Cupid commands a song in praise of love, then statues leap from their pedestals and dance, cupids rise, strew the stage with flowers, and fly away. (1961a: 30)

Sybil Rosenfeld comments that the elaborate spectacle of *Psyche* 'for the first time rivalled those of the court masques. . . . It was eight years before such another spectacle was seen' (1973: 53). Holman points up the crucial aspects of *Psyche*'s historical and musicological import: 'It has more than a dozen musical episodes . . . [and] requires a huge orchestra, including trumpets and drums, cornett and sackbuts, six types of woodwind instrument, strings, and continuo instruments – many of which must have been played by royal musicians' (1994: 191–2).

Purcell's semi-operas

In June 1690 the managers of the Theatre Royal produced *The Prophetess, or The History of Dioclesian* (known as *Dioclesian*) at Dorset Garden with music by Henry Purcell. For the first new semi-opera since Davenant and Banister's *Circe* (1677) and the first grand musico-dramatic work since the accession of William and Mary, Betterton adapted a play nearly seventy years old, Fletcher and Massinger's *The Prophetess* (Price 1984: 263). The catalyst for the action is Delphia the prophetess's enigmatic statement that Diocles, a Roman soldier, will become emperor after killing a boar; the 'boar' turns out to be Volutius Aper (Latin for boar), who has murdered the emperor Numerianus. Charinus, Numerianus's brother and heir, offers half the empire and his sister Aurelia in marriage to anyone who kills Aper. Diocles obliges and accepts the senate's offer of half the empire, but then with misguided humility passes the reward on to his unworthy nephew Maximinian. Downes remembered that 'being set out with Coastly Scenes, Machines and Cloaths... [*Dioclesian*] gratify'd the Expectation of Court and City; and got the Author great Reputation'. Milhous argues that *Dioclesian* 'remained the standard of operatic grandeur for some fifteen years' (Milhous 1984: 57). It established Purcell in the theatre, who, as the dedication to the handsomely printed folio score (1691) boasts, studied the Italian style – music's 'best Master' – as well as the '*French* air, to give it somewhat more of Gayety and Fashion'. In fact, *Dioclesian* was frequently revived well into Garrick's regime. The only dissenting eighteenth-century voice is as comical as it is churlish. The author of *A Comparison Between the Two Stages* (1702) objected to the 'absurd Impertinence' of the Act 2 musical celebration of Diocles's killing of Aper: 'How ridiculous is it in that Scene... where the great action of the *Drama* stops, and the chief Officers of the Army stand still with their Swords drawn to hear a Fellow Sing – *Let the Soldiers rejoice* – 'faith in my mind 'tis as unreasonable as if a Man shou'd call for a Pipe of Tobacco just when the Priest and his Bride are waiting for him at the Altar'.

Holman calls the work 'a landmark in the history of English theatre music', praising particularly the brilliant Act 5 pastoral masque that Delphia conjures in honour of the hero:

> There was a vast machine... representing the palaces of Flora, Pomona, Bacchus, and the Sun God; it was in four tiers, with singers and dancers on each level, like some extravagant 1930s musical.... The musical interest is kept up by constant changes of rhythmic and harmonic direction, and by the varied scoring: strings for Cupid, trumpets and strings for the 'entry of Heroes', oboes for Bacchus; the full orchestra is reserved for the chaconne 'Triumph victorious Love', with its spectacular antiphonal writing for trumpets, double reed quartet, and strings – probably the first time such effects had been heard in a London theatre. (1994: 202–3)

Dent comments more generally that *Dioclesian* shows Purcell clearly 'determined to spare no pains in the matter of finished workmanship and careful attention to detail' (1965: 203).

The United Company presumably undertook Dryden and Purcell's next effort, *King Arthur, or The British Worthy* (1691), on the strength of *Dioclesian*, which, along with *The Tempest* and *Psyche*, served as its model. Downes notes of the premiere that *King Arthur* was 'Excellently Adorn'd with Scenes and Machines:... The Play and Musick pleas'd the Court and City, and being well perform'd, 'twas very Gainful to the Company'. Dryden invented the plot, making *King Arthur* the only one of Purcell's semi-operas not adapted from an earlier play, although some of the personages recall those of Dryden and Davenant's *Tempest* (1667) adapted to medieval romance and history. Arthur plans to take back the west of England from Oswald, the invading

Saxon king of Kent. With the help of the evil wizard Osmond, Oswald offers a human sacrifice to the gods Woden, Thor and Freya, but Arthur defeats them nonetheless. The 'fierce earthy spirit' Grimbald (Caliban?), disguised as a shepherd, tries to dupe the Britons by leading them into marshes, but the 'airy spirit' Philidel (Ariel?) intervenes (singing the charming air 'Come follow me') and Grimbald vanishes amid flames. The Saxons capture Arthur's rather callow fiancée Emmeline (Miranda/ Dorinda?), the blind daughter of Conon, Duke of Cornwall; Merlin (Prospero?) tries to free her but can only restore her vision. Osmond tries to seduce Emmeline by showing her a '*Prospect of Winter in Frozen Countries*' where Cupid warms a chorus of Cold People 'in spite of cold weather'. This is the famous Frost Scene, a masque that the eighteenth century considered one of Purcell's greatest works and occasionally produced as a freestanding piece. Now Arthur tries to save Emmeline. Osmond distracts him momentarily with a vision of a magic grove, but Arthur frees his love and routs the Saxons. In a final masque, Merlin conjures a vision of Saxons and Britons harmoniously united, the future 'Glories of our Isle'; this includes the famous song for Venus, 'Fairest Isle', and ends with a song celebrating St George and the Order of the Garter. The music in *King Arthur* is more substantial than that of *Dioclesian*. Furthermore, it is better integrated; for example, like Venus in *Psyche*, Grimbald and Philidel sing as well as speak. Moore calls *King Arthur* 'a dazzlingly hued composition in a bold epic manner that puts one in mind of a ceiling by Rubens or Tiepolo' (1961a: 212).

Purcell's third, longest and most extravagant semi-opera, *The Fairy Queen*, premiered in May 1692 at Dorset Garden under Betterton. Downes wrote that 'The Court and Town were wonderfully satisfy'd with it; but the Expences in setting it out being so great, the Company got very little by it'. The anonymous playbook was adapted from Shakespeare's *A Midsummer Night's Dream*, and Josias Priest acted as choreographer. Although not a word of Shakespeare's verse was sung (instead it was cut, compressed and rewritten to accommodate the music – both facts have disturbed critics), *The Fairy Queen* boasted no fewer than four elaborate masques (a fifth was added for the 1693 revival): the first (Act 2), a lullaby for Titania; the second (Act 3), representing Titania's adoration of the braying Bottom; the next (Act 4), a threefold celebration of Titania and Oberon's reconciliation; and the last (Act 5), Oberon's demonstration of magic's power (via a spectacular *chinoiserie* scene) to the doubting Theseus as well as a paean to marriage (Price 1984: 322–46).

Holman argues that *The Fairy Queen* features Purcell's 'most consistently inspired theatre music', but that much of it is

> devoted to episodes only tangentially connected to the drama, with few dramatic qualities of their own. Also, it cannot be said that the adaptor or adaptors provided Purcell with a wide range of dramatic opportunities, or that Purcell made an effort to provide the range of characters with appropriate musical idioms. He has been praised for finding a special tone for *The Fairy Queen*, a musical equivalent of Shakespeare's *faery* – Curtis Price diagnoses a partiality for augmented chords and minor dominants – but it does tend to be applied indiscriminately throughout the work. Nevertheless, *The Fairy*

Queen can be a wonderful evening in the theatre, as a few sympathetic modern productions have shown. (1994: 214)

Moore offers more effusive praise from a slightly different point of view:

> It is not by the feeble spoken dialogue but through the music and its visual accompaniment in stage movement and dance that the fairy world is brought alive to the audience. Purcell has created the midsummer night's dream before our eyes and ears and enabled it to enter into the mind and heart. Before speaking of 'dramatic irrelevance' in connexion with these masques, one might ask what would be left were they removed. (1961a: 111)

Dryden and Purcell's *The Indian Queen* premiered following Betterton and other members of the United Company's rebellion against the notorious Christopher Rich, and probably not long before Purcell's death in November 1695 (the first *recorded* performance – for the Venetian ambassadors – took place on 29 April 1696). Its scenic effects were probably hampered by this unlucky turn of events, as its unfinished score and incoherent text certainly were (Pinnock 1990: 7–19). Moreover, Daniel Purcell was brought in to supplement his brother's dark, tragic score with an incongruously upbeat afterpiece masque of Hymen and Cupid. Yet though it 'bears the wounds inflicted by a slipshod first production', Price opines that 'the score is of the highest quality throughout' (1984: 125). Holman concurs, deeming *The Indian Queen* 'Purcell's greatest late theatre work' (1994: 219).

Adapted anonymously from Dryden and Howard's quintessential heroic drama of the mid-1660s, the plot involves the usurping Mexican (Aztec) Queen Zempoalla and her unrequited love for Montezuma, general to her enemy the Inca of Peru. Musical high points include the allegorical prologue between an Indian Boy and Girl prophesying an end to 'Native Innocence'; the Act 2 Masque of Fame, featuring Envy's sibilant snakes; and especially, the incantation scene in Act 3, scene 2, in which the desperate Zempoalla, tormented by a nightmare, seeks the advice of her high priest Ismeron. The conjuror summons the God of Dreams to pronounce her destiny. Holman offers a fine analysis of this scene, beginning with Ismeron's 'awe-inspiring' bass *tour de force*, 'You twice ten hundred deities':

> [Ismeron] starts in conventional recitative, addressing all the gods 'to whom we daily sacrifice'. [When he invokes the God of Dreams], the music becomes more and more laden with dissonance, reaching an anguished chromatic conclusion at the words 'what strange fate must on her dismal vision wait'. . . . In the air he recites a litany of charms, each one dispatched by a sinister, jerky figure in the violins. The voice mostly alternates with the violins, so that the singer can extract every ounce of vocal colour and menace from his voice without having to compete with them. Suddenly, the second violin begins a slow chromatic ascent, and we know that the charms have worked: the god is starting to rise through the trapdoor. Ismeron joins in, ascending an octave in a largely chromatic line, and ending with a shattering, dissonant climax at the words 'open thy unwilling eyes'. (1994: 219)

Price argues that 'the composer has . . . contributed as much to the drama as the poet', for 'although the Conjurer refuses to reveal in words what fate awaits the queen, Purcell's G minor recitative leaves little doubt. It is a catalogue of musical symbols for death' (1984: 125, 136). Charles Burney believed 'You twice ten hundred deities' to be 'the best piece of recitative in our language'. It is surely one of the pinnacles of Restoration theatre.

The British Enchanters

Just as Shadwell had done with *Psyche*, Granville designated *The British Enchanters, or, No Magick like Love* a 'Tragedy'; and as Shadwell had based *Psyche* on a Lullian *tragédie-ballet*, Granville adapted the Quinault/Lully *tragédie-lyrique Amadis* (1684). Eccles and Bartholomew Issack contributed the vocal music; William Corbett, the instrumental. Price reveals the differences between this work and ostensibly similar works by Purcell:

> Although [*The British Enchanters*] is, strictly speaking, an English semi-opera . . . Granville's musical scenes are not self-contained masques placed at the ends of acts, but are lyrical glosses on the main plot itself. They occur squarely in the middle of scenes, and Act 3 in fact consists largely of music and ballet in which the *dramatis personae* mime their parts. In every scene meaningful magic and magnificent spectacle abound. Nothing is incidental. (1987: 122)

Granville's semi-opera also strongly influenced the plot and characterization of Handel's first London opera, *Rinaldo* (1711), showing the latter to be far less foreign than scholars have traditionally assumed:

> a beautiful, vengeful sorceress (Arcabon in *The British Enchanters*, Armida in *Rinaldo*) is in dynastic conflict with a morally superior order (the Britains led by King Celius, the Christians led by Goffredo); through magic, the sorceress ensnares a cocksure though ultimately ineffectual hired hero (Amadis, Rinaldo), falling helplessly in love with her unyielding captive and thereby alienating her comrade in arms (Arcalaus, Argante). (Price 1987: 123)

Still, *The British Enchanters* itself looks back to *King Arthur* in ancient British themes and close parallels of language, so in a sense the original inspiration, here as elsewhere for Handel and his collaborators, comes from Dryden.

As noted earlier, the work was quite popular when it premiered at Vanbrugh's new Queen's theatre, Haymarket, on 21 February 1706. In *The Poetical Register* (1719) Granville's contemporary Giles Jacob admires *The British Enchanters*, confirms its immediate success and decries the Lord Chamberlain's edict that confined all-sung opera and spoken plays to Drury Lane and the Haymarket, respectively, discouraging similar ventures:

[Granville] had taken an early Dislike to the *French* and *Italian* Operas, consisting meerly of Dancing, Singing, and Decorations, without the least Entertainment for any other Sense but the Eye or the Ear. [He] seems to have applied himself to reconcile the Variety and Magnificence essential to Operas, to a more reasonable Model, by introducing something more substantial.... The Success in the Representation every way answer'd; but all future Entertainments of this kind were at once prevented, by the Division of the Theatre, and a Prohibition to that House [i.e., the Haymarket] where Dramatick Pieces were [formerly] allow'd to receive Musical Performers; which was intended for the better Encouragement of the *Italian* Opera's [at Drury Lane], at that time the prevailing Passion of the Town.

In fact, in December 1706 Granville himself tried to have a revival of *The British Enchanters* suppressed, for he believed the genre division, which prevented the performance from including 'singing & dancing mauger the necessity thereof' could only be interpreted as 'a design to murder the Child of my Brain'. He can scarcely be blamed for his petulance, since the scenes and machines, songs and dances were instrumental in the success of the first run.

All-sung Opera

Contrasting and competing with the English genres was the Italian or all-sung opera, first heard in London in 1705 in the form of Motteux (after Tomaso Stanzani) and Clayton's *Arsinoe*. Vanbrugh had intended to open his new opera house in the Haymarket with this work until Rich took it and mounted it at Drury Lane using his regular troupe (Hume 1984: 84). *Arsinoe* was a pastiche sung in English to undistinguished music; however, this did not hinder its success. The novelty of music drama performed wholly in recitative and air proved sufficiently bewitching that the obvious flaws went largely unnoticed, though not by Cibber: 'The *Italian* Opera began first to steal into *England* ... in as rude a disguise, and unlike itself as possible; in a lame, hobling Translation into our own Language, with false Quantities, or Metre out of Measure to its original Notes, sung by our own unskilful Voices, with Graces misapply'd to almost every Sentiment, and with action lifeless and unmeaning through every Character'. Bononcini's *Camilla* – an inherently better and ultimately more enduring opera – followed to similar acclaim in 1706, and all-sung opera had carved itself a niche in London. When the Italians themselves started to feature in performances – in bilingual versions (*Thomyris*, 1707, was the first), and then wholly in Italian with *L'Idaspe Fedele* (*Hydaspes*, 1710) – they added still more cachet to the foreign art. Yet in spite of the popularity of Italian opera, at no point did this translate into economic viability, the demise of the Royal Academy of Music in 1728 being only the most famous of a series of financial embarrassments. The English produced just one all-sung opera between 1660 and 1705, Dryden and Grabu's *Albion and Albanius* (1685) – and this practically by chance. In the fifteen years between Italian opera's arrival and the opening of the Royal Academy of Music, a few other English attempts emerged: Addison and Clayton's *Rosamond* (1707), Congreve and Eccles's *Semele*, and Hughes and Galliard's *Calypso and Telemachus* (Galliard also reset Charles Davenant's *Circe* in an all-sung version in 1719, but little is known of this).

Albion and Albanius

Dryden's first attempt at music drama took the form of an all-sung opera. It had been planned in the early to mid-1680s as a sung prologue (representing the restoration of Charles II via a series of allegorical scenes) to a semi-opera. Dryden's preface to *Albion and Albanius* states that Charles had wanted a Frenchified opera but that the play-wright concocted instead an English variety on the model of Shadwell and Locke's operatic *Tempest*. The semi-opera portion was postponed, Dryden says, due to 'some intervening accidents', and the prologue filled out to become the three-act *Albion and Albanius*. (Only after six years had passed would the semi-opera portion – Dryden and Purcell's *King Arthur* – emerge, and then as an independent work; Price 1984: 289.)

In 1668 the French-trained Catalan Grabu had been appointed master of the King's Violins, causing resentment among certain English musicians (notably Banister and Humfrey), but he returned to Paris in the late 1670s and was promptly forgotten. In 1683, however, Charles sent Betterton to Paris, according to a letter from Lord Preston to the Duke of York, 'to endeavour to carry over the Opera'. Betterton brought back not an opera but Grabu, who, because he had trained under Lully and had previously enjoyed Charles's indulgence, Preston thought capable of producing 'something at least like an Opera in England for his Majesty's diversion'. Purcell was no doubt insulted at being passed over for the honour of composing such a work, and scholars regard *Dioclesian* as a triumphant retort to the workmanlike Grabu.

In its musical form, *Albion and Albanius*, though all-sung, was not modelled on Italian opera (nor, of course, on English semi-opera as *King Arthur* was to be); rather, it conformed (as Preston had hoped) to the French operatic style of Lully which, unfamiliar as it was to many Englishmen, could not have helped the opera's chances of success. As Price notes, Grabu's 'misfortune was to have created the only kind of opera he could, a *tragédie lyrique*' (1984: 267). Still, the United Company's opera failed – and lost much money – after six nights at Dorset Garden more because of political circumstances than its intrinsic merit: first, it was postponed because of Charles's death on 6 February 1685 (necessitating last-minute changes to the ending to incorporate the new king and Albion's ascent to heaven), and then it was interrupted by Charles's illegitimate son the Duke of Monmouth's rebellion (13 June), which meant closing the theatres.

In fact, *Albion and Albanius* has its charms, as Anthony Rooley's successful revival (at the Dartington International Summer School, Devon, August 1997) showed. When Dryden's text offers adequate inspiration, Grabu rises to the occasion. For example, as Price notes, in Act 2, scene 2, when Albion (Charles II) is forced to decide whether to exile his own brother (the Duke of York and future James II):

Faced with the difficult task of consoling Albion and at the same time counselling Albanius's banishment . . . Grabu [has Hermes] deliver the bitter pill with a shift from plain recitative to lush *accompagnato*. When [Hermes] warns the king of dire consequences should his brother remain, the music conveys an agitation worthy of Purcell . . . [who] must have viewed it with more envy than contempt . . . [and] marvelled at the complete control in the five-part symphonies, whose inner voices show a suavity rivalling the finest continental music of the day. (1984: 267–8)

The scenes and machines in this £4,000 undertaking must also have been impressive. Dryden notes that 'Mr. *Betterton* . . . has spar'd neither for industry, nor cost, to make this Entertainment perfect, nor for Invention of the Ornaments to beautify it'. At one point, for example, the clouds divide to reveal Juno in a chariot drawn by peacocks; as it descends the tail of one peacock opens and almost fills the stage by means of a fan machine copied from the Florentine fête of 1586 (Rosenfeld 1973: 53). As Milhous notes, 'Even satirical comments admit that the production was eye-catching' (1984: 53–5).

Rosamond

Clayton, having succeeded with *Arsinoe*, decided to try another Italianate music drama, *Rosamond*, this time with an original English libretto by Joseph Addison and new music in imitation of the Italian style. Roger Fiske recounts how 'in September 1699 [Addison] sailed for France and was abroad for four years and a half. In Paris he saw operas by Lully, and in Venice and Florence operas by various forgotten Italians. By 1703 he was in Vienna, and later that year in Hamburg where he saw an opera by Keiser and perhaps met Handel. He came back to England in February 1704' (1986: 45). It was thus apparently Addison's experience of foreign opera that led him to contemplate his English counterpart. He felt that native opera should have an English story that would be more probable and comprehensible than those associated with Italian opera, but that it should be all-sung. The full-length, all-sung opera premiered on 4 March 1707 at Drury Lane. It lasted only three nights, apparently because of Clayton's execrable music. J. Merrill Knapp argues that Addison must share the blame: 'the verse is elegant and mellifluous, as both Dr. Johnson and Macaulay have pointed out, but the story [involving the popular legend of Henry II's mistress] lacks force. . . . It is difficult to get excited about the *dramatis personae* lost in a garden maze in Woodstock Park' (1961: 5). It would be well to remember when reading Addison's famous *Spectator* essays satirizing Handel's and others' more successful endeavours that the critic was hardly impartial.

Semele

It is sad to consider that a few Englishmen at this time were prepared to adapt the all-sung convention to their native musical drama – even to infuse it with English poetic beauty – but failed in the end to make their ideas fly. *Rosamond* was not the only victim. In fact Congreve and Eccles's *Semele* suffered an even more dismal fate, for though it boasted the musical writing of a native talent who was thoroughly familiar with Italian musico-dramatic convention (unlike the mediocre Clayton, or even some of his more competent native predecessors) it was never performed, lost in the shuffle when the Haymarket and Drury Lane were competing fiercely for audiences at an early peak in foreign opera's popularity.

Combined with a story derived from Greek mythology (as early Italian operas often had been) but infused with episodes recalling *Psyche*, *King Arthur* and *The Indian Queen*, we see in *Semele* an eclectic attitude towards the formulation of English opera. Eccles's recitative, which is distinctly unlike the Italian *secco* variety, also merits consideration. Eccles differs in this respect from his contemporaries in England – Daniel Purcell, Pepusch and Galliard – all of whom, when they wrote recitative, adhered to the Italian model. Eccles's style rather resembles the declamatory, arioso style of recitative that we encounter in Blow's *Venus and Adonis* and Purcell's *Dido and Aeneas*. That *Semele* was all-sung suggests that under more favourable conditions it might have exploited the vogue for such musical drama while promoting native talent and other characteristics of English opera.

Calypso and Telemachus

John Hughes, English poet and playwright, was intimately acquainted with writers such as Addison, Steele, Pope, Rowe, Congreve and Southerne; composers including Handel, Pepusch, Daniel Purcell, Clayton and Galliard; and singers Jane Barbier, Catherine Tofts and Margherita de l'Epine. Adapting an episode from Fénelon's *Télémaque* (1699), Hughes and Galliard, like Congreve and Eccles, made 'a genuine attempt to prove that opera in English was as feasible as opera in Italian' by means of their all-sung opera *Calypso and Telemachus* (1712) (Knapp 1961: 16). Supporters of Italian opera appear to have sabotaged the work before it even opened, managing to convince the Lord Chamberlain 'to take off the Subscription for it, and to open the House at the lowest Prices, or not at all' (William Duncombe, quoted in Knapp 1961: 7). *Calypso and Telemachus* played only five nights and was not revived until 1717, a fate only slightly less discouraging to promoters of English opera than those of *Semele* and *Rosamond*. The work surely merited better treatment: in 1813 William Kitchener wrote that 'Dr. Arnold told me Mr Handell had so high an opinion of Calypso and Telemachus as to have declared he would sooner have composed it than any one of his own Operas', and some of Hughes's songs clearly influenced Gay in *Acis and Galatea* (to which Hughes himself contributed a song). Burney pronounced Hughes's contributions 'very superior to those of any translated opera of that period'. Hume, echoing Price's eulogy for *Semele*, laments the demise of a second work that 'represented a possibility of return to opera in English, and with it an opportunity for rejoining opera and theater' (1988: 429). Each English opera attempted between 1705 and the opening of the Royal Academy ultimately failed, but each for a different reason, and

London was forced to wait until 1732 for the next wave of native operas, which would begin with Henry Carey and John Frederick Lampe's *Amelia*.

REFERENCES AND FURTHER READING

Burden, Michael (1995). 'Purcell and his Contemporaries', in Michael Burden (ed.), *The Purcell Companion*. Portland, OR: Amadeus Press, 52–98.

Corman, Brian and Gilman, Todd S. (1996). 'The Musical Life of Thomas Shadwell', *Restoration* 20, no. 2, 149–64.

Dean, Winton (1959; 1990). *Handel's Dramatic Oratorios and Masques*. Oxford: Clarendon Press.

Dent, Edward J. (1928; 1965). *Foundations of English Opera*. New York: Da Capo Press.

Fiske, Roger (1964). 'The "Macbeth" Music', *Music and Letters* 45, 114–25.

Fiske, Roger (1986). *English Theatre Music in the Eighteenth Century*. 2nd rev. ed. New York: Oxford University Press.

Gilman, Todd S. (1995). 'Augustan Criticism and Changing Conceptions of English Opera', *Theatre Survey* 36, no. 2, 1–35.

Holman, Peter (1994). *Henry Purcell*. Oxford: Oxford University Press.

Hume, Robert D. (1984). 'Opera in London, 1695–1706', in Shirley Strum Kenny (ed.), *British Theatre and the Other Arts, 1660–1800*. Toronto: Associated University Presses, 67–91.

Hume, Robert D. (1988). 'The Sponsorship of Opera in London, 1704–1720', *Modern Philology* 85, no. 4, 420–32.

Kenny, Shirley Strum (ed.). (1984). *British Theatre and the Other Arts, 1660–1800*. Toronto: Associated University Presses.

Knapp, J. Merrill (1961). 'A Forgotten Chapter in English Eighteenth-century Opera', *Music and Letters* 42, 4–16.

Laurie, A. Margaret (1963–4). 'Did Purcell Set *The Tempest?*', *Proceedings of the Royal Musical Association* 90, 43–57.

Lincoln, Stoddard (1972). 'A Congreve Masque', *Musical Times* 113, 1078–81.

Luckett, Richard (1977). 'Exotick But Rational Entertainments: The English Dramatick Operas', in Marie Axton and Raymond Williams (eds), *English Drama: Forms and Development*. New York: Cambridge University Press, 123–41.

Milhous, Judith (1979). *Thomas Betterton and the Management of Lincoln's Inn Fields, 1695–1708*. Carbondale: Southern Illinois University Press.

Milhous, Judith (1984). 'The Multimedia Spectacular on the Restoration Stage', in Shirley Strum Kenny (ed.), *British Theatre and the Other Arts, 1660–1800*. Toronto: Associated University Presses, 41–66.

Milhous, Judith and Hume, Robert D. (1999). 'Heidegger and the Management of the Haymarket Opera, 1713–17', *Early Music* 27, no. 1, 65–84.

Moore, Robert Etheridge (1961a). *Henry Purcell and the Restoration Theatre*. London: Heinemann.

Moore, Robert E. (1961b). 'The Music to *Macbeth*', *Musical Quarterly* 47, no. 1, 22–40.

Pinnock, Andrew (1990). 'Play into Opera: Purcell's *The Indian Queen*', *Early Music* 18, no. 1, 3–21.

Plank, Steven E. (1990). '"And Now about the Cauldron Sing": Music and the Supernatural on the Restoration Stage', *Early Music* 18, no. 3, 392–407.

Price, Curtis A. (1979). *Music in the Restoration Theatre*. Ann Arbor, MI: UMI Research Press.

Price, Curtis Alexander (1984). *Henry Purcell and the London Stage*. Cambridge: Cambridge University Press.

Price, Curtis (1987). 'English Traditions in Handel's *Rinaldo*', in Stanley Sadie and Anthony Hicks (eds), *Handel Tercentenary Collection*. Ann Arbor, MI: UMI Research Press, 120–37.

Rosenfeld, Sybil (1973). *A Short History of Scene Design in Great Britain*. Oxford: Blackwell.

Spink, Ian (1986). *English Song, Dowland to Purcell*. Rev. ed. London: Batsford.

APPENDIX: A NEW REGISTER OF FIRST PERFORMANCES OF ENGLISH OPERAS AND
RELATED GENRES, 1660–1719

All Dates in this Register are given in new style.

Format

Date of first performance. Place of first performance. *Title of work*. Playwright/librettist(s). Composer(s).
Genre, from title-page of the playbook/libretto whenever possible; [followed by suggested editorial
designation]

*c.*1663. Duke's theatre, Lincoln's Inn Fields. *Macbeth*. Sir William Davenant, after Shakespeare and
Middleton. Matthew Locke. Robert Johnson? 'Tragedy'; [semi-opera]

2 or 3 July 1663. Court. *A Great Masque*. Anonymous. Anonymous. Unpublished; [?]

October 1663. Duke's theatre, Lincoln's Inn Fields. *The Step-Mother*. Sir Robert Stapylton. Matthew
Locke. 'Tragi-comedy'; [semi-opera]

18 February 1667. Court. *A Masque*. Anonymous. Anonymous. Unpublished; [?]

3 February 1668. Court. *A Masque*. Anonymous. Anonymous. Unpublished; [?]

6 or 9 February 1671. Court. *The Queen's Masque*. Anonymous. Anonymous. Unpublished; [?]

18 February 1673. Duke's theatre, Dorset Garden. *Macbeth*. Sir William Davenant, after Shakespeare and
Middleton. Matthew Locke and Robert Johnson. 'Tragedy: With all the Alterations, Amendments,
Additions, And New Songs' (augmentation of 1663 version); [semi-opera]

March or April/3 July 1673. Court/Duke's theatre, Dorset Garden. *Orpheus and Euridice*. Elkanah Settle.
Matthew Locke. 'Masque' (interpolated into Elkanah Settle's tragedy *The Empress of Morocco*); [all-sung
masque]

July or August 1673. Duke's theatre, Lincoln's Inn Fields. *The Empress of Morocco*. Thomas Duffett. Music,
some taken from Locke, arranged by Duffett. 'Farce'; [burlesque of Settle's *Empress of Morocco*, with an
Epilogue burlesquing *Macbeth*]

15 March–30 April 1674. Duke's theatre, Dorset Garden. *The Tempest, or The Enchanted Island*. Thomas
Shadwell, after the 1667 adaptation of Shakespeare's play by Davenant and Dryden. Matthew Locke,
Robert Smith, John Banister, Giovanni Battista Draghi, James Hart, Pelham Humfrey and Pietro
Reggio. 'Comedy'; [semi-opera]

?Late spring 1674. Drury Lane. *The Mock-Tempest, or The Enchanted Castle*. Thomas Duffett. Music, some
of it from *The Tempest*, arranged by Duffett. (No genre given in title); [burlesque]

{Spring 1674, intended for Drury Lane. Unacted. *The State of Innocence, and Fall of Man*. John Dryden,
after Milton's *Paradise Lost*. Not set to music. 'Opera'; [semi-opera]}

?May 1674–27 February 1675. Duke's theatre, Dorset Garden. *Psyche*. Thomas Shadwell, after the
Molière, Corneille, Quinault and Lully *tragédie-ballet Psyché* (1671). Matthew Locke and Giovanni
Battista Draghi. 'Tragedy'; [semi-opera]

22 February 1675. Court. *Calisto, or The Chaste Nimph*. John Crowne. Nathaniel Staggins. 'Masque';
[semi-opera]

August 1675. Drury Lane. *Psyche Debauch'd*. Thomas Duffett. Music arranged by Duffett from *Psyche* and
traditional tunes. 'Comedy'; [burlesque]

18 November 1676. Boarding School at Chelsea. *Beauties Triumph*. Thomas Duffett. John Banister [and
others?]. 'Masque'; [masque with spoken dialogue]

May 1677. Duke's theatre, Dorset Garden. *Circe*. Charles Davenant. John Banister. 'Tragedy'; [semi-opera] *c.*January 1678. Duke's theatre, Dorset Garden. *The History of Timon of Athens, The Man-Hater*. Thomas Shadwell, after Shakespeare's tragedy. Louis Grabu and James Paisible. 'Masque' in Act 2 of the 'Play'; [all-sung masque]

{1679. Unacted. *Noah's Flood, or The Destruction of the World*. Edward Ecclestone, after Milton, *Paradise Lost* and Dryden, *The State of Innocence*. Not set to music. 'Opera'; [semi-opera]}

*c.*March–June 1681. Duke's theatre, Dorset Garden. *The Lancashire Witches and Tegue O'Divelly the Irish Priest*. Thomas Shadwell. John Eccles. 'Comedy'; [semi-opera]

?1681–2. Court. *Venus and Adonis*. Anonymous. John Blow. 'A Masque for the Entertainment of the King', 'Opera'; [all-sung masque]

? Court. *Dido and Aeneas*. Nahum Tate. Henry Purcell. 'Opera'; [all-sung masque]

3 June 1685. Queen's theatre, Dorset Garden. *Albion and Albanius*. John Dryden. Louis Grabu. 'Opera'; [all-sung opera]

3 June 1690. Queen's theatre, Dorset Garden. *The Prophetess, or The History of Dioclesian*. Thomas Betterton, after Fletcher and Massinger. Henry Purcell. 'After the Manner of an Opera'; [semi-opera]

4–8 June 1691. Queen's theatre, Dorset Garden. *King Arthur, or The British Worthy*. John Dryden. Henry Purcell. 'Dramatick Opera'; [semi-opera]

2 May 1692. Queen's theatre, Dorset Garden. *The Fairy Queen*. Anonymous, after Shakespeare, *A Midsummer Night's Dream*. Henry Purcell. 'Opera'; [semi-opera]

17 June 1693. York Buildings. *English Dialogues and Songs…with Instrumental Musick proper to them*. Peter Anthony Motteux. Johann Wolfgang Franck. Only musical excerpts published, indicating four characters and chorus, recitative and aria; [all-sung masque]

?February 1694. ?Queen's theatre, Dorset Garden. *The Rape of Europa by Jupiter*. Peter Anthony Motteux. John Eccles. 'Masque' (interpolated into Rochester's revision [1685] of John Fletcher's *Valentinian*); [all-sung masque]

?1695. Lincoln's Inn Fields. *Macbeth*. Sir William Davenant (1664), after Shakespeare and Middleton. John Eccles and Godfrey Finger. 'Tragedy'; [semi-opera]

May or June 1695. Drury Lane. *The History of Timon of Athens, or The Man-Hater*. Peter Anthony Motteux, altered from Shadwell's 1678 adaptation of Shakespeare's tragedy. Henry Purcell. 'Masque' in Act 2 of the 'Play'; [all-sung masque]

*c.*September 1695. Lincoln's Inn Fields. *The Taking of Namur and His Majesty's Safe Return*. Peter Anthony Motteux. John Eccles. 'Musical Entertainment'; [all-sung masque]

*c.*September 1695. Drury Lane. *Bonduca, or The British Heroine*. Anonymous, after Fletcher. Henry Purcell. 'Tragedy…With a New Entertainment of Musick, Vocal and Instrumental'; [semi-opera]

Autumn 1695. Drury Lane. *The Indian Queen*. John Dryden(?), after Dryden and Sir Robert Howard's tragedy (1665). Henry Purcell. Unpublished; [semi-opera]

?26 October 1696. Dorset Garden. *Brutus of Alba, or Augusta's Triumph*. Anonymous. Daniel Purcell. 'New Opera'; [semi-opera]

By 14 November 1696. Lincoln's Inn Fields. *The Loves of Mars and Venus*. Peter Anthony Motteux. Godfrey Finger and John Eccles. 'A Play set to Music' (three acts interpolated into and alternated with the three acts of Edward Ravenscroft's farce *The Anatomist, or The Sham Doctor*); [all-sung masque]

?16 January 1697. Drury Lane. *Cinthia and Endimion, or The Loves of the Deities*. Thomas Durfey. Daniel Purcell, Richard Leveridge, Jeremiah Clarke, Henry Purcell and David Underwood. 'New Opera'; [semi-opera]

8 June 1697. Lincoln's Inn Fields. *Hercules*. Peter Anthony Motteux. John Eccles. 'Masque' (Act 3 of Motteux's medley *The Novelty*); [all-sung masque]

25 or 26 June 1697. Dorset Garden. *The World in the Moon*. Elkanah Settle. Daniel Purcell, Jeremiah Clarke, Henry Purcell. 'Opera'; [semi-opera]

3 July 1697. Great Room, Lambeth Wells. *A Masque*. Anonymous. Anonymous. Unpublished; advertised as 'A New Mask of Vocal and Instrumental Musick, Consisting of about thirty Instruments and Voices'; [all-sung masque?]

September 1697. Drury Lane. *Endimion The Man in the Moon*. George Powell. Thomas Morgan. 'Masque' (interpolated into Act 5 of Powell's comedy *The Imposture Defeated, or A Trick to Cheat the Devil*); [all-sung masque]

October 1697. Boarding School at Besselsleigh, Berkshire. *Orpheus and Euridice*. Anonymous. Richard Goodson and John Weldon. 'Mask' (only musical excerpts published); [all-sung masque]

4 November 1697. Court and Lincoln's Inn Fields. *Europe's Revels for the Peace, and His Majesties Happy Return*. Peter Anthony Motteux. John Eccles and Thomas Morgan. 'Musical Interlude'; [all-sung masque]

November or December 1697. Lincoln's Inn Fields. *Ixion*. Edward Ravenscroft? John Eccles. 'Masque' (interpolated into Act 3 of Edward Ravenscroft's tragedy *The Italian Husband*); [all-sung masque]

?1–5 December 1698. Lincoln's Inn Fields. *Rinaldo and Armida*. John Dennis, after Tasso. John Eccles. 'Tragedy'; [semi-opera]

?7 February 1699. Drury Lane. *The Island Princess, or The Generous Portuguese*. Peter Anthony Motteux, after Fletcher (1621) and Nahum Tate (1687). Jeremiah Clarke, Richard Leveridge, Daniel Purcell. 'Opera'; [semi-opera]

?7 February 1699. Drury Lane. *The Four Seasons, or Love in Every Age*. Peter Anthony Motteux. Jeremiah Clarke. 'Musical Interlude' (following the last act of *The Island Princess* [q.v.]); [all-sung masque]

March 1699. Lincoln's Inn Fields. *Love and Riches Reconcil'd*. Joseph Harris. Samuel Akeroyde. 'Masque' (interpolated into Act 3 of Joseph Harris's farce *Love's a Lottery and a Woman the Prize*); [all-sung masque?]

Late January or February 1700. Drury Lane. *The Grove, or Love's Paradice*. John Oldmixon. Daniel Purcell. 'Opera'; [semi-opera]

Late April 1700. Drury Lane. *The Secular Masque*. John Dryden. Daniel Purcell and Godfrey Finger. 'Masque' (interpolated into Sir John Vanbrugh's adaptation of Fletcher's comedy *The Pilgrim*); [all-sung masque]

8 May 1700. York Buildings. *A Masque*. Anonymous. Anonymous. Unpublished; advertised as 'A new Mask set to Musick, with an Extraordinary entertainment of other Vocal and Instrumental Musick for the benefit of Mr Gouge and Miss Bradshaw'; [all-sung masque?]

?February 1701. Lincoln's Inn Fields. *Peleus and Thetis*. George Granville, Lord Lansdowne. John Eccles. 'Masque' (interpolated into Granville's comedy, *The Jew of Venice*, an adaptation of Shakespeare's *Merchant of Venice*); [all-sung masque]

?February 1701. Lincoln's Inn Fields. *The Mad Lover*. Peter Anthony Motteux, after John Fletcher (1617). John Eccles and Daniel Purcell. Unpublished – called 'New Opera' in word-book to *Acis and Galatea* (1701) (q.v.), a masque interpolated into the last act; [semi-opera]

?February 1701. Lincoln's Inn Fields. *Wine and Love*. Peter Anthony Motteux. John Eccles. 'Masque' (interpolated into the 'New Opera' *The Mad Lover* [q.v.]); [all-sung masque]

?February 1701. Lincoln's Inn Fields. *Acis and Galatea*. Peter Anthony Motteux. John Eccles. 'Masque' (interpolated into the 'New Opera' *The Mad Lover* [q.v.]); [all-sung masque]

20 February 1701. Drury Lane. *Alexander the Great*. Anonymous, after Nathaniel Lee's tragedy *The Rival Queens, or The Death of Alexander the Great* (1677). Godfrey Finger and Daniel Purcell. Unpublished; [semi-opera]

21 March 1701. Dorset Garden. *The Judgment of Paris*. William Congreve. John Eccles. 'Masque'; [all-sung masque]

28 March 1701. Dorset Garden. *The Judgment of Paris*. William Congreve. Godfrey Finger. 'Masque'; [all-sung masque]

11 April 1701. Dorset Garden. *The Judgment of Paris*. William Congreve. Daniel Purcell. 'Masque'; [all-sung masque]

6 May 1701. Dorset Garden. *The Judgment of Paris*. William Congreve. John Weldon. 'Masque'; [all-sung masque]

12 May 1701. Drury Lane. *The Virgin Prophetess, or The Fate of Troy*. Elkanah Settle. Godfrey Finger. 'Opera'; [semi-opera]

23 August 1701. Drury Lane. *Orpheus and Euridice*. Elkanah Settle. Anonymous. 'The original Mask set to new Musick' (interpolated into Elkanah Settle's 1673 tragedy *The Empress of Morocco*); [all-sung masque]

4 February 1702. York Buildings. *The Judgment of Paris*. William Congreve. Johann Wolfgang Franck. 'Masque . . . Compos'd for three Quires, and in quite a different way to the others, not used here before'; [all-sung masque]

21 November 1702. Drury Lane. *Macbeth*. Sir William Davenant, after Shakespeare and Middleton. Richard Leveridge and Matthew Locke. 'Tragedy . . . With Vocal and Instrumental Musick, all new Compos'd'; [semi-opera]

22 February 1704. Drury Lane. *Britain's Happiness*. Peter Anthony Motteux. John Weldon and Charles Dieupart. 'Musical Interlude'; [all-sung masque]

7 March 1704. Lincoln's Inn Fields. *Britain's Happiness*. Peter Anthony Motteux. Richard Leveridge. 'Musical Interlude'; [all-sung masque]

?18 January 1705. Drury Lane. *The Mountebank, or The Humours of the Fair*. Peter Anthony Motteux? Anonymous. 'Musical Interlude' (interpolated in and published with Motteux's comedy *Farewel Folly* [1707]); [all-sung masque]

{Published 1705. ?Unacted. *Orpheus and Euridice*. Martin Bladen. Not set to music? 'Masque'; [all-sung masque?]}

21 February 1706. Queen's theatre, Haymarket. *The British Enchanters, or No Magic Like Love*. George Granville, Lord Lansdowne. John Eccles, Bartholomew Issack and William Corbett. 'Tragedy'; [semi-opera]

5 April 1706. Queen's theatre, Haymarket. *Wonders in the Sun, or The Kingdom of the Birds*. Thomas Durfey. John Smith, Samuel Akeroyde, John Eccles, Giovanni Battista Draghi, Lully, Durfey. 'Comick Opera'; [semi-opera]

{Intended for 1706–7 season – libretto published in February 1707 in *The Muses Mercury*. *The Masque of Orpheus and Euridice*. John Dennis. Daniel Purcell. 'Masque'; [all-sung masque]}

4 March 1707. Drury Lane. *Rosamond*. Joseph Addison. Thomas Clayton. 'Opera'; [all-sung opera]

{Rehearsed at Drury Lane before April 1707. Unacted. *Semele*. William Congreve. John Eccles. 'Opera'; [all-sung opera]}

12 February 1708. Drury Lane. *Prunella*. Richard Estcourt. Estcourt, arranging current opera airs from *Arsinoe*, *Camilla* and *Thomyris*. 'Interlude' (interpolated into a revival of Buckingham's *The Rehearsal*); [burlesque]

{Published 4 February 1709. Unacted. *Alarbas*. 'Written by a Gentleman of Quality'. Not set to music. 'Dramatick Opera'; [semi-opera]}

c.1710. York Buildings. *A Pastoral Masque*. Anonymous. Thomas Clayton. 'Masque'; [all-sung masque]

11 April 1710. Queen's theatre, Haymarket. *Roger's Wedding*. Anonymous. Anonymous. 'A Comical Masque of Music' (the comic subplot of Motteux's *Acis and Galatea*?); [all-sung masque?]

24 May 1711. York Buildings. *The Passion of Sappho*. William Harrison. Thomas Clayton. 'Entertainment'; [all-sung masque?]

1712. Drury Lane. *The Tempest*. Shadwell's 1674 revision of the Dryden–Davenant adaptation of Shakespeare's *Tempest*. John Weldon? 'Comedy'; [semi-opera]

17 May 1712. Queen's theatre, Haymarket. *Calypso and Telemachus*. John Hughes (after Fénelon). John Ernest Galliard. 'Opera'; [all-sung opera]

{Written 1715? Unacted. *Cupid and Hymen's Holiday*. John Hughes. Not set to music? 'Pastoral Masque'; [all-sung masque]}

11 February 1715. Lincoln's Inn Fields. *The Beau Demolish'd*. Anonymous. Anonymous. Unpublished; advertised as 'a musical entertainment'; [?]

12 March 1715. Drury Lane. *Venus and Adonis*. Colley Cibber. John Christopher Pepusch. 'Masque'; [all-sung masque]

26 April 1715. Lincoln's Inn Fields. *Alexander the Great*. Anonymous, after the unpublished *Alexander the Great* of 20 February 1701? Anonymous. 'Opera'; [semi-opera]

5 November 1715. Drury Lane. *Myrtillo*. Colley Cibber. John Christopher Pepusch. 'Pastoral Interlude'; [all-sung masque]

21 December 1715. Lincoln's Inn Fields. *The Mountebank, or The Country Lass*. Anonymous, after Motteux's (?) 'Musical Interlude' *The Mountebank, or The Humours of the Fair* (1707)? Richard Leveridge. Unpublished; [all-sung masque]

12 January 1716. Drury Lane. *Apollo and Daphne*. John Hughes. John Christopher Pepusch. 'Masque'; [all-sung masque]

10 March 1716. Lincoln's Inn Fields. *Presumptuous Love*. William Taverner. William Turner. 'Dramatick Masque' (interpolated into Taverner's comedy, *Every Body Mistaken*); [all-sung masque]

11 April 1716. Lincoln's Inn Fields. *The Comick Masque of Pyramus and Thisbe*. Richard Leveridge, after Shakespeare, *A Midsummer Night's Dream*. Composed by the librettist. 'A Comic Masque, compos'd in the high Style of Italy'; [burlesque masque framed by *Rehearsal*-type farce]

17 April 1716. Drury Lane. *The Death of Dido*. Barton Booth. John Christopher Pepusch. 'Masque . . . Compos'd to Musick, after the Italian Manner'; [all-sung masque]

3 January 1718. Lincoln's Inn Fields. *The Professor of Folly*. Anonymous. Anonymous. 'New Dramatick Entertainment of Vocal and Instrumental Musick after the Italian manner'; [all-sung masque?]

14 January 1718. Lincoln's Inn Fields. *Pan and Syrinx*. Lewis Theobald. John Ernest Galliard. 'Opera of One Act'; [all-sung masque]

24 January 1718. Lincoln's Inn Fields. *Amadis*. Anonymous. Anonymous. 'New Dramatick Opera in Dancing'; [all-sung masque?]

4 March 1718. Lincoln's Inn Fields. *Love and a Bumper*. Unpublished; advertised as a 'New musical interlude' performed with a revival of *The Provok'd Wife*; [all-sung masque?]

22 March 1718. Lincoln's Inn Fields. *The Lady's Triumph*. Elkanah Settle/Lewis Theobald. John Ernest Galliard. 'Comi-Dramatick Opera' (performed with Act 5 abridged masque of *Decius and Paulina* [q.v.]); [semi-opera?]

22 March 1718. Lincoln's Inn Fields. *Decius and Paulina*. Lewis Theobald. John Ernest Galliard. 'Masque'; [all-sung masque]

?Summer 1718. Cannons Park. *Acis and Galatea*. John Gay, John Hughes and others. George Frideric Handel. Contemporary libretto unpublished – in 1722 score, 'Opera'; in *c*.1730 score, 'Masque'; in 1732 libretto, 'English pastoral opera'; [all-sung masque]

?Summer 1718. Cannons Park. *Esther*. ?Alexander Pope and John Arbuthnot, after Thomas Brereton's adaptation (1715) of Racine's tragedy (1689). George Frideric Handel. Contemporary libretto unpublished – in 1732 libretto, 'Oratorio, or Sacred Drama'; [oratorio]

11 April 1719. Lincoln's Inn Fields. *Circe*. Charles Davenant (adapted anonymously from 1677 version). John Ernest Galliard. Unpublished; [all-sung opera?]

11 April 1719. Lincoln's Inn Fields. *Decius and Paulina*. Lewis Theobald. John Ernest Galliard. 'Masque' (interpolated into *Circe* [q.v.]); [all-sung masque]

27 May 1719. Lincoln's Inn Fields. *Harlequin Hydaspes, or The Greshamite*. Mr Aubert. Music arranged by the librettist. 'Mock-Opera'; [musical burlesque of *L'Idaspe Fedele* (1710) with spoken dialogue]

16

Shakespeare and Other Adaptations

Sandra Clark

When the king returned to London in 1660, it was an important gesture at the start of the new regime to get theatres re-established. As lines from a new prologue to *Epicœne*, the first play to be performed in his presence at the Cockpit at Whitehall in November, put it:

> This truth we can to our advantage say,
> They that would have no KING, would have no *Play*.

In August 1660 patents had been issued to Thomas Killigrew and William Davenant, both active as playwrights in Caroline times, to erect, purchase or hire a playhouse and organize a troupe of actors. But what were they to perform? No new playwrights appeared until 1668, when Dryden became the first. Both companies fell back on pre-Restoration plays, and soon took steps to secure the rights to a number of them. Killigrew's company, the King's Men, who included several professionals from the Caroline era among their number, obtained the rights to the plays of the former King's Company, including most of Shakespeare's and those of Beaumont and Fletcher. Davenant and his company, the Duke's Men, made up of inexperienced actors, were less fortunate in respect of repertoire, initially having the rights to only two old plays, along with Davenant's own works, Middleton and Rowley's *The Changeling* and Massinger's *The Bondman*. But Davenant, a key figure in early Restoration theatre, had strong connections with pre-Restoration theatre, and he responded by presenting the Lord Chamberlain with a 'proposition of reformeing some of the most ancient Playes that were playd at Blackfriers and makeinge them fitt, for the Company of Actors'. In the repertoires of both companies Shakespeare's plays formed an important staple from the start. While Killigrew's company had the right to present them in their original form, Davenant's was obliged, from the terms of its patent, to 'improve' them. This obligation in no way proved a setback, since, as it soon turned out, Shakespeare's plays were generally preferred in adapted forms, and only a few, including *Julius Caesar, 1 Henry IV, Hamlet* and *Othello*, did well unaltered. It is worth noting that 'adaptation' was not a contemporary term; the usual word was alteration or imitation. And the attitude to this process was very different from that of some twentieth- and twenty-first-century commentators who regard Shakespeare's text as a sacred object and any modification of it at all as sacrilege.

In the period 1660–1700 revivals and adaptations of pre-Restoration playwrights constituted a large part of the dramatic repertoire. Out of 957 recorded performances, 486 were of old plays, 473 of new (Vickers 1974: 6). In the mid-eighteenth century, the popularity of Shakespeare actually increased, and by 1740 25 per cent of the performances in London were of his works. Three oeuvres stand out: those of Shakespeare, the Beaumont and Fletcher team, and Jonson. Of Shakespeare's work, twenty-eight plays were put on in some form or other; of Beaumont and Fletcher's, thirty-nine, in 342 separate revivals (Wilson 1928: 7), and of Jonson's, eight, though the most popular, *Volpone, Epicæne, The Alchemist* and *Bartholomew Fair*, many times each. Plays by the now neglected Caroline writers, Shirley, Brome and Suckling, also proved popular at particular times, Shirley's and Suckling's mainly in the first decade of the new regime, Brome's *The Jovial Crew* in the early eighteenth century. A range of individual plays by other writers also appeared, sometimes in adapted versions: Kyd's *The Spanish Tragedy*, Marlowe's *Dr Faustus*, Marston's *The Dutch Courtesan*, Middleton and Rowley's *The Changeling*, and Webster's *The White Devil* and *The Duchess of Malfi* were all staged at least once, and some of them more often. But Shakespeare, Beaumont and Fletcher, and Jonson, the only playwrights to have had their work published in great single-volume folio editions, were pre-eminent, both in the theatre and in the eyes of critics such as Flecknoe, Dryden, Rymer and Dennis. Flecknoe, in 1664, typically singles out Shakespeare, Jonson, and Beaumont and Fletcher as the most representative dramatists, out of a list running from Marlowe to Ford. Dryden groups them together constantly, as when he notes in the *Essay of Dramatic Poetry* (1668) 'two [of Beaumont and Fletcher's plays] being acted through the year for one of Shakespeare's or Jonson's', or calls Shakespeare and Fletcher Jonson's 'rivals in poetry'. In 1687 William Winstanley called them 'the happy *Triumvirate*'.

Restoration audiences did not respond with equal fervour to all of these plays. Shakespeare's tragedies were much preferred to his comedies, most of which met with little enthusiasm, due in part to 'too much romance ... and too chaotic plots', as Allardyce Nicoll laconically puts it (1923: 162). Only four of Jonson's many plays, not including his tragedies, achieved any stage success, though his tragedies won some critical admiration. Beaumont and Fletcher's plays were much more evenly appreciated, comedies such as *The Humorous Lieutenant* and *Rule a Wife and Have a Wife* vying with the tragedies *The Maid's Tragedy* and *The Bloody Brother* and the tragicomedies *Philaster* and *The Island Princess* for popularity. In many ways the work of Beaumont and Fletcher, perhaps more specifically the tragicomedies written by Fletcher, often in conjunction with the less acknowledged Massinger, proved more congenial to the times, and in consequence more influential as dramatic models.

Though this was a very different age, audiences were initially conscious of living in the shadow of the past, which partly accounts for the strong taste for tragicomedy with its themes of providential restoration and restitution, and also for the desire for contemporary parallels within plays. As Gary Taylor says, 'Restoration plays and audiences habitually interpreted plays in terms of contemporary politics. Many new plays depended upon implied parallels between onstage characters or events and their contemporary offstage counterparts' (1990: 23). Despite a climate of theatrical censorship in which too specific identifications might be dangerous, audiences sought out, and playwrights supplied, topical references. For several reasons, including the greater intimacy of the theatrical spaces and the more homogeneous nature of the audience, relations between actors, text and audience were of a different nature. This was a self-consciously new age, 'a pleasant, well-bred, complaisant, free, frolic, good-natured, pretty age', as Hippolyta says in Wycherley's *The Gentleman Dancing Master*, against which the era of Shakespeare and his contemporaries was regarded as rude, 'gothic', unrefined. 'The times were ignorant in which they lived', stated Dryden flatly.

Shakespeare in the Restoration

As soon as the theatres reopened, Shakespeare's plays began again to be performed. Between 1660 and 1667, sixteen of the thirty-seven were revived in some form. *Othello*, revived in 1660 with the first recorded appearance of an actress, *1 Henry IV* and *The Merry Wives of Windsor*, the only comedy that was liked in its original form, became staples of the repertoire of the King's Men; *Hamlet*, the only 'stock' Shakespeare play granted to Davenant, was performed in 1661 by the Duke's Men and regularly thereafter, although John Evelyn found it old-fashioned, commenting after one performance, 'Now the old playe began to disgust this refined age; since his Majestie being so long abroad'. *Pericles, Romeo and Juliet, Richard III, King Lear, A Midsummer Night's Dream* and *Twelfth Night* all appeared in the early years. Davenant lost no time in producing his adaptations, the first being the experimental *The Law Against Lovers* (1662); this was an ingenious combination of *Measure for Measure* and *Much Ado About Nothing*, in which Beatrice and Benedict are transplanted to Turin, and the Duke from *Measure for Measure* disguises himself to oversee events under a (temporary) Puritan government headed by Angelo. This curiosity was succeeded by the operatic *Macbeth* (1663–4), also an adaptation with strong reference to Interregnum politics, but one with other features which enabled it to hold the stage until the mid-eighteenth century. The most successful of Davenant's adaptations was *The Tempest, or The Enchanted Island*, on which he collaborated with the young Dryden in 1667. The plays of this early Restoration period are often thought to mark the first of three phases in Shakespeare adaptation; the second phase is deemed to consist of those adaptations of histories or tragedies between 1677 and 1683, produced in response to the Exclusion Crisis, and the third, of comedies and histories, at the turn of the century. Although less popular than Beaumont and Fletcher, Shakespeare's plays were performed frequently. Pepys's *Diary* for 1660–9 records twelve different Shakespeare plays seen on forty-one separate occasions; between 1703 and 1710. About 11 per cent of all performances in London were of Shakespeare and the proportion steadily increased in the course of the eighteenth century.

Although Shakespeare was venerated, his reputation was not unblemished and his plays were criticized in several respects: their language was considered archaic and incorrect, their plotting and construction clumsy, and their morality defective in its lack of poetic justice. Shakespeare was thought natural, but careless. Although Dryden was generous in his tributes to Shakespeare's stature in his preface to *All for Love* (1678), he took a very different tone in his *The Grounds of Criticism in Tragedy* (1679), attached to his version of *Troilus and Cressida*; he called the language 'so pestered with figurative expressions' as to be obscure, and Shakespeare's play so awkwardly constructed that 'the later part of the tragedy is nothing but a confusion of drums and trumpets, excursions and alarms'. That 'Cressida is false and not punished' was deemed a disastrous flaw. But because Dryden detected some signs 'of admirable genius' in the play, he undertook 'to remove that heap of rubble under which many excellent thoughts lay buried'. He felt himself obliged, not only to refine the language, remodel the plot and discard 'many unnecessary persons', but also to make 'with no small trouble, an order and connection of all the scenes' to provide 'a coherence of 'em with one another and a dependence on the main design'. This outspoken account of his revision of the play so as to bring it into line with contemporary tastes is typical in its dramatic principles. Nahum Tate in the same vein called Shakespeare's *King Lear* 'a Heap of Jewels, unstrung and unpolisht'; Thomas Ravenscroft, adapting *Titus Andronicus*, called it 'the most incorrect and indigested piece in all his works . . . rather a heap of Rubbish than a structure'. It is not surprising, then, that the adaptations were commonly presented in the spirit of improvements, doing a service to a long-dead writer from a primitive past. This view is confidently put forward in the Prologue to *The Jew of Venice* (1701) by George Granville, Lord Lansdowne. To open this neo-classical version of *The Merchant of Venice*, Shakespeare's ghost is resurrected to congratulate the reviser on his achievement:

> These Scenes in their rough Native Dress were mine,
> But now improv'd with nobler Lustre shine;
> The first rude Sketches *Shakespeare's* Pencil drew,
> But all the Shining Master stroakes are new.
> This Play, ye Criticks, shall your Fury 'stand,
> Adorn'd and rescu'd by a faultless Hand.

Adaptations and rewritings of Shakespeare's plays took many forms, and adapters worked with considerable freedom. Davenant illustrates two extremes of the spectrum, with his *Hamlet* (1661) at one end, which consists of Shakespeare's play in a cut version, with its diction modernized and simplified, and his *The Law Against Lovers*, which splices together two generically disparate plays, at the other. He was not the only writer to adopt this method. Some adapters retain the order of Shakespeare's scenes but rewrite the dialogue, as in *Sauny the Scot* (1667), a version of *The Taming of the Shrew* made by the comic actor John Lacy, which turns the play into contemporary prose. Others, like Dryden's *Troilus and Cressida*, change almost all aspects: plot-line, organization of scenes, characters, language, even genre. Tate's *King Lear* (1681) disposes of several characters, most significantly the Fool, provides Cordelia with a confidante, and reorders the plot to produce a happy ending. Tate in his dedicatory epistle pointed proudly to the simple device which achieved so many purposes at once:

> 'Twas my good Fortune to light on one Expedient to rectifie what was wanting in the Regularity and Probability of the Tale, which was to run through the whole, *A Love* betwixt *Edgar* and *Cordelia*, that never chang'd word with each other in the Original. This renders *Cordelia's* Indifference and her Father's passion in the first Scene probable. It likewise gives Countenance to *Edgar's* Disguise, making that a generous Design that was before a poor Shift to save his Life. . . . This Method necessarily threw me on making the Tale conclude in a Success to the innocent distrest Persons; Otherwise I must have incumbred the Stage with dead Bodies, which Conduct makes many Tragedies conclude with unseasonable Jests.

He retained a certain amount of Shakespeare's language where he could, tampering with it much less than Dryden did, but sometimes simplifying and even prettifying it. For example, the blinded Gloucester soliloquizes in Miltonic style:

> All Dark and Comfortless!
> Where are those various Objects that but now
> Employ'd my busie Eyes? Where those Eyes?
> Dead are their piercing Rays that lately shot
> O're flowry vales to distant Sunny Hills,
> And drew with joy the vast Horizon in.
>   (3.5.68–73)

Some adaptations, which use a high proportion of Shakespeare's language, indicate the author's concern to separate out his own contribution, employing typographical conventions in the published play text to do so. Colley Cibber in the Preface to *Richard III*, anxious to avoid any confusion over authorship, wrote that

> I have caus'd those [lines] that are intirely *Shakespear's* to be Printed in this *Italick Character*; and those lines with this mark (') before 'em, are generally his thoughts, in the best dress I could afford 'em: What is not so mark'd, or in a different Character is intirely my own.

Granville in *The Jew of Venice* marked out his own lines with inverted commas 'that nothing may be imputed to Shakespear which may seem unworthy of him'. The demarcations were not always accurate, and in *The Jew of Venice* the lines ostensibly

Shakespeare's are in fact often rewritten or redistributed to different characters. The great Betterton played Bassanio, and Granville gives him many new lines, some from Lorenzo's speeches. But nonetheless these acknowledgements by Cibber and Granville are significant in the history of Shakespeare's role as an author, and were perhaps deliberately intended to refute charges that were sometimes made against playwrights who stole wholesale from others' works without shame, 'our modern Plagiaries' as Langbaine called them in 1691.

Many adaptations introduce new material in ways which transform the play radically. Otway's *Caius Marius* (1679) is an extreme example, setting the story of Romeo and Juliet in republican Rome of the first century. The adaptation came about as a political intervention in contemporary affairs at the time of the Popish Plot and the Exclusion Crisis, which accounts for the new slant given to Shakespeare's tragedy of young love. For similar reasons Tate reset *Richard II* in Italy, calling it *The Sicilian Usurper* (1681) and renaming the characters appropriately, in the misguided hope that a play about the downfall of a rightful English monarch deposed by a usurper would escape censorship. Another late and radical adaptation of a history play was Aaron Hill's *King Henry the Fifth; or, the Conquest of France by the English* (1723), in which the king is followed to France by his abandoned ex-mistress, Harriet, disguised as a page. Adaptation may not seem to be a suitable term for such drastically changed texts as these, where the Shakespearean original is used largely as a pretext for the creation of a new work with an agenda all of its own. But it is not easy, maybe not appropriate, to categorize Restoration dramatic offshoots of Shakespeare according to modern standards of fidelity to the original. Davenant's *Macbeth*, revised 'in the nature of an opera' as John Downes puts it, is infamous for its scenes with flying witches and elaborate musical effects. Pepys, having attended a performance of it in January 1667, although admiring these aspects, was conscious of some incongruity: '*Macbeth* . . . though I saw it lately, yet appears a most excellent play in all respects, but especially in divertisement, though it be a deep tragedy; which is a strange perfection in a tragedy, it being most proper here, and suitable'. The version given at the Dorset Garden theatre in 1673 was probably even more elaborate; its special effects were satirically alluded to by Thomas Duffett in the Epilogue he attached to his burlesque *The Empress of Morocco* (1673), 'being a new Fancy after the old, and most surprising way of MACBETH, Perform'd with new and costly MACHINES'. This version, first printed in 1674, seems obviously remote from Shakespeare; yet *Hamlet*, often regarded as one of the few Shakespeare plays able to succeed with only minimal alterations, was 'done with scenes', as Pepys records in August 1661, and 'adorned and embellished with curious dances between the acts'. The diversification of tragedies with musical interludes was common; *The True and Ancient History of King Lear* was performed in 1703 with 'dancing By the Devonshire Girl and Mr Claxton, her Master', and in 1706 the dancing was supplemented by 'comical songs and dialogues from *Wonders in the Sun*' (Van Lennep 1965: 225).

Many plays were adapted with the primary intention of creating spectacular theatre. An anonymous commentator wrote:

> Yet tis too true that most who now are here,
> Come not to feast their Iudgment, but their Ear.
> Musicke, which was by Intervals design'd
> To ease the weary'd Actors voice and mind,
> You to the Play judiciously prefer,
> 'Tis now the bus'ness of the Theatre.

Davenant's version of *The Tempest* is also a case in point here. *The Tempest* was well received in 1667, when Davenant and Dryden first revised it, but it was even more popular in the operatic version of 1674, probably by Shadwell. It was given still further musical embellishment in a sumptuous production of 1695, with a score by Purcell. In this instance, unlike *Macbeth*, Shakespeare's own play provides the initial inspiration for the musical development, and Ariel's songs had originally been set by the well-known composer Robert Johnson. The set for the play also became increasingly elaborate. The first illustration for Rowe's edition of 1709 suggests what might have been achieved from the stage directions of the Shadwell text. The comment of Downes in *Roscius Anglicanus* makes a clear link between spectacle and commercial success; he describes

> *The Tempest, or Enchanted island*, made into an Opera by Mr Shadwell, having all New in it; as Scenes, machines; particularly, one Scene painted with *Myriads* of *Ariel* spirits; and another flying away, with a Table Furnisht out with Fruits, Sweet-meats, and all sorts of Viands; just when Duke *Trinculo* and his companions going to dinner; all things performed in it so Admirably well, that not any succeeding Opera got more Money. (1929: 35)

Another aspect of Restoration theatricality which Shakespeare was adapted to exploit was, of course, the appeal of actresses. Roles for women were enlarged, and where necessary, invented. Davenant's *Macbeth* expands the role of Lady Macduff, partly to create a greater symmetry of plot, so that the Macduffs can be developed as a virtuous couple in contrast to the Macbeths, but also to make a better part for the actress. In Tate's *King Lear* Cordelia is now a choice part, played by the celebrated Elizabeth Barry, and later by Colley Cibber's wife, who was painted in the role. She is now a romantic ingénue; she longs to take an active part in restoring her father to the throne, but feels prevented by a sense of feminine decorum. She secretly loves Edgar, but cannot admit to this until, in an exciting new scene, he rescues her from abduction by two ruffians whom Edmund has hired to procure her. She declares her passion for him, regardless of his disguise as Poor Tom:

> By the dear Vital Stream that baths my Heart,
> These hallow'd Rags of Thine, and naked Vertue,
> . . .
> To me are dearer than the richest Pomp
> Of purple Monarchs.
>
> (3.5.96–102)

Romantic love was an important ingredient for popular appeal. With this in mind, Shadwell in *Timon of Athens, or The Man-Hater* (1678) provided several new roles: Melissa, whom Timon is to marry although she really loves Alcibiades, her maid Chloe, and Evandra, Timon's faithful mistress who follows him to the woods and kills herself over his dead body. From such evidence as exists, this version was better received in its own day than Shakespeare's. Dryden's *Troilus and Cressida* also celebrates faithful love in the character of Andromache, Hector's wife, who gets two new scenes with her husband, in one of which she tragically envisages his death. In his *All for Love*, the role of Octavia, Antony's wife, is much enlarged, to transform the character into a forceful figure quite unlike the 'swan's down feather' in Shakespeare; this was perhaps done to suit the commanding actress Katherine Corey, who played the part, and to contrast with the image of Cleopatra, played by the more delicate and girlish Betty Bowtell. In Act 3, after Octavia, appearing with her children, seems to have regained the heart of Antony, she is given an emotional scene with Cleopatra which exploits the stereotype of the jealous, competitive, woman-as-bitch:

> *Octavia* (coming up nearer): I would view nearer
> That face, which has so long usurp'd my right,
> To find th'inevitable charms, that catch
> Mankind so sure, that ruin'd my dear Lord.
> *Cleopatra*: O, you do well to search: for had you known
> But half these charms you had not lost his heart.
> *Octavia*: Far be their knowledge from a *Roman* Lady,
> Far from a modest Wife. Shame of our Sex,
> Dost thou not blush, to own those black endearments
> That make sin pleasing?
> *Cleopatra*: You may blush, who want 'em.
>
> (3.435–45)

Dryden was obviously rather proud of this scene, for he draws attention to it in his preface by appearing to apologize for it. 'The French poets', he says, 'being attentive to historical accuracy would not have allowed Octavia and Cleopatra to meet, or if they had, would only have permitted them some cold civilities, not eager repartee, for fear of offending against the greatness of their characters, and the modesty of their sex'. But he justified his invention, claiming it to be 'both natural and probable' that Octavia would seek an occasion to gloat to Cleopatra over her regaining of Antony, and 'the two exasperated rivals should use such satire as I have put into their mouths: for after all, though the one were a Roman, and the other a queen, they were both women'.

One of the most successful exploitations of the actress's sexual appeal is in the Davenant/Dryden *Tempest*, in the transvestite role of Hippolyto. He is an entirely new character, the man who had never seen a woman, the invention of which Dryden ascribed admiringly in his preface to Davenant. The role was designed to be played by a woman, possibly by Mary Davis, famed for her legs, who attracted the king's attention in the part, and subsequently became his mistress. Hippolyto, who embodies the Restoration conception of masculinity as inherently promiscuous, falls in love with Dorinda, Miranda's sister and another addition to the dramatis personae, but also desires Miranda. Delighted to discover that there are other women in the world than Dorinda, he declares his intention to possess as many as he can:

> I must have all of that kind, if there be a hundred of 'em.
> . . . I must love where I like, and I believe I may like all,
> All that are fair.
>
> (3.6.53, 61–2)

Such lines – and they are typical of the play's risqué dialogue – spoken by an attractive woman in a man's role dressed so as to exploit her figure, in the presence, or at least knowledge, of a monarch of well-known prodigious sexual appetite, must have created a considerable *frisson* in the audience. And the transvestite convention, here boldly expressed through a character representing unsocialized male sexual desire, operates cleverly throughout the play to destabilize conceptions of gender.

To a greater degree than in Shakespeare's time parts were created and developed with particular performers in mind, and the relationship between audience and performers was a more intimate one. This is especially evident in the case of actresses, but it also applies to actors, some of whom laid claim to specific roles or types of role with which they became identified. Betterton, for example, was Hamlet in this period, and his success in the part contributed significantly to the financial well-being of the King's Men. Astonishingly, he played it from 1661 to 1709, stopping only a year before his death at the age of 75. Downes recorded that his 'exact Performance of [Hamlet] gain'd him Esteem and Reputation, Superlative to all other Plays. . . . No succeeding Tragedy for several Years got more Reputation, or Money to the Company than this' (1929: 21). James Nokes, the comic actor, early distinguished himself as Polonius, but became particularly associated with the part of the Nurse in *Caius Marius* and known as 'Nurse Nokes'. John Lacy capitalized on his reputation for dialect roles by writing himself a large part as Petruchio's servant, transformed into a foul-mouthed Scot, in *Sauny the Scot*. Cibber's adaptation of *Richard III*, including seven new soliloquies for Richard, was also designed to create a prize role for a particular actor, in this case Samuel Sandford. But Sandford was not available to play the part, being contracted to the rival company, so Cibber did it himself. His acting was not universally admired; he was said by one unimpressed observer to have 'screamed through four acts without Dignity or Decency'. But this adaptation itself became very popular, and held the stage until the later half of the nineteenth century.

It is not surprising that theatrical interests of one kind or another should lie behind the adaptation and revision of many Shakespeare plays. Although the plays were commonly criticized for defects of structure or language, his skill in the creation of character was always acknowledged and valued in an age which set great store by the consistency of characterization. But what may seem more unexpected initially is the perceived usefulness of Shakespeare as the basis of much political theatre. Many adaptations of the early years can be seen to reflect topical political concerns; for example, as Nancy Klein Maguire has shown, Davenant's *The Law Against Lovers* demonstrates how 'irreconcilable dilemmas . . . become an occasion to show how under the stern but benevolent Duke (Charles II) the state could be made secure, peaceful succession assured, and the effects of the act of regicide mended'. The Dryden/ Davenant *Tempest* comments on a number of current issues, 'ranging from regicide, usurpation, republicanism, and restoration to the present problems of royal lechery and royal treachery' (Maguire 1992: 63, 132). Its great contemporary popularity has been ascribed to its topicality, and to the fact that it was seen as a play 'determinedly about government' (Maus 1982: 144), though this does not account for the fact that it held the stage, in one form or another, until well into the next century. For all its wealth of possible parallels – Prospero as Charles II, or Clarendon, Hippolyto as Charles II, or James, Duke of York, or the Duke of Monmouth, or even Charles I – it does not take a specific political stance, and though recent critics are agreed on the fact that Shakespeare's play was revised with issues of the 1660s specifically in mind, they offer a variety of different, and sometimes contradictory, readings of it.

The most obvious examples of politically inflected adaptations are the outcrop that appeared during the period of intense ideological upheaval caused by the Popish Plot and the Exclusion Crisis. Michael Dobson counts nine Shakespeare adaptations in this new wave, constituting a marked revival of interest in his work: Edward Ravenscroft's *Titus Andronicus, or, The Rape of Lavinia* (1678); Dryden's *Troilus and Cressida* (1679); Otway's *Caius Marius* (1679); John Crowne's *The Misery of Civil-War* (1680), taken from *3 Henry VI*, and his *Henry the Sixth, the First Part* (1681); Tate's *The History of King Lear* (1681), *The Sicilian Usurper* (1680) and *The Ingratitude of a Common-wealth: Or the Fall of Caius Martius Coriolanus* (1681); and Thomas Durfey's *The Injured Princess* (1682), a version of *Cymbeline*. All these plays were royalist in their political perspective. This was an extraordinary period in the history of the British constitution, with fear and paranoia rife, and dramatists responded to it by writing new plays, such as Nathaniel Lee's *Lucius Junius Brutus* and Otway's *Venice Preserv'd*. But clearly Shakespeare's work was found to fill a need. All plays at this time were subject to especially vigilant censorship, and no doubt the adapting of the work of so old and respected a playwright, such a staple of the popular theatre, might have been thought to accord some degree of protection. This was not necessarily the case. New plays and adaptations alike fell foul of the censor. Lee's *Lucius Junius Brutus* was banned as too republican in its bias, but the same fate befell Tate's royalist *The Sicilian Usurper*, thought tactless in its depiction of the deposition of a monarch, and Crowne's *Henry the Sixth*, which suffered for comic satire of Catholics. A high degree of political tact was required to negotiate the delicate balance of official interests (Owen 1996).

Beaumont and Fletcher in the Restoration

Despite the cultural significance of Shakespeare in the Restoration period it was undeniably the plays of Beaumont and Fletcher that were most popular in the theatre, particularly in the early years. It has been calculated that between 1660 and 1671 they constituted twenty-eight of the 105 revivals of older plays (Maguire 1992: 56). Dryden's famous comment that they were twice as popular as Shakespeare's or Jonson's plays was made in 1668; he added by way of explanation, 'the reason being that there is a certain gaiety in their comedies, and pathos in their more serious plays, that suits generally with all men's humours'.

   In a sense, the ground had already been prepared during the years of the Interregnum; the publication of the Folio in 1647, perceived as an important act of royalist propaganda, made many plays newly available. Some Beaumont and Fletcher plays, printed earlier, were reprinted, including *A King and No King* in 1655, 'now for the fifth time Printed', as its title-page proclaimed. In Francis Kirkman's collection of drolls, *The Wits, or Sport upon Sport* (1652), fourteen of the twenty-seven pieces were taken from Beaumont and Fletcher plays, several of them specially shaped so as to focus on issues to do with kingship and authority. There were surreptitious performances of at least three plays in the late 1640s and the 1650s. A production of *The Spanish Curate* was staged by the Rhodes company in 1659, and just before the theatres officially opened in August 1660 *The Woman's Prize*, Fletcher's play based on *The Taming of The Shrew*, was performed at the Red Bull, with a newly written epilogue, emphasizing its status as a piece for the new regime. But of course the plays would not have been so popular and so influential in the theatre had they not in important ways spoken to the cultural needs of the time. In contemporary critical accounts of them certain aspects stand out. Their wit and verbal refinement were particularly admired, and linked, as by Dryden, with their ability to reproduce 'the conversation of gentlemen'. The appeal of these plays to class interest is significant, and they have often been thought to influence the tone of what Nicoll called 'aristocratic licentiousness' (1923: 170), typical of much Restoration comedy. Their wit was characterized by innuendo and double entendre, as Flecknoe noticed, when he compared Fletcher's 'witty obscenity' to 'a poison infused in pleasant liquor . . . always the more dangerous the more delightful'. That delight of this sort formed part of the appeal of the repartee in comedies such as *The Scornful Lady* or *Rule a Wife and Have a Wife* (both frequently revived in the period) is very probable, along with the handling of sexuality more generally. The element of titillation implicit in their treatment of transvestite roles, such as Bellario in *Philaster*, or their outspoken and sexually forthright women characters, like Evadne in *The Maid's Tragedy*, may have elicited some reproof from critics conscious of decorum. Yet although *The Custom of the Country* seems to have been something of a byword for its obscenity, when Colley Cibber adapted it as *Love Makes a Man* (1700) this was in fact an aspect he chose to play up rather than down. The Restoration versions of *The Chances*, by George Villiers,

Duke of Buckingham (1682), and *The Sea Voyage*, by Thomas Durfey as *A Common-wealth of Women* (1686), are, if anything, more bawdy than the originals. Thomas Scott's adaptation of the risqué *A Wife for a Month* as *The Unhappy Kindness* (1697) elaborates on the theme of sexual anticipation.

Another formative aspect of the Beaumont and Fletcher dramaturgy is pointed to by Flecknoe when he mentions that 'Beaumont and Fletcher first writ in the Heroick way'. Their handling of themes of honour, nobility, self-sacrifice and the competing moral claims of love and friendship, particularly in *Philaster*, *The Maid's Tragedy* and *A King and No King*, was highly influential on new playwrights, and also successful in the theatre. Waller, who wrote an adaptation of *The Maid's Tragedy*, probably around 1664 (see Hume 1982), later noted that 'Of all our elder Plays, This and *Philaster* have the lowdest fame'. Many critics have discussed the attractions that the moral debates and declamations of passion held for the Restoration, and it was often the combination in a single play of a sexual 'low' plot with a solemn and heroic 'upper' plot that provided the formal model for new comedy and tragicomedy. This latter mode especially, often now regarded as the typical royalist genre of the early Restoration period in its celebration of providential restoration and unexpected reconciliation plucked out of conflict, reversals of fortune and potential disaster, drew heavily on styles of plot established in the Beaumont and Fletcher plays. It is not surprising that *A King and No King* was extremely successful. Five or six editions of the play were published during the Commonwealth, and there were five productions during the Restoration decade. The royalist Sir Roger L'Estrange cited the play's title: 'we are now upon the very *Crisis*, of *King* or *No King*'. Nancy Klein Maguire distinguishes between the way that playwrights 'instinctively adapted the structure of Carolean tragicomedy from Fletcher', because it addressed the deep-seated psychological needs of theatregoers who might see the restoration of Charles II as the most unlikely of happy endings to the tragicomedy of the Interregnum years, and their more deliberate adoption of forms and techniques from the Beaumont and Fletcher plays which had proved commercially successful. In the latter regard she cites the frank tribute paid by Waller:

> *Fletcher*, to thee we do not only owe
> All our Good Plays, but all those other too,
> Thy wit repeated, does support the Stage
> Credits the last, and entertains this Age.
> (Maguire 1992: 123)

Although it is often stressed that far more of the Beaumont and Fletcher plays, particularly the comedies, were revived in their original form than was the case with Shakespeare, nonetheless a number of them were adapted. Interestingly, one of the earliest was *The Two Noble Kinsmen*, now accepted as a collaboration between Fletcher and Shakespeare, which was rewritten by Davenant as *The Rivals* in 1664. This play, accepted in its own time as an original piece of work, was well received and as Downes recorded, 'lasted uninterruptly Nine Days, with a full Audience'. It has strong political undertones, with the tyrant Harpacus (Creon) representing a Cromwell figure at the beginning of the play, and the Arcadians (the Athenians), the royalists. Formally it is converted from a tragicomedy into a comedy, largely due to the device of socially elevating the jailer's daughter, now named Cleania and daughter to a Provost, so that she can properly marry Philander (Palemon) at the end, leaving the other kinsman, Theocles, to Heraclia (Emilia), thus neatly avoiding the dark and violent end to the story both in *The Two Noble Kinsmen* and its source, Chaucer's *The Knight's Tale*. There is much more music and song, including 'a very fine Interlude ... of vocal and Instrumental Musick, mixt with very Diverting Dances' (Downes 1929: 63–4), and the complexities and tonal difficulties of the original play are smoothed over. Particularly characteristic of Restoration changes to older plays are the regularizing of the plot and the neatening of the dramatic structure. Dryden was typical of his time in objecting to the defective and irregular plotting of both Shakespeare and Fletcher. The anonymous preface to the Earl of Rochester's adaptation of Fletcher's unwieldy tragedy, *Valentinian*, notices that Rochester imposed a unity of action absent from the original; this was largely achieved by omitting the complexities of Fletcher's last act. As with Shakespeare adaptations, the Beaumont and Fletcher plays were also augmented with music and spectacle. *The Island Princess*, one of the most popular of the old plays for many years, was adapted in 1687 by Tate, who found in it 'defects in Manners' as he had done with *King Lear*, and then by Pierre Motteux, who turned it into an opera in 1699. Motteux, following Tate, also changed the characterization to create more consistency. Dryden, in the preface to 'The Grounds of Criticism in Tragedy' (1679), had complained, with some justification, that in tragedy Fletcher sacrificed his characters to his plots: 'They [the characters] are either good, bad, or indifferent as the scene requires it'. So in Motteux's version, Princess Quisara is made unequivocally high-minded and virtuous, which fitted in with Restoration ideas of social decorum in the presentation of rulers; as Rymer put it, 'all crown'd heads by *Poetical right* are Heroes'.

Adaptations of the popular plays *Philaster* and *The Maid's Tragedy* followed the same principles. Both were performed in the original versions in the early years of the Restoration by the King's Men with great success; *Philaster* figured prominently in the first two years, and was revived in 1667, possibly with Nell Gwyn as Bellario, while *The Maid's Tragedy* in 1660 featured Edward Kynaston as the king's mistress, Evadne. *Philaster* was adapted twice, as *The Restoration, or Right will Take Place*, by the Duke of Buckingham in 1683, a version which may never have been staged, and by Elkanah Settle in 1695. Settle made *Philaster* more obviously noble than the original somewhat ambivalent figure, removing his wounding of Arethusa and Bellario; he also modified the political tone of the play in keeping with the troubled history of recent years by a strong insistence on the impiety of rebellion. It was claimed that Waller's adaptation of *The Maid's Tragedy*, published in 1690, but possibly written much earlier, was 'alter'd to please the Court' (Sorelius 1966: 57). In effect, this involved rewriting the last act so as to avoid the situation, delicate in the 1660s, of an amorous king being killed by his mistress. Waller reforms the king, allowing him to show both magnanimity to his enemies and repentance for his sins, which fits him to survive; his mistress, Evadne, in one of two variant versions, leaves the island and goes into retreat with the Vestal Virgins. The play concludes by celebrating the friendship of the king with his brother, perhaps glancing at the relationship of Charles II and the Duke of York. Political considerations were significant in other adaptations: in Rochester's *Valentinian* (1685), in which measures are taken to heighten the emperor's tyranny and thus to discourage any equation with the English monarchy, and in Thomas Scott's tragic version of *A Wife for a Month* (1697), retitled *The Unhappy Kindness: or a Fruitless Revenge*, in which the cuckolded husband refrains from revenge on the tyrannical ruler because he cannot contemplate killing a king.

The Beaumont and Fletcher comedies were less subject to revision than the tragedies; and when they were revised, as was done by established playwrights such as Durfey, Vanbrugh, Farquhar and Cibber, it was as much in the spirit of plundering good material as in the desire to reform and refine. Adapters often preferred to conceal the extent of their borrowing, rather than displaying or providing a rationale for it. It may be significant that the majority of the adaptations were carried out in the latter part of the period, after 1680; in one or two cases, as with Rochester's *Valentinian* and *Bonduca* (by George Powell, 1695), this meant the introduction to the Restoration stage of plays not seen in any form earlier, but mostly the plays, the property of the King's Men, had already enjoyed some theatrical success in their original forms. And it was not until the early eighteenth century that the most extreme form of adaptation, the combining of two plays into one, was carried out, with Colley Cibber's *Love Makes a Man* (1701), constructed from *The Elder Brother* and *The Custom of the Country*, and *The City Ramble, or The Playhouse Wedding*, made by Elkanah Settle from *The Knight of the Burning Pestle* and *The Coxcomb*. By this time the high reputation that the Beaumont and Fletcher plays had enjoyed in the early years of the Restoration was in irreversible decline.

Jonson and Other Playwrights

The position occupied by Ben Jonson, third of Dryden's great 'rivals in poetry', was distinctively different from those of Shakespeare or Beaumont and Fletcher. Flecknoe's comparison typifies the critical position on their relationship:

> To compare our English Dramatick Poets together, without taxing them, *Shakespear* excelled in a natural vein, *Fletcher* in Wit, and *Johnson* in Gravity and ponderousness of Style, whose onely fault was he was too elaborate, and had he mixt less erudition with his Playes, they had been more pleasant and delightful then they are. Comparing him with *Shakespear*, you shall see the difference betwixt Nature and Art; and with *Fletcher*, the difference betwixt Wit and Judgment.

Jonson enjoyed the greatest critical prestige of the three. The erudition that may have marred his plays in the theatre – and the fact that so small a proportion of his large opus was regularly performed in the period supports this view – won him the admiration of critics like Dryden, who claimed of his classical borrowings that 'he invades authors like a monarch; and what would be theft in other poets, is only victory in him'. By comparison with the plays of Shakespeare and other pre-Restoration dramatists, Jonson's plays were seen as 'regular' and 'correct' in their plotting. His espousal of neo-classical principles in both his theory and his theatrical practice appealed to the tastes of the time, but also help raise the literary prestige of pre-Restoration theatre.

In the *Essay of Dramatic Poetry* Dryden takes *Epicœne* as 'the pattern of a perfect play' in its observation of the unities of time, place and action, and its variety of characters and humours; he also commended Jonson's depiction of 'the conversation of gentlemen' with 'more gaiety, air, and freedom' than in his other comedies. It was popular in the theatre from the start, four performances taking place in 1660, and more in 1661, when Pepys saw Kynaston as Epicœne and admired his beauty. Such was the box-office appeal of actresses that Mrs Knepp took over the part, one of the least appropriate for a woman, in 1663, when Kynaston played Dauphine. *Volpone* too was a popular success, mainly in the first twenty years. At its revival in 1705 at Drury Lane, it was felt by one of the actors to be obsolete:

'Volpone', or 'Tamerlane', will hardly fetch us a tolerable audience, unless we stuff the bills with long entertainments of dances, songs, scaramouched entries, and what not.

The Alchemist also enjoyed many early revivals, despite the implication, in a prologue newly written for it, that the actors felt themselves 'young beginners' in the face of such demanding parts as those of Face, Subtle and Doll Common. In 1663 Mrs Corey overcame the difficulties of playing Doll Common, and became known by this name, but the view that Jonson's roles demanded skills no longer available persisted. James Wright in *Historica Histrionica* (1699) noted the actors' belief that Jonson's plays were not revived because 'there are none now living, who can rightly humour those parts: for all who [were] related to the "Blackfriars" (where they were acted in perfection) are now dead, and almost forgotten'. Nonetheless, they continued to be performed during the eighteenth century, their true decline being thought to date from Garrick's retirement.

Downes noted among the 'Principal Old Stock Plays' of the King's Men *Volpone, The Alchemist, Epicœne* and also *Catiline, Bartholomew Fair, Everyman in his Humour, Everyman out of his Humour, Sejanus* and *The Devil is an Ass*, though these last six were 'Acted but now and then' (1929: 9). *Bartholomew Fair* was in fact popular, again in the first two decades; Pepys saw its first revival in June 1661, but thought it 'much too prophane and abusive', and the puppet-show had initially to be omitted. He saw it several times more, and continued to 'love the wit of it', a feature for which Jonson was generally admired, but considered the anti-Puritan satire dated. The characters of Ursula the Pig-Woman and Rabbi Busy entered popular mythology. But as for the remaining plays, few performances are recorded. Despite the critical adulation of his work, Jonson's plays were not absorbed into the theatrical mainstream of the Restoration to the same extent as those of Shakespeare and Beaumont and Fletcher. His comic humours influenced the work of new playwrights, the best known of whom are Shadwell and Wycherley, and, later, Susanna Centlivre; but his plays were never adapted or 'improved', perhaps because, as Dryden said, 'in his works you find little to retrench or alter'.

Of Shakespeare's other contemporaries only a few were notably popular or influential. Marlowe's *Dr Faustus* failed to impress Pepys in 1662, even though it probably had additional scenes; it was reworked as a farce by William Mountfort in 1688. Webster was one of the most successful: *The White Devil* was performed in 1661, and *The Duchess of Malfi* in 1662 with Betterton as Bosola, in a production which, Downes related, 'fill'd the House 8 days Successively, it proving one of the Best of Stock Tragedies' (1929: 25), and was admired by Pepys. Other productions of both plays are recorded, and even revised versions: in 1707 '*The Unfortunate Dutchess of Malfy, or the Unnatural Brothers*, revised with alterations' was performed, and in the same year Tate's *Injur'd Love, or, The Cruel Husband*, a version of *The White Devil*, appeared in print without mention of the original, though there is no record of performance. In 1669 Betterton adapted *Appius and Virginia* as *The Roman Virgin*. These tragedies influenced writers like Otway and Southerne with their portrayals of lust and violence. Webster's *A Cure for a Cuckold* was reworked by Joseph Harris as *The City Bride* in 1696, with music and song. Several of Massinger's plays were staged, of which *The Bondman*, put on in 1661 as a vehicle for Betterton, was particularly successful; this play also had political relevance in its handling of a slave revolt quelled by masters. The 'heroic' quality of plays like this and also *The Virgin Martyr*, also staged in 1661, guaranteed their appeal. Langbaine detected a number of plagiarisms from Massinger's work, by Aphra Behn among others, and felt that 'Authors not so generally known as Murston [*sic*], Middleton, Massinger' were particularly vulnerable to unacknowledged theft.

Pre-Restoration plays served as a storehouse of treasures for new playwrights to rifle, and Langbaine was not alone in accusing his contemporaries of stealing; a character in Lacy's *Sir Hercules Buffoon* (1684) denounces current practice: 'Ay, and some of 'em will filch and steal out o'th'old plays, and cry down the authors when they've done'. But on the other hand, adaptations were accepted and welcomed. Dryden, Tate, Ravenscroft and others believed themselves to be doing Shakespeare a service in improving his plays to suit the new standards, and the editor of the 1711 *Works* of Beaumont and Fletcher thought that the adaptations of their plays by aristocratic writers such as Rochester and Buckingham 'adds not a little to their reputation'. The history of Restoration theatre is unimaginable without the old plays, in whatever form, and their contribution to the culture of the period is not insignificant.

REFERENCES AND FURTHER READING

Dobson, Michael (1992). *The Making of the National Poet: Shakespeare, Adaptation, and Authorship*. Oxford: Clarendon Press.

Downes, John (1929). *Roscius Anglicanus*, ed. Montague Summers. New York and London: Benjamin Blom.

Dryden, John (1962). *Of Dramatic Poesy and Other Critical Essays*, ed. George Watson. 2 vols. London and New York: Dent.

Hume, R. D. (1982). '*The Maid's Tragedy* and Censorship in the Restoration Theatre', *Philological Quarterly* 61, 484–90.

Langbaine, Gerard (1691). *An Account of the English Dramatic Poets*.

Maguire, Nancy Klein (1992). *Regicide and Restoration: English Tragicomedy, 1660–1671*. Cambridge: Cambridge University Press.

Maus, Katherine Eisamen (1982). 'Arcadia Lost: Politics and Revision in the Restoration *Tempest*', *Restoration Drama* n.s. 13, 189–209.

Merchant, W. Moelwyn (1965). 'Shakespeare Made Fit', in John Russell Brown and Bernard Harris (gen. eds), *Restoration Theatre*. London: Edward Arnold, 195–219.

Nicoll, Allardyce (1923). *A History of Restoration Drama, 1660–1700*. Cambridge: Cambridge University Press.

Noyes, Robert Gayle (1935). *Ben Jonson on the English Stage, 1660–1776*. Cambridge, MA: Harvard University Press.

Odell, G. C. (1920–1). *Shakespeare from Betterton to Irving*. 2 vols. London and New York: Constable.

Owen, Susan J. (1996). *Restoration Theatre and Crisis*. Oxford: Clarendon Press.

Pepys, Samuel (1970–83). *The Diary of Samuel Pepys*, ed. Robert Latham and William Matthews. 11 vols. Berkeley: University of California Press.

Raddadi, Mongi (1979). *Davenant's Adaptations of Shakespeare*. Uppsala: Almqvist and Wiksells.

Sorelius, Gunnar (1966). '*The Giant Race before the Flood*': Pre-Restoration Drama on the Stage and in the Criticism of the Restoration. Uppsala: Almqvist and Wiksells.

Spencer, Christopher (ed.). (1965). *Five Restoration Adaptations of Shakespeare*. Urbana: University of Illinois Press.

Spencer, Hazelton (1927). *Shakespeare Improved: The Restoration Versions in Quarto and on the Stage*. Cambridge, MA: Harvard University Press.

Spingarn, J. E. (ed.). (1908). *Critical Essays of the Seventeenth Century*. Oxford: Clarendon Press.

Taylor, Gary (1990). *Reinventing Shakespeare: A Cultural History from the Restoration to the Present*. London: Hogarth Press.

Van Lennep, William (ed.). (1965). *The London Stage, 1660–1800*. Part I: *1660–1700*, ed. Emmett L. Avery and Arthur H. Scouten. Carbondale: Southern Illinois University Press.

Vickers, Brian (1974). *Shakespeare: The Critical Heritage*. Vol. 1: *1623–1692*. London and Boston: Routledge and Kegan Paul.

Wikander, Matthew (1986). 'The Spitted Infant: Scenic Emblem and Exclusionist Politics in Restoration Adaptations of Shakespeare', *Shakespeare Quarterly* 37, 91–108.

Wilson, J. H. (1928). *The Influence of Beaumont and Fletcher on Restoration Drama*. Columbus: Ohio State University Press.

Wright, James (1699). *Historica Histrionica: An Historical Account of the English-Stage*.

17

Rakes, Wives and Merchants: Shifts from the Satirical to the Sentimental

Kirk Combe

The following poem, entitled 'Régime de Vivre' (regime of life), is either by John Wilmot, second Earl of Rochester, or about him.

> I rise at eleven, I dine about two,
> I get drunk before seven, and the next thing I do,
> I send for my whore, when for fear of a clap,
> I spend in her hand, and I spew in her lap;
> Then we quarrel and scold, till I fall fast asleep,
> When the bitch growing bold, to my pocket does creep.
> Then slyly she leaves me, and to revenge the affront,
> At once she bereaves me of money and cunt.
> If by chance then I wake, hot-headed and drunk,
> What a coil do I make for the loss of my punk!
> I storm, and I roar, and I fall in a rage.
> And missing my whore, I bugger my page.
> Then crop-sick all morning I rail at my men,
> And in bed I lie yawning till eleven again.

Whether censure or boast, this portrait of a young aristocrat of the 1670s is not a flattering one. Besides his privileged indolence, his practice of safe sex unfortunately also subjects the prostitute he engages to being the target of his drunken vomiting. After she unceremoniously leaves him passed out in his rooms, his anger over no longer having a sexual plaything for the evening leads him to homosexual use, and possibly abuse, of his page, a young male attendant. Finally, hung over the next morning, he yells at his other servants until it is time to get out of bed to begin his daily course of debauchery anew. Thus we have a verse snapshot of Rochester, the leading rake of Charles II's libertine court, that includes too much time and money on his hands, sexual predatoriness and classism in the extreme. The poem also involves, however, the perplexities of satire. Is such a lifestyle being praised or blamed? If Rochester wrote the piece, does he display wry insight or blind inanity regarding himself? Or are such extremes our only choices for interpretation? Might not Rochester, as the arch-signifier for the patrician man-about-Town, both mock and flaunt his social power simultaneously? Might he not also set a poetic trap for all those would-be rakes-about-Town who, uncritically reading his and similar satiric productions of the day, aspire to this level of fashionable hedonism – and thereby show themselves to be fools? And might not Rochester also be seen as fooling himself, that is, deriding a way of life that he seemed unable to resist? After all, Rochester died in 1680 at the age of 33, the victim of perhaps the most celebrated case of burning the candle at both ends in English literary history.

The satiric perspective of Restoration literature is indeed complex. Social, political and economic circumstances were in flux after 1660 as the nation renegotiated itself following the turbulence of the Civil War and the novelty of Cromwell's republic. During Charles II's reign, the king's dissimulative manner in dealing with Parliament coupled with his penchant for a French-style, pleasure-seeking court produced an atmosphere among the power elite characterized by 'a sensation of distrust and alienation' (Hutton 1989: 458; see his ch. 16). In one of his best-known works, *A Satire Against Mankind*, Rochester aptly describes this high-born masquerade.

> Look to the bottom of his vast design,
> Wherein man's wisdom, power, and glory join:
> The good he acts, the ill he does endure,
> 'Tis all from fear, to make himself secure.
> Merely for safety after fame they thirst,
> For all men would be cowards if they durst.
> And honesty's against all common sense,
> Men must be knaves, 'tis in their own defence.
> Mankind's dishonest: if you think it fair
> Among known cheats to play upon the square,
> You'll be undone.
> Nor can weak truth your reputation save,
> The knaves will all agree to call you knave.
> Wronged shall he live, insulted o'er, oppressed,
> Who dares be less a villain than the rest.
> Thus sir, you see what human nature craves,
> Most men are cowards, all men should be knaves;
> The difference lies, as far as I can see,
> Not in the thing itself, but the degree;
> And all the subject matter of debate
> Is only, who's a knave of the first rate?

Like 'Régime de Vivre', this passage is both droll and chilling. It depicts a society so ruled by fear and competition that its members, in splendid oxymoron, don't even dare be cowards. Instead, all are forced to be knaves – unprincipled and dishonest schemers – out of a desperate need for self-defence. Surrounded by scoundrels, one dares be nothing less: individual truth has little chance against corporate lies. Therefore human nature is a pathetic business. While we long to be snivellers, we're compelled to be miscreants. The only really valid inquiry into human behaviour, then, is who, in our constant struggle for self-preservation, lies, cheats and manipulates others with utmost skill. Who *is* the knave of the first rate? As if all this isn't bad enough, by implication, we are all also fools for subjecting ourselves to this enervating charade. If collectively we could just muster the courage to be humane, we might escape this jungle. At once, then, Rochester's satire asserts and condemns such a brutal and absurd social scene. Arguably, it partakes in the senseless contest as well. Isn't Rochester in this polished attack showing himself to be the freethinker of the first rate? Isn't his poem a formidable display of linguistic and manipulative power itself? Really thought-provoking satire normally brings with it the element of self-examination, of self-irony. Few writers of the period rivalled Rochester's exasperatingly slippery critique of English society (see Combe 1998).

I've opened this chapter on the satiric and the sentimental in Restoration drama with poems by Rochester because his labyrinthine satiric point of view epitomizes much of the comedic drama of the early Restoration period, particularly that of the 1670s. In comedies by Wycherley, Etherege, Behn and Shadwell, for example, we see such hero-rakes as Horner, Dorimant, Willmore, Longvil and Bruce personate this same combination of sensualism and egoism treated in Rochester's works. Available as well in these leading men is the interpretive possibility for both celebration and reproach – and all points in between – of their libertine ways. Not surprisingly, each of these stage playboys is, to some degree, either suggestive of Rochester or in fact modelled upon that notorious man of the Town. Dorimant in particular, from Etherege's *The Man of Mode*, is taken to be a stage portrait of the Earl. Thus the most widely known type of Restoration drama, the so-called 'comedy of manners' or 'sex comedy' or 'laughing comedy', begins the era fundamentally in the sphere of Rochesterian social satire.

A half-century later, however, a very different comic ethos could be seen on the stage. In the *Tatler*, no. 219 of 1 September 1710, Richard Steele complains of an evening ruined by the uninvited company of two men of wit – the very rake types discussed above. Writes Steele: 'These people are the more dreadful, the more they have of what is usually called wit: for a lively imagination, when it is not governed by a good understanding, makes such miserable havoc both in conversation and business, that it lays you defenseless, and fearful to throw the least word in its way that may give it new matter for its further errors'. Rejecting this modish behaviour of 'coxcombs', Steele declares instead for a new manner of social interaction. 'From hence it is, that from long experience I have made it a maxim, that however we may pretend to take satisfaction in sprightly mirth and high jollity, there is no great pleasure in any company where the basis of the society is not mutual good-will.' In his ideal gathering of men, Steele insists that there 'is not a man among them has any notion of distinction of superiority to one another, either in their fortunes or their talents, when they are in company' (cited in McMillin 1997: 482–3). Obviously, we are a long way removed from Rochester's well-born society described in *A Satire Against Mankind* or depicted in the comedies of Wycherley and Etherege; that society dealt in little else but wit and contentions of superiority. And Steele's different conception of fellowship is visible in the comedy of the late seventeenth and early eighteenth centuries. In the epilogue to *The Lying Lover* (1703), Steele shuns the Rochesterian and Hobbesian mirth of earlier Restoration comedies.

> For laughter's a distorted passion, born
> Of sudden self-esteem and sudden scorn;
> Which, when 'tis o'er, the men in pleasure wise
> Both him that moved it and themselves despise.

The harsh satiric laughter of rake-driven comedy produces only empty pleasure, according to Steele, and a pleasure that is in reality shameful and destructive. Steele has placed at the heart of his comedy something quite dissimilar.

> While generous pity of a painted woe
> Make us ourselves both more approve and know.
> What is that touch within, which nature gave
> For man to man, e'er fortune made a slave?
> Sure it descends from that dread power alone
> Who levels thunder from His awful throne,
> And shakes both worlds – yet hears the wretched groan.
>   (Cited in McMillin 1997: 481)

Rather than show us a comedic society of pack hunters featuring the dominant beast, Steele founds his comedy on depictions of virtuous people in distress (but in the end preserved from harm) in order to evoke feelings of pity in his audience as well as an accompanying sensation of moral improvement. That 'touch within' producing such empathy and mutual good-will towards our fellow being is, in a word, sentiment, a fascinating and complicated phenomenon of early modern culture. The purpose of the present chapter is to discuss this shift away from a predominantly satiric brand of comedy found on the English stage soon after 1660 and towards a great deal of sentimental comedy produced there by the turn of the century and beyond.

  That there was a shift from the satirical to the sentimental in English drama, and in particular comedy, during the period 1660–1710 is unmistakeable. Reading *The Country Wife* and *The Man of Mode* at the beginning of this period compared to reading *The Careless Husband* and *The Lying Lover* by its end clearly marks the change. However, exactly why or when such a shift took place is not so easy to pinpoint. Neither is the shift really a changeover in the sense that one type of drama replaced a previous type; by the end of the eighteenth century both 'laughing' and 'weeping' comedy shared the stage. Nor is either type of comedy easy to define; in fact, both 'satirical' and 'sentimental' as literary terms come maddeningly close to defying definition. In short, it is a convoluted path – if it is even a passageway – from dramatic productions featuring elements of social satire to productions featuring elements of social sensibility. One scholar of sentimental comedy has observed that most writers about sentimental literature 'have been more interested in the origins and history than in the nature of sentimental literature' (Ellis 1991: 120). Heeding this caution, I will not attempt to provide here hard answers regarding this historical shift in dramatic attitude. To do so would not only be misleading, but it would do damage, via simplification, to the intricate cultural productions that are Restoration drama. Instead, I will present and explore a range of factors that reasonably seem to influence the move. Though perplexing, explanations of satiric and sentimental drama, already begun above, will be offered. Along with these provisional definitions, significant cultural circumstances, such as the moral reform movement of the 1690s, will be considered as well. Concluding my deliberations will be a discussion of the way the comedic drama of the period reflects a crucial transformation in the dominant ideology of English society. That is, as England moved from an aristocratic, land-based political economy to a mercantile, capitalistic one during the early modern period, the worldview of playwright and audience duly altered as well. I believe this alteration had much to do with the shift in drama from the satirical to the sentimental. Specifically, I will look into the changing comedic portrayal of the aristocratic rake in his relationships with two types of characters on stage: the women he seduces, courts and sometimes marries; and the new merchant class emerging around him. These social interactions involving sexual and class politics provide, I think, a useful venue in which to ponder issues not only of the early modern state, but of satire and sentiment in the early modern drama.

Satirical to Sentimental

As should be evident from the preceding discussion of Rochester's verse, satire presents a reader with multiple difficulties of interpretation (see Connery and Combe 1995). The satiric comedy of the early Restoration period similarly supports a variety of readings; however, perhaps some common characteristics can be cited. Typically, such plays centre around young aristocratic men of fashion and wit as they course after sex and money – normally in that order, but if they can combine the hunt into a single target heroine of good estate, all the better. While marriage is always a concern of comedy, these young rakes seldom wind up well matched by the end of the play. A few just merrily play the field (Horner), while some promise to steer their courtship towards matrimony in the vague future (Dorimant, Longvil, Bruce), while some engage to marry young aristocratic women in what would seem to be less than judicious relationships (Willmore). Marriages of true minds are few in the satiric drama of the 1670s; rather, unions based on superficial attraction and, more to the point, a wife bringing to the marriage funds sufficient to shore up a husband's flagging estate are the order of the day. Nor does the married state guarantee that the groom will suspend his womanizing ways. In fact, it seems fairly certain that he won't. Moreover, these hero-rakes exude personal charm and social entitlement. All women are attracted to them; all rival gentlemen fall victim to their superior machinations; all fops merely accentuate their essential brilliance. These blades move with ease and discernment in the stylish world of the Town. They are the master players of the cynical libertine power game. Often a nice young couple also appears in these plays via subplots involving a young man and woman more conventionally in love. However, compared to the wit couple of the play (that is, the rake and his feisty heiress), these lovers, while wholesome, are also dull. If their winding up happily married is intended to serve as an example of true love compared to the problematic relationship of the main couple, the lesson is easily lost amid the dash and dazzle of satiric wit comedy. But maybe that's the point. Maybe, as with Rochester's satire, that's the trap of these plays: to lure an unsuspecting audience into the glitter of a vain and brutal society, a society that is in fact their own mirrored on stage. In admiring the knave of the first rate — that is, the hero-rake — viewers condemn themselves as fools. The prologues and epilogues to these comedies frequently call attention to the element of social critique in a play, many flatly telling the audience that it is their own follies that they see performed on stage. At this point we encounter once more the complexities of satire. If satire, as Swift noted, is a mirror in which people see everybody's face but their own, how do we know if these plays chastened or enchanted their audiences? How do we know if the figure of the rake was taken as a pattern for emulation or as an admonition against vice and hypocrisy? And again, those extremes certainly are not our only choices.

Scholars of Restoration drama have come to no set interpretation of these satiric comedies. A variety of different shades of rakes and forms of comedy have been proposed (e.g. Hume 1983: chs 5 and 7). Wycherley's *The Country Wife*, for example, has been read as everything from a celebration of sensualism to a denunciation of a degenerate society (see also Hume 1981). At least one critic sees that play fitting squarely into the traditionally accepted function of classical formal verse satire, namely, to reprimand vice (Horner as lusty and deceitful satyr) and to recommend virtue (embodied in the dull couple of Alithea and Harcourt; see Zimbardo 1965: 154–64). After the death of Charles II and the removal of his brother, James II, from the throne, the controversy that started to stir around these comedies commonly took the shape of this same virtue/vice debate. The moral reform movements of the 1690s began to target earlier Restoration comedy as immoral, and in particular as licentious. The most famous of these attacks on the stage is Jeremy Collier's *A Short View of the Immorality and Profaneness of the English Stage*, published in 1698. There Collier asserts that:

> The business of plays is to recommend virtue and discountenance vice; to show the
> uncertainty of human greatness, the sudden turns of fate, and the unhappy conclusions
> of violence and injustice; 'tis to expose the singularities of pride and fancy, to make folly

and falsehood contemptible, and to bring everything that is ill under infamy and neglect. (Cited in McMillin 1997: 493)

According to Collier and many other reformers, the stage productions of the era of Charles II did not fulfil this properly upright and instructional function of drama. His specific charges against these pieces are several: 'their smuttiness of expression; their swearing, profaneness, and lewd application of Scripture; their abuse of the clergy; their making their top characters libertines and giving them success in their debauchery'. While Collier takes all of these offences seriously and expounds upon each one at length, the final crime named above, that of making rakes the heros of such comedies, might upset him most. Summing up his case against this dramatic practice, he writes with the passion of irony:

> A fine gentleman is a fine whoring, swearing, smutty, atheistical man. These qualifications, it seems, complete the idea of honor. They are the top improvements of fortune and the distinguishing glories of birth and breeding! This is the stage-test for quality, and those that can't stand it ought to be disclaimed. The restraints of conscience and the pedantry of virtue are unbecoming a cavalier.... Here you have a man of breeding and figure that burlesques the Bible, swears, and talks smut to ladies, speaks ill of his friend behind his back, and betrays his interest. A fine gentleman that has neither honesty nor honor, conscience nor manners, good nature nor civil hypocrisy; fine only in the insignificancy of life, the abuse of religion, and the scandals of conversation. (ibid.: 500)

Thus vice, to Collier, was being held up as virtue in the form of these attractive stage rogues. Whatever the merits of Collier's particular arguments, their vocalization looks to be part of a wider cultural movement that helped shift comedy away from the satirical and towards the sentimental. Of the many playwrights and literary men who responded to Collier's attacks, few denied the indelicacy of the early Restoration stage and most protested that Collier was making the mistake of shooting the messenger. That is, comedians were merely plying their trade, according to the dictates of the genre, in putting on stage representations of the worst sort of people. Congreve's response to Collier that same year is typical. Citing Aristotle, he writes in *Amendments of Mr. Collier's False and Imperfect Citations*:

> But the vices most frequent, and which are the common practice of the looser sort of livers, are the subject matter of comedy. He tells us farther, that they must be exposed after a ridiculous manner. For men are to be laughed out of their vices in comedy; the business of comedy is to delight as well as to instruct; and as vicious people are made ashamed of their follies or faults by seeing them exposed in a ridiculous manner, so are good people at once both warned and diverted at their expense. (Cited in McMillin 1997: 515)

Well-drawn *portraits* of vice, then, are the stuff of comedy. Delightful and ridiculous at once, these depictions of a promiscuous upper-crust society do in fact carry out a moral purpose, that of correction and caution. Whatever the validity of this counter-assertion by Congreve – the debate is an old one about satire – a changed theatrical and social scene already had begun to move English comedy away from such satiric aims in comedy and towards those of what would become known as sentimental.

Along with societies dedicated to the reform of morals and manners emerging after 1689 under the distinctly more sober-minded monarchs of William and Mary, several other cultural developments warrant mention here. After the 'Glorious Revolution' that had removed James II, obviously a new model of polity was operating in England, one where the balance of power had tipped away from the monarch and towards the Parliament and the House of Commons. Rule by aristocracy was giving way to rule by plutocracy. This new wealthy class – a mixture of the old land-owning money and the new business-generated money – brought with it outlooks and tastes different from the courtly elite of the previous generation. For example, the absolutist political theories of Hobbes and Filmer were superseded by the mixed constitution or limited monarchy tenets of Locke, who saw government as a blend of monarchy, oligarchy and democracy dedicated to the acquisition and preservation of property. Similarly, there was an intellectual movement away from the sceptical and acrid materialist views of Hobbes that had so influenced the court culture (including Rochester) of Charles II. Coming into currency were the more utilitarian rational philosophies of Locke as well as the optimistic moral philosophies of Anthony Ashley Cooper, third Earl of Shaftesbury. In his writings, collected in 1711 as *Characteristicks of Men, Manners, Opinions, Times*, Shaftesbury's method, like that of Locke, is self-examination; however, whereas Locke explores the human mind, Shaftesbury makes 'a formal Descent on the Territorys of *the Heart*' (1.355). There he finds human nature to be naturally virtuous and benevolent. Shaftesbury claims that humans are endowed with a moral sense and natural faculty that, when refined by education and reflection, enable them to distinguish right from wrong intuitively – just as the eye immediately can distinguish beauty from ugliness or the ear harmony from discord. Virtue thus comes from following our natural affections, namely, those 'founded in Love, Complacency, Good-will, and in a Sympathy with the Kind or Species' (2.99). Shaftesbury's ideas represent a shift in attitude towards human nature during this period. While certainly not embraced by everyone (see, for example, the political-economic thought of Mandeville), this utopian and sentimental perspective had a profound impact on eighteenth-century English culture and literature. Animating Pope's *Essay on Man* is a combination of Locke's psychology and Shaftesbury's optimistic cosmology. In their journalistic prose, Steele and Addison popularize not only a middle-class ethics based in the principles of optimism (see, for example, their attack on wit in the *Spectator*, nos 58–63), but champion as well the merchant as a new kind of English hero whose distinguishing attributes are natural good sense, probity of mind and indefatigable industry (see their creation, Sir Andrew Freeport, in the *Spectator*, nos 2 and 549). Thus, as the make-up of the English ruling class was recast, altered as well was the temperament of its dominant ideology. Inevitably, this transition had an effect on theatre audiences and productions.

John Dennis complains in 1702 that the quality and the tastes of the spectators had seriously declined since the audiences of Charles II's playhouse. That former time 'was an age of Pleasure, and not of Business', and therefore audiences were dominated by gentlemen who had both the ease and the learning to appreciate the finer points of the drama. In contrast, the newer audiences were controlled by spectators 'who have had no education at all; and who were unheard of in the Reign of Charles the Second'. Fundamentally, Dennis means people who had risen 'from a state of obscurity' to a 'condition of distinction and plenty' – that is, the *nouveaux riches*. He declares: 'there are ten times more Gentlemen now in business, than there were in King Charles his Reign'. Pressed by their business affairs, these new gentlemen have neither the leisure nor the understanding to appreciate sophisticated art. They are 'too full of great and real events, to receive due impressions from the imaginary ones of the Theatre'. Rather than coming to the playhouse to see excellent drama, then, these people come 'merely... to unbend', that is, to relax (1.293–4). Although Dennis indulges in nostalgia about the high-minded quality of earlier Restoration audiences, by the turn of the century it seems clear that a distinctly less courtly and more middle- and upper-middle-class playgoer attended the theatre. As one theatre historian observes: 'The post-1688 audience is patently more bourgeois and Whiggish, as one would expect after the accession of William and Mary' (Hume 1976: 488; see also ibid.: ch. 9). It also seems clear that this new audience wanted to see performed not only the aristocratic productions of the last age, but dramas that reflected their different cultural experiences, tastes and sensibilities as well.

Under these changing cultural circumstances we see sentimentality on the increase in English drama. Since the 1680s, the pathetic tragedy of Otway in *Venice Preserv'd* and the so-called 'she-tragedies' of John Banks had been popular. Such tragic pathos came much into vogue with the 'domestic tragedies' of Nicholas Rowe. In *The Fair Penitent* (1703), *Jane Shore* (1714) and *Lady Jane Grey* (1715), Rowe combines emotionalism and edification as he tells a story of a lady in distress. Instead of focusing on the usual subject matter for tragedy, the fate of kings and empires, Rowe asserts in the Dedication and Prologue to *The Fair Penitent* that 'We ne'er can pity what we ne'er can share'; therefore, a humbler theme was selected for his play: 'A melancholy tale of private woe' wherein the audience will find 'sorrows like your own' (cited in Bevis 1988: 130). Here is the aristocratic form of tragedy being both feminized and made middle class. From Rowe's plays it would be an easy step to George Lillo's bourgeois tragedy, *The London Merchant* (1731). The elements of that popular hit were melodrama, the glorification of commerce, extended moralizing and a notorious villainess in the character of Millwood. In the genre of comedy similar trends are evident. Domesticated, in the sense of dealing with current middle-class concerns, is the former aristocratic, satiric and Aristotelian comedy of the 1670s. Important to reiterate here, however, is the fact that no sudden or striking changeover occurred from satirical to sentimental comedy. For a number of years, what one critic calls 'hard' as opposed to 'humane' comedy competed and coexisted on the English stage, and audiences and playwrights alike were attracted to both. While undeniably the tone of comedy started to change during the 1690s, 'to discuss "sentimental" drama as an independent entity in the period 1660–1710 is to give further currency to nonsense' (Hume 1976: 382, 143). Since the latter part of the seventeenth century, quite a critical debate has transpired over the literary history and dramatic qualities of satirical versus sentimental comedy (for a brief overview of these quarrels, see Bevis 1988: 98–9). Perhaps the most basic difference between the two dramatic dispositions, though, is this. Whereas satirical comedy, motivated by fundamental beliefs in the corrupt nature of humanity, reveals vice, sentimental comedy, viewing people motivated to ethical behaviour by innate feelings of sympathy towards one another, presents instead behaviour worthy of emulation. As Collier's attacks on the immorality of the former comedy seem to signal, audiences of and after the 1690s were ready to see more of what they believed to be themselves on stage.

The very concept of 'sentimental' is a vexed one, and has been from the start. Its base word, sentiment, comes from the Latin *sentire*, to feel. Dictionary definitions of 'sentimental', therefore, feature notions of being extravagantly emotional, susceptible to tender, romantic or nostalgic feelings, and arising from feeling rather than reason. Whether these traits are good or bad, however, depends upon whom one reads. During the eighteenth century, writers and critics lined up on either side of the debate. At the same time, the term became so in vogue as to practically lose its meaning. In 1749, Lady Bradshaigh writes to Samuel Richardson asking him to define 'sentimental' for her.

> In letters and in common conversation, I have asked several who make use of it, and have generally received for an answer, it is – it is – *sentimental*. Everything clever and agreeable is comprehended in that word; but am convinced a wrong interpretation is given, because it is impossible everything clever and agreeable can be so common as this word. I am astonished to hear such a one is a *sentimental* man; we were a *sentimental* party; I have been taking a *sentimental* walk. (Cited in Sherbo 1957: 2)

Twentieth-century literary critics were in the same quandary over definition (for an account of both contemporary and more recent views on the sentimental, see Sherbo 1957: ch. 1). In the early twentieth century, Ernest Bernbaum offered a solid definition of the 'drama of sensibility' found in early modern sentimental comedy and domestic tragedy. In such productions, it is implied

> that human nature, when not, as in some cases, already perfect, was perfectible by an appeal to the emotions. It refused to assume that virtuous persons must be sought in a romantic realm apart from the everyday world. It wished to show that beings who were good at heart were found in the ordinary walks of life. It so represented their conduct as to arouse admiration for their virtues and pity for their sufferings. In sentimental comedy, it showed them contending against distresses but finally rewarded by morally deserved happiness. In domestic tragedy, it showed them overwhelmed by catastrophes for which they were morally not responsible. A new ethics had arisen, and new forms of literature were thereby demanded. (1915: 10)

A decade later, Joseph Wood Krutch conducted a thorough study of the historical origins and the salient features of sentimental comedy. He offers the following summary of a typical plot for this type of play: a virtuous person meets with a vicious one; our sympathies side, of course, with virtue; through a series of circumstances the vicious person is shown the error of (usually) his ways and reforms; the audience shares in the joy of the triumph of virtue. Krutch concludes that the point of such drama is 'to present conventional virtue in an attractive light, to convey the impression that uprightness is rewarded, that repentance brings happiness and reconciliation, and that the ideal gentleman is not a selfish rake but a kind and even soft-hearted philanthropist' (1924: 194).

By 1722 and the production of Steele's *The Conscious Lovers* – the very model of the sentimental comedy – such a characterization appears justified. In the preface to his play, Steele asserts that 'anything that has its foundation in happiness and success must be allowed to be the object of comedy, and sure it must be an improvement of it to introduce a joy too exquisite for laughter, that can have no spring but in delight' (cited in McMillin 1997: 323). In the prologue, written by Leonard Welsted, the new theatregoing bourgeoisie is entreated, via flattery and an appeal to national pride, to help establish a new brand of wholesome comedy on the English stage.

> Your aid, most humbly sought, then, Britons, lend,
> And lib'ral mirth like lib'ral men defend:
> No more let ribaldry, with license writ,
> Usurp the name of eloquence or wit;
> No more let lawless farce uncensured go,
> The lewd dull gleanings of a Smithfield show.
> 'Tis yours with breeding to refine the age,
> To chasten wit, and moralize the stage.
> Ye modest, wise and good, ye fair, ye brave,
> Tonight the champion of your virtues save,
> Redeem from long contempt the comic name,
> And judge politely for your country's fame.
>
> (Cited in ibid.: 324–5)

Before 1710, however, such a clear vision of sentimental comedy is unavailable. Three plays often cited as the first of this kind, Cibber's *Love's Last Shift* (1696) and *The Careless Husband* (1704) as well as Steele's *The Lying Lover* (1703), are all problematic productions judged by Krutch's definitions. Both of Cibber's plays hinge on the convention of the rake reformed by the good and long-suffering wife. In *Love's Last Shift*, though, the rake-husband Loveless is quite entertainingly rakish in the old 1670s mode right up until the very end of the play when he undergoes a histrionic rebirth as the devoted husband; moreover, his modest wife, Amanda, behaves rather too immodestly in her scheme to reform him. In *The Careless Husband*, Cibber presents us with the familiar sex-play of aristocratic society just on the perimeter of the court circle. After four acts where people of birth and education engage in witty, titillating intrigue, Lady Easy, feeling the secret pride of superior innocence, forgives her philandering husband, Sir Charles, for dallying with their maid, and another curtain falls on a flimsy tableau of conjugal accord. Finally, while Steele's early reform comedy certainly strives to give its audience proper entertainment for a Christian commonwealth, the duel between Young Bookwit and Lovemore and the resulting crisis of a supposed death apparently was too contrived, and the characters' motivations too obscure, to please spectators. Unlike the overwhelming success of *The Conscious Lovers* twenty years later, *The Lying Lover* suffered a short run.

At mid-twentieth century, Arthur Sherbo accepts the views of Bernbaum and Krutch as working definitions for sentimental drama, with some few additions, such as an improbability of plot, the presence of a moral element, an emphasis on pity, and characters drawn from domestic life – whether of the middle class or the nobility (1957: 11–14). When dissecting plays of the period to decide which are sentimental and which are not, however, Sherbo discovers his task to be impossible.

> The question of what constitutes sentimental drama is complex, and attempts at rigid definition are fruitless. . . . There are so many plays in which a definite decision – this is a sentimental play, or this is not a sentimental play – would involve one in endless argument. . . . No one criterion, taken alone, can be complete justification for deciding whether a play is sentimental. (1957: 140)

Krutch similarly had complained that a sentimental view of life 'was the result of many causes interacting upon one other, and like any important intellectual movement it was too complex ever to be fully explained' (1924: 256). In the 1970s and 1980s, Robert D. Hume applauds Sherbo's caution and asserts that no clear-cut genre called 'sentimental comedy' can be isolated. He maintains that this type of drama is 'a complicated phenomenon comprising some fairly disparate sorts of plays', and that sentimental traits appear in varying degrees: 'Typically, these traits amount to eschewal of humor and the bawdy, repetition and prolongation of certain kinds of scenes, and an emphasis which brings sensibility to the fore' (1983: 354, 321). Most recently, Frank H. Ellis concludes that something called sentimental comedy indeed exists. He is at a loss, however, really to define it.

> Sentimental comedy is not *sui generis*; there are many examples of it. Nor is it a genre, like satire or romance; it exists on a different level of generalization. It is 'a certain determinate kind' of comedy, a subgenre of comedy, like comedy of manners or romantic comedy. (1991: 118)

According to Ellis, this amorphous subgenre can only be identified ad hoc via the sentimental reactions it arouses. He lists a great many of these. In the literature of the eighteenth century, subjects treated sentimentally include: the universe; man; woman; parents; children; the lower orders – servants, peasants, foreigners, the poor; animals, vegetables and minerals; the emotions; evil, crime and death; money; the past and the elsewhere (Ellis 1991: 10–11). Secondary but non-essential characteristics of the subgenre might include: a sprinkling of tender melancholy conversation; reckless, self-sacrificing virtue; undeserved distress; overt moralizing (ibid.: 19–20). Ellis bases his investigation into the phenomenon of sentimentality, then, on the psychology of sentimentality. This sensation he explains as the passive observation of seemingly senseless acts of irrational generosity, devotion and love. What is needed, contends Ellis, is not another account of the literary history or the formal attributes of sentimental comedy, but a simple analysis of the cognitive and emotional mechanism of sentimentality (1991: 3–4). Whether the sentimental response in us triggers an unrealistic attitude towards the world, and thus should be treated as a disorder, or if pity towards anything from rocks to our fellow humans brings with it humanitarian impulses, and thus might represent, as Ellis suggests, 'man's last chance on this ravaged planet' (1991: 123), is a question that remains unresolved. In fact, in most regards the deliberation over sentimental comedy remains unsettled. The shift from satirical to sentimental impulses in early modern English drama stands as a rich, messy and productive area of cultural inquiry.

Rakes, Wives and Merchants

As suggested earlier, observation of the changing depiction of three comedic types from the period 1660 to 1710 enmeshes us in issues of stage satire and sentiment as well as the early modern transition from an aristocratic to a bourgeois hegemony. Visible in this comedy is a decline in the personal allure and the social power of the patrician rake coupled with a synchronous rise in the celebration of the merchant. Also signalling new cultural trends is a detectable shift in focus, or at least a significant sharing of the focus, from the young male hero of comedy to his object of attention, the young woman he woos and weds. Comedic heroines begin to enjoy more agency with regard to whom and how they marry. By the turn of the century, comedies regularly deal as well with the state of marriage rather than the process of courtship (for example, in the plays of Cibber and Farquhar). Problems of men and women staying together replace the frolic of men and women getting together. Such domestic concerns inherently highlight the circumstances and interests of women at a time when they were gaining, if not yet true empowerment, measurably more voice. This modified interaction among rakes, wives and merchants suggests, I believe, that during a period of modernization in governmental structure and national ideology, innovation took place as well with regard to who wrote plays and, more important, for whom they were written. As the seventeenth century came to a close, an established English taste for well-bred, sexually charged stage satire began, perforce, to share the boards with an emerging taste for bourgeois, edifying stage sentiment. Space allows for only two comedies briefly to be considered in this light, Sir George Etherege's *The Man of Mode* (1676) and Mary Pix's *The Beau Defeated* (1700).

In Etherege's comedy, Dorimant is the high-born arch-rake who, in most respects, represents Collier's worst nightmare regarding this attractive and powerful character type. Only love (as opposed to lust) seems to threaten the armour of Dorimant's fashion and privilege; in an aside he confesses the problem with his tender feelings for Harriet: 'I love her and dare not let her know it; I fear sh'as an ascendant o'er me and may revenge the wrongs I have done her sex' (4.1.172–4). Dorimant is quite successful at thwarting this threat, however, as he simultaneously pursues Harriet as a comely and witty young woman whose fortune, once they are married, will mend his own ruined estate, casts off his current mistress, Mrs Loveit, whom he has tired of, and seduces yet another young woman, Bellinda, in the process. Moreover, as the comedic heroine, Harriet is strangely acquiescent in the rake's plots. Although a young woman of wit, social acumen and rebellious tendencies who has no illusions regarding Dorimant's dissolute reputation in the Town, she is smitten with him and willingly participates in his schemes of courtship. While cautious of Dorimant and, unlike the other women of the play, adamant about protecting her virginity from him, Harriet nonetheless succumbs to what might be considered her comedic flaw: rake love. Upon hearing Dorimant proclaim that he will take even the drastic step of leaving London to travel into the boorish countryside to pursue his love for her, Harriet coyly accedes.

> *Harriet*: When I hear you talk thus in Hampshire I shall begin to think there may be some little truth enlarged upon.
> *Dorimant*: Is this all? Will you not promise me – ?
> *Harriet*: I hate to promise; what we do then is expected from us and wants much of the welcome it finds when it surprises.
> *Dorimant*: May I not hope?
> *Harriet*: That depends on you and not on me, and 'tis to no purpose to forbid it.
>   (5.2.179–88)

Though the course of true debauchery never runs smooth, Dorimant is well on his way to wedding his good estate.

Yet even in this satiric, rake-centric comedy of the 1670s, interesting hints of trends to come are visible. In the nearly tragic character of Mrs Loveit, we see a woman with genuine insight into the predatory nature of the rake. She aptly describes Dorimant as 'Exquisite fiend' (5.1.285), sees through his schemes and manoeuvres, 'I know you' (2.2.288), but is nonetheless helpless in her fatal love for him: 'I know he is a devil, but he has something of the angel yet undefaced in him, which makes him so charming and agreeable that I must love him, be he never so wicked' (2.2.18–21). Loveit's insights and threats of revenge against the rake, though, do her no good. In the end both Dorimant and Harriet humiliate her, and she withdraws, powerless, from the stage. To recall the passage from Rochester's *Satire Against Mankind*, Loveit has been the honest fool who, among 'known cheats', has made the mistake of playing 'upon the square'. As a result, her 'weak truth' – that is, her recognition of Dorimant for the rogue he really is – could not save her or her reputation. The knaves have all agreed to call her knave. Regardless of her undoing, however, in Loveit we catch a glimpse of a woman with authentic discernment and at least impulses of autonomy. Indications of the conflict brewing between rakes and merchants occur in Etherege's comedy as well, albeit in similarly tenuous form. In the opening scene showing us Dorimant in his rooms dressing for the day (pursuing his *régime de vivre*), two business people appear, an Orange-Woman (fruit-seller) and a Shoemaker. Dorimant owes them both money. As the aristocrat banters with these small-time entrepreneurs, some interesting notions arise. For one thing, the Orange-Woman, just like Mrs Loveit, instantly sees through Dorimant as he targets Harriet for his next conquest. Thus the antics of rakes do not seem particularly to fool the lower classes. She and Dorimant also engage in a bartering session (1.1.81–192) wherein their respective markets – his the marriage market and hers the mercantile trade – collide: he won't pay her until she tells him everything she knows about this 'heiress, vastly rich' newly come to London. Oddly, then, their two situations of economic need are not so different. In their light yet uneasy exchange, though, Dorimant clearly still holds the upper hand as the blue-blood. The Shoemaker also must work to please Dorimant in order to collect his fees, yet in their raillery the tradesman scores some deft hits of satire against the aristocrat. Being advised to mend his morals, the Shoemaker retorts: "Zbud, I think you men of quality will grow as unreasonable as the women. You would ingross the sins of the nation; poor folks can no sooner be wicked but th'are railed at by their betters'. At this impertinent suggestion that the upper classes monopolize sin, Dorimant rejoins, 'Sirrah, I'll have you stand i'the pillory for this libel!' (1.1.300–6). Next told to get himself home and treat his wife better, the Shoemaker comments wryly on the genteel married state: "Zbud, there's never a man i'the town lives more like a gentleman with his wife than I do. I never mind her motions, she never inquires into mine; we speak to one another civilly, hate one another heartily, and because 'tis vulgar to lie and soak together, we have each of us our several settle-bed' (1.1.336–42). In other words, his working-class marriage is every bit as estranged, alcoholic and loveless as those of the husbands and wives of the *beau monde*. While of course mockery of the lower orders is available in these two depictions of tradespeople, behind some double masks of satire Etherege certainly smirks at his cosmopolitan audience, too.

Two decades later in Pix's *The Beau Defeated* we can find a very different social interaction portrayed among rakes, wives and merchants. First, the nature of the comedic hero has changed radically. A rake – the Beau of the title – appears in the play, but, as the title alerts us, he is defeated; his subterfuges of lust and acquisition are all foiled. Sir John Roverhead looks and speaks and acts the part of Dorimant, but by the end of the play not only do his wit and charm bring him nothing, he is exposed as a fraud as well. He is in fact a servant of the Roverhead family come to London to hoodwink his way into wealth and position. His accomplice, Lady La Basset, is a cony-catcher as well, the cast mistress of one Sir Francis Basset. In this pair of *faux beau monde* perhaps we descry an early likeness of the criminalized underclass of the modern state. Replacing the rake as the hero of the comedy is Younger Clerimont, a second son unfairly dispossessed of his inheritance. Far from being a libertine, Clerimont is a man of conviction and feeling, in every way fitting the description of an ideal lover as spoken by the comedic heroine of the play, Lady Landsworth:

> He should be genteel, yet not a beau; witty, yet no debauchee; susceptible of love, yet abhorring lewd women; learned, poetical, musical, without one dram of vanity; in fine, very meritorious, yet very modest; generous to the last degree, and master of no estate; mightily in love with me, and not so much as know I am worth the clothes I wear. (169 [1.1])

Clerimont, then, is the new sentimental man. Once united by kind Fate and true hearts, he and Lady Landsworth form the new sentimental couple. Declares Clerimont: 'To look on thee secures a heart like mine from roving: to hear thee talk, will fix me for ever in the chains of love. But, oh! To have thee all; there words cannot aim, there breath is lost in ecstasy' (229 [5.2]). A second key difference in Pix's drama is that her comedic heroine is not hopelessly in love with a lout, as were Harriet and Loveit, but rather actively pursues, in the form of testing his character, a man of her choosing. At one point in the play Lady Landsworth is deceived into believing Clerimont to be, in fact, a rake. She instantly rejects him: 'Yonder he stands, methinks I hate him, now he has lost that modest sweetness which caught my soul, his looks are wild and lewd, and all I ever feared in men appears in that deceitful face: I would I were away' (215 [4.3]). Not only is this woman young, pretty, wealthy and witty, then, she is also level-headed, self-reliant, experienced and self-fashioning. These qualities are made all the more tangible in the circumstance of her being a widow. In English society at this time, widows were women of some real autonomy within the patriarchal system.

Finally, strikingly different as well in Pix's comedy is her depiction of the merchant. In the character of Mr Rich, a powerful City capitalist, we see the ascendancy of the modern businessman on stage. In the sense that all of his stratagems come to fruition, Mr Rich, more so than Clerimont, replaces Dorimant as the alpha male of the drama. He defeats the pseudo-rake, Sir John, in a knavish attempt to elope with his daughter, Lucinda.

> *Mr Rich*: Thou trifling coxcomb, all wig and no brains, begone this very instant, or I'll lead thee thus by the nose, I'll lead thee to a she-fop [Lady La Basset] of thy acquaintance, coxcomb, I will, therefore make use of thy heels.
> *Sir John*: Egad, this is very uncivil.
> *Mr Rich*: I meant it so.
> *Sir John*: I'll lampoon thee, till your friends shall fly ye, your neighbours despise ye, and the world laugh at ye.
> *Mr Rich*: I believe your wit's as dangerous as your courage, begone, insect.
> *Lucinda*: Pretend to be a Lord, and baulk a young woman's expectations!
> *Betty* [a busybody servant]: Ah poor Sir John, ha, ha.

Sir John: Has she been a spectator, I shall be jeered to death. I will study a revenge shall make you tremble, I will, thou barbarous Cit.
Mr Rich: Go set your periwig to rights fop, ha, ha.
Sir John: Curses, curses, ah I shall choke.

(224 [5.2])

In this exchange the comedic tables have been turned for these two social groups: no longer is the City merchant the standard butt of aristocratic jokes; instead, the man of mode of the fashionable Town is rendered a ridiculous and insignificant dandy. Mr Rich also brings under control the women in his life. He re-secures oversight of his daughter's fortune from his flighty sister-in-law, Mrs Rich. He also brings to heel that social-climbing City widow by engineering a deception that safely remarries her – and her fortune – to Elder Clerimont, a booby but earnest country squire. The trickery revealed to her, the feisty Mrs Rich exclaims: 'Oh, my cursed stars! First a citizen's, and then a country squire's wife. Ah! I shall never endure him, that's certain' (231 [5.2]). Pix ends her play with Mr Rich lecturing his daughter and sister-in-law about the character of 'the truly great' of their nation. They are not the *beau monde*, as both women had foolishly aspired to via the guile of Sir John. Instead:

> The glory of the world our British nobles are,
> The ladies too renowned, and chaste and fair:
> But to our City, Augusta's sons,
> The conquering wealth of both the Indias runs;
> Though less in name, of greater power by far,
> Honours alone, but empty 'scutcheons are;
> Mixed with their coin, the title sweetly sounds,
> No such allay as twenty thousand pounds.
>
> (234 [5.2])

The lesson of the play is clear. The libertine aristocracy that was the glory of Charles II's reign is mere swindle. England's future lies in the sober-minded combination of the landed nobility with, pivotally, the vast new wealth of the merchant class. Therein is the formula for empire. And from that alliance our modern world, at its core more sentimental than satirical, commenced.

REFERENCES AND FURTHER READING

Bernbaum, E. (1915). *The Drama of Sensibility*. Boston: Ginn.
Bevis, R. W. (1988). *English Drama: Restoration and Eighteenth Century, 1660–1789*. London and New York: Longman.
Birdsall, V. O. (1970). *Wild Civility: The English Comic Spirit on the Restoration Stage*. Bloomington: Indiana University Press.
Brown, L. (1981). *English Dramatic Form, 1660–1760*. New Haven, CT: Yale University Press.

Combe, K. (1998). *A Martyr for Sin: Rochester's Critique of Polity, Sexuality, and Society*. Newark: University of Delaware Press; London: Associated University Presses.

Connery, B. A. and Combe, K. (1995). 'Theorizing Satire: A Retrospective and Introduction', in B. A. Connery and K. Combe (eds), *Theorizing Satire: Essays in Literary Criticism*. New York: St Martin's Press, 1–15.

Cooper, Anthony Ashley, third Earl of Shaftesbury. (1711; 1900). *Characteristics of Men, Manners, Opinions, Times*, ed. J. M. Robertson. 2 vols. London: Grant Richards.

Dennis, J. (1943). *Critical Works*, ed. E. N. Hooker. 2 vols. Baltimore: Johns Hopkins University Press.

Ellis, F. H. (1991). *Sentimental Comedy: Theory and Practice*. Cambridge: Cambridge University Press.

Etherege, G. (1676; 1969). *The Man of Mode; or, Sir Fopling Flutter*, in G. H. Nettleton and A. E. Case (eds), *British Dramatists from Dryden to Sheridan*, revised by G. W. Stone, Jr. Carbondale and Edwardsville: Southern Illinois University Press.

Gill, P. (1994). *Interpreting Ladies: Women, Wit, and Morality in the Restoration Comedy of Manners*. Athens: University of Georgia Press.

Hume, R. D. (1976). *The Development of English Drama in the Late Seventeenth Century*. Oxford: Clarendon Press.

Hume, R. D. (1981). 'William Wycherley: Text, Life, Interpretation', *Modern Philology* 78, 399–415.

Hume, R. D. (1983). *The Rakish Stage: Studies in English Drama, 1660–1800*. Carbondale and Edwardsville: Southern Illinois University Press.

Hutton, R. (1989). *Charles II: King of England, Scotland, and Ireland*. Oxford: Clarendon Press.

Krutch, J. W. (1924). *Comedy and Conscience after the Restoration*. New York: Columbia University Press.

Loftis, J. (1963). *The Politics of Drama in Augustan England*. Oxford: Clarendon Press.

McDonald, C. O. (1964). 'Restoration Comedy as Drama of Satire: An Investigation into Seventeenth-century Aesthetics', *Studies in Philology* 61, 522–44.

McMillin, S. (ed.). (1997). *Restoration and Eighteenth-century Comedy*. 2nd ed. New York and London: W. W. Norton.

Pearson, J. (1988). *The Prostituted Muse: Images of Women and Women Dramatists, 1642–1737*. New York: St Martin's Press.

Pix, M. (1700; 1991). *The Beau Defeated; or, The Lucky Younger Brother*, in P. Lyons and F. Morgan (eds), *Female Playwrights of the Restoration: Five Comedies*. London and Rutland, VT: J. M. Dent and Charles E. Tuttle.

Sherbo, A. (1957). *English Sentimental Drama*. East Lansing: Michigan State University Press.

Traugott, J. (1986). 'Heart and Mask and Genre in Sentimental Comedy', *Eighteenth-century Life* 10, no. 3, 122–44.

Wilmot, John, second Earl of Rochester (1993). *Rochester: Complete Poems and Plays*, ed. P. Lyons. London and Rutland, VT: J. M. Dent and Charles E. Tuttle.

Zimbardo, R. (1965). *Wycherley's Drama: A Link in the Development of English Satire*. New Haven, CT: Yale University Press.

Part III
Dramatists

18

William Davenant and John Dryden

Richard Kroll

In the middle of the fourth act of Part 2 of William Davenant's *The Siege of Rhodes*, performed in 1656, and universally considered the first English opera, the audience is treated to the spectacle of 'Roxalana's Rich Pavilion, wherein is discern'd at a distance, *Ianthe* sleeping on a Couch; *Roxalana* at one end of it, and *Haly* at the other; Guards of Eunuchs are discover'd at the wings of the Pavilion; *Roxalana* having a *Turkish* Embroidered Handkerchief in her left hand, and a naked Ponyard in her right' (Davenant, *Works* 2: 51). It is my central argument in this chapter that, at this moment of English theatrical history – which established the conventions of the proscenium, perspective scenery and actresses that were to last into the twentieth century – Davenant creates a charged representational scene which was, in significant ways, to determine the course of Dryden's career as a playwright. Davenant's concoction of exoticism, spectacular display, erotic danger and allusions to Shakespeare, whose illegitimate son he was sometimes reputed to be, moves, I believe, in the explicitly political direction which had already formed the basis of his critical exchange with Hobbes (discussed further below). *The Siege of Rhodes* is centrally about an issue that occupied Davenant from the mid-1620s onwards, namely, the relationship between the art of virtuous rule and the rhetorical devices that make it viable in an epistemologically and morally compromised world. One of Davenant's many bequests to Dryden was the assumption that the theatre provided a particularly sensitive climate within which to discuss the question, since drama – more than any other genre, and like the polity imagined in Hobbes's *Leviathan* – forges a compromise among many competing points of view, a compromise that, in Hobbes, becomes the institution of the state, but in drama can range from the conventions of stage setting itself, to the second-order languages that characters use about their circumstances, to the resolutions demanded by the five-act structure of English plays.

At the moment we catch Roxalana, the Ottoman queen, wielding a poignard, she is indeed tempted to kill the sleeping Ianthe, because Ianthe, representing at this point the beseiged Rhodians, is both, in an absolute sense, virtuous and beautiful. The entire plot of the play or opera is arranged around a chiasmus, whereby the virtuous ruler is Roxalana's husband, Solyman the Magnificent, while the virtuous woman is the Christian Ianthe, married to the Rhodian Alphonso. Because they each embody the self-possession of true virtue, in Part 1, Solyman frees Ianthe to return to Rhodes, and in Part 2, Ianthe risks returning to his camp to ask him to expand his private benefits to her into the general and public benefit of lifting the siege altogether. Thus, as in *The Conquest of Granada* (1671), which owes so much to it, *The Siege of Rhodes* must be read entire, for the personal agreements prompting the action in Part 1 become infinitely more complicated in Part 2, now that the issue is the fate of states, not individuals. These complications stem in large part from Roxalana and Alphonso, for just as Roxalana cannot credit her husband with a disinterested response to Ianthe's appeal, so Alphonso cannot credit Solyman with anything but the basest of motives. The opera represents a highly charged balance between ontology (Solyman and Ianthe are virtuous) and epistemology (circumstances persuade Roxalana and Alphonso that Solyman must have compromised Ianthe); and an equally charged balance between an interest conceived of as the public good (Solyman and Ianthe) and passion (Roxalana and Alphonso). Evidently, rather than our having to wait until the eighteenth century to develop a political economy of mutually balanced interests – as some historians have argued – the seventeenth century had already developed the distinction between interest and passion, and was capable, at a theoretical level, of squaring the one off against the other. It is in large part the purpose of *The Siege of Rhodes* to do precisely that, in order to derive the possibility of what Davenant insistently calls 'civil' order from the turgid passions that define human responses to history. Because Ianthe is, for Davenant's opera, the image *par excellence* of virtue – this is an actual woman on stage whose beauty strikes all onlookers – Davenant launches Roxalana into a therapeutic response to her own desire to kill her. Crucially for my argument, this therapeutic response occurs in terms which comment on the very stage conditions set before us, so that Roxalana literally dramatizes her responses to Ianthe. In the process, Davenant makes us aware of how all knowledge involves the kinds of perspectives that only the stage can, in materializing them, render uniquely three-dimensional. And although to speak of the moral action of the scene as therapeutic might invoke the biologism of Aristotle's *Poetics*, with its famous emphasis on the medical effects of plot, Davenant invokes the possibility of pity as a motive for action only in order to dismiss it in favour of an ocular, imagistic and, in that sense, aesthetic or locally spectacular reading of how stage events affect us. It is specifically the image of Ianthe's beauty that creates the irritant which all characters must explain, so that the scene opens with a kind of syllogism:

> *Roxalana*: Thou dost from beauty, *Solyman*
> And as much refrain as Nature can;
> Who making Beauty, meant it should be lov'd.
> (*Works* 2: 51)

Consequently, the inadequacy of pity as a motive is marked by Haly's rather feeble appeal, 'Oh let pity stay your hand!' (ibid.). Roxalana's intensity swamps such objections in favour of a melodramatic mode by which she comments on the physiology that, at least by the conventions of seventeenth-century dramaturgy, governs or expresses emotion on stage. It is as if by pointing inwards at her own body as a vehicle of dramatic action, she can then, by allusion as it were, project and choreograph the structure of emotions which gather around the idea of her imagined victim:

> *Sultan*, I will not weep, because my tears
> Cannot suffice to quench thy Loves false flame;
> Nor will I to a paleness bleed,
> To show my Loves true fears,
> Because I rather need
> More blood to help to blush away thy shame.
>
> (Ibid.)

And when Haly reminds her of the difference between Solyman's possible intentions and his overt acts – between *mens rea* and *actus reus* – Roxalana asks him to recount the effects of her incriminating letter to Alphonso, whose responses Haly records by reference to another kind of theatre, namely, the drama of the passions:

> With silence first he did his sorrows bear;
> Then anger raised him, till he fell with fear;
> At last, said she was now past Counsel grown;
> Or else could take no better than her own.
>
> (Ibid.: 52).

Because it externalizes knowledge, as Roxalana remarks, this moment thrusts judgement into the realm of the merely inferential ('His thoughts a double Vizard wear, / And only lead me to suspence' [ibid.]). When Ianthe wakes, Roxalana experiences a revolution from envy to shame, and it is now Ianthe's turn to theatricalize the event, prompting an exchange which also invokes the analogy between moral and stage 'distance':

> *Ianthe*: What dangers should I fear?
>   Her brow shows smooth and clear;
>   Yet so much greatness cannot want disguise.
>   The Great live all within;
>   And are but seldom seen
>   Looking abroad through the Casements of their Eyes.
> *Roxalana*: Have courage fair *Sicilian*, and come near. –
> *Ianthe*: My distance shews my Duty more than Fear.
>
> (Ibid.)

Perhaps paradoxically, the relative poverty of Davenant's poetic reveals a great strength of the dramatic tradition with which Dryden came to associate him, as well as his crucial role in mediating the connections between early and late Stuart theatre. For virtually at every turn, *The Siege of Rhodes* reveals the impress of Davenant's own schooling in the masque tradition – his *Salmacida Spolia* was the last masque produced before the closing of the theatres in 1642 – and, more importantly, to the playwrights who both competed with and succeeded Shakespeare and Jonson. Rhetorically, this is visible in two aspects of speech in the opera: the self-consciousness about its own conditions of staging, extending, on the one hand, to the characters' inclination to spatialize, by summoning an architectural metaphor, their relation to their own bodies as vehicles of dramatic meaning; and, on the other, to reminding the audience of its assent to all the other artifices of production, such as their relative distance and proximity on stage. What, furthermore, appears to us as a kind of poetic failure echoes a common criticism of revenge tragedy and of early Stuart tragicomedy, namely, that they indulge too often in a kind of verbal and stylistic excess. If Shakespeare, we are told, is nature's child, then Beaumont and Fletcher are entirely too artificial. If Shakespeare represents the power of absorption into the dramatic moment, his rivals invoke the psychologically alienating force of theatricality itself. And if Jonson's character types represent a kind of ideal coherence – in the precise sense – then his successors' characters explode their own apparent verbal integrity by stumbling too frequently into hyperbole and catachresis. But such criticisms ignore the fact that, in extending this alternative tradition of theatrical representation, and providing it with actual and material vehicles of expression, Davenant enriched the capacity for this drama to become what both he and Dryden intended it to be, namely, a political forum for discussing the conditions and limitations of power.

This political point can be made by analogy to Davenant's role in the development of changeable scenery on the English stage. His career followed hard on the heels of what Richard Southern dubs 'the great scenic controversy', in which Inigo Jones and Ben Jonson almost came to blows over the relative merits of staging and text in the masques they mounted. Southern's commentary is telling, because the role of scenery at this stage was anti-illusionistic (Southern 1952: 96), and Davenant's revolutionary adaptation of scenery in *The Siege of Rhodes* remained true to the Jonesian preference for exposing its mechanics to the audience. Part of the thrill of production was, in an indoor theatre whose candle-lighting blended the world of the audience with that of the stage, to witness often elaborate changes of scene during the course of a play, a feature of the opera underscored in its original title: 'THE SIEGE OF RHODES *Made a Representation by the Art of Prospective in Scenes*'. Commenting that 'such an attitude had probably existed in no English playwright before' (1952: 111), Southern expands: 'This particular attitude to scenery as a decorative adjunct to a theatrical presentation or as an accompaniment to the progress of the mood of the play, and not as a representation of the background of the characters, is of importance in assessing the original estimate in which it was held' (1952: 112). And just as, under these conditions, the *mise-en-scène* becomes an object of speculation in its own right, so the subject of the opera dissects and examines the artifice of political institutions.

I therefore disagree with some implications of Martin Butler's excellent book on the drama of the 1630s, *Theatre and Crisis* (1984). Butler makes a convincing case that the theatres closed in 1642 because the criticisms of Charles I issuing from the commercial theatre, epitomized by figures like Richard Brome, created ambivalence at court. But he implies that this tradition of dissent was permanently muffled not only by the subsequent eighteen years of war and Interregnum, but by the reinvention of the theatres after 1660. In this argument, in obtaining theatrical monopolies that stifled opposition and commercial competition after the Restoration, and in playing to a largely coterie audience, Davenant and Killigrew continued the essentially propagandistic work of Cavalier drama. However, Butler relies in part on an outmoded attitude to Restoration audiences, since scholars have long demonstrated that those audiences were socially diverse, even though Charles II patronized the theatre; and he ignores the extent to which royalist drama in the hands of Davenant and his successor as poet laureate, Dryden, served the purposes of literature rather than propaganda, where the motive is hortatory rather than epideictic. Whereas Butler tends to reveal the political differences between Brome and Davenant by providing thematic readings of their plays, I would argue that the extreme epistemological and representational self-consciousness equally of Davenant and Dryden serves as a deliberation on the means by which power achieves its effects, on the view that those means are always artificial, and its effects not uniformly benign. Thematic reading often presupposes a kind of narrative coherence and even linguistic transparency whose ends the second-order language I have analysed above seeks to deflect or frustrate, with the purpose of emphasizing how things are put as much as what is said. This tendency to arrest narrative movement is in part what makes it so difficult to read Davenant's heroic poem, *Gondibert* (1651), and can help explain our modern difficulties with the episodic and emblematic tendencies of heroic drama, especially *The Conquest of Granada*. At the same time, however, the activity of self-scrutiny in turn imports its own form of political allegory, not least because under that aegis, literature deliberates on its own exemplary force. It is no accident that Davenant and Hobbes were personal friends, and that there is a recognizably Hobbesian (rather than Hobbist) account of power in Dryden because for them both good rule depends on good counsel.

Dryden himself, I think, makes many of these points when he admits his debts to Davenant in *The Conquest of Granada*. If we treat both parts of the play as a single text, then it appears sandwiched between two of Dryden's more sustained critical pronouncements, namely, the Preface, comprising 'Of Heroic Plays. An Essay', and the Epilogue, namely, 'Defence of the Epilogue. Or, An Essay on the Dramatic Poetry of the Last Age'. Given Davenant's parlous position in English literary history, and given that Dryden owed his post as laureate to the fact that Davenant had died in 1668, slightly over two years before the first performance, it may be tempting to minimize Dryden's appreciation of his predecessor as merely conventional. But part of the thrust of this essay is to argue that Dryden's construction of his role in literary history, a kind of knowledge he arguably did most to invent, must be taken seriously, and in the terms which he presents. Taken together, and considered along with Dryden's Dedication to the Duke of York, who appears as an heroic figure, these two essays represent a profound meditation on Dryden's relation to Davenant, and on their relations to their predecessors, namely, Shakespeare, Jonson and, most critically, Fletcher. Because our literary history and tastes are so infused with Wordsworthian and Coleridgean preconceptions, modern critics have instinctively ignored Dryden's almost obsessive relation to this particular triumvirate, excepting Shakespeare, though it has long been known that Beaumont and Fletcher represent the single most performed body of work in the decade following the Restoration. Thus when Dryden concludes his sortie, he urges his readers to 'ascribe to the gallantry and civility of our age the advantage which we have above' Shakespeare, Jonson and Fletcher; and in the earlier essay, probably conscious that Davenant's plays from the 1630s were largely Fletcherian in manner, implies that *The Conquest of Granada* addresses some of the deficiencies of *The Siege of Rhodes*. There he writes, 'For heroick Plays . . . the first light we had of them on the English Theatre was from the late Sir *William D'avenant*' (Dryden, *Works* 11: 9). The music and staging, Dryden says, derived from the Italians, and the heightened examples of moral virtue from '*Corneille* and some *French* Poets' (ibid.), but I would argue that the subsequent essay supplies a native genealogy, which accounts for Davenant's relation to Fletcher and to the masque tradition, both of which help explain his comfort with theatrical artifice. What implicitly allows Davenant to improve on his predecessors, and Dryden on Davenant, is the parallel growth of a social and political artifice he associates with 'conversation', 'gallantry and civility', which he ascribes to the example of Charles II, whose exile on the Continent made him 'conversant in the most polish'd Courts of *Europe*' (ibid.: 216).

The reference to Charles II and the Dedication to the Duke of York raise a central issue provoking the storm of criticism aimed at Almanzor, that most hyperbolic of literary heroes. This is of course the topic of Davenant's groundbreaking critical exchange with Hobbes in 1650, occasioned by the imminent publication of *Gondibert*, in which the defining role of literature is declared to be exemplary. Thus Davenant contrasts 'Truth narrative', the province of the historian, to 'truth operative', whose 'effects [are] continually alive' (Spingarn 1963, 2: 11). Contemporaries were awake to the problem of how literature could successfully present us with moral examples, as John and Mary Evelyn's responses to *The Conquest of Granada* attest. John Evelyn comments on the dramatic vehicle in ways that, by now, we should expect, writing that 'there were indeede very glorious scenes & perspectives, the worke of Mr. Streeter, who well understands it'; and I believe that Mary remains true to that ocular and perspectival attitude when she writes that Dryden's play was 'a play so full of ideas that the most refined romance I ever read is not to compare with it', although she injects a critical note into her response, when she adds that 'love is made so pure, and valor so nice, that one would imagine it designed for an Utopia rather than our stage' (cited in *Works* 11: 411). Mary Evelyn's use of the word *ideas*, I would argue, carries some of the freight of its Greek etymology, which assumes that knowledge is mediated by images (*eidolon*), so that the point at issue is how the image of Almanzor persuades us to moral improvement. Evidently she would concur with Buckingham that Almanzor strayed too far beyond the bounds of probability; but undoubtedly all would agree on the need for moral examples, which – as Johnson points out in *Rambler* no. 4 – requires us to depart from the merely quotidian, so that an element of the extraordinary is a virtual requirement. In that sense literature plays out a suspicion we normally entertain, namely, that things as they are are not quite as they should be; and the demand for alterity then raises the question of how positively we imagine a state that is sufficiently like ours to invite response, yet sufficiently unlike ours to summon us to finer things.

Once again, Davenant set the stage for Dryden, because, in his practice, he suggests that the right kind of alterity – truth operative indeed – can energize the dramatic plot by recourse to either of two devices: the choice of an exotic locale, and – in the tradition of English tragicomedy – a double plot. Thus in *The Siege of Rhodes*, Solyman the Magnificent initiates what becomes something of a habit of using Muslim culture as a means of criticizing the failures of Christians (and vice versa); and the differential necessitated by an exemplary theory of literature is served both by the chiastic structure of the plot, as well as the relation between the two parts. Davenant had pursued his challenge to the Interregnum prohibition on theatrical entertainment in the wake of *The Siege of Rhodes* by mounting *The Cruelty of the Spaniards in Peru* (1658) and *The History of Sir Francis Drake* (1658), dramatic vignettes he later incorporated into a curious framing device called *The Play House to be Let* (1663), in which entirely different genres jostle with each other in a kind of goulash, and explicitly locate the new-world plays in a history of the commercial theatre which, by 1673, the date of Davenant's *Works*, was an established fact. Dryden arguably paid homage to those plays by also setting two of his very first – *The Indian Queen* (1663) and *The Indian Emperour* (1665), in which the exotic hero is Montezuma – in the new world.

As a theory of the relationship between politics, rhetoric, exemplarity, poetry and drama, Davenant's critical exchange with Hobbes over the impending *Gondibert* is an extraordinary affair. In his reply to Davenant, Hobbes makes a suggestion Dryden was to adopt in his Preface to *The Conquest of Granada*, namely, that Davenant's heroic poem assumes many features of the drama: 'methinks the Fable is not much unlike the Theater', Hobbes writes (Spingarn 1963, 2: 60), a view Dryden echoes: 'this, I think, is rather a Play in Narration (as I may call it) than an Heroick Poem' (*Works* 11: 11). And since Davenant holds – not unlike Shelley – that poetry is the precondition of law and civil society, it follows that drama has a special status in culture: 'the Grecian Laws, – Laws being the gravest endevor of humane Councels for the ease of Life, – were long before the dayes of *Lycurgus*, to make them more pleasant to memory, published in Verse' (Spingarn 1963, 2: 48). The exemplary force of dramatic action is such, Davenant proposes, that it plays the central suasive role in the arts of rule. The argument is at once epistemological and political: because drama prefers examples over precepts, the people will submit to its blandishments both reasonably and willingly, so that the rhetorical indirections of drama have an exact corollary in Davenant's almost Miltonic rejection of force as a means of securing political harmony. Davenant's royalism is explicitly opposed to tyranny where he prefers a rational and obedient populace to an oppressed and resentful multitude. He writes, for example, 'the Perswasions of Poesy, in stead of menaces, are Harmonious and delightful insinuations, and never any constraint, unless the ravishment of Reason may be call'd Force' (ibid.: 46).

In preferring poetic indirection to force as a means of rule – Hobbes also defends the necessity of metaphor as a vehicle of knowledge – both Davenant and Hobbes comment on the substance of their arguments at a second-order level. Davenant's text proceeds by constant allusions to an architectural image, which, as we have seen, connoted for him the three-dimensional nature of the dramatic stage, of which his own critical text is implicitly a model; and Hobbes concludes his reply with an extended deliberation on the perspectival machinery of Davenant's poem:

> I beleeve, Sir, you have seen a curious kinde of perspective, where he that looks through a short hollow pipe upon a picture containing divers figures sees none of those that are there painted, but some one person made up of their parts, conveyed to the eie by the artificial cutting of a glass. I finde in my imagination an effect not unlike it from your Poem. The vertues you distribute there amongst so many noble Persons represent in the reading the image but of one mans vertue to my fancy, which is your own, and that so deeply imprinted as to stay for ever there, and govern all the rest of my thoughts and affections in the way of honouring and serving you to the utmost of my power. (Ibid.: 66–7)

Although Hobbes argues that their friendship reconciles the competing perspectives of different characters in *Gondibert*, his selection of the perspectival image renders his scepticism patent. And it is precisely this kind of scepticism, as well as the practical need for plays to stage after 1660, which urged Davenant and his successors to revise Shakespeare. In Davenant's own version of *Macbeth* (1664), for example, the sceptical pressure registers pervasively at an almost microscopic level, so that whereas Shakespeare's witches cry 'fair is foul, and foul is fair' (1.1.11), Davenant undercuts the metaphorical conflation of terms by converting the seemingly absolute into a purely phenomenological description of the world: 'to us fair weather's foul, and foul is fair!' (1.1.11). Consequently, when it came to Davenant and Dryden collaborating on *The Tempest, or The Enchanted Island* (1667), the additional characters do not serve the purposes that some critics have been tempted to imagine. In providing Miranda with a sister, Dorinda, Ferdinand with a double, Hippolyto ('one that never saw Woman, right Heir of the Dukedom of Mantua' [*Works* 10: 8]), and Caliban with a sister, Sycorax, the effect is less a sterile neo-Palladian balance than a series of competitive responses to events in the play. Competing points of view are very much the point of Shakespeare's original – who, after all, has the right story about the island when Prospero and Miranda first appeared? – but Davenant and Dryden seem intent on generalizing those difficulties. Early in the play, for example, Dorinda and Miranda discuss the effects of the storm in terms that Robert Hooke might have used about Royal Society experimentalism:

> *Dorinda*: Oh sister! What have I beheld?
> *Miranda*: What is it moves you so?
> *Dorinda*: From yonder Rock,
>   As I my Eyes cast down upon the Seas,
>   The whistling winds blew rudely on my face,
>   And the waves roar'd; at first I thought the War
>   Had bin between themselves, but strait I spy'd
>   A huge great Creature.
>
> (1.2.293–300)

In the exchange with Davenant, Hobbes has introduced the conundrum of scientific instrumentation. It transpires that Galileo's optick tube, in bringing objects nearer yet by the same token mechanically intensifying the problem of perspective, prevents as much as assists our grasp of scientific facts. Here the problem migrates to Dorinda's consciouness of her own body as a spatialized vehicle of knowledge, so that her speech, like that of Roxalana, regards the speaker as much as the world outside. In this way, knowledge-as-such yields to a discussion of the conventions and processes of knowing. And lest we impugn Davenant's and Dryden's intelligence in daring to reform Shakespeare, what occurs in their new play exemplifies, spatializes and stages their own sense of their place in the history of Stuart drama. Shakespeare is to the history of English drama what the magical notion of kingship is to the restored Charles II, whose behaviour is embarrassingly close to Hippolyto's, who, once having seen women, wants them all to himself. The differential introduced in the act of doubling, whose political applications are painfully obvious, is reproduced in Davenant's and Dryden's sense of the greater artifices informing their theatrical techniques, artifices they ascribe jointly to Jonson and Fletcher. In their Prologue, Shakespeare appears as a natural and magical king, a kind of Puck or Green Knight or even Charles I, whose laws are above criticism, yet by the same token incapable of proving a methodical guide to his successors. This may be perceived as a fall, but it is a necessary descent into a forum where knowledge can be athletically contested. The conventions associated with Jonsonian and Fletcherian stagecraft, which can be debated and developed by legitimate heirs, must, ideally prompted by the example of this play, and if Charles II is similarly to secure a succession, find their equivalent in a more artificial knowledge of statecraft:

> As when a Tree's cut down the secret root
> Lives under ground, and thence new Branches shoot;
> So, from old *Shakespear*'s honour'd dust, this day
> Springs up and buds a new reviving Play:
> *Shakespear*, who (taught by none) did first impart
> To *Fletcher* Wit, to labouring *Johnson* Art.

> He Monarch-like gave those his subjects law,
> And is that Nature which they paint and draw.
> *Fletcher* reach'd that which on his heights did grow,
> Whilst *Johnson* crept and gather'd all below.
>
> . . . *Shakespear*'s Magick could not copy'd be,
> Within that Circle none durst walk but he.
> I must confess 'twas bold, nor would you now,
> That liberty to vulgar Wits allow,
> Which works by Magick supernatural things:
> But *Shakespear*'s pow'r is sacred as a King's.
> Those Legends from old Priest-hood were receiv'd,
> And he then writ, as people then believ'd.
>
> (*Works* 10: 6)

Even in a play as early as *The Cruel Brother* (1626–7), Davenant's Fletcherian tendencies encourage a running parallel between the art of the stage and the arts of rule – one that Thomas Carew mentions in his dedication to *The Just Italian* – on the view that an unself-critical attitude to power finds its corollary in an unself-consciousness about the perspectival conditions of stage meaning. The cruel brother of the title is Forreste, who, discovering that the Duke of Sienna has raped his sister, Corsa (married to Lucio, a count), murders her as an example to the body politic. Corsa is of course that female figure of abstracted virtue, whose image becomes the object of speculation by the different men who believe that they can control and possess it. The perspectival problem surfaces throughout the play, so that early in Act 1, Lucio remarks, 'where sight is young and clear, there Spectacles are troublesome; and rather hide than shew the object' (*Works* 2: 467), whereas the Duke in the same exchange insists on his singularity: ''Tis cheap and base for Majesty not to be singular in all effects' (ibid.), the irony of course being that in being singular, and raping Corsa, he has merely repeated Tarquin's crime. In Act 5, as Forreste is preparing to murder his sister, they debate how and whether the example might take effect: if Corsa remains alive, she asks, what 'constructions [will] the world . . . make of my sinister chance'? To which her brother replies:

> I there's the point. The giddy multitude have neither skill nor leisure to convince supposition, with arguments of strength and charity. Their quick censure brings such effect as Spectacles, when us'd in haste; which then do rather aggravate the shape: then give distinction of the form. Who, who would live to be an argument for them? (Ibid.: 482)

Having killed her, Forreste now meditates on her spiritual state, recognizing that even an act of faith supplies no guarantee:

> Faith's a Perspective; through whose narrow lane; little things (far of) seem so much too great, too near: that what was first unknown is more estrang'd from knowledge than it was before. (Ibid.: 483)

Although if Lucio secures a just response to his wife's death, Forreste promises that 'you shall behold my heart without a perspective' (ibid.: 484), the Duke's assumption of divine right is untroubled by any such question, since evidently the Duke remains oblivious to the dramatic frame of his assertions: 'Did not high providence treble the assurance of my safety, by Guards invisible, when I was first predestinate to this supream function? And dar'st thou tempt the strength of heaven?' (ibid.: 485). And although this provokes a reluctance to murder the anointed sovereign, within a few lines the Duke falls prey to a murderous trap of his own devising, so that public justice is served.

Plays like *The Just Italian* (1630) and *Love and Honour* (1634) engage in similar debates between self-justifying attitudes to authority and the public compromises and scrutiny of the kind necessitated by the stage, whether, in the former case, it is imagined as the king's confidence in his own personal dispensation of justice as opposed to something regulated by custom, or in the latter, it is visible in the tension between a crude code of military honour and the highly mediated protocols of civil society. (At one point, we are reminded, 'you are not here / I'th'Camp, but in a civil Common-wealth' [ibid.: 238].) Like *The Cruel Brother*, *Love and Honour* focuses on the problem of the female image or 'Idea' (ibid.: 253) – here Evandra, taken prisoner by the virtuous Prospero according to the rules of war – as a potential moral example, an issue the play stylizes and pictorializes by numerous stage effects, setting characters in a cave, within the frame of a window, and at one point lifting Evandra from below through a trap. This emblematic tendency is orchestrated by many kinds of musical effects, as well as a running commentary on characters' potential significance either within this plot or within some imagined history which would endow them with value. In fact, the tension between private and public value is itself spoken of as the possibility of different kinds of narratives:

> The Warrior seeks great dangers for proud story;
> Where he records each day when he prevails:
> The Lover walks through greater with less glory;
> And of his perils makes but Winter Tales.
>> (Ibid.: 236)

And that the human body itself must always answer to the conditions of public knowledge is curiously argued by a comment about the widow who appears in Act 3: 'Her skin is Parchment, but not large enough / To hold half her Annals; she has liv'd / So long already' (ibid.: 245). A happy series of disguises and reversals helps to reconcile the motives of love and honour, at which point one character declares, 'I'll buy me an Optick, study Astrology, / And visit [the stars] in Moon-shine on my House Leads' (ibid.: 271).

It should not surprise us, therefore, that *The Platonick Lovers* (1636) serves as something of an affectionate spoof of the court of Charles I, which imagined the relationship between the king and the country in neo-Platonic terms. The basic premise is that the conditions of the theatre, requiring a consciousness of physical space and of the body, expose the absurdities of neo-Platonic love, which seeks to abstract itself from corporeal desires. Theander and Phylomont are two young dukes engaged to each other's sisters, but whereas Phylomont welcomes the carnal obligations marriage will impose, Theander remains comically blind to the delights and effects of sex. This circumstance alone allows for much play with the oxymoron of Platonic love, as Buonatelle remarks at one point:

> My Lord, I beseech you not to wrong my good old Friend *Plato*, with this Court calumny; they father on him a fantastick love he never knew, poor Gentleman, upon my knowledge, Sir, about two thousand years ago, in the high street yonder at *Athens*, just by the corner as you pass to *Diana*'s Conduit (a Haberdashers house) it was (I think) he kept a wench. (Ibid.: 393)

The comedy assumes another twist when Theander takes a medicinal draft which fires his blood, and at this point, I think Davenant alludes to Harveian physiology, of which Theander has at first no account, since he treats his fever as a private malady that the public ritual of marriage can cover, if not cure. The point is that Buonatelle's urban and sartorial imagination and this Harveian view of the body spatialize and incarnate knowledge much like the theatre itself. Of course Act 5 proposes a reconciliation between public and private, love and honour, body and soul, a resolution anticipated in Theander's opening speech: 'the sickness of my blood is gone, my hot and eager thoughts grow temp'rate now, my veins are cool within, as silver Pipes replenish'd from a Spring' (ibid.: 408).

I will conclude this chapter by arguing that Dryden's greatest plays – *Marriage A-la-Mode*, *All for Love*, *Don Sebastian* and *Amphitryon* – owe a fundamental debt to Davenant's theatrical politics, yet with a seriousness and coherence that only a great writer could have achieved. In all cases, Dryden's royalism, like Davenant's, his predecessor as poet laureate, is shot through with the recognition that monarchy must respect the epistemological compromises epitomized in the proscenium stage, an institution that, as Congreve recalls in *The Way of the World*, English playwrights owed to the reforms of *The Siege of Rhodes*. Having, in the Preface and Epilogue to *The Conquest of Granada*, paid homage to the Fletcherian tradition as mediated by Davenant, I also think that Dryden realized that in Almanzor he had presented a hero – an image of value – insufficiently compromised by the theatrical vehicle, and that Buckingham's criticisms in *The Rehearsal* had some grounds. There is too much rant and too little of Davenant's self-consciousness about the epistemological problems involved: it is less a question of whether we like Almanzor, more of knowing who he is from perspectives other than his own.

Thus in *Marriage A-la-Mode* (1671–2), Dryden largely takes up where *The Platonick Lovers* (also set in Sicily) had left off, for it is possible that from that play he imported the chiastic structure of the low plot, in which Rhodophil, Palamede, Melantha and Doralice mutually compete for satisfactory compromises in marriage; that from that play, the self-regarding tendencies of power occur as a form of pastoral (in Dryden, Leonidas and Palmyra filtered entirely through a romance mode), punctured in both cases by observers who can ironize it; that from that play, the desire to gain access to power expresses itself by the need to learn French – Dryden exploits Mrs Bowtell's comic abilities as Melantha, 'an affected lady'; and from Davenant in general, the powers of perspective scenery also amplified by the masquerade. Thus Melantha's bittersweet obsession about gaining access to the court – the 'presence' she calls it – is comically rendered by her suddenly leaping into the wings, as she sees the courtiers pass by. Thus the ability to spatialize the difference between private and public value on stage, as the four lovers in the low plot gather outside a cave for an assignation. And thus the desire to suggest that although Leonidas as true heir comes into his own, he does so in terms that his own self-regarding manner simply ignores. As in Davenant, the comic resolution does not imply an uncritical endorsement of the monarch, while the stage itself serves to point up the artifice of the institution.

Charles II's narcissistic and self-regarding inclinations – imagined as Davidic indulgence in *Absalom and Achitophel* – become the central topic of *All for Love* (1677), for in this play, Antony and Cleopatra's obsession with staging themselves for each other's pleasure aggressively ignores the sense – embodied in Ventidius – that staging an argument calls for competing interpretations or points of view. Everything about Antony and Cleopatra resists mobility, whether imagined as the mobility of decision, the mobility of history (whether past or imagined), the mobility of trade, or the future mobility of a great emperor – Octavius approaches Egypt throughout the play – so that, in exploiting the most theatrical possibilities of the perspective stage, they cast themselves into tableau after tableau. But these are tableaux without any proper sense of audience, so that the power of theatrical perspective becomes entirely inverted or hollowed out. According to this logic, the only conclusion could be the stylized tableau of death into which Antony first arranges himself, and into which Cleopatra then arranges herself and her dead lover.

Both *Don Sebastian* (1689) and *Amphitryon* (1690) come in the wake of another kind of death altogether, namely, the 1688 Revolution and the expulsion of James II. Dryden's return to heroic drama in the one play, and his courting of farce in the other, ride in each case on a double plot, whose stage possibilities Dryden indulges to the full. In both cases, the artifice of monarchy becomes the object of scrutiny once again, an artifice which in this case argues that the actual king – whether James II or William III – can never correspond to the ideal of true kingship. In *Amphitryon* that point is brilliantly achieved in the figure of the false Amphitryon – Jupiter in disguise – whose lustfulness alludes to Charles II and James II, but whose attempt to usurp the lawful Amphitryon alludes to William III. *Don Sebastian* continues the tradition of placing Muslim and Christian values into competition, and the affairs of the heart (in the low plot) against affairs of state (in the high plot). At a critical juncture and at a purely stage level, events in the Mufti's garden (the low plot) spill over into events at the palace, just as Antonio's finally becoming betrothed to his Muslim lover resolves the question of whether Muslim women have souls – as in *The Platonick Lovers*, body and soul are reconciled. But Don Sebastian himself repeats the romance fallacy that the political drama I have described so clearly satirized from early in the century: he has had a homosexual affair as a young man, and commits incest in the course of the play, both of which symbolize a stylized self-regard that corresponds to the character of the historical Portuguese monarch. His punishment is evacuation from the plot, so that Dryden's suggestion is that the ambivalence of even moderate loyalist Catholics like himself prefers to entertain the legitimate king at a safe distance from English shores. As Freud describes this particular cultural neurosis in *Totem and Taboo*, the loyalist prefers to guarantee the patriarchy at a metaphysical level by reference to an absent or murdered king, since too great a scrutiny of the actual monarch can only foment disappointment or hostility in his subjects. Because he was writing with a knowledge of Stuart fortunes, Freud curiously captures something about the ironic structure of the dramatic tradition Dryden consciously adopted from Davenant; and one could argue that this theatrical history contributes substantially to seventeenth-century political theory, since, like Hobbes, what Davenant and Dryden brought as playwrights to their political commitments forced them – at a theoretical level – to treat all human institutions as conventional.

REFERENCES AND FURTHER READING

Bordinat, Philip and Blaydes, Sophia B. (1981). *Sir William Davenant*. Boston: Twayne.

Butler, Martin (1984). *Theatre and Crisis, 1632–1642*. Cambridge: Cambridge University Press.

Davenant, William (1673; reprinted 1968). *The Works of Sir William Davenant*. 2 vols. New York and London: Benjamin Blom.

Dryden, John (1956–). *The Works of John Dryden*, ed. Edward Niles Hooker, H. T. Swedenberg, Jr, et al. 20 vols in progress. Berkeley: University of California Press.

Edmond, Mary (1987). *Rare Sir William Davenant: Poet Laureate, Playwright, Civil War General, Restoration Theatre Manager*. Manchester: Manchester University Press.

Freud, Sigmund (1989). *Totem and Taboo*. New York: Norton.

Harbage, Alfred (1964). *Cavalier Drama: An Historical and Critical Supplement to the Study of the Elizabethan and Restoration Stage*. New York: Russell and Russell.

Harbage, Alfred (1935; reprinted 1971). *Sir William Davenant, Poet, Venturer, 1606–1668*. New York: Octagon.

Hotson, Leslie (1928; reprinted 1962). *The Commonwealth and Restoration Stage*. New York: Russell and Russell.

Kavenick, Frances M. (1995). *British Drama, 1660–1779: A Critical History*. New York: Twayne.

Kroll, Richard (1990). 'Emblem and Empiricism in Davenant's *Macbeth*', *ELH* 57, 835–64.

Kroll, Richard (1995). 'Instituting Empiricism: Hobbes's *Leviathan* and Dryden's *Marriage a la Mode*', in J. Douglas Canfield and Deborah C. Payne (eds), *Cultural Readings of Restoration and Eighteenth-century Theater*. Athens: University of Georgia Press, 39–66.

Kroll, Richard (2000). 'The Double Logic of *Don Sebastian*: The Oedipal Conscience at the Glorious Revolution', *Huntington Library Quarterly* 63.

Markley, Robert (1988). *Two-Edg'd Weapons: Style and Ideology in the Comedies of Etherege, Wycherley, and Congreve*. Oxford: Clarendon Press.

Maus, Katherine Eisaman (1982). 'Arcadia Lost: Politics and Revision in the Restoration *Tempest*', *Renaissance Drama* n.s. 13, 189–209.

Randall, Dale B. J. (1995). *Winter Fruit: English Drama, 1642–1660.* Lexington: University of Kentucky Press.

Rothstein, Eric (1967). *Restoration Tragedy: Form and the Process of Change.* Madison: University of Wisconsin Press.

Southern, Richard (1952). *Changeable Scenery: Its Origin and Development in the British Theatre.* London: Faber and Faber.

Spencer, Christopher (ed.). (1965). *Five Restoration Adaptations of Shakespeare.* Urbana: University of Illinois Press.

Spingarn, J. E. (ed.). (1963). *Critical Essays of the Seventeenth Century.* 3 vols. Bloomington: Indiana University Press.

Summers, Montague (1934; reprinted 1964). *The Restoration Theatre.* New York: Humanities Press.

Summers, Montague (1935; reprinted 1964). *The Playhouse of Pepys.* New York: Humanities Press.

Wilson, John Harold (1928). *The Influence of Beaumont and Fletcher on Restoration Drama.* Columbus: Ohio State University Press.

19

'Still on the Criminal's Side, against the Innocent': Etherege, Wycherley and the Ironies of Wit

Robert Markley

Over the course of the last three centuries, the plays of Sir George Etherege and William Wycherley have both benefited and suffered from being treated as though they exemplify and yet somehow transcend the concerns of wit comedy in the 1660s and 1670s. According to many critics, the two dramatists perfected the 'comedy of manners', a genre that lays bare the pretences of false wit and secures for its heroes and heroines some sense of emotional and financial stability in a world of glittering social forms, sexual hypocrisy and deception. Responses to Etherege's and Wycherley's seven plays have run the gamut from denunciations of their immorality by Thomas Babington Macaulay, to defences of what Charles Lamb characterized as a 'utopia of gallantry', to arguments in the 1960s and 1970s that their plays exhibited the philosophical seriousness that distinguishes great literature.[1] Trotted out by critics such as Dale Underwood and Norman Holland to demonstrate the New Critical significance of Restoration comedy, Etherege and Wycherley were often excised with near-surgical precision from the context of the 1670s and celebrated to the exclusion of contemporaries such as Aphra Behn, Sir John Vanbrugh, George Farquhar, Thomas Otway, Thomas Shadwell and even John Dryden.

More recently, the privileged position of Etherege and Wycherley in the canon of Restoration drama has been qualified, and occasionally challenged, by three broad movements: approaches that historicize the drama by paying close attention to the complex relations between party politics and the theatre (Canfield 1997; Owen 1996); efforts to situate their plays (and five hundred others) within a comprehensive generic history of the late seventeenth-century stage (Hume 1976; Hughes 1996); and analyses that draw on feminist theory to explore the ways in which both playwrights reinscribe, and test, the gendered ideology of a patrilineal society (Gill 1994; Velissariou 1995). In practice, these approaches often overlap, producing reassessments of Etherege's and Wycherley's work and metacritical debates about particular aesthetic and ideological approaches. Several other developments have contributed to a relative decline in their status among critics. The fate of Etherege's and Wycherley's plays on the eighteenth-century stage has led some theatre historians to qualify traditional views of their representative or exemplary status. Paulina Kewes, for example, calls attention to the disparity between Wycherley's critical reputation in the early eighteenth century and the fact that there were 'only five known perform-ances of *Country Wife* and nine of *The Plain-Dealer*' (1998: 223). Because much recent criticism has concentrated on the role of the drama during the Exclusion Crisis in the early 1680s, Etherege and Wycherley, who both left the theatre in 1676, have had to share the spotlight with dramatists such as John Dryden, John Crowne, Aphra Behn and Elkanah Settle who wrote polemical comedies that shed a good deal of light on the complex intersections between theatrical performance and political intrigue.[2] Finally, Robert Hume and Derek Hughes, who survey the entire drama of the late seventeenth century to outline trends and map generic transformations from season to season, argue persuasively that the achievements of individual playwrights can be appreciated only within the context of the period as a whole.

Nevertheless, the attention that Etherege and Wycherley have received since their own day suggests that their comedies play significant *ideological* roles in late seven-teenth-century literary culture. In brief, their plays display the ironies that they themselves seem to have experienced in Restoration London: the prospect of trying to get ahead in a fashionable world without displaying any effort beneath the dignity of a gentleman, and the comic ambiguities of libertine existence in a culture whose moral and politico-sexual authority they flout, satirize, manipulate and pay court to for their sustenance. In a sense, both men revel in and exploit the ironies of a generation of playwrights and theatregoers who seemingly can't live with the folly and hypocrisy of Restoration society and can't live without it. Their works register the ideological complexities of interpellation – the always impure process of internalizing cultural restrictions and prohibitions as the bases of one's own social, moral and emotional identity.[3] Both playwrights present for comic scrutiny the spectacle of characters either complicit with or resigned to social and economic practices that work *against* their own interests. In short, their plays, in a variety of ways, dramatize the ideological tensions within a class-stratified, patrilineal society by revealing – in very funny ways – the cultural fantasies that take self-interested and mercenary values for time-transcendent truths.

A theoretically sophisticated and historically situated conception of ideology is crucial to understanding the contributions that feminist criticism has made to the reinterpretation of Restoration comedy. Pat Gill argues that the ambiguities of representation on the stage – the gap between signs and what they attempt to signify – reflect the values and assumptions of a profoundly misogynistic society. 'Restoration comic satire', she maintains, 'revolves around the female figure as the prototype of problematic signification' (Gill 1994: 11). In this respect, the misogynistic depiction of women as either hypocrites or prudes acts as both the enabling condition and the satiric consequence of masculine conceptions of 'wit' and 'manners' that are deployed to police social behaviour and to ensure the stability of property relations. The feminist re-readings of the plays of Etherege and Wycherley question some of the basic premises of formalist interpretations. Some critics, Laura Brown, for example, have read the romantic subplots of Wycherley's plays, notably the courtship of Harcourt and Alithea in *The Country Wife*, as an effort to anchor his comedies in traditional conceptions of satiric correction: Harcourt's devotion to Alithea represents a moral norm – true love – that rises above the deception rampant elsewhere in the play. In such scenarios, however, 'morality' is effectively indistinguishable from a deeply ingrained anti-feminism that renders women either chaste vessels for the transmission of property among men (Alithea) or whores (all the other women). This dichotomy, however, is more apparent than real because women are always constructed as sexual beings who must be controlled by male guardians and husbands, even as women in the audience must be sexually minded enough to understand the incessant double entendres that characterize rakish wit. 'There can be no innocent women' in plays such as *The Country Wife*, says Gill, because the masculinist dialectic of virgin and whore is irrevocably undermined by any hint of female sexuality and desire – ironically, the very ingredients that are essential to get the plot of almost any comedy under way (Gill 1994: 73).

As valuable as feminist approaches to the comedies of Etherege and Wycherley have been, it would be going too far to make either dramatist the avatar of a monochromatic misogyny and type their plays as theatrical demonstrations of a conservative ideology, a right-way, wrong-way manual of masculine wit and feminine vulnerability. The endemic anti-feminism of seventeenth-century society is itself riddled by paradoxes, tensions and contradictions – and the comic drama as a whole delights in spectacles of women violating decorum in order both to call into question and to justify the reimposition of moral and social codes that govern a patrilineal society. The popularity of *The Man of Mode* and *The Country Wife* suggests that the critical controversies which swirl around these works reflect complexities that inhere within the plays themselves. The more critics try to pigeonhole these works as demonstrations of this or that critical orthodoxy, the more the plays seem to slip out from under definitive readings of what their authors intended or what they might mean.

The critical and theatrical fortunes of the two playwrights have depended on the willingness of readers and audiences to offer themselves as targets of satire, to recognize, if only intuitively, their complicity in the ironies of social forms and cultural fantasies. Those who look to literature for moral guidance or romantic sustenance historically have either been outraged by Dorimant's seductive wit and Horner's stratagem or have tried to prove that the spectacle of twenty-something heroes zeroing in on teenage heiresses can be shoehorned into one philosophical orthodoxy or another. A more historically situated approach might see their plays not as the embodiments of abstract systems of thought but as a selective rendering of the dilemmas, ironies and opportunities that arise from young men and women of the gentry testing the limits of social and sexual decorum without relinquishing their positions in society. The contemporary popularity of Etherege's and Wycherley's comedies can be attributed to the dramatists' convincing staging of the problems posed by younger sons and members of the minor gentry whose desire to live like gentlemen in a fashionable – and expensive – world threatens to overtax the networks of seventeenth-century patronage and privilege (see Goldstone 1991: 63–167). In this regard, Horner and Dorimant may be less dangerous as cuckold-makers than they would be as disgruntled seekers of court patronage, as 'men of business' like Sir Jasper Fidget. The sexual adventures of Wycherley's and Etherege's heroes offer a kind of compensatory mechanism for young men who can triumph sexually over a foolish older generation even if their incomes, lodgings and lifestyles suffer in comparison. The ideal rakes are those who live by their wits, seek rich heiresses to repair the estates they, almost inevitably, seem to have wasted, and never mention hunting for patronage positions: to seek preferment on stage in the 1670s is to risk bad form at a time when the king was chronically short of money. The rakes' dilemma – a lifestyle in search of the resources to maintain it – underwrites the ideology and ironies of wit in the 1660s and 1670s.

It is not surprising that Etherege and Wycherley have engendered such various responses to their work because, in some measure, their careers reflect the dilemmas that plagued many offspring of the gentry who lived to the limits of their incomes. Both men used their comic genius to try to secure positions that would provide them with the recognition, access and patronage to cement their status as members of the fashionable elite. The son of a Berkshire gentleman, Etherege studied law at Clement's Inn from 1658 to 1663. His first play, *The Comical Revenge* (1664), brilliantly parodies the fashion for heroic couplets and recasts the premises of Jacobean city comedy and Fletcherian wit comedy to fashion a multi-plot extravaganza that, like other plays of the 1660s, identifies Cavalier carousing with loyalty to the Stuart monarchy. By the mid-1660s the former clerk was a fixture among the wits – including Sir Charles Sedley and the Earl of Rochester – who moved in fashionable circles, and he became a Gentleman of the Privy Chamber in Ordinary. *She Wou'd if She Cou'd* in 1668 was not as successful as *The Comical Revenge*; Etherege blamed the actors, but eventually the play was successful enough to confirm his status as a leading, if usually idle, comic dramatist. Etherege parlayed his theatrical success into a diplomatic post; from 1668 to 1671 he served as the Secretary to Sir Daniel Harvey, the Ambassador Extraordinary in Constantinople. Back in London, Etherege reverted to a dissolute existence, and the historical record before and after the first production of *The Man of Mode* includes tavern fights, run-ins with the watch, a reputation for idleness, and allusions to his venereal disease. *The Man of Mode* in 1676 was a resounding success. By 1680 Etherege had married for money and in 1682 was awarded a pension of £100 per annum. From 1685 to 1689 he was the English Resident in Ratisbon, where he carried on a public affair with an actress, gambled, drank to all hours, and celebrated the birth of James II's heir in 1688. In a letter dated February 1687, Dryden addressed him as 'thou imortal source of Idleness'. After James fled England, Etherege fades from history, though he seems to have died in Paris in 1691. 'Loose, wandring, *Etherege*, in wild Pleasures tost' is how Thomas Southerne described him a year later.

This overview of Etherege's career is suggestive: playwriting was, at best, a sometime occupation that Etherege seems to have regarded (like his apparently loveless marriage and diplomatic posts) as a means to support a gentlemanly lifestyle. Without down-playing his achievement, we should recognize that authorship for Etherege carries little of the romantic baggage that it acquires a century later. In a letter from Ratisbon in 1688, the retired dramatist offers this self-characterization: 'nature you know intended me for an idle fellow, and gave me passions and qualities fit for that blessed calling, but fortune has made a Changeling of me, & necessity now forces me to set up for a fop of business'. In his fifties, Etherege still values the 'passions and qualities' of an existence of gentlemanly leisure – of drinking, sex and gambling – without having to suffer the consequences of age and dissolution. To always remain the successful rake, even in one's imagination, is to avoid giving in to the pleasure-denying world of 'business' and its responsibilities.

It seems fitting, then, that Etherege's first comic hero, Sir Frederick in *The Comical Revenge*, enters commenting wittily on his hangover:

> I am of the opinion that drunkenness is not so damnable a sin to me as 'tis to many; Sorrow and Repentance are sure to be my first Work the next morning: 'Slid, I have known some so lucky at this recreation, that, whereas 'tis familiar to forget what we do in drink, have even lost the memory, after sleep, of being drunk: Now do I feel more qualms than a young woman in breeding. (1.1.21–7)

Sir Frederick becomes both the subject and object of his wit; he parodies and appropriates a familiar moral rhetoric of sin and repentance by rendering the consequences of drinking in amoral, physical terms. In large measure, his jokes come at his own expense – by comparing himself to a pregnant woman, he plays with the idea of his physical weakness and anticipates his fate in marrying the widow: 'breeding' heirs and managing estates will intrude on his hedonistic lifestyle. Wit may become a means to forestall time and responsibility, but marrying money is essential to Sir Frederick's maintaining his gentlemanly existence.

The ironies of Sir Frederick's rhetorical pose are suggestive of Etherege's comic practice in his second play. *She Wou'd if She Cou'd*, like *The Comical Revenge*, offers paradoxical images of the relations between men and women: the main plot takes the form of a love story, in which the heroes talk their way into the heroines' hearts, if not their beds, even as they and the other male characters bandy about conventional misogynist images of women as animals, temptresses and illusory 'Juglers Tricks...meer cheats' (1.1.179, 181). Precisely because women are barred, legally and ideologically, from full participation in seventeenth-century social life, Etherege is able to use his witty heroines, Gatty and Ariana, as a means to tweak the hypocrisy of masculinist authority. Their rebellion against restrictive gender roles, however, has no socio-political ramifications, leaving intact the patrilineal control of property that restricts women to talking about rather than acting on their frustrations. Gatty and Ariana appropriate traditional misogynistic imagery to signal their recognition of the ways in which women are debased by comparisons to 'Rooks' (2.1.27), 'Deer' (2.1.69), 'skittish Fillies' (2.2.132), 'Trouts' (3.1.100), 'Chickens' (3.3.30) and 'Horse-flesh'

(4.2.152). When they are deceived by Lady Cockwood into questioning their lovers' fidelity, they claim that the men 'daily hover about these Gardens, as a Kite does about a back-side, watching an opportunity to catch up the Poultry' (4.2.189–91). If, as Gill suggests, women cannot remain innocent in such a misogynistic society, they nonetheless can try to delay or manoeuvre around the difficult choices that confront them: to be pursued like poultry, ignored or ridiculed like Lady Cockwood. Rather than relinquish their bodies and estates, they can forestall such decisions by imposing a trial period of good behaviour on the heroes.

The endings of both *She Wou'd* and *The Man of Mode* resist aesthetic and ideological closure. Etherege's heroines prolong their fashionable lives of witty banter and comparative freedom, of stylistic rather than political rebellion, by acknowledging their love for their suitors but extending the trials of courtship and demanding good behaviour. Both plays, then, offer a masculinist fantasy of feminine sexuality: the women remain poised indefinitely between experience and innocence, between sexual corruption and their integrity as vessels for the transmission of property. In an important sense, there can be no Act 6 to either *She Wou'd* or *The Man of Mode* because the ironies of fashionable opposition to moral, economic and legal strictures that cannot be overthrown admit of no real resolution. The plays end without weddings because the underlying fantasy that the audience must both acknowledge and repress is that of the rake's ongoing rebellion against a killjoy morality. Courtall, Freeman and Dorimant exit still maintaining the 'passions and qualities' that allow them to resist becoming 'fop[s] of business', that leave them free from the consequences of lawsuits and loveless marriages which, outside the theatre, attend the pursuit of idleness.

If Etherege owes much of his contemporary popularity to dramatizing the comic tensions of a wished-for existence, he also calls into question some of the fundamental premises of libertine life in a class-stratified world. In a telling scene in *The Man of Mode*, Sir Fopling Flutter preens for the collected company by bandying the brand names of his Parisian tailor, shoemaker and wigmaker as infallible signs of his good breeding (3.3.220–33). The antithetical qualities of Sir Fopling's social identity – 'Brisk and insipid' (Dorimant), and 'Pert and dull' (Medley) (3.2.261–2) – suggest the paradox of the fop who seems both a kind of childlike innocent, fascinated by all he sees, and a fashionable fraud who cannot play the role he wants to assume. At stake in this scene is an ideology of interpretation – not simply learning to read the signs by which observers can distinguish true from false wit, but the underlying belief that such scrutiny can produce definitive judgements of men's fashion and women's virtue. Sir Fopling's list of designer labels, in this respect, discloses reciprocal fantasies at work: the idea that one can distinguish the fop from the true man of elegance or wit, and that the codes which enable characters and members of the audience to make this distinction can be revealed or somehow acquired. At the beginning of Act 5, Pert tries to comfort the jilted Mrs Loveit by observing that her new suitor, Sir Fopling, is 'as handsom a man as Mr *Dorimant*, and as great a Gallant' (5.1.4–5). Although Loveit finds this comparison 'intolerable' and 'false', she never challenges directly Pert's view of the social and physical similarities between the two men. To confuse the two is to threaten the ideological distinctions between true and false wit that fashionable society strives to maintain. For Etherege to introduce this comparison is to question comically the fictions of inherent worth, of stable identities that endure regardless of the social performances that bring them into being.

Dorimant is a consummate actor. At the end of the play, his protestations of love for Harriet – the woman who has parodied and mimicked him throughout their wit battles – elicit her aesthetic judgements of his performance. 'Hold – Though I wish you devout, I would not have you turn Fanatick' (5.2.146–7). Although Harriet puts him on romantic probation for a month at her aunt's country estate, the audience can never be quite sure that his love is genuine enough to withstand temptation or that it can be separated from his self-interest. In an aside later in the scene, Dorimant confides to Loveit that he is only seeking 'a Wife, to repair the ruines of my estate that needs it' (5.2.292–3), even as he lies to her to conceal his affair with Bellinda. He then tells the latter that "tis as unreasonable to expect we [men] should perform all we promise then, as do all we threaten when we are angry' (5.2.299–301). In the theatre, the audience is unlikely to keep running totals of Dorimant's true and false declarations, even if his motives were easily decipherable. Dorimant does not have a single, monological identity, and his claims of sincerity can never transcend the ironies of his performance. His reform can only be deferred, not dramatized. Because *The Man of Mode* resists universalizing as moral truths the characters' efforts to distinguish love from lust, honour from corruption, and substance from pretence, it offers only a performative ethics, an opportunity to traverse the fantasies that structure society and thereby to recognize that one cannot opt out of a social existence of fashion, pretence and gendered rules of play.

Wycherley's plays, even more than Etherege's, seem intent on disrupting and frustrating the audience's ability to impose value judgements of the kind on which satire supposedly insists. The son of a litigious Shropshire gentleman, Wycherley went to Paris as a teenager, briefly converted to Catholicism, and then in 1660 returned to London and read law at the Inner Temple. He may have seen naval action in 1665 in the Second Dutch War. His first two plays, *Love in a Wood* (1671) for the King's Men and *The Gentleman Dancing-Master* (1672) at Dorset Garden, established his reputation as a comic dramatist. Like Etherege, Wycherley lived a fashionable existence beyond his means. Although both *The Country Wife* (1674) and *The Plain Dealer* (1676) were extremely successful, he eventually ended up in debtors' prison while his father spent the better part of two decades involved in lawsuits, depleting the estate that, at age 50, the satirist was to inherit. In 1679 Wycherley married the widowed Countess of Drogheda, apparently for her money; she was violently jealous and the marriage was not a happy one. After her death in 1681, Wycherley found himself embroiled in lawsuits with her relatives that dragged on for years. Although Wycherley basked in his reputation as a satirist for the last forty years of his life, a long illness that affected his memory apparently left him unwilling or unable to return to the stage. In 1715, almost on his deathbed, he was coerced into marrying his cousin's mistress; he died eleven days later and she and her lover received the jointure that Daniel Wycherley had provided should his son ever remarry.

If Etherege's characters – Sir Frederick Frolick, Dorimant and Harriet – embody the ambiguities of social existence in a patrilineal culture, Wycherley's men and women are more aggressive in venting their frustrations with the corruption of the society in which they must live. In *Love in a Wood*, Wycherley undermines familiar distinctions among wits, fops and fools. Language and action, character and situation frequently work at cross purposes. The noble lovers, Valentine and Christina, are undone by the illusions they hold about each other. Valentine is the first of Wycherley's jealous neurotics: his language of absolute certainty blinds him to Christina's virtue so that he is convinced she will betray him even before he has any reason to suspect her. For her part, Christina remains faithful to her idealized view of Valentine, isolating herself from society and, in her continued praises of his virtues, confirming his narcissistic vision of himself as an honourable man beset by a corrupt world. In a play that gets its laughs from the welter of competing idioms of love, wit and honour, this inability to perceive one's own best interests ensures that all the characters remain 'in a wood' – that is, blindly stumbling over obstacles that they themselves create. For characters from the fop Dapperwit to hypocrites such as Lady Flippant and Gripe, the world of the play is self-referential. The Town – fashionable London society – becomes both a comic ideal and a satiric target, the theatrical reflection of a society in which declarations of love and honour become forms of self-deception.

The rigidity of moral values and the tyranny of fashion are mocked as well in *The Gentleman Dancing-Master*: Sir James Formal, obsessed with all things Spanish, styles himself Don Diego; his nephew, Nathaniel Paris, has transformed himself into the Frenchified Monsieur; and both are outwitted by Hippolita, a 14–year-old eager to find 'any man, though he were but a little handsomer than the Devil' (1.131), and Gerrard, a gentleman who pretends to be a dancing master to gain access to the closely guarded heroine. As James Thompson has argued, the play takes advantage of the ambiguous social status of dancing masters – men who marketed their skill, deportment and grace to all comers – to explore the comic possibilities of the characters' belief that moral and social virtues can be acquired, developed, performed and even faked. If the funny but repetitive routines in this play mock the irrationality of patriarchal authority – satirically exaggerated in Don Diego – they also give comic form to anxieties about social position and privilege in the late seventeenth century. Gerrard's assumed role as a dancing master to secure an heiress worth £2,000 a year is a fantasy solution to the prospect of younger sons and gentlemen with shrinking or limited incomes faced with life on the fringes of fashionable society.

If Dorimant embodies the seductive qualities of a performative masculine identity, Horner in *The Country Wife* is, as I have suggested, a kind of walking pun: the cuckold-maker, a standard of masculine sexuality, and almost the satyr that Olivia in *The Plain Dealer* says he is (Markley 1988: 159–60). He is, at once, a foil to expose the impotence and stupidity of failed exemplars of masculine sexuality, notably Sir Jasper Fidget and Pinchwife, and a deceptive ironist who verges on becoming the butt of his own joke. In the deservedly famous china scene, Horner enters after having had sex with Lady Fidget in his china closet and is unable, for the time being, to satisfy Squeamish, who is intent on dragging him back among his porcelain to 'have some China too' (4.329). His 'stratagem' of feigning impotence to gain access to the fashionable women of the Town, at least temporarily, becomes real enough to prevent more 'toiling and moiling' for china (ibid.). Although Horner may have to wait to satisfy his partners in sexual deception, he is never unmasked and suffers no legal or dramatic justice at the end of the play. His seduction of Margery does not signal an end to his role-playing or a solution to her miserable marriage but initiates her into a community of fashionable deception.

Helen Burke offers an important feminist corrective to those critics, such as Eve Kosofsky Sedgwick, who read *The Country Wife* as an anti-feminist play that privileges male homosocial desire at the expense of passive women. Although Horner's opening dialogue with Harcourt and Dorilant in Act 1 is replete with conventional truisms about women as sexual objects that hinder male fellowship, many readers miss the point of the scene: the hero's friends, Harcourt and Dorilant, do not know about his ploy and remain ignorant of it throughout the play. At the end of the play, Harcourt is willing to fight the hero over the offence to Alithea's honour that he presumes Horner is willing and capable of having made. The alienation that Horner cultivates in the play is from men, not women, and despite his claim to Quack that he can use his feigned impotence to get new mistresses and get rid of old ones, he does not break off with any of the women he seduces. His ongoing affairs with Margery, Lady Fidget, Squeamish and Dainty make him seem ultimately, as Gerald Weales puts it, 'more like a chain smoker than a great lover' (Wycherley 1966: xii). If Horner, as he tells Lady Fidget, is 'a *Machiavel* in love' (4.325), it is never clear exactly what he gains by his frenetic sexual activity. Although he may be intrigued by possibilities of ideological and aesthetic control, all his triumphs are ambiguous.

In a sense, though, Horner embodies the rake's fantasy that one can ridicule patrilineal authority and cuckold much of fashionable London society without suffering any social consequences. Unlike Dorimant, Horner has no designs on marriageable women or the estates that their bodies might convey to him. The targets of Horner's deception are men of business like Sir Jasper and married former rakes, like Pinchwife. Etherege's hero seduces unmarried women; Horner cuckolds men who have titles. Sparkish complains that previously dramatists 'were contented to make Serving-men only their Stage-Fools, but these Rogues must have Gentlemen, with a Pox to 'em, nay Knights: . . . you shall hardly see a Fool upon the Stage, but he's a Knight' (3.297). The overdetermined satire directed against Sparkish may be seen as a compensatory mechanism, a displacement onto an outright fool of the antagonisms that inhere in a hierarchical and rigid system that pits men against each other. *The Country Wife*, in this regard, satirically violates the homosocial bonds that bind upper-class men in networks of familial alliances, patronage obligations and patrilineal privilege. However compulsive Horner's sexual conquests may appear, he abandons Harcourt and Dorilant very quickly and places himself in the company and confidence of the 'women of honour'. Because homosocial antagonisms have no ideological outlet in a theatre that catered to the elite classes, they surface as satiric judgements directed against older men of business, property and titles: economic hostility within the elite classes is rewritten as theatrical rebellion against socio-sexual authority.

In Act 5, when it seems Horner must falsely compromise Alithea's honour to protect Margery, he declares that such deception is 'no new thing with me; for in these cases I am still on the criminal's side, against the innocent' (5.355). Although some critics have read this admission as means to validate conservative moral standards, it might be more useful to consider this confession as a kind of romanticized self-portrait that reveals Horner's investment in his status as a Machiavel wreaking havoc from within the patrilineal system. Horner never openly offers anything resembling a political critique of gender or social relations. In this sense, he may be more a safety valve than a 'criminal', a fantasy figure to reconcile desirous women to a socio-economic system that hypocritically demands their chastity and compliance. Rather than a satiric revelation of the corrupt nature of womankind, then, Horner's stratagem ironically confirms what the audience 'already knows': women are always on the verge of turning from country wives to fashionable hypocrites. Since jealous husbands such as Pinchwife and fools like Sir Jasper drive their wives into Horner's arms, they are the ultimate butts of Wycherley's satiric jokes. These men fail because they try to control the sexual desire and unmask the social hypocrisy that are essential for women to play along with a repressive socio-economic system.

Wycherley dedicated his final play, *The Plain Dealer*, to a well-known bawd, Mother Bennet, and this gesture is at once brutally satiric and profoundly ironic. It initiates the play's readers into a satiric world that savages hypocrisy, yet offers no alternative to the corruption of law, language and even love. In the opening scenes, the dramatist allows Manly, the play's hero, to denounce the world around him and to get the better of the compliant wits and hangers-on in verbal duels that make him a poster boy for plain-dealing. In characteristic fashion for such a satire, Olivia, the faithless woman who has conned Manly into letting her hold his sea-captain's fortune, and the litigious Widow Blackacre become scapegoats for the failings of a hypocritical society. Yet both women, it seems, act in accordance with the values and expectations of a masculinist realm that forces them to mimic the self-interest and hypocrisy they see around them. Manly, the intransigent moralist who cannot recognize his complicity in a double-dealing society, and Freeman, who pursues the Widow simply for her estate, can claim no moral high ground. In a telling exchange that leaves the audience wondering how the hero could have been duped by such a scene-stealing hypocrite, Olivia taunts Manly for his 'spirit of contradiction' (2.427) and later anatomizes his character for the disguised Fidelia: 'I knew he lov'd his own singular moroseness so well, as to dote upon any Copy of it; wherefore I feign'd a hatred to the World too, that he might love me in earnest' (4.482). Righteous indignation is itself a form of delusion. The Plain Dealer's inability to detect the outlandish hypocrisy of Olivia and Vernish or to recognize the merit of Freeman and Fidelia suggests that his 'singular moroseness' stems from a narcissistic obsession with his own desires; even as spectators may identify with his moralistic stance, he seems less a Timonian moralist than the heir of satiric butts such as Valentine in *Love in a Wood* or even Pinchwife. By sneaking into Olivia's bedroom to take the place of the disguised Fidelia, Manly relinquishes any claim to satiric correction.

Although *The Plain Dealer* is a darkly satiric play, it is also extremely funny. Much of its humour comes from attacking the very figure – the wit – who dominates the conventional comedy of manners. In the Prologue, 'Spoken by the PLAIN-DEALER', the audience learns that the playwright 'wou'd not have the Wits pleas'd here to Day', and that the play's 'men of Wit, and Pleasure of the Age, / Are as dull Rogues, as ever cumber'd Stage' (385–6). This rejection of the values and assumptions of wit comedy, spoken by Charles Hart, who had recently played Horner and Dorimant, comes close to a kind of satiric self-effacement. It is difficult in such a world to rely on the conventional meting out of rewards and punishments as indications of poetic justice at work. If the female characters embody the antithetical typing of seventeenth-century morality – the whore Olivia set against the chaste and loyal Fidelia – such distinctions do not do much to salvage a sense of love triumphant at the end of the play. The marriage of Manly and Fidelia rewards him beyond what he deserves, and Fidelia, who claims that she fell in love with Manly 'having in several publick places seen you, and observ'd your actions thoroughly, with admiration' (5.514), seems as blind as her future husband. Her dedication to a man who justifies his sleeping with Olivia to satisfy his sense of injured merit suggests that her 'virtue' comes close to a kind of masochism. The ironic wit that distinguishes rake-heroes such as Sir Frederick Frolick gives way in Wycherley's final play to a comedy of solipsistic projection, to the fantasies that characters can make the world conform to their visions of what it should be.

John Dennis's description of *The Plain Dealer*'s premiere suggests that Wycherley deliberately pushed the limits of comedy as far as they could go: 'And when upon the first representation of the *Plain Dealer*, the Town, as the Authour has often told me, appeared Doubtfull what Judgment to Form of it; [Sir John Denham, Edmund Waller, the Duke of Buckingham, the Earls of Rochester, Dorset and Mulgrave, and several other upper-class wits] by their loud approbation of it, gave it both a sudden and lasting reputation'. Wycherley's apparent pride in repeating this story reveals a dramatist's delight in forcing his audience to recognize and even revel in brutal send-ups of the corruption of the society in which they live. In the close-knit circles of the Restoration theatre, Wycherley is saved by the 'approbation' of a group of wits who applaud the spectacle of their own complicity in the double-dealing that they habitually condemn. To appreciate his achievement, it seems, it helps to have almost as thick a skin as the playwright. Wycherley signed his dedication to the play 'The Plain-Dealer', and the label stuck. Southerne refers to him as '*Manly Witcherley*', and the identification of playwright and hero served to protect Wycherley when almost all of his contemporaries – Etherege, Dryden and Congreve included – were attacked by Jeremy Collier in 1698. Ironically, this conflation of hero and creator serves as both a romanticized self-image of the satirist rising above the corruption of his times and an ultimate image of ironies of interpellation.

When Etherege left Ratisbon in 1689 following the flight of James II, his secretary appended a list of books that he left behind. Along with editions of Shakespeare and Cowley was a translation of Procopius's *Secret History*. Procopius wrote the official history of the campaigns of Belisarius, the *History of the Wars of Justinian* (551–3), which celebrates victories in Persia, Africa and Italy; his *Secret History* covers the same period (527–40) but offers a condemnation of the political, sexual and moral corruption of Justinian's court. It is, in some ways, a fitting work for Etherege to have left behind because it details the corruption and bankruptcy of a polity of which Procopius remained an integral part. The historian and satirist became a Prefect of the City of Constantinople a decade after his savage attack on the court. It would be a mistake to read Etherege's or Wycherley's plays, even *The Plain Dealer*, as generic successors to the *Secret History*, but the book that Etherege forgot may serve as an emblem for the ways in which cultural complicity and social satire, pension-seeking and ironic distance, resist being resolved into a dialectical view of the world. It is revealing that both playwrights, having taken the conventions of wit comedy to their limits, drifted away from the theatre while they were still in their thirties. Their final plays offer, at once, comic deferral, satiric defiance and gentlemanly disinterest. Etherege and Wycherley leave the stage still on the criminal's side, even as they seek the patronage and estates that, they hope, will secure their futures as men of 'idleness'.

NOTES

1   Macaulay (1900, 3: 156–63); Lamb (1899, 2: 277–89). On the history of responses to Etherege and Wycherley see Markley (2000) and Harwood (1982).
2   On the politics of the theatre in this period, see Markley (1995) and Owen (1996).
3   On interpellation see Althusser (1986) and Žižek (1989). Ideology, in this regard, differs from overtly articulated political positions; it is neither a consciously held set of beliefs nor the bad faith imposition of false consciousness on those who are victimized by a corrupt system. Rather, ideology can be defined as the complex of discourses and practices that naturalize historically contingent conditions of property, gender, political authority, truth, civility and identity as the ways of the world, as 'just the way things are', as what 'everybody knows'. Ideology does not, therefore, take the form of external modes of repression but of the processes of internalizing the strictures that enjoin us to police ourselves – what Behn terms in her poem 'The Golden Age' 'those Politick Curbs to keep man in'.

REFERENCES AND FURTHER READING

Althusser, Louis (1986). *For Marx*. London: Verso.
Berglund, Lisa (1990). 'The Language of the Libertines: Subversive Morality in *The Man of Mode*', *Studies in English Literature, 1500–1900* 30, 369–86.
Brown, Laura (1981). *English Dramatic Form, 1660–1760*. New Haven, CT: Yale University Press.
Burke, Helen (1988). 'Wycherley's "Tendentious Joke": The Discourse of Alterity in *The Country Wife*', *The Eighteenth Century: Theory and Interpretation* 29, 227–41.

Canfield, J. Douglas (1997). *Tricksters and Estates: On the Ideology of Restoration Comedy*. Lexington: University Press of Kentucky.

Gill, Pat (1994). *Interpreting Ladies: Women, Wit and Morality in the Restoration Comedy of Manners*. Athens: University of Georgia Press.

Goldstone, Jack A. (1991). *Revolution and Rebellion in the Early Modern World*. Berkeley and Los Angeles: University of California Press.

Harwood, John (1982). *Critics, Values, and Restoration Comedy*. Carbondale: Southern Illinois University Press.

Hawkins, Harriett (1972). *Likenesses of Truth in Elizabethan and Restoration Drama*. Oxford: Clarendon Press.

Holland, Norman (1959). *The First Modern Comedies: The Significance of Etherege, Wycherley, and Congreve*. Cambridge, MA: Harvard University Press.

Holland, Peter (1979). *The Ornament of Action*. Cambridge: Cambridge University Press.

Hughes, Derek (1996). *English Drama, 1660–1700*. Oxford: Clarendon Press.

Hume, Robert (1976). *The Development of English Drama in the Late Seventeenth Century*. Oxford: Clarendon Press.

Husboe, Arthur (1987). *Sir George Etherege*. Boston: Twayne.

Hynes, Peter (1996). 'Against Theory? Knowledge and Action in Wycherley's Plays', *Modern Philology* 94, 163–89.

Kaufman, Anthony (1979). 'Idealization, Disillusion, and Narcissistic Rage in Wycherley's *The Plain Dealer*', *Criticism* 21, 119–33.

Kewes, Paulina (1998). *Authorship and Appropriation: Writing for the Stage in England, 1660–1710*. Oxford: Clarendon Press.

Lamb, Charles (1899). 'On the Artificial Comedy of the Last Century', in *The Life and Works of Charles Lamb*, ed. Alfred Ainger. 12 vols. London: Macmillan.

Macaulay, Thomas Babington (1843; reprinted 1900). *Critical and Historical Essays*, ed. Israel Gollancz. London: Dent.

McCarthy, B. Eugene (1979). *William Wycherley: A Biography*. Athens: University of Ohio Press.

Markley, Robert (1988). *Two-Edg'd Weapons: Style and Ideology in the Comedies of Etherege, Wycherley, and Congreve*. Oxford: Clarendon Press.

Markley, Robert (1995). '"Be Impudent, Be Saucy, Forward, Bold, Touzing and Leud": The Politics of Masculine Sexuality and Feminine Desire in Behn's Tory Comedies', in J. Douglas Canfield and Deborah Payne (eds), *Cultural Readings of Restoration and Eighteenth-century English Theater*. Athens: University of Georgia Press, 114–40.

Markley, Robert (2000). 'The Canon and Its Critics', in Deborah Payne Fisk (ed.), *The Cambridge Companion to Restoration Drama*. Cambridge: Cambridge University Press, 226–42.

Morrow, Laura (1990). 'The Right Snuff: Dorimant and the Will to Meaning', *Restoration* 14, 15–21.

Neill, Michael (1983). 'Heroic Heads and Humble Tails: Sex, Politics, and the Restoration Comic Rake', *The Eighteenth Century: Theory and Interpretation* 24, 115–39.

Neill, Michael (1988). 'Horned Beasts and China Oranges: Reading the Signs in *The Country Wife*', *Eighteenth-century Life* 12, 3–17.

Owen, Susan J. (1996). 'Sexual Politics and Party Politics in Behn's Drama, 1678–1683', in Janet Todd (ed.), *Aphra Behn Studies*. Cambridge: Cambridge University Press, 15–29.

Payne, Deborah C. (1986). 'Reading the Signs in *The Country Wife*', *Studies in English Literature, 1500–1900* 26, 403–19.

Rogers, Katharine M. (1972). *William Wycherley*. New York: Twayne.

Sedgwick, Eve Kosofsky (1984). 'Sexualism and the Citizen of the World: Wycherley, Sterne, and Male Homosocial Desire', *Critical Inquiry* 11, 226–45.

Thompson, James (1984). *Language in Wycherley's Plays: Seventeenth-century Language Theory and Drama*. University, AL: University of Alabama Press.

Thompson, Peggy (1992). 'The Limits of Parody in *The Country Wife*', *Studies in Philology* 89, 100–14.

Underwood, Dale (1957). *Etherege and the Seventeenth-century Comedy of Manners*. New Haven, CT: Yale University Press.

Velissariou, Aspasia (1995). 'Patriarchal Tactics of Control and Female Desire in Wycherley's *The Gentleman Dancing-Master* and *The Country Wife*', *Texas Studies in Language and Literature* 37, 115–26.

Weber, Harold (1986). *The Restoration Rake-Hero: Transformations in Sexual Understanding in the Seventeenth Century*. Madison: University of Wisconsin Press.

Wycherley, William (1966). *The Complete Plays of William Wycherley*, ed. Gerald Weales. New York: Doubleday.

Zimbardo, Rose (1965). *Wycherley's Drama: A Link in the Development of English Satire*. New Haven, CT: Yale University Press.

Žižek, Slavoj (1989). *The Sublime Object of Ideology*. London: Verso.

20

'Who Vices Dare Explode': Thomas Shadwell, Thomas Durfey and Didactic Drama of the Restoration

Christopher J. Wheatley

No companion to Restoration drama of thirty years ago would have given a separate chapter to Durfey and Shadwell. The mud spattered on their names by such figures as Dryden, Swift, Pope and Johnson effectively killed interest in their plays for modern scholars, even though their works had remained popular for much of the eighteenth century (Pope and Swift were even nominally friends of Durfey when they mocked his writing). Indeed, other than Congreve, Dryden, Etherege, Farquhar, Vanbrugh and Wycherley among comic playwrights, and Dryden, Otway (and maybe Lee) among tragic playwrights, most dramatists of the Restoration received little attention in the first two-thirds of the twentieth century, even among specialists of Restoration and eighteenth-century English literature. 'Comedy of manners' dominated critical discussion of comedy, and 'heroic' and 'pathetic' were the common designations for serious plays. Neither Shadwell's nor Durfey's plays fit comfortably in any of these categories. A shift in scholarly emphasis slowly brought attention to playwrights other than those usually anthologized. The publication of *The London Stage, 1660–1800* made available the performance records for the entire period and made clear how complicated the picture of theatrical movements actually was. Robert Hume, in his seminal work *The Development of English Drama in the Late Seventeenth Century* (1976), created an extended taxonomy of dramatic genres which made it necessary for other scholars to read many more plays than they had previously, and required a greater willingness to consider the dramatists who did not fit the largely artificial critical template that had developed since the Restoration (all dates for the premieres of plays in this chapter are from Hume).

Shadwell and Durfey well repay extended study, although it is not self-evident that they should be paired in a critical discussion, since they differed in social class, contemporary regard and political affiliation. Durfey's background is clouded in obscurity. Sir Richard Steele, a friend of Durfey in his later life, asserted that Durfey's father was a grandnephew of Honoré d'Urfé, the author of *L'Astrée* and a member of a noble family, and that his mother was a gentlewoman named Marmion, and thus he was related to the playwright Shackerley Marmion (the DLB account is derived from Steele 1959: 138–42). However, no one, including Cyrus Lawrence Day, who did extensive work on the biographical problems of Durfey in his edition of *The Songs of Thomas Durfey*, has found supporting evidence for these claims, and the chronology represents significant difficulties. Durfey did not attend university, and while Langbaine declared Durfey to have been bred for the law, there is more contemporary evidence that he was a scrivener's apprentice. Indeed, Durfey's probably humble origins are a useful corrective to the generalization that the Restoration playwrights were an aristocratic group.

Shadwell, on the other hand, was from the gentry, and a not insignificant family. His father was a royalist during the Civil War and suffered financially for it, but although Shadwell grew up in limited financial circumstances his family's rank was assured. John Shadwell, Thomas's father, became an early version of the roving colonial administrator, serving as recorder of Galway, attorney-general for Connaught and attorney-general for Tangier. Shadwell himself attended Gonville and Caius at Cambridge and studied at the Middle Temple for the bar. Although he married an actress and ended up writing for the theatre, Shadwell's social rank was well above Durfey's.

Shadwell's and Durfey's reputations were also by no means equal. John Wilmot, Earl of Rochester, paired Shadwell with Wycherley as the writers of 'true comedy':

> Shadwell's unfinished works do yet impart
> Great proof of force of nature, none of art:
> With just, bold strokes he dashes here and there,
> Showing great mastery, with little care,
> And scorns to varnish his good touches o'er
> To make the fools and women praise 'em more.

At least one of the reasons Dryden came to dislike Shadwell was this favourable estimation in a poem that begins 'Well, sir, 'tis granted I said Dryden's rhymes / Were stol'n, unequal, nay dull many times'. In contrast to the socially clumsy Dryden, Shadwell was comfortable with the wits. Etherege, while ambassador to the Imperial court at Ratisbon, specifically asked for Shadwell's latest play, *The Squire of Alsatia*:

> Tho' I have given over writing plays, I shou'd be glad to read a good one, wherefore pray lett Will: Richards send me Mr. Shadwells when it is printed, that I may know what follies are in fashion. The fops I know are grown stale, and he is likely to pick up the best collection of new ones.

As it happens Etherege did not like the play, but it is striking that he admires Shadwell's sharp eye for folly. And Langbaine writes in *An Account of the English Dramatic Poets* that Shadwell's comedies are 'Better than Mr. *Dryden*'s; as having more variety of Characters, and those drawn from the Life; I mean Men's Converse and Manners, and not from other Men's ideas, copied out of their publick Writings'.

Durfey had his friends among the nobility, but only Charles Sackville, Earl of Dorset, was comfortable among the court wits called 'the merry band' (Dorset was also a patron of Shadwell and primarily responsible for Shadwell becoming poet laureate after Dryden). James Butler, Duke of Ormond, was an admirer of Durfey's work, and Philip Sidney, third Earl of Leicester, was a patron. But if Durfey's aristocratic friends were not numbered with the gentlemen who wrote with ease, and literary evaluations of his work were largely negative, he nevertheless had friends who in terms of success mattered more than Rochester, Dryden and Shadwell combined. Charles II admired *A Fond Husband* so much he asked Dryden to write a play like it, a request which Kirk Combe is surely right in suggesting must have driven Dryden nearly round the bend (Combe 1995: 159). Nevertheless, Dryden wrote to Lord Latimer that he was complying with Charles II's request with the help of the king himself: 'it will be almost such another piece of business as the fond Husband, for such the King will have it, who is parcell poet with me in the plott; one of the designs being a story he was pleasd formerly to tell me; and therefore I hope he will keep the jest in countenance by laughing at it'. The resulting play, *Mr Limberham*, although praised by modern critics, had nothing like the success of *A Fond Husband*. After the Glorious Revolution, Queen Mary greatly admired Durfey's *The Comical History of Don Quixote*. Still, while the patronage of monarchs and wealthy noblemen was doubtless both financially and socially gratifying, Durfey had nothing like Shadwell's critical reputation as a playwright.

Certainly for much of their careers their political differences made them open enemies. Shadwell was by far the most important of the Whig playwrights; as such he believed in the primacy of parliamentary control of the British government. Durfey was a Tory until the Glorious Revolution of 1688; that is, he supported the claims of Charles II and James II that Parliament was usurping some of the rightful prerogatives of the monarch. The Whigs tended to be violently anti-Catholic, while Tories, particularly those with close ties to the Stuart monarchy, tended to support religious tolerance (the Stuarts hoped to add Catholics and Dissenters to their list of supporters). Of course after 1688 Durfey decided he really had nothing against William III and his wife Mary and become a firm supporter of the revolutionary settlement.

Shadwell's political convictions were deeply felt – so much so that his explosive *The Lancashire Witches* (*c*.October 1681) led to his being tacitly barred from the stage for seven years (with the possible exception of work he may have done on his brother-in-law Thomas Jevon's *The Devil of a Wife* [1686] – see Richards 1906). In the play Sir Edward, the model of a country gentleman, educated, tolerant and sceptical, is placed in opposition to Catholic cruelty and lechery, and Anglican intolerance (Munns 1996; Owen 1996). When Shadwell became laureate in 1688, replacing the Tory Dryden, it was at least partially a recognition for the poverty he had endured for his support of Whig ideology. Durfey, on the other hand, was flexible in his political positions, although by modern standards a conservative who believed that the status quo was worth preserving whenever possible. This was not an unusual position at the time.

William III, the beneficiary of the Glorious Revolution, and an admirer of Durfey's songs, described himself to Halifax as a trimmer.

Shadwell satirized Durfey and his successful play, *The Fond Husband* (May 1677), with a hilarious play within a play in *The True Widow* (probably March 1678). When the play is disrupted by bravos, the normative character Carlos says, 'there is no loss in the Play; this *Prickett* can write none but Low Farce, and his fools are rather odious than ridiculous'. Subsequently, Shadwell's enmity became overtly political during the tensions of the Exclusion Crisis. In *The Tory-Poets: a Satyr* (1682), Durfey follows Dryden, Otway and Behn, in descending order of offences against liberty and taste:

> As Toads spue poyson he doth libels vent,
> Of Villainy the very Excrement;
> A brave court mixture; for he is at once,
> A *Debauchee*, *Buffoon*, a *Knave*, a *Dunce*,
> Here hold my Muse! the Task's too hard for thee,
> To bow so low, even below Infamy:
> Thou never yet to write with dirt hadst skill,
> Or from a Dunghill tookst a stinking quill.

Michael Alssid regards the pairing of Juvenalian and Horatian standpoints as characteristic of Shadwell's comedies in general (1967: 57). Here, the vituperation is characteristic of Juvenalian satire, in that moderation is not a virtue when confronting vice. At the same time in the Horatian mode, Durfey is beneath the contempt of a man of the world. Durfey is an object of satire for his politics, but not worth the lashing of Juvenalian satire because of his ineptitude as a writer. This was, of course, the tone that Dryden had taken with Shadwell in *MacFlecknoe*, but there Dryden's extended attack, despite its affectation of urbanity, indicates a genuine anger not perceptible in Shadwell's brief sallies against Durfey (there is a real rage in Shadwell's attacks against his former acquaintances, Dryden and Otway).

No shrinking violet himself, Tom Durfey launched his own fusillade at Shadwell. In particular Durfey uses *Sir Barnaby Whig* (*c.*October 1681) to attack Shadwell's *The Lancashire Witches* (Owen 1996: ch. 6). *The Lancashire Witches* was printed with italicized passages to indicate what had to be cut from production to avoid political offence, particularly a satire on an Anglican priest. Durfey's dedication complains that 'in this Age, 'tis not a Poets Merit, but his Party that must do his business; so that if his Play consist of a witch, a Devil, or a Broomstick, so he have but a Priest at one end of the Play; and a Faction at 'tother end of the Pit, it shall be fam'd for an excellent piece'. The title character is a 'huge fat fellow' who writes propaganda for the Whigs; Wilding rails at Sir Barnaby when he affects wit, 'thou double Traytor, dar'st thou assasinate that too – thou contrary to Wit as Loyalty'. Sir Barnaby is also depicted as lacking any religious belief, and willing to become a Puritan, an Anglican, a Catholic or a Muslim if he sees financial advantage, and Shadwell's religious beliefs were an object of suspicion at that time. Durfey is at his best where Shadwell's offences are itemized in a song the title character sings about himself:

> Farewell my Lov'd Science, my former delight,
> Moliere is quite rifled, then how should I write?
> My fancy's grown sleepy, my quibbling is done:
> And design and invention, alas! I have none.
> But still let the Town never doubt my condition:
> Though I fall a damn'd Poet, I'le mount a Musician.
>
> I got Fame by filching from Poems and Plays,
> But my Fidling and Drinking have lost me the Bays;
> Like a Fury I rail'd, like a Satyr I writ,
> Thersite my humour, and Fleckno my Wit.
> But to make some amends for my snarling and lashing
> I divert all the Town with my Thrumming and Thrashing.

Plagiarism is, of course, a standard charge that Restoration dramatists traded with each other when annoyed, but Shadwell's early plays *The Humorists* and *The Miser* were partially derived from Molière, so he was vulnerable. More damaging is the claim that Shadwell has the ill temper of a satirist but not the wit. Worse is the imputation that Shadwell is not really a gentleman, as Thersite is the only completely unheroic character in the *Iliad*. Even in this passage, however, there is a double-edged insult. It is true that Shadwell prided himself on his musicianship – so, too, did Durfey, and in introducing the subject Durfey invites direct comparison to his own advantage, having sung with Charles II (he would eventually sing for William III). In fact, one of the similarities Shadwell and Durfey share is the importance of music to their careers and their conception of drama.

Durfey and Shadwell clearly found each other's politics pernicious prior to 1688, but there seems, at least to me, to be little personal animus towards each other. To a great extent this is probably a function of Shadwell's awareness that Durfey was beneath him, not merely in rank and achievement, but in terms of dramatic subjects. Shadwell wrote comedy and Durfey frequently wrote the lowest subcategory of comedy, farce, where humour arises from mistaken identities and slapstick. They were, however, artistically related at times as the two foremost practitioners of Jonsonian humours comedy. Moreover, although each writes one interesting 'serious' play, their works are almost exclusively comic in nature. Durfey ends up writing a prologue to Shadwell's posthumous *The Volunteers* (November 1692), and sums up what the two playwrights have in common:

> So, shall I to his *Genius* give just due,
> And pleasure what, still strove to pleasure you:
> I mean all you that can good *Satyr* bear,
> Let th' rest look grum, make mouths, and sweat for fear.

Although in the 1670s Shadwell flirted with the celebration of the libertine ethos that I have elsewhere called the comic sublime, and Durfey contributed to it greatly, for most of their careers Durfey and Shadwell consistently dramatized the danger to society of the witty, promiscuous rake, and asserted the necessity of his domestication in marriage to a virtuous woman. That is, their gay couples must escape the pleasure of witty combat and accept a relationship based on mutual affection. As a consequence, when many playwrights reduce their women characters to mere objects of prey, Shadwell and Durfey present women who were frequently intellectually and morally superior to the rakes who seek to seduce them; indeed, in the case of Durfey, in several crucial cases the men are too inferior to the women, and no marriage occurs at the end to provide dramatic closure. When the rake does marry the virtuous heroine, he assumes his rightful place in society as the defender of order.

Shadwell makes several attempts at serious drama, including his adaptation of John Fountain's unstaged drama of 1661, *The Rewards of Virtue. The Royal Shepherdesse* (February 1669), as indicated by its title, was a pastoral romance, and reasonably successful (it ran for six nights and, according to Pepys, emptied the rival house of the King's Men, who tried to compete with Fletcher's *The Faithful Shepherd*); the original appealed to Shadwell because 'the Rules of Morality and good Manners are strictly observed in it'. He also does a workmanlike adaptation of Shakespeare with *The History of Timon of Athens* (*c.*January 1678), adding a plot involving a choice for Timon between Evandra, who is beautiful and good, yet whom Timon has already enjoyed, and Melissa, a virgin with a corrupted mind. The morality of the play is prudential, although it attacks marriages of economic convenience.

But Shadwell's most interesting so-called 'serious' play is *The Libertine* (June 1675). Variously seen as a horror play, a satire on the libertine ethos in Restoration comedy, or as a black comedy itself, the play engages the popular subject of Don Juan, previously treated by Tirso de Molina in *El Burlador de Seville y convidado de piedra* and Molière's *Dom Juan*, among others. In Shadwell's version, Don John and his friends Lopez and Antonio commit numerous crimes in between speeches extolling appetite. Don John has killed his father and rapes nuns. Lopez has killed his older brother, and Antonio has made his sisters pregnant. At times Don John seems like a character out of Sade in that vicious crimes are discussed with elaborate philosophical justification:

> Nature gave us our Senses, which we please:
> Nor does our Reason war against our Sense.
> By Nature's order, Sense should guide our Reason,
> Since to the mind all objects Sense conveys.

Coleridge, when discussing the Don Juan character, takes all his examples from Shadwell and presents the character as both an abstract of pure materialism and an example of the confusion of means and ends:

In fine the character of *Don John* consists in the union of every thing desirable to human nature, as *means*, and which therefore by the well known law of association become desirable on their own account. On their own account, and in their own dignity they are here displayed, as being employed to *ends* so *un*human, that in effect, they appear almost as *means* without an *end*.

Don John has the characteristics of the heroes of Restoration comedy: courage, wit, wealth and good looks. However, he cannot practise virtue, since for the materialist the only true virtue is satisfaction of appetite. Shadwell finally has Don Juan hauled off to Hell, but, in a sense, he is destroyed for the audience by showing the absurdity of fashionable hedonism (a theme that recurs in *The Woman Captain*, *c*.September 1679).

Durfey's first effort at serious drama is the eminently forgettable *The Siege of Memphis* (*c*.September 1676), but in 1700 he writes the unique and powerful two-part *The Famous History of the Rise and Fall of Massaniello* (*c*.May 1699). The play did badly, but then, few plays did well in the season of 1700. The subject of the play is the 1647 peasant rebellion in Naples led by the fisherman Thomas Aiello. The members of the nobility speak verse and the peasants speak prose, but both sides are corrupted by power. While the play is sometimes seen as a 'Tory' portrayal of the grim consequences of mob rule, in fact Durfey builds sympathy for the peasant rebellion, only to show that no one in ascendancy is capable of self-denial (Wheatley 1992: 233). Massaniello is initially a hero defending the starving and impoverished peasants; by the end he tells Aurelia, the former vice-queen, 'I am Mad too, and so are all my People; the Times are Mad, we should be in the Fashion'. In an inversely parallel development, Mataloni, one of the exploitative nobility at the beginning of the play, becomes a sympathetic romantic hero, who at least recognizes his failure in power: 'Pray, Sir, not too much of your Trust, I may deceive ye; for what I have done, perhaps I had my Reasons, but if you burthen me with Place and Office – I shall do like most of the rest in such Cases; I shall serve my self in the first place'. Ultimately the play suggests that the English should be grateful for the social stability that was a consequence of the Glorious Revolution, but the play's energy comes from its portrayal of a society where all class relations are adversarial and no political structure exists to restrain those in power.

Shadwell's and Durfey's place in the history of musical theatre assures them a place in any serious discussion of the Restoration stage even aside from their efforts to write morally instructive drama. Brian Corman and Todd S. Gilman argue that 'no dramatist or composer is more important in determining the course of English opera and musical theatre in the late seventeenth century' than Shadwell (1996: 150). Shadwell played the lute and composed both music and lyrics. Shadwell reworked Dryden and Davenant's *Tempest* into the first semi-opera on the English stage. More importantly, his play *Psyche* (February 1675), with music by Matthew Locke and Draghi, featured the first dramatic musical score to be printed in England, and 'is as close as the English came to producing an all-sung native opera before the abortive *Semele* of Congreve and Eccles in 1707' (Corman and Gilman 1996: 153). Shadwell's eclectic taste made him comfortable with both English and Continental music, and songs figure prominently in his plays.

If Shadwell is not the most important figure in the integration of music on the English stage prior to Gay, then Durfey is. Durfey was a prolific songwriter who worked with the best composers of his time, including Henry Purcell from 1688 to 1695, and his lyrics were widely popular on every social level. According to Carolyn Kephart, Durfey virtually invented the form of musical comedy in *The Comical History of Don Quixote* (Parts 1 and 2, May 1694, and Part 3, November 1695) with the addition of pertinent songs to Cervantes's novel, because prior to *The Comical History* semi-operas were invariably serious (Kephart 1989: 88). Throughout his career, his songs are not incidental to his plays but a commentary on the action. Above all, his six-volume collection, *Wit and Mirth: or, Pills to Purge Melancholy* (1719–20), preserved and established a canon of traditional English lyrics that playwrights such as Gay and John O'Keeffe could draw on for ballad operas later in the century.

Aside from the paucity of their serious drama and their importance to musical theatre, Shadwell and Durfey are the two foremost descendants of Jonsonian humours comedy. It is a truism of Restoration criticism that Fletcher was the most important influence on Restoration comedy. Fletcher's plays possessed 'Breeding', 'Courtly Elegance', 'quickness of wit in repartees', 'gentile familiarity of style', and accurately portrayed the conversation of gentlemen (Markley 1984: 92). Jonsonian comedy, on the other hand, emphasized plot construction, urban settings and the humours character himself. The Renaissance theory of humours posited that when the bodily fluids were imbalanced the individual acted immoderately, whether in anger, envy, lust or misanthropy. This is more of a metaphor than a psychological theory in the plays of Jonson: moderation and virtue characterize the normative characters in Jonson's comedies, uncontrolled passions and exaggerated language the diseased.

Although Rothstein claims that Shadwell's drama too is Fletcherian in character (1989: 189), Shadwell repeatedly asserted his allegiance to Jonson. In the preface to his first play, *The Sullen Lovers* (May 1668), he writes,

> I have endeavour'd to represent variety of Humours (most of the persons of the Play differing in their Characters from one another) which was the practice of *Ben Jonson*, whom I think all Dramatick *Poets* ought to imitate, though none are like to come near; he being the onely person that appears to me to have made perfect Representations of Humane Life, most other Authors that I ever read, either have wilde Romantick *Tales* wherein they strein Love and Honour to that Ridiculous height, that it becomes Burlesque.

Here variety of humours indicates Shadwell's interest in delineating distinct characters rather than dramatic types. That is, while there are gay couples, cuckolded citizens, hypocritical Puritans and sexually voracious older women scattered throughout Shadwell's plays, there are also characters who are 'original' to the stage; however, at the same time as the audience recognizes them as unusual, they should also recognize them as an imitation of particular kinds of flawed characters who threaten society.

A True Widow (March 1678) represents an example of how the humours character functions for comic effect and moral instruction. The play failed, although it may be Shadwell's best and is certainly his most complex, and he justifies in the dedication to Sir Charles Sedley both the failure and his theatrical practice:

> Satyr will be always unpleasant to those that deserve it. It was not my design in this Play to please a Bawd of Quality, a vain *Selfish*, a senseless, noisie *Prig*, a methodical Blockhead, having only a form of Wisdom, or a Coxcomb that's run stark mad after wit, which uses him very unkindly, and will never be won by him; nor did I think to please the Widdows in the Name. The three first of these Characters are wholly new, not so much touch'd upon before, and the following ones are new in the greatest part.

The characters are comical in their lack of self-knowledge. Young Maggot is 'an Inns of Court-Man, who neglects his Law and runs mad after Wit, pretending much to Love, and both in spight of Nature, since his face makes him unfit for one, and his brains for the other'. There is a poetic justice involved when he marries Gartrude, the second daughter of the true widow, Lady Cheatly, of the title. Gartrude is so stupid as to be virtually mentally retarded, of a whorish disposition (at one point she copulates with Selfish and Stanmore in quick succession), and she has no fortune, for Lady Cheatly has deceived the citizens of the town in a successful effort to get herself and her daughters married. Shadwell invites no sympathy for either bride or groom.

But the danger of the mentally and socially unbalanced, both to individuals and to society, is real. Lady Busy, 'half bawd, Half Match-maker', is perfectly willing to help Isabella, Lady Cheatly's virtuous daughter, into either marriage or keeping, but thinks the latter more likely in the state of things:

> Now I say, since Custom has so run down Wedlock, what remains? but that we should make use of the next thing to it – good – Nay, not but that Vertue is a rare thing, – Heaven forbid I should detract from that; – But, I say the main is to be respected, a good deal of Money, there's the point. –

The problem is that not merely does Lady Cheatly think this is perfectly normal, but Bellamour, who loves Isabella, prefers keeping as well:

> *Bellamour*: What will nothing down, but to have and hold? I'll marry no body else, and when my inclination dies, leave you its wealthy Widow, you may marry after it.
> *Isabella*: I'll bring no infamy, where I bring my person.
> *Bellamour*: This coldness inflames me more: consent to my desires, and none of the Ladies shall outshine, no Equipage exceed yours.

Isabella: And I the while shall be a part of your equipage, be kept; what is it but to wear your Livery, and take Board-wages?

An individual must recognize his or her role in society and live up to it. Isabella, along with the exemplary male Carlos, knows that economics are not the basis of fully realized human relations. A mistress is a servant of the appetites of her keeper, while a wife is nearly an equal in the most important of social relationships. Fornication is not only a vice in itself, but threatens the future, for Bellamour is a gentleman with an estate. Satire lashes vice in the play, but positive moral instruction comes from Bellamour, who must realize his errors. After nearly losing Isabella, he finally takes her even without a dowry: 'When I made these offers, I did not know half your worth: I was a fair Chapman for your Beauty; but your Vertue, and other Perfections, are inestimable'. Characters' faults must be amendable to be an object of satire, and the amelioration takes place in the audience as well (Corman 1984: 135).

Durfey's explicit and extensive debt to Jonson was documented by C. B. Graham (1947). Despite Durfey's affinity for farce, when Charles Gildon praises Durfey's *The Marriage Hater Match'd* (January 1692) in a letter prefaced to the first edition, he does so in terms that indicate what the appropriate standards of critical judgement should be: 'in spight of all the disadvantages it labour'd under of Action, and Audience, [it] pleas'd on, after several times Repitition, and will as long as *Wit*, *Humour*, and *Plot* shall be esteem'd as necessary Materials to compose a good *Play*'. 'Wit' no longer bears any Fletcherian overtones as many significantly wittier playwrights had come and gone, but so far as I know no Restoration critic disputed Jonson's mastery of plot and humour.

Durfey adapted three plays by Fletcher: *Trick for Trick* (c.March 1678) from *Monsieur Thomas* (1615), *A Commonwealth of Women* (August 1685) from *The Sea Voyage* (1622), and *A Fool's Preferment* (April 1688) from *The Noble Gentleman* (1626). Nevertheless, these plays show a consistent rejection of the plasticity of character identified by Rothstein and Kavenik (1988: 46) as central to Fletcherian comedy (Wheatley 1996). In both Fletcher's *Monsieur Thomas* and Durfey's *Trick for Trick*, the central character Thomas enrages his father by pretending to reform, but tells his sister Dorothy not to worry for he can calm their father if need be. In Durfey's play, the point is he cannot. Thomas's father is a former rake, his betrothed Cellide insistent that he reform, and he cannot satisfy both. As his tricks spin out of his control, he attempts to rape Cellide in front of her father, pass the gentlewoman Sabina to his servant Launce, and all this happens in the house of his friend Valentine, under whose protection the women are. By the end of the play only Valentine is partially placated, while Cellide and her father Sir Peregreene are swearing vengeance. Fletcher's witty gentleman is translated by Durfey into a character inclined to vice by his corrupt upbringing, and this is reflected both in his behaviour and his language (Hughes 1996: 204). In his adaptations of Fletcher, Durfey is at his most Jonsonian.

Shadwell and Durfey both in the 1670s bowed to the prevailing interest in sex comedies. Indeed, Durfey was one of the most successful practitioners of it. In *The Fond Husband* he combines sexual intrigue with elevated language to start a vogue for what I have elsewhere referred to as 'the comic sublime' (Wheatley 1993a). Emilia, according to her cuckolded husband, Peregrine Bubble, is 'one of the pearls of Eloquence. – And Pop, – by the way let me tell you, there's ne'er an Orator in Christendom has more Tropes and Figures, take her when her hands in'. On one level the association of the elevated style with adultery is comic, a mismatching of elements that mirrors the mismatching of Bubble with the beautiful and witty Emilia. On another level, Emilia's victories over Bubble, Ranger (another rake in love with Emilia) and Maria (Bubble's sister and in love with Rashley, the rake with whom Emilia is having an affair) show a splendid indifference to convention, a nobly irregular attitude towards mercenary marriages.

Shadwell's flirtation with positive portrayals of libertinism in *Epsom Wells* (December 1672) and *The Virtuoso* (May 1676) remains ambiguous, although the rakes are clearly less censored than in the rest of his plays, and no moral exemplars are present. In *Epsom Wells* Bevil has an affair with the wife of his friend Woodly, only bad luck keeps Rains from enjoying Mrs Woodly as well, and a surprising demand for marriage keeps Rains from having his way with Mrs Jilt. Nevertheless, at the end Bevil and Rains are still accepted as the 'servants' of the virtuous and witty Carolina and Lucia. In *The Virtuoso*, Bruce and Longvil are philosophical libertines; the play opens with Bruce quoting Lucretius on the indifference of the divine to man and saying approvingly 'Thou reconcil'st Philosophy with Verse, and dost, almost alone, demonstrate that Poetry and Good Sence may go together'. Their philosophical detachment stands them in good stead, because the plot complication is that while Bruce loves Clarinda and Longvil Miranda, Miranda loves Bruce and Clarinda Longvil. Happily for them both women are 'handsome, rich, and honest', so they can cheerfully switch the object of their affections.

Paralleling the successful courtship of Bevil and Rains in *Epsom Wells* is the dissolution of their friend Woodly's marriage. As much a rake as either of them, he attempts Carolina's virtue unsuccessfully, while Mrs Woodly cheerfully commits adultery with Bevil and seeks it with Rains. In *The Virtuoso* Bruce and Longvil each commit adultery with Lady Gimcrack under the impression that they are fornicating with their friend's beloved. This brings them nearly to a duel which highlights the only real danger to the rake of Restoration comedy: his social equal. As I have argued elsewhere at length, in these plays Shadwell shows that the natural tendency to seek pleasure and indulge one's own self-interest is ultimately not satisfying (Wheatley 1993c: 129–45), and Canfield is surely right when he says Shadwell in *The Virtuoso* creates his best Jonsonian characters in Sir Formal Trifle and Sir Samuel (1997: 103). However, there is no denying that *Epsom Wells* and *The Virtuoso* look more like Wycherley and Etherege than any other plays in Shadwell's corpus.

Nevertheless, throughout Shadwell's career he insisted that drama was supposed to be morally instructive and that his was. There seems no reason to doubt his sincerity; Shadwell was attacked for his politics and, by Dryden, for dullness, but no one accused him of hypocrisy. Durfey, on the other hand, was accused of hypocrisy, and he defended himself in *The Moralist*:

> That I pretend to't [virtue] shall appear in this,
> Justice and Honour with regard I prize,
> And Virtues Laws have still before my Eyes;
> And tho Offences cannot be withstood
> By the frail Government of Flesh and Blood,
> Yet reason daily glittering in my Sight,
> Still makes me take in Folly less delight.

When Jeremy Collier attacked the profanity of the English stage, Durfey was among those singled out. Durfey responded angrily in the preface to *The Campaigners* (June 1698), accusing Collier of selectivity in his choice of plays:

> nay, tho by his Book we may suppose he has read a thousand, yet amongst twenty of my Comedies Acted and Printed, he never heard of the *Royalist*, the *Boarding School*, the *Marriage Hater Match'd*, the *Richmond Heiress*, the *Virtuous Wife*, and others, all whose whole Plots and designs I dare affirm, tend to that principal instance, which he proposes, and which we allow, *viz.* the depression of Vice and encouragement of Virtue.

Not all of Durfey's plays qualify as didactic drama, but only Durfey approaches Shadwell in terms of number of plays that anticipate the movement away from unrepentant rakish heroes that culminated in what is sometimes called 'sentimental' drama in the eighteenth century, after a belief that moral behaviour begins in feelings of revulsion for vice, sympathy for suffering and attraction to virtue (Smith 1966; Lynch 1930). Neither Shadwell nor Durfey writes sentimental drama; their protagonists reform because of a recognition that what is forgivable in youth becomes inappropriate and aesthetically unpleasant in men and women who have social roles to fill.

In Durfey's *The Virtuous Wife* (September 1679) Beverly, who early in the play defends drunkenness as the great liberator of man from natural and social order, dons a mask to escape his wife and seek his mistress, Jenny. His wife Olivia also dons the disguise of a rake to bring him to his senses by seducing Jenny. Far from being liberating, the carnival of disguise reveals Beverly's failure in judgement. By the end of the play even Beverly sees that his decision is wrong not just on moral grounds, but by aesthetic standards as well: 'this piece of Countrey dirt was once my Mistriss, Lady of my Heart, of all my Love, my Honour, whose face made me forget a virtuous Wife, to fawn and doat upon her hypocrysie'. The desire for novelty, characteristic of Etherege's Dorimant, here indicates deficient taste and judgement, as Beverly confesses to Olivia: 'all base drossy thoughts, that soil'd the life and lustre of my Judgement, shall vanish; and instead of those, thy Beauty, Love, Constancy, and Wit, shall crown my heart'.

In most of Shadwell's plays, an exemplary male character is paired with a hero who must reform. Thus the audience is always aware of the standards of moral judgement. In Shadwell's most successful comedy, *The Squire of Alsatia* (May 1688), he varies the normal dramatic structure to contrast two brothers, one raised in the country far from fashionable dissipations by his father, and the other in the city as a gentleman of fortune by his uncle. Both educational schemes on the face of it appear to be failures. The country brother, Belfond Sr, is helpless against the sharpers of Alsatia, a 'liberty' in London, and enamoured of vice when finally introduced to it. The city brother, Belfond Jr, has one cast mistress (Termagant) seeking his head, seduces another (Lucia), the daughter of a respectable lawyer who is heart-broken by his child's fall, and assumes that a lie well told can get him out of most kinds of trouble. But Belfond Jr's education has made him, as his guardian Sir Edward says, 'a Compleat Gentleman, fit to serve his Country in any capacity'. After Belfond Jr has sown his wild oats (a natural drive virtuous or vicious only by its social consequences), like the energetic young man he is, his marriage to Isabella locks him into the social position for which he was born and trained. The individual learns to tell the difference between short- and long-term interests, and, under the guidance of a wise and benevolent father-figure – common in Shadwell's plays from *The Lancashire Witches* to the posthumous *The Volunteers* – recognize obligations to society that are larger than his own personal desires. Morality is to some extent prudential; probable consequences shape ethical judgement.

Ethical behaviour is closely related to political obligation for a gentleman. In Shadwell's *The Volunteers, or The Stock-jobbers* (November 1692) – a scene from which is borrowed by Caryl Churchill to open her farce, *Serious Money*, on business excesses in England under Thatcher in the 1980s – a virtuous gentleman like Hackwell Jr serves his country as a volunteer in the war in Ireland, while a buffoon like Sir Timothy is indifferent to political turmoil: 'tis all one to me who Reigns, if I can keep my 2000 Pound a Year, and enjoy myself with the Ladies'. In Durfey's *Love for Money* (January 1691), Lady Addleplot (a cross-dressing part) comically embodies the extremism inherent in Jacobitism because of its acceptance of Stuart absolutism: a man acts the part of a woman who seeks the aid of Catholics and Dissenters (both conventional scapegoats after the Glorious Revolution) because she cannot tell the difference between natural hierarchies (male authority over women) and superstitious veneration (for the Pope and James II). Both Shadwell and Durfey thus help to define public-interest patriotism at the end of the seventeenth century (Wheatley 1993b).

The consequences of an ethical system based on one's role in society are not necessarily attractive for women, and Shadwell was aware of the difficulties. Reclaiming wealthy libertines for the good of society and themselves may be a laudable activity, but it is still a risky business for the heroine. Torn between love and the need to marry well to ensure that children will be raised and supported, pressured by the rakes and the heroine's own desires while at the same time aware of what honour and family require, the heroine can only find an appropriate role (in a patriarchal society) in marriage, while marriage itself threatens to tie her to an uncongenial and unappreciative fop or bumpkin. Gertrude is addressing the wrong audience in Lord Bellamy in *Bury-Fair* (*c*.April 1689), for he is the exemplary figure in the play, but she accurately depicts the function of women in marriage: 'indeed it makes me smile, to think of a grave Mother, or, for want of her, a wise Father, putting a Daughter into a Room, like a Hare out of a Basket, and letting him loose; that is, to act the Part of a Lover before Marriage, and never think of it afterward'. The metaphor is drawn from the sport of coursing, where greyhounds run down a hare. Women are prey, valuable for dowry and reproductive capacity, and, after marriage captive in potentially brutal relationships. Gertrude does accept Wildish at the end of *Bury-Fair*, but his reformation seems tenuous.

Durfey goes much further than Shadwell. Although Marsden (1990) argues that in *The Injured Princess* (1682) – an adaptation of *Cymbeline* – Durfey creates a heroine whose passivity anticipates the pathetic heroines of later she-tragedies, Eugenia, the central character of that play, is not characteristic of women in Durfey's works as a whole. Indeed, as Derek Hughes says, 'Durfey suggests that the mentality of institutionalized finance is fundamental to all human relationships, and he comes closer than any other male dramatist to Aphra Behn in portraying prostitution as the essential model of dealings between the sexes' (1996: 406). In *The Royalist* (January 1682), Aurelia is seduced by Heartall and then married to the vicious Justice Eitherside, whom she promptly cuckolds with Heartall, even though she realizes that a known score is the primary satisfaction of the rake: 'Nay I see it is not in your power to forbear insulting, for you men always love the Triumph above the Conquest'. Although she attacks the double standard in judgements about promiscuity in society, her situation, a loveless marriage and a liaison with a rake, offers no possibility of amelioration. In *The Richmond Heiress* (April 1693), a group of fortune hunters pursue the heiress Fulvia, including the rake Frederick, who disregards his previous object Sophronia. Ultimately Durfey indulges in idealism, as Fulvia refuses all of her suitors:

> My eyes in contradiction to the World, have ever (scorning Interest) fix'd on Merit, and led by Love and Generous inclination, have strove to make that Sentiment appear by a free present of my Heart and Fortune to one I thought as nobly had deserv'd 'em. but, Oh! the Race of Men are all Deceivers, and my relief, is my resolve to shun 'em.

But Fulvia has a fortune of 50,000 pounds; few real women could afford her ideals.

In exceptionally prolific careers, Durfey (thirty plays, depending on how we count those that had multiple parts) and Shadwell (around nineteen plays) experimented with the forms and subjects of comedy perhaps more than any of their peers. If they lack the studied polish of Etherege and Congreve, and the disturbing ambiguities of Wycherley and Vanbrugh, and perhaps the arguable radical social critique of Behn and Southerne, they nonetheless possess a comic energy that surpasses their more frequently revived contemporaries. Still stageable, their plays are the refutation of most generalizations about Restoration comedy.

REFERENCES AND FURTHER READING

Alssid, Michael W. (1967). *Thomas Shadwell*. New York: Twayne.
Canfield, J. Douglas (1997). *Tricksters and Estates: On the Ideology of Restoration Comedy*. Lexington: University Press of Kentucky.

Combe, Kirk (1995). '"But Loads of Sh__ Almost Choked the Way": Shadwell, Dryden, Rochester, and the Summer of 1676', *Texas Studies in Literature and Language* 37, 127–64.

Combe, Kirk (1996). 'Introduction: Considering Shadwell', in Judith Bailey Slagle (ed.), *Thomas Shadwell Reconsider'd: Essays in Criticism*. Special issue of *Restoration: Studies in English Literary Culture* 20, no. 2 (autumn), 88–100.

Corman, Brian (1984). 'Thomas Shadwell and the Jonsonian Comedy of the Restoration', in Robert Markley and Laura Finke (eds), *From Renaissance to Restoration: Metamorphoses of the Drama*. Cleveland: Bellflower Press, 127–52.

Corman, Brian and Gilman, Todd S. (1996). 'The Musical Life of Thomas Shadwell', in Judith Bailey Slagle (ed.), *Thomas Shadwell Reconsider'd: Essays in Criticism*. Special issue of *Restoration: Studies in English Literary Culture* 20, no. 2 (autumn), 149–64.

Graham, C. B. (1947). 'The Jonsonian Tradition in the Comedies of Thomas D'Urfey', *MLQ* 8, 47–52.

Hughes, Derek (1996). *English Drama, 1660–1700*. Oxford: Clarendon Press.

Hume, Robert D. (1976). *The Development of English Drama in the Late Seventeenth Century*. Oxford: Clarendon Press.

Kephart, Carolyn (1989). 'Thomas Durfey', in Paula Backscheider (ed.), *Dictionary of Literary Biography 80: Restoration and Eighteenth-century Dramatists*. First series. Detroit: Gale Research, 81–93.

Lynch, Kathleen M. (1930). 'Thomas D'Urfey's Contribution to Sentimental Comedy', *Philological Quarterly* 9 (July), 249–59.

Markley, Robert (1984). '"Shakespeare *To Thee Was Dull*": The Phenomenon of Fletcher's Influence', in Robert Markley and Laura Finke (eds), *From Renaissance to Restoration: Metamorphoses of the Drama*. Cleveland: Bellflower Press, 89–126.

Marsden, Jean I. (1990). 'Pathos and Passivity: D'Urfey's *The Injured Princess* and Shakespeare's *Cymbeline*', *Restoration: Studies in English Literary Culture* 14, no. 2, 71–81.

Munns, Jessica (1996). '"The Golden Days of Queen Elizabeth": Thomas Shadwell's *The Lancashire-Witches* and the Politics of Nostalgia', in Judith Bailey Slagle (ed.), *Thomas Shadwell Reconsider'd: Essays in Criticism*. Special issue of *Restoration: Studies in English Literary Culture* 20, no. 2 (autumn), 195–216.

Owen, Susan J. (1996). *Restoration Theatre and Crisis*. Oxford: Clarendon Press.

Richards, Alfred E. (1906). 'A Literary Link between Thomas Shadwell and Christian Felix Weiss', *PMLA* 21, 803–30.

Rothstein, Eric (1989). 'Thomas Shadwell', in Paula Backscheider (ed.), *Dictionary of Literary Biography 80: Restoration and Eighteenth-century Dramatists*. First series. Detroit: Gale Research, 181–95.

Rothstein, Eric and Kavenik, Frances M. (1988). *The Designs of Carolean Comedy*. Carbondale: Southern Illinois University Press.

Smith, John Harrington (1966). 'Shadwell, the Ladies, and the Change in Comedy', in John Loftis (ed.), *Restoration Drama: Modern Essays in Criticism*. New York: Oxford University Press, 236–52.

Steele, Richard (1959). *Richard Steele's Periodical Journalism, 1714–16*, ed. Rae Blanchard. Oxford: Clarendon Press.

Wheatley, Christopher J. (1992). '"Power Like New Wine": The Appetites of Leviathan and Durfey's *Massaniello*', in Patricia B. Craddock and Carla H. Hay (eds), *Studies in Eighteenth-century Culture*, vol. 22. East Lansing: Colleagues Press, 231–51.

Wheatley, Christopher J. (1993a). 'Thomas Durfey's *A Fond Husband*, Sex Comedies of the Late 1670s and Early 1680s, and the Comic Sublime', *Studies in Philology* 90, no. 4 (autumn), 371–90.

Wheatley, Christopher J. (1993b). 'Thomas Shadwell's *The Volunteers* and the Rhetoric of Honor and Patriotism', *ELH* 60, 397–418.

Wheatley, Christopher J. (1993c). *Without God or Reason: The Plays of Thomas Shadwell and Secular Ethics in the Restoration*. Lewisberg: Bucknell University Press.

Wheatley, Christopher J. (1996). '"But Speak Every Thing in its Nature": Influence and Ethics in Durfey's Adaptations of Fletcher', *Journal of English and Germanic Philology* 95, 515–33.

21

Otway, Lee and the Restoration History Play

Paulina Kewes

Thomas Otway and Nathaniel Lee are generally thought of as writers of tragedy. There is, however, another, more revealing, way of considering them: as writers not so much of tragedy as of history. While many contemporary playwrights employed historical plots at one time or another, Otway and Lee were unique in the scope and seriousness of their preoccupation with the past. Virtually all of their rhymed and blank verse tragedies were history plays. That is, not only were they set in the past: they had a known historical setting and had known historical characters.

Why this preoccupation with history? To begin with, the past held authority and fascination for early modern writers and audiences, and mattered far more to them than it does to us. People went to the past, in ways that we do not, for guidance to the present. The minds of dramatists, audiences and readers moved easily across time, detecting parallels between past and present or noting examples of general historical laws which applied to all periods and thus applied to their own. Throughout the seventeenth century the conception of history remained didactic. Yet the split in society and ideology produced by the Civil War in the 1640s made it much harder for people to agree about what the lessons of history were. Whereas before the Civil War there was a degree of consensus, now there was polarization. The restoration of the Stuart monarchy in 1660 reduced the area of disagreements but did not remove them. In the late 1670s, with the onset of the Popish Plot and Exclusion Crisis, interpretations of history were polarized once more.

Of all Restoration dramatists, Otway and Lee are the two leading writers of topical and partisan history plays. However, the stock identification of Otway as a Tory and Lee as a Whig is far too limiting to explain the ideological and political slant of their individual plays. In this chapter I shall look at most of Otway's and Lee's dramatic output. My focus will be on their rhymed heroic dramas and blank verse tragedies founded on history. By situating these plays in their politico-historical contexts, I shall explore the uses they made of the past.

Before I begin the investigation of particular plays, I would like to consider some general questions. What kind of constraints and expectations were Restoration writers of history plays working with? What was allowed and permissible, and what was likely to cause offence? How did the proprieties of historical drama change over time? The mid-seventeenth-century conflict between king and Parliament, which led to Civil War, regicide, republic and restoration of the monarchy, had a lasting impact on politics, drama and history writing. Charles II's return from exile in 1660 was followed by the Act of Oblivion, which ruled that past offences (other than the actual regicide) be forgiven and forgotten. The regime's desire to exorcise and annihilate the past is manifest in the decision to count the new king's reign not from 1660 but from 1649, the year of his father's death on the block. Yet the memory of the recent trauma lived on, shaping the views of the present and determining the course of the future.

Restoration drama had a part in this process. Susan Owen's contribution to this volume discusses the role of censorship and usefully surveys a variety of topical plays. Owen reminds us that the drama was highly political *throughout* the period, becoming even more so during the Popish Plot and Exclusion Crisis (1678–82). What was the influence of ideology and politics on the dramatizations of history? Whether set in Peru, Turkey or medieval England, early Restoration tragicomedies and heroic plays by Roger Boyle, Earl of Orrery, John Dryden and many others retold the story of regicide and restoration, for the most part offering reassuringly happy endings (Maguire 1992). The specificity of the historical settings of those plays was all but obliterated in the service of loyalist and royalist ideology. But the political honeymoon did not last. When Otway and Lee launched their playwriting careers in the early 1670s, the Restoration settlement was under increasing strain. No longer a mere tool for recalling and condemning the mid-century rebellion, history was once again being used by playwrights to reflect on the present. Lee was the pioneer; Otway and others followed shortly. The analogies Lee and Otway drew between the past and the present testify to the relevance of history. Their conflicting and contradictory interpretations of the past point to the erosion of ideological (and political) consensus.

Let me now turn to specifics. I shall start by considering how Otway and Lee appropriated episodes from the history of ancient Rome and early modern Spain, Italy and France. Some of those episodes, notably those selected for dramatization by Lee in *Nero*, *Gloriana*, *Caesar Borgia*, *The Massacre of Paris* and *Lucius Junius Brutus*, had previously furnished sources for Elizabethan and Jacobean plays. How Lee depicts Roman, Italian and French history, and in what ways his depictions resemble or depart from those of pre-Civil War history plays, will be one theme of this chapter. Another will be Otway's figuration of history, ranging from the politically neutral depiction of the past in *Alcibiades* and *Don Carlos* to the complex and equivocal topicality of *Caius Marius* and *Venice Preserv'd*.

Though they portrayed a vast array of historical figures and events, and though they often used radically divergent theatrical vocabularies and means of expression, Otway and Lee were keenly responsive to each other's work so that individual plays can be seen as artistic and ideological retorts to their immediate predecessors, as was Lee's *Lucius Junius Brutus* (1680) to Otway's *Caius Marius* (1679). Otway's and Lee's competing versions of the past were firmly rooted in the here and now of late Restoration England; however, as we shall see, the two writers' implicit, and at times explicit, debate on the status and prerogative of kings, the duties and rights of subjects, the role of religion and the relative merits of different forms of government cannot be reduced to a mere dialogue between the Whig Lee and the Tory Otway. The partisan reception of Lee's and Otway's historical tragedies written during the Popish Plot and Exclusion Crisis is a case in point. We shall ask why Lee's foregrounding of 'repetition with a difference' as a fundamental law of history proved, on at least two occasions, highly politically sensitive and why, by contrast, Otway's profoundly ambiguous representation of history was seen by his contemporaries as innocuous in *Caius Marius*, and as loyalist and Tory in *Venice Preserv'd*.

Lee's *Nero*: Imperial Rome and Carolean England

Written in resounding rhyming couplets, Lee's first play, *The Tragedy of Nero* (1674), recounts the incest, matricide, fratricide and genocide committed by the eponymous Roman tyrant prior to his enforced suicide in the face of treason and rebellion. Replete with topical allusions, *Nero*, soon to be followed by *Gloriana* (1676), *The Rival Queens* (1677) and *Mithridates* (1678), initiates a series of Lee's plays set in the ancient world, which, though not overtly anti-monarchical or anti-Stuart, are covertly critical of aspects of Charles II's personality and government.

How does Lee's representation of imperial despotism in *The Tragedy of Nero* compare with the depictions of Roman tyrants by pre-Civil War playwrights? More broadly, what is the significance of imperial Rome in the early and late Stuart drama? In the early part of the seventeenth century James I and Charles I had deployed imperial iconography to shore up the authority and dignity of monarchical rule; their critics had seized on that iconography to expose the two kings' shortcomings. Voicing the growing concern about the absolutist leanings of the first two Stuart rulers, playwrights such as Ben Jonson, Thomas May, Philip Massinger and Nathaniel Richards drew parallels between imperial Rome and early Stuart England. In doing so they appropriated the rhetoric of contemporary parliamentary polemic and anti-court pamphleteering to anatomize the rise and fall of successive Roman tyrants, from Tiberius to Domitian (Butler 1985). Yet though their Roman plays were written and produced in the climate of mounting political tension, and though at least some of them denounced courtly corruption and favouritism, Jacobean and Caroline drama for the most part refrained from personal satire or immediate topicality. Thus the Nero in the anonymous *The Tragedy of Nero* (c.1623) is *not* James I, nor is the Domitian in Massinger's *The Roman Actor* (1626) a satirical portrait of Charles I. However, by the time Nathaniel Lee came to dramatize the fate of Nero in his first historical tragedy, the connections between Stuart monarchs and Roman tyrants had been long established and long exploited to devastating effect by the opponents of the Crown (Butler 1985; Hammond 1991; Kewes 2002).

The flood of printed polemic which followed the temporary collapse of censorship in the early 1640s transformed the grammar and vocabulary of political controversy. Even though the Puritan authorities strove to halt the unrestrained outpouring of polemical literature in the 1650s, and even though the restored Stuart regime reimposed censorship in the form of the periodically renewed Licensing Act, the channels for publication and dissemination of controversial materials in both manuscript and printed form had been too deeply entrenched to be wholly eradicated (Harris 1987: 28ff.). Possibly the most obvious area where this can be seen was the proliferation of the so-called 'Poems on Affairs of State', which ranged from subtle, accomplished and politically incisive to scurrilous, vulgar and crude. Drawing on a body of such ephemeral but nonetheless vastly influential writings, Paul Hammond has shown that though the Stuart Restoration of 1660 seemed to mark the triumph of royalist ideology, the *cachet* of the monarchy had been deeply eroded, a process which rapidly accelerated in the 1670s. Nathaniel Lee's choice of Nero as the villain, and of the old script (which was shortly to be revived on the Restoration stage as *Piso's Conspiracy*) as the source of his piece, was telling. Lee was aware that his tragedy would be part of the intertextual universe created by a range of literary and non-literary writings in which Charles II had been figured as Tarquin, Nero, Commodus, Tiberius, Domitian, Heliogabalus, Sardanapalus and Agathocles, and satirized for his indolence, lust and lack of political backbone (Hammond 1991: 24ff.).

Lee's method in *Nero* is twofold. First, his tragedy significantly departs from the historical record. For example, it features a fictional subplot, revolving around the love of Nero's half-brother Britannicus for the Parthian princess Cyara, which Lee is likely to have found in a Continental romance. Among other blatant deviations from history are: the elimination of Piso's conspiracy against Nero, the historical leaders of which had been apprehended and punished by death; the turning of Petronius, whose historical prototype had been ordered by Nero to commit suicide, into the emperor's most loyal friend and favourite; and the retributive murder of Nero's queen Poppea by her brother and her betrayed former husband rather than by Nero, who had been the nemesis of her historical counterpart.

Second, Lee is deliberately topical, inserting passages which alert the spectators to similarities between Nero and Charles II (Barbour 1940; Kastan 1977). Both rulers love sensual pleasure and both have empty coffers. Like Charles, who publicly flaunted his countless amours, Nero is easily fired by Petronius's description of Poppea's beauty and promptly makes her his. And like Charles's finances, which were in perennial shambles, Nero's 'Treasures are consum'd with late expence' (5.2.43). The memory of the Great Rebellion that had toppled Charles's father is evoked through the figuration of an unhistorical popular rising against Nero: 'The rabble, Sir, with wine and rage inspir'd / With Trayt'rous hands your Palace would have fir'd' (4.4.47–8). The emperor retaliates by ordering the city to be burnt, an event that establishes a further connection between Neronian Rome and Carolean London: 'Nothing but flames can quench my kindled Ire: / Blood's not enough; Fire I'le revenge with fire. / Fierce as young Phaeton I will return: / Great ROME, the World's Metropolis, shall burn' (4.4.55–8). The burning of Rome recalls the Great Fire of London of 1666 that enemies of the king construed as divine punishment for his immorality and ungodliness. The Roman populace may have been frightened into temporary submission, but within a short time Nero is confronted by a fresh challenge: the revolt in the provinces. Oblivious to the gravity of his situation – the troops of the rebellious Galba are already at the gates of Rome – and concerned solely about sexual gratification ('Do you consult, while I my pleasures mind' [5.2.46]), Nero loses everything: his pleasure, his throne and his life.

Charles II was no Nero, yet given the proliferation of pointed allusions to him in the play, we might expect *Nero* to have been unpalatable even to the Merry Monarch. And yet we know that Charles saw the tragedy on at least one occasion and found nothing objectionable in it. Why was he prepared to tolerate it? The king saw neither himself nor his father as a tyrant. Even so, we may surmise that the arguments in favour of tyrannicide which are made by several virtuous characters would have reminded both him and his subjects of the arguments made by mid-century Round-heads that had led to Charles I's execution in 1649: 'some noble Roman should / Dare to be glorious, dangerously good, / And kill this Tyrant', urges the noble Drusus, 'kill him gorg'd with wine, / Forcing a day, and making black night shine, / Debauch'd, and sordidly ambitious grown, / Midst all his Revels, would the deed were done' (2.1.17–22). Similarly, Piso styles himself as an instrument of divine vengeance and extols the killing of the imperial monster as 'An act so great, pale Brutus shall desire / To see, Cato and Cassius shall admire' (3.2.97–8). Such tyrannicidal sentiments, which go unchallenged in the context of the play, demonstrate what has been described by modern scholars as the deconsecration of sovereignty (Moretti 1982). The divinity of kings, on which both early and late Stuarts and their apologists forcefully insisted, comes to be severely tested if not undercut when Piso, the would-be regicide, exclaims: 'Nero, prepare; for, when so're I come, / Immortal as thou art, I bring thy doom. / I'le make that Cedar tremble like a reed: / Nero shall dye; that vaunting God shall bleed' (3.2.105–8). In 1674 when *Nero* was written and per-formed, Charles II still felt relatively secure about his position, and though, with the debacle of the Third Dutch War and widespread accusations of mismanagement of funds, strains were beginning to show, he could afford to be indulgent of, and amused by, what may strike us as quite outrageous verse and prose portrayals of him. Nero's self-incriminating outbursts in Lee's tragedy, whose dedicatee was the Earl of Roches-ter, deliberately echo his patron's satiric poem 'On King Charles', in which the king's 'sceptre and his prick are of a length' (1.11):

> *Nero*: My Scepter, like a charming rod, shall raise
> Such sports, as would old Epicures amaze:
> Pleasures so rich, so various, and so new,
> As never yet the Gods, my great fore-fathers, knew.
>
> (1.2.144–7)

Already with his first play (and first foray into historical drama), Lee establishes himself as no Stuart apologist or glorifier of divine right kingship.

Lee's Ancient Worlds

Far less topical than its predecessor, Lee's next Roman tragedy, *Sophonisba, or Hannibal's Overthrow* (1675), shifts the action back in time to the Punic Wars. Some of the familiar elements of Lee's dramatic method are here, notably the unhistorical romantic entanglements. For example, Lee provides the Carthaginian general Hannibal with a Roman mistress Rosalinda ('A Man so great, I, though a Roman born, / Can for his sake, my Friends, and Countrey scorn' [3.1.22–3]). Once again Lee shows a sharp awareness of early seventeenth-century Roman drama, drawing upon earlier treatments of the story in both John Marston's *The Wonder of Women, or Sophonisba* (1605–6) and Thomas Nabbes's *Hannibal and Scipio* (1635), and gleaning hints from Shakespeare's *Antony and Cleopatra* and *Macbeth*. Despite his departures from fact and romantic embroideries upon the past, Lee's epilogue for a performance in Oxford anticipates the appreciation of the play by those who know the story, that is, the erudite academic audience: 'Knowing th' Original, you the Copy praise, / And Crown the Artist with deserved Bayes' (ll. 16–17).

Displaying such trademarks of Lee's dramatic style as fire, passion and heroic rant, *Sophonisba* provides a contrast to *Nero*, for instead of imperial corruption and decay we see old Roman virtue, restraint, self-control and courage epitomized in the figure of the Roman general Scipio Africanus. However, Scipio's inexorable drive towards victory and the glory of Rome comes into conflict with the very human passions of love and friendship. In what is perhaps one of the most moving instances of the clash between honour and love and friendship to be found in Restoration heroic drama, Scipio acknowledges that he is moved by the Numidian prince Massinissa's passionate love for the Carthaginian lady Sophonisba, yet Rome's greater good requires that she be sacrificed. It is a measure of his humanity that having witnessed the lovers' double suicide, he is touched so deeply that he resolves not to pursue the Carthaginians but return to Rome and relinquish his military career. Once described by Hannibal as someone who 'to the management of all aspires. / Alone the scepter of the world would sway, / Alone would rule the heaven and drive the day' (4.1.161–3), Scipio retires to the country a broken man, and, with his withdrawal, Rome's imperial project is temporarily halted.

In his third rhymed heroic tragedy and his third engagement with ancient Rome, Lee returns to the period of the early empire. As its subtitle indicates, *Gloriana, or The Court of Augustus Caesar* (1676) is located in the courtly setting of Augustan Rome. Based as much on La Calprenède's prose romance *Cléopâtre* as on Classical historians Plutarch and Suetonius, *Gloriana* portrays the ageing Augustus consumed by lust for the (fictional) daughter of Pompey the Great, the titular Gloriana, herself in love with and beloved of the son of Julius Caesar and Cleopatra, Cesario. The young and innocent if headily heroic and passionate protagonists both die at the end. Of interest for the purposes of this essay is Lee's treatment of Augustus Caesar. Seventeenth-century Englishmen were hardly unanimous in their assessment of the role of Augustus in Rome's transition from republic to empire. Some hailed him for bringing peace after years of turmoil and civil war, held up as exemplary his administration of the empire, and extolled the literary and artistic patronage extended by him and Maecenas to Virgil and Horace; others condemned him for destroying the republican heritage and instituting autocratic government which would turn tyrannical under his successors Tiberius, Caligula and Nero (Weinbrot 1978). Yet nothing in even the most critical appraisals of Augustus prepares us for Lee's ageing despot: lustful, degenerate, suspicious, fearful and cruel. Threatening violence to Gloriana, who rejects his unwanted advances, he compares himself to that prototypical Roman rapist, Tarquin: 'I'le come by Moon-light which my flame shall feed, / Like Tarquin pale resolv'd upon the deed' (3.2.157–8). And when Agrippa disingenuously praises him as 'the best of Kings', Augustus is disturbingly forthright about his own shortcomings, a forthrightness he can afford given the absolute sway he enjoys: 'No, I'm the worst, / Stupid, morose, tyrannical, accurst' (1.1.282–3).

A vast ideological divide separates the pre- and post-Civil War representations of the early Roman empire. In his comical satire *Poetaster*, written late in Queen Elizabeth's reign, Ben Jonson had portrayed the court of Augustus as a place where major and minor abuses can be rectified, and where the very presence of Augustus, a wise, just and benign monarch, effects the reformation of manners and morals. By contrast, Lee's Rome is a state governed by terror in which things can only get worse, as they undoubtedly will under Augustus's heir Tiberius, who is already waiting in the wings. There is a further contrast between pre- and post-1642 figurations of imperial tyranny. Where late Jacobean and Caroline tragedies set in imperial Rome contain a powerful republican subtext, the virtues of Brutus, Cassius and other champions of the republic being repeatedly held up against the corrupt morals and dwindling stature of present-day Romans, in Lee's play the republic is not so much as mentioned. It is no small irony that Gloriana, the daughter of the republic's last great military leader Pompey, styles herself as 'Royal' (3.2.243); while Cesario resents Augustus's usurpation of what he sees as his rightful inheritance: 'Yes, my renown'd extraction I declare, / I am by birth what you adopted are, / The King of Kings, and the World's lawfull Heir' (4.1.216–18). The question of whether the republic should be restored never arises; all that matters is who should be king and whose claim – backed by heredity or sheer force – is stronger. The debunking of Rome reaches its apogee when, in a parody of Caesar's assassination by Brutus and Cassius, Cesario is stabbed by Augustus's henchmen over the body of Gloriana. Dying for love rather than empire – 'I'le grasp her all, and Love shall last be mine; / Give me but this, Caesar, the world is thine' (5.2.205–6) – Cesario leaves Augustus despoiled of his sexual prey and shaken in the conviction of his omnipotence. Ludicrously staggering across the stage 'in his Night-gown', this very un-divine Augustus is now ready to bequeath the throne to the wily Tiberius, and the audience know full well what that portends for the future of Rome.

The Historical Settings of Otway's Rhymed Heroic Plays

Like Lee, Otway chose historical subjects for his first three rhymed heroic tragedies. He took up the history of ancient Athens and Sparta, sixteenth-century Spain and second-century Rome in *Alcibiades* (1675), *Don Carlos* (1676) and *Titus and Berenice* (1676), respectively. His approach to the dramatization of the past differs from Lee's. Where Lee's early heroic dramas provide striking revaluations of ancient Roman history and politics that, as in the case of *Nero* and to a lesser extent *Gloriana*, possess a distinctly topical resonance, Otway deploys historical settings of *Alcibiades* and *Don Carlos* as a mere backdrop for the tales of passion, love and incest that are predicated on contests between tyrannical fathers and virtuous sons. For example, in *Alcibiades* the war between Athens and Sparta in which the latter is victorious could be a war between any two states (and indeed in the preface to *Don Carlos* Otway himself acknowledges that '[he] might without offence to any person in the Play, as well have call'd it *Nebuchadnezzar*' [ll. 23–4]). The Spartan king and queen, it is true, insist on the superiority of the Spartan monarchy to the Athenian democracy: 'Thus must proud States submit when Monarchs claim: / They govern in a rude disorder'd frame' (3.1.9–10). Yet this endorsement of monarchical government rings hollow not only because the Spartan victory is made possible by the defection of the Athenian general Alcibiades, but also because throughout the play we see the corruption and blatant disregard for the public good destroying the Spartan body politic. The essential similarity of Sparta and Athens signals the irrelevance of such systemic distinctions, or at least Otway's indifference to them.

The historical setting of *Don Carlos* is likewise curiously disembodied. The play centres on the tragic love of the French princess Elizabeth and the Spanish prince Don Carlos. Elizabeth had been contracted to Don Carlos before his ageing father, King Philip II, decided to marry her himself. Now the young couple's love is doubly illicit, for its consummation would entail both adultery and incest. The peculiarity of *Don Carlos* is not that it is largely unhistorical in having Elizabeth and Don Carlos die horrific deaths and King Philip descend into madness; after all, Lee's Roman tragedies were hardly true to fact. Yet there is nothing 'Spanish' about Philip's court, and even the references to the conflict in Flanders, in which Don Carlos intends to get involved, are abstract and unspecific. The grievances of the Flemish rebels are never explained, and the Spanish Inquisition is not so much as mentioned. What is at stake is the politics of the passions, not the politics of the state, unless we take Otway's preoccupation with vitiated fatherhood and kingship as a sign of his uneasiness about, or perhaps lack of faith in, the patriarchal structure of monarchical government.

Otway's choice of the Spanish setting is likely to have been dictated by the Franco-Spanish rivalry in the north of Europe and the Netherlands. Yet the prologue's claim that 'He found the Fame of *France* and *Spain* at stake, / Therefore long paus'd and fear'd which part to take; / Till this his judgment safest understood, / To make 'em both Heroick as he cou'd' (ll. 11–14) is doubly disingenuous. First, the pathologically jealous Philip and the masochistically self-lacerating Don Carlos are hardly the stuff heroes are made of. Second, the international ramifications of the love triangle are never explored; the atmosphere at the Spanish court is so stifling and claustrophobic as to obliterate any sense of a world elsewhere, let alone of a wider European context.

Only in his third play (and the first one that is set in ancient Rome) does Otway's historico-political vision begin to shape his presentation of the protagonists' passions. In *Titus and Berenice* (1676) Otway does more than translate and compress Jean Racine's five-act *Bérénice* (1670) into a three-act piece of affective theatre; he offers a wholesale reinterpretation of Racine's protagonists and their historical antecedents, especially the Roman emperor Titus. Like Lee (who turned the exemplary or, at worst, controversial ruler Augustus into a ranting despot in *Gloriana*), Otway transforms the clement Titus of story and history into a tyrant *in statu nascendi*. The love of Titus and Berenice which is the driving force behind Racine's play appears secondary to the process of Titus's political maturation, or, rather, degeneration. Having been brought up at Nero's court and having participated in his debauches, Titus has been temporarily redeemed and reformed by the salutary influence and love of the Jewish Queen Berenice. (What has become, we might ask, of the vaunted Roman *virtus* if moral values have to be learnt from a Jew and a female?) He reciprocates Berenice's love, yet since the Roman law forbids the emperor to marry a foreigner, Titus sacrifices personal happiness for the sake of retaining imperial sway: 'dearest *Berenice* we must part. / And now I would not a dispute maintain, / Whether I lov'd, but whether I must Reign' (3.1.79–81). This, then, is hardly an exemplary subordination of private passion to the public good; at the play's conclusion Titus ominously emerges as another Nero to whom, in any event, he has repeatedly compared himself: 'I hate my self. *Nero*, so much abhor'd, / That bloody Tyrant, whom I blush to name; / Was never half so cruel as I am' (3.1.206–8).

Otway's unexpected association of Rome, its emperor, its people and its laws with barbarism and cruelty rather than civilization and moral order is integral to his portrayal of the Roman polity as precariously poised between two systems of government: republic and monarchy. The country's republican past is implicit in the recurrent allusions to its people's deeply entrenched anti-monarchical sentiments – 'To Kingly Power still enemies th'ave been, / Nor will, I fear, admit of you a Queen' (1.1.160–1); '*Rome* that to Kings so long a foe has been, / Will not admit my marriage with the Queen' (2.1.96–7). Though the transition to the rule by one man has been accomplished significantly before his time, Titus is acutely aware of the power that resides in the multitude. He bows to popular pressure, emblematically expressed through offstage shouts, and complies with the Roman law not because he believes that this is the right thing to do, but because the mob demands that he do so. In sharp contrast to the abstract and generalized Athens, Sparta and Spain of Otway's earlier heroic dramas, the Rome of *Titus and Berenice* is a forceful presence, its ascendancy over the individual, even one as great as the emperor, being underscored by the proliferation of references to 'Rome' and all things Roman. Although nominally a monarchy, this Rome experiences a resurgence of popular politics, the voice of 'that clamorous

Rout' (3.1.241) as Titus contemptuously dubs them, carrying the day. Yet for all its preoccupation with the demands placed upon the ruler by his subjects and his country's laws, *Titus and Berenice* closes with that ruler's ringing assertion of his arbitrary power: 'let *Rome* of her great Emp'ror boast. / Since they themselves first taught me cruelty, / I'le try how much a Tyrant I can be' (3.1.473–5). The populace and the senators remain offstage, and the only Rome the audience are allowed to see is the Rome of the imperial palace and its various chambers, corridors and ante-chambers. Such decorous restraint was shortly to disappear with the eruption of political turmoil that brought rioting crowds to the streets of London and to the boards of its theatres.

Caius Marius, *Lucius Junius Brutus* and the Roman Republic

In sharp contrast to *Titus and Berenice*, the action of Otway's second (and last) Roman play, *The History and Fall of Caius Marius* (1679), unfolds in the city's public spaces such as the street, the forum and the senate, with a few scenes being set in the private spaces of homes, gardens and a family tomb, and one taking place in the country. Produced in the autumn of 1679 when the hysteria surrounding Titus Oates's allegations of a Catholic conspiracy against king and nation was at its highest, and set in the Rome torn by a bloody civil war, this blank verse tragedy dramatizes the struggle for power between two factions: the patricians headed by Metellus and the popular faction headed by Marius Senior (who, however, counts among his supporters several young men from noble families).

Otway's political loyalties in the troubled years of the Popish Plot and the Exclusion Crisis remained firmly royalist. Yet this does not mean that his plays from that period are mere exercises in Tory propaganda. On the contrary, as *Caius Marius* and the slightly later *Venice Preserv'd* demonstrate, Otway's explorations of political life under republican regimes, whether Roman or Venetian, were subtle and open-ended, thus providing a counterpoint to his personal political views as expressed in prologues, epilogues and dedications. For example, the prologue to *Caius Marius*, which was written in the autumn of 1679 when anxieties about succession were exacerbated by Charles II's sudden illness, mourns '*Cæsar*'s Absence' and eagerly anticipates the king's return, figuring him as 'The Lord of Hearts, and President of Wit' (ll. 35, 39). Yet the play which follows is hardly an unreserved celebration of royalist or Tory values. Based on Plutarch's Life of Marius and Shakespeare's *Romeo and Juliet*, whose star-crossed loves it appropriates, *Caius Marius* transforms a family feud into a conflict between the populist Marius, father of Marius Junior (Romeo), and the patrician Metellus, father of Lavinia (Juliet) and ally of Sylla. Given the fancifulness of history as represented on the Restoration stage, Otway could easily have vested Tory ideals in the patricians and figured the ascendancy of Sylla as providential, demonizing Marius's rabble-rousing as Whiggish. However, the play's treatment of Roman politics precludes such facile identifications. For the Metellans, as much as the Marians, are prone to corruption, bribery, election-rigging and exploitation of mob politics (Munns 1995: 107ff.). Their political rhetoric, moreover, is as specious as that of their opponents, and the political vision that informs *Caius Marius* is unrelentingly bleak. The tragic fate of the lovers is deeply moving, their deaths being made even more pathetic than in Shakespeare as Lavinia-Juliet wakes up in the family tomb from the drug-induced sleep only to have her Romeo die in her arms and to see her father murdered by her father-in-law before stabbing herself with her lover's sword. In contrast to the Elizabethan play, which offered the prospect of a reconciliation between the Capulets and the Montagues, the conclusion of *Caius Marius* intimates that worse is yet to come. The moral of the story as spelled out by Marius Senior – 'Be warn'd by me, ye Great ones, how y' embroil / Your Country's Peace, and dip your Hands in Slaughter / Ambition is a Lust that's never quencht' (5.477–9) – is as irrelevant to the play the audience have just seen as it is to the political reality to which they are about to return. In *Caius Marius* Otway transfers from contemporary England to late republican Rome the political rhetoric of rights, liberties and royal privilege *and* the political practices deployed by both the Whigs and the Tories in their efforts to secure parliamentary majority and to win public opinion, without explicitly directing the spectators' sympathies to either faction. Metellus's plea to the gods – 'That we may once more know each other; know / Th' extent of Laws, Prerogatives and Dues; / The Bounds of Rules and Magistracy; who / Ought first to govern, and who must obey?' (1.1.3–6) – which has opened the play remains conspicuously unanswered at its end.

The dark and dispiriting ending of *Caius Marius* is in stark contrast to the more optimistic outcome of Lee's slightly later *Lucius Junius Brutus* (1680), which centres on the pivotal moment in Rome's early history: the expulsion of the Tarquin kings and the foundation of the consular republic in the sixth century BC. In the intervening period Lee had written three more tragedies set in the ancient world: *The Rival Queens* (1677) about Alexander the Great; *Mithridates* (1678) about the king of Pontus; and *Theodosius* (1680) about the emperor of fifth-century Byzantium. All three were studies of vitiated kingship, blackening their protagonists by comparison with the historical record in ways which imply oblique criticism of Charles II's personal character and policy making, notably his promiscuity, prodigality and lack of diplomatic and military successes. *The Rival Queens* shows Alexander as a weak man driven by passions, fickle, changeable, unpredictable, by turns generous and cruel to his friends and supporters, his former military glory being eclipsed by conflicts of the bedchamber that make him blind to treasonable plotting against his person and that ultimately lead to his downfall. Like Alexander, Mithridates brings about the ruin of himself, his family and his kingdom by giving free reign to his passion – in his case it is the desire for his son's beloved, Semandra, whom he forcibly marries and rapes.

Theodosius is another of Lee's flawed monarchs. Though less of a tyrant than either Alexander or Mithridates, he is nonetheless shown to be unequal to the task of governing the empire he has inherited. Abuses are rife at Theodosius's court, which teems with sycophants – 'Guilded Flies' (2.1.28); his army is only tardily paid, if at all, which makes them discontented and ready to rebel; and religious tension between Christianity and paganism divides his subjects. Even that epitome of old Roman virtues, the steadfast general Marcian, is sorely tempted to rise against the slothful Theodosius and himself assume imperial dignity:

> What hinders now, but that I mount the Throne?
> And make to that this purple Youth my Footstool?
> . . .
> Did not the former Brutus for the Crime
> Of Sextus drive old Tarquin from his Kingdom?
> And shall this Prince too, by permitting others
> To act their wicked Wills and lawless pleasures,
> Ravish from the Empire it's dear health,
> Well being, happiness, and ancient glory,
> Go on in this dishonourable rest?
>
> (4.2.142–3, 153–9)

Though ultimately Marcian's loyalty prevails, we have seen that even the most constant of subjects may contemplate rebellion *not* for selfish reasons but for the greater good of the country. This lesson could very well apply to the situation of the English king: by 1680, Charles II had lost much of the good will of the subjects who had welcomed him so enthusiastically on his return from exile twenty years earlier.

Marcian's seditious soliloquy contains an explicit reference to the expulsion of Tarquin from Rome by Lucius Junius Brutus; another such reference occurs in a speech of Lucius, Marcian's lieutenant, who urges him to seize the opportunity created by Theodosius's indolence and depose him: 'Methinks like Junius Brutus I have watcht / An Opportunity, and now it comes!' (2.1.238–9). (In the event Marcian and Lucius let the opportunity pass; Theodosius soon abdicates of his own accord; and Marcian peacefully ascends the throne by marrying Theodosius's sister Pulcheria.) In Lee's next play we see Lucius Junius Brutus in action. Banned for its allegedly 'very Scandalous Expressions & Reflections upon ye Government', *Lucius Junius Brutus; or, The Father of his Country* shows the abolition of the monarchy and the institution of the republic, at once recalling the fate of Charles I and issuing a warning to Charles II.

The play is Lee's considered answer to Otway's *Caius Marius*. Lee signals his aim by choosing a Roman setting and by appropriating the motif of love across familial and political divides: in *Lucius Junius Brutus*, Titus, the son of the eponymous enemy of the Tarquins and leader of the rebellion against them, marries Teraminta, the illegitimate daughter of the king. In both plays political allegiances are complex and divided. Like Otway's young men who turn against their patrician fathers and side with the populist Marius, Lee's young men turn against their republican fathers and side with the tyrannical Tarquins. Yet here the similarities between the two tragedies end. *Caius Marius* and *Lucius Junius Brutus* dramatize radically opposed moments in Roman history, the former focusing on the demise of the Roman republic, the latter on its rise. The atmosphere of Otway's tragedy is gloomy and depressing throughout; by contrast, however tragic the outcome of Lee's love plot (Titus and Teraminta die public and humiliating deaths), the political conclusion of his play ushers in what appears to be a heroic vision of a republican future. Otway chronicles the corruption and disintegration of Rome's republican institutions and offices (the senate, the consulship and the tribuneship) and the moral degeneration of its citizens, twin processes that produce civil war and anarchy; at the same time, he does not so much as allude to a republican past of political integrity and moral health. Lee provides a corrective to this historical 'amnesia' by reminding his audience of the principles and values upon which the Roman republic had been founded. To drive the message home and underscore its contemporary relevance, he infuses his Roman world with analogues to England's recent past and its current problems, a tactic which led to the play's suppression by the authorities.

The politics of *Lucius Junius Brutus* have been much debated. Some critics see it as an unqualified endorsement of republicanism (Owen 1991); others point to the political machinations and virtually gratuitous cruelty of its hero, Lucius Junius Brutus, traits that cannot but compromise the republican cause he espouses (Hughes 1996: 293–300; Hayne 1996). Not only the dubious morality of its main character but also the pattern of topical allusions scattered throughout the play undercut the possibility of reading *Lucius Junius Brutus* as staunchly and unreservedly republican. Even so, the republican solution, albeit flawed and imperfect, is presented as *preferable* to degenerate monarchy.

Early in the play Lee evokes the memory of the English Civil War, explicitly associating the plebeians headed by Vinditius with the Good Old Cause:

> *Vin.*: . . . look you, Sirs, I am a true Commonwealth's-man, and do not naturally love Kings, tho they be good; for why should any one man have more power than the People? (2.1.41–3)

Aside from satirizing unthinking anti-monarchism, this passage introduces a double historical perspective upon the action by creating a correspondence between the early Roman republic and the English Commonwealth. The effect of this correspondence is twofold. Vinditius, the rabble and, to a lesser extent, Lucius Junius Brutus himself become tainted by the reminiscence of Civil War and regicide. Yet, paradoxically, the connection with Rome's republican past and its worthies seems retrospectively to redeem the English regicides and to salvage what was noble and idealistic in their enterprise. This reading is confirmed by a third kind of historical allusion which points directly to the reality of 1680 when Lee wrote the play. That year witnessed successive attempts by Whig parliamentarians to exclude the Catholic heir to the throne, James, Duke of York, from succession. Though these attempts had failed so far, the Crown was by no means assured of victory: in Parliament as in the country at large, the loyalists, or Tories as they came to be called, were on the defensive. Although there was a republican wing to the Whigs, mainstream Whigs did not want to abolish the monarchy; they were concerned simply to remove the threat of Catholic succession and to prevent the king's arrogation of what they dubbed arbitrary power. Yet elements of their political rhetoric, notably the insistence on the rights and liberties of the subject and the protection of property, lent themselves easily to republican constructions. By placing that political language in the mouths of his revolutionaries, and by making the adherents of Tarquin speak the language of Tory propaganda, Lee invites his audience to contemplate the relevance of both Rome's and England's republican past to the present. History need not repeat itself, he suggests; the knowledge and understanding of the past can help avoid the pitfalls into which others have fallen and point a way for the future.

Lee's dramatization of Rome's transition from monarchy to consular republic in *Lucius Junius Brutus* raises the question about the status of historical representation in the Restoration theatre. As in *Nero*, *Sophonisba* and *Gloriana*, here too Lee recycles historical materials which had appeared on the early seventeenth-century stage. To understand the new historical sensibility that developed after the Restoration and recover its effect on the drama, we may usefully compare *Lucius Junius Brutus* with Thomas Heywood's *The Rape of Lucrece* (c.1607), an early Jacobean play which, like Lee's, focuses on the foundation of the Roman republic. There are important differences between Heywood's and Lee's depictions of the Tarquins and their enemies. In *The Rape of Lucrece* the victorious rebels are presented as unambiguously virtuous, not, as in Lee, as partially compromised by the political means they employ. Where Heywood turned the Roman past on its head by figuring an unhistorical regicide and having Tarquin and his queen, Tullia, slaughtered in full view of the audience, Lee was more cautious and more historically accurate: his Tarquins are exiled 'without Damage to their persons' (2.1.229). They are also kept offstage throughout: neither Tarquin nor Tullia nor Sextus makes an appearance; and the only members of the Tarquin family that we see are the pathetic Teraminta and the wronged Collatinus.

Heywood's play, through extensive use of anachronism, had invited the audience and readers to contemplate general correspondences between late monarchical Rome and early Jacobean England, without, however, encouraging them to draw specific parallels between the two (Kewes 2002). Contrariwise, Lee introduced a number of allusions to England's recent past and its current crisis which positively demanded topical application. We have already noted Lee's references to the English Commonwealthmen and the Good Old Cause, and his deployment of the partisan rhetoric characteristic of the Tory–Whig debates. He also evokes and discredits the memory of the Stuart Restoration, for he portrays the royalist conspiracy to reinstate the tyrannical Tarquin as a restoration. According to Brutus's son Tiberius, the goal of the plotters is 'the Restauration / Of our most Lawful Prince' (3.1.71–2). Yet we know that Tiberius's royalism is specious and self-serving, and that the king's return would result in yet more violence and injustice. By metaphorically equating Charles II with Tarquin, Lee seems not only to advocate Charles's deposition but also, retrospectively, to cast doubt on the rationale for and desirability of the Stuart Restoration which for two decades had been hailed by preachers, poets and playwrights as blessed and providential (and which seemed less so with every passing year).

Lucius Junius Brutus was duly banned, yet we must ask whether the ban was prompted solely by Lee's tendentious treatment of the Roman past or whether the historical moment he chose to dramatize was likely in itself to cause offence irrespective of the spin that was put on it. More generally, we have to enquire into the proprieties of dramatizing history after the Restoration. In what ways were the theatrical representations of the past shaped by the mid-century upheaval? How did they change when the Stuart regime came once again under threat? The range of the historical incidents and personages that provided materials for late seventeenth-century drama was rich and diverse. It is marked, however, by a few significant omissions. The omissions pertain to two moments of critical importance for the political history of ancient Rome and two for medieval England. They are: the abolition of Tarquinian monarchy, the assassination of Julius Caesar, and the depositions of Edward II and Richard II, respectively. These four moments had come to be seen as crucial precedents for, and imaginative equivalents to, the English Civil War and regicide; any play that took up the story of Tarquin's or Caesar's, Edward's or Richard's fall would have elicited a definite set of expectations from the audience. Given Lee's transparent association of the Stuart rule with tyranny and popery, the authorities' decision to suppress *Lucius Junius Brutus* is hardly surprising. But there is reason to suppose that the play would not have been allowed even if its spectrum of anti-Stuart allusions had been eliminated, for by then this episode in Rome's history had come to be perceived as far too sensitive for dramatic rendition. As late as 1703, Charles Gildon's much-toned-down adaptation of Lee's *Lucius Junius Brutus*, called *The Patriot*, was refused a licence by the Master of the Revels; and Gildon was obliged to relocate the action from ancient Rome to the Florence of the Medici.

Blackening a reportedly good ruler is always easier than redeeming a reportedly bad one. The historical record afforded no scope to improve Tarquin's character and dramatize his deposition in such a way as to make the audience sympathetic to his plight; hence the authorities' firm line on dramatic representations of that event. Yet the authorities were no less firm with respect to plays which portrayed key figures in English or Roman history such as Richard II and Julius Caesar about whom posterity was hotly divided. By the later seventeenth century competing accounts of Caesar and Richard were in abundance, figuring them as good, bad or, at best, liable to more than one interpretation. However controversially the two rulers might have been depicted in prose historiography, political pamphlets and verse, their representation on the stage was subject to stringent scrutiny, for in the nation's political imagination their fates had become inextricably linked with that of the Royal Martyr, Charles I. When, in 1681, Nahum Tate undertook to revise Shakespeare's *Richard II* and, at the expense of doing 'Violence to . . . *Truth*', recuperate Richard as 'an Active, Prudent Prince', he designed his adaptation as a loyalist warning against rebellion. However, Tate's scheme backfired spectacularly. *The History of King Richard the Second* was banned, hastily rejigged and illicitly acted under the title of *The Sicilian Usurper*, and ultimately suppressed by the Lord Chamberlain on the third night of its opening run. Albeit condemned in Tate's play as criminal and irreligious, the deposition and murder of the 'good' King Richard II were judged too touchy a subject to be handled at a time of crisis. In a climate so alive to potential topical resonances of historical figures and events, that regicide of regicides, the killing of Julius Caesar by Brutus, Cassius and others, was likewise withheld from the stage. So far as we know, Shakespeare's *Julius Caesar* was not revived between 1678 and 1682; and no new play on the subject materialized until John Sheffield, Duke of Buckingham, adapted and expanded the Shakespearean original into two plays – *The Tragedy of Julius Caesar* and *The Tragedy of Marcus Brutus* (*c.*1716) – which, however, were never performed (Dobson 1991). In the age of Shakespeare the deposition and murder of Julius Caesar, Tarquin, Edward II and Richard II had been acceptable subjects for plays; during the crisis that followed the real-life deposition and execution of an English king, they emphatically ceased to be so. This shift illustrates the difference between the use of history as a warning or even a threat to the current regime, and its deployment as a warning, a threat *and* an ominous recollection of that regime's recent crisis.

Popery and Arbitrary Government: Lee's Italy and France

In his early plays Lee adapted historical materials to explore vitiated kingship and relations between kings and subjects. His choice of fifth-century Byzantium in the process of transition from paganism to Christianity as the setting for *Theodosius* signals an incipient interest in the interaction between politics and religion. That interest comes to the fore in a series of historical tragedies composed between 1679 and 1682 when the latent fears of popery and arbitrary government turned into widespread anti-Catholic hysteria. In this atmosphere any reference to matters of religion in works of the literary imagination was potentially suspect and open to political construction. The rhetoric of anti-Catholicism, which earlier scholars have attributed exclusively to the Whigs, was, in the initial stages of the Crisis, a weapon in the Tory arsenal too (Harris 1987: 129). Only as the Exclusion Crisis progressed did anti-Catholicism disappear from the Tory propaganda. The fortunes of Lee's historical dramas set in Catholic Italy and France – *Caesar Borgia*, *The Massacre of Paris* and *The Duke of Guise* (the last written jointly with John Dryden) – are a good illustration of the changing political uses of anti-Catholicism. With two plays banned and his livelihood in jeopardy, Lee performed a remarkable volte-face and, relinquishing Whig tropes, shifted to Tory ones.

Conceived when 'an Universal Consternation spread . . . through the Kingdom', *Caesar Borgia* (1679) exposes the corruption of the papacy by retailing the lurid story of Pope Alexander VI and his bastard son Caesar Borgia. That story had served to whip up anti-Catholic sentiment once before, in Barnaby Barnes's *The Devil's Charter* (1606), a play written in the aftermath of the Gunpowder Plot of 1605 when a group of Catholic conspirators had narrowly missed blowing up James I and his Parliament. *The Devil's Charter* centres on the downfall of the Pope, *Caesar Borgia* on that of his son. Though separated by more than half a century, the two plays share a number of themes and tropes. Both emphasize the degeneration of the Catholic clergy that manifests itself in their promiscuity and sexual deviancy (having fathered several illegitimate children, Barnes's Pope commits homosexual rape and arranges for his victim's murder; Lee's Cardinal Ascanio Sforza is an acknowledged lecher and a bisexual), political treachery (in Lee, as in Barnes, the Pope and his son plot to gain political control over the whole of Italy, which involves them in a series of perjuries, betrayals and murders), bribery (Lee's Ascanio Sforza has purchased his cardinalship) and irreligion (in a quasi-Faustian deal, Barnes's Pope has sold his soul to the Devil and is haled off to Hell amid thunder and lightning; Lee's Pope is a self-confessed atheist). Through the sensationalism of their portrayal of the Borgias, which occasionally borders on the grotesque, Barnes and Lee remind the spectators of what they might expect should Britain succumb to the forces of the Antichrist.

Yet there is a difference in perspective: *The Devil's Charter* is intensely moral and religious in tone, *Caesar Borgia* amoral and secular. That difference is reflected in the contrasting uses Barnes and Lee make of the figures of two Florentine historians and political thinkers, Francesco Guicciardini and Niccolò Machiavelli, on whose accounts their plays are based. In the Jacobean tragedy Guicchiardine functions as a chorus, commenting on the action, bridging gaps in the narrative and pointing out the poetically just outcome of the story he has presented in 'this tragike myrrour'. No such narratorial guidance is proffered in Lee's play. Gone, too, is Barnes's supernatural machinery of magic, ghosts and devils. Instead, a thoroughly this-worldly Machiavel becomes the controlling figure in the plot. He purveys an outrageously corrupt political philosophy extracted from the writings of the historical Machiavelli, in particular *The Prince*. Acting as Borgia's mentor, Machiavel instructs the young man in the arts of political dissimulation so as to make him fit to subdue and rule all of Italy – 'A Prince! who, by the vigor of this brain, / Shall rise to the old height of Roman Tyrants' (1.1.85–6). The sense of divine justice, so prominent at the end of *The Devil's Charter*, is entirely absent at the conclusion of *Caesar Borgia*. With his pupil dead and his schemes in ruins, Machiavel faces not the wrath of heaven but trial and punishment by the course of law. The moral he tenders at parting is the product of rational deliberation rather than spiritual illumination and repentance: 'I here resolve on this, as my last Judgment; / No Power is safe, nor no Religion good, / Whose Principles of growth are laid in Blood' (5.3.370–2). Lee himself spells out the contemporary application of his tale in the epilogue: 'He says 'twas done two hundred years ago: / He only points their ways of murdering then; / If you must damn, spare the Historian's Pen, / And damn those Rogues that act 'em o're again' (ll. 19–22). The rogues in question are, of course, the home-grown popish plotters whose grisly schemes are no more than a slavish re-enactment of timeworn and equally grisly schemes of their Continental brethren.

Caesar Borgia capitalized on the anti-Catholic sentiment that had seemingly united the nation. Yet when Lee tried to repeat the trick by dramatizing the Catholic massacre of the Huguenots on St Bartholomew's Day in 1572, he suffered a serious setback. Although postdating *Caesar Borgia* by no more than two or three months, *The Massacre of Paris* (June 1679?) was banned outright. As far as the authorities were concerned, it was one thing to allow a play which, however critical of the papacy and subversive in its representation of Borgia's Machiavellian statesmanship, entailed no *direct* attack on Charles II and his government, quite another to permit one which combined rabid anti-Catholicism with an assault on the monarchy and its major ally, France. In *The Massacre of Paris* the weakness, vacillation and duplicity of the French King Charles IX, who authorizes the slaughter of the Protestants, contrast vividly with the loyalty, integrity and virtue of the Protestant subject Chastillon, Admiral of France. The inference that the English Charles might be complicit in the slaughter of *his* Protestant subjects is virtually inescapable.

The oppositional slant of Lee's play is thrown into relief when we compare it with Christopher Marlowe's treatment of the same episode in *The Massacre at Paris* (*c*.1593). Written shortly after the defeat of the Spanish Armada in 1588, this jingoistically patriotic piece presupposes an audience united in their hatred of popery and in their love of the queen. Even her erstwhile enemies recognize Queen Elizabeth's superior worth: in the closing scene of the play King Henry III, dying by an assassin's hand, launches into a lavish encomium of the English queen, exhorting his successor, the Protestant Henry of Navarre, to ally France with Elizabeth's England. Lee's outlook is diametrically different. Addressing a polarized and factious audience, he figures the Catholic threat as domestic, *not* external. Unlike Marlowe, who pays tribute to his queen by holding her up against degenerate French royalty, Lee reflects critically on his king by implicitly identifying him with his devious French namesake. And he warns the English Protestants to keep on their guard against the enemy within.

Initiated in *Caesar Borgia* and continued in two plays the authorities saw fit to suppress (*The Massacre of Paris* and *Lucius Junius Brutus*), Lee's use of anti-Catholicism as an oppositional trope undergoes a striking transformation in *The Duke of Guise* (1682), on which Lee collaborated with the Stuart poet laureate and leading Tory propagandist, John Dryden. A historical tragedy set in late sixteenth-century France, *The Duke of Guise* is a self-professed parallel play: 'Our Play's a Parallel', says the prologue, 'The Holy League / Begot our Cov'nant: *Guisards* got the Whigg' (ll. 1–2). In a telling reversal of his earlier practice, Lee joins Dryden to produce a piece whose satiric portrayal of the Catholic clergy is not aimed at stigmatizing the papists, but at exposing the Whig Dissenters. The erstwhile Catholic threat has now become a Protestant threat, and in place of anti-Catholic tropes we find vilification of seditious non-conformists. Desperate of ever obtaining a licence for the *Massacre*, Lee went so far as to cannibalize passages from that play for inclusion in *The Duke of Guise*. In the process, he transferred a number of speeches from villains to heroes and vice versa, a move which neatly illustrates the instability of topical meaning and historical application in late seventeenth-century drama.

Initially Lee's sensational defection to the Tory camp seemed not to have paid off: *The Duke of Guise* was banned by the Lord Chamberlain due to its explicit attack on the king's illegitimate son the Duke of Monmouth, who was shadowed under the character of the rebellious Guise. However, within a few months the political situation changed, the king lost patience with his wayward son and the ban was revoked. Belatedly premiered in November 1682, *The Duke of Guise* enjoyed a successful run in the theatre and was soon available in printed form. By far the most controversial play of the period, it incited a venomous paper war whose target was John Dryden, Lee escaping virtually scot free. Reviled as a Tory stooge and timeserver, Dryden was charged with leading astray the innocent Lee and misappropriating his unacted tragedy. One oppositional pamphleteer fumed:

> This Play, at first … was written by another, intending to expose that unparallel'd Villany of the *Papists* in the most horrid *Parisian Massacre* … But … [Dryden] tempts his Friend, poisons and perverts his good Intentions, and by his wicked Management of the Play, turns it from the honest Aim of the first Author, to so diabolical an End, as methinks it should make a Civil Government blush to suffer it, or not to put the highest mark of Infamy upon it.

And he further accused Dryden of distorting history for partisan ends: 'See now the impudent Knavery as well as Folly of this Sycophant to falsify a *History* so common that it is read by all *Gentlemen* that pretend to Reading'. Given the volatility and uncertainty of the times, the slightest departure from fact in a publicly performed play was likely to be noticed and interpreted as a sign of topical intent on the part of the author. Ironically, the Tory message of this collaborative work was credited to Dryden alone.

An effective piece of propaganda rather than of theatre, *The Duke of Guise* vanished from the repertory once the circumstances to which it was responding, and the figures it was satirizing, had faded away. By contrast, its suppressed predecessor and partial source, Lee's *The Massacre of Paris*, was destined to make an unexpected comeback. Cutting short the reign of the Catholic James II and installing the firmly Protestant William and Mary as joint sovereigns, the Revolution of 1688–9 had altered the political landscape yet again. With the Church of England once more in control at home and the persecution of the Huguenots mounting in France, *The Massacre of Paris* was performed 'in its first Figure', its savage anti-Catholicism relevant more than ever. At long last Lee could come clean about his political aims: 'The Play cost me much pains, the Story is true, and I hope the Object will display Treachery in its own Colours' (1954–5, 2: 153).

Encoding Ambiguity: Otway's *Venice Preserv'd*

Although we might quibble about the moral stature of its titular hero, the Whiggish (and republican) slant of *Lucius Junius Brutus* is not in question. The virulent anti-Catholicism of *Caesar Borgia* and *The Massacre of Paris* is equally plain, the suppression of the latter play being surely caused by its pointed criticism of popishly inclined royalty. What is less readily explicable is the partisan reception of Otway's most acclaimed tragedy, *Venice Preserv'd; or, A Plot Discover'd* (1682). Set in republican Venice, this highly emotive drama depicts a failed conspiracy against the senate and the state at large. Were the senators presented as patriots and the plotters as seditious ruffians, the adoption of the play by the Tories would come as no surprise. But given that the Venetian government is shown to be as corrupt as its opponents, its preservation is hardly cause for rejoicing. So what made the play so appealing to the Tories? How can so ambiguous a piece have been proclaimed a loyalist manifesto?

Venice Preserv'd has elicited a number of competing interpretations, some critics locating its Toryism in the satiric representation of rebellion, others pointing to vitiated fatherhood as a sign of contradictions within Otway's Tory stance, and still others proffering essentially apolitical readings that focus on the role of pathos and the sentimental (for an overview see Owen 1996: 236–8). A comparison with the slightly earlier *Caius Marius* supports the view that the play's ideology is fractured and uncertain, but also helps to explain its co-option as a pro-Stuart drama. Both *Caius Marius* and *Venice Preserv'd* are set in republican regimes and both document civil disorder, the opposing sides (the patricians and the populists in the former, the senate and the conspirators in the latter) being presented as equally compromised. In both cases Otway manipulates audience response through suggestive prologues and epilogues that proclaim his political loyalties to be Tory. By refraining from glamorizing the values of military republicanism (Rome) or commercial republicanism (Venice), Otway implicitly declares himself in favour of monarchical government and royal sovereignty. His assessment of England's predicament is disillusioned: 'The publick Stock's a Beggar; one *Venetian* / Trusts not another... Empty Magazines, / A tatter'd Fleet, a murmuring unpaid Army, / Bankrupt Nobility, a harrast Commonalty, / A Factious, giddy, and divided Senate' (2.265–70). Yet England has one clear advantage over Venice (and republican Rome): above the 'Factious, giddy, and divided Senate' there is a king who can still put things to right. To someone looking for a ringing endorsement of the Stuart regime, this might seem a disappointing and ultimately demoralizing message. Yet we should at least entertain the possibility that the play's ambiguous portrayal of Venetian politics, and its overlaying of history with sentiment, enhanced rather than diminished its effectiveness as a Tory piece. Precisely because *Venice Preserv'd* avoided divisive partisanship and transparent parallels *à la Duke of Guise*, tellingly refraining from bringing seditious crowds on to the stage, and because it placed so much freight on the emotional states of its protagonists, it was less likely to alienate the Whig section of the audience and more likely to win middle-ground opinion. So complex a play was also less likely to drop out of the repertory once its topical allure had passed. The impressive stage history of *Venice Preserv'd* is potent testimony to lasting appeal.

The choice of the Spanish-inspired plot against the state of Venice, a historical episode which exploited the current agitation with plots but which did *not* possess the ideological charge that made native and ancient Roman past so sensitive and tricky to handle, was a stroke of genius. If the admiration of his contemporaries and the admiration of (and interpretive split among) modern scholars be evidence of success, Otway was successful.

How, then, do Otway and Lee differ in their treatment of history and how do their methods and aims change over time? Lee, as we have seen, appropriates historical subjects which had supplied themes for pre-Civil War drama, whereas Otway chooses themes which were for the most part new to the English stage. From the outset of his career Lee builds on pre-existing parallels and associations such as the equivalence between the Stuarts and the Tarquins or England and imperial Rome, and reuses historical figures and events previously deployed by Elizabethan and Jacobean play-wrights to expose papist atrocities, for example in *The Massacre of Paris* and *Caesar Borgia*. In his early heroic plays Otway presents history in non-partisan ways before moving on to politicized dramatizations of the past in *Caius Marius* and *Venice Preserv'd*. Yet this juxtaposition of the two writers' methods does not entail a contrast between the imitative Lee and the original Otway. If anything, the striking interpretive twists with which Lee furnishes his historical tragedies, the obvious example being his representation of Augustus in *Gloriana*, attest to the power of his historical and artistic imagination.

More broadly, how do the uses of the past in late seventeenth-century drama compare with those in pre-1642 drama? Restoration history plays, especially those of the Popish Plot and Exclusion Crisis period, are far more explicit about their engagement in contemporary politics than earlier plays had been. More erudite and better versed in native and foreign history than their predecessors, contemporary audiences had come to expect representations of the past to carry topical meaning and had been conditioned to look for discrepancies between the historical record and the dramatic treatment. Renaissance plays are often said to be wildly anachronistic and free with the past; Restoration plays are no less so, although the motivations for their departures from fact are different. In most cases they arise out of a desire to exploit the romantic potential of the story, something that had rarely been at stake in earlier drama, and to offer a partisan commentary on the political situation at home, a trend which had begun in earnest under James I, but which became widespread only after the Restoration. Neo-classical critical doctrine, too, was a factor. The claims made by French neo-Aristotelians and their English followers about the need to sacrifice truth to decorum had been accepted by some playwrights, who modified their historical sources accordingly (Kewes 1998: 81–5).

Paradoxically, even as historical plays, poems and prose narratives proliferated the authority of the past began to dwindle. History writing was becoming more profes-sional and scientific; at the same time, the demand for hack accounts of the past and partisan historiography was on the rise. Given the multiplicity of rival and contradict-ory accounts of the past, to insist on objectivity and universality of history writing, and to hold on to the providential view of history, was becoming increasingly difficult. Otway, Lee and their fellow playwrights responded to current political anxieties and concerns, though they were unlikely to have told their audiences anything they did not already know or think. The value of history plays as topical vehicles was for the most part that of reinforcement of political opinions already held by the target audience, although plays such as *Venice Preserv'd* endorse the effectiveness of ambiguity as a mode of conveying political outlook. By the close of the seventeenth century the long-standing perception of history as a storehouse of *universal* truths was itself becoming history.

REFERENCES AND FURTHER READING

Armistead, J. M. (1979). *Nathaniel Lee*. Boston: Twayne.

Barbour, Frances (1940). 'The Unconventional Heroic Plays of Nathaniel Lee', *University of Texas Studies in English* 20, 109–16.

Brown, Richard E. (1986). 'Nathaniel Lee's Political Dramas, 1679–1683', *Restoration* 10, 41–52.

Butler, Martin (1985). 'Romans in Britain: *The Roman Actor* and the Early Stuart Classical Play', in Douglas Howard (ed.), *Philip Massinger: A Critical Reassessment*. Cambridge: Cambridge University Press, 139–70.

Dobson, Michael (1991). '"Accents Yet Unknown": Canonisation and the Claiming of *Julius Caesar*', in Jean I. Marsden (ed.), *The Appropriation of Shakespeare: Post-Renaissance Reconstructions of the Works and the Myth*. New York: Harvester Wheatsheaf, 11–28.

Hammond, Paul (1991). 'The King's Two Bodies: Representations of Charles II', in Jeremy Black and Jeremy Gregory (eds), *Culture, Politics and Society in Britain, 1660–1800*. Manchester and New York: Manchester University Press, 13–49.

Harris, Tim (1987). *London Crowds in the Reign of Charles II: Propaganda and Politics from the Restoration until the Exclusion Crisis*. Cambridge: Cambridge University Press.

Hayne, Victoria (1996). '"All Language then is Vile": The Theatrical Critique of Political Rhetoric in Nathaniel Lee's *Lucius Junius Brutus*', *English Literary History* 63, 337–65.

Hughes, Derek (1996). *English Drama, 1660–1700*. Oxford: Clarendon Press.

Hume, Robert D. (1976a). *The Development of English Drama in the Late Seventeenth Century*. Oxford: Clarendon Press.

Hume, Robert D. (1976b). 'The Satiric Design of Nat. Lee's *The Princess of Cleve*', *Journal of English and Germanic Philology* 75, 117–38.

Hume, Robert D. (1976c). 'Otway and the Comic Muse', *Studies in Philology* 73, 87–116.

Kastan, David Scott (1977). '*Nero* and the Politics of Nathaniel Lee', *Papers on Language and Literature* 13, 125–35.

Kewes, Paulina (1998). *Authorship and Appropriation: Writing for the Stage in England, 1660–1710*. Oxford: Clarendon Press.

Kewes, Paulina (2002). 'Roman History and Early Stuart Drama: Thomas Heywood's *The Rape of Lucrece*', *English Literary Renaissance*, forthcoming.

Lee, Nathaniel (1954–5). *The Works of Nathaniel Lee*, ed. Thomas B. Stroup and Arthur L. Cooke. 2 vols. New Brunswick: Scarecrow Press.

MacGillivray, Royce (1973). *Restoration Historians and the English Civil War*. The Hague: Martinus Nijhoff.

Maguire, N. K. (1992). *Regicide and Restoration: English Tragicomedy, 1660–1671*. Cambridge: Cambridge University Press.

Moretti, Franco (1982). '"A Huge Eclipse": Tragic Form and the Deconsecration of Sovereignty', *Genre* 15, 7–48.

Munns, Jessica (1995). *Restoration Politics and Drama: The Plays of Thomas Otway, 1675–1683*. Newark: University of Delaware Press.

Otway, Thomas (1932; reprinted 1968). *The Works of Thomas Otway: Plays, Poems, and Love-Letters*, ed. J. C. Ghosh. 2 vols. Oxford: Clarendon Press.

Owen, Susan J. (1991). '"Partial Tyrants" and "Freeborn People" in *Lucius Junius Brutus*', *Studies in English Literature* 31, 463–82.

Owen, Susan J. (1996). *Restoration Theatre and Crisis*. Oxford: Clarendon Press.

Owen, Susan J. (2001). 'Restoration Drama and Politics: An Overview', in Susan J. Owen (ed.), *A Companion to Restoration Drama*. Oxford: Blackwell, 126–39.

Wallace, John M. (1988). 'Otway's *Caius Marius* and the Exclusion Crisis', *Modern Philology* 85, 363–72.

Weinbrot, Howard D. (1978). *Augustus Caesar in 'Augustan' England: The Decline of a Classical Norm.* Princeton, NJ: Princeton University Press.

Woolf, R. D. (1990). *The Idea of History in Early Stuart England*. Toronto: University of Toronto Press.

22

Elkanah Settle, John Crowne and Nahum Tate

Don-John Dugas

The literary and professional interests of Elkanah Settle, John Crowne and Nahum Tate intersected or ran parallel at several points during their careers. In the early 1670s, both Settle and Crowne got their starts writing rhymed heroic plays that employed spectacular effects and featured expensive, state-of-the-art scenes. The former's greatest success, *The Empress of Morocco*, touched off a controversy in which Settle was forced to defend himself against the critical assault of John Dryden, Thomas Shadwell and Crowne. During the Popish Plot and Exclusion Crisis, all three wrote propagandistic drama for their respective factions. And all hoped to parlay their professional success into salaried offices, though only Tate achieved this goal. Settle and Crowne died in poverty and obscurity.

But perhaps the closest bond these playwrights share today is the fact that their early twenty-first-century literary reputations reflect hardly at all the success they enjoyed during the late seventeenth century. Indeed, the critical picture that we have inherited presents a severely distorted view of their relative popularity and importance during their own lifetimes, for while Tate is now the most famous, he wrote fewer plays (more than half of which are adaptations) and had a shorter, less distinguished theatrical career than either Settle or Crowne.

My goal is to reconstruct the contemporary impact and reputations of Settle, Crowne and Tate in order to present a fresh picture of these playwrights. While the career summaries I offer are by no means detailed, they are comprehensive in their coverage of each author's professional theatrical output. A popular success and a favourite of the court by the age of 22, Settle was one of the most commercially successful dramatists of the 1670s. In a career that spanned nearly fifty years, he wrote more than twenty-five plays, operas, pageants and shows that were attended by literally hundreds of thousands of Londoners. Settle's first play, *Cambyses*, established his popularity almost overnight, while the success of and controversy surrounding *The Empress of Morocco* secured that popularity and made his reputation as the critic who exposed the shortcomings of Dryden's heroic dramatic theory. Another court favourite, Crowne wrote some nineteen plays – including the hugely popular *City Politiques* and *Sir Courtly Nice* – during a career that lasted almost thirty years. Tate was appointed poet laureate after the death of Shadwell but, while he is better known today than either Settle or Crowne, he wrote only ten plays and operas, seven of which are adaptations. Indeed, Tate's importance now has little to do with his laureateship or the popularity of his two most successful plays, *The History of King Lear* and *A Duke and No Duke*, but with the rather dubious position he came to occupy in the field of Shakespeare studies in the nineteenth and twentieth centuries. Because Tate's notoriety is the product of scholarship and not of his contemporary reputation, I consciously downplay modern critical assessments of his Shakespeare adaptations here. (Readers interested in a discussion of these should consult chapter 16 in this volume.)

Elkanah Settle

The son of a barber and innkeeper, Elkanah Settle was born in Dunstable on 1 February 1648. A precocious boy, Settle attended Westminster School and matriculated at Trinity College, Oxford, in 1666. While he was certainly gifted, there is no evidence to support F. C. Brown's assertion that the 17-year-old Settle completed his first play before the end of his first term at Oxford (1910: 9). We know that Settle left the university without taking a degree, but not when he departed.

Settle's first performed play, *Cambyses, King of Persia*, received its premiere by the Duke of York's Company in early autumn 1670 (Downes 1987: 59–60). A tragicomedy in heroic couplets, the play was one of the greatest heroic blood- and-thunder spectaculars on the Carolean stage, at least a contemporary of – and probably a predecessor to – Dryden's more famous *The Conquest of Granada*. *Cambyses* is the first play to feature Settle's heady mix of heroic love, pathos, an exotic oriental court setting, political intrigue, capture, imprisonment, assassination, suicide, single combat, surprise plot twists, dance, music and manifestations of the supernatural – all presented in rhyming couplets. This formula included another element that scholars have overlooked: state-of-the-art scenic and mechanical effects *devised by Settle himself*. As Settle's later work for the Pope-burning pageants, Lord Mayor's Shows and the fairs suggests, the playwright was not only mechanically minded but gifted. Probably more than any other late seventeenth-century playwright, Settle embraced the use and understood the technical aspects of what we would now call 'special effects'. I would suggest that much of Settle's appeal was the result of his mechanical and theatrical inventiveness; audiences came to expect that, while other playwrights reused the same stock mechanical effects, Settle would give them something new. *Cambyses* proved a tremendous success. John Downes, the prompter of the Duke's, remarked that it 'Succeeded six Days with a full Audience', while the playwright and critic John Dennis remarked in 1717 that the play ran for three weeks, which, if true, was an extremely unusual achievement by the standards of the time. *Cambyses* was published in four separate editions by the end of the century and may have been revived in the mid-1670s and the early 1690s, a testament to its enduring appeal.

The tremendous success of *Cambyses* changed Settle's life. Almost overnight, he received the patronage of such courtiers as the Duchess of Monmouth, the Earl of Norwich and the Earl of Rochester. Dennis observed that Settle's new-found fashionability and popularity at court enabled him to have his next play acted by the members of the court at the king's private theatre in Whitehall. That play, another spectacular tragicomedy, would prove both more popular and more controversial than *Cambyses*.

The Empress of Morocco is one of the most theatrically effective plays in the history of English drama and arguably the most lavish heroic spectacular of the 1670s. It received its first public performance by the Duke's at the company's new home at the Dorset Garden theatre – the most technologically advanced theatre in England – by July 1673. (Unless otherwise indicated, all performance dates are taken from Van Lennep et al. 1960–8, Parts 1 and 2.) *The Empress of Morocco* features all of the same elements that made *Cambyses* a hit, only with a simpler plot and more elaborate scenes and effects. Settle's oriental intrigue and horror formula works to maximum effectiveness here. Noteworthy elements include the evil queen mother who plots to murder her own son, a wife who inadvertently murders her disguised husband, an elaborate masque of Hell, and the famous death-by-impalement of the arch-villain, Crimalhaz, in the final scene. Four pieces of evidence testify to the play's tremendous success. First, Dennis claimed that it ran for a month, which, if true, is a feat unmatched on the late seventeenth-century London stage. Second, it was the first English play whose quarto edition was published with multiple illustrations, one of which was oversized – a feature so costly that we must conclude that Settle's publisher must have been absolutely certain of high returns in order to have hazarded such a venture. Third, the play was published in three separate editions by the end of the century. Finally, the play spawned a parody almost immediately: Thomas Duffett's play of the same name was performed by the King's Company in December 1673.

The success of *The Empress of Morocco* stirred the jealousy of Dryden (who had already exchanged barbs with Settle), Shadwell and Crowne. The three playwrights collaborated on an anonymous tract entitled *Notes and Observations on The Empress of Morocco* (1674), in which they condemned Settle's plot as incoherent and absurd, declared the playwright's characters ill chosen and one-dimensional, and accused Settle of being devoid of learning and wit. The entire pamphlet smacks of pettiness and envy (particularly of the illustrations in *The Empress*'s quarto edition) masquerading as objective criticism. Dryden's contributions may have been the product of his own doubts regarding rhymed heroic drama, a genre which he abandoned in 1675 (Winn 1987: 259–60).

Settle struck back in 1675 with his *Notes and Observations on The Empress of Morocco Revised*. After attacking his 'anonymous' commentators, Settle applies to some of Dryden's plays the very critical method used by his detractors, making even Dryden's best lines look silly. Settle emerged from the exchange victorious: his opponents' obvious jealousy and his spiritedly learned defence only served to enhance the playwright's reputation and literary respectability, if at the expense of the entire genre of rhymed heroic drama (Hume 1976: 289).

Unfortunately, the unprecedented success of Settle's first two plays and his victory over his detractors seem to have gone to the young playwright's head. He became so arrogant that Dennis used him as a cautionary tale to readers some forty-three years later: 'The Fortune that has happen'd to Mr. SETTLE . . . ought to be a lesson to All . . . not to grow insolent upon Success'. That insolence would ultimately cost Settle his court patronage and, for a while, deny him an outlet for his plays.

Settle's next piece for the stage was an adaptation of Heminge's *The Fatal Contract*. A blank verse tragicomedy, *Love and Revenge* (by November 1674) is reminiscent of late sixteenth- and early seventeenth-century revenge tragedies. Like its forebears, *Love and Revenge* is a formulaic exercise in lust, revenge, murder, ghosts and pretended madness. Settle, however, deviates from his model by providing a 'happy' ending of sorts, allowing the virtuous romantic couple, Aphelia and Lewis, to survive the obligatory bloodbath. The Prologue gives us an important insight into the playwright's conception of what constituted a popular play (scenes, machines, dance and wit) and his frankly commercial outlook: he likens properly constructed plays to vivacious, painted, urban courtesans who continue to allure and tantalize after a few nights' enjoyment – unlike their dull, unpainted country sisters. While *Love and Revenge* did not enter the repertory, recorded performances both in November 1674 and on 9 December of the same year suggest that its initial run was somewhat successful.

Judging by Settle's next performed play, *The Conquest of China by the Tartars* (by 28 May 1675), the principal lesson the playwright seems to have drawn from the success of *The Empress of Morocco* was that horror sells. Another lavish, heroic tragicomedy employing Settle's oriental intrigue formula, *The Conquest of China* also features a particularly large dose of the horrific at the expense of the vigorous dialogue and action that had animated *The Empress of Morocco*. The king of China stabs himself, then writes his will with his own blood before he dies. His wives commit mass suicide, and their bodies are displayed on stage with swords and daggers thrust through them. *The Conquest of China* appears to have been unsuccessful on the boards; its wearisome speeches and sluggish pace may well have been a disappointment to audience members eager for the energy of *Cambyses* or *The Empress of Morocco*.

Settle's next play, *Ibrahim the Illustrious Bassa*, almost certainly fared better than *The Conquest of China*. Originally acted privately for an aristocratic audience, this heroic tragicomedy was produced for the public stage by the Duke's *c*.March 1676. While lacking the intensity of *The Empress of Morocco*, *Ibrahim* is certainly one of the playwright's best offerings. Modifying his formula slightly, the playwright emphasizes the romantic and downplays the violent. The poetry here is workmanlike (if not inspired), and the psychological characterization is unusually good. The publication of a second edition in 1694 (and the revival it implies) suggests that the play was successful, if not wildly so.

Produced later that year, Settle's next dramatic work departed even more radically from the heroic spectaculars upon which his reputation was based. Founded upon a recent translation of Guarini's *Il Pastor Fido*, Settle's *Pastor Fido; or, The Faithful Shepherd* (c.December 1676) is a pastoral in rhymed heroic verse. Featuring the playwright's best poetry, an Arcadian setting and a simple romantic plot, the play is different from anything Settle had written or would write again. The public seems to have responded quite favourably to *Pastor Fido*: three editions of the play had been published by 1700, suggesting two revivals and very keen interest from play readers.

We know little of Settle's activities between 1676 and 1679. Owing, no doubt, to an inauspicious combination of changing taste and Settle's arrogance, the playwright's courtly connections and fashionability had evaporated by the end of the 1670s. Deserted by his patrons, the playwright attached himself to the Earl of Shaftesbury and the Whigs. In 1679, the Whigs were lobbying for the passage of a bill to exclude the Duke of York from the succession. The principal means by which Shaftesbury's followers gathered popular support for the bill was by fanning anti-Catholic sentiments, and Settle was at the forefront of attempts to do so through the drama.

Late in 1679, the first of Settle's three Pope-burning pageants was staged. These spectacular anti-Catholic ceremonies were as inflammatory as they were popular: upwards of 200,000 people are thought to have attended the first (Owen 1996: 143n). Settle, the chief engineer and mechanic for them, was now using London as his stage to reach a wholly different magnitude of audience. The playwright returned to the boards in 1680 with *The Female Prelate: Being the History of the Life and Death of Pope Joan*. His first original blank verse tragedy, the play is similar in many respects to *Love and Revenge* in its reliance upon pre-Commonwealth revenge tragedy. Dedicated to Shaftesbury, the play received its premiere by the ailing King's Company on 31 May 1680. The most vitriolically anti-Catholic play of the late seventeenth century, *The Female Prelate* is a delightfully outrageous exhibition of revenge, intrigue, imprisonment, torture, ghastly murders, the supernatural and sexual depravity served up with considerable relish by the master of spectacle. The play proved very successful, but the author's benefit performance was spoiled by an influential Catholic aristocrat whom Settle had offended: the Newdigate Newsletters reported that the 'Duchess of Portsmouth to disoblige Mr Settle the Poet carryed all the Court with her to the Dukes house to see Macbeth'.

Comparatively devoid of political content, Settle's next play, *Fatal Love, or The Forc'd Inconstancy*, fared considerably worse than *The Female Prelate* when the King's Company performed it c.September 1680. While fully stocked with tragi-romantic devices, the play is marred by flat dialogue, shabby characterization and an almost complete lack of scenic interest. It failed utterly.

In the autumn of 1681, Settle agreed to 'write or compose a certain Interlude or Stage Play [based] upon A certain Subject or Theme' provided by Elizabeth Leigh (presumably the actress) and to pay her £20 and half of all profits over £40. Settle never paid Leigh, and so Leigh had Settle arrested in 1687. In the legal battle that ensued, Leigh claimed that Settle agreed to pay her the £20 by 1 June 1682. Settle claimed that he agreed to pay Leigh only if the play was performed, which it never was. Leigh also claimed that Settle entered into another such agreement with her in 1681, this time for a play about a woman who 'contracts her soul to the Devil to make her a beauty, and afterwards seduces a certain Prince . . . from the affection & bed of his Princess and causes the said Prince to murder the said princess'. As this is the plot of Settle's *The Ambitious Slave* (performed 1694), we must conclude that that play was composed in the early 1680s (Hotson 1928: 277). Settle and Leigh probably worked out an amicable compromise out of court, for we know that Leigh and her mother, Mrs Lynn, paid Settle an annual salary in the 1700s and 1710s to write drolls for their booths at Bartholomew and Southwark Fairs.

Settle returned to the spectacular in 1682 with his last heroic drama, *The Heir of Morocco: With the Death of Gayland*, the sequel to his masterpiece. Three factors contributed to the play's failure. First, the King's Company was in its final death-throes (the brawl that precipitated the company's dissolution occurred less than a fortnight after *The Heir of Morocco* received its premiere) and was nearly incapable of delivering a respectable performance. Second, the play is formulaic: the plot is too familiar (it is, in fact, very similar to that of *Ibrahim*) and is devoid of the grandeur and exuberance that distinguish Settle's earlier heroic spectaculars. Third and perhaps most important, horror tragedy was dead by 1682. In order to continue pleasing audiences, Settle would have to switch to a more fashionable genre such as pathetic tragedy, city comedy or farce. Surprisingly, a second edition of *The Heir of Morocco* was published in 1694, which suggests that readers, if not theatregoers, had not altogether tired of Settle's formula.

On 21 March 1682, an argument between the senior and junior members of the King's brought to a head almost fifteen years of mismanagement, embezzlement, disaster and dissent. Later that year, the company was absorbed into the Duke's and formed what became the United Company. While the Duke's almost certainly saw the elimination of competition as a wonderful thing, the impact of the union on playwrights, the market for new plays, English dramatic literature and Elkanah Settle was profoundly negative. Without competition, there is no need for novelty and innovation. Without the need for novelty and innovation, who needs new plays – especially ones written by an arrogant playwright who was so outspoken about the heir apparent to the Crown and the patron of the company?

Settle became a creature of politics during the 1680s, devoting his creative energies to one thing: ingratiating himself with whomever was in power. To further this end, he wrote confessionals explaining his change of political allegiance, lauding high-placed Tories in verse, and wrote tracts attacking prominent Whigs. So zealous were Settle's efforts on behalf of his new masters that he failed to see which way the wind was blowing as the decade came to a close. William and Mary accepted the throne in 1689, and Settle switched camps once more. His *A View of the Times. With Britain's Address to the Prince of Orange* praising the new monarch was published later that year, but William III was unlikely to forget Settle's efforts on behalf of James II.

Settle's next play was *Distress'd Innocence: or, The Princess of Persia* (October 1690). The title indicates that the playwright knew that he must write in a genre then in vogue (pathetic tragedy in this case) if he wanted to be successful. Settle delivers plenty of pathos (not to mention bloodshed) with his depiction of the struggle of the nobly Christian hero against the nefarious schemes of the arch-villain and the plight of the hero's wife after the villain captures, drugs and marries her. The playwright seems to have gauged the temperament of his new audience nicely: Settle's dedication indicates that *Distress'd Innocence* was well received, helped no doubt by an overture and seven tunes written for it by Henry Purcell.

Settle was appointed city poet of London *c.*1691. In this capacity, the playwright was required to devise a pageant for the Lord Mayor's Show every October, which suggests that Settle's appointment was the result of the successes of his Pope-burning pageants. While a salaried office was every late seventeenth-century playwright's ultimate ambition, this post seems to have been unsalaried. Instead, the city poet was paid a sum after each year's pageant by whichever company the Lord Mayor belonged to, a sum based entirely upon how well that company had enjoyed it. Settle apparently earned little money from his pageants, but seems to have enjoyed styling himself 'City Poet' on the title-pages of his plays. We know that the playwright wrote at least ten such pageants (1691–5, 1698–1702 and 1708), all but one of which were entitled *The Triumphs of London*. Unfortunately, we can account neither for the missing years' pageants nor for Settle's apparent abandonment of pageant-writing after 1708.

Settle's *The New Athenian Comedy*, a bawdy but listless satire, was published in 1693 but never performed. The next work the playwright presented for performance on the public stage was *The Ambitious Slave; or, A Generous Revenge*, which, as we have already seen, was written in the 1680s. A tragedy of revenge, the work is a morass of impenetrable intrigue, subplots and multiple conflicts of emotion tarted up with Settle's by then cliché oriental settings, heroic love, ambition, imprisonment, ghosts, madness and death. The day after the play received its premiere at Drury Lane (21 March 1694), an anonymous audience member dismissed it as 'a mere babel, [that] will sink for ever' and noted that the United Company thought the play so bad that it refused to produce it under the normal arrangement whereby the author would receive a third-night benefit.

In the autumn of 1694, the United Company lost most of its actors as the result of the rebellion of three of its most prominent members. Two companies – Christopher Rich's at Dorset Garden and Drury Lane, and Betterton's new company at Lincoln's Inn Fields – emerged from the turmoil and began to play in 1695. Late in 1695, Rich's Company performed Settle's next play, *Philaster, or Love Lies a Bleeding*, an adaptation of Beaumont and Fletcher's enduringly popular tragicomedy. The play seems to have enjoyed some success, for we know it was revived in 1711.

In late June 1697, Rich's Company performed *The World in the Moon*, a split-plot comic opera with a libretto by Settle and music by Daniel Purcell. The playwright's flair for spectacular scenes and effects was well suited to opera: *The World in the Moon* features a huge moon that 'wanes off by degrees', twelve golden chariots flying through the clouds, and two gigantic and lavish palaces, to name but a few. Settle's first opera was quite successful: two editions of it as well as a separate edition of the songs were published in 1697, and the *Post Boy* reported that it 'is acting with great applause'. I say 'first opera' because, while Brown attributes the 1692 opera, *The Fairy-Queen*, to Settle (1910: 95–6), Milhous and Hume conclude that there is no persuasive evidence that the work should be regarded as anything but anonymous (1983: 15).

Four years later, Settle reprised his operatic success with *The Virgin Prophetess: or, The Fate of Troy* (15 May 1701). The opera is a tragedy, but, like *The World in the Moon* before it, the story is of secondary importance to the music, dancing, costumes and spectacular scenes and effects. Settle dazzles again: Helen and Paris are drawn in a 20 ft-high chariot by two white elephants, Cassandra summons the Furies from beneath the stage to perform a dance of Hell, and Troy is burned by the Greeks. With two editions published as well as a separate edition of the score, *The Virgin Prophetess* seems to have been as successful as *The World in the Moon*, although the overall degree of success of either opera is hard to determine because so few performance records from this particular period survive.

Settle returned to traditional drama with his next play, *The City-Ramble*, which received its premiere at Drury Lane on 17 August 1711. The ten-year lapse between *The Virgin Prophetess* and *The City-Ramble* and the fact that the latter received its premiere during the August doldrums suggest that Settle was having considerable difficulty getting his works produced by this point in his career. A comedy, *The City-Ramble* is founded upon two plays by Beaumont and Fletcher: *The Knight of the Burning Pestle* and *The Coxcomb*. From the former, the playwright borrows the device of having 'audience-member' commentators sit on the stage. Settle updates his commentators by making them proper moral censors of their age: in an amusing sendup of Jeremy Collier and his adherents, Common-Council-Man and his wife attend the play in order to criticize and reform the profane and immoral stage. While well written and engaging, the play was only performed three times.

The last of the playwright's works to be produced on the public stage, *The Lady's Triumph* is a domestic comedy-cum-opera. (Avery is in error when he attributes the play to Lewis Theobald in Van Lennep et al. 1960–8, Part 2, 2: 488.) The main plot is simple: a husband and wife devise several humorous schemes in order to punish a rake who is attempting to seduce the wife. With witty dialogue, slapstick, spectacular scenic and mechanical effects, a trip to Bedlam featuring a dance of madmen, music by Galliard and an act-long masque by Theobald, the piece is varied and entertaining. Like full-blown operas of the period, tickets to the first three performances of *The Lady's Triumph* cost considerably more than normal theatre tickets and all tickets were purchased by subscription. The play received its premiere at Lincoln's Inn Fields on 22 March 1718 and proved successful. While it was performed a total of eight times, it yielded but one benefit for Settle.

In addition to his work for the public theatres, Settle also devised commercial entertainments for the fairs for which he was paid an annual salary. *St George for England* may have been the first of these, for a droll of that name was performed at

Bartholomew Fair in 1688. *The Siege of Troy* was Settle's greatest work for the fairs and proved one of the most enduring works in the history of the genre. A three-act droll based on *The Virgin Prophetess*, *The Siege of Troy* features the low comic scenes of the rambunctious Trojan workmen while omitting almost entirely the scenes of emotional seriousness found in its source. It played throughout the first half of the eighteenth century and was immortalized by Hogarth in *Southwark Fair* (1733), which depicts a performance. *The Siege of Troy* had already been reprinted more than half a dozen times by 1750.

Settle wrote one more play, now lost, *The Expulsion of the Danes from Britain*. A tragedy, the play may have been offered for production shortly before his death, but it was never performed. Almost six years after the success of *The Lady's Triumph*, Settle died destitute in the Charterhouse on 12 February 1724.

John Crowne

The son of a military officer and land speculator, John Crowne was probably born in England (possibly in Shropshire) *c*.1640 (White 1922: 22–4). In 1657, Crowne's family moved to lands his father had acquired in what is now Maine and New Brunswick. Crowne attended Harvard College from 1657 to 1660, but returned to England sometime late in 1660 or early in 1661 without taking a degree. Almost nothing is known of his life until 1665, when he published a lumbering heroic romance entitled *Pandion and Amphigeneia*.

In the early 1670s, Crowne turned his attention to the drama – certainly the most financially promising field of literary activity for an aspiring writer at that time. His first dramatic effort, the semi-satirical tragicomedy *Juliana; or The Princess of Poland*, was performed by the Duke's at Lincoln's Inn Fields *c*.June 1671. While the play apparently did not fare well (Crowne blamed its failure on a heat wave), the young playwright was not deterred. Later that year, Crowne's next play, *The History of Charles the Eighth of France, or The Invasion of Naples by the French* (late November 1671), received its premiere at the newly opened Dorset Garden theatre. A rhymed heroic tragicomedy patterned closely upon Dryden's *The Conquest of Granada*, *Charles the Eighth* features much the same kind of violence, political and domestic intrigue, and exaggerated emphasis upon love and honour as its model. Despite the opulence of its venue, the new costumes that had been made specifically for the play, and the greatest actor of the age, Thomas Betterton, in the title role, Downes reported that it was not quite as successful as the company hoped: 'it was all new-Cloath'd, yet lasted but 6 Days together, but 'twas Acted now and then afterwards'.

Crowne's next offering, a rather bald and uninspired translation of Racine's *Andromache* (1674), fared much worse. The tragedy was performed during the summer vacation season when, as the translator notes in his preface, 'the Play-houses are willing to catch at any Reed to save themselves from Sinking'. As far we as know, it was never revived.

Crowne co-authored *Notes and Observations on The Empress of Morocco* with Dryden and Shadwell that same year. While Crowne later claimed that he wrote three-quarters of the pamphlet, scholars have been unable to determine each author's specific contribution. Crowne might have been well advised to remain silent, however, for his inexperience and the indifferent success of his first three plays enabled Settle to attribute his participation to 'Vain Glory of being in Print, knowing himself to be so little a Reptile in Poetry, that hee's beholding for a Lampoon for giving the World to know, that there is such a writer in being'.

But Crowne's fortunes were about to improve. Between December 1674 and February 1675, his musical spectacular, *Calisto; or, The Chaste Nymph*, was rehearsed and performed at court by a cast of aristocratic amateurs. With characteristic maliciousness, Rochester seems to have recommended Crowne to Charles II to write the entertainment – a preferment that would simultaneously have humiliated both Settle (who had been enjoying the favour of the court since *The Empress of Morocco* had been performed at Whitehall) and Dryden (who, as poet laureate, would normally have been assigned such a task). Whatever animus Crowne's preferment served, the playwright became an intimate of the court and a friend of Charles II as a result. And, thanks to the detailed accounts kept by various courtiers involved with the preparations, *Calisto* has the distinction of being the seventeenth-century dramatic production about which we possess the most information.

Possibly encouraged by his new environment and the recent success of Wycherley's *The Country Wife*, Crowne decided to try his hand at comedy. Written as the vogue for London sex comedy was nearing its apogee, *The Countrey Wit; or, Sir Mannerly Shallow* (March? 1675) is a skilful fusion of Crowne's own material and parts of Molière's *Le Sicilien* and *Tartuffe*. The result is an enjoyable gulling farce that is actually quite restrained compared to some of the more famous exemplars of its genre. Crowne's dedication states that the play withstood the criticism of 'a whole party, who did me the honour to profess themselves my enemy'. The play enjoyed lasting, if not exuberant, success (it was revived into the 1720s), and was said to have been a particular favourite of Charles II.

The Destruction of Jerusalem by Titus Vespasian (Parts 1 and 2, both January 1677) marks an important juncture in Crowne's career. Like *The History of Charles the Eighth*, *The Destruction of Jerusalem* was also patterned on *The Conquest of Granada*, only more so: ten grand acts, a foreign setting in which two exotic cultures are shown in conflict, a siege during which the besieged squabble amongst themselves, and a wildly super-heroic protagonist are all there. While Crowne's couplets, characterization and emotional depth are not of the same quality as Dryden's, both parts of Crowne's play (particularly Part 2) are so resplendent with elaborate scenes and effects that we should not be surprised that contemporaries enjoyed it. Ironically, Dryden had abandoned rhymed heroic drama in 1675; Crowne was writing in a genre now dominated by the man he had attacked in *Notes and Observations on The Empress of Morocco*: Elkanah Settle. That Crowne's play succeeded largely on the strength of its scenes and effects suggests that the author was not above imitating the 'unlearned' Settle.

Unfortunately, the Duke's Company was unwilling to produce *The Destruction of Jerusalem*, perhaps because it had performed Otway's *Titus and Berenice* (a play quite similar to Part 2 of Crowne's work) in December 1676. The Duke's refusal resulted in Crowne's defection to the King's Company. Because it produced a play written by an author under contract to the other company, the King's was later compelled to buy Crowne's contract as well as to reimburse the Duke's for the money Crowne had personally invested in *The Destruction of Jerusalem* before the Duke's decided not to mount it – monies amounting to the considerable sum of £152. So while *The Destruction of Jerusalem* proved a dazzling success for the King's and established Crowne's reputation in the genre of rhymed heroic spectacular, it was not as profitable as it might otherwise have been.

The Destruction of Jerusalem signalled the end of Crowne's use of the heroic couplet: in the epilogue to Part 2, he announced that, like Dryden, he would 'ring those chimes no more'. Crowne's next play, his first blank verse tragedy, *The Ambitious Statesman*, received its premiere at Lincoln's Inn Fields *c*.March 1679. While *The Ambitious Statesman* was innovative in its prefiguration of the politically oriented tragedies of the 1680s (Hume 1976: 326), it did poorly in the theatre. Crowne blamed the play's failure on the unrest in London at the time of the Popish Plot.

The political and religious turmoil in England reached fever pitch in 1680 and 1681. During this time, Crowne focused his efforts on adapting three tragedies, to all of which he added topical political references. The first, an improved version of Seneca's *Thyestes* (*c*.March 1680), is a recipe-book of horrors that puts *Titus Andronicus* to shame, with anti-Catholic sentiments and comments about brotherly succession thrown in for good measure. While Nicoll reports that the play was very well received, he offers no evidence to support this assertion (1952–9, 1: 150).

Crowne's second and third adaptations, *The Misery of Civil-War* (a condensed version of Acts 4–5 of Shakespeare's *2 Henry VI* and all of *3 Henry VI*) and *Henry the Sixth, The First Part* (a revision of Acts 1–3 of Shakespeare's *2 Henry VI*), almost certainly fared worse than *Thyestes*. Both plays bristle with topical references and parallels. *The Misery of Civil-War* (1680) is the less overtly allusive of the two, offering royalist warnings about the dangers of religious factionalism (Owen 1996: 76–82). In it Crowne depicts a regicide, but clearly establishes that this act is the direct result of the deposition of a true king. But in *Henry the Sixth* (1681), the playwright was not so discreet. After only one performance, the Lord Chamberlain suppressed it, almost certainly because the playwright depicted a successful rebellion against a true king. While we know of only one performance of each of these plays, in 1691 Gerard Langbaine reported that the original audience had enjoyed *Henry the Sixth* before the Lord Chamberlain's interdiction: 'This Play was oppos'd by the Popish Faction, who by their Power at Court got it supprest: however it was well receiv'd by the Rest of the Audience'. As far as we know, neither play was performed again.

In 1682, the King's collapsed and was absorbed into the Duke's to form the United Company. Because of its monopoly on public drama in London, the United Company mounted only a handful of new plays each year. Specifically, it produced, on average, only three new plays a year during the first five years of its thirteen-year existence. The fact that Crowne wrote two of them is a testament to his talent and contemporary reputation.

Those two plays are the two for which he is best known today: *City Politiques* (1682) and *Sir Courtly Nice* (1685). Both a delightful sex-farce and a biting political, social and personal satire, *City Politiques* was originally banned before performance in late June 1682. It was allowed in January 1683 following the Tory victory in the government, but only, according to Dennis, after the personal intervention of Charles II. The Newdigate Newsletters list some of Crowne's satiric targets: 'A Ld Mayor Sheriffs & some Aldermen with their wives . . . buffooned & Reviled a great Lawyer with his young Lady Jeared and Intreagued Dr Oates pfectly represented berogued & beslaved the papist plott Egregiosuly Rediculed . . . the Whiggs totally vanquished & undon'. The play seems to have been a success at the time it received its premiere, and it was revived as late as 1718 – a testament to how enjoyable the sex-farce part of the play is, considering that most of Crowne's political allusions would have been meaningless by that time.

Sir Courtly Nice; or, It Cannot Be (May 1685) proved even more successful and enduring than *City Politiques*, despite the unusual circumstances of its creation. Charles II promised a salaried office to Crowne if the playwright would provide the ailing monarch with an adaptation of Moreto's influential comedy, *Non puede ser.* Crowne dutifully complied, but his dream of a regular income was shattered when Charles II died a few days after the dress rehearsal, his promise to the author unfulfilled. The play itself is witty, straightforward and effective. With characters like the scheming Crack and the amiably idiotic Sir Courtly, Crowne was able to breathe new life into a lighthearted love and honour plot that was obsolete by the comedic standards of the 1680s. Punning dreadfully, Downes remarked that 'This Comedy being justly Acted, and the Characters in't new, Crown'd it with a general applause', while Langbaine noted that 'This play is accounted an excellent Comedy, and has been frequently acted with good Applause'. *Sir Courtly Nice* remained a repertory staple throughout the eighteenth century.

During the remaining years of his career, Crowne alternated between tragedy and comedy, despite comedy's fashionability and the fact that the playwright's comic gifts outweighed his tragic abilities. Following a severe bout of depression, Crowne returned to blank verse tragedy for his next play, *Darius, King of Persia* (1688). A listless attempt at the pathetic style popularized by the likes of Lee and Otway in the early 1680s, *Darius* seems to have closed after three performances. Fortunately for Crowne, James II attended the author's benefit performance on the third night, boosting the playwright's profits by £20.

Crowne returned to comedy with *The English Frier* (1690), a decidedly romantic and moral comedy that attacks hypocrisy and *coquetterie*. It is also satirizes many of the same groups that Crowne had lashed in *City Politiques*. More specifically, *The English Frier* is resoundingly anti-Catholic. In works such as *The Ambitious Statesman* and the adaptations of the early 1680s, the playwright had hinted at his strong anti-Catholic sentiments. Writing after the flight of James II and the accession of William and Mary, Crowne was able to give full voice to those beliefs in *The English Frier*. A riot almost broke out in the pit during the first night, causing so much noise that the actors could not be heard. The play seems to have lasted but three performances.

Using the ancient past for inspiration as he had for *Darius*, Crowne's next play was another tragedy, *Regulus* (June 1692). Based loosely on the French tragedy of the same name by Pradon, *Regulus* is a study of heroic stoicism intermixed with comic elements of Crowne's own devising. The overall effect is strange, stiff and unmoving. *Regulus* was a commercial failure.

Returning to comedy, Crowne's next offering was *The Married Beau; or, The Curious Impertinent*, which received its premiere in April 1694. Inspired by Cervantes's novel, *El curioso Impertinente*, *The Married Beau*, like *The English Frier*, is romantic and moral, encouraging virtue and attacking *coquetterie*. The play proved popular and profitable, if not enduringly successful. An overture and songs by Henry Purcell no doubt enhanced its appeal.

After a severe bout of physical and mental illness, Crowne found himself drawn again towards tragedy and the ancient world. His penultimate play, *Caligula*, was performed by Rich's Company in February 1698. Observing the unities and written largely in obsolete heroic couplets, the play is clearly patterned on the French neo-classical tragedy that came into vogue in England during the last years of the 1690s. Unfortunately, Crowne's plot is thin, the action cool, and the nature of the protagonist and his actions are decidedly unheroic. Like the rest of Crowne's tragedies, *Caligula* proved a failure.

Crowne returned to comedy for his final play, *Justice Busy, or The Gentleman Quack* (*c*.1699–1700), which was performed by Betterton's Company but is now lost. Downes wrote that "twas well Acted, yet prov'd not a living Play', suggesting that, while it may have been performed on more than one occasion, it did not enjoy a long run.

Between 1697 and 1706, Crowne focused most of his energies on recovering lands in North America that his father had laid claim to in the 1640s but that had since been surrendered to France. While his attempts proved unsuccessful, his petitions brought him to the attention of various powerful figures in the government who initially responded by granting the ageing and destitute playwright £50, but eventually stopped responding altogether. Crowne died in poverty and obscurity in April 1712.

Nahum Tate

The son of a Puritan minister, Nahum Tate was born, probably in Ireland, *c*.1652. He attended Trinity College, Dublin, and took a BA in 1672. Like Crowne, Tate first tried his hand at another literary genre (the first edition of his melancholy, Miltonic *Poems* was published in 1677) before turning to the drama.

Tate's first play, *Brutus of Alba or, The Enchanted Lovers*, received its premiere by the Duke's at Dorset Garden *c.*June 1678. A quasi-heroic blank verse tragedy based upon the Dido and Aeneas story from the *Aeneid*, the play was patterned on Dryden's recent triumph, *All for Love*. Unfortunately, Tate's style is forced, his exposition clumsy, his dialogue riddled with cliché, and his action rendered almost comic with ineffective histrionics. The play was a failure.

The Duke's performed the playwright's next offering, *The Loyal General*, in December 1679. With a complex plot involving a weak old king who would like to give up his throne, a loyal and beautiful daughter and a family conspiracy against the king, *The Loyal General* shows that Tate contemplated the Lear story for some time before writing his (now) infamous adaptation. While the plot of *The Loyal General* is complex, it is fast-paced and far more engaging than that of *Brutus of Alba*. Tate does much to compensate for his occasional bouts of bombast through his handling of sensation and spectacle. The play was no success, but it probably fared better than *Brutus*.

Tate's three Shakespeare adaptations appeared at the very height of the Exclusion Crisis. The first, *The History of King Richard the Second*, gained him some notoriety for it was refused a licence before it could be performed. When it was acted (as *The Sicilian Usurper*) in January 1681, the Lord Chamberlain silenced the theatre and did not permit it to reopen for ten days – the longest silencing in the late seventeenth century. We should not be surprised the Lord Chamberlain denied *Richard the Second* a licence: the deposition and murder of a dissolute English king devoted to ease and luxury was not a topic he would tolerate during this period.

Tate's second and best-known Shakespeare adaptation, *The History of King Lear*, received its premiere at Dorset Garden two months later, in March 1681. Modern scholars have commented extensively upon the political motivations underlying Tate's alterations, but I would suggest that the staggering success of the play was not the product of its rather dangerous topicality but of its symmetrical, aesthetically less challenging structure. By regularizing the action, emphasizing the romantic, heightening the pathos and imposing a happy ending, Tate transformed Shakespeare's original into a distributive justice tragicomedy. In this type of play, poetic justice requires that evil characters be punished and good characters rewarded once they have seen the error of their ways. Notwithstanding the outrage of Bardophiles, Tate's *Lear* is an appealing pattern tragicomedy whose long-term success is quite understandable. The play proved one of the most popular, longest-running Shakespeare adaptations ever written, holding the stage (and keeping the original from it) from 1681 to 1838. Even Samuel Johnson believed it to be superior to Shakespeare's original.

Late in 1681, the King's Company performed Tate's last Shakespeare adaptation, *The Ingratitude of a Common-wealth*, based on *Coriolanus*. Tate added elements of horror and pathetic tragedy to the final act, which becomes a frenzy of battle, attempted rape, suicide, madness, mutilation and death. While drawing contemporary political parallels is an important part of Tate's message, he pre-empted in the dedication any objections the Lord Chamberlain may have had: 'The Moral thereof of these Scenes being to Recommend Submission and Adherence to Establisht Lawful Power, which in a word, is LOYALTY'. Unfortunately for Tate, neither loyalty nor the popularity of *The History of King Lear* guaranteed success: *The Ingratitude of a Common-wealth* disappeared without comment after its second known performance in January 1682.

Tate's next offering, *A Duke and No Duke* (August 1683), was an adaptation of Cokain's *commedia dell'arte*-inspired *Trappolin creduto Principe; or, Trappolin Suppos'd a Prince*. A mistaken-identity farce, *A Duke and No Duke* was a radical departure for Tate, but a most auspicious one. Tate not only streamlines Cokain's material, but introduces new action and dialogue in order to burlesque the high-minded love and honour sentiments of heroic drama. The play enjoyed great success during its initial run and was regularly revived into the 1780s.

Unlike Crowne, Tate understood that the best way to maximize commercial success after a hit was to give theatregoers another play written in the same genre. Tate followed up the success of *A Duke and No Duke* with *Cuckolds-Haven: or, An Alderman No Conjurer* (1685), an abridged version of Jonson, Marston and Chapman's *Eastward Ho!* combined with parts of Jonson's *The Devil is an Ass*. The playwright also added a few farcical and bawdy elements for good measure, but the resulting hybrid lacks the wonderful escapism and satisfying resolution of *A Duke and No Duke*. Tate blamed the play's failure on the unavailability of the actor for whom he had written the part of Touchstone, but I would suggest that much of the blame can be laid on the script.

Tate's next play, *The Island Princess*, received its premiere by the United Company on 25 April 1687. For this play, Tate chose a source with a much more distinguished track record than that of *Cuckold's-Haven*, for Fletcher's original tragicomedy of the same name was a perennial favourite, being revised or adapted no fewer than three times during the seventeenth century. In his streamlined version of the 1668 revision, Tate enhances the romance and melodrama. He also heightens and purifies the religious motivations of the play, probably in a reaction to the contemporary religious crisis in which the most important member of his courtly audience, James II, was embroiled (Golden 1954: 259). That the play was revived for public performance during the season 1690–1 suggests that it was well received at court.

For his penultimate dramatic offering, Tate returned to the source of his first play: the *Aeneid*. While one of his most famous works, the lyrics he contributed to Henry Purcell's masterpiece, *Dido and Aeneas*, are seldom considered by students of literature. Italian opera had become a force to be reckoned with in London by the early 1670s, and by the middle of the decade the indigenous dramatic companies were mounting English operas in response to the foreign competition. Musicologists credit Tate's libretto for the work's simple clarity and emotional range. Moore reads it as the creation of a playwright who understood that his verse must be subordinate to the music, and that exposition, not action, is necessary for an opera to be effective dramatically (1961: 59–60). While the poetry is not Tate's best ('So fair the game, so rich the sport, / Diana's self might to these woods resort'), it complements Purcell's score beautifully. The first recorded performance of *Dido and Aeneas* occurred in 1689, although music historians now believe that it was composed and probably performed sometime between 1682 and 1688 (see Wood and Pinnock 1992; Price 1994; Walkling 1994). The opera was revived commercially in 1700 as a four-part masque performed in another Shakespeare adaptation, *Measure for Measure, or Beauty the Best Advocate*, which remained a stock play into the 1730s.

In December 1692, Tate was appointed poet laureate by William III. The playwright remained staunchly loyal until the king's death in 1702, despite the fact that Tate's annual salary was £100 – some £200 a year less than the preceding laureates, Dryden and Shadwell, had been paid (Spencer 1972: 32). Now salaried and literarily respectable by royal decree, Tate did what many late seventeenth-century playwrights did if they were fortunate enough to attain financial security: he retired from writing plays. Tate devoted himself to religious and political verse for most of the twenty-three remaining years of his life. For reasons unknown, he returned to the drama one last time in the first decade of the eighteenth century. *Injur'd Love: Or, The Cruel Husband* (published 1707) was an adaptation of Webster's *The White Devil*. Conforming to the moral reforms proposed by Collier, Tate altered his source so as to refashion Vittoria – Webster's adulterous, husband-murdering 'White Devil' – into a model of wifely fidelity and virtue. If *Injur'd Love* was ever performed, there is no record of it. Further, a phrase on the title-page – 'Design'd to be Acted at the Theatre Royal' – implies that it was intended to be performed, but was not. Significantly, the title-page advertises Tate as the 'Author of the Tragedy call'd King Lear' (rather than 'Poet Laureate') in order to enhance the desirability of *Injur'd Love*. To this day, Tate's name is still linked to his Shakespeare adaptation, although not usually with the positive connotations assumed so enthusiastically by the publisher of his final play. Tate died on 30 July 1715.

Conclusions

While fashions and fortunes changed throughout the period under consideration, these authors exhibited particular characteristics that emerged again and again. Regardless of the genre he wrote in, Settle was a scenic and mechanical innovator who understood the importance of spectacle and how to maximize its effect. He was also an impressively versatile playwright. While Settle's contemporary reputation was founded upon his staggering early successes in the genre of heroic drama (*Cambyses*, *The Empress of Morocco*), he abandoned that genre some thirty-six years before his last play received its premiere. That Settle would turn to opera (*The World in the Moon*, *The Virgin Prophetess*) to exhibit his unique talents and would be successful in that genre seems natural. More surprising from our perspective are his successes in the genres of tragedy (*The Female Prelate*), pathetic tragedy (*Distress'd Innocence*), tragicomedy (*Philaster*) and domestic comedy (*The Lady's Triumph*). Arrogant as he no doubt was, Settle knew how to delight generations of theatre and fair audiences.

John Crowne's career reveals a playwright who seems to have been desperate to achieve success in a genre in which he was not gifted: tragedy. While Crowne's 'big break' came in the form of one musical spectacular (*Calisto*) and one heroic drama (*The Destruction of Jerusalem*), his reputation, then and now, was and is based on his considerable talents as a comic playwright (most obviously *City Politiques* and *Sir Courtly Nice*, but also *The Countrey Wit* and *The Married Beau*). Despite the audience's manifest preference for his comedies (and the financial rewards their approval brought him), Crowne returned to tragedy again and again without achieving a single success.

The least prolific of the three playwrights, Nahum Tate was also fondest of adaptation. More important, he was the most professionally and politically savvy of the three. That Tate was able to parlay nine plays (only two of which – *The History of King Lear* and *A Duke and No Duke* – were hits) and a scattering of poems into the laureateship in 1692 is a testament to the artful way he marketed his literary accomplishments to the people that mattered. Tate's Puritan upbringing no doubt enhanced his candidacy, for his personal religious views may well have prevented him from engaging in the dicey flip-flopping of religious and party allegiances that spelled political disaster for authors like Dryden and Settle in the 1680s. William III probably had little difficulty giving the laureateship to the comfortingly Protestant Tate, whose *Lear* and *Dido and Aeneas* were, after all, so proper and so enjoyable.

REFERENCES AND FURTHER READING

Brown, F. C. (1910). *Elkanah Settle: His Life and Works*. Chicago: University of Chicago Press.

Dennis, John (1939–43). *The Critical Works of John Dennis*, ed. Edward Niles Hooker. 2 vols. Baltimore: Johns Hopkins Press.

Downes, John (1708; 1987). *Roscius Anglicanus*, ed. Judith Milhous and Robert D. Hume. London: Society for Theatre Research.

Golden, Samuel A. (1954). 'Nahum Tate', doctoral dissertation, Trinity College, Dublin.

Hotson, Leslie (1928). *The Commonwealth and Restoration Stage*. Cambridge, MA: Harvard University Press.

Hume, Robert D. (1976). *The Development of English Drama in the Late Seventeenth Century*. Oxford: Clarendon Press.

Hume, Robert D. (1998). 'The Politics of Opera in Late Seventeenth-century London', *Cambridge Opera Journal* 10, no. 1, 15–43.

Milhous, Judith and Hume, Robert D. (1983). 'Attribution Problems in English Drama, 1660–1700', *Harvard Library Bulletin* 31, 5–39.

Moore, Robert E. (1961). *Henry Purcell and the Restoration Theatre*. Cambridge, MA: Harvard University Press.

Nicoll, Allardyce (1952–9). *A History of English Drama, 1660–1900*. Rev. ed. 6 vols. Cambridge: Cambridge University Press.

Owen, Susan J. (1996). *Restoration Theatre and Crisis*. Oxford: Clarendon Press.

Price, Curtis (1994). '*Dido and Aeneas*: Questions of Style and Evidence', *Early Music* 22, 115–25.

Spencer, Christopher (1972). *Nahum Tate*. New York: Twayne.

Van Lennep, William, Avery, Emmett L., Scouten, Arthur H., Winchester Stone, Jr, George and Beecher Hogan, Charles (eds). (1960–8). *The London Stage, 1660–1800*. 5 parts in 11 vols. Carbondale: Southern Illinois University Press.

Walkling, Andrew R. (1994). 'The Dating of Purcell's *Dido and Aeneas*?': A Reply to Bruce Wood and Andrew Pinnock', *Early Music* 22, 469–81.

White, Arthur Franklin (1922). *John Crowne: His Life and Dramatic Work*. Cleveland, OH: Case Reserve University Press.

Winn, James Anderson (1987). *John Dryden and His World*. New Haven, CT: Yale University Press.

Wood, Bruce and Pinnock, Andrew (1992). '"Unscarr'd by Turning Times"? The Dating of Purcell's *Dido and Aeneas*', *Early Music* 20, 373–90.

23

Two Female Playwrights of the Restoration: Aphra Behn and Susanna Centlivre

Cynthia Lowenthal

In a moment I will never forget, back in the dark ages of the early 1970s, a scholar of Restoration literature was asked by a member of an audience to say a few words by way of introduction about 'this Aphra Behn person' to whom so many male writers refer in their works. With an airy and dismissive wave of his hand, the scholar said, 'Oh, she was a whore . . . and a sometime second-rate playwright'. Thus was one of the major writers of the Restoration banished that night, as she had been for centuries before, from the legitimate realms of scholarly inquiry. Since those dark days, however, there has been an explosion of scholarship concerning the first British woman playwright to make a living by her pen. And subsequent students of Restoration literature have 'rediscovered' a host of women playwrights whose works were as valued by contemporary audiences as were those of their male counterparts, chief among them, in the early eighteenth century, Susanna Centlivre.[1]

In this chapter, I will examine the kinds of marriage plots, especially stories of forced marriages, that both Behn and Centlivre produce in order to discover how the heroes or heroines of these comedies win their freedom from a coercive social system that forces them to marry partners not of their own choosing. What emerges from an examination of two plays in particular, Behn's *Rover* and Centlivre's *Bold Stroke for a Wife*, is that each playwright uses 'feigning' or 'dissembling', two seventeenth-century terms for 'pretending', very differently and they do so especially in terms of the limits of pretence allowed each gender and the extent of the individual agency that results.

When certain events are staged – such as a woman's attempts to control her own sexual destiny through donning a disguise and acting on her desire – the result is an increased degree of agency for that woman but also a diffuse form of anxiety for everyone else, an anxiety that interrogates and even subverts certain seventeenth-century social truisms, as often happens in Behn's works. When other events are staged – such as a man's cleverness in outwitting other men through disguise and acting on his desire – a very different result is achieved: his deceit and increased agency merely reinforce certain cultural assumptions, and the comedy produced is less edgy, less anxiety-producing and less provocative, as often happens in Centlivre's work. The danger presented by Behn and the questions she poses about performance, deceit and agency become muted in the early eighteenth century in the plays of Susanna Centlivre, who is more interested in commenting on the power of illusion to break through coercive economic structures than on the power of representation to liberate a sometimes dangerous desire.

The First Professional Women Writers

'The stature and significance of Aphra Behn in the early years of Restoration drama cannot be underestimated', writes Ros Ballaster (1996: 278), even though, according to Catherine Gallagher, Behn was also 'a colossal and enduring embarrassment to the generations of women who followed her into the literary marketplace' (1988: 23). As the first woman to make her living by the pen, she was the first woman to endure some of the harshest criticism ever levelled against a writer – *because* she was a woman. And yet Behn initially burst on to the Restoration literary scene as a talent to be reckoned with, not as an example of female shame. She was the only woman dramatist, with the exception of 'Ephelia' (whose identity remains unknown), to write and to have her plays performed on the public stage from the period 1671 to her death in 1689. In the 1670s and 1680s she was second only to Dryden in the number of plays she produced, and she wrote very successfully in other genres as well: she produced an impressive body of poetry; one of the earliest novels, *Love-Letters between a Nobleman and his Sister*; and the text that has come today to be known as one of the most powerful novellas in the entire English language, *Oroonoko: or, The Royal Slave*.

Why, then, was Behn a powerful figure during her lifetime and an 'embarrassment' to future generations of women writers? The events of her personal life are not particularly helpful in allowing us to answer these questions, since the facts remain rather murky, even after the publication of a number of biographies.[2] What most agree on is that Behn lived an extraordinary life. She spent a portion of her youth in Surinam, where her father, who died on the voyage, was to have been Lieutenant-General and where she experienced some of the events that she later incorporates into her novella, *Oroonoko*. After she returned to London in 1664 and married Mr Behn (about whom we know almost nothing), she spied for the British on the Dutch during the Dutch War. Upon her return to England, completely uncompensated for that work, she was thrown into debtors' prison. Alone, destitute and without regular employment, Behn turned to playwriting, which produced for her rather quick success. Her first play, *The Forced Marriage*, was produced in 1670 at the Duke of York's theatre, but it was *The Rover*, in 1677, that secured her a place among the writers of the day. From 1670 to 1689, the date of her death, Behn wrote at least eighteen plays, and her last productions, *The Lucky Chance* (1686) and *The Emperor of the Moon* (1687), are two of her best – a dark comedy about sex and money and a bright farce about extraterrestrials, respectively. They, along with a posthumous production of *The Widow Ranter* in 1689, secured her fame during her lifetime.

But for all her success among her contemporaries, her critical stature began to erode almost immediately upon her death. The changing nature of cultural norms was largely responsible, since the early eighteenth century saw a rejection of the licentiousness that was typical not only of Behn's comedy, but also of Restoration comedy generally. There were also 'objections to a woman's success in a world so inimical to emergent ideals of feminine delicacy', according to Jane Spencer (1996: 84). Thus Behn suffered criticism simply for being the first woman writer to earn a living by writing. Up until the latter half of the seventeenth century, there had been no 'professional' women writers because no such category existed, and thus women were forced into one of two classes of writers that Paula Backscheider describes this way: 'the new position of the shameless, crass, fallen woman jostling with men and willing to live by her illicitly gained sexual knowledge, a place in stark contrast to the other, which was the long-accepted practice of the aristocrat writing for herself and her circle tastefully circulating manuscripts' (1993: 81).

Behn, writing as one of those 'jostling' women, did not circulate her work in private manuscripts but presented it in the most public forum there is: the theatre. Angeline Goreau reminds us that seventeenth-century culture heard very distinctly the 'public' in 'publication', and Catherine Gallagher tells us why that matters: 'The woman who shared the contents of her mind instead of reserving them for one man was literally, not metaphorically, trading her *sexual* property. If she were married, she was selling what did not belong to her, because in *mind and body* she should have given herself to her husband' (1988: 27). The seventeenth century therefore saw an easy equation of the woman writer with the prostitute, or 'the poetess with the punk', as seventeenth-century satirist Robert Gould put it. Never one to be content with allowing others to define or categorize her, Behn took that insult and used it against her critics by creating for herself a new persona, 'the professional woman writer as a newfangled whore', in Gallagher's words (1988: 24). Thus in the Prologue to *The Forc'd Marriage*, the very first prologue Behn ever penned, she aligns the poetess with the prostitute by suggesting that the woman writer sends out prostitutes, in black velvet masks, as scouts, to celebrate the woman writer's play, no matter its quality, and thus to stave off the criticism sure to come: 'The Poetess too, they say, has spyes abroad, / Which have dispos'd themselves in every road, / I'th' upper Box, Pit, Galleries, every face / you find disguis'd in a black Velvet-Case'.

Public women, then, in the late seventeenth century, occupied a precarious position, one that allowed them almost no room to fashion a persona beyond that of the poetess or punk. Susanna Centlivre, who wrote only ten years after Behn died, is usually described in very different terms and thus faced a different audience reaction: not infamous for her own personal, sexual exploits, as was Behn, Centlivre is presented as a respectable middle-class married woman whose comedies relied far less often on highly charged sexual situations for their humour.[3] She was therefore less likely to be accused of displaying too great a personal understanding of sexual matters. The events of Centlivre's life are, like those of Behn's, not altogether clear, but we do know that she was born sometime between 1667 and 1677 and, when she travelled as an actor with a group of strolling players, she met and married Joseph Centlivre, a man who would ultimately rise to the secure, middle-ranking position of cook to Queen Anne (his title was an official but unfortunate one: Yeoman of the Mouth). From 1700 to her death in 1723, and from the economic and social security of a successful marriage she wrote nineteen plays, some of which enjoyed command performances.

Unlike Behn, Centlivre's reputation remained strong for the next century and a half, and she has been called, in contemporary scholarship, 'the premiere woman dramatist of the first quarter of the eighteenth century' (Frushell 1986: 16). Three of her plays – *The Busie Body, The Wonder* and *A Bold Stroke for a Wife* – remained in repertory for years after their debuts and were produced by some of the best actors and managers of the eighteenth century, including David Garrick, Kitty Clive and Charles Kemble. But perhaps the most influential event to shape the content of Centlivre's and other early eighteenth-century playwrights' work was the Collier controversy, the particulars of which are traced in chapters 2 and 3 in this volume. One result of the controversy was a change in direction of the modes of eighteenth-century comedy. The post-Collier comedy – sometimes called 'humane', 'benevolent', 'sentimental' or 'genteel' comedy – was of a new kind, one that shunned the cynicism and libertine excesses of 'classic' Restoration comedy and featured instead much greater restraint in all matters sexual and much more focus on matters economic. Susan Owen summarizes the changes this way, with special reference to changing gender norms: 'The early eighteenth century sees the relocation of ideas of honour and personal worth from the aristocracy to the virtuous woman; the rise of the cult of sensibility and of female-authored sentimental literature gave women a voice and a certain moral authority, despite the need for framing moral protestations; and eighteenth-century notions of the feminine played a strong role in developing ideas of modern subjectivity' (1996: 161).

In the short space of time separating Behn and Centlivre, the social, literary and cultural conditions of the nation had begun a slow but radical shift, and Centlivre is one of the earliest important playwrights in whose works the effects of this critical shift can be seen, argues Brian Corman. Corman claims that Centlivre was aware of the impera- tive to keep 'the moral attitudes represented in her plays in line with the standards imposed by her audience, especially by sanitizing dramatic language to free it of the growing number of words and phrases that were no longer tolerated in the theater' (1993: 127, 123). These shifts in the nature of comedy can best be traced in the way each of these women playwrights treats the forced marriage plot and in the strategies of deceit, illusion and impersonation each employs in the production of individual agency.

Forced Marriages: Passions v. Portions

The single most important event in Behn's and Centlivre's comedies is the marriage chase, usually a complicated set of incidents meant to resolve or eliminate the problem of a forced marriage or the barriers present between young lovers. Forced marriages were all too real for seventeenth-century men and women of a certain class who would not have had the option to choose their mates. Marriages were arranged according to the needs of the families involved and thus were in essence dynastic arrangements. Often in the plays of Centlivre and Behn, drawn from patriarchal cultures, old men act as obstacles to the desires of the young lovers. These 'blocking characters' become the focus of attention as young lovers attempt to circumvent the power these coercive fathers and/or brothers wield as they secure their dominion over the problem of 'disposing' of a woman to a man.

Behn and Centlivre treat this same problem very differently, however. In what Susan Staves has called the 'passion v. portion' problem, young women had to negotiate a way to secure the particular husband they desired – their passion –without forfeiting their rights to money they would bring to the marriage – the portion (or what modern terminology calls 'the dowry'). This was money controlled by others, usually fathers, uncles, brothers or guardians, who would negotiate the marriage settlement. The first panel of Hogarth's *Marriage à la Mode* (1745) shows how the negotiation of a marriage settlement, focused on the portion but lacking any passion, would proceed. The gouty, aristocratic father, sitting with the scroll of the family tree rolled out on the floor, proudly displays a lineage that stretches back to the medieval world of knights and swords. The other father, a merchant, sits with bags of money at his feet. These images indicate that a genuine sale and purchase are being negotiated – the young heiress's body in exchange for a title. The couple to be married, sitting with their backs to one another, understand that theirs is not a love match: the young heiress looks pale and frightened, rolling the wedding ring on her handkerchief; the young aristocrat, wearing a patch on his neck to cover what could be either a fit of fashion or an outbreak of syphilis sores, looks bored beyond belief, taking snuff from his snuffbox and grimacing. Neither young person has a say in what would amount, in modern terms, to a corporate merger.

Behn and Centlivre also represent older men as having control over young women's bodies – including their movement outside domestic spaces, their opportunities to meet and converse with young men, and their final destinies as nuns or wives. Behn's *Feign'd Curtizans* provides a very strong example of this control. The heroines in this play have their futures plotted for them by their uncle, Morisini: Marcella has been contracted to a gentleman, Octavio, described as a 'deform'd revengeful' young count; Cornelia, who has been 'bred' in and is destined for a nunnery, is in Rome to attend her sister's wedding. Marcella, the more restrained sister, is willing to admit that any injury to her reputation is dangerous: 'A too forward Maid Cornelia, hurts her own fame, and that of all her sex'. When Marcella muses that 'there's such charms, in wealth and Honour too', Cornelia opts for love: 'None half so powerfull as Love, in my opinion, life Sister thou art Beautifull, and hast a Fortune too, which before I wou'd lay out upon so shamefull a purchase as such a Bedfellow for life as Octavio; I wou'd turn errant keeping Curtizan, and buy my better fortune'. When presented with the opportunity to be freed, in Marcella's case, from a deplorable marriage and, in

Cornelia's case, from constant surveillance, the sisters decide to play the 'errant keeping Curtizan' and so don the attire of women who sell their bodies for money, impersonations of women whose real characters are supposedly at farthest remove from that of these young virgins.

Cross-dressed by 'type' of woman, not gender (even though Cornelia does play 'the breeches part', that is, she disguises herself as a man at one point in the drama), the sisters create for themselves much greater freedom of movement; they create, too, the opportunity for conversation and flirtation that wealthy and well-bred daughters of a gentleman would normally be denied. Cornelia celebrates the freedoms of the courtesan: 'there are a thousand satisfactions to be found, more than in a dull virtuous life! Oh the world of dark Lanthorn men we shou'd have; the Serinades, the Songs, the sighs, the Vows, the presents, the quarrels, and all for a look or a smile'. One might think that going unchaperoned out into the world would present actual danger to these women, especially the danger of sexual assault, but in the world of this Behn drama a woman whose honour is supposedly not only lost but for sale is far safer than her virginal sister, who is vulnerable to predation by libertine men; dressed as courtesans, the sisters have no need to protect their maidenheads because they are not under siege.

Behn's heroes are wits and rovers and Cavaliers, men invested in maximizing their own pleasures and minimizing the restraints on their behaviour. According to Melinda Zook, Behn's political position on this question of gender is quite specific: 'her political philosophy centered around a celebration of the young elite male, the cavalier, the epitome of individual freedom. . . . True freedom was freedom from want, freedom from customary behavior, and freedom from religious fanaticism' (1998: 78). Thus Galliard, one of the heroes in *The Feign'd Curtizans*, is filled with an animal vitality and reckless pleasure-seeking that prompt him to redefine the 'lawful enjoyment' of women: 'Lawful enjoyment! Prethee what's lawful enjoyment, but to enjoy 'em according to the generous indulgent Law of Nature; enjoy 'em as we do Meat, Drink, Ayr and Light, and all the rest of her common blessings'. And at the end of the play, when Galliard realizes that the courtesan he has been chasing is in fact a gentleman's daughter, he asks, unkindly, 'have I been dreaming all this Night, of the possession of a new gotten Mistress, to wake and find my self nooz'd to a dull wife in the morning?' To this disheartening question Cornelia responds wittily, with just an undertone of a threat: 'I do here promise to be the most Mistriss-like wife, – you know Signior I have learnt the trade, though I had not stock to practice, and will be as expensive, Insolent, vain, Extravagant, and Inconstant, as if you only had the keeping part, and another the Amourous Assignations'. J. Douglas Canfield argues that such language forms 'a counterdiscourse to the traditional code of sexual virtue, underwritten by religious language and underwriting the merchandising of bodies for the perpetuation of estates and titles' (1997: 40), a discourse, I would add, that more than hints at a future full of conflict and contention about the very female agency that produced mistress-like behaviour and the mimicking of the 'trade' she has learned.

Centlivre's heroines and heroes, and the blocking characters who attempt to force them into unwanted marriages, are very different. In *The Busie Body*, the two blocking characters are merchants, not aristocrats. The first is Sir Jealous Traffick who, as his name implies, buys and sells goods. His 'humour' is that he admires all things Spanish. Desiring that his daughter Isabinda marry only a Spanish merchant, he keeps her entirely locked up and away from prying eyes, as is the Spanish custom. The second plot involves Miranda, who is sequestered by her guardian, Sir Francis Gripe, because he wants to control more than her thirty thousand pounds a year: he has designs on her himself.

On the surface, the coercion in *The Busie Body* seems more threatening and dangerous than that found in Behn's plays: Isabinda must negotiate a father's irrational whims, ones that keep her positively hidden from life outside her room, while Miranda has an even more desperate task: to escape the clutches of a powerful and predatory older man. But in fact Centlivre's audience would have understood that no harm will come to anyone in this dramatic world, for two reasons. First, Centlivre's heroines are willing to risk very little by way of their reputations and their economic security. While they are cheerful, good-natured and pliable, they would rather trust the men in their lives to win for them what they deserve. They are less aggressive, sometimes less intelligent, and always less witty than Behn's heroines, especially in the ways they demand to shape their lives. For instance, Isabinda in Centlivre's *Busie Body* resists Charles's suggestion that they run away together because she fears poverty: 'I fear if I consult my Reason, Confinement and Plenty is better than Liberty and Starving. I know you'd make the Frolick pleasing for a little time, by Saying and Doing a World of tender things; but when our small substance is once Exhausted, and a Thousand Requisits for Life are Wanting; Love, who rarely dwells with Poverty, would also fail us'.

The second, more substantive reason for the less threatening atmosphere of Centlivre's plays, which all seem to have the hallmarks of danger and intrigue, is the more profound change one sees in Restoration and eighteenth-century definitions of masculinity, a new movement towards 'feminization' and away from the violent and the hyperaggressive. The shift in the cultural norms for men's behaviour generally can be seen not only on stage, but also in the periodicals of the time. Sir Richard Steele – an aristocrat, a fine playwright in his own right, and one of the first essayists of repute to succeed in the new print culture burgeoning in England – contributes to the rewriting of these gender norms in one of his most famous essays, *Tatler* no. 25, by urging men to put up their swords and to give up the practice of duelling on city streets, 'so fatal a folly', he calls it. A bump or jostle on a seventeenth-century street was likely to precipitate the drawing of swords, and moderating that behaviour would lessen the generalized aura of violence surrounding early modern men and move male behaviour towards greater restraint, more passivity, greater reflection – all virtues associated with women. Centlivre's young heroes are just such men, willing to battle the external obstacles to their beloveds but never posing any kind of real threat, especially the threat of sexual violence, to young women. Richard Frushell appreciates that Centlivre's heroes are never knaves among fools; instead they are men smarter than their competition who participate because they enjoy the sport, while Douglas Butler notes perhaps the salient difference between rakish heroes in libertine comedy and Centlivre's gentler heroes: they want to *marry*, not to *bed*, the women they love (1991: 366). Towards that end in *The Busie Body*, Sir Charles cross-dresses as a Spaniard, not to trick his beloved into giving up her virtue, but to trick an older man into surrendering his control over her destiny.

Centlivre's *Busie Body* ends without the edginess and gestures towards future conflict found at the conclusions of many of Behn's dramas. Isabinda marries Charles, who has unbeknownst to him inherited his uncle's estate and thus no longer needs to depend on his father. Miranda marries Sir George Airy, taking with her the thirty thousand pounds due to her. Sir Jealous Traffick, the merchant who proves to be gracious after being duped, gets to speak the play's concluding triplet, one that celebrates the freedom to choose in marriage: 'By my Example let all Parents move, / And never strive to cross their Childrens Love; / But still submit that Care to Providence above'.

Thus the forced marriage plot allows us to see some salient differences between these two playwrights, especially in terms of agency. Behn's sprightly heroines win the day by disguising and multiplying their identity. They will cross-dress as persons very different from themselves, producing a fluidity of identity that is open to modification and exchange, one not essential and binding but playful and performative. No such fluidity of identity, no such forms of deceit, are available to Behn's heroes: the men in *The Feign'd Curtizans* are essentially as they appear – good-natured English gentlemen. In Centlivre's plays, the opposite is true in terms of gender: deceit is an activity generally given over to men, while women are essentially what they appear to be. In *The Busie Body*, Charles and Sir George are the ones who don disguises: they do not cross-dress their gender positions; they instead cross-dress outside their national and class identities, as a Spaniard and a merchant, respectively. Centlivre's heroines aid and abet this behaviour, but it is the heroes who are active, aggressive and bold in their masquerades.

Deceit and Disclosure: Representations of Desire

All of this seems, on the surface, very tidy: Behn's heroines and Centlivre's heroes are the best dissemblers. Also superficially, these elements suggest a narrative of progress in the history of the moral development of women: they are represented as becoming more honest, more straightforward and more reliable than their male counterparts. But in terms of their power as theatrical subjects, women thus represented appear less complex, less multi-dimensional and, finally, less interesting. Indeed, if the ability to manipulate one's image – to 'be' something one 'is' not – signals agency, then in Centlivre's plays such control for women dwindles precipitously. More important for our purposes here, in the theatrical world of illusion, the act of donning a disguise – of representing oneself to the world through a creative act – produces power because it cultivates desire, a fact Behn not only recognizes but exploits. As a comment on the world of representation and on the potential doubleness, if not multiplicity, of identity available to characters with agency, Behn penned one of the most fascinating characters to be found in all of Restoration drama, one who speaks explicitly to the questions of performance and its relationship to one's representation. Centlivre, too, presents a powerful dissembling character whose actions thematize and problematize the limits of both performance and desire. An examination of these two characters teaches us even subtler lessons about what constitutes identity and how we recognize it, and about the gendered limits of both deceit and desire.

Behn's character is Angellica Bianca – a real, not a feigned, courtesan – in *The Rover; or, The Banish'd Cavaliers*. Her plot begins when Willmore, the hero of the play and the 'rover' in the seventeenth-century sense of the word (that is, a playboy), becomes 'acquainted' with her because her fame has preceded her in the rapturous descriptions offered up by men who have seen her: 'She's now the only ador'd beauty of all the youth in Naples, who put on all their charms to appear lovely in her sight: their coaches, liveries, and themselves all gay as on a monarch's birthday to attract the eyes of this fair charmer, while she has the pleasure to behold all languish for her that see her'. Her price is as extreme as her beauty: 'she's exposed to sale, and four days in the week she's yours, for so much a month'.

In an extraordinarily important moment in the play, one that makes concrete the theme of desire as it is provoked by a doubling of identity, two of Angellica Bianca's servants arrive and hang one very large and two small paintings of the courtesan outside her window. Willmore is unprepared for the powerful impact that seeing her picture will have on him. Gazing at her painted representation, he becomes both enraptured and enraged: 'How wondrous fair she is! A thousand crown a month? . . . A plague of this poverty, of which I ne'er complain but when it hinders my approach to beauty which virtue ne'er could purchase'. As a courtesan, Angellica Bianca manipulates promises of her sexual availability in publicly displayed painted representations of herself intended to garner for her economic power. Hers is an image replicated and repeated, offered up for public scrutiny, intended to produce desire in those who behold the image, and ultimately placed outside her window as an equivalent to her body itself. The images are deployed in order to seduce men, to woo them into desiring her and thus paying her to satisfy that desire. In such a moment, Behn displays both her understanding and her anxiety about the public availability of women's images and their bodies, especially as those 'items' are for sale, an anxiety made concrete as the plot progresses.

The scene ends with an eroticized violence breaking out below Angellica Bianca's window between men who are generally covetous of the courtesan's body, but ostensibly between a Spaniard who can afford to purchase the courtesan and Willmore who, in his poverty, can only afford to steal a small picture of her and clutch it to his breast. Seeing Willmore injured in the fight over her, Angellica Bianca invites him into her house, where the plot then takes a curious turn: Angellica Bianca ends up not hurting Willmore but falling in love with him. That act places her less in line with the desiring, freedom-seeking Restoration heroines Behn has penned, such as Cornelia and Marcella, and more in line with new sentimentalized heroines, who seek not financial independence but love.

We know, even if Angellica Bianca does not, that she cannot regain her lost 'honour', when the word designates chastity, a fact Willmore quite cruelly points out to her when he says,

> Yes, I am poor. But I'm a gentleman,
> And one that scorns this baseness which you practice.
> Poor as I am I would not sell myself,
> No, not to gain your charming high-prized person.
> Though I admire you strangely for your beauty,
> Yet I contemn your mind.
> And yet I would at any rate enjoy you;
> At your own rate; but cannot.

She is smart enough to call his hand on this complaint about the sale of gentle-women's bodies in the marriage market: 'Pray tell me, sir, are not you guilty of the same mercenary crime? When a lady is proposed to you for a wife, you never ask how fair, discreet, or virtuous she is, but what's her fortune; which, if but small, you cry "she will not do my business", and basely leave her, though she languish for you. Say, is this not poor?' This scene ends with Angellica Bianca's directing Willmore to 'put up thy gold', and to take her for free because, as she professes, she loves him. Thus she makes the very mistake that chaperones fear giddy, chaste virgins will make if left unsupervised – she gives her body to a man without being compensated for it: for a virgin, that means acting on her passion without securing her portion through marriage, and, for a courtesan, it means falling in love without securing more immediate financial arrangements.

The courtesan's plot ends badly, as one might suspect, when Willmore does not return her love. Seeking revenge, she bursts onstage during the fifth act, and wielding a pistol she threatens to shoot Willmore. Dagny Boebel calls her 'the phallic enforcer of chastity' who unmasks Willmore's role as a 'proponent of male domination' (1996: 67–8). When Antonio disarms her but offers to shoot Willmore himself, she relents but banishes the rover forever from her sight, bereft of her self-respect and her unexamined belief that 'all men were born [her] slaves':

> But when love held the mirror, the undeceiving glass,
> Reflected all the weakness of my soul, and made me know
> My richest treasure being lost, my honor,
> All the remaining spoil could not be worth
> The conqueror's care or value.
> Oh, how I fell, like a long-worshiped idol,
> Discovering all the cheat.

Having professed her love and having been betrayed in that love, Angellica Bianca turns to look at herself, and there the mirror reveals only weakness and dishonour. Behn produces a moment on stage that every woman in the audience would recognize: a woman wields power in a libertine culture as long as she remains chaste, and thus sexually desirable and emotionally aloof. But Behn fully recognizes the irony of Angellica Bianca's situation: her 'honour' – which in a young virgin would be her untouched body, her chastity, the thing sacrificed and given up in the marriage bargain – here Behn stages as a virginal, pure, untouched heart. In a play that features desire as radiating from and returning to illusion, desire is not constituted by the profession of an unrepresentable love; instead, the surface is both the source and the result of desire.

Centlivre cannot produce a character as marginal and transgressive as Angellica Bianca; changing times and an altered literary taste simply prevent it. Centlivre can, however, pen the artful, adept and dissembling Colonel Fainwell, in *A Bold Stroke for a Wife*, who manipulates his image, controls the plot and ultimately secures his desires through the agency of illusion in ways the courtesan cannot. The fact that the character most likely to masquerade and impersonate in this drama is a *man* signals an important shift, a new moment in the relationship between deceit and desire.

The Colonel's part is an actor's dream, since he gets to wear five different disguises, put on five different accents and perform five different identities through the course of one play. The plot concerns the beautiful, young, unmarried Ann Lovely, whose fortune is thirty thousand pounds a year but whose father has attempted to ensure she will not marry by putting her fate into the hands of four different guardians, all of whom must consent to the same marriage partner: 'he left her in the Care of four Men, as opposite to each other as Light and Darkness: Each has his quarterly Rule, and three Months a Year she is oblig'd to be subject to each of their Humours'. Ann Lovely, however, has fallen in love with Colonel Fainwell, who reciprocates her feelings, but they are barred from marriage by the guardians' contradictory demands for Ann's future. Therefore, the Colonel hatches a plan to win consent from each guardian by disguising himself as four different men, each of whom would be attractive to one guardian, even if repulsive to the others; the Colonel will then trick each man into signing his consent to the marriage. Richard C. Frushell writes, 'there is no courting Anne, since her love for Fainwell was already communicated to him at the start of the play. . . . The main action has nothing to do with wooing' (1986: 31). In the strictest sense of that word, this assertion is true. But I would like to suggest, in another sense, there is *only* wooing going on in this play; it is just, however, a form of male-to-male seduction, a desire predicated on illusion but, more importantly, on an appeal to likeness, to a self represented to the self from outside, a seduction that does not culminate in sexual union but in the parting of a man from his money.

In his first impersonation, Colonel Fainwell visits Sir Philip, an old beau who 'admires nothing but new Fashions, and those must be *French*; loves, Operas, Balls, Masquerades, and is always the most tawdry of the whole Company on a Birth day'. The Colonel's first impersonation is important because it encodes the vital elements in Centlivre's comments on desire and disguise, and because it allows us to see more clearly the differences between the Colonel's and Angellica Bianca's status: we discover that the courtesan's identity, which would appear to suggest multiplicity in its repeated representations of painted images, actually always returns to the singular: she *is* the courtesan; for all her protestations of love, beyond the paint, she is her tainted body. The Colonel, actively exploiting the same possibilities for the division of the self, the same self-alienation found in Angellica Bianca's painted representations, produces truly multiple identities; the Colonel uses his body – not painted representations – to produce desire, and he does so in a different way: by becoming *likeness* to 'woo' the objects of his desire into desiring in return.

For Sir Philip, Fainwell dresses in the cast-off velvet and gold brocade clothing pawned by a destitute French count and never recovered. As he enters the park he spots the old beau sitting on a park bench with a masked woman. Fainwell takes a seat, not next to the woman but next to the old beau, and at this moment the real nature of the encounter begins to develop: if wooing and seduction are the order of the day, then Fainwell has his sights set on the old man and the sacrifice of his financial interest in Ann Lovely, and not on the young woman and the sacrifice of her body. In a masterful performance, the Colonel allows himself to be thought all of the things the old man values: French, uninterested in politics, and passionate only for the dress and pleasures of a gentleman. And in a powerfully theatrical moment that makes concrete the thematic import of the exchange, when Sir Philip disparages the English as a nation incapable of producing a real man of quality, the Colonel disagrees by holding up his pocket mirror to Sir Philip's face and making 'real' the image of such an Englishman of quality.

In this scene, then, Sir Philip does not 'recognize' and value the Colonel for what and who he *is*. More important, he doesn't even appreciate the man the Colonel *pretends* to be. In fact, Sir Philip recognizes what he really wants: an image of himself – a narcissism reflected, replicated and reproduced in multiple images before him in the forms of the mirror's reflection, his own image and that of the Colonel. Unlike the repetition of the images of Angellica Bianca, this scene becomes an object lesson in the ways that likeness and similarity flatter and persuade, how seduction is predicated on an appreciation of one's own reflected image. In the mirror, the old beau does not see weakness and dishonour, as Angellica Bianca does; he sees only his own pleasing image. More provocative, this scene suggests how little it takes to produce that likeness, how few external cues – of dress and bearing, language and gesture – are needed to secure this image and to be wooed and won by one's own image. Indeed, a few modifications on the outside signal all.

The Colonel performs four other acts of impersonation to win Ann Lovely's hand, while she stays 'safely' sequestered in the house of her current guardian. To woo Tradelove, a merchant, the Colonel presents himself in the clothing and accents of a Dutchman named Jan van Timtamtirelereletta Heer van Fainwell, and in a wager, rigged by the Colonel's friend Freeman, Tradelove 'loses' and must recoup his loss by selling his stock in the Ann Lovely 'corporation' to the *faux* Dutchman. To woo Periwinkle – described as a 'a Traveller and man of fine Speculation', that is, one obsessed with empiricism and the observing and collection of data and specimens – the Colonel dons Egyptian dress and feigns a love of all things marvellous. When that ploy fails, he engages in yet another impersonation, of Periwinkle's steward. That ruse succeeds in fooling the collector into signing away his consent.

The final act of feigning is the most revealing. It requires that the Colonel pretend to be a Quaker, Simon Pure, who has come to visit the Prims, a Quaker family who are Ann Lovely's current guardians. Thorough-going hypocrites, the Prims are more interested in the fashions of Miss Lovely's clothes than in the state of her soul, a fact Ann forthrightly resists: when Mrs Prim insists that Ann don the trappings of a more 'modest' woman, Ann asks, 'Pray what are they? Are the pinch'd Cap, and formal Hood, the Emblems of Sanctity? Does your Virtue consist in your Dress, Mrs. Prim?' Still wearing the fashionable clothes Sir Philip had allowed her to wear, including bodices that allow glimpses of her breasts, Ann suffers from the stares of Obediah Prim: 'Verily, thy naked Breasts troubleth my outward Man; I pray thee hide 'em, Ann; put on a Handkerchief, Ann Lovely'. When she responds that she wears a handkerchief only outdoors to protect her from the sun, Obediah names his desire more explicitly: 'If thou cou'd'st not bear the Sun-beams, how dost thou think Man shou'd bear they Beams? Those Breasts inflame Desire, let them be hid, I say'.

On the surface, this 'battle' about clothing only superficially mimics the questions of value found in the Colonel's disguises, because gender plays such a vital and distinguishing role. When the female body is displayed, it provokes intense emotions, the 'enflaming of desire'. Like Angellica Bianca, Ann Lovely is too available, too much her body. And yet the Colonel's body is similarly on display, only draped and covered in clothing that variously signifies. It invites scrutiny and becomes the insistent focal point of others' vision, the subject of minute observation, but his performance produces a very different form of desire: a narcissistic impulse towards likeness from male observers and a willingness to surrender control. More important, unlike the Colonel who can become an infinite number of men – a beau, a trader, a traveller, a steward and a Quaker – Ann Lovely has only two identities available to her: the chaste woman or the sexually promiscuous woman, each of whom is signalled by the clothing she wears.

The play concludes inside the Prims' house where the Colonel, disguised as the expected visitor, Quaker Simon Pure, tricks Obediah Prim into signing away his consent, and thus when the other guardians arrive, the Colonel has signatures from them all. When he reveals the ruse to them, Tradelove asks the question about identity that they should all have asked of the man standing before them in the incongruous costume of the Quaker: 'Well, since you have outwitted us all, pray you *what*, and *who* are you, Sir?' (emphasis mine). The Colonel gets the last word in the play, describing himself this way: 'I have had the Honour to serve his Majesty, and headed a Regiment of the bravest Fellows that ever pushed Boyonet in the Throat of a Frenchman; and notwithstanding the Fortune this Lady brings me, whenever my Country wants my Aid, this Sword and Arm are at her Service'. The play thus ends with an 'essential' kernel of an identity uncovered and revealed. The play does not ask, as Behn would have asked, whether the Colonel's new role, as Her Majesty's loyal soldier, is not just the next in a series of impersonations. Instead, the moment authorizes a singular and stable identity for the Colonel, even though all the evidence runs to the contrary. Moreover, the Colonel achieves his double objectives: he secures not just Ann Lovely's body, but Ann Lovely *and* her money. These are objectives she herself shares: she plans not just to escape from a bad match or the nunnery, as it would be for Marcella or Cornelia, but to escape with the Colonel *and* all of her financial resources. Desire seems an afterthought.

If desire does indeed radiate from and attract those who feign – from courtesans (feigned or otherwise), colonels and other humans able to embrace a certain lability of identity, contingency and metamorphosis – then the Colonel is certainly a desirable fellow, and like Angellica Bianca, he makes himself publicly available to men who desire him. But he does so by leading the guardians to recognize likeness and to desire themselves. Angellica Bianca deploys desire very differently. She initially appeals to and secures a more violent and ultimately more destructive desire, one predicated on what appears to be multiplicity of the kind we see in the Colonel, but ultimately one which always returns to replication and repetition: images of the 'dishonoured' state of her unchaste body. The disguises and impersonations that Behn's virginal heroines participate in are, like the Colonel's, multiple and liberatory; they produce the same agency for Marcella and Cornelia, who ultimately direct the course of their marriage settlements. Thus in a curious twist of character and history, Centlivre's heroine, Ann Lovely, turns out to resemble Behn's courtesan, Angellica Bianca: both women understand that they possess only two identities, signalled by their clothing in a public performance – the virgin or the whore.

This fact brings me back to the beginning of this chapter, and to those references from Behn's contemporaries and 1970s scholars which labelled her, but not Centlivre, 'a whore'. Understanding the precarious place of the woman playwright in the changing culture of the late seventeenth century, Behn chose to meet the criticism by acknowledging that desire is generated by the seeming division of identity predicated on illusion and deceit. Thus she creates fictionalized identities for her heroines and for herself that point to an agency-producing self-alienation in writing that exceeds its designated spaces, both the heroines' dressing rooms and the theatrical space. Centlivre, living under different social conditions and existing less under personal siege, is content to confirm the status quo in writing bordered by the boundaries of women's closets and the stage itself. Thus we see, in the late seventeenth- to early eighteenth-century theatre, a shift in all the power to be found in deceit and desire from women to men, and the subsequent transference of the equivalent powers of agency.

NOTES

1 For students interested in the women playwrights who followed Aphra Behn, there is much still to investigate. Chief among the playwrights are the following: Delarivier Manley, Catharine Trotter and

Mary Pix. These women were skilled writers in many genres, including comedies, heroic tragedies and prose. They became so famous that a farce, *The Female Wits*, which in satirizing them implicitly acknowledges the threat they present to the status quo, was produced in 1696. For more on the earliest women playwrights, see Ballaster (1996); Clark (1986); Cotton (1980); Mann and Mann (1996); and Morgan (1981, 1991).

2   For early biographies of Behn, see Woodcock (1948) and Cameron (1961). For more up-to-date accounts of Behn's life, see Duffy (1977); Goreau (1980); Mendelson (1987: ch. 3); and Todd (1996).

3   The four contemporary biographies of Centlivre are incomplete or inaccurate; included in that group are those written by Giles Jacob (1719), Abel Boyer (1723), John Mottley (1747) and William Rufus Chetwood (1750). Both Boyer and Mottley relate stories that would seem to indicate at least one sexual adventure for Centlivre before she married, but as her modern biographer F. P. Lock argues, there is no way to prove the veracity or the falsehood of such stories. See Lock (1979: 13–30; see also the 'Chronology'). For other modern accounts of Centlivre's life see Bowyer (1952) and Morgan (1991: vii–xx).

REFERENCES AND FURTHER READING

Backscheider, Paula (1993). *Spectacular Politics: Theatrical Power and Mass Culture in Early Modern England*. Baltimore: Johns Hopkins University Press.

Ballaster, Ros (1996). 'The First Female Dramatists', in Helen Wilcox (ed.), *Women and Literature in Britain, 1500–1700*. Cambridge: Cambridge University Press, 267–90.

Boebel, Dagny (1996). 'In the Carnival World of Adam's Garden: Roving and Rape in Behn's *Rover*', in Katherine M. Quinsey (ed.), *Broken Boundaries: Women and Feminism in Restoration Drama*. Lexington: University Press of Kentucky, 54–69.

Bowyer, John Wilson (1952). *The Celebrated Mrs. Centlivre*. Durham, NC: Duke University Press.

Butler, Douglas (1991). 'Plot and Politics in Susanna Centlivre's *A Bold Stroke for a Wife*', in Mary Anne Schofield and Cecilia Macheski (eds), *Curtain Calls: British and American Women in the Theatre, 1660–1820*. Athens: Ohio University Press, 357–70.

Cameron, W. J. (1961). *New Light on Aphra Behn*. Auckland: University of Auckland Press.

Canfield, J. Douglas (1997). *Tricksters and Estates: On the Ideology of Restoration Comedy*. Lexington: University Press of Kentucky.

Canfield, J. Douglas and Payne, Deborah (eds). (1995). *Cultural Readings of Restoration and Eighteen-century English Theater*. Athens: University of Georgia Press.

Clark, Constance (1986). *Three Augustan Women Playwrights*. New York: Peter Lang.

Corman, Brian (1993). *Genre and Generic Change in English Comedy*. Toronto: University of Toronto Press.

Cotton, Nancy (1980). *Women Playwrights in England, 1363–1750*. Lewisburg: Bucknell University Press.

Diamond, Elin (1989). 'Gesture and Signature in Aphra Behn's *The Rover*', *ELH* 56, no. 3, 519–41.

Duffy, Maureen (1977). *The Passionate Shepherdess, Aphra Behn, 1640–89*. London: Jonathan Cape.

Frushell, Richard C. (1986). 'Marriage and Marrying in Susanna Centlivre's Plays', *Papers on Language and Literature* 22, no. 1 (winter), 16–38.

Gallagher, Catherine (1988). 'Who Was That Masked Woman? The Prostitute and the Playwright in the Comedies of Aphra Behn', *Women's Studies* 15, 23–42.

Gallagher, Catherine (1994). *Nobody's Story: The Vanishing Acts of Women Writers in the Marketplace: 1670–1820*. Berkeley: University of California Press.

Goreau, Angeline (1980). *Reconstructing Aphra*. New York: Dial Press.

Hutner, Heidi (ed.). (1993). *Rereading Aphra Behn: History, Theory and Criticism*. Charlottesville: University of Virginia Press.

Kinney, Suz-Anne (1994). 'Confinement Sharpens the Invention: Aphra Behn's *The Rover* and Susanna Centlivre's *The Busie Body*', in Gail Finney (ed.), *Look Who's Laughing: Gender and Comedy*. Pennsylvania: Gordon and Breach, 81–98.

Lock, F. P. (1979). *Susanna Centlivre*. Boston: Twayne.

Mann, David and Mann, Susan Garland (1996). *Women Playwrights in England, Ireland, and Scotland, 1660–1823*. Bloomington: University of Indiana Press.

Mendelson, Sara (1987). *The Mental World of Stuart Women*. Amherst: University of Massachusetts Press.

Morgan, Fidelis (1981). *The Female Wits: Women Playwrights on The London Stage, 1660–1720*. London: Virago.

Morgan, Fidelis (1991). *Female Playwrights of the Restoration: Five Comedies*. London: Dent.

Owen, Susan J. (1996). *Restoration Theatre and Crisis*. Oxford: Clarendon Press.

Quinsey, Katherine M. (ed.). (1996). *Broken Boundaries: Women and Feminism in Restoration Drama*. Lexington: University Press of Kentucky.

Roberts, David (1989). *The Ladies: Female Patronage of Restoration Drama, 1660–1700*. Oxford: Clarendon Press.

Spencer, Jane (1996). '*The Rover* and the Eighteenth Century', in Janet Todd (ed.), *Aphra Behn Studies*. Cambridge: Cambridge University Press, 84–106.

Staves, Susan (1990). *Married Women's Separate Property in England, 1660–1833*. Cambridge, MA: Harvard University Press.

Straub, Krista (1992). *Sexual Suspects: Eighteenth-century Players and Sexual Ideology*. Princeton, NJ: Princeton University Press.

Stone, Lawrence (1977). *The Family, Sex and Marriage in England, 1500–1800*. New York: Harper and Row.

Todd, Janet (1996a). 'Introduction', in Janet Todd (ed.), *Aphra Behn Studies*. Cambridge: Cambridge University Press, 1–12.

Todd, Janet (1996b). *The Secret Life of Aphra Behn*. Rutgers: Rutgers University Press.

Todd, Janet (ed.). (1999). *Aphra Behn: New Casebooks*. New York: St Martin's Press.

Woodcock, George (1948). *The Incomparable Aphra*. London: Boardman.

Zook, Melinda (1998). 'Contextualizing Aphra Behn: Plays, Politics, and Party: 1679–1689', in Hilda L. Smith (ed.), *Women Writers and the Early Modern British Political Tradition*. Cambridge: Cambridge University Press, 75–94.

24
William Congreve and Thomas Southerne
Miriam Handley

When once a Poet settles an ill Name,
Let him Write well, or ill, 'tis all the same:
For Criticks now a days, like Flocks of Sheep,
All follow, when the first has made the leap.

(Prologue to *The Fatal Marriage* by Thomas Southerne)

Although spoken by Mrs Bracegirdle and written from the actress's point of view, Southerne's prologue describes the playwright's perception of his reputation. In the years preceding *The Fatal Marriage* (1694), Southerne had seen 'criticks' at Drury Lane 'leap' to condemn *The Wives' Excuse* (1691–2) and *The Maid's Last Prayer* (1692–3). He also watched as Congreve's first comedy, *The Old Batchelour* (1693), was applauded by the same audiences that had rejected his own work. Within a few years Southerne's 'ill Name' was being used to emphasize Congreve's critical success. When Congreve for example decided to write a tragedy without a comic subplot, it was hailed as 'the most perfect Tragedy that has been wrote in this Age' and was compared favourably to Southerne's tragicomedies (Blackmore 1697: vii). Ignoring the fact that Congreve had praised Southerne's mixture of 'grief and mirth' in *Oroonoko* (1695) and had encouraged him to disregard criticism of his split plots, critics such as Sir Richard Blackmore expressed the hope that 'slovenly writers' would now abandon the 'obscene and prophane Pollutions' of tragicomedy. Thus, in the two years that separated the writing of *Oroonoko* from Congreve's tragedy, *The Mourning Bride* (1697), Southerne's decision to mix comedy and tragedy was transformed from an aesthetic choice into an 'obscene' moral failing.

If, as Southerne maintained, his reputation already amounted to an 'ill Name' by 1694, he would hardly be surprised at the subsequent reception of his plays. A survey of criticism reveals that Congreve is praised and Southerne reproved even when their writing practice does not differ. This is particularly evident in the critical presentation of the playwrights' relationship with their audiences. Critics have agreed for example that *The Old Batchelour* is 'derivative', but have argued that this indicates Congreve's early sensitivity to theatrical tradition and his audience's taste. When Southerne's attention to the audience's taste is discussed however it is more commonly represented as commercially motivated crowd-pleasing.

Later in the Restoration period it might have appeared to Southerne that Congreve's fortunes were about to change. Collier's much discussed attack on Restoration drama in his *Short View of the Immorality and Profaneness of the English Stage* (1698) focused on Congreve's plays but took little notice of Southerne's. One hundred and fifty years later, when Macaulay launched his broadside against Restoration drama in the *Edinburgh Review*, Southerne's plays again escaped castigation. In both cases however the short-term damage of adverse criticism was offset by the attention it attracted to Congreve's works. Southerne may have felt the benefit of being over-looked by Collier during the final years of the seventeenth century, but by the mid-nineteenth century Collier's oversight had been converted into a more thorough-going critical neglect of Southerne's plays.

In effect, the differing fortunes of the two playwrights comes to this: Congreve was hailed at the outset of his career as the playwright who would refresh the traditions of Restoration drama and Southerne was not. The attention paid to Congreve by his peers reconstituted the individual playwright as a literary institution, and in consequence his plays have been closely analysed by any admirer or detractor of Restoration drama. Southerne's experience of critical commentary has been very different. From the moment that Dryden referred to Southerne as one of Congreve's 'foil'd Contemporaries', the playwright began to suffer from the comparison (Dryden, cited in Congreve 1982: 101). His plays were marginalized by his contemporaries, by the eighteenth-century actors who adapted his work and presented lopped halves of his tragicomedies to their audiences, and by critics who have been hard pressed to fit him into their discussions of Restoration drama.

Returning to Southerne's prologue to *The Fatal Marriage* we find a playwright who, justifiably or otherwise, believed that his 'ill Name' was fixed whatever he wrote. Since, unlike the women discussed in Southerne's play *Sir Anthony Love* (1690), the playwright did not outlive his first reputation and achieve a more favourable second (4.4.51–2), this chapter will attempt to discover how Southerne's and Congreve's respective reputations were decided and how this has affected their subsequent reception. To do this the plays will be discussed in the order in which they were performed, and their representation of the playwrights' offstage negotiation of a place in the theatrical succession of Restoration authors will be examined.

The Loyal Brother (1682) to *The Old Batchelour* (1693)

In March 1693 Southerne wrote a dedicatory poem to Congreve's first play in which he presented the younger playwright as Dryden's heir. The poem describes Dryden's search for a successor amongst living and recently deceased Restoration dramatists such as Wycherley, Etherege, Lee and Otway, and claims that Congreve had been chosen to protect the older playwright's posthumous reputation. Southerne's support of Congreve had of course begun some time before he wrote his dedication to *The Old Batchelour*. In 1692 he provided Congreve with his first opportunity to publish a dramatic composition when he included one of his songs in *The Maid's Last Prayer*. Shortly afterwards Southerne read Congreve's first play, 'engagd Mr Dryden in its favour', and formed part of a literary consortium that shaped *The Old Batchelour* to suit 'the fashionable cutt of the Town' (Southerne, cited in Hodges 1964: 151). If we look earlier in the playwrights' careers we find other potential points of communication between them. Southerne was born in Dublin in February 1660, Congreve in York-shire in January 1670, but both attended Trinity College, Dublin and came into contact with the same tutor. In 1680 and 1689 respectively, Southerne and Congreve left Dublin and travelled to England where they subsequently became members of the Middle Temple.

Neither playwright appears to have been keen to study law although much has since been made of the legal knowledge demonstrated in Congreve's later plays. Instead the playwrights gravitated towards the literary cliques gathering in London's coffee houses, where each came to Dryden's attention. At this point in their respective careers however their fortunes diverge. While Congreve quickly impressed Dryden with his abilities as a classical scholar, Southerne had to work harder for the laureate's approval. In fact the first reference to Southerne's relationship with Dryden is an account of their negotiations over money.

> [Dryden's] usual price till then had been four guineas: But when Southern came to him for the Prologue he had bespoke, Dryden told him he must have six guineas for it; 'which (said he) young man, is out of no disrespect to you, but the Players have had my goods too cheap'. (William Warburton, cited in Southerne 1988, 1: xiv–xv)

This anecdote could merely refer to Dryden's avarice and what this implies about his relationship with the King's Company actors in 1682, but it might also suggest that Dryden raised his prices because he did not like Southerne's play. If this is the case, Southerne's critics have tended to share the laureate's opinion. Some have noted that *The Loyal Brother* is 'imitative', but given their generosity to Congreve's first 'derivative' work it is best to look elsewhere to explain their cool reception of the play. The answer seems to lie in the play's explicit references to the attempts to exclude James, Charles II's Catholic brother, from the throne. Criticizing a play for making topical allusions has become increasingly rare but many of Southerne's critics appear to believe this to be sufficient reason for passing over *The Loyal Brother* to his more accessible second play, *The Disappointment* (1684). Nicoll for example notes that *The Loyal Brother* is 'spoilt by political references', and his conclusion is shared by Hume who objects not to the political allusions in the play but to the crudity of their expression (Nicoll 1928: 143; Hume 1990: 280).

Although critics have noted the broad political parallels in *The Loyal Brother*, recent work on the theatre's reflection of and participation in the Restoration's political upheavals encourages us to flesh out the detail of the play's contemporary references. When we look at Ismael's rabble-rousing in *The Loyal Brother* for example (5.2.71–135), it is not difficult to recognize in a character described as a *'villainous Favourite'* a Tory representation of Shaftesbury inciting a new generation of rebels to agitate for civil war. Within moments of Ismael's arrival in the Persian street, its citizens are chorusing 'we'r all for Rebellion' (5.2.107). This simple identification of *The Loyal Brother*'s dramatis personae with key figures in the Exclusion Crisis does not however explain Dryden's reference to Southerne as 'neither yet a Whigg, nor a Tory boy' (Dryden, cited in Southerne 1988, 1: 72). Indeed Southerne gave voice to some distinctly non-Tory ideas with his depiction of ungoverned citizens attacking officers and calling in debts. These could be references to the 1681 dissolution of Parliament and rumours of the king's negotiations with France over money for a standing army. For Charles II, who watched the play on 4 February 1682, Act 5, scene 2 of Southerne's first play could have looked like a critique of his policies.

Southerne retreated from overt political commentary in his second play, *The Disappointment* and correspondingly we find more detailed readings of the text. Nicoll famously noted that *The Disappointment* heralded 'the development of a new type of sentimental, moral, problem drama', but other critics have been less certain about ways of interpreting the play (Nicoll 1928: 144). Hume points to Southerne's unusual decision to designate *The Disappointment* 'a Play' and examines the 'odd' fusion of wit comedy in the Angelline plot and heroic drama in the Erminia plot (Hume 1990: 280–1). The discomforting juxtaposition of characters who disagree over the seriousness of adultery introduces a theme that informs Southerne's later comedies and split-plot tragedies. Also indicating future developments in Southerne's plays is Erminia whose behaviour, language and loyalty render her incapable of coping with the world in which she finds herself. Southerne represents her isolation spatially, for in contrast to other characters Erminia spends the play within her chamber. In this she recalls *The Loyal Brother*'s Semanthe, *'melancholy in her Apartment'* (4.2.0), an allusion supported by Sarah Cook's performance of both roles. Doubted and played upon by every character she meets, Erminia ends the play with her husband Alphonso holding a dagger to her throat; he withdraws it only to conclude that while his wife's innocence may have been proved, he still anticipates the 'forked Fortune' of a cuckold (5.2.339).

Southerne's depiction of Erminia as hopelessly disabled amongst a cast of rakes and duplicitous maids introduces into the play an early indication of his exploration of the tension between character and stereotype. This tension is dramatized by Alphonso, who polices the boundaries between the two plots. Having spent most of the play in *'an open garden'* outside his own house (3.1.0), or in 'the next room' in Rogero's home (4.1.272), his action is punctuated by bouts of violence that suggest his intention of turning *The Disappointment* into a tragedy rather than continuing to live in the generic confusion of Southerne's 'Play'.

Given the bewilderment of Southerne's dramatis personae over the type of play in which they find themselves, it is not surprising that audiences were unenthusiastic about *The Disappointment*. Shortly after the play's production, Southerne abandoned the theatre and established his credentials as a 'Tory boy' by accepting an ensign's commission to a regiment raised to deal with Monmouth's rebellion. He left the theatre in 1685 for five years and although he wrote a portion of a play that would become *The Spartan Dame* (1719), its support of James II became inappropriate after the Glorious Revolution installed William and Mary on the throne in 1689. Like Dryden, who was stripped of his laureateship upon William's accession, Southerne found himself obliged to foreground his political adaptability in the first plays he wrote after leaving the army.

Recent editors of Southerne's most popular play of his early career, *Sir Anthony Love* (1690), argue that the entire text demonstrates the playwright's willingness to adapt to the new political climate. They point to Sir Anthony's comment, 'I am always of the Religion of the Government I am in' (1.1.184–5), and to the careful balancing of a song by the 'troublesome' Jacobite Sir Edward Sackvile with Southerne's satire on the Catholicism of the Abbé (Southerne 1988, 1: 165). If we look closer, however, it is possible to argue that these interpretations of Southerne's political adaptability are unsafe.

At first glance it seems that even the text of *Sir Anthony Love* celebrates the adaptability of its characters. Sir Anthony's ability to shift between male and female personae for example is reflected in the play's stage directions. When the Pilgrim tells Sir Anthony that he knows her true gender he is described as '*Squeezing and kissing her hand*' (3.1.113), but when Ilford takes hold of Sir Anthony's arm in the following scene he is described as '*Bringing him back by the hand*' (3.2.9) (my emphasis). This textual adaptability is further demonstrated in the depiction of that other shape-shifter, the Pilgrim. When the Pilgrim's disguise is discovered he assumes with his new costume a different speech designation, 'Palmer'. This does not happen however when Sir Anthony's identity is revealed at the end of the play. In the final scene Sir Anthony appears in a borrowed dress, married to the wrong man and referred to as Mistress Lucy, but she retains her 'Sir Anthony' speech designation. Perhaps, as Weber suggests, Sir Anthony's 'disguise has come to dominate her personality', but it is also possible to argue that Southerne has used his text to cast doubt on the extent to which Sir Anthony will adapt to her new situation (Weber 1984: 129).

When we turn to consider the Abbé's decision to sing and dance to Sackvile's 'In vain *Clemene*' (5.4.42) it is clear that the Jacobite's song is initially shown to be astonishingly inappropriate to the situation. The Abbé appears to have chosen the song for its theme 'I'm lost if you deny / A quick possession', but he wilfully ignores the fact that the song addresses a female subject and sings it instead to Sir Anthony, whom he believes to be male. When Sir Anthony reveals herself to be a woman however the song suddenly becomes more appropriate to the situation. Sir Anthony is now 'Mistress Lucy' and the Abbé is indeed lost when she denies him 'quick possession', for she forces him to disturb the foundations of his society. The Abbé puts aside familial loyalty to his brother, marries his niece to a libertine, and conducts a ceremony in which Sir Gentle Golding is tricked into marrying Sir Anthony. Having breached family loyalty, performed a sham ceremony and been revealed as homosexual, Southerne's Abbé is forced to acknowledge that he is out of step with Sir Anthony's world. He says, 'I'm an old Fellow...upon my last Leggs' (5.4.159–60). Sackvile's song in contrast is more readily adapted to the context in which it is sung. This is significant, for in demonstrating the relevance of a Jacobite song to a play performed in the 1690s, Southerne's play casts doubt on an interpretation of *Sir Anthony Love* as an implicit assertion of the playwright's own political adaptability.

Southerne's success with *Sir Anthony Love* was remarkable. Unlike his two earlier plays, it ran for six nights and yielded two benefit nights for the playwright. His next two plays were less successful with audiences but critics have argued that *The Wives' Excuse* (1691–2) and *The Maid's Last Prayer* (1692–3) represent Southerne's most interesting work. The first of Southerne's plays to be set in London, *The Wives' Excuse* contrasts the familiar settings of Rosamund's Pool and the Piazza with an opening scene that prevents the audience's identification with the characters. As Holland has noted, Act 1, scene 1 serves as a frame to the play (1979: 165–7). It introduces the main characters' footmen and pages and allows them to voice their opinion of their employers before they revert to their silent movement through the remainder of the scenes. Act 1, scene 1 describes a different view of the play's world and implies that this commentary continues offstage. As Thompson notes, this distinction between public and private speech is emphasized by the stage directions describing the shift between whispered conversations and speeches made '*to the company*' (Thompson 1993: 84).

The Wives' Excuse continues to explore the distinction between public and private concerns by articulating a tension between the unhappily married Mrs Friendall and the stereotype to which she is expected to conform. Cordner points out that all the characters surrounding Mrs Friendall, from her husband's friends to her footman, expect her to counter the effect of her miserable marriage by making her husband a cuckold; hence the play's subtitle, 'Cuckolds Make Themselves' (Cordner 1990: 274–7). Mrs Friendall's refusal to cuckold her deserving husband has serious consequences for the play: she separates from Friendall, resists the rake and renders the play's subtitle irrelevant.

Holland adds to critical accounts of the play by analysing the theatrical context informing the audience's response to it. He cites the offstage rumours that linked Mr Mountfort to the alluring actress Mrs Bracegirdle and argues that the 'on-stage pursuit of Bracegirdle/Sightly' by Mr Mountfort's character, Mr Friendall, 'becomes part of a theatrical relationship as well as a dramatic one' (Holland 1979: 143). Jordan continues this kind of analysis by reading Southerne's next play, *The Maid's Last Prayer*, as a companion piece to *The Wives' Excuse* (1991: 99–100). Performed at Drury Lane without great success, the play's characters move through familiar scenes but present a very different picture of the life they lead. The lack of male characters in the play could be interpreted as another intersection with its theatrical context. After

Mountfort's murder, Leigh's heartbroken death and Betterton's unexplained absence from the cast, *The Maid's Last Prayer* describes a world in which the women outnumber and outmanoeuvre the men. Southerne archly depicts both Mountfort's widow and Mrs Bracegirdle as lacking a significant man in the play, but focuses the contrast between the two texts on his casting of Mrs Barry. As Mrs Friendall the actress protested that she would not cuckold her husband but in her role as Lady Malepert in *The Maid's Last Prayer* she is introduced as an adulterous 'whore' (1.1.57).

Within a few months of *The Maid's Last Prayer* being performed, Southerne wrote his dedicatory poem to Congreve's *The Old Batchelour*. At this stage in his career the first five of Southerne's ten plays had been performed and only one, *Sir Anthony Love*, had been successful with audiences. Southerne's depiction of characters trapped in alien environments and isolated from the rest of the dramatis personae introduces a theme that he would develop in his subsequent plays. In his later work however he eschewed the attempt to portray these isolated characters in 'comedies'. Instead he represented their failure to adapt as a tragedy.

Congreve, the Rightful Heir and Money, Southerne's Mistress

By the time Congreve's first play, *The Old Batchelour*, was performed at Drury Lane in March 1693, the playwright had already started to rehearse his role as a Restoration author. He claimed that he had written his novel *Incognita* 'in the idler hours of a fortnight's time' and that *The Old Batchelour* was produced 'to amuse myself in a slow Recovery from a Fit of Sickness' (Congreve 1964: 9). In his third play, *Love for Love* (1695), Congreve also depicted Valentine musing on a career as a dramatist to the counterpoint of duns knocking at his door for money (1.1). Congreve's biographical and theatrical accounts of his own writing practice look back to Etherege's and Wycherley's, who, as Markley argues elsewhere in this volume, had attempted 'to get ahead in a fashionable world without displaying any effort beneath the dignity of a gentleman' (see chapter 19).

There are other parallels between Congreve, Wycherley and Etherege. All three abandoned the theatre in their thirties and both Etherege and Congreve provided themselves with lucrative government posts. All three also scandalized their peers on their deathbeds. Although Macaulay interpreted Wycherley's last actions as 'prompted by obdurate malignancy', he depicted Congreve's will, which bequeathed his wealth to his illegitimate daughter in the form of a diamond necklace, as 'absurd and capricious' (Macaulay 1841: 528).

In a 1997 article Weber argues that the success of Congreve's attempts to promote and maintain an image of Restoration dramatic authorship was guaranteed by Southerne's and Dryden's dedications to *The Old Batchelour* and *The Double Dealer* (1997: 359). Both poems name Congreve as Dryden's heir, and both Southerne and Dryden indicate their abdication in his favour. Southerne wrote,

> His eldest *Wycherley*, in wise Retreat,
> Thought it not worth his quiet to be great.
> Loose, wand'ring *Etherege*, in wild Pleasures tost,
> And foreign Int'rests, to his hopes long lost;
> Poor *Lee* and *Otway* dead! CONGREVE appears,
> The Darling, and last Comfort of his Years.
> (Cited in Congreve 1982: 4)

Southerne's poem presents Dryden's abdication as a natural process of succession but Southerne's reason for omitting his own name from this list of potential heirs is less clear. His abdication in Congreve's favour is however central to an understanding of the relationship between the two playwrights and the way in which critical responses to their works have developed.

In his dedication to *The Old Batchelour* Southerne writes,

> We timely court the rising Hero's Cause
> And on his side, the Poet wisely draws; . . .
> The days will come, when we shall all receive,
> Returning Interest from what we now give.
> (Cited in ibid.: 3–4)

While it would be possible to interpret 'Returning Interest' without reference to a financial context, these words give the impression of Southerne lavishing praise on the younger playwright in the hope of reward. Discounting for a moment this ungenerous reading of Southerne's motivation, there appear to be two reasons for his decision to obscure his place in the theatrical succession. First, as Dryden's dedication to *The Wives' Excuse* reveals, Southerne's difference from other Restoration playwrights had already been noted. Dryden advised,

> The Standard of thy Style, let *Etherege* be:
> For Wit, th'Immortal Spring of *Wycherly*.
> Learn after both, to draw some just Design,
> And the next Age will learn to Copy thine.
> (Cited in Southerne 1988, 1: 271)

As Southerne's later work makes clear however the playwright was not attempting to write the kind of plays that Etherege and Wycherley had popularized. Although he utilized the stereotypes of Restoration comedy in his plays, Southerne's depiction of heroic characters trapped in the wrong genre suggests that he was attempting to subvert rather than emulate the 'just Designs' that Dryden noticed in Wycherley's and Etherege's plays.

A more pressing reason for Southerne's omission of his name from Dryden's theatrical succession can be located in the similarity of their situations. Having demonstrated their Jacobite allegiance, both playwrights found themselves in a very different theatrical and political climate after William and Mary's accession in 1689. Their only collaboration, on the final act of Dryden's tragedy *Cleomenes* (1692), produced a text whose performance was vigorously opposed by the government. As a Protestant Whig however Congreve had access to patrons from whom Dryden and Southerne were alienated. In the light of the political and theatrical implications of his situation, Dryden, who required an heir to rehabilitate his reputation, could not have chosen Southerne for the position. Nevertheless he drew Southerne back into the theatrical lineage in his dedication to Congreve's second play, *The Double Dealer*. In this poem, Dryden praises Southerne's 'purity'. Kaufman, who has researched other appearances of this word in Dryden's corpus, suggests that the poet equated the term with linguistic 'blandness' (1973: 36–7). In effect, Dryden complimented Southerne on his ability to write plays that appeared to conceal his political allegiance.

Congreve's reaction to Dryden's patronage can be seen in the decisions he subsequently made about the presentation of his work. Dryden noticed for instance the innovative inclusion of Congreve's name on the playbill for *The Double Dealer*, and others have since discussed Congreve's attempts to formulate alternative theatrical lineages for himself. Lindsay and Erskine-Hill have suggested that Congreve voluntarily adopted the role of laureate, continuing in William's reign the part Dryden had performed in Charles II's (1989: 6). Congreve's contemporary, Catharine Trotter, also indicated her awareness of the literary significance of the playwright's decision to write a tragedy,

> This only part was wanting to thy name
> That wit's whole empire thou mightst justly claim.
>
> (1751: 564)

Congreve's attention to the development of his writing career thus paints a very different picture of playwriting than that provided by Valentine, Jeremy and Scandal in *Love for Love*. Their depiction of the shame attached to modern writing encompassed the possibility of disinheritance, social shame, the necessity for servility to great men and the prospect of sexual misfortune. The social triumphs of Congreve's career disprove this depressing vision of authorship, but Southerne's experience was less happy. As his reference to 'Returning Interest' in his dedication to *The Old Batchelour* suggests, Southerne was forced to foreground his connection of writing and its reward.

Critical descriptions of Southerne's career revel in his remarkable assiduity in reaping the financial rewards of his authorship. Dodds lingers over Southerne's success in pursuing recompense for his work, contrasting it with Dryden's and Congreve's more reticent approach. Referring to the £36 Southerne made from the copyright of *The Fatal Marriage*, Dodds quotes a contemporary's comment that 'this kind of usage... will vex huffing Dryden and Congreve to madness' (1933: 26). Theophilus Cibber makes a similar comparison when he describes Dryden's chagrin on hearing that Southerne made £700 from a play in comparison to the £100 that he had come to expect. 'The secret is,' concludes Cibber, 'Mr Southerne was not beneath the drudgery of sollicitation . . . a degree of servility which perhaps Mr Dryden thought was much beneath the dignity of a poet' (1753: 329). These representations of Southerne as financially driven also lie behind other interpretations of his life. Southerne chose to marry a wealthy wife, made a name for himself as a 'Cat in Pan' when he shifted his political allegiance to the Whigs in 1704, and worst of all continued to write plays until he became too deaf to hear the audiences hissing his last, *Money the Mistress* (1726). This presentation of Southerne's financial motivation for writing could be interpreted as connected to his abdication from Dryden's theatrical succession. In placing himself outside the genealogy of 'dignified' Restoration authors, Southerne allowed himself to be depicted as an 'underplayer'. To determine whether this is another example of Southerne's 'ill Name' shaping critical responses to his career, we can compare the playwrights' attitudes to literary inheritance and financial fortune as this is suggested in the plays produced between Congreve's debut and the end of the Restoration period.

The Old Batchelour (1693) to *The Fate of Capua* (1700)

So much has been said about the significance of *The Old Batchelour* as the occasion of Congreve's literary accession that it has become difficult to disjoin the play from its reception. Bevis and Davis for instance analyse the play in terms of its own references to other writers, an approach recommended by its many allusions. *The Old Batchelour* certainly conveys an impression of its author negotiating a place for himself in the literary landscape. Yet in its references to Wycherley's *The Plain Dealer* (4.4.219), Seneca, Jonson and Dryden (5.1.192), Dryden's *Amphitryon* (5.1.363–4) and, indirectly, to Dryden again in an allusion to Buckingham's *The Rehearsal* in the epilogue, Congreve's play suggests a specific approach to inherited literary texts.

Congreve provides two examples of the wrong way of using texts in *The Old Batchelour*. The first is Silvia's forgery of a letter from Araminta to Vainlove in which she makes explicit her rival's affection as a means of driving the couple apart. Although Silvia's letter initially has the effect she intends, Araminta is able to regain Vainlove's interest by claiming indifference to him. The forgery fails because it makes explicit Araminta's true feelings and flouts the convention of emotional disguise that governs the characters' behaviour in Congreve's dramatic world. The same point is made when Bellmour uses a book to make explicit his adulterous intentions in Act 4, scene 2. Bellmour disguises himself as the superb unseen character Tribulation Spintext but whilst dressing himself in the garb of this 'Fanatick, one-ey'd Parson' (1.1.92–3), he replaces Spintext's prayer book with Scarron's lewd novel, *The Innocent Adultery*. Although this book is appropriate to Bellmour's seduction of Laetitia Fondlewife, it violates Congreve's rules of disguise by pointing out Bellmour's satire on the stereotype of lustful clergymen.

Congreve's first play indicates that texts should not be used to explain the subtext of a situation, and this representation of his attitude to his literary heritage is replicated in his later work. In *The Way of the World* (1700) Millamant uses a poem by Suckling to inform Mirabell of her fear that he will become indifferent to her if they marry but Mirabell demonstrates his Congrevian pedigree by politely pretending to misunderstand her 'pretty artifice' (Bruce 1987: 334). Later in the play Marwood and Fainall indicate a more serious abuse of texts when they satirize the piety of swearing an oath on a prayer book by replacing it with a volume of Messalina's poems. The maids who swear the oath however take note of the substitution and perceive themselves to be free to reveal vital information to Mrs Fainall, thereby frustrating Fainall's and Marwood's plans.

Congreve uses *The Old Batchelour* to indicate that his work will not rely on simple borrowings from his theatrical forebears. In his second play, performed later in 1693, Congreve extends his preoccupation with literary inheritances to the transfer of money between generations. Set in 'A *Gallery in* Lord Touchwood's *home, with Chambers adjoining*' (1.1.0), the enclosed world of *The Double Dealer* is rendered both verbally and spatially confusing. Characters eavesdrop on conversations taking place in the main gallery, and Maskwell moves duplicitously through the play using his asides and soliloquies as a linguistic parallel to the side rooms in which he makes his plans.

With two fortunes at stake, the confined setting of the play becomes significant. By placing two generations of characters in close proximity to each other, Congreve uses cross-generational desire to threaten the patrilinear transference of wealth. Lady Touchwood's attraction to her husband's nephew Mellefont may be incestuous, but Lady Plyant's attraction to him is presented as perverse. Having demonstrated her unwillingness to provide Sir Paul with an heir by swaddling him in blankets and tying his hands and feet together when they are in bed (3.1.316–17), Lady Plyant revels in the prospect of an affair with her step-daughter's fiancé. Unconvincingly protesting her inviolable virginity, she says:

> Marrying the Daughter only to make a cuckold of the Father! . . . To my thinking, now, I could resist the strongest temptation. – But yet I know 'tis impossible for me to know whether I could or not; there is no certainty in the things of this life. (2.1.340–1, 354–5)

The women are not alone in desiring affairs with the younger generation. Sir Paul suggests an imaginative equivalent of incest to Cynthia in Act 4, scene 1. Attempting to influence the family features of his future grandchild by offering money, he promises '500 *l.* for every inch of his that resembles me' (4.1.268). To ensure the transmission of family features Sir Paul encourages his daughter to imagine him as she is conceiving her child, 'Think on thy old Father, Heh? Make the young rogue as like as you can . . . Let [thy Father's leer] be transmitted to the young Rogue by help of imagination' (4.1.254–5, 261–2).

The confusingly related families of *The Double Dealer* introduce Congreve's interest in analysing the larger complexities of his society. In his second and third plays,

Congreve establishes the importance of unravelling family relationships by referring to the significance of characters that are unborn or dead. Mellefont for example is justifiably afraid that he will be disinherited if Lady Touchwood has a child in *The Double Dealer*, and in *Love for Love* Valentine's extravagance with money is explained by an exchange between Ben and Sir Sampson in which it is suggested that Valentine only became heir to his father's inheritance after the death of his elder brother, Dick (3.1.306–17). Although as Woolf noticed it is almost impossible to understand the relationship between Congreve's characters, the playwright represents this as basic to their ability to survive in their environment and ally themselves to those most likely to inherit wealth (Woolf 1982: 95).

Congreve waited until April 1695 before staging his next play, *Love for Love*, but in the intervening period Southerne produced *The Fatal Marriage* and *Oroonoko*. For two centuries after their first performances in February 1694 and March 1695 these plays were considered Southerne's finest, and although both were shorn of their comic subplots during the eighteenth century, they continued to be performed and praised until the mid-nineteenth century. *The Fatal Marriage* and *Oroonoko* return us to Southerne's theme of characters disabled by the environment in which they find themselves, but the plays use split plots to indicate the contiguity of tragedy to Restoration comic plots. In *The Fatal Marriage* for example Southerne's comic subplot rehearses incidents that reappear as tragic later in the play. In Act 4, scene 1 Fabian's and Victoria's tyrannical father is drugged and, upon waking in the '*Monastery Burying-Place*' (4.1.0), is led to believe that he has returned from the dead. His children effectively frighten him into sharing out his estate, welcoming his daughter and her lover into the family and being kinder to his second wife. In the following scene Isabella's husband Biron also returns from the dead but having discovered that his wife is remarried and his servants do not recognize him, he is swiftly despatched back to the grave by his younger brother. Both plots put an estate at stake, but the contrast established between them demonstrates Southerne's sense of the tragic potential inherent in this familiar Restoration scenario.

The Fatal Marriage's preoccupation with estates is replaced in *Oroonoko* by Southerne's emphasis on the indiscriminate sale of princes, women and slaves. Hughes argues that Southerne makes use of the contrast between the heroic and comic plots to suggest that 'sale' is now 'the primary mode of human relationships' (Hughes 1996: 344), but Rich and Vermilion produce other interpretations of *Oroonoko*'s split plot. Rich for example notes that, 'the Prince's and Imoinda's heroism in the play is not intended as a rejection of those values; [but] rather . . . as a critique of that world in which heroic value has no place' (1983: 174). Vermilion's approach to Southerne's play rests on her belief that it articulates Southerne's response to Aphra Behn, whose novel he was adapting. She argues that Southerne rejected Behn's attempt to construct parallels between herself, her narrator and Oroonoko. In analysing Southerne's version of Behn's novel, Vermilion argues that Behn and her narrator are represented as the avaricious, morally defunct Charlott Welldon. She concludes that Southerne's depiction of the breeches-wearing Charlott provides an indication of his response to Behn's attempts to enter the male domain of authorship: '[Southerne's] use of the split-plot form is indicative of the relationship between literary convention and the anti-feminism of Eighteenth-century literary culture' (Vermilion 1992: 29).

These articles are integral to the reappraisal of Southerne's work. Rich's conclusions allow us to see Southerne's tragedies as an endpoint in his examination of political adaptability. Instead of depicting characters such as Erminia, Mrs Friendall, Isabella and Oroonoko as unable to adapt to their environments, *The Fatal Marriage* and *Oroonoko* suggest that it is now impossible for such characters to survive. As Hughes notes Southerne's plays demonstrate 'the power of money to dissolve orders based on faith and the word' (Hughes 1996: 456). The application of such conclusions to Southerne's works returns us to his connection of heroic drama with the old royalist values. Southerne's tragedies critique the comic worlds with 1690s London and mark the point at which society barters heroic values for money.

It is possible to argue that Vermilion's conclusions are overstated but her argument is significant for its discussion of Southerne's anxiety in acknowledging his debt to Behn, both in *Oroonoko* and in his earlier works. Southerne displays his nervousness in his dedication to *Oroonoko*, in which he criticizes every aspect of the source text. The reasons for Southerne's anxiety in acknowledging Behn as his literary forebear are compellingly listed by Lowenthal. If, as Lowenthal argues, Behn's contemporaries thought of her as a financially driven punk using her 'illicitly gained sexual knowledge' as theatrical currency, it is not surprising that Southerne wanted to maintain a critical distance from the playwright (see chapter 23).

Oroonoko and Congreve's third play *Love for Love* were performed within a month of each other but the difference between the plays and the context of their performance emphasizes the difference between the playwrights. Both plays were ready for performance when Betterton, enraged by the parsimony of the United Company's manager, established his rival company at Lincoln's Inn Field's theatre. Southerne's play was produced at Drury Lane but Congreve's became the first play to be performed at Betterton's theatre. While Southerne's decision to remain at Drury Lane has been seen as his privileging of financial security over aesthetic considerations, Congreve's choice has been interpreted more favourably.

The plays' themes also reveal the playwrights' political and ideological differences. While *Oroonoko* laments the devaluing of heroic qualities, *Love for Love* celebrates Valentine's triumph over his tyrannical father, Sir Sampson. The moment of Valentine's succession represents a starting point for Congreve's later preoccupation with legal documents and wills in *The Way of the World*. Sir Sampson, a personification of a 'capricious and tyrannical' older generation, is confounded by Valentine's and Angellica's manipulation of legal occasions. Valentine's inheritance is punctuated by the sound of Angellica tearing the deed with which Sir Sampson hoped to disinherit both of his sons from their fortune. As in *The Double Dealer*, Congreve uses cross-generational desire to symbolize the threat to the transmission of inheritance. Having torn up Sir Sampson's deed, Angellica rebukes Valentine's father for attempting to marry her, saying, 'learn to be a good Father, or you'll never get a second Wife' (5.1.620–1).

Although it is very different from *Love for Love*, Congreve's well-received tragedy *The Mourning Bride* continues the theme of succession. As Congreve's audience noticed however it was written to assert the legality of William and Mary's accession to the throne. Congreve parallels the political situation by foregrounding his own theatrical lineage. By setting his tragedy in Granada Congreve locates *The Mourning Bride* against the theatrical context of Dryden's *The Conquest of Granada* (1670–1). In effect, Congreve appropriated the milieu of *The Conquest of Granada* and its association with Dryden's valorization of the Stuart line, and used it to assert the legality of the new royal succession. Although it may be an overstatement to suggest that this refashioning of Dryden's play constituted an attempt to rehabilitate the older playwright's fortunes, it is clear that *The Mourning Bride* makes reference to Dryden's play and to Congreve's status as his 'heir' for political purposes. Southerne's unsuccessful tragedy, *The Fate of Capua*, represents a rather less adept attempt to capitalize on Congreve's political dexterity and theatrical success. Abandoning his much-maligned comic subplots, Southerne seems once again to be attempting to indicate his aesthetic and ideological adaptability.

The Fate of Capua was the last of the two playwrights' plays to be performed during the Restoration period but it seems more appropriate to conclude with a discussion of Congreve's finest comedy, *The Way of the World*. The criticism interpreting this play is extensive but it consistently attempts to explain Congreve's reasons for writing a play that audiences and readers find so difficult to follow. In this play, far from sharing the main characters' thoughts, the audience is better represented onstage by Witwoud who is woken by Mirabell to take his part in the play's dénouement and is last heard expostulating, 'Gad, I understand nothing of the matter' (5.1.649).

The audience's association with Witwoud can also be interpreted as politically nuanced. If, as Hughes asserts, Fainall is intended as a representative of the old Tory order of tyranny and Mirabell personifies government by contract, then Witwoud's unwitting signature on Mrs Fainall's deed of interest integrates him in the new world that Mirabell constructs for the play's characters (Hughes 1996: 138). When we compare this situation to that of Britain in 1689 it becomes clear that Congreve is attempting to conclude the debate over the legality of the royal succession. Despite the details of the document's preparation and the legal dexterity needed to prove its validity, Congreve's characters accept its authority. The playwright suggests in this point that his audience of Witwouds have made the right decision in excluding the tyrannical Fainall from power.

The play's preoccupation with Millamant's six thousand pounds and her future inheritance of Lady Wishfort's estate emphasizes the political allusions implicit in Fainall's and Mirabell's attempts to appropriate this inheritance. Braverman argues that the outcome of the men's manoeuvring is predicated in the opening card-playing scene, for although the play begins with Fainall winning the hand, we later discover that the game is Mirabell's because he has possession of a deed that gives him access to Mrs Fainall's estate (Braverman 1985: 134). Congreve's use of the opening card game looks back to Southerne's *The Wives' Excuse* where Mrs Teazall's and Mrs Friendall's inability to win at cards symbolizes their exclusion from society. Old Mrs Teazall comments,

> I must be playing with Company so much younger than my self, but I shall be wiser for the future and play the fool in my own form, where I cheat in my turn. (4.1.368–70)

Mrs Teazall realizes that her age and status disbars her from understanding the games played in *The Wives' Excuse* but in *The Way of the World* Fainall is forced to see that his skills as a card player define him as redundant in a world that has turned its attention to playing with legal documents.

This depiction of generations is marked in *The Way of the World* by the arrival of a new breed of wits. Fainall's failure to understand the intricacies of the legal contracts associates him with Lady Wishfort. These characters are relics from comedies written by Congreve's forebears, Wycherley and Etherege, but they also recall Southerne's characters. Lady Wishfort resembles Oroonoko, for the beliefs and mannerisms of both characters explain their irrelevance to the world of the 1690s. Fainall recalls Alphonso from *The Disappointment*. Both men draw their swords on their wives but in Mrs Fainall's case, a legal document renders her husband's sword powerless and allows his threats of revenge to be characterized as a 'Bear-Garden flourish' (5.1.617). By the end of the seventeenth century therefore both Congreve and Southerne have presented their response to the issue of literary inheritance: both playwrights suggest that the old theatrical lineage is both implicit in and redundant to the new theatrical and political context.

A comparison of Southerne's and Congreve's work has indicated compelling non-dramatic reasons for their different critical fortunes. Southerne's politically motivated decision to remove himself from a theatrical inheritance that passed from Dryden to Congreve was instrumental in marginalizing his work. Southerne's ungracious acknowledgement of a different theatrical forebear, Aphra Behn, also seems to have had its effect on the reception of his plays because both playwrights were depicted by their contemporaries as driven to write by a desire for money. Southerne's plays however describe the sacrifices required to satisfy this need for money as tragic. As Hughes argues, the plays set out 'a shift in values, a triumph of economic forces over older and more sacred bonds, of which the Revolution and its aftermath are a prime and archetypal example' (2000: 138). The distinction between Southerne's perception of money and the necessities he faced to obtain it during his lifetime articulates most clearly an example of critics using biography to skew an interpretation of a playwright's reputation and writing. There is now however a new interest in the very fact of Southerne's marginalization. Critics have noticed the variety of his generic choices, the sheer length of his life, and are now seeking to reappraise Southerne's 'ill Name'. As the Royal Shakespeare Company's 1995 production of *The Wives' Excuse* proves though, more can be done to counter the view that performing Southerne's plays on the modern stage is itself an heroic act.

Despite indications to the contrary, Congreve's reputation as a literary institution has also had its effect on the criticism that greets his plays. Collier's and Macaulay's thorough-going condemnation of the plays and the twentieth century's admiring rehabilitation of their critical significance produce a criticism that, at times, seems monolithic. Recent articles have indicated new avenues of approach by looking more closely at the social and material context of the plays. Loftis's article on *The Way of the World* and popular criminal literature is refreshing because it contrasts the familiar discussions of sparkling wit with evidence of the dirty press and the nasty gossip that anatomized Restoration life. In disclosing the seriousness of Marwood's threat to publish Lady Wishfort's private affairs to the world, Loftis uncovers textual evidence to support Woolf's sense of the vulgar noise that rises from the streets to replace the foul air escaping the open windows of the Restoration drawing room.

> Drays roar on the cobbles ...; the brawling of the street hucksters and tavern rioters comes in at the open windows ... these ladies and gentlemen speak so freely, drink so deeply, smell so strong. (Woolf 1982: 97)

REFERENCES AND FURTHER READING

Bevis, Richard (1988). *English Drama: Restoration and Eighteenth Century, 1660–1789*. London: Longman.

Blackmore, R. (1697). 'Preface', in *King Arthur: An Heroic Poem*. London.

Braverman, Richard (1985). 'Capital Relations and *The Way of the World*', *ELH* 52, no. 1, 133–58.

Bruce, D. W. (1987). 'Why Millamant Studies Sir John Suckling', *Notes and Queries* 34, 334–5.

Cibber, Theophilus and [Shiels, Robert] (1753). *The Lives of the Poets of Great Britain and Ireland*. London, vol. 3.

Congreve, William (1964). *The Complete Works of William Congreve*, ed. Montague Summers. New York: Russell and Russell.

Congreve, William (1982). *The Comedies of William Congreve*, ed. Anthony G. Henderson. Cambridge: Cambridge University Press.

Cordner, Michael (1990). 'Marriage Comedy after the 1688 Revolution: Southerne to Vanbrugh', *Modern Language Review* 85, no. 2, 273–89.

Dodds, John Wendell (1933). *Thomas Southerne Dramatist*. London: Oxford University Press.

Hodges, John C. (ed.). (1964). *William Congreve: Letters and Documents*. London: Macmillan.

Holland, Peter (1979). *The Ornament of Action. Text and Performance in Restoration Comedy*. Cambridge: Cambridge University Press.

Hughes, Derek (1996). *English Drama, 1660–1700*. Oxford: Clarendon Press.

Hughes, Derek (2000). 'Restoration and Settlement: 1660–1688', in Deborah Payne Fisk (ed.), *Cambridge Companion to English Restoration Theatre*. Cambridge: Cambridge University Press, 127–41.

Hume, Robert D. (1990). 'The Importance of Thomas Southerne', *Modern Philology* 87, no. 3, 275–90.

Jordan, Robert (1991). 'Inversion and Ambiguity in *The Maid's Last Prayer*', *Restoration Studies in English Literary Culture* 15, no. 2, 99–110.

Kaufman, Anthony (1973). ' "This Hard Condition of a Woman's Fate": Southerne's *The Wives' Excuse*', *Modern Language Quarterly* 34, 36–47.

Lindsay, Alexander and Erskine-Hill, Howard (eds). (1989). *William Congreve: The Critical Heritage*. London and New York: Routledge and Kegan Paul.

Loftis, John (1996). 'Congreve's *Way of the World* and Popular Criminal Literature', *Studies in English Literature, 1500–1900* 36, no. 3, 561–78.

Macaulay, Thomas Babington (1841). 'Comic Dramatists of the Restoration', *Edinburgh Review* 72, 490–528.

Nicoll, Allardyce (1928). *A History of Restoration Drama, 1660–1700*. 2nd ed. London: Cambridge University Press.

Rich, Julia A. (1983). 'Heroic Tragedy in Southerne's *Oroonoko*: An Approach to Split-plot Tragicomedy', *Philological Quarterly* 62, no. 2, 187–200.

Southerne, Thomas (1988). *The Works of Thomas Southerne*, ed. Robert Jordan and Harold Love. 2 vols. Oxford: Clarendon Press.

Thompson, Peggy (1993). 'Facing the Void in *The Wives' Excuse*', *Papers in Language and Literature* 31, no. 1, 78–98.

Trotter, Catharine (1751). *The Works of Mrs. Catharine Cockburn, Theological, Moral, Drama, and Poetical.* London, vol. 2.

Vermilion, Mary (1992). 'Buried Heroism: Critiques of Female Authorship in Southerne's Adaptations of Behn's *Oroonoko*', *Restoration Studies in English Literary Culture* 16, no. 1, 28–37.

Weber, Harold (1984). 'The Female Libertine in Southerne's *Sir Anthony Love* and *The Wives' Excuse*', *Essays in Theatre* 2, no. 2, 125–39.

Weber, Harold (1997). 'A "Double Portion of his Father's Art": Congreve, Dryden, Jonson and the Drama of Theatrical Succession', *Criticism* 39, no. 3, 359–82.

Woolf, Virginia (1937; 1982). 'Speed, Stillness and Meaning', in Patrick Lyons (ed.), *Congreve: Comedies.* London and Basingstoke: Macmillan.

25

Sir John Vanbrugh and George Farquhar in the Post-Restoration Age

John Bull

That the names of Sir John Vanbrugh and George Farquhar are frequently linked is an acknowledgement of the fact that, after William Congreve had abruptly ended his theatrical career in 1700, they were the last great writers of the comic renaissance that had started in the immediate post-Restoration period. And, indeed, their plays do have important points of contact. Both playwrights were subject to much the same general cultural determinants, but they lived in very different areas of a non-homogeneous society, and they experienced those areas from almost totally opposite perspectives. As Farquhar was working on *The Recruiting Officer*, set – after the bloody battle of Blenheim – in Shrewsbury where the playwright had himself been stationed as a soldier, Vanbrugh was planning the great monument to the glory of the victorious general, Marlborough – Blenheim Palace. To understand the reasons for these differences, and to come to terms with the impulses shaping their work, contributes towards an understanding not only of the way in which British theatre was changing as it entered the eighteenth century, but also of how the formation of British society was altering as it evolved towards a modern capitalist state. The questions and problematics of ideology are never very far away from the work of either writer.

There is an obvious distinction to be made between their two careers. Vanbrugh came to prominence with his first two plays, *The Relapse* (1696) and *The Provok'd Wife* (1697); both plays, though conjuring with contemporary issues, look defiantly back to the heyday of Restoration comedy. Although Vanbrugh continued to produce further plays, they are – with the wonderful exception of his 'city comedy', *The Confederacy* (1705) – all minor works. In contrast, Farquhar can be seen to have served an apprenticeship. His early plays are heavily dependent on the conventions of the earlier drama, and it is only with his two final plays, *The Recruiting Officer* (1706) and *The Beaux' Stratagem* (1707), that he really comes of age, with work that at last announces the end of the post-Restoration comedy tradition and looks forward to, in particular, John Gay's *The Beggar's Opera*. The writers' different social origins and their resultant ambitions played a large part in this, committing Vanbrugh to an examination of essentially the same world of fashionable society that had chiefly preoccupied his predecessors, whilst Farquhar, in his last two great plays, opened up the stage to a wider social milieu.

For what would have seemed most immediately surprising to contemporary audiences of both *The Recruiting Officer* and *The Beaux' Stratagem* is that neither play is set in London but in the provinces, upon which scorn was so consistently poured by the wits and ladies of the earlier drama. Moreover, Farquhar is at great pains to create a realized locale for his audience, stressing that the action really is set away from the familiar world of the metropolis. This change of locale is the single most obviously innovatory, and subsequently influential, aspect of *The Recruiting Officer*. 'Critics generally agree that in forsaking the London drawing-room for the country air of Shrewsbury, Farquhar was introducing a new kind of atmosphere into comedy which was to affect not only *The Beaux' Stratagem* but other subsequent comedy as well' (Kenny 1988, 2: 6–7). It is not just the shift of location to the provinces that marks out *The Recruiting Officer*, however. What really signifies the final break with the post-Restoration tradition and places the play in an essentially eighteenth-century context that will lead to, among other things, the depiction of Tom Jones in Henry Fielding's novel is the treatment afforded the new theatrical territory and its inhabitants. For, as Farquhar argues in his Dedication, his intention was 'to write a Comedy, not a Libel', and consequently he writes not from a satirical, London-oriented perspective but with the sympathy and engagement of the open-minded tourist – the tourist being both Farquhar himself and his theatrical counterpart, Captain Plume. But Farquhar is more than a neutral observer of the scene. The conflicting class interests in the community may not be central to the play's narrative, but they figure importantly in the way in which justice is meted out to the members of the underclass who have been tricked by Plume and his assistant, Sergeant Kite, into enrolling in the army (see Bull 1998: 112–22).

This sense of a society with opposed class interests received more formal recognition in Farquhar's last play, *The Beaux' Stratagem*. Not only are there two socially distinct groups of characters, but the play moves between two carefully defined locales, each of which is the specific property of one of those groups. The play opens in the courtyard of an inn, and it is not until the second act that the action is transferred to the more traditional arena of the country house. Furthermore, the action alternates between inn and country house in an absolutely regular pattern, until after the first scene of the final act, when the ultimate supremacy of the landed and would-be landed class is confirmed in their capture of the stage space. The first characters we are confronted with in the play are, then, as in *The Recruiting Officer*, not the beaux and ladies of the earlier comedy but figures from the lower orders, in this instance the landlord Boniface and his daughter Cherry. The way in which the inn will operate in the play is immediately apparent, as the pair bustle around to prepare themselves for the coach passengers from whom they derive their income. It provides an arena in which the two social groupings can meet. That the values of the country house will eventually prevail over those of the public inn is inevitable, but what is remarkable is the extent to which Farquhar insists on the validity of voices largely unheard in the earlier post-Restoration drama. While Vanbrugh's plays do little to challenge the expectations of narrative location, Vanbrugh does share with Farquhar a strong sense of the changing audience constituency; and in this respect a qualified sense of a common inheritance is important.

Vanbrugh and Farquhar were both born after the restoration of Charles II, which alone separates them from the earlier generation of post-Restoration playwrights whose ideological presuppositions were formed in an atmosphere dominated by the issues raised by the Civil War and the restoration of the monarchy. However, that they wrote in the shadow of this earlier generation is at least as important as the fact that they were writing in the context of a new kind of society. Both playwrights' careers started after the organized accession of William III and Mary in 1689, an accession that was predicated on the acceptance of a limitation of the monarch's power and an extension of the power of Parliament. The fondly remembered days of Charles II's extensive royal patronage of the arts, and in particular the theatre, were long gone.

Farquhar's career as a dramatist is in stark contrast to that of Vanbrugh. Whilst Vanbrugh aspired to a world of aristocratic privilege, seeing playwriting as virtually incidental to his other careers of architect and politician, Farquhar's attitude was straightforwardly economic. Farquhar was born in Dublin in 1677 or 1678, and acted there with the Smock Alley Company without any great success, culminating in a near-disastrous accident on stage during a sword fight. According to an early biographer he was encouraged by his fellow actor and lifelong friend, Robert Wilks, to 'quit the stage and write a comedy'. Wilks helped out financially while Farquhar wrote a draft of what was to be his first production, *Love in a Bottle* (O'Bryan 1732: 13–14). Shortly afterwards he arrived in London, and the theatre impresario Christopher Rich was persuaded to find a place for the play in the 1698 season at the Drury Lane theatre. Farquhar achieved early success with *The Constant Couple* (1699), but even his attempt at a sequel, *Sir Harry Wildair* (1701), failed to bring him significant financial reward and he died in penury, before the public acclaim that was to be accorded his final play, *The Beaux' Stratagem*, in 1707.

Vanbrugh's first production had also been staged at the Drury Lane theatre two years earlier, but the circumstances of his arrival there are somewhat different. Vanbrugh was born into a large and prosperous family in 1664. At the age of 19 Vanbrugh was sent to France, where he remained for about three years, returning to England in 1685, the year of Charles II's death. The following year he bought a commission in the Earl of Huntingdon's regiment which, in 1688, enthusiastically supported the arrival of the Protestant William of Orange (William III). On the death of his father soon after, Vanbrugh, as the oldest surviving child, received a significant percentage of the family wealth.

By 1690 he was again in France and was imprisoned as a suspected spy, not being released until 1692. Vanbrugh probably started work on *The Provok'd Wife* while in the Bastille. Certainly, his extended times in France were to make him far more familiar than Farquhar with Continental drama. For instance, Vanbrugh's *The Confederacy* of

1705 is based on Dancourt's *Les Bourgeoisies à la Mode*, which was first performed in Paris in the month of Vanbrugh's release; indeed, more than any of the post-Restoration playwrights, Vanbrugh was responsible for introducing direct versions of French drama to the London stage. His income was derived largely from his work as an architect, and it was his financial involvement with the management of the new theatre that he had designed in the Haymarket that prompted the production of most of his later plays.

Back in England, Vanbrugh was stationed in Dorset near the home of Sir Thomas Skipwith, who was one of the patentees of the Drury Lane theatre. Offered friendship and patronage by Sir Thomas, Vanbrugh produced a play, *The Relapse*, by way of thanks. With this play Vanbrugh not only announced himself as a playwright, but directly entered the fray that was developing within the rapidly changing world of the theatre.

Changes were being instigated from outside the theatre rather than from within, and in this they are genuinely representative of the larger changes in society that were taking place, in particular the increasing influence and power of its newly enriched elements whose natural environment might be thought of as the City rather than the court. Historically, the momentum for change has always been associated with the publication of Jeremy Collier's *A Short View of the Immorality and Prophaneness of the English Stage* in 1698. Collier's *Short View* was a vitriolic attack on the blasphemies and licentiousness of the contemporary comedies, most significant for its detailed and illustrated accounts of these shortcomings that Collier drew from the plays. Amongst others, Vanbrugh attempted a defence in his *A Short Vindication of The Relapse and The Provok'd Wife from Immorality and Prophaneness*. Collier's reaction to these counterblasts was swift. In 1699, now riding a wave of public and royal popularity, he published *A Defence of the Short View of the Immorality and Prophaneness of the English Stage*, forty-two pages of which were devoted to Vanbrugh.

In his anonymously published *The Adventures of Covent Garden* (1699), Farquhar was probably right when he had his group of playgoers conclude 'that the best way of answering Mr Collier was not to have replied at all', although his rider was evidently not true, 'for there was so much fire in his book, had not his adversaries thrown in fuel, it would have fed upon itself, and so have gone out in a blaze' (Kenny 1988, 2: 269). The reason why Collier's attack would not have 'gone out in a blaze' is that, although Collier has become almost solely associated with the backlash against the stage, he was in truth by no means the only person to launch such attacks, and certainly was not the initiator of them. He caught the public mood but did not create it. That Collier's attack should have proved so popular demonstrates that there was already a strong Puritan distaste for the excesses of a theatre that was identified, rightly or wrongly, with celebrating the hedonistic activities associated with, and thus protected by, the court of King Charles. Public taste, even amongst theatre audiences, was changing before Collier's broadside, and the subsequent activities of organizations such as the Society for the Reformation of Manners created an umbrella for the organized utterance of such demands for change. So it was not that there had been no signs of a Puritan opposition to the post-Restoration theatrical celebration of excess before this time; rather, with the accession of William and Mary, and thus the removal of the previous Stuart royal patronage, it became a less problematic public utterance. Shortly after the accession a royal proclamation against immorality was published, and many more were to follow (see Collier 1987: lxxvii ff.). It was a movement strongly connected with the growth of a pro-Whig mercantile class whose roots lay in the English Revolution, and whose interests in the new world of money and commerce did nothing to undermine their hostility to the old world of aristocratic privilege. For it would undoubtedly be more sensible to see the opposition to the theatre as a symbol of an essentially political opposition than as somehow a purely moral one. Indeed, Farquhar makes the connection quite explicitly in *The Constant Couple*, first performed the year after Collier's *Short View* was published, in which he has the 'old Merchant' Smuggler, the representative of a corrupt City world, 'reveal' that the attack had been paid for by City money: 'Tis a hard matter now, that an honest sober man can't sin in private for this plaguey stage. I gave an honest Gentleman five guineas myself towards writing a book against it, and it has done no good' (5.2).

The tide of reaction looked unstoppable at the time. 'The phrase "reformation of manners" appeared everywhere' in the 1690s (Bahlman 1957: 14), and it is clear that the theatre could no longer afford to ignore the growing swell of opposition to it. In January 1695 the Lord Chamberlain had issued an order that all plays be fully licensed – that is, vetted for approval before performance – and by 1699, the poet laureate Nahum Tate put forward a *Proposal for Regulating the Stage and Stage-Players*, a work written with a clear belief that a total ban on the theatres was being considered if such reforms did not occur.

The reform movement was, then, to directly affect the way in which new plays modified dramatic traditions, and it also provided the inspiration for a new form of drama, the sentimental comedy, in which the excesses of the post-Restoration tradition were excised and a morally correct happy ending provided in a way that began to bring in new elements to audiences. The first of these new sentimental comedies, Colley Cibber's *Love's Last Shift* (1696), was actually produced two years before Collier's published outburst and was to provide the model for Vanbrugh's first staged play. Cibber's conclusion, in which the married couple are successfully reunited after the wife has effected a moral about-turn on the part of the philandering husband, was followed by the aptly titled *The Relapse*, in which Vanbrugh takes the pair back into the familiar earlier territory of adultery and intrigue. In his *Short Vindication* of 1698, he talks of the genesis of *The Relapse* as 'a pleasure to indulge a musing fancy, and suppose myself' in Loveless's place at the end of Cibber's play.

To this end Vanbrugh brings the married couple, Loveless and Amanda, back to London and has the supposedly morally repentant husband stumble at the very first hurdle, falling in love with a woman during a visit to the playhouse, where he has been watching a play whose plot mirrors his own 'relapse'. It transpires that the woman, Berinthea, is a distant relative of Amanda's and, after a first visit, she is invited to lodge with them. They are immediately visited by Worthy, 'a gentleman of the town', who, we quickly learn, is not only besotted by Amanda but is an ex-lover of Berinthea. The pair join forces against the married couple, the better to further their individual interests. By Act 4 Loveless has crept secretly back into his own house and to Berinthea's chamber, where, after the shortest of verbal foreplay, he sets about the most comically unprotesting ravishment of the entire post-Restoration theatre:

> *Puts out the candles.*
> *Berinthea*: O Lord! are you mad? What shall I do for light?
> *Loveless*: You'll do as well without it.
> *Berinthea*: Why, one can't find a chair to sit down.
> *Loveless*: Come into the closet, madam, there's moonshine upon the couch.
> *Berinthea*: Nay, never pull, for I will not go.
> *Loveless*: Then you must be carried.
> *Carrying her.*
> *Berinthea* (*very softly*): Help, help. I'm ravished, ruined, undone. O Lord, I shall never be
>   able to bear it.
>
>   *{Exeunt.}* (4.3)

This is not the end of the play, or indeed, of this strand of the plot; but the playwright has further issue to take with *Love's Last Shift*. In a beautifully economical stroke Vanbrugh collapses the action in Cibber's play concerned with the fop, Sir Novelty Fashion, and with the two Worthy brothers in pursuit of wives into a single secondary plot. The elder Worthy does not appear in *The Relapse*, and the younger brother, still married to a Narcissa who neither appears nor is mentioned in the sequel, is subsumed into the main plot in pursuit of an adulterous affair with Amanda. The newly made-up knight now becomes Lord Foppington. Lord Foppington acquires a younger brother, Young Fashion, who is as strapped for cash as the younger Worthy was in *Love's Last Shift*.

Lord Foppington resolutely refuses to help his brother; and it is left to a rogue character, Coupler, to suggest a way of duping his brother and achieving financial security at a stroke. A marriage has been arranged, for money, between Lord Foppington and Miss Hoyden, the country house-bound daughter of Sir Tunbelly Clumsey, a man as savagely caricatured as a member of the rural gentry as Foppington is as a representative of the urban aristocracy. In order to gain credence with the audience as a decent chap at heart, Young Fashion gives his brother one final chance to redeem himself. When he is again rebuffed, he willingly embraces the plan to impersonate Foppington. Miss Hoyden is a headstrong girl who is only too willing to marry Young Fashion in his assumed guise as Lord Foppington; willing, indeed, to take any man to whom she can be allowed access by the father who keeps her locked in her room. She is a supreme example of Vanbrugh's dictum of the urgency of the sexual itch – imprisoned against temptation, she is jealous that 'the young greyhound bitch can run loose about the house all day long' (3.4) – and willingly accepts an immediate marriage. When, after Lord Foppington has arrived, been trussed and imprisoned by her father, the truth is revealed, she happily embarks on a secret second marriage, having enjoyed a first taste of sexual pleasure and looking for further adventures in London.

It is the character of Lord Foppington, however, who gives the play its real comic heart, chiefly because of the unusually prominent role that he plays in *The Relapse*. The foppish forerunners, not only Sir Novelty Fashion, on whom Vanbrugh draws so heavily had all been peripheral to the real action of the plays in which they appeared; their main function was to entertain by their outrageously satirized *nouveaux riches* behaviour, which was set against the 'model' of the polished beau of the old order – a Sir Fopling Flutter against a Dorimant in *The Man of Mode*, most obviously. Not only does Lord Foppington's access to all parts of the play allow virtually the only point of actual connection between the two plots – when he visits Loveless and Amanda in their town house and is first slapped by the wife, then cut with a sword by the husband after he has attempted a public seduction of the woman – but he is a properly active protagonist throughout the play. The result is a more brilliantly rounded, albeit still satirized, fop than in any other post-Restoration play. The sincerity of Cibber's commitment to a morally reformed stage in *Love's Last Shift* was, incidentally, more than somewhat compromised by the fact that he willingly took on, and embellished, the part of Lord Foppington in Vanbrugh's sequel.

Foppington's visit to Amanda and Loveless in Act 2, scene 1, for instance, is a piece of comic business without parallel. For what is most remarkable about the fop that Vanbrugh has created is his absolute certainty. Having introduced himself, uninvited, into their house, he captures the conversation and proves utterly impervious to all attempts to put him down. His dialogue with the virtuous Amanda and the very unvirtuous Berinthea is wonderful in its depiction of a confrontation between two completely different moral codes: the more Foppington blunders into what in Amanda's mind are increasingly outrageous assertions, the more he thinks he is conquering her, not only by the external appearance of his dress and manner, on which he places so much importance, but by the force of his logic.

Lord Foppington is, then, the summation of the fop characters of the earlier comedy, and the play is a last bow towards the earlier drama and its mores. In many other ways, however, the sequel that Vanbrugh produced looked more of the new age than Cibber's attempt to modify the comedy tradition. For in Miss Hoyden he created an unmarried female character whose sexual appetite is every bit as voracious as that of the predatory males, both single and married, of the earlier comedy; and in the somewhat unhappy resolution of the main plot – hurried through doubtless because Vanbrugh wanted his play to appear in the same season as *Love's Last Shift* – he leaves the situation of the married Amanda surrounded by greater confusion than had been customary. The force of Vanbrugh's attack on Cibber's presentation of the reformed husband rests on the need for Amanda herself not to change, to remain faithful and chaste, otherwise the significance of the 'relapse' is lost and Loveless and Amanda become just another post-Restoration comedy couple going through the adulterous routine. That she should be so resolutely courted by a man with the name of Worthy serves only to highlight Amanda's very different, and moral, sense of the concept of worthiness to that more worldly one understood by the Town at large.

Consequently, in Act 5, scene 4, when Worthy is finally afforded the opportunity of directly propositioning Amanda, the attempt must be doomed to failure. We know that she is attracted to him already, and there is much in the scene that allows an actress scope to show a woman caught between loyalty and sexual interest, especially since she has been given firm proof of her husband's infidelity by Berinthea. But she cannot give in, and so the scene is concluded with Amanda extracting a promise from Worthy that he may love her only 'if, from this moment, you forbear to ask whatever is unfit for me to grant'. It is, as she immediately adds, a problematic concession: 'I doubt, on such hard terms, a woman's heart is scarcely worth the having'. Eventually Worthy, somewhat surprisingly, agrees to her terms, and Amanda is left to rebuild her marriage as best she can.

However, we need to remember just what Worthy's track record has been to date. Vanbrugh has inherited him from *Love's Last Shift*, where his marriage to Narcissa seemed more than in part prompted by the estate she would bring a penniless younger brother and was accompanied by no sense that he would cease to play the field. Although, obviously, Vanbrugh is free to discard what he wishes of this Worthy's past – including Narcissa, who does not and could not ever appear – nothing we learn of him does much to alter the record. Now married to a woman about whom he never talks, he has had Berinthea as a mistress and now courts another man's wife, with the willing contrivance of that ex-mistress. Small wonder that Vanbrugh should leave affairs at that juncture. That is the last we hear from Amanda and Worthy, and Loveless has but one more sentence in the play. As Foppington mistakenly celebrates his marriage to Miss Hoyden in the final scene, he invites Loveless to take revenge on him for his attempt on his wife in the traditional manner, by cuckolding him. Loveless's reply, 'You need not fear, sir, I'm too fond of my own wife to have the least inclination to yours', is unfathomable.

What all these uncertainties of resolution do is to foreground the problematics of marriage within the context of revisiting the earlier conventions of the comedy tradition. Clearly Vanbrugh has been forced to take on, in particular, the situation of the sinned-against wife by his decision to provide a sequel to Cibber's offering, and he is certainly not the first to do so (see Cordner 1995: xli–xlix). However, the success of both Cibber's and Vanbrugh's plays points to a change in the audience constituency. From 1703 onwards the 'ladies' in the audience were able to request revivals of plays; from their choice it is apparent that, for the wives, the issue was marriage in a patriarchal society (see Bull 1998: 25–39). In his next original play, *The Provok'd Wife* (1697), Vanbrugh was to tackle the issue head-on.

In *The Provok'd Wife* Vanbrugh again concentrates the interest on an unhappy marriage. Given that most plays in the earlier comedy tradition used marriage as the necessary resolution of the plot, the particular focus of interest is significant. There are precedents for this, but none considers with quite the same degree of seriousness as Vanbrugh the problems attendant on what is shown from the outset to be a totally misguided union. In addition, the fact that *The Provok'd Wife* differs from virtually all the earlier plays in having nothing that can be properly defined as a secondary plot strengthens the emphasis, drawing the activities of all the other characters into its plot resolution.

That the husband in question should be a Sir John Brute gives a further indication of the novelty of Vanbrugh's intent. For, from the opening words, we are left in no doubt that our sympathies will not be made to engage with the man. Sir John starts the action alone on stage. His attack on marriage, both in general and in particular, sets him up as a stereotyped bully who will experience adultery as a victim rather than as a protagonist.

Vanbrugh quickly generates sympathy for the 'provoked wife' in ways which suggest that, if she does eventually take her revenge, we will think none the worse of her for it. Left alone after his blunt abuse of her and her sex, she immediately reflects aloud on the possibility of obtaining a legal separation – 'these are good times; a woman may have a gallant, and a separate maintenance too' – or a divorce, an exceedingly difficult undertaking at the time, despite Lady Brute's attempts to invoke a new world of social contracts as evidenced by the 1688 settlement that had brought William and Mary to the throne: 'What opposes? My matrimonial vow? Why, what did I vow? I think I promised to be true to my husband. Well; and he promised to be kind to me. But he hasn't kept his word. Why then I'm absolved from mine. Ay, that seems clear to me. The argument's good between the king and the people, why not between the husband and the wife?' (1.1).

Lady Brute's invocation of the concept of marriage as a contract is already placed by her in a larger political context in which the notion of contract was central to the entire post-Restoration period, but in particular to the period after the Glorious Revolution of 1688. The introduction of the legal possibility of civil marriages during the Commonwealth period was but a first stage in the secularization of the contract; but it is necessary to consider the particular implications of her connected argument, since it is more than an analogy. Susan Staves quotes a contemporary judicial ruling: '"When the wife departs from her husband against his will, she forsakes and deserts his Government . . . Therefore . . . this offence should put her in the same plight in the petit commonwealth of the household, that it puts the subjects for the like offence in the great commonwealth of the realm"' (Staves 1979: 111). The use of the term 'Commonwealth' here brings a particular edge to the general principle enunciated: that a wife owes the same absolute allegiance to her husband as the subject does to the monarch. The wife's desertion is thus presented as akin to the action of the New Model Army *et alia* in their formal separation from the monarch. However, the notion of contract – which is of central import to all political debate of the late seventeenth and eighteenth centuries, as particularly exemplified in the work of Hobbes and Locke – was already implicit at the time of the Restoration. In 1688 it was established as a fundamental tenet of the agreement by which Parliament accepted William as monarch. So, Lady Brute's linkage of the two areas must be seen as a part of a larger questioning of the contractual nature of marriage – if the king has to debate terms, then so logically must the husband – and, more specifically, of the position of women in those arranged and contractual marriages, a perfect example of which is that of the Brutes. It is, then, no accident that the position of married women, and in particular unhappily married women, should be foregrounded in the major plays of both Vanbrugh and Farquhar.

We learn from the opening of Lady Brute's soliloquy that she had been warned of her future husband's likely conduct before she accepted the match, 'but I thought I had charms enough to govern him, and that where there was an estate, a woman must needs be happy; so my vanity has deceived me, and my ambition has made me uneasy' (1.1). In accepting Sir John, then, she had weighed the acquisition of an estate, with its consequent raising of her financial and social status, as a positive to be set against her knowledge of his bad qualities. And in the following act Sir John, bemoaning the fact of his marriage to Constant and Heartfree, is asked by them why, if he is not happy with 'one of the best wives in the world', he should have married her. His reply is blunt: 'I married because I had a mind to lie with her, and she would not let me'. And to Heartfree's 'why did you not ravish her?', he pleads the fear of recriminations from her relatives, and the fact that he then kept 'bad' company – 'fellows that went to church, said grace to their meat, and had not the least tincture of quality about 'em' (2.1).

This latter explanation of his refusal to play the role of courtly rake as a bachelor helps us to place Sir John in the panorama of post-Restoration society. He is not a member of the traditional landed gentry, whose interests and exploits were the chief object of celebration in earlier comedies. His lineage derives from the Commonwealth period, like that of Sir Nicholas Cully in Etherege's first play, *The Comical Revenge* (1664) – a man sneeringly described by the knight of the old order, Sir Frederick Frolick, a defiantly non-Puritan beau, as having been made up by Cromwell 'for the transcendent knavery and disloyalty of his father'. Heartfree's question, and the nature of Sir John's response, create an important distinction between the interests of these two worlds and add to the significance of Lady Brute's error in marrying for this particular estate.

Thus, although the particular ramifications of this marriage are now somewhat dimmed, Vanbrugh's audiences would have had a much more acute sense of the nature of this arranged union and would readily be able to read into it not only an account of an individual misalliance, but issues of far greater social import. Sir John is to be viewed not only as a brute but as an outsider figure, a trespasser on the proper concerns of the traditional courtly rake as represented most obviously by Heartfree (who woos Sir John's wife), and he stands in for the *nouveau*-fop figure of the earlier comedies, a figure of key significance in Vanbrugh's first play and importantly missing from this one.

The plot set in motion by Vanbrugh is concerned with much more than the dilemma of a particular couple. It raises questions that were crucial to the perpetuation of a changing order and the family politics of arranged marriages; and it offers to do so in ways that highlight the particular dilemma of the women who were effectively sold off in order to facilitate the workings of such arrangements. No previous playwright had taken the debate so far, although, as Jacqueline Pearson points out, Vanbrugh is unable to provide any formal resolution to the dilemma in terms of the plot:

> Amanda in *The Relapse* and Lady Brute in *The Provoked Wife* are trapped in oppressive marriages by their very virtues, which forbid them to take the only possible escape-route, an affair with a sympathetic lover. Consequently in these plays Vanbrugh cannot find a satisfactory comic idiom in which to conclude the main plot, and in the final scenes of both plays, he concentrates almost exclusively on the more conventional resolutions of the subplots. Only so can he prevent the comic ending from being completely disrupted by the pathos of his unhappily married women. (Pearson 1988: 79)

Farquhar tried to deal with a related problem in *The Twin Rivals* (1702). This play provides a bridge from the earlier immediate post-Restoration comedy to the more socially concerned milieu of his final works. The problem for contemporary audiences was that they clearly found the transition difficult to comprehend. Farquhar attempts to celebrate the continuance of debauchery even as he is apparently offering a critique of it. The play's two central male characters, Benjamin Wouldbe and Richmore, are uncompromisingly reprobate figures, and Farquhar's intention to bend with what he took to be the new moral tone of the age results in a plot resolution that sees the total failure of their various designs. But the main dynamism of the play centres precisely around these designs in a way that makes the denouement unconvincing and somewhat tacked on.

That the play does end with an apparently satisfactory ending, from the point of view of the criticisms levelled by Collier and others at the immoralities of the contemporary stage, was obviously one of the major reasons for its lack of success. Farquhar makes this point rather bitterly in his published Preface to the play. He claims to have taken the moral objections to the earlier comedies perfectly seriously, and to have tried to 'improve upon his invective, and to make the stage flourish, by virtue of that satire by which he thought to suppress it'. By showing the failure of Wouldbe's and Richmore's designs, 'I thought indeed to have soothed the splenetic zeal of the city, by making a gentleman a knave, and punishing their great grievance – a whoremaster'.

In his final play, *The Beaux' Stratagem* (1707), Farquhar was to take the process a stage further. One of the central characters is Mrs Sullen, newly and unhappily married to a husband who has many of Sir John's attributes, a drunken sot who cares nothing for her and who carefully avoids her company and the necessity of communicating with her: 'There's some diversion in a talking blockhead; and since a woman must wear chains, I would have the pleasure of hearing them rattle a little', she tells Dorinda, and her comically grotesque description of her husband's belated possession of the marital bed is confirmed by the arrival of the sore-headed man himself:

He came home this morning at his usual hour of four, wakened me out of a sweet dream of something else, by tumbling over the tea-table, which he broke all to pieces, after his man and he had rowled around the room like sick passengers in a storm, he comes flounce into bed, dead as a salmon into a fishmonger's basket; his feet cold as ice, his breath hot as a furnace, and his hands and his face as greasy as his flannel night-cap – Oh Matrimony – He tosses up the clothes with a barbarous swing over his shoulders, disorders the whole economy of my bed, leaves me half naked, and my whole night's comfort is the tuneable serenade of that wakeful nightingale, his nose. (2.1)

In Lady Sullen, Farquhar has created one of his most remarkable roles, and her continual cry for help dominates the action of the play. That the best lines of the play should be given to a female character signifies more than simply a growing awareness of the potential for defining the actress's role as not automatically a passive foil to the male leads – a steady development through the entire period. The particular circumstances of her marriage are used by the playwright to question the more general problematics of marriage as an institution.

The plot of *The Beaux' Stratagem* is structured around the arrival into a rural community of two penniless fortune hunters, Aimwell and Archer, who have been taking it in turns to act as master and servant, with Aimwell having the ascendancy on this occasion. Farquhar makes the marriage question central by having Aimwell potentially paired off with Mrs Sullen's sister-in-law Dorinda, whilst Archer makes his play for the married woman. The narrative is concluded in a way that is both predictable and yet deliberately surprising.

Dorinda and Aimwell are allowed to slip quietly off into a romantic partnership, whilst that of the Sullens, a coupling of mutual antipathy, increasingly becomes the play's centre of interest. It is not that there were no married couples in the earlier comedies – and certainly there was adultery aplenty – but nowhere previously had the predicament of a Lady Sullen, trapped by the inflexibilities of contemporary marriage laws, received such a full and, indeed, sympathetic treatment. So intent is Farquhar on pursuing the theme that by the end of the third act he has Lady Sullen quoting passages from John Milton's *Doctrine and Discipline of Divorce*, a tract written in 1643 which argued the case for divorce in the event of unsatisfactory alliances.

Lady Sullen enlarges on this theme in the opening scene of the fourth act, a continuation of the action that had concluded the previous act. Musing on the fact that her country has a female ruler (Queen Anne, whose power as a woman is stressed in the play's Prologue), she puts her own situation in the larger context of all women in her society: 'Were I born a humble Turk, where women have no soul or property there I must sit contented – But in England, a country whose women are its glory, must women be abused, where women rule, must women be enslaved? nay, cheated into slavery, mocked by a promise of comfortable society into a wilderness of solitude' (4.1).

There is no single way of describing Lady Sullen's position at this point, which makes the irresolution of the relationship between her and her husband the more dramatically interesting. At one extreme, it could be said that Farquhar is teasing his audience, promising them something that could not possibly occur; at another, that Lady Sullen is more than willing to be pushed over the edge into adultery. The ambiguity is something that can only be resolved in performance, and will certainly be resolved in different ways throughout the play's stage history and in the context of changing social mores.

The two strands of the plot are resolved somewhat arbitrarily by the introduction of Mrs Sullen's brother, the suitably named Sir Charles Freeman. Having already brought news that Aimwell's elder brother is dead and that the young adventurer is actually entitled to the estate he had falsely appropriated – and is thus now a suitable match for Dorinda – Freeman sets about giving Mrs Sullen a divorce on the grounds that both parties desire it; and Archer concludes affairs with a direct address to the audience, ending with a final 'Consent is law enough to set you free' (5.5).

The play's final word 'free' is, of course, extremely problematic. Lady Sullen may end the play separated from her husband, but would not have done so in her contemporary society. The obvious trick of the happy ending serves to reinforce the seriousness of Farquhar's theme; that for all the Lady Sullens of his world there was no way out of the tyranny of an unhappy marriage.

There is no such direct consideration of the role of women, and specifically married women, in Farquhar's penultimate and greatest play, *The Recruiting Officer* (1706). For all that the various rituals of courtship predictably shape the progress of the plot, *The Recruiting Officer* is, as its title suggests, as much concerned with the process of recruitment in the town. The central male character is Captain Plume, the recruiting officer. In the first scene, having learned that he has just become a father as a result of a fling with his 'old friend Molly at the Castle' on his last recruitment drive, he settles the matter by agreeing to provide for the child and prevailing upon his assistant, Sergeant Kite, to take Molly as the sixth of his wives dotted around the country. Plume is thus set up from the outset as a traditional womanizer and is contrasted with his friend Worthy, who had, for a financial consideration, been about to install the delightful Melinda as his mistress at the time of their previous meeting. In this play money can 'recruit' both men and women.

However, Melinda has had a change of fortune which means that Worthy is no longer able to court her as a mistress: and, as Plume surmises, 'she grew haughty, and because you approached her as a goddess, she used you like a dog'. Melinda is, then, in her newly enriched state, well able to hold out for suitable terms, including marriage.

During the course of the play, Plume is to have a rather similar switch deployed on him. For, in addition to Melinda, there is another unmarried lady, Silvia, the daughter of Plume's old friend Justice Balance. The Captain is anxious that she shall not hear of the business with Molly, for he has long had designs on her person:

Plume: 'Tis true, Silvia and I had once agreed to go to bed together, could we have adjusted preliminaries; but she would have the wedding before consummation, and I was for consummation before the wedding – We could not agree, she was a pert obstinate fool, and would lose her maidenhead her own way, so she may keep it for Plume.

Worthy: But do you intend to marry upon no other conditions?

Plume: Your pardon, Sir, I'll marry upon no conditions at all, if I should, I'm resolved
never to bind myself to a woman for my whole life, till I know whether I shall like
her company for half an hour – Suppose I married a woman that wanted a leg? Such a
thing might be, unless I examined the goods before-hand; if people would but try
one another's constitutions before they engaged, it would prevent all those elope-
ments, divorces, and the Devil knows what. (1.1)

However, Silvia is no easy catch. Already firm in her intent to have Plume, and with a
father only concerned that the Captain's intentions are to make an honest woman of
her, she sets about testing her prospective husband. Although parts for female actors
were beginning to be less automatically stereotyped, Silvia is still an unusually
strong-willed character to be found wearing skirts; a fact she herself comments on
to her friend Melinda. She is frustrated by the limitations placed upon her as a
woman, declaring not only that can she 'do everything with my father but drink and
shoot flying', but also that the kind of man she finds attractive will not have 'confined
thoughts', a quality she has already had cause to observe in Plume, given that she had
sent financial assistance to Molly after the birth:

> *Silvia*: I think a petticoat a mighty simple thing, and I'm heartily tired of my sex.
> *Melinda*: That is, you are tired of an appendix to our sex, that you can't so handsomely
> get rid of in petticoats as if you were in breeches – O my conscience, Silvia, hadst
> thou been a man, thou hadst been the greatest rake in Christendom.
> *Silvia*: I should endeavour to know the world, which a man can never do thoroughly
> without half a hundred friendships, and as many amours. But now I think on it, how
> stands your affair with Mr Worthy? (1.2)

Farquhar is interested in liberating the 'courtship' of Silvia and Plume from the
conventional male/female demarcations of the earlier drama. Thus, Silvia's desire to be
rid of her petticoats is soon fulfilled, as the playwright has her disguise herself as a
would-be recruit to be enlisted by the Captain. She is then able to take on the role of the
predatory lover, one which is, as she has ruefully remarked, usually reserved for the
male. Furthermore – in the breeches role – she finds herself well on the way to becoming
the rake that Melinda had jibed her about; for, to persuade her to enlist with him,
Plume assigns a young girl, Rose, to the disguised Silvia as a bed-companion. She
accepts the offer, having first asked for assurance that Rose is still a virgin.

> *Plume*: I can't tell you how you can be certified in that point, till you try, but upon my
> honour she may be a vestal for ought that I know to the contrary. ...
> *Silvia*: So you only want an opportunity for accomplishing your designs upon her?
> *Plume*: Not at all, I have already gained my ends, which were only the drawing in one or
> two of her followers. ... So kiss the prettiest country wenches, and you are sure of
> listing the lustiest fellows. Some people may call this artifice, but I term it stratagem.
> (4.1)

Plume's is a rather dubious rationalization. His stratagem is certainly seen to work in the play, but he has already admitted that only the jealous intervention of his landlady had prevented him from coupling with Rose; and he tells the disguised Silvia that the tedium of recruiting must be alleviated with some pleasure. However, the arrangement does ensure that Rose remains unmolested and that Silvia is able to share quarters with the Captain, the better to consider the conduct of her future husband.

The ambiguity is crucial, for it allows Farquhar to present Plume as both the dashing rake and as the faithful lover, if only during the course of this play's narrative in the latter case. Having relinquished all claim to Rose, he assures the disguised Silvia, 'I am not that rake that the world imagines, I have got an air of freedom, which people mistake for lewdness in me, as they mistake formality in others for religion'. The significance of this is directly related to the paralleling of Silvia and Melinda's change of fortune. Worthy starts the play aware of the reason for Melinda's refusal to be bought as a mistress. The first meeting between Justice Balance and Captain Plume (2.1) is dominated by the father's attempts to ensure that the recruiting officer's intentions are honourable: 'would you not debauch my daughter if you could?' He stresses his willingness for the pair to be married, telling Plume that she will come with £1,500. However, the following scene brings the news that Balance's son and heir has died, and Silvia learns that she will inherit his estate. The father undergoes a rapid change of heart. 'I liked him well enough for a bare son-in-law, I don't approve of him for an heir to my estate and family, fifteen hundred pound, indeed, I might trust in his hands, and it might do the young fellow a kindness, but . . . twelve hundred pound a year would ruin him, quite turn his brain. A Captain of Foot worth twelve hundred pound a year' (2.2).

Silvia is sent to the country and away from temptation. However, the impending change of fortune makes no difference to her. Again the audience is directed to regard her more sympathetically than Melinda, who is actually quite reasonably intent on making Worthy jealous as a punishment for what she now regards as his previously ungallant behaviour – behaviour which, in their first meeting in the play (1.2), Silvia tells Melinda that she had in fact actively encouraged, unlike her own determination for marriage, and the pair fall out over the accusation. Having accepted her father's declaration that he will not marry her against her will, and having given her promise that she will not marry against his, Silvia then resorts to disguise and returns to the fray as the appropriately named Jack Wilfull.

From this point, the disguised Silvia is firmly in control of the plot. Having agreed to be recruited by Plume, she is single-mindedly determined to 'recruit' her man. There is little doubt about the outcome. Having ensured that Melinda and Worthy will marry, Farquhar allows Justice Balance to discover that he has forced his own daughter to enlist. However, Silvia is not, of course, without the ability to maintain herself financially and, her discharge having generously been granted by Plume, the pair receive the father's blessings. It is left to Plume to first take care of Rose, by having her engaged by Silvia as a servant, and then to resign from the service, handing over to Brazen – his rival as recruiting officer and as suitor for the hand and dowry of

Silvia – the twenty recruits he has enlisted in place of the twenty thousand pounds he had hoped for. The related themes of recruitment, marriage and money are thus brought neatly together at the end.

What is fundamentally different about Farquhar's treatment of the gender debate is that he is acutely aware of the significance of class and money, as is evidenced most obviously by the way in which Melinda's status is seen to alter on the acquisition of a settlement. In contrast, the Mollys and the Roses of the world depicted by Farquhar remain simply disposable goods, to be bought, sold and exchanged in the market-place. Nor are his observations confined to the women in this play.

A theatre audience can easily be brought to accept the brisk way in which Farquhar achieves his resolution; it is, after all, a comedy. However, the conclusion is arrived at by largely glossing over the fates of the play's more minor characters, those unfortu-nates whose future will lie not in financially comfortable marriages, but in foreign and bloody fields of war. The first man to be produced before the Court of Justice to appeal against his enlistment, for instance, may be thought to have a very different perspective on the outcome. Denied a voice in the scene by Farquhar, his circum-stances are presented in as bad a light as possible by Kite and Plume, and vainly protested by his wife. Learning from her that he has five children to support, Justice Scale is for letting the man go, until he is informed that he supports them by the unlawful activity of poaching. Plume reinforces the case against him by arguing that sending the man away will prevent the wife from producing further children to be a burden on the parish; at which point the wife denies the validity of his argument in a way which condemns both of them:

> *Wife*: Look'e, Mr Captain, the parish shall get nothing by sending him away, for I won't
>   lose my teeming-time if there be a man left in the parish.
> *Balance*: Send that woman to the House of Correction – and the man –
> *Kite*: I'll take care of him, if you please. (*Takes the man down*.) (5.5)

This emphasis on the way in which class interests determine the fate of individual characters is to be found in all the events concerning recruitment; although, of course, it was not very likely to have been perceived as a problem by early eighteenth-century audiences. But it is something quite new, which has assumed greater importance as the play's production history has moved towards the present day. This is the real measure of the play's move towards realism. It is not that the playwright wished to present a propagandist piece – far from it – but rather that in depicting the practicalities of recruitment, he introduces the possibility of seeing events from more than one class perspective. The plot resolutions satisfactorily reinforce the status quo, but the differing outcomes given to different individuals, and the way in which they are seen to be achieved, have come to seem increasingly significant.

Both playwrights started their careers attempting to come to terms with the new Puritanism. With the exception of *The Confederacy*, Vanbrugh always has half an eye on the past; realistic enough to know that circumstances have changed, he writes wishing that they hadn't. In his early work Farquhar found himself frequently squeezed between what he understood to be the conflicting demands of two ideologically divided audiences, but in his final two great plays he moved the drama on, widening the social context and introducing an at least qualified degree of realism to a genre that had reached its highpoint of mannered artificiality – albeit wonderfully expressed – in the work of Congreve. Had he lived, he might perhaps have made the break more acute. As it is, his real legacy is not to be found in the theatre, excepting occasional moments like Gay's *The Beggar's Opera*, but in the steady development of the social novel tradition as it moved towards its position of cultural supremacy in the nineteenth century.

REFERENCES AND FURTHER READING

Bahlman, Dudley (1957). *The Moral Revolution of 1688*. New Haven, CT: Yale University Press.

Berkowitz, Gerald M. (1981). *Sir John Vanbrugh and the End of Restoration Comedy. Costerus* 31. Amsterdam: Rodopi.

Bingham, Madelaine (1974). *Masks and Facades: Sir John Vanbrugh, the Man in his Setting*. London: Allen and Unwin.

Bull, John (1998). *Vanbrugh and Farquhar*. Basingstoke: Macmillan.

Burns, Edward (1987). *Restoration Comedy: Crises of Desire and Identity*. Basingstoke: Macmillan.

Collier, Jeremy (1987). *A Short View of the Immorality and Prophaneness of the English Stage: A Critical Edition*, ed. Bernard Hillinger. New York: Garland.

Connelly, Willard (1949). *Young George Farquhar: The Restoration Drama at Twilight*. London: Cassell.

Cordner, Michael (ed.). (1989). *Vanbrugh: Four Comedies*. Harmondsworth: Penguin.

Cordner, Michael (ed.). (1995). *Four Restoration Marriage Plays*. Oxford: Oxford University Press.

Craik, T. W. (ed.). (1976). *Revels History of Drama in English, 1660–1750*. London: Methuen.

Downes, Kerry (1987). *Sir John Vanbrugh: A Biography*. London: Sidgwick and Jackson.

Holmes, Geoffrey (1993). *The Making of a Great Power: Late Stuart and Early Georgian Britain, 1660– 1722*. London: Longman.

Hume, Robert D. (ed.). (1980). *The London Theatre World, 1660–1800*. Carbondale: Southern Illinois University Press.

Husboe, Arthur R. (1986). *Sir John Vanbrugh*. Boston: Twayne.

James, Eugene Nelson (1986). *George Farquhar: A Reference Guide*. Boston: Hall and Co.

Kenny, Shirley Strum (ed.). (1988). *The Works of George Farquhar*. 2 vols. Oxford: Clarendon Press.

McCormick, Frank (1991). *Sir John Vanbrugh: The Playwright as Architect*. Pennsylvania: Pennsylvania State University Press.

McCormick, Frank (1992). *Sir John Vanbrugh: A Reference Guide*. New York: Hall and Co.

O'Bryan, Daniel (1732). *Authentic Memoirs; or, the life and character of that most celebrated comedian... R.Wilks... To which is added, an elegy on his death*. London.

Pearson, Jacqueline (1988). *The Prostituted Muse: Images of Women and Women Dramatists, 1642–1737*. New York: St Martin's Press.

Roberts, David (1989). *The Ladies: Female Patronage of Restoration Drama, 1660–1700*. Oxford: Clarendon Press.

Staves, Susan (1979). *Players' Scepters: Fictions of Authority in the Restoration*. Lincoln: University of Nebraska Press.

Styan, J. L. (1986). *Restoration Comedy in Performance*. Cambridge: Cambridge University Press.

Thomas, David (ed.). (1989). *Restoration and Georgian England, 1660–1788*. Cambridge: Cambridge University Press.

Index